TRAVELS IN TARTARY, THIBET AND CHINA

TRAVELS IN TARTARY, THIBET AND CHINA

DURING THE YEARS 1844-5-6

BY

M. HUC

TRANSLATED FROM THE FRENCH BY W, HAZLITT
SECOND REPRINT EDITION

VOL. I

ILLUSTRATED WITH FIFTY ENGRAVINGS ON WOOD

GYAN

Published by

GYAN

Gyan Publishing House
5, Ansari Road
Daryaganj, New Delhi-110002
Phone: 011-47034999, 9811692060
E-mail: books@gyanbooks.com

Distribution Network
gyanbooks.com
India, USA, Canada, UK, Australia, France

ISBN : 978-81-212-4154-0 (Set)
ISBN : 978-81-212-4975-1 (HB)
First Published, 1900

2nd Impression 2020

Printed at: Gyan Press, Delhi.

The book at your disposal is the edition of an old book originally published long back. The Text quality of this book may not be at par as compared to our other books but many readers approached us to reprint this important book so that it could satiate their hunger. We request all the readers of this book to help us to improve its quality by providing the necessary text of those pages which are not properly visible. Your valuable support in this case will be highly appreciated and acknowledged and our future readers will be benefitted immensely.

Travels in Tartary, Thibet and China

DURING THE YEARS 1844–5–6

BY M. HUC

TRANSLATED FROM THE FRENCH BY W. HAZLITT

SECOND REPRINT EDITION

VOL. I

ILLUSTRATED WITH FIFTY ENGRAVINGS ON WOOD

CHICAGO
THE OPEN COURT PUBLISHING COMPANY
LONDON AGENTS
KEGAN PAUL, TRENCH, TRUEBNER & CO.
1900

MAP OF TARTARY, THIBET, AND CHINA.

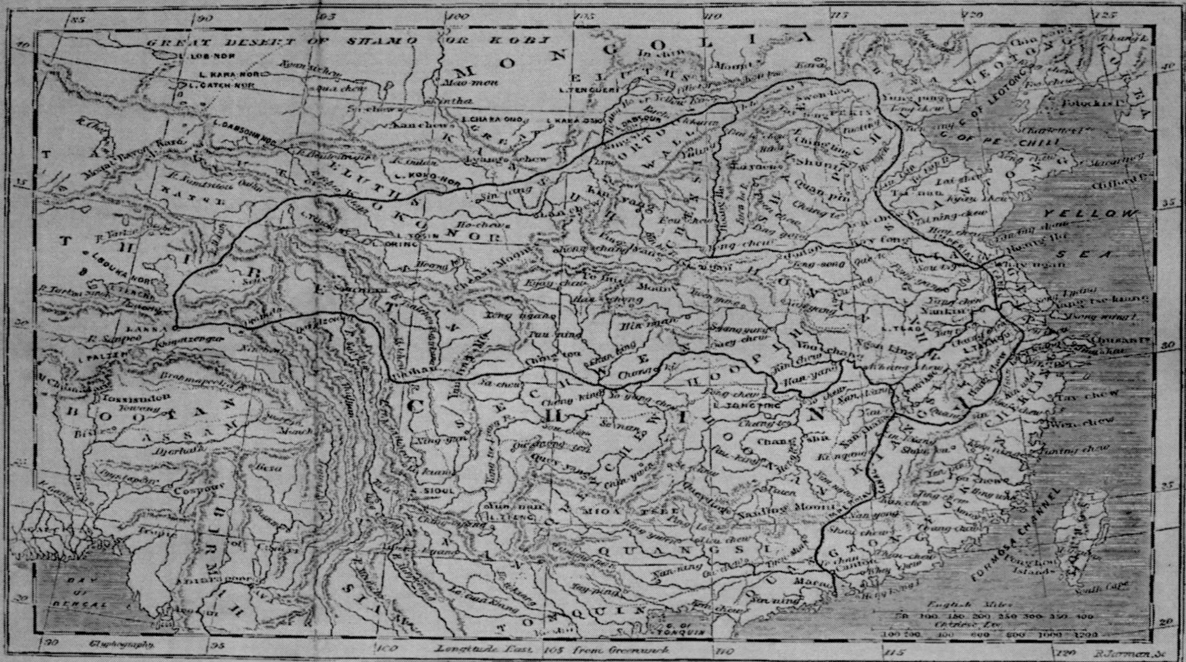

THE DARK LINE INDICATES THE ROUTE OF THE TRAVELLERS MM. HUC AND GABET.

TARTAR AND CHINESE COSTUMES.

TRAVELS

IN

TARTARY, THIBET, AND CHINA

ILLUSTRATED

MM. GABET AND HUC

CHICAGO
THE OPEN COURT PUBLISHING COMPANY
LONDON AGENTS
KEGAN PAUL, TRENCH, TRUEBNER & CO.

PUBLISHER'S PREFACE.

CONSIDERING the many myths that are now rife about Thibetan Mahatmas and the sensational reports of recent would-be travelers, whose fictitious discoveries are seriously accepted by many readers, it seems appropriate to remind the reading public of a famous but now almost forgotten book, "The Travels in Tartary, Thibet, and China" of the two Lazarist missionaries Huc and Gabet. These gentlemen did not find in Thibet lost manuscripts of the life of Jesus, nor do they describe the Thibetans as savages. Their half-dead servants did not take kodak pictures of them while being tortured on the rack. Nor did they use the powers of hypnotism in their dealings with the Lamas and while being subjected to outrageous tortures. There is, in fact, nothing incredible in M. Huc's story, and yet, perhaps because of this reason, the book is far more interesting than any report that has since appeared.

The sensation which M. Huc's book created on its first appearance has subsided, and it is now known only to scholars and historians. Indeed the book is out of print and can, both in its original French and in its German and English translations, be had only through second-hand book dealers, where the copies are at a high premium. Under these circumstances it seems desirable that the book should be reprinted and once more placed before the reading public. What a storehouse it is for the ethnologist, geographer, the scholar interested in religious customs, the reader of travels, and the student of human nature!

The book undoubtedly deserves a revision, and many things which were puzzling to MM. Huc and Gabet may, in the light of the better knowledge of to-day, have found their explanation. For instance, some botanist may be able to tell us what the tree of the ten thousand images is; ethnologists may now know much about the barbarous ceremony mentioned in Vol. I., Chap. IX., which is probably a mere trick played on a credulous audience for the purpose of extracting their money. Further, the reasons for the similarities which Huc and Gabet observed between Buddhist ceremonies and the rituals of the Roman Church are also better understood to-day. But what will be of keenest interest to us is the description of the personal character of the Thibetans and their Lamas. There is a certain family likeness between them and the Western nations. They also are kind-hearted and inspired with good intentions. It is true they fear invasions and are constantly on their guard against the English, on whom they look with extraordinary suspicion. The greatest crime for a traveler is to draw maps, which is taken as a sure sign of being a spy in the English service. In fact, the sole trouble which Messrs. Huc and Gabet encountered was on account of the maps which were discovered in their baggage, but they were at once released from captivity and protected against maltreatment when the court arrived at the conclusion that these maps were printed and could not have been drawn by the travelers for the purpose of betraying the country.

A careful reader will also notice that our French travelers are sometimes quick in their judgment.*

Being unable to give trustworthy information about all these and similar complications contained in M. Huc's reports, we prefer to leave the book as it stands and republish it without comments of our own, leaving this task to critics and readers who are better equipped for the purpose.

* Sandara, a young Lama of unusual talents and broad experience, who is suspected by his brethren in the Lamasery of being a freethinker, is engaged as a Thibetan teacher by the Lazarist missionaries. At first he is praised for the extraordinary interest he takes in Christianity by M. Huc, who sees him in a hopeful vision develop into a Thibetan Apostle. Later on, however, Sandara becomes impatient with his French pupils and addresses them with such words as these: "What! you learned fellows want to have the same thing told you three times over? Why, if I were to tell a donkey the same thing three times over he'd remember it." It is on this occasion that Messrs. Huc and Gabet change their opinion of their Thibetan teacher, declaring that, "All the fine things that they had imagined of Sandara vanished like a dream." He is now suspected of being "a dissipated knave" whose only aim was to ease the French missionaries of their money; yet they deemed it wise to submit, "For," says M. Huc, "his very rudeness we considered, would aid our progress in acquiring the Thibetan language." And "this system, though somewhat tedious and decidedly displeasing to our self-love was incomparably superior to the method practised by the (over-polite) Chinese Christians toward the European missionaries in giving them Chinese lessons." In spite of M. Huc's accusation, Sandara proves a faithful and honest friend in times of emergency. Not only does he see through the malicious lies of Samdadchiemba, when he claims to have been robbed of things which he stole himself, but also succeeds in recovering the tent of the missionaries which had been pawned by the rascally inn-keeper on New Year's day, for the sake of paying some debts. (See Vol. II., Chap. II.) In this instance, as on other occasions, M. Huc always depicts the situation from the point of view which he takes at the moment.

For similar reasons, the transcriptions of foreign names have been left as they stood in the original translation.

The Thibetans are a warlike race, but their military tendencies are subdued by an extreme religious devotion, which, far from being exclusively Buddhistic, seems among their educated men to be as broad as it is among the most scholarly philosophers of Europe and of America. Think only of the Thibetan custom, strongly reminding us of the Christian Angelus, of the whole people praying in common at certain hours! Think of the interest which the Regent of Lhassa took in the Christian religion! How he trembled when the maps were found, and how he triumphed when the innocence of our travelers was brought out! How eagerly he studied the Christian doctrines! With what humor he treated the ignorant Lamas and their superstition, typical of the popular Buddhism of the masses! Even when the Chinese Plenipotentiary urged to him the danger of Christianity's replacing Buddhism in Thibet, the attitude of the Regent of Lhassa towards the Lazarists remained unaltered. He said to them: "Religious persons, men of prayer, belonging to all countries, are strangers nowhere. Such is the doctrine taught by our holy books. Lhassa being the peculiar assembling place and abode of men of prayer, that title of itself should always secure for you liberty and protection." His answer to the Chinese Plenipotentiary is also characteristic: "If the doctrine which these men hold is a false doctrine, the Thibetans will not embrace it: if on the contrary it is true, what have we to fear? How can the truth be prejudicial to men."

And so this book, apart from its interest to the general reader, will also be welcome to all persons interested in Christian missions and to all students of Buddhism and its institutions.

THE OPEN COURT PUBLISHING CO.

PREFACE.

THE Pope having, about the year 1844, been pleased to establish an Apostolic Vicariat of Mongolia, it was considered expedient, with a view to further operations, to ascertain the nature and extent of the diocese thus created, and MM. Gabet and Huc, two Lazarists attached to the petty mission of Si-Wang, were accordingly deputed to collect the necessary information. They made their way through difficulties which nothing but religious enthusiasm in combination with French elasticity could have overcome, to Lha-Ssa, the capital of Thibet, and in this seat of Lamanism were becoming comfortably settled, with lively hopes and expectations of converting the Talé-Lama into a branch-Pope, when the Chinese Minister, the noted Ke-Shen, interposed on political grounds, and had them deported to China. M. Gabet was directed by his superiors to proceed to France, and lay a complaint before his Government, of the arbitrary treatment which he and his fellow Missionary had experienced. In the steamer which conveyed him from Hong Kong to Ceylon, he found Mr. Alexander Johnstone, secretary to Her Majesty's Plenipotentiary in China; and this gentleman perceived so much, not merely of entertainment, but of important information in the conversations he had with M. Gabet, that he committed to paper the leading features of the Reverend Missionary's statements, and on his return to his official post, gave his manuscripts to Sir John Davis, who, in his turn, considered their contents so interesting, that he embodied a copy of them in a despatch to Lord Palmerston. Subsequently the two volumes, here translated, were prepared by M. Huc, and published in Paris. Thus it is, that to Papal aggression in the East, the Western World is indebted for a work exhibiting, for the first time, a complete representation of countries previously almost unknown to Europeans, and indeed considered practically inaccessible; and of a religion, which, followed by no fewer than 170,000,000 persons, presents the most singular analogies in its leading features with the Catholicism of Rome.

CONTENTS OF VOLUME I.

CHAPTER I.

CHAPTER II.

CHAPTER III.

CHAPTER IV.

CHAPTER V.

CHAPTER VI.

CHAPTER VII.

CHAPTER VIII.

CHAPTER IX.

CHAPTER X.

CHAPTER XI.

CHAPTER XII.

LIST OF ILLUSTRATIONS

PEKING.

CHAPTER I.

French Mission of Peking—Glance at the Kingdom of *Ouniot* — Preparations for Departure—Tartar-Chinese Inn—Change of Costume—Portrait and Character of Samdadchiemba—*Sain-Oula* (the Good Mountain)—The Frosts on Sain-Oula, and its Robbers—First Encampment in the Desert—Great Imperial Forest—Buddhist monuments on the summit of the mountains—Topography of the Kingdom of *Gechekten*—Character of its Inhabitants—Tragical working of a Mine—Two Mongols desire to have their horoscope taken—Adventure of Samdadchiemba—Environs of the town of *Tolon-Noor*.

THE French mission of Peking, once so flourishing under the early emperors of the Tartar-Mantchou dynasty, was almost extirpated by the constant persecutions of Kai-King, the fifth monarch of that dynasty, who ascended the throne in 1799. The missionaries were dispersed or put to death, and at that time Europe was herself too deeply agitated to enable her to send succor to this distant Christendom, which remained for a time abandoned. Accordingly, when the French Lazarists reappeared at Peking, they found there scarce a vestige of the true faith. A great number of Christians, to avoid the persecutions of the Chinese authorities, had passed the Great Wall, and sought peace and liberty in the deserts of Tartary, where they lived dispersed upon small patches of land which the Mongols permitted them to cultivate. By dint of perseverance the missionaries collected together these dispersed Christians, placed themselves at their head, and hence superintended the mission of Peking, the immediate administration of which was in the hands of a few Chinese Lazarists. The French missionaries could not, with any prudence, have resumed their former position in the capital of the empire. Their presence would have compromised the prospects of the scarcely reviving mission.

In visiting the Chinese Christians of Mongolia, we more than once had occasion to make excursions into the Land of Grass, (*Tsao-Ti*), as the uncultivated portions of Tartary are designated, and to take up our temporary abode beneath the tents of the Mongols. We were no sooner acquainted with this nomadic people, than we loved them, and our hearts were filled with a passionate desire to announce the gospel to them. Our whole leisure was therefore devoted to acquiring the Tartar dialects, and in 1842, the Holy See at length fulfilled our desires, by erecting Mongolia into an Apostolical Vicariat.

Towards the commencement of the year 1844, couriers arrived at Si-wang, a small Christian community, where the vicar apostolic of Mongolia had fixed his episcopal residence. Si-wang itself is a village, north of the Great Wall, one day's journey from Suen-hoa-Fou. The prelate sent us instructions for an extended voyage we were to undertake for the purpose of studying the character and manners of the Tartars, and of ascertaining as nearly as possible the extent and limits of the Vicariat. This journey, then, which we had so long meditated, was now determined upon; and we sent a young Lama convert in search of some camels which we had put to pasture in the kingdom of Naiman. Pending his absence, we hastened the completion of several Mongol works, the translation of which had occupied us for a considerable time. Our little books of prayer and doctrine were ready, still our young Lama had not returned; but thinking he could not delay much longer, we quitted the valley of Black Waters (*Hé-Chuy*), and proceeded on to await his arrival at the Contiguous Defiles (*Piè-liè-Keou*), which seemed more favorable for the completion of our preparations. The days passed away in futile expectation; the coolness of the autumn was becoming somewhat biting, and we feared that we should have to begin our journey across the deserts of Tartary during the frosts of winter. We determined, therefore, to despatch some one in quest of our camels and our Lama. A friendly catechist, a good walker and a man of expedition, proceeded on this mission. On the day fixed for that purpose he returned; his researches had been wholly without result. All he had ascertained at the place which he had visited was, that our Lama had started several days before with our camels. The surprise of our courier was extreme when he found that the Lama had not reached us before himself. "What!" exclaimed he, "are my legs quicker than a camel's! They left Naiman before me, and here I am arrived before them! My spiritual fathers, have patience for another day. I'll answer that both Lama and camels will be here in that time." Several days, however, passed away, and we were still in the same position. We once more despatched the courier in search of the Lama, enjoining him to proceed to the very place where the camels had been put to pasture, to examine things with his own eyes, and not to trust to any statement that other people might make.

During this interval of painful suspense, we continued to inhabit the Contiguous Defiles, a Tartar district dependent on the kingdom of Ouniot.[1] These regions appear to have been affected by great revolutions. The present inhabitants state that, in the olden time, the country was occupied by Corean tribes, who, expelled thence in the course of various wars, took refuge in the peninsula which they still possess, between the Yellow Sea and the sea of Japan. You often, in these parts of Tartary, meet with the remains of great towns, and the ruins of fortresses, very nearly resembling those of the middle ages in Europe, and, upon turning up the soil in these places, it is not unusual to find lances, arrows, portions of farming implements, and urns filled with Corean money.

Towards the middle of the 17th century, the Chinese

[1] Notwithstanding the slight importance of the Tartar tribes, we shall give them the name of kingdoms, because the chiefs of these tribes are called *Wang* (King.)

began to penetrate into this district. At that period, the whole landscape was still one of rude grandeur; the mountains were covered with fine forests, and the Mongol tents whitened the valleys, amid rich pasturages. For a very moderate sum the Chinese obtained permission to cultivate the desert, and as cultivation advanced, the Mongols were obliged to retreat, conducting their flocks and herds elsewhere.

From that time forth, the aspect of the country became entirely changed. All the trees were grubbed up, the forests disappeared from the hills, the prairies were cleared by means of fire, and the new cultivators set busily to work in exhausting the fecundity of the soil. Almost the entire region is now in the hands of the Chinese, and it is probably to their system of devastation that we must attribute the extreme irregularity of the seasons which now desolate this unhappy land. Droughts are of almost annual occurrence; the spring winds setting in, dry up the soil; the heavens assume a sinister aspect, and the unfortunate population await, in utter terror, the manifestation of some terrible calamity; the winds by degrees redouble their violence, and sometimes continue to blow far into the summer months. Then the dust rises in clouds, the atmosphere becomes thick and dark; and often, at midday, you are environed with the terrors of night, or rather, with an intense and almost palpable blackness, a thousand times more fearful than the most somber night. Next after these hurricanes comes the rain: but so comes, that instead of being an object of desire, it is an object of dread, for it pours down in furious raging torrents. Sometimes the heavens suddenly opening, pour forth in, as it were, an immense cascade, all the water with which they are charged in that quarter; and immediately the fields and their crops disappear under a sea of mud, whose enormous waves follow the course of the valleys, and carry everything before them. The torrent rushes on, and in a few hours the earth reappears; but the crops are gone, and worse even than that, the arable soil also has gone with them. Nothing remains but a ramification of deep ruts, filled with gravel, and thenceforth incapable of being plowed.

Hail is of frequent occurrence in these unhappy districts, and the dimensions of the hailstones are generally enormous.

We have ourselves seen some that weighed twelve pounds. One moment sometimes suffices to exterminate whole flocks. In 1843, during one of these storms, there was heard in the air a sound as of a rushing wind, and therewith fell, in a field near a house, a mass of ice larger than an ordinary millstone. It was broken to pieces with hatchets, yet, though the sun burned fiercely, three days elapsed before these pieces entirely melted.

The droughts and the inundations together, sometimes occasion famines which well-nigh exterminate the inhabitants. That of 1832, in the twelfth year of the reign of *Tao-Kouang*,[1] is the most terrible of these on record. The Chinese report that it was everywhere announced by a general presentiment, the exact nature of which no one could explain or comprehend. During the winter of 1831, a dark rumor grew into circulation. *Next year*, it was said, *there will be neither rich nor poor; blood will cover the mountains; bones will fill the valleys* (Ou fou, ou kioung; hue man chan, kou man tchouan.) These words were in every one's mouth; the children repeated them in their sports; all were under the domination of these sinister apprehensions when the year 1832 commenced. Spring and summer passed away without rain, and the frosts of autumn set in while the crops were yet green; these crops of course perished, and there was absolutely no harvest. The population was soon reduced to the most entire destitution. Houses, fields, cattle, everything was exchanged for grain, the price of which attained its weight in gold. When the grass on the mountain sides was devoured by the starving creatures, the depths of the earth were dug into for roots. The fearful prognostic, that had been so often repeated, became accomplished. Thousands died upon the hills, whither they had crawled in search of grass; dead bodies filled the roads and houses; whole villages were depopulated to the last man. There was, indeed, *neither rich nor poor;* pitiless famine had leveled all alike.

It was in this dismal region that we awaited with impatience the courier, whom, for a second time, we had despatched into the kingdom of Naiman. The day fixed for his return came and passed, and several others followed, but brought no camels, nor Lama, nor courier, which seemed

[1] Sixth Emperor of the Tartar-Mantchou dynasty. He died in the year 1849.

to us most astonishing of all. We became desperate; we could not longer endure this painful and futile suspense. We devised other means of proceeding, since those we had arranged appeared to be frustrated. The day of our departure was fixed; it was settled, further, that one of our Christians should convey us in his car to *Tolon-Noor*, distant from the Contiguous Defiles about fifty leagues. At *Tolon-Noor* we were to dismiss our temporary conveyance, proceed alone into the desert, and thus start on our pilgrimage as well as we could. This project absolutely stupefied our Christian friends; they could not comprehend how two Europeans should undertake by themselves a long journey through an unknown and inimical country: but we had reasons for abiding by our resolution. We did not desire that any Chinese should accompany us. It appeared to us absolutely necessary to throw aside the fetters with which the authorities had hitherto contrived to shackle missionaries in China. The excessive caution, or rather the imbecile pusillanimity of a Chinese catechist, was calculated rather to impede than to facilitate our progress in Tartary.

On the Sunday, the day preceding our arranged departure, everything was ready; our small trunks were packed and padlocked, and the Christians had assembled to bid us adieu. On this very evening, to the infinite surprise of all of us, our courier arrived. As he advanced, his mournful countenance told us before he spoke, that his intelligence was unfavorable. "My spiritual fathers," said he, "all is lost; you have nothing to hope; in the kingdom of Naiman there no longer exist any camels of the Holy Church. The Lama doubtless has been killed; and I have no doubt the devil has had a direct hand in the matter."

Doubts and fears are often harder to bear than the certainty of evil. The intelligence thus received, though lamentable in itself, relieved us from our perplexity as to the past, without in any way altering our plan for the future. After having received the condolences of our Christians, we retired to rest, convinced that this night would certainly be that preceding our nomadic life.

The night was far advanced, when suddenly numerous voices were heard outside our abode, and the door was shaken with loud and repeated knocks. We rose at once; the Lama, the camels, all had arrived; there was quite a little revolution. The order of the day was instantly changed. We resolved to depart, not on the Monday, but on the Tuesday; not in a car, but on camels, in true Tartar fashion. We returned to our beds perfectly delighted; but we could not sleep, each of us occupying the remainder of the night with plans for effecting the equipment of the caravan in the most expeditious manner possible.

Next day, while we were making our preparations for departure, our Lama explained his extraordinary delay. First, he had undergone a long illness; then he had been occupied a considerable time in pursuing a camel which had escaped into the desert; and finally, he had to go before some tribunal, in order to procure the restitution of a mule which had been stolen from him. A lawsuit, an illness, and a camel hunt were amply sufficient reasons for excusing the delay which had occurred. Our courier was the only person who did not participate in the general joy; he saw it must be evident to every one that he had not fulfilled his mission with any sort of skill.

All Monday was occupied in the equipment of our caravan. Every person gave his assistance to this object. Some repaired our traveling-house, that is to say, mended or patched a great blue linen tent; others cut for us a supply of wooden tent pins; others mended the holes in our copper kettle, and renovated the broken leg of a joint stool; others prepared cords, and put together the thousand and one pieces of a camel's pack. Tailors, carpenters, braziers, rope-makers, saddle-makers, people of all trades assembled in active co-operation in the courtyard of our humble abode. For all, great and small, among our Christians, were resolved that their spiritual fathers should proceed on their journey as comfortably as possible.

On Tuesday morning, there remained nothing to be done but to perforate the nostrils of the camels, and to insert in the aperture a wooden peg, to use as a sort of a bit. The arrangement of this was left to our Lama. The wild piercing cries of the poor animals pending the painful operation, soon collected together all the Christians of the village. At this moment, our Lama became exclusively the hero of the expedition. The crowd ranged themselves in a circle around him; every one was curious to see how, by gently pulling the cord attached to the peg in its nose, our Lama could make the animal obey him, and kneel at his pleasure. Then, again, it was an interesting thing for the Chinese to watch our Lama packing on the camels' backs the baggage of the two missionary travelers. When the arrangements were completed, we drank a cup of tea, and proceeded to the chapel; the Christians recited prayers for our safe journey; we received their farewell, interrupted with tears, and proceeded on our way. Samdadchiemba, our Lama cameleer,

The Travelers setting out on their Journey.

gravely mounted on a black, stunted, meager mule, opened the march, leading two camels laden with our baggage; then came the two missionaries, MM. Gabet and Huc, the former mounted on a tall camel, the latter on a white horse.

Upon our departure we were resolved to lay aside our accustomed usages, and to become regular Tartars. Yet we did not at the outset, and all at once, become exempt from the Chinese system. Besides that, for the first mile or two of our journey, we were escorted by our Chinese Christians, some on foot, and some on horseback, our first stage was to be an inn kept by the Grand Catechist of the Contiguous Defiles.

The progress of our little caravan was not at first wholly successful. We were quite novices in the art of saddling and girthing camels, so that every five minutes we had to halt, either to rearrange some cord or piece of wood that hurt and irritated the camels, or to consolidate upon their backs, as well as we could, the ill-packed baggage that threatened, ever and anon, to fall to the ground. We advanced, indeed, despite all these delays, but still very slowly. After journeying about thirty-five lis,[1] we quitted the cultivated district and entered upon the Land of Grass. There we got on much better; the camels were more at their ease in the desert, and their pace became more rapid.

We ascended a high mountain, where the camels evinced a decided tendency to compensate themselves for their trouble, by browsing, on either side, upon the tender stems of the elder tree or the green leaves of the wild rose. The shouts we were obliged to keep up, in order to urge forward the indolent beasts, alarmed infinite foxes, who issued from their holes and rushed off in all directions. On attaining the summit of the rugged hill we saw in the hollow beneath the Christian inn of *Yan-Pa-Eul.* We proceeded towards it, our road constantly crossed by fresh and limpid streams, which, issuing from the sides of the mountain, reunite at its foot and form a rivulet which encircles the inn. We were received by the landlord, or, as the Chinese call him, the Comptroller of the Chest.

Inns of this description occur at intervals in the deserts of Tartary, along the confines of China. They consist almost universally of a large square enclosure, formed by high poles interlaced with brushwood. In the center of this enclosure is a mud house, never more than ten feet high. With the exception of a few wretched rooms at each extremity, the entire structure consists of one large apartment, serving at once for cooking, eating, and sleeping; thoroughly dirty, and full of smoke and intolerable stench. Into this pleasant place all travelers, without distinction, are ushered, the portion of space applied to their accommodation being a long, wide *Kang*, as it is called, a sort of furnace, occupying more than three-fourths of the apartment, about four feet high, and the flat, smooth surface of which is covered with a reed mat, which the richer guests cover again with a traveling carpet of felt, or with furs. In front of it, three immense coppers, set in glazed earth, serve for the preparation of the traveler's milk-broth. The apertures by which

[1] The Chinese *Li* is about equivalent to the quarter of an English mile.

Kang of a Tartar-Chinese Inn.

these monster boilers are heated communicate with the interior of the *Kang*, so that its temperature is constantly maintained at a high elevation, even in the terrible cold of winter. Upon the arrival of guests, the Comptroller of the Chest invites them to ascend the *Kang*, where they seat themselves, their legs crossed tailor-fashion, round a large table, not more than six inches high. The lower part of the room is reserved for the people of the inn, who there busy themselves in keeping up the fire under the caldrons, boiling tea, and pounding oats and buckwheat into flour for the repast of the travelers. The *Kang* of these Tartar-Chinese inns is, till evening, a stage full of animation, where the guests eat, drink, smoke, gamble, dispute, and fight: with nightfall, the refectory, tavern, and gambling-house of the day is suddenly converted into a dormitory. The travelers who have any bed-clothes unroll and arrange them; those who have none, settle themselves as best they may in their personal attire, and lie down, side by side, round the table.

When the guests are very numerous they arrange themselves in two circles, feet to feet. Thus reclined, those so disposed, sleep; others, awaiting sleep, smoke, drink tea, and gossip. The effect of the scene, dimly exhibited by an imperfect wick floating amid thick, dirty, stinking oil, whose receptacle is ordinarily a broken tea-cup, is fantastic, and to the stranger, fearful.

The Comptroller of the Chest had prepared his own room for our accommodation. We washed, but would not sleep there; being now Tartar travelers, and in possession of a good tent, we determined to try our apprentice hand at setting it up. This resolution offended no one, it was quite understood we adopted this course, not out of contempt towards the inn, but out of love for a patriarchal life. When we had set up our tent, and unrolled on the ground our goatskin beds, we lighted a pile of brushwood, for the nights were already growing cold. Just as we were closing our eyes, the Inspector of Darkness startled us with beating the official night alarum, upon his brazen *tam-tam*, the sonorous sound of which, reverberating through the adjacent valleys struck with terror the tigers and wolves frequenting them, and drove them off.

We were on foot before daylight. Previous to our departure we had to perform an operation of considerable importance—no other than an entire change of costume, a complete metamorphosis. The missionaries who reside in China, all, without exception, wear the secular dress of the people, and are in no way distinguishable from them; they bear no outward sign of their religious character. It is a great pity that they should be thus obliged to wear the secular costume, for it is an obstacle in the way of their preaching the gospel. Among the Tartars, a *black man*—so they discriminate the laity, as wearing their hair, from the clergy, who have their heads close shaved—who should talk about religion would be laughed at, as impertinently meddling with things, the special province of the Lamas, and in no way concerning him. The reasons which appear to have introduced and maintained the custom of wearing the secular habit on the part of the missionaries in China, no longer applying to us, we resolved at length to appear in an ecclesiastical exterior becoming our sacred mission. The views of our vicar apostolic on the subject, as explained in his written instructions, being conformable with our wish, we did not hesitate. We resolved to adopt the secular dress of the Thibetian Lamas; that is to say, the dress which they wear when not actually performing their idolatrous ministry in the Pagodas. The costume of the Thibetian Lamas suggested itself to our preference as being in unison with that worn by our young neophyte, Samdadchiemba.

We announced to the Christians of the inn that we were resolved no longer to look like Chinese merchants; that we were about to cut off our long tails, and to shave our heads. This intimation created great agitation: some of our disciples even wept; all sought by their eloquence to divert us from a resolution which seemed to them fraught with danger; but their pathetic remonstrances were of no avail; one touch of a razor, in the hands of Samdadchiemba, sufficed to sever the long tail of hair, which, to accommodate Chinese fashions, we had so carefully cultivated ever since our departure from France. We put on a long yellow robe, fastened at the right side with five gilt buttons, and round the waist by a long red sash; over this was a red jacket, with a collar of purple velvet; a yellow cap, surmounted by a red tuft, completed our new costume. Breakfast followed this decisive operation, but it was silent and sad. When the Comptroller of the Chest brought in some glasses and an urn, wherein smoked the hot wine drunk by the Chinese, we told him

The Missionaries in their Lamanesque Costume.

that having changed our habit of dress, we should change also our habit of living. "Take away," said we, "that wine and that chafing dish; henceforth we renounce drinking and smoking. You know," added we, laughing, "that good Lamas abstain from wine and tobacco." The Chinese Christians who surrounded us did not join in the laugh; they looked at us without speaking and with deep commiseration, fully persuaded that we should inevitably perish of privation and misery in the deserts of Tartary. Breakfast finished, while the people of the inn were packing up our tent, saddling the camels, and preparing for our departure, we took a couple of rolls, baked in the steam of the furnace, and walked out to complete our meal with some wild currants growing on the bank of the adjacent rivulet. It was soon announced to us that everything was ready—so, mounting our respective animals, we proceeded on the road to Tolon-Noor, accompanied by Samdadchiemba.

We were now launched, alone and without a guide, amid a new world. We had no longer before us paths traced out by the old missionaries, for we were in a country where none before us had preached Gospel truth. We should no longer have by our side those earnest Christian converts, so zealous to serve us; so anxious, by their friendly care, to create around us as it were an atmosphere of home. We were abandoned to ourselves, in a hostile land, without a friend to advise or to aid us, save Him by whose strength we were supported, and whose name we were seeking to make known to all the nations of the earth.

As we have just observed, Samdadchiemba was our only traveling companion. This young man was neither Chinese, nor Tartar, nor Thibetian. Yet, at the first glance, it was easy to recognize in him the features characterizing that which naturalists call the Mongol race. A great flat nose, insolently turned up; a large mouth, slit in a perfectly straight line, thick, projecting lips, a deep bronze complexion, every feature contributed to give to his physiognomy a wild and scornful aspect. When his little eyes seemed starting out of his head from under their lids, wholly destitute of eyelash, and he looked at you wrinkling his brow, he inspired you at once with feelings of dread and yet of confidence. The face was without any decisive character : it exhibited neither the mischievous knavery of the Chinese, nor the frank good-nature of the Tartar, nor the courageous energy of the Thibetian; but was made up of a mixture of all three. Samdadchiemba was a *Dchiahour.* We shall hereafter have occasion to speak more in detail of the native country of our young cameleer.

Samdadchiemba.

At the age of eleven, Samdadchiemba had escaped from his Lamasery, in order to avoid the too frequent and too severe corrections of the master under whom he was more immediately placed. He afterwards passed the greater portion of his vagabond youth, sometimes in the Chinese towns, sometimes in the deserts of Tartary. It is easy to comprehend that this independent course of life had not tended to modify the natural asperity of his character; his intellect was entirely uncultivated; but, on the other hand, his muscular power was enormous, and he was not a little vain of this quality, which he took great pleasure in parading. After having been instructed and baptized by M.-Gabet, he had attached himself to the service of the missionaries. The journey we were now undertaking was perfectly in harmony with his erratic and adventurous taste. He was, however, of no mortal service to us as a guide across the deserts of Tartary, for he knew no more of the country than we knew ourselves. Our only informants were a compass, and the excellent map of the Chinese empire by Andriveau-Goujon.

The first portion of our journey, after leaving Yan-Pa-Eul, was accomplished without interruption, sundry anathemas excepted, which were hurled against us as we ascended a mountain, by a party of Chinese merchants, whose mules, upon sight of our camels and our own yellow attire, became frightened, and took to their heels at full speed, dragging after them, and in one or two instances, overturning the wagons to which they were harnessed.

The mountain in question is called *Sain-Oula* (Good-Mountain), doubtless *ut lucus a non lucendo*, since it is notorious for the dismal accidents and tragical adventures of which it is the theater. The ascent is by a rough, steep path, half-choked up with fallen rocks. Midway up is a small temple, dedicated to the divinity of the mountain,

Mountain of Sain-Oula.

Sain-Nai, (the Good Old Woman;) the occupant is a priest, whose business it is, from time to time, to fill up the cavities in the road, occasioned by the previous rains, in consideration of which service he receives from each passenger a small gratuity, constituting his revenue. After a toilsome journey of nearly three hours we found ourselves at the summit of the mountain, upon an immense plateau, extending from east to west a long day's journey, and from north to south still more widely. From this summit you discern, afar off in the plains of Tartary, the tents of the Mongols, ranged semi-circularly on the slopes of the hills, and looking in the distance like so many beehives. Several rivers derive their source from the sides of this mountain. Chief among these is the *Chara-Mouren* (Yellow River—distinct, of course, from the great Yellow River of China, the *Hoang-Ho*)—the capricious course of which the eye can follow on through the kingdom of *Gechekten*, after traversing which, and then the district of *Naiman*, it passes the stake-boundary into Mantchouria, and flowing from north to south, falls into the sea, approaching which it assumes the name *Léao-Ho*.

The *Good Mountain* is noted for its intense frosts. There is not a winter passes in which the cold there does not kill many travelers. Frequently whole caravans, not arriving at their destination on the other side of the mountain, are sought and found on its bleak road, man and beast frozen to death. Nor is the danger less from the robbers and the wild beasts with whom the mountain is a favorite haunt, or rather a permanent station. Assailed by the brigands, the unlucky traveler is stripped, not merely of horse and money, and baggage, but absolutely of the clothes he wears, and then left to perish from cold and hunger.

Not but that the brigands of these parts are extremely polite all the while; they do not rudely clap a pistol to your ear, and bawl at you: "Your money or your life!" No; they mildly advance with a courteous salutation: "Venerable elder brother, I am on foot; pray lend me your horse —I've got no money, be good enough to lend me your purse—It's quite cold to-day, oblige me with the loan of your coat." If the venerable elder brother charitably complies, the matter ends with, "Thanks, brother;" but otherwise, the request is forthwith emphasized with the arguments of a cudgel; and if these do not convince, recourse is had to the saber.

The sun declining ere we had traversed this platform, we resolved to encamp for the night. Our first business was to seek a position combining the three essentials of fuel, water, and pasturage; and, having due regard to the ill reputation of the *Good Mountain*, privacy from observation as complete as could be effected. Being novices in traveling, the idea of robbers haunted us incessantly, and we took everybody we saw to be a suspicious character,

First Encampment.

against whom we must be on our guard. A grassy nook, surrounded by tall trees, appertaining to the Imperial Forest, fulfilled our requisites. Unlading our dromedaries, we raised, with no slight labor, our tent beneath the foliage, and at its entrance installed our faithful porter, Arsalan, a dog whose size, strength, and courage well entitled him to his appellation, which, in the Tartar-Mongol dialect, means, "Lion." Collecting some *argols*[1] and dry branches of trees, our kettle was soon in agitation, and we threw into the boiling water some Kouamien, prepared paste, something like Vermicelli, which, seasoned with some parings of bacon, given us by our friends at Yan-Pa-Eul, we hoped would furnish satisfaction for the hunger that began to gnaw us. No sooner was the repast ready, than each of us, drawing forth from his girdle his wooden cup, filled it with Kouamien, and raised it to his lips. The preparation was detestable—uneatable. The manufacturers of Kouamien always salt it for its longer preservation; but this paste of ours had been salted beyond all endurance. Even Arsalan would not eat the composition. Soaking it for a while in

[1] Dried dung, which constitutes the chief, and indeed in many places the sole fuel in Tartary.

cold water, we once more boiled it up, but in vain; the dish remained nearly as salt as ever; so, abandoning it to Arsalan and to Samdadchiemba, whose stomach by long use was capable of anything, we were fain to content ourselves with the *dry-cold*, as the Chinese say; and taking with us a couple of small loaves, walked into the Imperial Forest, in order at least to season our repast with an agreeable walk. Our first nomade supper, however, turned out better than we had expected, Providence placing in our path numerous *Ngao-la-Eul* and *Chan-ly-Houng* trees, the former, a shrub about five inches high, which bears a pleasant wild cherry; the other, also a low but very bushy shrub, producing a small scarlet apple, of a sharp agreeable flavor, of which a very succulent jelly is made.

The Imperial Forest extends more than a hundred leagues from north to south, and nearly eighty from east to west. The Emperor Khang-Hi, in one of his expeditions into Mongolia, adopted it as a hunting ground. He repaired thither every year, and his successors regularly followed his example, down to *Kia-King*, who, upon a hunting excursion, was killed by lightning at *Ge-ho-Eul*. There has been no imperial hunting there since that time—now twenty-seven years ago. *Tao-Kouang*, son and successor of *Kia-King*, being persuaded that a fatality impends over the exercise of the chase, since his accession to the throne has never set foot in *Ge-ho-Eul*, which may be regarded as the Versailles of the Chinese potentates. The forest, however, and the animals which inhabit it, have been no gainers by the circumstance. Despite the penalty of perpetual exile decreed against all who shall be found, with arms in their hands, in the forest, it is always half full of poachers and wood-cutters. Gamekeepers, indeed, are stationed at intervals throughout the forest; but they seem there merely for the purpose of enjoying a monopoly of the sale of game and wood. They let any one steal either, provided they themselves get the larger share of the booty. The poachers are in especial force from the fourth to the seventh moon. At this period, the antlers of the stags send forth new shoots, which contain a sort of half-coagulated blood, called *Lou-joung*, which plays a distinguished part in the Chinese *Materia Medica*, for its supposed chemical qualities, and fetches accordingly an exorbitant price. A *Lou-joung* sometimes sells for as much as a hundred and fifty ounces of silver.

Deer of all kinds abound in the forest; and tigers, bears, wild boars, panthers, and wolves are scarcely less numerous. Woe to the hunters and wood-cutters who venture otherwise than in large parties into the recesses of the forest; they disappear, leaving no vestige behind.

The fear of encountering one of these wild beasts kept us from prolonging our walk. Besides, night was setting in, and we hastened back to our tent. Our first slumber in the desert was peaceful, and next morning early, after a breakfast of oatmeal steeped in tea, we resumed our march along the great *Plateau*. We soon reached the great *Obo*, whither the Tartars resort to worship the Spirit of the Mountain.

Buddhist Monuments.

The monument is simply an enormous pile of stones, heaped up without any order, and surmounted with dried branches of trees, from which hang bones and strips of cloth, on which are inscribed verses in the Thibet and Mongol languages. At its base is a large granite urn in which the devotees burn incense. They offer, besides, pieces of money, which the next Chinese passenger, after sundry ceremonious genuflexions before the Obo, carefully collects and pockets for his own particular benefit.

These Obos, which occur so frequently throughout Tartary, and which are the objects of constant pilgrimages on the part of the Mongols, remind one of the *loca excelsa* denounced by the Jewish prophets.

It was near noon before the ground, beginning to slope, intimated that we approached the termination of the plateau. We then descended rapidly into a deep valley, where we found a small Mongolian encampment, which we passed without pausing, and set up our tent for the night on the margin of a pool further on. We were now in the kingdom of Gechekten, an undulating country, well watered, with abundance of fuel and pasturage, but desolated by bands of robbers. The Chinese, who have long since taken possession of it, have rendered it a sort of general refuge for malefactors; so that "man of Gechekten" has become a synonym for a person without fear of God or man, who will commit any murder, and shrink from no crime. It would seem as though, in this country, nature resented the encroachments of man upon her rights. Wherever the plough has passed, the soil has become poor, arid, and sandy, producing nothing but oats, which constitute the food of the people. In the whole district there is but one trading town, which the Mongols call *Altan-Somé*, (Temple of Gold). This was at first a great Lamasery, containing nearly 2000 Lamas. By degrees Chinese have settled there, in order to traffic with the Tartars. In 1843, when we had occasion to visit this place, it had already acquired the importance of a town. A highway, commencing at Altan-Somé, proceeds towards the north, and after traversing the country of the *Khalkhas*, the river *Keroulan*, and the *Khinggan* mountains, reaches Nertechink, a town of Siberia.

The sun had just set, and we were occupied inside the tent boiling our tea, when Arsalan warned us, by his barking, of the approach of some stranger. We soon heard the trot of a horse, and presently a mounted Tartar appeared at the door. "*Mendou*," he exclaimed, by way of respectful salutation to the supposed Lamas, raising his joined hands at the same time to his forehead. When we invited him to drink a cup of tea with us, he fastened his horse to one of the tent-pegs, and seated himself by the hearth. "Sirs Lamas," said he, "under what quarter of the heavens were you born?" "We are from the western heaven; and you, whence come you?" "My poor abode is towards the north, at the end of the valley you see there on our right." "Your country is a fine country." The Mongol shook his head sadly, and made no reply. "Brother," we proceeded, after a moment's silence, "the Land of Grass is still very extensive in the kingdom of Gechekten. Would it not be better to cultivate your plains? What good are these bare lands to you? Would not fine crops of corn be preferable to mere grass?" He replied, with a tone of deep and settled conviction, "We Mongols are formed for living in tents, and pasturing cattle. So long as we kept to that in the kingdom of Gechekten, we were rich and happy. Now, ever since the Mongols have set themselves to cultivating the land, and building houses, they have become poor. The *Kitats* (Chinese) have taken possession of the country; flocks, herds, lands, houses, all have passed into their hands. There remain to us only a few prairies, on which still live, under their tents, such of the Mongols as have not been forced by utter destitution to emigrate to other lands." "But if the Chinese are so baneful to you, why did you let them penetrate into your country?" "Your words are the words of truth, Sirs Lamas; but you are aware that the Mongols are men of simple hearts. We took pity on these wicked Kitats, who came to us weeping, to solicit our charity. We allowed them, through pure compassion, to cultivate a few patches of land. The Mongols insensibly followed their example, and abandoned the nomadic life. They drank the wine of the Kitats, and smoked their tobacco, on credit; they bought their manufactures on credit at double the real value. When the day of payment came, there was no money ready, and the Mongols had to yield, to the violence of their creditors, houses, lands, flocks, everything." "But could you not seek justice from the tribunals?" "Justice from the tribunals! Oh, that is out of the question. The Kitats are skilful to talk and to lie. It is impossible for a Mongol to gain a suit against a Kitat. Sirs Lamas, the kingdom of Gechekten is undone!" So saying, the poor Mongol rose, bowed, mounted his horse, and rapidly disappeared in the desert.

We travelled two more days through this kingdom, and

everywhere witnessed the poverty and wretchedness of its scattered inhabitants. Yet the country is naturally endowed with astonishing wealth, especially in gold and silver mines, which of themselves have occasioned many of its worst calamities. Notwithstanding the rigorous prohibition to work these mines, it sometimes happens that large bands of Chinese outlaws assemble together, and march, sword in hand, to dig into them. These are men professing to be endowed with a peculiar capacity for discovering the precious metals, guided, according to their own account, by the conformation of mountains, and the sorts of plants they produce. One single man, possessed of this fatal gift, will suffice to spread desolation over a whole district. He speedily finds himself at the head of thousands and thousands of outcasts, who overspread the country, and render it the theater of every crime. While some are occupied in working the mines others pillage the surrounding districts, sparing neither persons nor property, and committing excesses which the imagination could not conceive, and which continue until some mandarin, powerful and courageous enough to suppress them, is brought within their operation, and takes measures against them accordingly.

Calamities of this nature have frequently desolated the kingdom of Gechekten; but none of them are comparable with what happened in the kingdom of Ouniot, in 1841. A Chinese *mine discoverer*, having ascertained the presence of gold in a particular mountain, announced the discovery, and robbers and vagabonds at once congregated around him, from far and near, to the number of 12,000. This hideous mob put the whole country under subjection, and exercised for two years its fearful sway. Almost the entire mountain passed through the crucible, and such enormous quantities of metal were produced, that the price of gold fell in China fifty per cent. The inhabitants complained incessantly to the Chinese mandarins, but in vain; for these worthies only interfere where they can do so with some benefit to themselves. The King of Ouniot himself feared to measure his strength with such an army of desperadoes.

One day, however, the Queen of Ouniot, repairing on a pilgrimage to the tomb of her ancestors, had to pass the valley in which the army of miners was assembled. Her car was surrounded; she was rudely compelled to alight, and it was only upon the sacrifice of her jewels that she was permitted to proceed. Upon her return home, she reproached the King bitterly for his cowardice. At length,

Military Mandarin.

stung by her words, he assembled the troops of his two banners, and marched against the miners. The engagement which ensued was for a while doubtful; but at length the miners were driven in by the Tartar cavalry, who massacred them without mercy. The bulk of the survivors took refuge in the mine. The Mongols blocked up the apertures with huge stones. The cries of the despairing wretches within were heard for a few days, and then ceased forever. Those of the miners who were taken alive had their eyes put out, and were then dismissed.

We had just quitted the kingdom of Gechekten, and entered that of Thakar, when we came to a military encampment, where were stationed a party of Chinese soldiers charged with the preservation of the public safety. The hour of repose had arrived; but these soldiers, instead of giving us confidence by their presence, increased, on the contrary, our fears; for we knew that they were themselves the most daring robbers in the whole district. We turned aside, therefore, and ensconced ourselves between two rocks, where we found just space enough for our tent. We had scarcely set up our temporary abode, when we observed, in the distance, on the slope of the mountains, a numerous body of horsemen at full gallop. Their rapid but irregular evolutions seemed to indicate that they were pursuing something which constantly evaded them. By and by, two of the horsemen, perceiving us, dashed up to our tent, dismounted, and threw themselves on the ground at the door. They were Tartar-Mongols. "Men of prayer," said they, with voices full of emotion, "we come to ask you to draw our horoscope. We have this day had two horses stolen from us. We have fruitlessly sought traces of the robbers, and we therefore come to you, men whose power and learning is beyond all limit, to tell us where we shall find our property." "Brothers," said we, "we are not Lamas of Buddha; we do not believe in horoscopes. For a man to say that he can, by any such means, discover that which is stolen, is for them to put forth the words of falsehood and deception." The poor Tartars redoubled their solicitations; but when they found that we were inflexible in our resolution, they remounted their horses, in order to return to the mountains.

Samdadchiemba, meanwhile, had been silent, apparently paying no attention to the incident, but fixed at the fire-place, with his bowl of tea to his lips. All of a sudden he knitted his brows, rose, and came to the door. The horsemen were at some distance; but the Dchiahour, by an exertion of his strong lungs, induced them to turn round in their saddles. He motioned to them, and they, supposing we had relented, and were willing to draw the desired horoscope, galloped once more towards us. When they had come within speaking distance:—"My Mongol brothers," cried Samdadchiemba, "in future be more careful; watch your herds well, and you won't be robbed. Retain these words of mine on your memory: they are worth all the horoscopes in the world." After this friendly address, he gravely re-entered the tent, and seating himself at the hearth, resumed his tea.

We were at first somewhat disconcerted by this singular proceeding; but as the horsemen themselves did not take the matter in ill part, but quietly rode off, we burst into a laugh. "Stupid Mongols!" grumbled Samdadchiemba; "they don't give themselves the trouble to watch their animals, and then, when they are stolen from them, they run about wanting people to draw horoscopes for them. After all, perhaps, it's no wonder, for nobody but ourselves tells them the truth. The Lamas encourage them in their credulity; for they turn it into a source of income. It is difficult to deal with such people. If you tell them you can't draw a horoscope, they don't believe you, and merely suppose you don't choose to oblige them. To get rid of them, the best way is to give them an answer haphazard." And here Samdadchiemba laughed with such expansion, that his little eyes were completely buried. "Did you ever draw a horoscope?" asked we. "Yes," replied he, still laughing. "I was very young at the time, not more than fifteen. I was traveling through the Red Banner of Thakar, when I was addressed by some Mongols who led me into their tent. There they entreated me to tell them, by means of divination, where a bull had strayed, which had been missing three days. It was to no purpose that I protested to them I could not perform divination, that I could not even read. 'You deceive us,' said they; 'you are a *Dchiahour* and we know that the Western Lamas can all divine more or less.' As the only way of extricating myself from the dilemma, I resolved to imitate what I had seen the Lamas do in their divinations. I directed one person to collect eleven sheep's droppings, the dryest he could find. They were immediately brought. I then seated myself very gravely; I counted the droppings over and over; I arranged them in rows, and then counted them again; I rolled them up and down in threes; and then appeared to meditate. At last I said to the Mongols, who were impatiently awaiting the result of the horoscope:—'If you would find your bull, go seek him towards the north.' Before the words were well out of my mouth, four men were on horseback, galloping off towards the north. By the most curious chance in the world, they had not proceeded far, before the missing animal made its appearance, quietly browsing. I at once got the character of a diviner of the first class, was entertained in the most liberal manner for a week, and when I departed had a stock of butter and tea given me enough for another week. Now that I belong to Holy Church, I know that these things are wicked and prohibited; otherwise I would have given these horsemen a word or two of horoscope, which perhaps would have procured for us, in return, a good cup of tea with butter."

The stolen horses confirmed in our minds the ill reputation of the country in which we were now encamped; and we felt ourselves necessitated to take additional precaution. Before night-fall we brought in the horse and the mule, and fastened them by cords to pins at the door of our tent, and made the camels kneel by their side, so as to close up the entrance. By this arrangement no one could get near us without our having full warning given us by the camels, which, at the least noise, always make an outcry loud enough to awaken the deepest sleeper. Finally, having suspended from one of the tent-poles our traveling lantern, which we kept burning all the night, we endeavored to obtain a little repose, but in vain; the night passed away, without our getting a wink of sleep. As to the *Dchiahour*, whom nothing ever troubled, we heard him snoring with all the might of his lungs until daybreak.

We made our preparations for departure very early, for we were eager to quit this ill-famed place, and to reach *Tolon-Noor*, which was now distant only a few leagues.

On our way thither, a horseman stopped his galloping steed, and, after looking at us for a moment, addressed us: "You are the chiefs of the Christians of the Contiguous Defiles?" Upon our replying in the affirmative, he dashed off again; but turned his head once or twice, to have another look at us. He was a Mongol, who had charge of some herds at the Contiguous Defiles. He had often seen us there; but the novelty of our present costume at first prevented his recognizing us. We met also the Tartars who, the day before, had asked us to draw a horoscope for them. They had repaired by daybreak, to the horse-fair at *Tolon-Noor*, in the hope of finding their stolen animals; but their search had been unsuccessful.

The increasing number of travelers, Tartars and Chinese, whom we now met, indicated the approach to the great town of Tolon-Noor. We already saw in the distance, glittering under the sun's rays, the gilt roofs of two magnificent Lamaseries that stand in the northern suburbs of the town. We journeyed for some time through a succession of cemeteries; for here, as elsewhere, the present generation is surrounded by the ornamental sepulchers of past generations. As we observed the numerous population of that large town, environed as it were by a vast circle of bones and monumental stones, it seemed as though death was continuously engaged in the blockade of life. Here and there, in the vast cemetery which completely encircles the city, we remarked little gardens, where, by dint of extreme labor, a few miserable vegetables were extracted from the earth: leeks, spinach, hard bitter lettuces, and cabbages, which, introduced some years since from Russia, have adapted themselves exceedingly well to the climate of Northern China.

With the exception of these few esculents, the environs of Tolon-Noor produced absolutely nothing whatever. The soil is dry and sandy, and water terribly scarce. It is only here and there that a few limited springs are found, and these are dried up in the hot season.

City of Tolon-Noor.

CHAPTER II.

Inn at Tolon-Noor—Aspect of the City—Great Foundries of Bells and Idols—Conversation with the Lamas of *Tolon-Noor*—Encampment—Tea-Bricks—Meeting with Queen *Mourguevan*—Taste of the Mongols for Pilgrimages—Violent Storm—Account from a Mongol Chief of the War of the English against China—Topography of the Eight Banners of the *Tchakar*—The Imperial herds—Form and Interior of the Tents—Tartar Manners and Customs—Encampment at the Three Lakes—Nocturnal Apparitions—Samdadchiemba relates the Adventures of his Youth—Gray Squirrels of Tartary—Arrival at *Chaborté*.

Our entrance into the city of Tolon-Noor was fatiguing and full of perplexity; for we knew not where to take up our abode. We wandered about for a long time in a labyrinth of narrow, tortuous streets, encumbered with men and animals and goods. At last we found an inn. We unloaded our dromedaries, deposited the baggage in a small room, foddered the animals, and then, having affixed to the door of our room the padlock which, as is the custom, our landlord gave us for that purpose, we sallied forth in quest of dinner. A triangular flag floating before a house in the next street indicated to our joyful hearts an eating-house.

A long passage led us into a spacious apartment, in which were symmetrically set forth a number of little tables. Seating ourselves at one of these, a tea-pot, the inevitable prelude in these countries to every meal, was set before each of us. You must swallow infinite tea, and that boiling hot, before they will consent to bring you anything else. At last, when they see you thus occupied, the Comptroller of the Table pays you his official visit, a personage of immensely elegant manners, and ceaseless volubility of tongue, who, after entertaining you with his views upon the affairs of the world in general, and each country in particular, concludes by announcing what there is to eat, and requesting your judgment thereupon. As you mention the dishes you desire, he repeats their names in a measured chant, for the information of the Governor of the Pot. Your dinner is served up with admirable promptitude; but before you commence the meal, etiquette requires that you rise from your seat, and invite all the other company present to partake. "Come," you say, with an engaging gesture, "come my friends, come and drink a glass of wine with me; come and eat a plate of rice;" and so on. "No, thank you," replies everybody; "do you rather come and seat yourself at my table. It is I who invite you;" and so the matter ends. By this ceremony you have "manifested your honor," as the phrase runs, and you may now sit down and eat it in comfort, your character as a gentleman perfectly established.

When you rise to depart, the Comptroller of the Table again appears. As you cross the apartment with him, he chants over again the names of the dishes you have had, this time appending the prices, and terminating with the sum total, announced with especial emphasis, which, proceeding to the counter, you then deposit in the money-box. In general, the Chinese restaurateurs are quite as skilful as those of France in exciting the vanity of the guests, and promoting the consumption of their commodities.

Two motives had induced us to direct our steps, in the first instance, to Tolon-Noor: we desired to make more purchases there to complete our traveling equipment, and, secondly, it appeared to us necessary to place ourselves in communication with the Lamas of the country, in order to obtain information from them as to the more important localities of Tartary. The purchases we needed to make gave us occasion to visit the different quarters of the town. Tolon-Noor (Seven Lakes) is called by the Chinese *Lama-Miao* (Convent of Lamas). The Mantchous designate it the *Nadan-Omo*, and the Thibetians, the *Tsot-Dun*, both translations of Tolon-Noor, and, equally with it, meaning "Seven Lakes." On the map published by M. Andriveau-Goujon,[1] this town is called *Djo-Naiman-Soumé*, which in Mongol means, "The Hundred and Eight Convents." This name is perfectly unknown in the country itself.

Tolon-Noor is not a walled city, but a vast agglomeration of hideous houses, which seem to have been thrown together with a pitchfork. The carriage portion of the streets is a marsh of mud and putrid filth, deep enough to stifle and bury the smaller beasts of burden that not unfrequently fall within it, and whose carcases remain to aggravate the general stench; while their loads become the prey of the innumerable thieves who are ever on the alert. The foot-path is a narrow, rugged, slippery line on either side, just wide enough to admit the passage of one person.

Yet, despite the nastiness of the town itself, the sterility of the environs, the excessive cold of its winter, and the intolerable heat of its summer, its population is immense, and its commerce enormous. Russian merchandise is brought hither in large quantities by the way of Kiakta. The Tartars bring incessant herds of camels, oxen, and horses, and carry back in exchange tobacco, linen, and tea. This constant arrival and departure of strangers communicates to the city an animated and varied aspect. All sorts of hawkers are at every corner offering their petty wares; the regular traders, from behind their counters, invite with honeyed words and tempting offers, the passers-by to come in and buy. The Lamas, in their red and yellow robes, gallop up and down, seeking admiration for their equestrianism, and the skilful management of their fiery steeds.

The trade of Tolon-Noor is mostly in the hands of men from the province of *Chan-Si*, who seldom establish themselves permanently in the town; but after a few years, when their money-chest is filled, return to their own country. In this vast emporium, the Chinese invariably make fortunes,

[1] With the exception of a very few inaccuracies, this map of the Chinese empire is a most excellent one. We found it of the most valuable aid throughout our journey.—Huc.

An English version of the map is prefixed to this volume.—Ed.

and the Tartars invariably are ruined. Tolon-Noor, in fact, is a sort of great pneumatic pump, constantly at work in emptying the pockets of the unlucky Mongols.

The magnificent statues, in bronze and brass, which issue from the great foundries of Tolon-Noor, are celebrated not only throughout Tartary, but in the remotest districts of Thibet. Its immense workshops supply all the countries subject to the worship of Buddha with idols, bells, and vases employed in that idolatry. While we were in the town, a monster statue of Buddha, a present from a friend of Oudchou-Mourdchin to the Talè-Lama, was packed for Thibet, on the backs of six camels. The larger statues are cast in detail, the component parts being afterward soldered together.

Bell and Idol Foundry.

We availed ourselves of our stay at Tolon-Noor to have a figure of Christ constructed on the model of a bronze original which we had brought with us from France. The workmen so marvelously excelled, that it was difficult to distinguish the copy from the original. The Chinese work more rapidly and cheaply, and their complaisance contrasts most favorably with the tenacious self-opinion of their brethren in Europe.

During our stay at Tolon-Noor, we had frequent occasion to visit the Lamaseries, or Lama monasteries, and to converse with the idolatrous priests of Buddhism. The Lamas appeared to us persons of very limited information; and as to their symbolism, in general, it is little more refined or purer than the creed of the vulgar. Their doctrine is still undecided, fluctuating amidst a vast fanaticism of which they can give no intelligible account. When we asked them for some distinct, clear, positive idea what they meant, they were always thrown into utter embarrassment, and stared at one another. The disciples told us that their masters knew all about it; the masters referred us to the omniscience of the Grand Lamas; the Grand Lamas confessed themselves ignorant, but talked of some wonderful saint, in some Lamasery at the other end of the country: *he* could explain the whole affair. However, all of them, disciples and masters, great Lamas and small, agree in this that their doctrine came from the West: "The nearer you approach the West," said they unanimously, "the purer and more luminous will the doctrine manifest itself. When we expounded to them the truths of Christianity, they never discussed the matter; they contented themselves with calmly saying, "Well, we don't suppose that our prayers are the only prayers in the world. The Lamas of the West will explain everything to you. We believe in the traditions that have come from the West."

In point of fact there is no Lamasery of any importance in Tartary, the Grand Lama or superior of which is not a man from Thibet. Any Tartar Lama who has visited *Lha-Ssa* [Land of Spirits], or *Monhe-Dhot* [Eternal Sanctuary], as it is called in the Mongol dialect, is received, on his return, as a man to whom the mysteries of the past and of the future have been unveiled.

After maturely weighing the information we had obtained from the Lamas, it was decided that we should direct our steps towards the West. On October 1st we quitted Tolon-Noor; and it was not without infinite trouble that we managed to traverse the filthy town with our camels. The poor animals could only get through the quagmire streets by fits and starts; it was first a stumble, then a convulsive jump, then another stumble and another jump, and so on. Their loads shook on their backs, and at every step we expected to see the camel and camel-load prostrate in the mud. We considered ourselves lucky when, at distant intervals, we came to a comparatively dry spot, where the camels could travel, and we were thus enabled to readjust and tighten the baggage. Samdadchiemba got into a desperate ill temper; he went on, and slipped, and went on again, without uttering a single word, restricting the visible manifestation of his wrath to a continuous biting of the lips.

Upon attaining at length the western extremity of the town, we got clear of the filth indeed, but found ourselves involved in another evil. Before us there was no road marked out, not the slightest trace of even a path. There was nothing but an apparently interminable chain of small hills, composed of fine, moving sand, over which it was impossible to advance at more than a snail's pace, and this only with extreme labor. Among these sand-hills, moreover, we were oppressed with an absolutely stifling heat. Our animals were covered with perspiration, ourselves devoured with a burning thirst; but it was in vain that we looked round in all directions, as we proceeded, for water; not a spring, not a pool, not a drop presented itself.

It was already late, and we began to fear we should find no spot favorable for the erection of our tent. The ground, however, grew by degrees firmer, and we at last discerned some signs of vegetation. By and by, the sand almost disappeared, and our eyes were rejoiced with the sight of continuous verdure. On our left, at no great distance, we saw the opening of a defile. M. Gabet urged on his camel, and went to examine the spot. He soon made his appearance at the summit of a hill, and with voice and hand directed us to follow him. We hastened on, and found that Providence had led us to a favorable position. A small pool, the waters of which were half concealed by thick reeds and other marshy vegetation, some brushwood, a plot of grass: what could we under the circumstances desire more? Hungry, thirsty, weary as we were, the place seemed a perfect Eden.

The camels were no sooner squatted, than we all three, with one accord, and without a word said, seized, each man his wooden cup, and rushed to the pond to satisfy his thirst. The water was fresh enough; but it affected the nose violently with its strong muriatic odor. I remembered to have drunk water just like it in the Pyrenees, at the good town of Ax, and to have seen it for sale in the chemists' shops elsewhere in France: and I remembered, further, that by reason of its being particularly stinking and particularly nasty, it was sold there at fifteen sous per bottle.

After having quenched our thirst, our strength by degrees returned, and we were then able to fix our tent, and each man to set about his especial task. M. Gabet proceeded to cut some bundles of horn-beam wood; Samdadchiemba collected argols in the flap of his jacket; and M. Huc, seated at the entrance of the tent, tried his hand at drawing a fowl, a process which Arsalan, stretched at his side, watched with greedy eye, having immediate reference to the entrails in course of removal. We were resolved, for once and away, to have a little festival in the desert; and to take the opportunity to indulge our patriotism by initiating our *Dchiahour* in the luxury of a dish prepared according to the rules of the *cuisinier Français*. The fowl, artistically dismembered, was placed at the bottom of our great pot. A few roots of synapia, prepared in salt water, some onions, a clove of garlic, and some allspice, constituted the seasoning. The preparation was soon boiling, for we were that day rich in fuel. Samdadchiemba, by and by, plunged his hand into the pot, drew out a limb of the fowl, and, after carefully inspecting it, pronounced supper to be ready. The pot was taken from the trivet, and placed upon the grass. We all three seated ourselves around it, so that our knees almost touched it, and each, armed with two chopsticks, fished out the pieces he desired from the abundant broth before him.

When the meal was completed, and we had thanked God for the repast he had thus provided us with in the desert, Samdadchiemba went and washed the caldron in the pond. That done, he brewed us some tea. The tea used by the Tartars is not prepared in the same way as that consumed by the Chinese. The latter, it is known, merely employ the smaller and tenderer leaves of the plant, which they simply infuse in boiling water, so as to give it a golden tint; the coarser leaves, with which are mixed up the smaller tendrils, are pressed together in a mold, in the form and of the size of the ordinary house brick. Thus prepared, it becomes an article of considerable commerce, under the designation of Tartar tea, the Tartars being its exclusive consumers, with the exception of the Russians, who drink great quantities of it. When required for use, a piece of the brick is broken off, pulverized, and boiled in the kettle, until the water assumes a reddish hue. Some salt is then thrown in, and effervescence commences. When the liquid has become almost black, milk is added, and the beverage, the grand luxury of the Tartars, is then transferred to the teapot. Samdadchiemba was a perfect enthusiast of this tea. For our parts, we drank it in default of something better.

Next morning, after rolling up our tent, we quitted this asylum without regret indeed, for we had selected and occupied it altogether without preference. However, before departing, we set up, as an *ex-voto* of our gratitude for its reception of us for a night, a small wooden cross, on the site of our fireplace, and this precedent we afterwards followed, at all our encamping places. Could missionaries leave a more appropriate memorial of their journey through the desert!

We had not advanced an hour's journey on our way, when we heard behind us the trampling of many horses, and the confused sound of many voices. We looked back, and saw hastening in our direction a numerous caravan. Three horsemen soon overtook us, one of whom, whose costume bespoke him a Tartar mandarin, addressed us with a loud voice, "Sirs, where is your country?" "We come from the west." "Through what districts has your beneficial shadow passed?" "We have last come from Tolon-Noor." "Has peace accompanied your progress?" "Hitherto we have journeyed in all tranquillity. And you: are you at peace? And what is your country?" "We are Khalkhas, of the kingdom of Mourguevan." "Have the rains been abundant? Are your flocks and herds flourishing!" "All goes well in our pasture-grounds." "Whither proceeds your caravan?" "We go to incline our foreheads before the *Five Towers*." The rest of the caravan had joined us in the course of this abrupt and hurried conversation. We were on the banks of a small stream, bordered with brushwood. The chief of the caravan ordered a halt, and the camels formed, as each came up, a circle, in the center of which was drawn up a close carriage upon four wheels. "Sok! sok!" cried the camel drivers, and at the word, and as with one motion, the entire circle of intelligent animals knelt. While numerous tents, taken from their backs, were set up, as it were, by enchantment, two mandarins, decorated with the blue button, approached the carriage, opened the door, and handed out a Tartar lady, covered with a long silk robe. She was the Queen of the Khalkhas repairing in pilgrimage to the famous Lamasery of the Five Towers, in the province of *Chan-Si*. When she saw us, she saluted us with the ordinary form of raising both her hands: "Sirs Lamas," she said, "is this place auspicious for an encampment?" "Royal Pilgrim of Mourguevan," we replied, "you may light your fires here in all security. For ourselves, we must proceed on our way, for the sun was already high when we folded our tent." And so saying, we took our leave of the Tartars of Mourguevan.

Queen of Mourguevan.

Our minds were deeply excited upon beholding this queen

and her numerous suite performing this long pilgrimage through the desert: no danger, no distance, no expense, no privation deters the Mongols from their prosecution. The Mongols are, indeed, an essentially religious people; with them the future life is everything, the things of this world nothing. They live in the world as though they were not of it; they cultivate no lands, they build no houses, they regard themselves as foreigners traveling through life; and this feeling, deep and universal, develops itself in the practical form of incessant journeys.

The taste for pilgrimages which, at all periods of the world's history, has manifested itself in religious people, is a thing worthy of earnest attention. The worship of the true God led the Jews, several times a year, to Jerusalem. In profane antiquity, those who took any heed to religious belief at all repaired to Egypt, in order to be initiated in the mysteries of Osiris, and to seek lessons of wisdom from his priests. It was to travelers that the mysterious sphynx of Mount Phicæus proposed the profound enigma of which Œidpus discovered the solution. In the middle ages, the spirit of pilgrimage held predominant sway in Europe, and the Christians of that epoch were full of fervor for this species of devotion. The Turks, while they were yet believers, repaired to Mecca in great caravans; and in our travels in Central Asia, we constantly met numerous pilgrims going to or fro, all of them profoundly filled with and earnestly impelled by a sincere sentiment of religion. It is to be remarked that pilgrimages have diminished in Europe, in proportion as faith has become rationalist, and as people have taken to discuss the truths of religion. Wherever faith remains earnest, simple, unquestioning, in the breasts of men, these pilgrimages are in vigor. The reason is, that the intensity of simple faith creates a peculiarly profound and energetic feeling of the condition of man, as a wayfarer upon the earth; and it is natural that this feeling should manifest itself in pious wayfarings. Indeed the Catholic Church, which is the depository of all truth, has introduced processions into the liturgy, as a memorial of pilgrimages, and to remind men that this earth is a desert, wherein we commence, with our birth, the awful journey of eternity.

We had left far behind us the pilgrims of Mourguevan,

and began to regret that we had not encamped in their company upon the banks of the pleasant stream, and amid the fat pastures which it fed. Sensations of fear grew upon us, as we saw great clouds arise in the horizon, spread, and gradually obscure the sky. We looked anxiously around, in all directions, for a place in which we could commodiously halt for the night, but we saw no indication whatever of water. While we were deep in this perplexity, some large drops of rain told us that we had no time to lose. "Let us make haste, and set up the tent," cried Samdadchiemba vehemently. "You need not trouble yourselves any more in looking for water; you will have water enough presently. Let us get under shelter before the sky falls on our heads." "That is all very well," said we, "but we must have some water for the animals and ourselves to drink. You alone require a bucket of water for your tea every evening. Where shall we find some water?" "My fathers, you will very speedily have more water than you like. Let us encamp, that's the first thing to be done. As to thirst, no one will need to die of that this evening: dig but a few holes about the tent, and they'll soon overflow with rain-water. But we need not even dig holes," added Samdadchiemba, extending his right hand; "do you see that shepherd there and his flock? You may be sure water is not far off." Following with our eyes the direction of his finger, we perceived in a lateral valley a man driving a large flock of sheep. We immediately turned aside, and hastened after the man. The rain which now began to fall in torrents redoubled our celerity. To aggravate our distress, the lading of one of the camels just at this moment became loose, and slipped right round towards the ground, and we had to wait while the camel knelt; and Samdadchiemba readjusted the baggage on its back. We were, consequently, thoroughly wet through before we reached a small lake, now agitated and swollen by the falling torrent. There was no occasion for deliberating that evening as to the particular site on which we should set up our tent; selection was out of the question, when the ground all about was deeply saturated with the rain.

The violence of the rain itself mitigated; but the wind absolutely raged. We had infinite trouble to unroll our miserable tent heavy and impracticable with wet, like a large sheet just taken from the washing-tub. The difficulty seemed insuperable when we attempted to stretch it upon its poles, and we should never have succeeded at all, but for the extraordinary muscular power with which Samdadchiemba was endowed. At length we effected a shelter from the wind, and from a small cold rain with which it was accompanied. When our lodging was established, Samdadchiemba addressed us in these consolatory words:—"My spiritual fathers, I told you we should not die to-day of thirst; but I am not at all sure that we don't run some risk of dying of hunger." In point of fact, there seemed no possibility of making a fire. There was not a tree, not a shrub, not a root to be seen. As to argols, they were out of the question; the rain had long since reduced that combustible of the desert to a liquid pulp.

We had formed our resolution, and were on the point of making a supper of meal steeped in a little cold water, when we saw approaching us two Tartars, leading a small camel. After the usual salutations, one of them said: "Sirs Lamas, this day the heavens have fallen; you, doubtless, have been unable to make a fire." "Alas! how should we make a fire, when we have no argols?" "Men are all brothers, and belong each to the other. But laymen should honor and serve the holy ones; therefore it is that we have come to make a fire for you." The worthy Tartars had seen us setting up our tent, and conceiving our embarrassment, had hastened to relieve it by a present of two bundles of argols. We thanked Providence for this unexpected succor, and the Dchiahour immediately made a fire, and set about the preparation of an oatmeal supper. The quantity was on this occasion augmented in favor of the two friends who had so opportunely presented themselves.

During our modest repast, we noticed that one of these Tartars was the object of especial attention on the part of his comrade. We asked him what military grade he occupied in the Blue Banner. "When the banners of Tchakar marched two years ago against the Rebels of the South,[1] I held the rank of Tchouanda." "What! were you in that famous war of the South? But how is it that you, shepherds of the plains, have also the courage of soldiers? Ac-

[1] The English, then at war with the Chinese, were designated by the Tartars the *Rebels of the South*.

customed to a life of peace, one would imagine that you would never be reconciled to the terrible trade of a soldier which consists in killing others or being killed yourselves." "Yes, yes, we are shepherds, it is true; but we never forget that we are soldiers also, and that the Eight Banners compose the army of reserve of the Grand Master (the Emperor). You know the rule of the Empire; when the enemy appears, they send against them, first—the *Kitat* soldiers; next, the banners of the *Solon* country are set in motion. If the war is not finished then, all they have to do is to give the signal to the banners of the *Tchakar*, the mere sound of whose march always suffices to reduce the rebels to subjection."

The Emperor Tao-Kouang.

"Were all the banners of Tchakar called together for this southern war?" "Yes, all; at first it was thought a small matter, and every one said that it would never affect the Tchakar. The troops of Kitat went first, but they did nothing; the banners of Solon also marched; but they could not bear the heat of the South;—then the Emperor sent us his sacred order. Each man selected his best horse, removed the dust from his bow and quiver, and scraped the rust from his lance. In every tent a sheep was killed for the feast of departure. Women and children wept, but we addressed to them the words of reason. 'Here,' said we, 'for six generations have we received the benefits of the Sacred Master, and he has asked from us nothing in return. Now that he has need of us can we hold back? He has given to us the fine region of Tchakar to be a pasture-land for our cattle, and at the same time a barrier for him against the Khalkhas. But now, since it is from the South the rebels came, we must march to the South. Was not reason in our mouths, Sirs Lamas? Yes, we resolved to march. The Sacred Ordinance reached us at sunrise, and already by noon the *Bochehous* at the head of their men, stood by the *Tchouanda;* next to these were the *Nourou-Tchayn,* and then the *Ougourda.* The same day we marched to Peking; from Peking they led us to Tien-Tsin-Veï, where we remained for three months." "Did you fight," asked Samdadchiemba; "did you see the enemy?" "No, they did not dare to appear. The Kitat told us everywhere that we were marching upon certain and unavailing death. 'What can you do,' asked they, 'against sea-monsters? They live in the water like fish. When you least expect them, they appear on the surface, and hurl their fire-bombs at you; while, the instant your bow is bent to shoot them, down they dive like frogs.' Then they essayed to frighten us; but we soldiers of the Eight Banners know not fear. Before our departure the great Lamas had opened the Book of Celestial Secrets, and had thence learned that the matter would end well for us. The Emperor had attached to each Tchouanda a Lama learned in medicine, and skilled in all the sacred auguries, who was to cure all the soldiers under him of the diseases of the climate, and to protect us from the magic of the sea-monsters. What then had we to fear? The rebels, hearing that the invincible troops of Tchakar were approaching, were seized with fear, and sought peace. The Sacred Master, of his immense mercy, granted it, and we returned to the care of our flocks."

The narrative of this *Illustrious Sword* was to us full of intense interest. We forgot for a moment the misery of our position amid the desert. We were eager to collect further details of the expedition of the English against China ; but night falling, the two Tartars took their way homeward.

Thus left once more alone, our thoughts became exceedingly sad and somber. We shuddered at the idea so recalled to us of the long night just commencing. How were we to get any sleep ? The interior of the tent was little better than a mud heap; the great fire we had been keeping up had not half dried our clothes ; it had merely resolved a portion of the water into a thick vapor that steamed about us. The furs, which we used at night by way of mattress, were in a deplorable condition, not a whit better for the purpose than the skin of a drowned cat. In this doleful condition of things, a reflection, full of gentle melancholy, came into our minds, and consoled us ; we remembered that we were the disciples of Him who said, "The foxes have holes, and the birds of the air have nests ; but the Son of Man hath not where to lay his head."

We became so fatigued, after remaining awake the greater part of the night, that sleep conquering us, we fell into a restless doze, seated over the embers of the fire, our arms crossed, and our heads bent forward, in the most uncomfortable position possible.

It was with extreme delight that we hailed the termination of that long and dreary night. At daybreak, the blue, cloudless sky, presaged compensation for the wretchedness of the preceding evening. By and by, the sun rising clear and brilliant, inspired us with hope that our still wet clothes would soon get dry as we proceeded on our way. We speedily made all preparations for departure, and the caravan set forth. The weather was magnificent. By degrees, the large grass of the prairie raised its broad head, which had been depressed by the heavy rain ; the ground became firmer, and we experienced, with delight, the gentle heat of the sun's ascending rays. At last, to complete our satisfaction, we entered upon the plains of the Red Banner, the most picturesque of the whole Tchakar.

Tchakar signifies, in the Mongol tongue, *Border Land.* This country is limited, on the east by the kingdom of *Gechekten*, on the west by *Western Toumet*, on the north by the *Souniot*, on the south by the Great Wall. Its extent is 150 leagues long, by 100 broad. The inhabitants of the *Tchakar* are all paid soldiers of the Emperor. The foot soldiers receive twelve ounces of silver per annum, and the cavalry twenty-four.

The *Tchakar* is divided into eight banners—in Chinese *Pa-Ki*—distinguished by the name of eight colors : white, blue, red, yellow, French white, light blue, pink, and light yellow. Each banner has its separate territory, and a tribunal, named *Nourou-Tchayn*, having jurisdiction over all the matters that may occur in the Banner. Besides this tribunal, there is, in each of the Eight Banners, a chief called *Ou-Gourdha*. Of the eight *Ou-Gourdhas* one is selected to fill at the same time, the post of governor-general of the Eight Banners. All these dignitaries are nominated and paid by the Emperor of China. In fact, the Tchakar is nothing more or less than a vast camp, occupied by an army of reserve. In order, no doubt, that this army may be at all times ready to march at the first signal, the Tartars are severely prohibited to cultivate the land. They must live upon their pay, and upon the produce of their flocks and herds. The entire soil of the Eight Banners is inalienable. It sometimes happens that an individual sells his portion to some Chinese ; but the sale is always declared null and void if it comes in any shape before the tribunals.

It is in these pasturages of the Tchakar that are found the numerous and magnificent herds and flocks of the Emperor, consisting of camels, horses, cattle, and sheep. There are 360 herds of horses alone, each numbering 1200 horses. It is easy from this one detail, to imagine the enormous extent of animals possessed here by the Emperor. A Tartar, decorated with the white button, has charge of each herd. At certain intervals, inspectors-general visit the herds, and if any deficiency in the number is discovered, the chief herdsman has to make it good at his own cost. Notwithstanding this impending penalty, the Tartars do not fail to convert to their own use the wealth of the Sacred Master, by means of a fraudulent exchange. Whenever a Chinese has a broken-winded horse, or a lame ox, he takes it to the imperial herdsman, who, for a trifling consideration, allows him to select what animal he pleases in exchange, from among the imperial herds. Being thus always provided with the actual number of animals, they can benefit by their fraud in perfect security.

Never in more splendid weather had we traversed a more splendid country. The desert is at times horrible, hideous; but it has also its charms—charms all the more intensely appreciated, because they are rare in themselves, and because they would in vain be sought in populated countries. Tartary has an aspect altogether peculiar to itself: there is nothing in the world that at all resembles a Tartar landscape. In civilized countries you find, at every step, populous towns, a rich and varied cultivation, the thousand and one productions of arts and industry, the incessant movements of commerce. You are constantly impelled onwards, carried away, as it were, by some vast whirlwind. On the other hand, in countries where civilization has not as yet made its way into the light, you ordinarily find nothing but primeval forests in all the pomp of their exuberant and gigantic vegetation. The soul seems crushed beneath a nature all powerful and majestic. There is nothing of the kind in Tartary. There are no towns, no edifices, no arts, no indusrty, no cultivation, no forests; everywhere it is prairie, sometimes interrupted by immense lakes, by majestic rivers, by rugged and imposing mountains; sometimes spreading out into vast limitless plains. There, in these verdant solitudes, the bounds of which seem lost in the remote horizon, you might imagine yourself gently rocking on the calm waves of some broad ocean. The aspect of the prairies of Mongolia excites neither joy nor sorrow, but rather a mixture of the two, a sentiment of gentle, religious melancholy, which gradually elevates the soul, without wholly excluding from its contemplation the things of this world; a sentiment which belongs rather to Heaven than to earth, and which seems in admirable conformity with the nature of intellect served by organs.

You sometimes in Tartary come upon plains more animated than those you have just traversed; they are those, whither the greater supply of water and the choicest pastures have attracted for a time a number of nomadic families. There you see rising in all directions tents of various dimensions, looking like balloons newly inflated, and just about to take their flight into the air. Children, with a sort of hod at their backs, run about collecting argols, which they pile up in heaps round their respective tents. The matrons look after the calves, make tea in the open air, or prepare milk in various ways ; the men, mounted on fiery horses, and armed with a long pole, gallop about, guiding to the best pastures the great herds of cattle which undulate, in the distance all around, like waves of the sea.

All of a sudden these pictures, so full of animation, disappear, and you see nothing of that which of late was so full of life. Men, tents, herds, all have vanished in the twinkling of an eye. You merely see in the desert heaps of embers, half-extinguished fires, and a few bones, of which birds of prey are disputing the possession. Such are the sole vestiges which announce that a Mongol tribe has just passed that way. If you ask the reason of these abrupt migrations, it is simply this :—the animals having devoured all the grass that grew in the vicinity, the chief had given the signal for departure ; and all the shepherds, folding their tents, had driven their herds before them, and proceded, no matter whither, in search of fresh fields and pastures new.

Tartar Encampment.

After having journeyed the entire day through the delicious prairies of the Red Banner, we halted to encamp for the night in a valley that seemed full of people. We had scarcely alighted, when a number of Tartars approached, and offered their services. After having assisted us to unload our camels, and set up our house of blue linen, they invited us to come and take tea in their tents. As it was late, however, we stayed at home, promising to pay them a visit next morning ; for the hospitable invitation of our new neighbors determined us to remain for a day amongst them. We were, moreover, very well pleased to profit by the beauty of the weather, and of the locality, to recover from the fatigues we had undergone the day before.

Next morning, the time not appropriated to our little household cares, and the recitation of our Breviary, was devoted to visiting the Mongol tents, Samdadchiemba being left at home in charge of the tent.

We had to take especial care to the safety of our legs, menaced by a whole host of watchdogs. A small stick sufficed for the purpose; but Tartar etiquette required us to leave these weapons at the threshold of our host's abode. To enter a man's tent with a whip or a stick in your hand is as great an insult as you can offer to the family; and quite tantamount to saying, "You are all dogs."

Visiting amongst the Tartars is a frank, simple affair, altogether exempt from the endless formalities of Chinese gentility. On entering, you give the word of peace *amor* or *mendou*, to the company generally. You then seat yourself on the right of the head of the family, whom you find squatting on the floor, opposite the entrance. Next, everybody takes from a purse suspended at his girdle a little snuff-bottle, and mutual pinches accompany such phrases as these: "Is the pasturage with you rich and abundant?" "Are your herds in fine condition?" "Are your mares productive?" "Did you travel in peace?" "Does tranquillity prevail?" and so on. These questions and their answers being interchanged always with intense gravity on both sides, the mistress of the tent, without saying a word, holds out her hand to the visitor. He as silently takes from his breast-pocket the small wooden bowl, the indispensable *vade mecum* of all Tartars, and presents it to his hostess, who fills it with tea and milk, and returns it. In the richer, more easily circumstanced families, visitors have a small table placed before them, on which is butter, oatmeal, grated millet, and bits of cheese, separately contained in little boxes of polished wood. These Tartar delicacies the visitors take mixed with their tea. Such as propose to treat their guests in a style of perfect magnificence make them partakers of a bottle of Mongol wine, warmed in the ashes. This wine is nothing more than skimmed milk, subjected for awhile to vinous fermentation, and distilled through a rude apparatus that does the office of an alembic. One must be a thorough Tartar to relish or even endure this beverage, the flavor and odor of which are alike insipid.

The Mongol tent, for about three feet from the ground, is cylindrical in form. It then becomes conical, like a pointed hat. The woodwork of the tent is composed below of a trellis-work of crossed bars, which fold up and expand at pleasure. Above these, a circle of poles, fixed in the trellis-work, meets at the top, like the sticks of an umbrella. Over the woodwork is stretched, once or twice, a thick covering of coarse linen, and thus the tent is composed. The door, which is always a folding door, is low and narrow. A beam crosses it at the bottom by way of threshold, so that on entering you have at once to raise your feet and lower your head. Besides the door there is another opening at the top of the tent to let out the smoke. This opening can at any time be closed with a piece of felt fastened above it in the tent, and which can be pulled over it by means of a string, the end of which hangs by the door.

The interior is divided into two compartments; that on the left, as you enter, is reserved for the men, and thither the visitors proceed. Any man who should enter on the right side would be considered excessively rude. The right compartment is occupied by the women, and there you find the culinary utensils: large earthen vessels of glazed earth, wherein to keep the store of water; trunks of trees, of different sizes, hollowed into the shape of pails, and destined to contain the preparations of milk, in the various forms which they make it undergo. In the center of the tent is a large trivet, planted in the earth, and always ready to receive the large iron bell-shaped caldron that stands by, ready for use.

Behind the hearth, and facing the door, is a kind of sofa, the most singular piece of furniture that we met with among the Tartars. At the two ends are two pillows, having at their extremity plates of copper, gilt, and skilfully engraved. There is probably not a single tent where you do not find this little couch, which seems to be an essential article of

Interior of a Tartar Tent.

furniture; but strange to say, during our long journey we never saw one of them which seemed to have been recently made. We had occasion to visit Mongol families, where everything bore the mark of easy circumstances, even of affluence, but everywhere alike this singular couch was shabby, and of ancient fabric. But yet it seems made to last forever, and is regularly transmitted from generation to generation.

In the towns where Tartar commerce is carried on, you may hunt through every furniture shop, every broker's, every pawnbroker's, but you meet with not one of these pieces of furniture, new or old.

At the side of the couch, towards the men's quarter, there is ordinarily a small square press, which contains the various odds and ends that serve to set off the custom of this simple people. This chest serves likewise as an altar for a small image of Buddha. The divinity, in wood or copper, is usually in a sitting posture, the legs crossed, and enveloped up to the neck in a scarf of old yellow silk. Nine copper vases, of the size and form of our liquor glasses, are symmetrically arranged before Buddha. It is in these small chalices that the Tartars daily make to their idol offerings of water, milk, butter and meal. A few Thibetian books, wrapped in yellow silk, perfect the decoration of the little pagoda. Those whose heads are shaved, and who observe celibacy, have alone the privilege of touching these prayer-books. A layman, who should venture to take them into his impure and profane hands, would commit a sacrilege.

A number of goats' horns, fixed in the woodwork of the tent, complete the furniture of the Mongol habitation. On these hang the joints of beef or mutton destined for the family's use, vessels filled with butter, bows, arrows, and matchlocks; for there is scarcely a Tartar family which does not possess at least one fire-arm. We were, therefore, surprised to find M. Timkouski, in his Journey to Peking,[1] making this strange statement: "The sound of our fire-arms attracted the attention of the Mongols, who are acquainted only with bows and arrows." The Russian writer should have known that fire-arms are not so foreign to the Tartars as he imagined; since it is proved that already, as early as the commencement of the 13th century, *Tcheng-Kis-Khan* had artillery in his armies.

The odor pervading the interior of the Mongol tents, is, to those not accustomed to it, disgusting and almost insupportable. This smell, so potent sometimes that it seems to make one's heart rise to one's throat, is occasioned by the mutton grease and butter with which everything on or about a Tartar is impregnated. It is on account of this habitual filth, that they are called *Tsao-Ta-Dze* (Stinking Tartars), by the Chinese, themselves not altogether inodorous, or by any means particular about cleanliness.

Among the Tartars, household and family cares rest entirely upon the woman; it is she who milks the cows, and prepares the butter, cheese, etc.; who goes, no matter how far, to draw water; who collects the argol fuel, dries it, and piles it around the tent. The making of clothes, the tanning of skins, the fulling of cloth, all appertains to her; the sole assistance she obtains, in these various labors, being that of her sons, and then only while they are quite young.

The occupations of the men are of very limited range; they consist wholly in conducting the flocks and herds to

1 "Voyage à Peking, à travers la Mongolie, par M. G. Timkouski," chap. ii., p. 57.

pasture. This for men accustomed from their infancy to horseback is rather an amusement than a labor. In point of fact, the nearest approach to fatigue they ever incur, is when some of their cattle escape; they then dash off at full gallop, in pursuit, up hill and down dale, until they have found the missing animals, and brought them back to the herd. The Tartars sometimes hunt; but it is rather with a view to what they can catch than from any amusement they derive from the exercise; the only occasions on which they go out with their bows and matchlocks are when they desire to shoot roebucks, deer, or pheasants, as presents for their chiefs. Foxes they always course. To shoot them, or take them in traps, would, they consider, injure the skin, which is held in high estimation among them. They ridicule the Chinese immensely on account of their trapping these animals at night. "We," said a famous hunter of the Red Banner to us, "set about the thing in an honest straightforward way. When we see a fox, we jump on horseback, and gallop after him till we have run him down."

With the exception of their equestrian exercises, the Mongol Tartars pass their time in an absolute *far niente*, sleeping all night, and squatting all day in their tents, dozing, drinking tea, or smoking. At intervals, however, the Tartar conceives a fancy to take a lounge abroad; and his lounge is somewhat different from that of the Parisian idler; he needs neither cane nor quizzing glass; but when the fancy occurs, he takes down his whip from its place above the door, mounts his horse, always ready saddled outside the door, and dashes off into the desert, no matter whither. When he sees another horseman in the distance, he rides up to him; when he sees the smoke of a tent, he rides up to that; the only object in either case being to have a chat with some new person.

The two days we passed in these fine plains of the *Tchakar*, were not without good use. We were able at leisure to dry and repair our clothes and our baggage; but, above all, it gave us an opportunity to study the Tartars close at hand, and to initiate ourselves in the habits of the nomad peoples. As we were making preparations for departure, these temporary neighbors aided us to fold our tent and to load our camels. "Sirs Lamas," said they, "you had better encamp to-night at the Three Lakes; the pasturage there is good and abundant. If you make haste you will reach the place before sunset. On this side, and on the other side of the Three Lakes, there is no water for a considerable distance. Sirs Lamas, a good journey to you!" "Peace be with you, and farewell!" responded we, and with that proceeded once more on our way, Samdadchiemba heading the caravan, mounted on his little black mule. We quitted this encampment without regret, just as we had quitted preceding encampments; except indeed, that here we left, on the spot where our tent had stood, a greater heap of ashes, and that the grass around it was more trodden than was usual with us.

During the morning the weather was magnificent, though somewhat cold. But in the afternoon the north wind rose, and began to blow with extreme violence. It soon became so cutting, that we regretted we had not with us our great fur caps, to operate as a protector for the face. We hurried on, in order the sooner to reach the Three Lakes, and to have the shelter there of our dear tent. In the hope of discovering these lakes, that had been promised us by our late friends, we were constantly looking right and left, but in vain. It grew late, and, according to the information of the Tartars, we began to fear we must have passed the only encampment we were likely to find that day. By dint of straining our eyes, we at length got sight of a horseman, slowly riding along the bottom of a lateral valley. He was at some distance from us; but it was essential that we should obtain information from him. M. Gabet accordingly hastened after him, at the utmost speed of his tall camel's long legs. The horseman heard the cries of the camel, looked back, and seeing that some one was approaching him, turned his horse round, and galloped towards M. Gabet. As soon as he got within earshot: "Holy personage," cried he, "has your eye perceived the yellow goats? I have lost all traces of them." "I have not seen the yellow goats; I seek water, and cannot find it. Is it far hence?" "Whence came you? Whither go you?" "I belong to the little caravan you see yonder. We have been told that we should this evening on our way, find lakes, upon the banks of which we could commodiously encamp; but hitherto we have seen nothing of the kind." "How could that be? 'Tis but a few minutes ago you passed within a few yards of the water. Sir Lama, permit me to attend your shadow; I will guide you to the Three Lakes." And so saying, he gave his horse three swinging lashes with his whip, in order to put it into a pace commensurate with that of the camel. In a minute he had joined us. "Men of prayer," said the hunter, "you have come somewhat too far; you must turn back. Look" (pointing with his bow) "yonder; you see those storks hovering over some reeds: there you will find the Three Lakes." "Thanks, brother," said we; "we regret that we cannot show you your yellow goats as clearly as you have shown us the Three Lakes." The Mongol hunter saluted us, with his clasped hands raised to his forehead, and we proceeded with entire confidence towards the spot he had pointed out. We had advanced but a few paces before we found indications of the near presence of some peculiar waters. The grass was less continuous and less green, and cracked under our animals' hoofs like dried leaves; the white efflorescence of saltpetre manifested itself more and more thickly. At last we found ourselves on the bank of one lake, near which were two others. We immediately alighted, and set about erecting our tent; but the wind was so violent that it was only after long labor and much patience that we completed the task.

While Samdadchiemba was boiling our tea, we amused ourselves with watching the camels as they luxuriously licked up the saltpetre with which the ground was powdered. Next they bent over the edge of the lake, and inhaled long, insatiable draughts of the brackish water, which we could see ascending their long necks as up some flexible pump.

We had been for some time occupied in this not unpicturesque recreation, when, all of a sudden, we heard behind us a confused, tumultuous noise, resembling the vehement flapping of sails, beaten about by contrary and violent winds. Soon we distinguished, amid the uproar, loud cries proceeding from Samdadchiemba. We hastened towards him, and were just in time to prevent, by our cooperation, the typhoon from uprooting and carrying off our linen *louvre*. Since our arrival, the wind, augmenting in violence, had also changed its direction; so that it now blew exactly from the quarter facing which we had placed the opening of our tent. We had especial occasion to fear that the tent would be set on fire by the lighted argols that were driven about by the wind. Our first business therefore was to tack about; and after a while we succeeded in making our tent secure, and so got off with our fear and a little fatigue. The misadventure, however, put Samdadchiemba into a desperately bad humor throughout the evening; for the wind, by extinguishing the fire, delayed the preparation of his darling tea.

The wind fell as the night advanced, and by degrees the weather became magnificent; the sky was clear, the moon full and bright, and the stars glittered like diamonds. Alone, in this vast solitude, we distinguished in the distance only the fantastic and indistinct outline of the mountains which loomed in the horizon like gigantic phantoms, while the only sound we heard was the cries of the thousand aquatic birds, as, on the surface of the lakes, they contended for the ends of the reeds and the broad leaves of the water-lily. Samdadchiemba was by no means a person to appreciate the charms of this tranquil scene. He had succeeded in again lighting the fire, and was absorbed in the preparation of his tea. We accordingly left him squatted before the kettle, and went to recite the service, walking round the larger lake, which was nearly half a league in circuit. We had proceeded about half round it, praying alternately, when insensibly our voices fell, and our steps were stayed. We both stopped spontaneously, and listened intently, without venturing to interchange a word, and even endeavoring to suppress our respiration. At last we expressed to each other the cause of our mutual terror, but it was in tones low and full of emotion: "Did you not hear, just now, and quite close to us, what seemed the voices of men?" "Yes, a number of voices, speaking as though in secret consultation." "Yet we are alone here:—'tis very surprising. Hist! let us listen again." "I hear nothing; doubtless we were under some illusion." We resumed our walk, and the recitation of our prayers. But we had not advanced ten steps, before we again stopped; for we heard, and very distinctly, the noise which had before alarmed us, and which seemed the confused vague murmur of several voices discussing some point in under tones. Yet nothing was visible. We got upon a hillock, and thence, by the moon's light, saw, at a short distance, some human forms moving in the long grass. We could hear their voices too, but not distinctly enough to know whether they spoke Chinese or Tartar. We retraced our steps to our tent, as rapidly as was consistent with the maintenance of silence; for we took these people to be robbers, who, having perceived our tent, were deliberating as to the best means of pillaging us.

"We are not in safety here," said we to Samdadchiemba; "we have discovered, quite close to us, a number of men, and we have heard their voices. Go and collect the animals, and bring them to the tent." "But," asked Samdadchiemba, knitting his brows, "if the robbers come, what shall we do? May we fight them? May we kill them? Will Holy Church permit that?" "First go and collect the animals; afterwards we will tell you what we must do." The animals being brought together, and fastened outside the tent, we directed our intrepid Samdadchiemba to finish his tea, and we returned on tiptoe to the spot where we had seen and heard our mysterious visitors. We looked around in every direction, with eye and ear intent; but we could neither see nor hear any one. A well-trodden pathway, however, which we discovered among the reeds of tall grass on the margin of the greater lake, indicated to us that those whom we had taken to be robbers were inoffensive passengers, whose route lay in that direction. We returned joyfully to our tent, where we found our valorous Samdadchiemba actively employed in sharpening, upon the top of his leather boots, a great Russian cutlass, which he had purchased at *Tolon-Noor*. "Well," exclaimed he, fiercely, trying with his thumb the edge of his sword, "where are the robbers?" "There are no robbers; unroll the goatskins, that we may go to sleep." "'Tis a pity there are no robbers; for here is something that would have cut into them famously!" "Ay, ay, Samdadchiemba, you are wonderfully brave now, because you know there are no robbers." "Oh, my spiritual fathers, it is not so; one should always speak the words of candor. I admit that my memory is very bad, and that I have never been able to learn many prayers; but as to courage, I may boast of having as much of it as another." We laughed at this singularly expressed sally. "You laugh, my spiritual fathers," said Samdadchiemba. "Oh, you do not know the Dchiahours. In the west, the land of *San-Tchouan* (Three Valleys) enjoys much renown. My countrymen hold life in little value; they have always a saber by their side, and a long matchlock on their shoulder. For a word, for a look, they fight and kill one another. A Dchiahour, who has never killed any-one, is considered to have no right to hold his head up among his countrymen. He cannot pretend to the character of a brave man." "Very fine! Well, you are a brave man, you say: tell us how many men did you kill when you were in the Three Valleys?" Samdadchiemba seemed somewhat disconcerted by this question; he looked away, and broke out into a forced laugh. At last, by way of diverting the subject, he plunged his cup into the kettle, and drew it out full of tea. "Come," said we, "drink your tea, and then tell us about your exploits."

Samdadchiemba wiped his cup with the skirt of his jacket, and having replaced it in his bosom, addressed us gravely, thus: "My spiritual fathers, since you desire I should speak to you about myself, I will do so; it was a great sin I committed, but I think Jehovah pardoned me when I entered the holy Church.

"I was quite a child, not more, at the utmost, than seven years old. I was in the fields about my father's house, tending an old she-donkey, the only animal we possessed. One of my companions, a boy about my own age, came to play with me. We began quarreling, and from words fell to blows. I struck him on the head with a great root of a tree that I had in my hand, and the blow was so heavy that he fell motionless at my feet. When I saw my companion stretched on the earth, I stood for a moment as it were paralyzed, not knowing what to think or to do. Then an awful fear came over me, that I should be seized and killed. I looked all about me in search of a hole wherein I might conceal my companion, but I saw nothing of the kind. I then thought of hiding myself. At a short distance from our house there was a great pile of brushwood, collected for fuel. I directed my steps thither, and with great labor made a hole, into which, after desperately scratching myself, I managed to creep up to my neck, resolved never to come out of it.

"When night fell, I found they were seeking me. My mother was calling me in all directions; but I took good care not to answer. I was even anxious not to move the brushwood, lest the sound should lead to my discovery, and, as I anticipated, to my being killed. I was terribly frightened when I heard a number of people crying out and disputing, I concluded, about me. The night passed away; in the morning I felt devouringly hungry. I began to cry; but I could not even cry at my ease, for I feared to be discovered by the people whom I heard moving about, and I was resolved never to quit the brushwood."—"But were you not afraid you should die of hunger?"—"The idea never occurred to me; I felt hungry indeed, but that was all. The reason I had for concealing myself was that I might not die; for I thought that if they did not find me, of course they could not kill me."—"Well, and how long did you remain in the brushwood?"—"Well, I have often heard people say that you can't remain long without eating; but those who say so, never tried the experiment. I can answer for it, that a boy of seven years old can live, at all events, three days and four nights without eating anything whatever.

"After the fourth night, early in the morning, they found me in my hole. When I felt they were taking me out, I struggled as well as I could and endeavored to get away. My father took me by the arm. I cried and sobbed, 'Do not kill me, do not kill me,' cried I; 'it was not I who killed *Nasamboyan*.' They carried me to the house, for I would not walk. While I wept, in utter despair, the people about me laughed. At last they told me not to be afraid, for that Nasamboyan was not dead, and soon afterwards Nasamboyan came into the room as well as ever, only that he had a great bruise on his face. The blow I had struck him had merely knocked him down, and stunned him."

When the Dchiahour had finished this narrative, he looked at us in turns, laughing and repeating, again and again, "Who will say people cannot live without eating?" "Well," said we, "this is a very good beginning, Samdadchiemba; but you have not told us yet how many men you have killed." "I never killed any one; but that was merely because I did not stay long enough in my native Three Valleys; for at the age of ten they put me into a great Lamasery. I had for my especial master a very rough cross man, who gave me the strap every day, because I could not repeat the prayers he taught me. But it was to no purpose he beat me; I could learn nothing: so he left off teaching me, and sent me out to fetch water and collect fuel. But he continued to thrash me as hard as ever, until the life I led became quite insupportable, and at last I ran off with some provisions, and made my way towards Tartary. After walking several days, haphazard, and perfectly ignorant where I was, I encountered the train of a Grand Lama who was repairing to Peking. I joined the caravan, and was employed to take charge of a flock of sheep that accompanied the party, and served for its food. There was no room for me in any of the tents, so I had to sleep in the open air. One evening I took up my quarters behind a rock, which sheltered me from the wind. In the morning, waking somewhat later than usual, I found the encampment struck, and the people all gone. I was left alone in the desert. At this time I knew nothing about east, west, north, or south; I had consequently no resource but to wander on at random, until I should find some Tartar station. I lived in this way for three years—now here, now there, exchanging such slight services as I could render for my food and tent-room. At last I reached Peking and presented myself at the gate of the Great Lamasery of *Hoang-Sse*, which is entirely composed of Dchiahour and Thibetian Lamas. I was at once admitted, and my countrymen having clubbed together to buy me a red scarf and a yellow cap, I was enabled to join the chorus in the recitation of prayers, and, of consequence, to claim my share in the distribution of alms."—We interrupted Samdadchiemba at this point, in order to learn from him how he could take part in the recitation of prayers, without having learned either to read or pray.—"Oh," said he, "the thing was easy enough. They gave me an old book; I held it on my knees, and mumbling out some gibberish between my lips, endeavored to catch the tone of my neighbours. When they turned over a leaf, I turned over a leaf; so that, altogether, there was no reason why the leader of the chorus should take any notice of my maneuver.

"One day, however, a circumstance occurred that very

nearly occasioned my expulsion from the Lamasery. An ill-natured Lama, who had remarked my method of reciting the prayers, used to amuse himself with mocking me, and creating a laugh at my expense. When the Emperor's mother died, we were all invited to the *Yellow Palace* to recite prayers. Before the ceremony commenced, I was sitting quietly in my place, with my book on my knees, when this roguish fellow came gently behind me, and looking over my shoulder mumbled out something or other in imitation of my manner. Losing all self-possession, I gave him so hard a blow upon the face, that he fell on his back. The incident excited great confusion in the *Yellow Palace*. The superiors were informed of the matter, and by the severe rules of Thibetian discipline, I was liable to be flogged for three days with the black whip, and then my hands and feet in irons, to be imprisoned for a year in the tower of the Lamasery. One of the principals, however, who had taken notice of me before, interposed in my favor. He went to the Lamas who constituted the council of discipline, and represented to them the fact that the disciple who had been struck was a person notorious for annoying his companions, and that I had received extreme provocation from him. He spoke so warmly in my favor that I was pardoned on the mere condition of making an apology. I accordingly placed myself in the way of the Lama whom I had offended: 'Brother,' said I, 'shall we go and drink a cup of tea together?' 'Certainly,' replied he; 'there is no reason why I should not drink a cup of tea with you.' We went out, and entered the first tea-house that presented itself. Seating ourselves at one of the tables in the tea-room, I offered my snuff-bottle to my companion, saying: 'Elder brother, the other day we had a little disagreement; that was not well. You must confess that you were not altogether free from blame. I, on my part, admit that I dealt too heavy a blow. But the matter has grown old; we will think no more about it.' We then drank our tea, interchanged various civilities, and so the thing ended."

These and similar anecdotes of our Dchiahour had carried us far into the night. The camels, indeed, were already up and browsing their breakfast on the banks of the lake. We had but brief time before us for repose. "For my part," said Samdadchiemba, "I will not lie down at all, but look after the camels. Day will soon break. Meantime I'll make a good fire, and prepare the *pan-tan*."

It was not long before Samdadchiemba roused us with the intimation that the sun was up, and the *pan-tan* ready. We at once rose, and after eating a cup of *pan-tan*, or, in other words, of oatmeal diluted with boiling water, we planted our little cross upon a hillock, and proceeded upon our pilgrimage.

It was past noon when we came to a place where three wells had been dug, at short distances, the one from the other. Although it was early in the day, we still thought we had better encamp here: A vast plain, on which we could discern no sort of habitation, stretched out before us to the distant horizon; and we might fairly conclude it destitute of water, since the Tartars had taken the trouble to dig these wells. We therefore set up our tent. We soon found, however, that we had selected a detestable encampment. With excessive nastiness of very brackish and very fetid water was combined extreme scarcity of fuel. We looked about for argols, but in vain. At last Samdadchiemba, whose eyes were better than ours, discerned in the distance a sort of enclosure, in which he concluded that cattle had been folded. He took a camel with him to the place in the hope of finding plenty of argols there, and he certainly returned with an ample supply of the article; but unfortunately the precious manure-fuel was not quite dry; it absolutely refused to burn. The Dchiahour essayed an experiment. He hollowed out a sort of furnace in the ground, surmounting it with a turf chimney. The structure was extremely picturesque, but it labored under the enormous disadvantage of being wholly useless. Samdadchiemba arranged and rearranged his fuel, and puffed, and puffed, with the full force of his potent lungs. It was all lost labor. There was smoke enough, and to spare; we were enveloped in smoke, but not a spark of fire: and the water in the kettle remained relentlessly passive. It was obvious that to boil our tea or heat oatmeal was out of the question. Yet we were anxious, at all events, to take the chill off the water, so as to disguise, by the warmth, its brackish flavor and its disagreeable smell. We adopted this expedient.

You meet in the plains of Mongolia with a sort of gray squirrel, living in holes like rats. These animals construct, over the opening of their little dens, a sort of miniature dome, composed of grass, artistically twisted, and designed as a shelter from wind and rain. These little heaps of dry grass are of the form and size of mole-hills. The place where we had now set up our tent abounded with these gray squirrels. Thirst made us cruel, and we proceeded to level the house-domes of these poor little animals, which retreated into their holes below as we approached them. By means of this vandalism we managed to collect a sackful of efficient fuel, and so warmed the water of the well, which was our only aliment during the day.

Our provisions had materially diminished, notwithstanding the economy to which the want of fire on this and other occasions had reduced us. There remained very little meal or millet in our store bags, when we learned, from a Tartar whom we met on the way, that we were at no great distance from a trading station called *Chaborté* (Slough). It lay, indeed, somewhat out of the route we were pursuing; but there was no other place at which we could supply ourselves with provisions, until we came to Blue-Town, from which we were distant a hundred leagues. We turned therefore obliquely to the left, and soon reached Chaborté.

Russian Convent at Peking.

CHAPTER III.

Festival of the Loaves of the Moon—Entertainment in a Mongol tent—*Toolholos,* or Rhapsodists of Tartary—Invocation to Timour—Tartar Education—Industry of the Women.—Mongols in quest of missing animals—Remains of an abandoned City—Road from Peking to Kiaktha—Commerce between China and Russia—Russian Convent at Peking—A Tartar solicits us to cure his mother from a dangerous Illness—Tartar Physicians—The intermittent Fever Devil—Various forms of Sepulture in use among the Mongols—Lamasery of the Five Towers—Obsequies of the Tartar Kings—Origin of the kingdom of Efe—Gymnastic Exercises of the Tartars—Encounter with three Wolves—Mongol Carts.

WE arrived at Chaborté on the fifteenth day of the eighth moon, the anniversary of great rejoicings among the Chinese. This festival, known as the *Yué Ping* (Loaves of the Moon), dates from the remotest antiquity. Its original purpose was to honor the moon with superstitious rites. On this solemn day, all labor is suspended; the workmen receive from their employers a present of money; every person puts on his best clothes; and there is merrymaking in every family. — Relations and friends interchange cakes of varous sizes, on which is stamped the image of the moon; that is to say, a hare crouching amid a small group of trees.

Since the fourteenth century, this festival has borne a

political character, little understood, apparently, by the Mongols: but the tradition of which is carefully preserved by the Chinese. About the year 1368, the Chinese were desirous of shaking off the yoke of the Tartar dynasty, founded by Tcheng-Kis-Khan, and which had then swayed the empire for nearly a hundred years. A vast conspiracy was formed throughout all the provinces, which was simultaneously to develop itself, on the 15th day of the eighth moon, by the massacre of the Mongol soldiers, who were billeted upon each Chinese family, for the double purpose of maintaining themselves and their conquest. The signal was given by a letter concealed in the cakes which, as we have stated, are on that day, mutually interchanged throughout the country. The massacre was effected, and the Tartar army dispersed in the houses of the Chinese, utterly annihilated. This catastrophe put an end to the Mongol domination; and ever since, the Chinese, in celebrating the festival of *Yué-Ping*, have been less intent upon the superstitious worship of the moon, than upon the tragic event to to which they owed the recovery of their national independence.

The Mongols seem to have entirely lost all memory of the sanguinary revolution; for every year they take their full part in the festival of the Loaves of the Moon, and thus celebrate, without apparently knowing it, the triumph which their enemies heretofore gained over their ancestors.

At a gunshot from the place where we were encamped, we perceived several Mongol tents, the size and character of which indicated easiness of circumstances in the proprietors. This indication was confirmed by the large herds of cattle, sheep, and horses, which were pasturing around. While we were reciting the Breviary in our tent, Samdadchiemba went to pay a visit to these Mongols. Soon afterwards, we saw approaching an old man with a long white beard, and whose features bespoke him a personage of disstinction. He was accompanied by a young Lama, and by a little boy who held his hand. "Sirs Lamas," said the old man, "all men are brothers: but they who dwell in tents are united one with another as flesh with bone. Sirs Lamas, will you come and seat yourselves, for a while, in my poor abode? The fifteenth of this moon is a solemn epoch; you are strangers and travelers, and therefore cannot this evening occupy your places at the hearth of your own noble family. Come and repose for a few days with us; your presence will bring us peace and happiness." We told the good old man that we could not wholly accept his offer, but that, in the evening, after prayers, we would come and take tea with him, and converse for a while about the Mongol nation. The venerable Tartar hereupon took his leave; but he had not been gone long, before the young Lama who had accompanied him returned, and told us that his people were awaiting our presence. We felt that we could not refuse at once to comply with an invitation so full of frank cordiality, and accordingly, having directed our Dchiahour to take good care of the tent, we followed the young Lama who had come in quest of us.

Upon entering the Mongol tent, we were struck and astonished at finding a cleanliness one is little accustomed to see in Tartary. There was not the ordinary coarse fireplace in the center, and the eye was not offended with the rude dirty kitchen utensils which generally encumber Tartar habitations. It was obvious, besides, that everything had been prepared for a festival. We seated ourselves upon a large red carpet; and there was almost immediately brought to us, from the adjacent tent, which served as a kitchen, some tea with milk, some small loaves fried in butter; cheese, raisins, and jujubs.

After having been introduced to the numerous Mongols by whom we found ourselves surrounded, the conversation insensibly turned upon the festival of the Loaves of the Moon. "In our Western Land," said we, "this festival is unknown; men there adore only Jehovah, the Creator of the heavens, and of the earth, of the sun, of the moon, and of all that exists." "Oh, what a holy doctrine!" exclaimed the old man, raising his clasped hands to his forehead; "the Tartars themselves, for that matter, do not worship the moon; but seeing that the Chinese celebrate this festival, they follow the custom without very well knowing why." —"You say truly; you do not, indeed, know why you celebrate this festival. That is what we heard in the land of the *Kitat* (Chinese). But do you know why the Kitat celebrate it?" and thereupon we related to these Mongols what we knew of the terrible massacre of their ancestors. Upon the completion of our narrative, we saw the faces of all our audience full of astonishment. The young men whispered to one another; the old man preserved a mournful silence; his head bent down, and big tears flowing from his eyes. "Brother rich in years," said we, "this story does not seem to surprise you as it does your young men, but it fills your heart with emotion."—"Holy personages," replied the elder, raising his head, and wiping away the tears with the back of his hand, "the terrible event which occasions such consternation in the minds of my young men was not unknown to me, but I would I had never heard of it, and I always struggle against its recollection, for it brings the hot blood into the forehead of every Tartar, whose heart is not sold to the Kitat. A day known to our great Lamas will come, when the blood of our fathers, so shamefully assassinated, will at length be avenged. When the holy man who is to lead us to vengeance shall appear, every one of us will rise and follow in his train; then we shall march, in the face of day, and require from the Kitat an account of the Tartar blood which they shed in the silence and dark secrecy of their houses. The Mongols celebrate every year this festival, most of them seeing in it merely an indifferent ceremony; but the Loaves of the Moon-day ever recalls, in the hearts of a few amongst us, the memory of the treachery to which our fathers fell victims, and the hope of just vengeance."

After a brief silence, the old man went on: "Holy personages, whatever may be the associations of this day, in other respects it is truly a festival for us, since you have deigned to enter our poor habitation. Let us not further occupy our breasts with sad thoughts. Child," said he to a young man seated on the threshold of the tent, "if the mutton is boiled enough, clear away these things." This command having been executed, the eldest son of the family entered, bearing in both hands a small oblong table, on which was a boiled sheep, cut into four quarters, heaped one on the other. The family being assembled round the table, the chief drew a knife from his girdle, severed the sheep's tail, and divided it into two equal pieces, which he placed before us.

With the Tartars, the tail is considered the most delicious portion of their sheep, and accordingly the most honorable. These tails of the Tartarian sheep are of immense size and weight, the fat upon them alone weighing from six to eight pounds.

The fat and juicy tail having thus been offered a homage to the two stranger guests, the rest of the company, knife in hand, attacked the four quarters of the animal, and had speedily, each man, a huge piece before him. Plate or fork there was none, the knees supplied the absence of the one, the hands of the other, the flowing grease being wiped off, from time to time, upon the front of the jacket. Our own embarrassment was extreme. That great white mass of fat had been given to us with the best intentions, but, not quite clear of European prejudices, we could not make up our stomachs to venture, without bread or salt, upon the lumps of tallow that quivered in our hands. We briefly consulted, in our native tongue, as to what on earth was to be done under these distressing circumstances. Furtively, to replace the horrible masses upon the table would be imprudent; openly to express to our Amphytrion our repugnance to this *par excellence* Tartarian delicacy, was impossible, as wholly opposed to Tartar etiquette. We devised this plan: we cut the villainous tail into numerous pieces, and insisted, in that day of general rejoicing, upon the company's partaking with us of this precious dish. There was infinite reluctance to deprive us of the treat; but we persisted, and by degrees got entirely clear of the abominable mess, ourselves rejoicing, instead, in a cut from the leg, the savor of which was more agreeable to our early training. The Homeric repast completed, a heap of polished bones alone remaining to recall it, a boy, taking from the goat's-horn on which it hung a rude three-stringed violin, presented it to the chief, who, in his turn, handed it to a young man of modest mien, whose eyes lighted up as he received the instrument. "Noble and holy travelers," said the chief, "I have invited a Toolholos to embellish this entertainment with some recitations." The minstrel was already preluding with his fingers upon the strings of his instrument. Presently he began to sing, in a strong, emphatic voice, at times interweaving with his verses recitations full of fire and animation. It was interesting to see all those Tartar faces bent towards the minstrel, and accompanying the meaning of his words with the movements of their features. The *Toolholos* selected, for his subjects, national traditions, which warmly excited the feelings of his audience. As to ourselves, very slightly acquainted with the history of Tartary, we took small interest in all those illustrious unknown, whom the Mongol rhapsodist marshaled over the scene.

When he had sung for some time, the old man presented to him a large cup of milk-wine. The minstrel placed his instrument upon his knees, and with evident relish proceeded to moisten his throat, parched with the infinitude of marvels he had been relating. While, having finished his draught, he was licking the brim of his cup: "*Toolholos*," said we, "the songs you have sung were all excellent. But you have as yet said nothing about the Immortal Tamerlane: the 'Invocation to Timour,' we have heard, is a famous song, dear to the Mongols." "Yes, yes," exclaimed several voices at once, "sing us the 'Invocation to Timour.'" There was a moment's silence, and then the Toolholos, having refreshed his memory, sang, in a vigorous and warlike tone, the following strophes:—

"When the divine Timour dwelt within our tents, the Mongol nation was redoubtable and warlike; its least movements made the earth bend; its mere look froze with fear the ten thousand peoples upon whom the sun shines.

"O divine Timour, will thy great soul soon revive?
Return! return! we await thee, O Timour!

"We live in our vast plains, tranquil and peaceful as sheep; yet our hearts are fervent and full of life. The memory of the glorious age of Timour is ever present to our minds. Where is the chief who is to place himself at our head, and render us once more great warriors?

"O divine Timour, will thy great soul soon revive?
Return! return! we await thee, O Timour!

"The young Mongol has arms wherewith to quell the wild horse, eyes wherewith he sees afar off in the desert the traces of the lost camel. Alas! his arms can no longer bend the bow of his ancestors; his eye cannot see the wiles of the enemy.

"O divine Timour, will thy great soul soon revive?
Return! return! we await thee, O Timour!

"We have burned the sweet smelling wood at the feet of the divine Timour, our foreheads bent to the earth; we have offered to him the green leaf of tea and the milk of our herds. We are ready; the Mongols are on foot, O Timour! And do thou, O Lama, send down good fortune upon our arrows and our lances.

"O divine Timour, will thy great soul soon revive?
Return! return! we await thee, O Timour!"

When the Tartar Troubadour had completed this national song, he rose, made a low bow to the company, and, having suspended his instrument upon a wooden pin, took his leave. "Our neighbors," said the old man, "are also keeping the festival, and expect the Toolholos: but, since you seem to listen with interest to Tartar songs, we will offer some other melodies to your notice. We have in our own family a brother who has in his memory a great number of airs, cherished by the Mongols; but he cannot play; he is not a Toolholos. Come, brother Nymbo, sing; you have not got Lamas of the West to listen to you every day."

A Mongol, whom, seated as he was in a corner, we had not before noticed, at once rose, and took the place of the departed *Toolholos*. The appearance of this personage was truly remarkable; his neck was completely buried in his enormous shoulders; his great dull staring eyes contrasted strangely with his dark face half-calcined as it were by the sun; his hair, or rather a coarse uncombed mane, straggling down his back, completed the savageness of his aspect. He began to sing; but his singing was a mere counterfeit, an absurd parody. His grand quality was extreme longwindedness, which enabled him to execute roulades, complicated and continuous enough to throw any rational audience into fits. We soon became desperately tired of his noise, and watched with impatience a moment's cessation, that might give us an opportunity of retiring. But this was no easy matter; the villain divined our thoughts, and was resolved to spite us. No sooner had he finished one air than he dovetailed another into it, and so started afresh. In this way he went on, until it was really quite late in the night. At length he paused for a moment to drink a cup of tea; he threw the beverage down his throat, and was just clearing his throat to commence anew, when we started up, offered to the head of the family a pinch of snuff, and having saluted the rest of the company, withdrew.

You often meet in Tartary these Toolholos, or wandering singers, who go about from tent to tent, celebrating in their melodies national events and personages. They are generally very poor; a violin and a flute, suspended from the girdle, are their only property; but they are always received by the Mongol families with kindness and honor; they often remain in one tent for several days, and on their departure are supplied with cheese, wine, tea, and so on, to support them on their way. These poet-singers, who remind us of the minstrels and rhapsodists of Greece, are also very numerous in China; but they are, probably, nowhere so numerous or so popular as in Thibet.

The day after the festival, the sun had scarcely risen, when a little boy presented himself at the entrance of our tent, carrying in one hand a wooden vessel full of milk, and in the other hand a rude rush basket, in which were some new cheese and some butter. He was followed soon after by an old Lama, attended by a Tartar who had on his shoulder a large bag of fuel. We invited them all to be seated. "Brothers of the West," said the Lama, "accept these trifling presents from my master." We bowed in token of thanks, and Samdadchiemba hastened to prepare some tea, which we pressed the Lama to stay and partake of. "I will come and see you this evening," said he; "but I cannot remain at present; for I have not set my pupil the prayer he has to learn this morning." The pupil in question was the little boy who had brought the milk. The old man then took his pupil by the hand, and they returned together to their tent.

The old Lama was the preceptor of the family, and his function consisted in directing the little boy in the study of the Thibetian prayers. The education of the Tartars is very limited. They who shave the head, the Lamas, are, as a general rule, the only persons who learn to read and pray. There is no such thing throughout the country as a public school. With the exception of a few rich Mongols, who have their children taught at home, all the young Lamas are obliged to resort to the Lamaseries, wherein is concentrated all that exists in Tartary, of arts, or sciences, or intellectual industry. The Lama is not merely a priest; he is the painter, poet, sculptor, architect, physician; the head, heart, and oracle of the laity. The training of the young Mongols, who do not resort to the Lamaseries, is limited, with the men, to perfecting the use of the bow and arrow and matchlock, and to their obtaining a thorough mastery of equestrianism. When a mere infant the Mongol is weaned, and as soon as he is strong enough he is stuck upon a horse's back behind a man, the animal is put to a gallop, and the juvenile rider, in order not to fall off, has to cling with both hands to his teacher's jacket. The Tartars thus become accustomed, from a very early age, to the movements of the horse, and by degrees and the force of habit, they identify themselves, as it were, with the animal.

There is, perhaps, no spectacle more exciting than that of Mongol riders in chase of a wild horse. They are armed with a long, heavy pole, at the end of which is a running knot. They gallop, they fly after the horse they are pursuing down rugged ravines, and up precipitous hills, in and out, twisting and twining in their rapid course, until they come up with their game. They then take the bridle of their own horses in their teeth, seize with both hands their heavy pole, and bending forward throw, by a powerful effort, the running knot round the wild horse's neck. In this exercise the greatest vigor must be combined with the greatest dexterity, in order to enable them to stop short the powerful untamed animals with which they have to deal. It sometimes happens that pole and cord are broken; but as to a horseman being thrown, it is an occurrence we never saw or heard of.

The Mongol is so accustomed to horseback that he is altogether like a fish out of water when he sets foot on the ground. His step is heavy and awkward; and his bowed legs, his chest bent forward, his constant looking around him, all indicate a person who spends the greater portion of his time on the back of a horse or a camel.

When night overtakes the traveling Tartar, it often happens that he will not even take the trouble to alight for the purpose of repose. Ask people whom you meet in the desert where they slept last night, and you will as frequently as not have for answer, in a melancholy tone, "*Temen dero*" (on the camel). It is a singular spectacle to see caravans halting at noon, when they come to a rich pasturage. The camels disperse in all directions, browsing upon the high grass of the prairie, while the Tartars, astride between the two humps of the animal, sleep as profoundly as though they were sheltered in a good bed.

This incessant activity, this constant traveling, contributes to render the Tartars very vigorous, and capable of supporting the most terrible cold without appearing to be in the least affected by it. In the deserts of Tartary, and especially in the country of the Khalkhas, the cold is so intense, that for a considerable portion of the winter the thermometer will not act, on account of the congelation of the mercury. The whole district is often covered with snow; and if at these times the southwest wind blows, the plain wears the aspect of a raging sea. The wind raises the snow in immense waves, and impels the gigantic avalanches vehemently before it. Then the Tartars hurry courageously to the aid of their herds and flocks, and you see them dashing in all directions, exciting the animals by their cries, and driving them to the shelter of some rock or mountain. Sometimes these intrepid shepherds stop short amid the tempest, and stand erect for a time, as if defying the cold and the fury of the elements.

The training of the Tartar women is not more refined than that of the men. They are not, indeed, taught the use of the bow and the matchlock; but in equitation they are as expert and as fearless as the men. Yet it is only on occasions that they mount on horseback; such, for example, as traveling, or when there is no man at home to go in search of a stray animal. As a general rule, they have nothing to do with the care of the herds and flocks.

Their chief occupation is to prepare the family meals, and to make the family clothes. They are perfect mistresses of the needle; it is they who fabricate the hats, boots, coats, and other portions of the Mongol attire. The leather boots, for example, which they make are not indeed very elegant in form, but, on the other hand, their solidity is astonishing. It was quite unintelligible to us how, with implements so rude and coarse as theirs, they could manufacture articles almost indestructible in their quality. It is true they take their time about them, and get on very slowly with their work. The Tartar women excel in embroidery, which, for taste and variety of pattern and for excellence of manipulation, excited our astonishment. We think we may venture to say, that nowhere in France would you meet with embroidery more beautiful and more perfect in fabric than that we have seen in Tartary.

The Tartars do not use the needle in the same way as the Chinese. In China they impel the needle perpendicularly down and up; whereas the Tartars impel it perpendicularly up and down. In France the manner is different from both; if we recollect right, the French women impel the needle horizontally from right to left. We will not attempt to pronounce as to the respective merit of the three methods; we will leave the point to the decision of the respectable fraternity of tailors.

On the 17th of the moon, we proceeded very early in the morning to the Chinese station of *Chaborté*, for the purpose of laying in a store of meal. *Chaborté*, as its Mongol name intimates, is built upon a slough. The houses are all made of mud, and surrounded each by an enclosure of high walls. The streets are irregular, tortuous, and narrow; the aspect of the whole town is somber and sinister, and the Chinese who inhabit it have, if possible, a more knavish look than their countrymen anywhere else. The trade of the town comprehends all the articles in ordinary use with the Mongols—oatmeal and millet, cotton manufactures, and brick tea, which the Tartars receive in exchange for the products of the desert, salt, mushrooms, and furs. Upon our return, we hastened to prepare for our departure. While we were packing up our baggage in the tent, Samdadchiemba went in search of the animals which had been put to pasture in the vicinity. A moment afterwards he returned with the three camels. "There are the camels," said we, with gloomy anticipation, "but where are the horse and mule; they were both at hand just now, for we tied their legs to prevent their straying." "They are stolen, in all probability. It never does to encamp too near the Chinese, whom everybody knows to be arrant horse stealers." These words came upon us like a clap of thunder. However, it was not a moment for sterile lamentation; it was necessary to go in search of the thieves. We each mounted a camel, and made a circuit in search of the animals, leaving our tent under the charge of Arsalan. Our search being futile, we resolved to proceed to the Mongol encampment, and inform them that the animals had been lost near their habitation.

By a law among the Tartars, when animals are lost from a caravan, the persons occupying the nearest encampment are bound either to find them or to replace them. It seems, no doubt, very strange to European views, that because, without their consent or even knowledge, without being in the smallest degree known to them, you have chosen to pitch your tent near those of a Mongol party, you and your animals, and your baggage are to be under their responsibility; but so it is. If a thing disappears, the law supposes that your next neighbor is the thief, or at all events an accomplice. This it is which has contributed to render the Mongols so skilful in tracking animals. A mere glance at the slight traces left by an animal upon the grass, suffices to inform the Mongol pursuer how long since it passed, and whether or not it bore a rider; and the track once found, they follow it throughout all its meanderings, however complicated.

We had no sooner explained our loss to the Mongol chief, than he said to us cheerfully: "Sirs Lamas, do not permit sorrow to invade your hearts. Your animals cannot be lost; in these plains there are neither robbers nor associates of robbers. I will send in quest of your horses. If we do not find them, you may select what others you please in their place, from our herd. We would have you leave this place as happy as you came to it." While he was speaking eight of his people mounted on horseback, and dashed off in as many directions, upon the quest, each man trailing after him his lasso, attached to the long, flexible pole we have described. After a while they all collected in one body, and galloped away, as hard as they could, towards the town. "They are on the track now, holy sirs," said the chief, "who was watching their movements by our sides, and you will have your horses back very soon. Meanwhile come within my tent, and drink some tea."

In about two hours, a boy appeared at the entrance of the tent, and announced the return of the horsemen. We hastened outside, and in the track which we had pursued saw something amid a cloud of dust which seemed horsemen galloping like the wind. We presently discovered the eight Tartars, dashing along, like so many mad centaurs, our stray animals each held by a lasso, in the midst of them. On their arrival, they alighted, and with an air of satisfaction said: "We told you nothing was ever lost in our country." We thanked the generous Mongols for the great service they had rendered us; and, bidding adieu to them, saddled our horses, and departed on our way to the Blue City.

On the third day we came, in the solitude, upon an imposing and majestic monument of antiquity,—a large city utterly abandoned. Its turreted ramparts, its watch towers, its four great gates, facing the four cardinal points, were all there perfect, in preservation, except that, besides being three-fourths buried in the soil, they were covered with a thick coating of turf. Arrived opposite the southern gate, we directed Samdadchiemba to proceed quietly with the animals, while we paid a visit to the Old Town, as the Tartars designate it. Our impression, as we entered the vast enclosure, was one of mingled awe and sadness. There were no ruins of any sort to be seen, but only the outline of a large and fine town, becoming absorbed below by gradual accumulations of wind-borne soil, and above by a winding-sheet of turf. The arrangement of the streets and the position of the principal edifices, were indicated by the inequalities of ground. The only living things we found here were a young Mongol shepherd, silently smoking his pipe, and the flock of goats he tended. We questioned the former as to when the city was built, by whom, when abandoned, and why? We might as well have interrogated his goats; he knew no more than that the place was called the Old Town.

Such remains of ancient cities are of no unfrequent occurrence in the deserts of Mongolia; but everything connected with their origin and history is buried in darkness. Oh, with what sadness does such a spectacle fill the soul! The ruins of Greece, the superb remains of Egypt,—all these, it is true, tell of death; all belong to the past; yet when you gaze upon them, you know what they are; you can retrace, in memory, the revolutions which have occasioned the ruins and the decay of the country around them. Descend into the tomb, wherein was buried alive the city of Herculaneum,—you find there, it is true, a gigantic skeleton, but you have within you historical associations wherewith to galvanize it. But of these old abandoned cities of Tartary, not a tradition remains; they are tombs without an epitaph, amid solitude and silence, uninterrupted except when the wandering Tartars halt, for a while, within the ruined enclosures, because there the pastures are richer and more abundant.

Although, however, nothing positive can be stated respecting these remains, the probabilities are, that they date no earlier back than the 13th century, the period when the Mongols rendered themselves masters of the Chinese empire, of which they retained possession for more than 100 years. During their domination, say the Chinese annals, they erected in Northern Tartary many large and powerful cities. Towards the middle of the 14th century the Mongol dynasty was expelled from China; the Emperor *Young-Lo*, who desired to exterminate the Tartars, invaded their country, and burned their towns, making no fewer than three expeditions against them into the desert, 200 leagues north of the Great Wall.

After leaving behind us the Old Town, we came to a broad road crossing N. S. that along which we were traveling E. W. This road, the ordinary route of the Russian embassies to Peking, is called by the Tartars *Koutcheon-Dcham* (Road of the Emperor's Daughter), because it was constructed for the passage of a princess, whom one of the Celestial Emperors bestowed upon a King of the Khalkhas. After traversing the *Tchakar* and *Western Souniot*, it enters the country of the *Khalkhas* by the kingdom of *Mourguevan;* thence crossing N. S. the great desert of *Gobi*, it traverses the river *Toula*, near the *Great Couren*, and terminates with the Russian factories at *Kiaktha*.

This town, under a treaty of peace in 1688 between the Emperor *Khang-Hi*, and the *White Khan of the Oros*, i. e. the Czar of Russia, was established as the entrepôt of the trade between the two countries. Its northern portion is occupied by the Russian factories, its southern by the Tartaro-Chinese. The intermediate space is a neutral ground, devoted to the purposes of commerce. The Russians are not permitted to enter the Chinese quarter, nor the Chinese the Russian. The commerce of the town is considerable, and apparently very beneficial to both parties. The Russians bring linen goods, cloths, velvets, soaps, and hardware; the Chinese tea in bricks, of which the Russians use large quantities; and these Chinese tea-bricks being taken in payment of the Russian goods at an easy rate, linen goods are sold in China at a lower rate than even in Europe itself. It is owing to their ignorance of this commerce of Russia with China that speculators at Canton so frequently find no market for their commodities.

Under another treaty of peace between the two powers, signed 14th of June, 1728, by Count Vladislavitch, Ambassador Extraordinary of Russia, on the one part, and by the Minister of the Court of Peking on the other, the Russian government maintains, in the capital of the celestial empire, a monastery, to which is attached a school, wherein a certain number of young Russians qualify themselves as Chinese and Tartar-Mantchou interpreters. Every ten years, the pupils, having completed their studies, return with their spiritual pastors of the monastery to St Petersburg, and are relieved by a new settlement. The little caravan is commanded by a Russian officer, who has it in charge to conduct the new disciples to Peking, and bring back the students and the members who have completed their period. From Kiaktha to Peking the Russians travel at the expense of the Chinese government, and are escorted from station to station by Tartar troops.

M. Timkouski, who in 1820 had charge of the Russian caravan to Peking, tells us, in his account of the journey, that he could never make out why the Chinese guides led him by a different route from that which the preceding ambassadors had pursued. The Tartars explained the matter to us. They said it was a political precaution of the Chinese government, who conceived that, being taken by all sorts of roundabout paths and no-paths, the Russians might be kept from a knowledge of the regular route;—an immensely imbecile precaution, since the Autocrat of all the Russias would not have the slightest difficulty in leading his armies to Peking, should he ever take a fancy to go and beard the Son of Heaven in his celestial seat.

This road to Kiaktha, which we thus came upon unexpectedly amid the deserts of Tartary, created a deep emotion in our hearts: "Here," said we to each other, "here is a road which leads to Europe!" Our native land presented itself before our imagination, and we spontaneously entered upon the road, which connected us with our beloved France. The conversation that rose to our lips from our hearts was so pleasing, that we insensibly advanced. The sight of some Mongol tents, on an adjacent eminence, recalled us to a sense of our position, and at the same moment a loud cry came from a Tartar whom we saw gesticulating in front of the tents. Not understanding the cry to be addressed to us, we turned, and were proceeding on our route when the Tartar, jumping on his horse, galloped after us: upon reaching us, he alighted and knelt before us: "Holy sirs," said he, raising his hands before Heaven, "have pity upon me, and save my mother from death. I know your power is infinite: come and preserve my mother by your prayers." The parable of the good Samaritan came before us, and we felt that charity forbade us to pass on without doing all we could in the matter. We therefore turned once more, in order to encamp near the Tartars.

While Samdadchiemba arranged our tent, we went, without loss of time, to tend the sick woman, whom we found in a very deplorable state. "Inhabitants of the desert," said we to her friends, "we know not the use of simples, we are unacquainted with the secrets of life, but we will pray to Jehovah for this sick person. You have not heard of this Almighty God—your Lamas know him not; but, be assured, Jehovah is the master of life and of death." Circumstances did not permit us to dwell on the theme to these poor people who, absorbed in grief and anxiety, could pay little attention to our words. We returned to our tent to pray, the Tartar accompanying us. When he saw our Breviary; "Are these," asked he, "the all-powerful prayers to Jehovah, of which you spoke?" "Yes," said we; "these are the only true prayers; the only prayers that can save." Thereupon he prostrated himself successively before each of us, touching the ground with his forehead; then he took the Breviary, and raised it to his head in token of respect. During our recitation of the prayers for the sick, the Tartar remained seated at the entrance of the tent, preserving a profound and religious silence. When we had finished, "Holy men," said he, again prostrating himself, "how can I make acknowledgments for your great benefits? I am poor; I can offer you neither horse nor sheep." "Mongol brother," we replied, "the priests of Jehovah may not offer up prayers for the sake of enriching themselves; since thou art not rich, accept from us this trifling gift;" and we presented to him a fragment of a tea-brick. The Tartar was profoundly moved with this proceeding; he could not say a word, his only answer to us was tears of gratitude.

We heard next morning with pleasure that the Tartar woman was much better. We would fain have remained a few days in the place, in order to cultivate the germ of the true faith thus planted in the bosom of this family; but we were compelled to proceed. Some of the Tartars escorted us a short distance on our way.

Medicine in Tartary, as we have already observed, is exclusively practised by the Lamas. When illness attacks any one, his friends run to the nearest monastery for a Lama, whose first proceeding, upon visiting the patient, is to run his fingers over the pulse of both wrists simultaneously, as the fingers of a musician run over the strings of an instrument. The Chinese physicians feel both pulses also, but in succession. After due deliberation, the Lama pronounces his opinion as to the particular nature of the malady. According to the religious belief of the Tartars, all illness is owing to the visitation of a *Tchutgour* or demon; but the expulsion of the demon is first a matter of medicine. The Lama physician next proceeds, as Lama apothecary, to give the specific befitting the case; the Tartar pharmacopœia rejecting all mineral chemistry, the Lama remedies consist entirely of vegetables pulverized, and either infused in water or made up into pills. If the Lama doctor happens not to have any medicine with him, he is by no means disconcerted; he writes the names of the remedies upon little scraps of paper, moistens the papers with his saliva, and rolls them up into pills, which the patient tosses down with the same perfect confidence as though they were genuine medicaments. To swallow the name of a remedy, or the remedy itself, say the Tartars, comes to precisely the same thing.

The medical assault of the usurping demon being applied, the Lama next proceeds to spiritual artillery, in the form of prayers, adapted to the quality of the demon who has to be dislodged. If the patient is poor, the *Tchutgour* visiting him can evidently be only an inferior *Tchutgour*, requiring merely a brief, off-hand prayer, sometimes merely an interjectional exorcism. If the patient is very poor, the Lama troubles himself with neither prayer nor pill, but goes away, recommending the friends to wait with patience until the sick person gets better or dies, according to the decree of *Hormoustha*. But where the patient is rich, the possessor of large flocks, the proceedings are altogether different. First, it is obvious that a devil who presumes to visit so eminent a personage must be a potent devil, one of the chiefs of the lower world; and it would not be decent for a great *Tchutgour* to travel like a mere sprite; the family, accordingly, are directed to prepare for him a handsome suit of clothes, a pair of rich boots, a fine horse, ready saddled and bridled, othewise the devil will never think of going, physic or exorcise him how you may. It is even possible, indeed, that one horse will not suffice, for the demon, in very rich cases, may turn out, upon inquiry, to be so high and mighty a prince, that he has with him a number of courtiers and attendants, all of whom have to be provided with horses.

Everything being arranged, the ceremony commences. The Lama and numerous co-physicians called in from his own and other adjacent monasteries, offer up prayers in the rich man's tents for a week or a fortnight, until they perceive that the devil is gone—that is to say, until they have exhausted all the disposable tea and sheep. If the patient recovers, it is a clear proof that the prayers have been efficaciously recited; if he dies, it is a still greater proof of the efficaciousness of the prayers, for not only is the devil gone, but the patient has transmigrated to a state far better than that he has quitted.

The prayers recited by the Lamas for the recovery of the sick are sometimes accompanied with very dismal and alarming rites. The aunt of Tokoura, chief of an encampment in the Valley of Dark Waters, visited by M. Huc, was seized one evening with an intermittent fever. "I would invite the attendance of the doctor Lama," said Tokoura, "but if he finds that there is a very big *Tchutgour* present, the expenses will ruin me." He waited for some days; but as his aunt grew worse and worse, he at last sent for a Lama; his anticipations were confirmed. The Lama pronounced that a demon of considerable rank was present, and that no time must be lost in expelling him. Eight other Lamas were forthwith called in, who at once set about the construction, in dried herbs, of a great puppet, which they entitled the *Demon of Intermittent Fevers*, and which, when completed, they placed on its legs by means of a stick, in the patient's tent.

The ceremony began at eleven o'clock at night; the Lamas ranged themselves in a semicircle round the upper portion of the tent, with cymbals, sea-shells, bells, tambourines, and other instruments of the noisy Tartar music. The remainder of the circle was completed by the members of the family, squatting on the ground close to one another, the patient kneeling, or rather crouched on her heels, opposite the *Demon of Intermittent Fevers*. The Lama doctor-in-chief had before him a large copper basin filled with millet, and some little images made of paste. The dung-fuel threw, amid much smoke, a fantastic and quivering light over the strange scene.

Upon a given signal, the clerical orchestra executed an overture harsh enough to frighten Satan himself, the lay congregation beating time with their hands to the charivari of clanging instruments and ear-splitting voices. The diabolical concert over, the Grand Lama, opened the Book of Exorcisms, which he rested on his knees. As he chanted one of the forms, he took from the basin, from time to time, a handful of millet, which he threw east, west, north, and south, according to the Rubric. The tones of his voice, as he prayed, were sometimes mournful and suppressed, sometimes vehemently loud and energetic. All of a sudden, he would quit the regular cadence of prayer, and have an outburst of apparently indomitable rage, abusing the herb puppet with fierce invectives and furious gestures. The exorcism terminated, he gave a signal by stretching out his arms, right and left, and the other Lamas struck up a tremendously noisy chorus, in hurried, dashing tones; all the instruments were set to work, and meantime the lay congregation, having started up with one accord, ran out of the tent, one after the other, and tearing round it like mad people, beat it at their hardest with sticks, yelling all the while at the pitch of their voices in a manner to make ordinary hair stand on end. Having thrice performed this demoniac round, they re-entered the tent as precipitately as they had quitted it, and resumed their seats. Then all the others covering their faces with their hands, the Grand Lama rose and set fire to the herb figure. As soon as the flames rose, he uttered a loud cry, which was repeated with interest by the rest of the company. The laity immediately rose, seized the burning figure, carried it into the plain, away from the tents, and there, as it consumed, anathematized it with all sorts of imprecations; the Lamas meantime squatted in the tent, tranquilly chanting their prayers in a grave, solemn tone.

Upon the return of the family from their valorous expedition, the praying was exchanged for joyous felicitations. By and by, each person provided with a lighted torch, the whole party rushed simultaneously from the tent, and formed into a procession, the laymen first, then the patient, supported on either side by a member of the family, and lastly, the nine Lamas, making night hideous with their music. In this style the patient was conducted to another tent, pursuant to the orders of the Lama, who had declared that she must absent herself from her own habitation for an entire month.

After this strange treatment, the malady did not return. The probability is, that the Lamas, having ascertained the precise moment at which the fever-fit would recur, met it at the exact point of time by this tremendous counter-excitement, and overcame it.

Though the majority of the Lamas seek to foster the ignorant credulity of the Tartars, in order to turn it to their own profit, we have met some of them who frankly avowed that duplicity and imposture played considerable part in all their ceremonies. The superior of a Lamasery said to us one day : "When a person is ill, the recitation of prayers is proper, for Buddha is the master of life and death; it is he who rules the transmigration of beings. To take remedies is also fitting, for the great virtue of medicinal herbs also comes to us from Buddha. That the Evil One may possess a rich person is credible, but that, in order to repel the Evil One, the way is to give him dress, and a horse, and what not, this is a fiction invented by ignorant and deceiving Lamas, who desire to accumulate wealth at the expense of their brothers."

The manner of interring the dead among the Tartars is not uniform. The Lamas are only called in to assist at extremely grand funerals. Towards the Great Wall, where the Mongols are mixed up with the Chinese, the custom of the latter in this particular, as in others, has insensibly prevailed. There the corpse is placed, after the Chinese fashion, in a coffin, and the coffin in a grave. In the desert, among the true nomadic tribes, the entire ceremony consists in conveying the dead to the tops of hills or the bottoms of ravines, there to be devoured by the birds and beasts of prey. It is really horrible to travelers through the deserts of Tartary to see, as they constantly do, human remains, for which the eagles and the wolves are contending.

The richer Tartars sometimes burn their dead with great solemnity. A large furnace of earth is constructed in a pyramidical form. Just before it is completed, the body is placed inside, standing, surrounded with combustibles. The edifice is then completely covered in, with the exception of a small hole at the bottom to admit fire, and another at the top, to give egress to the smoke, and keep up a current of air. During the combustion, the Lamas surround the tomb and recite prayers. The corpse being burnt, they demolish the furnace and remove the bones, which they carry to the Grand Lama; he reduces them to a very fine powder, and having added to them an equal quantity of meal, he kneads the whole with care, and constructs, with his own hands, cakes of different sizes, which he places one upon the other, in the form of a pyramid. When the bones have been thus prepared by the Grand Lama, they are transported with great pomp to a little tower built beforehand, in a place indicated by the diviner.

They almost always give to the ashes of the Lamas a sepulture of this description. You meet with a great number of these monumental towers on the summits of the mountains, and in the neighborhood of the Lamaseries; and you may find them in countries whence the Mongols have been driven by the Chinese. In other respects these countries scarcely retain any trace of the Tartars: the Lamaseries, the pasturages, the shepherds, with their tents and flocks, all have disappeared, to make room for new people, new monuments, new customs. A few small towers raised over graves alone remain there, as if to assert the rights of the ancient possessors of these lands, and to protest against the invasion of the Kitat.

The most celebrated seat of Mongol burials is in the province of Chan-Si, at the famous Lamasery of Five Towers (*Ou-Tay*). According to the Tartars, the Lamasery of the Five Towers is the best place you can be buried in. The ground in it is so holy, that those who are so fortunate as to be interred there are certain of a happy transmigration thence. The marvelous sanctity of this place is attributed to the presence of Buddha, who for some centuries past has taken up his abode there in the interior of a mountain. In 1842 the noble Tokoura, of whom we have already had occasion to speak, conveying the bones of his father and mother to the Five Towers, had the infinite happiness to behold there the venerable Buddha. "Behind the great

Lamasery of the Five Towers.

monastery," he told us, "there is a very lofty mountain, which you must climb by creeping on your hands and feet. Just towards the summit you come to a portico cut in the rock: you lie down on the earth, and look through a small aperture not larger than the bowl of a pipe. It is some time before you can distinguish anything, but by degrees your eye gets used to the place, and you have the happiness of beholding, at length, in the depths of the mountain, the face of the ancient Buddha. He is seated cross-legged, doing nothing. There are around him Lamas of all countries, who are continually paying homage to him."

Whatever you may think of Tokura's narrative, it is certain that the Tartars and the Thibetians have given themselves up to an inconceivable degree of fanaticism, in reference to the Lamasery of the Five Towers. You frequently meet, in the deserts of Tartary, Mongols, carrying on their shoulders the bones of their parents, to the Five Towers, to purchase, almost at its weight in gold, a few feet of earth, whereupon they may raise a small mausoleum. Even the Mongols of Torgot perform journeys occupying a whole year and attended with immense difficulty, to visit for this purpose the province of Chan-Si.

The Tartar kings sometimes make use of a sepulture which is the height of extravagance and barbarism. The royal corpse is conveyed to a vast edifice, constructed of bricks, and adorned with numerous statues representing men, lions, elephants, tigers, and various subjects of Buddhic mythology. With the illustrious defunct, they bury in a large cavern, constructed in the center of the building, large sums of gold and silver, royal robes, precious stones, in short, everything which he may need in another life. These monstrous interments sometimes cost the lives of a great number of slaves. They take children of both sexes, remarkable for their beauty, and make them swallow mercury till they are suffocated; in this way they preserve, they say, the freshness and ruddiness of their countenance, so as to make them appear still alive. These unfortunate victims are placed upright, round the corpse of their master, continuing, in this fashion, to serve him as during life. They hold in their hands the pipe, fan, the small phial of snuff, and the numerous other knick-knacks of the Tartar kings.

To protect these buried treasures, they place in the cavern a kind of bow, capable of discharging a number of arrows, one after the other. This bow, or rather these several bows joined together, are all bent, and the arrows ready to fly. They place this infernal machine in such a manner that, on opening the door of the cavern, the movement causes the discharge of the first arrow at the man who enters; the discharge of the first arrow causes the discharge of the second, and so on to the last—so that the unlucky person, whom covetousness or curiosity should induce to open the door, would fall, pierced with many arrows, in the tomb he sought to profane. They sell these murderous machines, ready prepared by the bow-makers. The Chinese sometimes purchase them, to guard their houses in their absence.

After a march of two days, we entered the district called the Kingdom of Efe; it is a portion of the territory of the Eight Banners, which the Emperor Kin-Loug dismembered in favor of a prince of the Khalkhas. *Sun Tché*, founder of the Mantchou dynasty, laid down this maxim: "In the south, establish no kings; in the north, interrupt no alliances." This policy has ever since been exactly pursued by the court of Peking. The Emperor *Kien-Long*, in order to attach to his dynasty the prince in question, gave him his daughter in marriage, hoping by this means to fix him at Peking, and thus to weaken the still dreaded power of the Khalkha sovereigns. He built for him, within, the circuit of the Yellow Town itself, a large and magnificent palace, but the Mongol prince could not adapt or reconcile himself to the stiff arbitrary etiquette of a court. Amid the pomp and luxury accumulated for his entertainment, he was incessantly absorbed with the thought of his tents and his herds: even the snows and frosts of his country were matters of regret. The attentions of the court being altogether inadequate to the dissipation of his ennui, he began to talk about returning to his prairies in the Khalkhas. On the other hand, his young wife, accustomed to the refinements of the court of Peking, could not bear the idea of spending the rest of her days in the desert, amongst milkmaids and shepherds. The Emperor resorted to a compromise which sufficiently met the wishes of his son-in-law, without too violently disconcerting the feelings of his daughter. He dismembered a portion of the *Tchakar*, and assigned it to the Mongol prince; he built for him, amid these solitudes, a small but handsome city, and presented to him a hundred families of slaves skilled in the arts and manufactures of China. In this manner, while the young Mantchou princess was enabled to dwell in a city and to have a court, the Mongol prince, on his part, was in a position to enjoy the tranquillity of the Land of Grass, and to resume at will the pleasures of nomadic life, in which he had passed his boyhood.

The King of Efe brought with him into his petty dominions a great number of Mongol Khalkhas, who inhabit, under the tent, the country bestowed upon their prince. These Tartars fully maintain the reputation for strength and active vigor which is generally attributed to the men of their nation. They are considered the most powerful wrestlers in southern Mongolia. From their infancy, they are trained to gymnastic exercises, and at the public wrestling matches, celebrated every year at Peking, a great number of these men attend to compete for the prizes, and to sustain the reputation of their country. Yet, though far superior in strength to the Chinese, they are sometimes thrown by the latter, generally more active, and especially more tricky.

In the great match of 1843, a wrestler of the kingdom of Efe had overthrown all competitors, Tartars and Chinese. His body, of gigantic proportions, was fixed upon legs which seemed immovable columns; his hands, like great grappling irons, seized his antagonists, raised them, and then hurled them to the ground, almost without effort. No person had been at all able to stand before his prodigious strength, and they were about to assign him the prize, when a Chinese stepped into the ring. He was short, small, meager, and appeared calculated for no other purpose than to augment the number of the Efeian's victims. He advanced, however, with an air of firm confidence; the Goliath of Efe stretched out his brawny arms to grasp him, when the Chinese, who had his mouth full of water, suddenly discharged the liquid in the giant's face. The Tartar mechanically raised his hands to wipe his eyes, and at the instant, the cunning Chinese rushed in, caught him round the waist, threw him off his balance, and down he went, amid the convulsive laughter of the spectators.

This anecdote was told to us by a Tartar horseman who traveled with us a part of our way through the kingdom of Efe. From time to time he showed us children engaged in wrestling. "This," said he, "is the favorite exercise with all the inhabitants of our kingdom of Efe. We esteem in a man but two things,—his being a good horseman and his being a good wrestler." There was one group of youthful wrestlers whom, exercising as they were on the side of our road, we were enabled to watch closely and at leisure; their ardor redoubled when they saw we were looking at them. The tallest of the party, who did not seem more than eight or nine years old, took in his arms one of his companions, nearly his own height, and very fat, and amused himself with tossing him above his head, and catching him again, as you would a ball. He repeated this feat seven or eight times, and at every repetition we trembled for the life of the boy; but the rest of the children only gamboled about, applauding the success of the performers.

On the 22d day of the eighth moon, on quitting the petty kingdom of Efe, we ascended a mountain, on the sides of which grew thickets of fir and birch. The sight of these at first gave us great pleasure. The deserts of Tartary are in general so monotonously bare, that you cannot fail to experience a pleasurable sensation when you come upon some occasional trees on your way. Our first feelings of joy were, however, soon demolished by a sentiment of a very different nature; we were as though frozen with horror, on perceiving at a turn of the mountain, three enormous wolves, that seemed awaiting us with calm intrepidity. At sight of these villainous beasts we stopped suddenly and as it were instinctively. After a moment of general stupor, Samdadchiemba descended from his mule, and wrung the noses of our camels. The expedient succeeded marvelously; the poor beasts sent forth such piercing and terrible cries, that the scared wolves dashed off with all speed. Arsalan, who saw them flee, thinking undoubtedly that it was himself they were afraid of, pursued them at the utmost speed of his legs; soon the wolves turned round, and our tent-porter would have been infallibly devoured had not M. Gabet rushed to his aid, uttering loud cries, and wringing the nose of his camel; the wolves having taken flight a second time, disappeared without our again thinking of pursuing them.

Although the want of population might seem to abandon the interminable deserts of Tartary to wild beasts, wolves are rarely met with. This arises, no doubt, from the incessant and vindictive warfare which the Mongols wage against them. They pursue them, everywhere, to the death, regarding them as their capital enemy, on account of the great damage they may inflict upon their flocks. The announcement that a wolf has made its appearance in a neighborhood, is for every one a signal to mount his horse. As there are always near each tent horses ready saddled, in an instant the plain is covered with numerous cavalry, all armed with their long lasso-poles. The wolf in vain flees in every direction: it meets everywhere horsemen who rush upon it. There is no mountain so rugged or arduous, up which the Tartar horses, agile as goats, cannot pursue it. The horseman who is at length successful in passing round its neck the running knot, gallops, off at full speed, dragging the wolf after him to the nearest tent; there they strongly bind its muzzle, so that they may torture it securely; and then, by way of finale, skin it alive, and turn it off. In summer, the wretched brute lives in this condition several days; but in winter, exposed without a skin to the rigors of the season, it dies forthwith, frozen with cold.

Some short time after we had lost sight of our three wolves, we had a singular encounter enough. We saw advancing towards us, on the same road, two chariots each drawn by three oxen. To each chariot were fastened, with great iron chains, twelve dogs of a terrible and ferocious aspect, four on each side, and four behind. These carriages were laden with square boxes, painted red; the drivers sat on the boxes. We could not conjecture what was the nature of the load, on account of which they thought it essential to have this horrible escort of Cerberuses. In accordance with the customs of the country, we could not question them on this point. The slightest indiscretion would have made us pass in their eyes for people actuated by evil intentions. We contented ourselves with asking if we were still very far from the monastery of Tchortchi, where we hoped to arrive that day; but the baying of the dogs, and clanking of their chains, prevented us from hearing the answer.

As we were going through the hollow of a valley, we remarked on the summit of an elevated mountain before us a long line of objects without motion, and of an indefinite form. By and by these objects seemed to resemble a formidable battery of cannons, ranged in line, and the nearer we advanced, the more were we confirmed in this impression. We felt sure that we saw distinctly the wheels of the carriages, the sponge-rods, the mouths of the cannons pointed towards the plain. But how could we bring ourselves to think that an army, with all its train of artillery could be there in the desert, amid this profound solitude? Giving way to a thousand extravagant conjectures, we hastened our progress, impatient to examine this strange apparition closely. Our illusion was only completely dissipated when we arrived quite at the top of the mountain. What we had taken for a battery of cannons was a long caravan of little Mongol chariots. We laughed at our mistake, but the illusion was not an unnatural one. These small two-wheeled chariots were all standing still on their frames, each laden with a sack of salt, covered with a mat, the ends of which extended beyond the extremities of the sacks so as to resemble exactly the mouths of cannon; the Mongol wagoners were boiling their tea in the open air, whilst their oxen were feeding on the sides of the mountain. The transport of merchandise, across the deserts of Tartary, is ordinarily effected, in default of camels, by these small two-wheeled chariots. A few bars of rough wood are the only materials that enter into their construction, and they are so light that a child may lift them with ease. The oxen that draw them, have all a little iron ring passed through their nostrils; to this ring is a cord, which attaches the animal to the preceding chariot; thus all the carriages, from the first to the last, are connected together, and form a long uninterrupted line. The Mongol wagoners are generally seated on the oxen, very rarely on the carriage, and scarcely ever on foot. On all the chief roads you meet with these long lines of carriages, and long before you see them, you hear the lugubrious and monotonous sound of the iron bells, which the oxen carry suspended from their neck.

After drinking a cup of tea with the Mongols whom we had met in the mountain, we proceeded on our way; the sun was on the point of setting, when we set up our tent on the margin of a stream about a hundred yards from the Lamasery of Tchortchi.

Lamasery of Tchortchi.

CHAPTER IV.

Young Lama converted to Christianity—Lamasery of Tchortchi—Alms for the Construction of Religious Houses—Aspect of the Buddhist Temples—Recitation of Lama Prayers—Decorations, Paintings, and Sculptures of the Buddhist Temples—Topography of the *Great Kouren* in the country of the *Khalkhas*—Journey of the *Guison-Tamba* to Peking—The *Kouren* of the Thousand Lamas—Suit between the Lama-King and his Ministers—Purchase of a Kid—Eagles of Tartary—Western Toumet—Agricultural Tartars—Arrival at the Blue Town—Glance at the Mantchou Nation—Mantchou Literature—State of Christianity in Mantchouria—Topography and productions of Eastern Tartary—Skill of the Mantchous with the Bow.

ALTHOUGH we had never visited the Lamasery of Tchortchi, we, nevertheless, knew a good deal about it from the information that had been given us. It was here that the young Lama was educated who came to teach M. Gabet the Mongol language, and whose conversion to Christianity gave such great hopes for the propagation of the gospel among the Tartar tribes. He was twenty-five years of age when he quitted his Lamasery, in 1837; there he had passed fourteen years in the study of Lama books, and had become well acquainted with Mongol and Mantchou literature. He had as yet but a very superficial knowledge of the Thibetian language. His tutor, an old Lama, well-educated and much respected, not merely in the Lamasery, but throughout the whole extent of the Yellowish Banner, had cherished great hopes of his disciple; it was, therefore, very reluctantly that he had consented to a temporary separation, which he limited to a month. Before his departure the pupil prostrated himself, according to custom, at the feet of his master, and begged him to consult for him the Book of Oracles. After having turned over some leaves of a Thibetian book, the old Lama addressed to him these words: 'For fourteen years thou hast remained by thy master's side like a faithful Chabi (disciple). Now, for the first time thou art about to go from me. The future fills me with anxiety; be careful then to return at the appointed time. If thy absence is prolonged beyond one moon thy destiny condemns thee never more to set foot in our holy Lamasery." The youthful pupil departed, resolved to obey to the letter the instructions of his tutor.

When he arrived at our mission of Si-Wan, M. Gabet chose, as the subject of his Mongol studies, an historical summary of the Christian religion. The oral and written conferences lasted nearly a month. The young Lama, subdued by the force of truth, publicly abjured Buddhism, received the name of Paul, and was ultimately baptized, after a long course of study. The prediction of the old Lama had its perfect accomplishment; Paul, since his conversion, has never again set foot in the Lamasery which he quitted.

About 2,000 Lamas inhabit the Lamasery of Tchortchi, which, it is said, is the favorite Lamasery of the Emperor, who has loaded it with donations and privileges. The Lamas in charge of it each receive a pension from the court of Peking. Those who absent themselves from it by permission, and for reasons approved by the superiors, continue to share in the distributions of money and the provisions that are made during their absence; on their return they duly received the full amount of their share. Doubtless that air of ease pervading the Lamasery of Tchortchi is to be attributed to the imperial favors. The houses in it are neat, sometimes even elegant; and you never see there, as in other places, Lamas covered with dirty rags. The study of the Mantchou language is much cultivated there, an incontestable proof of the great devotion of the Lamasery to the reigning dynasty.

With some rare exceptions the imperial benefactions go very little way towards the construction of the Lamaseries.

Those grand and sumptuous monuments, so often met with in the desert, are due to the free and spontaneous zeal of the Mongols. So simple and economical in their dress and manner of living, these people are generous, we might say, astonishingly prodigal in all that concerns religious worship and expenditure. When it is resolved to construct a Buddhist temple, surrounded by its Lamasery, Lama collectors go on their way forthwith, provided with passports, attesting the authenticity of their mission. They disperse themselves throughout the kingdom of Tartary, beg alms from tent to tent in the name of the Old Buddha. Upon entering a tent and explaining the object of their journey, by showing

Buddhist Temple.

the sacred basin in which the offerings are placed, they are received with joyful enthusiasm. There is no one but gives something. The rich place in the "badir" ingots of gold and silver; those who do not possess the precious metals, offer oxen, horses, or camels. The poorest contribute according to the extent of their means; they give lumps of butter, furs, ropes made of the hair of camels and horses. Thus, in a short time, are collected immense sums. Then in these deserts, apparently so poor, you see rise up, as if by enchantment, edifices whose grandeur and wealth would defy the resources of the richest potentates. It was, doubtless, in the same manner, by the zealous co-operation of the faithful, that were constructed in Europe those magnificent cathedrals whose stupendous beauty is an abiding reproach to modern selfishness and indifference.

The Lamaseries you see in Tartary are all constructed of brick and stone. Only the poorest Lamas build for themselves habitations of earth, and these are always so well whitewashed that they closely resemble the rest. The temples are generally built with considerable elegance, and with great solidity; but these monuments always seem crushed, being too low in proportion to their dimensions. Around the Lamasery rise, numerous and without order, towers or pyramids, slender and tapering, resting generally on huge bases, little in harmony with the tenuity of the constructions they support. It would be difficult to say to what order of architecture the Buddhic temples of Tartary belong. They are always fantastical constructions of monstrous colonnades, peristyles with twisted columns, and endless ascents. Opposite the great gate is a kind of altar of wood or stone, usually in the form of a cone reversed; on this the idols are placed, mostly seated cross-legged. These idols are of colossal stature, but their faces are fine and regular, except in the preposterous length of the ears; they belong to the Caucasian type, and are wholly distinct from the monstrous, diabolical physiognomies of the Chinese Pou-Ssa.

Before the great idol, and on the same level with it, is a gilt seat where the living Fô, the Grand Lama of the Lamasery is seated. All around the temple are long tables almost level with the ground, a sort of ottomans covered with carpet; and between each row there is a vacant space, so that the Lamas may move about freely.

When the hour for prayer is come, a Lama, whose office it is to summon the guests of the convent, proceeds to the great gate of the temple, and blows, as loud as he can, a sea-conch, successively towards the four cardinal points. Upon hearing this powerful instrument, audible for a league round, the Lamas put on the mantle and cap of ceremony and assemble in the great inner court. When the time is come the sea-conch sounds again, the great gate is opened, and the living Fô enters the temple. As soon as he is seated upon the altar all the Lamas lay their red boots at the vestibule, and advance barefoot and in silence. As they pass him they worship the living Fô by three prostrations, and then place themselves upon the divan, each according to his dignity. They sit cross-legged; always in a circle.

As soon as the master of the ceremonies has given the signal, by tinkling a little bell, each murmurs in a low voice a preliminary prayer, whilst he unrolls, upon his knees, the prayers directed by the rubric. After this short recitation, follows a moment of profound silence; the bell is again rung, and then commences a psalm in double chorus, grave and melodious. The Thibetian prayers, ordinarily in verse, and written in a metrical and well-cadenced style, are marvelously adapted for harmony. At certain pauses, indicated by the rubric, the Lama musicians execute a piece of music, little in concert with the melodious gravity of the psalmody. It is a confused and deafening noise of bells, cymbals, tambourines, sea-conches, trumpets, pipes, etc., each musician playing on his instrument with a kind of ecstatic fury, trying with his brethren who shall make the greatest noise.

The interior of the temple is usually filled with ornaments, statues, and pictures, illustrating the life of Buddha, and the various transmigrations of the more illustrious Lamas. Vases in copper, shining like gold, of the size and form of teacups, are placed in great numbers on a succession of steps, in the form of an amphitheater, before the idols. It is in these vases that the people deposit their offerings of milk, butter, Mongol wine, and meal. The extremities of each step consist of censers, in which are ever burning aromatic plants, gathered on the sacred mountains of Thibet. Rich silk stuffs, covered with tinsel and gold embroidery, form, on the heads of the idols, canopies from which hang pennants and lanterns of painted paper or transparent horn.

The Lamas are the only artists who contribute to the ornament and decoration of the temples. The paintings are quite distinct from the taste and the principles of art as understood in Europe. The fantastical and the grotesque

Interior of Buddhist Temple.

predominate inside and out, both in carvings and statuary, and the personages represented, with the exception of Buddha, have generally a monstrous and satanic aspect. The clothes seem never to have been made for the persons upon whom they are placed. The idea given is that of broken limbs concealed beneath awkward garments.

Amongst these Lama paintings, however, you sometimes come across specimens by no means destitute of beauty. One day, during a visit in the kingdom of Gechekten to the great temple called *Alton-Somné* (Temple of Gold), we saw a picture which struck us with astonishment. It was a large piece representing, in the center, Buddha seated on a rich carpet. Around this figure, which was of life size, there was a sort of glory, composed of miniatures, allegorically expressing the Thousand Virtues of Buddha. We could scarcely withdraw ourselves from this picture, remarkable as it was, not only for the purity and grace of the design, but also for the expression of the faces and the splendor of the coloring. All the personages seemed full of life. We asked an old Lama, who was attending us over the place, what he knew about this admirable work. "Sirs," said he, raising his joined hands to his forehead in token of respect, "this picture is a treasure of the remotest antiquity; it comprehends within its surface the whole doctrine of Buddha. It is not a Mongol painting; it came from Thibet, and was executed by a saint of the *Eternal Sanctuary*."

The artists here are, in general, more successful in the landscapes than in the epic subjects. Flowers, birds, trees, mythological animals, are represented with great truth and with infinitely pleasing effect. The coloring is wonderfully full of life and freshness. It is only a pity that the painters of these landscapes have so very indifferent a notion as to perspective and chiaro-oscuro.

The Lamas are far better sculptors than painters, and they are accordingly very lavish of carvings in their Buddhist temples. Everywhere in and about these edifices you see work of this class of art, in quantity bespeaking the fecundity of the artist's chisel, but of a quality which says little for his taste. First, outside the temples are an infinite number of tigers, lions, and elephants crouching upon blocks of granite; then the stone balustrades of the steps leading to the great gates are covered with fantastic sculptures representing birds, reptiles, and beasts, of all kinds, real and imaginary. Inside, the walls are decorated with *rilievos* in wood or stone, executed with great spirit and truth.

Though the Mongol Lamaseries cannot be compared, in point either of extent or wealth, with those of Thibet, there are some of them which are highly celebrated and greatly venerated among the adorers of Buddha.

The most famous of all is that of the Great Kouren (enclosure), in the country of the Khalkhas. As we had an opportunity of visiting this edifice in one of our journeys into Northern Tartary, we will here give some details respecting it. It stands on the bank of the river Toula, at the entrance to an immense forest, which extends thence northwards, six or seven days' journey to the confines of Russia, and eastward, nearly five hundred miles to the land of the Solons, in Mantchouria. On your way to the Great Kouren, over the desert of Gobi, you have to traverse, for a whole month, an ocean of sand, the mournful monotony of which is not relieved by a single stream or a single shrub; but on reaching the Kougour mountains, the western boundary of the states of the Guison-Tamba, or King-Lama, the scene changes to picturesque and fertile valleys, and verdant pasture-hills, crowned with forests that seem as old as the world itself. Through the largest valley flows the river Toula, which, rising in the Barka mountains, runs from east to west through the pastures of the Lamasery, and then entering Siberia, falls into Lake Balkal.

The Lamasery stands on the northern bank of the river, on the slope of a mountain. The various temples inhabited by the Guison-Tamba, and other Grand Lamas, are distinguishable from the rest of the structure by their elevation and their gilded roofs. Thirty thousand Lamas dwell in the Lamasery itself, or in smaller Lamaseries erected about it. The plain adjoining it is always covered with the tents of the pilgrims who resort hither from all parts to worship Buddha. Here you find the U-Pi-Ta-Dze, or "Fish-skin Tartars," encamped beside the Torgot Tartars from the summits of the sacred mountains (Bokte-Oula), the Thibetians and the Péboum, of the Himalaya, with their long-haired oxen, mingling with the Mantchous from the banks of the Songari and Amor. There is an incessant movement of tents set up and taken down, and of pilgrims coming and going on horses, camels, oxen, mules, or wagons, and on foot.

Viewed from the distance, the white cells of the Lamas, built in horizontal lines one above the other on the sides of the mountain, seem the steps of a grand altar, of which the tabernacle is the temple of the Guison-Tamba. In the depths of that sanctuary, all resplendent with gold and bright coloring, the Lama-King, The Holy, as he is called, *par excellence*, receives the homage of the faithful, ever prostrate, in succession, before him. There is not a Khalkha Tartar who does not glory in the title of the *Holy One's Disciple*. Wherever you meet a man from the district of the Great Kouren, and ask him who he is, his proud reply is always this: *Koure Bokte-Ain Chabi* (I am a disciple of the Holy Kouren).

Half a league from the Lamasery, on the banks of the Toula, is a commercial station of Chinese. Their wooden or mud huts are fortified by a circle of high palisades to keep out the pilgrims, who, despite their devotion, are extremely given to thieving whenever the opportunity occurs. A watch and some ingots of silver, stolen during the night from M. Gabet, left us no doubt as to the want of probity in the Holy One's disciples.

A good deal of trade is carried on here, Chinese and Russian goods changing hands to a very large extent. The payments of the former are invariably made in tea-bricks. Whether the article sold be a house, a horse, a camel, or a bale of goods, the price is settled for in bricks of tea. Five of these represent, in value, an ounce of silver; the monetary system, therefore, which Franklin so much disliked, is not in use by these Northern Tartars.

The Court of Peking entertains several Mandarins at the Great Kouren, ostensibly for the purpose of preserving order among the Chinese traders, but in reality to keep a watch upon the Guison-Tamba, always an object of suspicion to the Chinese Emperors, who bear in mind that the famous Tching-Kis-Khan was a Khalkha, and that the memory of his conquests has not passed away from the hearts of this warlike people. The slightest movement at the Great Kouren excites alarm at Peking.

In 1839 the Guison-Tamba announced his intention of paying a visit to the Emperor Tao-Kouan. The Court of Peking became horribly alarmed, and negotiators were dispatched to divert, if possible, the Guison-Tamba from his journey; but all they could effect was, that he should be attended by only 3,000 Lamas, and that three other Khalkha sovereigns who were to have accompanied him should be left behind.

Immediately upon the Guison-Tamba's departure on his progress, all the tribes of Tartary put themselves in motion, and took up positions on the road he was to travel, in vast multitudes, each tribe bringing for his acceptance offerings of horses, oxen, sheep, gold and silver bullion, and precious stones. Wells were dug for him at intervals throughout the length of the great desert of Gobi, and at each of these were placed for his use, by the chieftain of the particular locality, a store of provisions of all sorts. The Lama King was in a yellow palanquin, carried by four horses, each led by a dignitary of the Lamasery. The escort of 3,000 Lamas were before, behind, and on each side of the palanquin, jovially dashing about on horses and camels. The road almost throughout was lined with spectators, or rather with worshippers, eagerly awaiting the arrival of the Holy, and upon his approach, falling, first on their knees, and then on their faces, before him, their hands crossed over the head. It seemed the progress of a divinity come upon earth to bless its people. On reaching the Great Wall, the Guison-Tamba, ceasing to be a divinity, became only the chief of some nomad tribes, scorned by the people of China, but feared by the Court of China, more alive to political contingencies. Only one half of the 3,000 Lamas were permitted to attend their chief further, the rest remaining encamped north of the Great Wall.

The Guison-Tamba sojourned at Peking for three months, receiving an occasional visit from the Emperor, and from the Grand Dignitaries. He then relieved the celestial city from his troublesome presence, and after paying visits to the Lamaseries of the Five Towers, and of the Blue Town, set out on his return to his own states when he died, the victim, it was asserted, of a slow poison that had been administered to him by order of the Emperor. The Khalkhas, however, were more irritated than intimidated by his death, for they are persuaded that their Guison-Tamba never actually dies. All he does, when he appears to die, is to transmigrate to some other country, whence he returns to them younger, more vigorous, more active than ever. In 1844, accordingly, they were told that their living Buddha was incarnate in Thibet, and they went thither, in solemn procession, to fetch the child of five years old who was indicated to them, and to place him on his imperishable throne. While we were encamped at Kou-Kou-Noor, on the banks of the Blue Sea, we saw pass by us the great caravan of Khalkhas, who were on their way to Lha-Ssa to bring home the Lama-King of the Great Kouren.

The Kouren of the Thousand Lamas—*Mingan Lamané Kouré*—is also a celebrated Lamasery, which dates from the invasion of China by the Mantchous. When Tchun-

Tche,[1] founder of the dynasty now reigning in China, descended from the forests of Mantchouria to march upon Peking, he met on his way a Lama of Thibet, whom he consulted as to the issue of his enterprise. The Lama promised him complete success, where upon Tchun-Tche ordered him to come and see him when he should be installed at Peking. After the Mantchous had rendered themselves masters of the capital of the empire, the Lama did not fail to keep his appointment. The Emperor at once recognized the person who had favored him with such an auspicious horoscope; and, in token of his gratitude, allotted to him a large extent of land whereon to construct a Lamasery, and revenues sufficient for the support of a thousand Lamas. From the time of its erection, however, the Lamasery of the Thousand Lamas has grown and grown, so that at present it contains more than four thousand Lamas, though its original designation still remains. By degrees, traders have established themselves around it, and have built a considerable town, jointly occupied by Chinese and by Tartars. The principal commerce of the place is in beasts.

The Grand Lama of the Lamasery is, at the same time, sovereign of the district. It is he who makes laws, who administers justice, and who appoints magistrates. When he dies, his subjects go and seek for him in Thibet, where he is always understood to metempsychose himself.

At the time of our visit to the Kouren of the Thousand Lamas, everything was in utter confusion, by reason of a suit between the Lama King and his four ministers, who are called, in the Mongol language, Dchassak. The latter had taken upon themselves to marry, and to build houses for themselves apart from the Lamasery, things altogether subversive of Lama discipline. The Grand Lama essayed to bring them to order; the four Dchassak, instead of submitting, had collected a whole heap of grievances, upon which they framed an accusation against their chief before the Tou-Toun, the high Mantchou Mandarin, who acts as Secretary-of-State for the Tartar department.

The suit had been under prosecution two months when

[1] The anecdote, which we give as we heard it, must have reference to Tchun-Tche's father, who died immediately after the conquest. Tchun-Tche himself was only four years old at the time.

we visited the Lamasery, and we soon saw how the establishment was suffering from the absence of its principals. Study or prayer there was none; the great outer gate was open, and seemed not to have been closed at all for some time past. We entered the interior; all we found there was silence and solitude. The grass was growing in the courts, and upon the walls. The doors of the temples were padlocked, but through the gratings we could see that the seats, the altars, the paintings, the statues, were all covered with dust; everything manifested that the Lamasery had been for some time in a state of utter neglect. The absence of the superiors, and the uncertainty as to the result of the suit, had unloosened all the bonds of discipline. The Lamas had dispersed, and people began to regard the very existence of the Lamasery as extremely compromised. We have since heard that, thanks to enormous bribery, the suit terminated in favor of the Lama King, and the four Dchassak were compelled to conform themselves in all respects to the orders of their sovereign.

We may add to the enumeration of the many celebrated Lamaseries, those of Blue Town, of Tolon-Noor, of Gé-Ho-Eul; and within the Great Wall, that of Peking, and that of the Five Towers in Chan-Si.

After quitting the Lamasery of Tchortchi, just as we were entering upon the Red Banner, we met a Mongol hunter, who was carrying behind him, on his horse, a fine roebuck he had just killed. We had been so long reduced to our insipid oatmeal, seasoned with a few bits of mutton fat, that the sight of the venison inspired us with a somewhat decided desire to vary our entertainment; we felt, moreover, that our stomachs, weakened by our daily privations, imperiously demanded a more substantial alimentation. After saluting the hunter, therefore, we asked him if he was disposed to sell his venison. "Sirs Lamas," replied he, "when I placed myself in ambush to await the deer, I had no thought of trading in my head. The Chinese carmen, stationed up yonder beyound Tchortchi, wanted to buy my game for four hundred sapeks, but I said no! But to you, Sirs Lamas, I speak not as to Kitat; there is my roebuck: give me what you please for it." We told Samdadchiemba to pay the hunter five hundred sapeks; and hanging the venison over the neck of one of the camels, we proceeded on our way.

Five hundred sapeks are equivalent to about 2*s.* 1*d.*, and this is the ordinary price of a roebuck in Tartary; the price of a sheep is thrice that amount. Venison is little esteemed by the Tartars, and still less by the Chinese; black meat, say they, is never so good as white. Yet in the larger cities of China, and especially at Peking, black meat has an honorable place on the tables of the rich and of the mandarins; a circumstance, however, to be attributed to the scarcity of the article, and a desire for variety. The Mantchous, indeed, do not come within the preceding observation; for, great lovers of hunting, they are also great lovers of its produce, and especially of bears, stags, and pheasants.

It was just past noon when we came to a spot marvelously beautiful. After passing through a narrow opening between two rocks, whose summits seemed lost in the clouds, we found ourselves in a large enclosure, surrounded by lofty hills, on which grew a number of scattered pines. An abundant fountain supplied a small stream, whose banks were covered with angelica and wild mint. The rivulet, after making the circuit of the enclosure, amid rich grass, had its issue thence by an opening similar to that by which we had entered the place. No sooner had a glance comprehended the attractions of the spot, than Samdadchiemba moved that we should at once set up our tent there. "Let us go no further to-day," said he; "let us encamp here. We have not gone far this morning, it is true, and the sun is still very high; but we have got the venison to prepare, and should therefore encamp earlier than usual." No one opposing the honorable gentleman's motion, it was put and carried unanimously, and we proceeded to set up our tent by the side of the spring.

Samdadchiemba had often talked of his great dexterity in the dissection of animals, and he was delighted with this opportunity of displaying his excellence in this respect. Having suspended the roebuck from a pine-branch, sharpened his knife upon a tent-pin, and turned up his sleeves to the elbow, he asked whether we would have the animal dismembered *à la Chinoise*, *à la Turque*, or *à la Tartare*. Unprovided with any reason for preferring any one of these modes to the other two, we left it to Samdadchiemba to obey the impulse of his genius in the matter. In a minute he had skinned and gutted the animal, and he then cut away the flesh from the bones, in one piece, without separating the limbs, so as to leave suspended from the tree merely the skeleton of the deer. This, it appeared, was the Turkish fashion, in use upon long journeys, in order to relieve travelers from the useless burden of bones.

This operation completed, Samdadchiemba cut some slices of venison and proceeded to fry them in mutton fat, a manner of preparing venison not perhaps in strict accordance with the rules of the culinary art; but the difficulty of the circumstances did not allow us to do better. Our banquet was soon ready, but, contrary to our expectations, we were not the first to taste it; we had seated ourselves triangularly on the grass, having in the midst the lid of the pot, which served us as a dish, when all of a sudden we heard, as it were, the rushing of a storm over our heads: a great eagle dashed, like a lightning stroke, upon our entertainment, and immediately rose with equal rapidity, bearing off in each claw a large slice of venison. Upon recovering from our fright at this sudden incident, we ourselves were fain to laugh at the ludicrous aspect of the matter, but Samdadchiemba did not laugh by any means; he was in a paroxysm of fury, not indeed at the loss of the venison, but because the eagle, in its flight, insolently dealt him a sound box on the ear with the extremity of its great wings.

This event served to render us more cautious on the following venison days. During our previous journeyings we had, indeed, on several occasions observed eagles hovering over our heads at meal-times, but no accident of this kind had occurred; probably the royal birds had scorned our mere oatmeal repasts.

You see the eagle almost everywhere throughout the deserts of Tartary; sometimes hovering and making large circles in the air, sometimes perched upon a rising ground, motionless as the hillock itself. No one in these countries hunts the eagle or molests it in any way; it may make its nest where it pleases, and there bring up its eaglets, and itself grow old, without being in the smallest degree interfered with by man. You often see before you an eagle resting on the plain, and looking there larger than a sheep; as you approach, before rising, it leisurely moves along the ground, beating its wings, and then, by degrees ascending, it attains the altitude where it can fly in all its grandeur and power.

After several days' journey we quitted the country of the Eight Banners and entered Western Toumet. At the time of the conquest of China by the Mantchous, the king of Toumet, having distinguished himself in the expedition as an auxiliary of the invaders, the conqueror, in order to evince his gratitude for the services which the prince had rendered him, gave him the fine districts situated north of Peking, beyond the Great Wall. From that period they have borne the name of Eastern Toumet, and Old Toumet took that of Western Toumet; the two Toumets are separated from each other by the Tchakar River.

The Mongol Tartars of Western Toumet do not lead the pastoral and nomadic life: they cultivate their lands and apply themselves to the arts of civilized nations. We had been for nearly a month traversing the desert, setting up our tent for the night in the first convenient place we found, and accustomed to see nothing but, above us the sky, and below and around us interminable prairies. We had long, as it were, broken with the world, for all we had seen of mankind had been a few Tartar horsemen dashing across the Land of Grass, like so many birds of passage. Without suspecting it, our tastes had insensibly become modified, and the desert of Mongolia had created in us a temperament friendly to the tranquillity of solitude. When, therefore, we found ourselves amid the cultivation, the movement, the bustle, the confusion of civilized existence, we felt, as it were, oppressed, suffocated; we seemed gasping for breath, and as though every moment we were going to be stifled. This impression, however, was evanescent; and we soon got to think that, after all, it was more comfortable and more agreeable, after a day's march, to take up our abode in a warm, well-stored inn, than to have to set up a tent, to collect fuel, and to prepare our own very meager repast, before we could take our rest.

The inhabitants of Western Toumet, as may well be imagined, have completely lost the stamp of their original Mongol character; they have all become, more or less, Chinese; many of them do not even know a word of the Mongol language. Some, indeed, do not scruple to express contempt for their brothers of the desert, who refuse to

Tartar Agriculturist.

subject their prairies to the ploughshare; they say, how ridiculous is it for men to be always vagabondizing about, and to have merely wretched tents wherein to shelter their heads, when they might so easily build houses, and obtain wealth and comforts of all kinds from the land beneath their feet. And, indeed, the Western Toumetians are perfectly right in preferring the occupation of agriculturist to that of shepherd, for they have magnificent plains, well watered, fertile, and favorable to the production of all kinds of grain crops. When we passed through the country, harvest was over; but the great stacks of corn that we saw in all directions told us that the produce had been abundant and fine. Everything throughout Western Toumet bears the impress of affluence; nowhere, go in what direction you may, do you see the wretched tumble-down houses that disfigure the highways and by-ways of China; nowhere do you see the miserable, half-starved, half-clothed creatures that pain the hearts of travelers in every other country: all the peasants here are well fed, well lodged, and well clothed. All the villages and roads are beautified with groups and avenues of fine trees; whereas, in the other Tartar regions, cultivated by the Chinese, no trees are to be seen; trees are not even planted, for everybody knows they would be pulled up next day by some miserable pauper or other, for fuel.

We had made three days' journey through the cultivated lands of the Toumet, when we entered *Kou-Kou-Hote* (Blue Town), called in Chinese *Koui-Hoa-Tchen*. There are two towns of the same name, five *lis* distant from one another. The people distinguish them by calling the one "Old Town," and the other "New Town," or "Commercial Town," and "Military Town." We first entered the latter, which was built by the Emperor Khang-Hi, to defend the empire against its northern enemies. The town has a beautiful, noble appearance, which might be admired in Europe itself. We refer, however, only to its circuit of embattled walls, made of brick: for inside, the low houses, built in the Chinese style, are little in unison with the lofty, huge ramparts that surround them. The interior of the town offers nothing remarkable but its regularity, and a large and beautiful street, which runs through it from east to west. A Kiang-Kian, or military commandant, resides here with 10,000 soldiers, who are drilled every day; so that the town may be regarded as a garrison town.

The soldiers of the New Town of Koukou Khoton are Mantchou Tartars; but if you did not previously know the fact, you would scarcely suspect it from hearing them speak. Amongst them there is perhaps not a single man who understands the language of his own country. Already two ages have passed away since the Mantchous made themselves masters of the vast empire of China, and you would say that during these two centuries they have been unceasingly working out their own annihilation. Their manners, their language, their very country—all has become Chinese. It may now be affirmed that Mantchou nationality has become irremediably annihilated. In order to account for this strange counter-revolution, and to understand how the Chinese have been able to fuse their conquerors with themselves, and to get possession of Mantchouria, we must look some way back, and enter somewhat into detail.

In the time of the Ming dynasty, which flourished in China from 1368 to 1644, the Mantchous, or Eastern Tartars, after a long series of internal wars, concurred in the selection of a chief, who united all the tribes into one, and

Chinese Soldier.

established a kingdom. From that time this ferocious and barbarian people insensibly acquired an importance which gave great umbrage to the Court of Peking; and in 1618 its power was so well established, that its king did not fear to transmit to the Emperor of China the statement of seven grievances which, he said, he had to avenge. The daring manifesto finished with these words: "*And in order to avenge these seven injuries, I will reduce and subjugate the dynasty of the Ming.*" Shortly afterwards the empire was convulsed with revolts in all directions; the rebel chief besieged Peking, and took it. Thereupon the Emperor, despairing of his fortune, hanged himself from a tree in the Imperial garden, leaving near him these words, written in his own blood : "*Since the empire is falling, the Emperor, too, must fall.*" Ou-San-Koueï, the Imperial general, called in the Mantchous to aid him in reducing the rebels. The latter were put to flight, and while the Chinese general was pursuing them southward, the Tartar chief returned to Peking, and finding the throne vacant, assumed it.

Previous to this event, the Great Wall, carefully maintained by the Ming dynasty, had kept the Mantchous from entering China, while, reciprocally, the Chinese were forbidden to enter Mantchouria. After the Mantchou conquest of the empire, however, there was no longer any frontier separating the two nations. The Great Wall was freely passed, and the communication between the two countries once thrown open, the Chinese populations of Pe-Tchi-Li and Chan-Toung, hitherto confined within their narrow provinces, burst like torrents upon Mantchouria. The Tartar chief had been considered the sole master, the sole possessor of the lands of his kingdom; but, established as Emperor of China, he distributed his vast possessions among the Mantchous, upon the condition that they should pay him heavy rents for them every year. By means of usury and cunning, and persevering machinations, the Chinese have since rendered themselves masters of all the lands of their conquerors, leaving to them merely their empty titles, their onerous statutory labor, and the payment of oppressive rents. The quality of Mantchou has thus by degrees become a very costly affair, and many, of consequence, seek altogether to abnegate it. According to the law, there is, every third year, a census made of the population of each banner, and all persons who do not cause their names to be inscribed on the roll, are deemed no longer to belong to the Mantchou nation; those, therefore, of the Mantchous whose indigence induces them to desire exemption from statute labor and military service, do not present themselves to the census enumerators, and by that omission enter the ranks of the Chinese people. Thus, while, on the one hand, constant migration has carried beyond the Great Wall a great number of Chinese, on the other, a great number of Mantchous have voluntarily abdicated their nationality.

The decline, or rather the extinction of the Mantchou nation, is now progressing more rapidly than ever. Up to the reign of Tao-Kouan, the regions watered by the Songari were exclusively inhabited by Mantchous: entrance into those vast districts was prohibited to the Chinese, and no man was permitted to cultivate the soil within their range. At the commencement of the present reign, these districts were put up for public sale, in order to supply the deficiency in the Imperial treasury. The Chinese rushed upon them like birds of prey, and a few years sufficed to remove everything that could in any way recall the memory of their ancient possessors. It would be vain for any one now to seek in Mantchouria a single town, a single village, that is not composed entirely of Chinese.

Yet, amid the general transformation, there are still a few tribes, such as the Si-Po and the Solon, which faithfully retain the Mantchou type. Up to the present day their territories have been invaded neither by the Chinese nor by cultivation; they continue to dwell in tents and to furnish soldiers to the Imperial armies. It has been remarked, however, that their frequent appearance at Peking, and their long periods of service in the provincial garrisons, are beginning to make terrible inroads upon their habits and tastes.

When the Mantchous conquered China, they imposed upon the conquered people a portion of their dress and many of their usages. Tobacco smoking, for example, and the manner of dressing the hair, now in use by the Chinese, came to them from the Mantchou Tartars. But the Chinese, in their turn, did far more than this; they managed to make their conquerors adopt their manners and their language. You may now traverse Mantchouria to the river Amour, without being at all aware that you are not traveling in a province of China. The local coloring has become totally effaced. With the exception of a few nomadic tribes no one speaks Mantchou: and there would, perhaps, remain no trace of this fine language, had not the Emperors Khang-Hi and Kien-Loung erected, in its honor, monuments imperishable in themselves, and which will ever attract the attention of European orientalists.

At one time the Mantchous had no writing of their own; it was not until 1624, that Tai-Tsou-Kao-Hoang-Ti, chief of the Eastern Tartars, directed several learned persons of his nation to design a system of letters for the Mantchous, upon the model of those of the Mongols. Subsequently, in, 1641, a man of great genius, named Tahai, perfected the work, and gave to the Mantchou system of letters the elegance, clearness, and refinement which now characterize it.

Chun-Tche had the finest productions of Chinese literature translated into Mantchou. Khang-Hi established an academy of learned persons, equally versed in the Chinese and Tartar languages, whom he employed upon the translation of classical and historical works, and in the compilation of several dictionaries. In order to express novel objects and the various conceptions previously unknown to the Mantchous, it was necessary to invent terms, borrowed, for the most part, from the Chinese, and adapted, by slight alterations, as closely as possible, to the Tartar idiom. This process, however, tending to destroy, by imperceptible degrees, the originality of the Mantchou language, the Emperor Kien-Loung, to avert the danger, had a Mantchou dictionary compiled, from which all Chinese words were excluded. The compilers went about questioning old men and other Mantchous deemed most conversant with their mother-tongue, and rewards were given to such as brought forward an obsolescent word or expression which was deemed worthy of revival and perpetuation in the dictionary.

Thanks to the solicitude and enlightened zeal of the first sovereigns of the present dynasty, there is now no good Chinese book which has not been translated into Mantchou; and all these translations are invested with the greatest possible authenticity, as having been executed by learned academies, by order and under the immediate auspices of several emperors: and as having, moreover, been subsequently revised and corrected by other academies, equally learned, and whose members were versed alike in the Chinese language and in the Mantchou idiom.

The Mantchou language has attained, by means of all these learned labors, a solid basis; it may, indeed, become no longer spoken, but it will ever remain a classic tongue, and ever be of most important aid to philologers applying their studies to the Asiatic tongues. Besides numerous and faithful translations of the best Chinese books, the Mantchou language possesses versions of the principal productions in the Lamanesque, Thibetian, and Mantchou literature. A few years' labor will thus suffice to place the diligent student of Mantchou in full possession of all the most precious monuments of Eastern Asiatic literature.

The Mantchou language is sonorous, harmonious, and, above all, singularly clear. Its study is now rendered easy and agreeable by H. Conon de la Gabelentz's "Elemens de la Grammaire Mantchou," published at Altemburg, in Saxony, and which develops, with happy lucidity, the mechanism and rules of the language. The excellent work of this learned orientalist cannot fail to be of great assistance to all who desire to apply themselves to the study of a language menaced with extinction in the very country which gave it birth, but which France, at least, will preserve for the use of the world of letters. M. Conon de la Gabelentz says, in the preface to his grammar: "I have selected the French language in the preparation of my work, because France is, as yet, the only European country in which Mantchou has been cultivated, so that it seems to me indispensable that all who desire to study this idiom should first know French, as being the tongue in which are composed the only European works which relate to Mantchou literature."

While the French missionaries were enriching their country with the literary treasures which they found in these remote regions, they were, at the same time, ardently engaged in diffusing the light of Christianity amid these idolatrous nations, whose religion is merely a monstrous medley of doctrines and practises borrowed at once from Lao-Tseu, Confucius, and Buddha.

It is well known that in the earlier years of the present dynasty, these missionaries had, by their talents, acquired great influence at court; they always accompanied the Emperors in the long and frequent journeys which at that period they were accustomed to make into the regions of their ancient rule. These zealous preachers of the gospel never failed on all such occasions to avail themselves of the protection and influence they enjoyed, as a means for sowing, wherever they went, the seeds of the true faith. Such was the first origin of the introduction of Christianity into Mantchouria. They reckoned at first but few neophytes; but the number of these was insensibly augmented afterwards by the migrations of the Chinese, in which were always to be found several Christian families. These missions formed part of the diocese of Peking until within a few years past; then the Bishop of Nanking, administrator of the diocese of Peking, finding himself nigh the close of his career, and fearing that the political commotions of which Portugal, his native country, was at that time the theater, would preclude the Portuguese church from sending an adequate number of laborers to cultivate the vast field which had been confided to him, communicated his apprehensions to the Sacred College de Propagandâ Fide, and earnestly entreated its members to take under their especial attention a harvest, already ripe, but which was under peril of destruction, for want of husbandmen to gather it in. The sacred congregation, touched with the anxiety of this venerable and zealous old man, among its other arrangements for meeting the requirements of these unfortunate missions, dismembered Mantchouria from the diocese of Peking, and erected it into an Apostolic Vicariat, which was confided to the charge of the Foreign Missionary Society. M. Verolles, Bishop of Colombia, was made the new Vicar Apostolic. Nothing less than the patience, the devotion, the every virtue of an apostle, was essential for the due administration of this Christendom. The prejudices of the neophytes, not as yet brought within the rules of ecclesiastical discipline, were, for M. Verolles, obstacles more difficult to overcome than even the ruggedness of heart of the pagans; but his experience and his wisdom soon triumphed over all impediments. The mission has assumed a new form; the number of Christians is annually augmenting; and there is now every hope that the Apostolic Vicariat of Mantchouria will become one of the most flourishing missions in Asia.

Mantchouria is bounded on the north by Siberia, on the south by the Gulf Phou-Hai and Corea, on the east by the sea of Japan, and on the west by Russian Dauria and Mongolia.

Moukden, in Chinese Chen-Yan, is the chief town of Mantchouria, and may be considered the second capital of the Chinese empire. The Emperor has a palace and courts of justice there on the model of those at Peking. Moukden is a large and fine city, surrounded by thick and lofty ramparts; the streets are broad and regular, and less dirty and tumultuous than those of Peking. One entire quarter is appropriated to the princes of the Yellow Girdle; that is, to the members of the Imperial family. They are all under the direction of a grand Mandarin, who is entrusted with the inspection of their conduct, and empowered summarily to punish any offenses they may commit.

After Moukden, the most remarkable towns are Ghirin, surrounded by high wooden palisades, and Ningouta, the native place of the reigning Imperial family. Lao-yan, Kai-Tcheou, and Kin-Tcheou, are remarkable for the extensive commerce their maritime position brings them.

Mantchouria, watered by a great number of streams and rivers, is a country naturally fertile. Since the cultivation has been in the hands of the Chinese, the soil has been enriched by a large number of the products of the interior. In the southern part, they cultivate successfully the dry rice, or that which has no need of watering, and the Imperial rice, discovered by the Emperor Khang-Hi. These two sorts of rice would certainly succeed in France. They have also abundant harvests of millet, of Kao-Léang or Indian corn (*Holcus Sorghum*), from which they distil excellent brandy: sesamum, linseed, hemp, and tobacco, the best in the whole Chinese empire.

The Mantchourians pay especial attention to the cultivation of the herbaceous-stemmed cotton plant, which produces cotton in extraordinary abundance. A Meou of these plants, a space of about one-sixth of an acre, ordinarily produces 2,000 lbs. of cotton. The fruit of the cotton tree grows in the form of a cod or shell, and attains the size of a hazelnut. As it ripens, the cod opens, divides into three parts, and develops three or four small tufts of cotton which contain the seeds. In order to separate the seed, they make use of a sort of little bow, firmly strung, the cord of which vibrating under the cotton tufts removes the seeds, of which a portion is retained for next year's sowing, and the rest is made into oil, resembling linseed oil. The upper portion of Mantchouria, too cold to grow cotton, has immense harvests of corn.

Besides these productions, common to China, Mantchouria possesses three treasures [1] peculiar to itself: jinseng, sable fur, and the grass Oula.

[1] The Chinese designate them San Pao: the Mantchous, Ilan Baobai: the Mongols, Korbanerdeni; and the Thibetans, Tchok-Soum.

The first of these productions has been long known in Europe, though our learned Academy there ventured some years ago to doubt its existence. Jin-seng is perhaps the most considerable article of Mantchourian commerce. Throughout China there is no chemist's shop unprovided with more or less of it.

The root of jin-seng is straight, spindle-shaped, and very knotty; seldom so large as one's little finger, and in length from two to three inches. When it has undergone its fitting preparation, its color is a transparent white, with sometimes a slight red or yellow tinge. Its appearance, then, is that of a branch of stalactite.

The Chinese report marvels of the jin-seng, and no doubt it is, for Chinese organization, a tonic of very great effect for old and weak persons; but its nature is too healing, the Chinese physicians admit, for the European temperament, already, in their opinion, too hot. The price is enormous, and doubtless its dearness contributes, with a people like the Chinese, to raise its celebrity so high. The rich and the Mandarins probably use it only because it is above the reach of other people, and out of pure ostentation.

The jin-seng, grown in Corea, and there called Kao-li-seng, is of very inferior quality to that of Mantchouria.

The second special treasure of Eastern Tartary is the fur of the sable, which, obtained by the hunters with immense labor and danger, is of such excessive price that only the princes and great dignitaries of the empire can purchase it. The grass called Oula, the third specialty of Mantchouria, is, on the contrary, of the commonest occurrence; its peculiar property is, that if put into your shoes, it communicates to the feet a soothing warmth, even in the depth of winter.

As we have said above, the Mantchou Tartars have almost wholly abdicated their own manners, and adopted instead those of the Chinese; yet, amid this transformation of their primitive characters, they have still retained their old passion for hunting, for horse exercise, and for archery. At all periods of their history, they have attached an astonishing importance to these various exercises; any one may convince himself of this by merely running his eye over a Mantchou dictionary. Every thing, every incident, every attribute relating to these exercises, has its special expression, so as to need no circumlocution to convey it. There are different names, not only for the different colors of the horse, for example, for its age and qualities, but for all its movements; and it is just the same with reference to hunting and archery.

The Mantchous are excellent archers, and among them the tribe Solon is particularly eminent in this respect. At all the military stations, trials of skill with the bow take place on certain periodical occasions, in presence of the Mandarins and of the assembled people. Three straw men, of the size of life, are placed in a straight line, at from twenty to thirty paces distance from one another; the archer is on a line with them, about fifteen feet off from the first figure, his bow bent, and his finger on the string. The signal being given, he puts his horse to a gallop, and discharges his arrow at the first figure; without checking his horse's speed, he takes a second arrow from his quiver, places it in the bow, and discharges it against the second figure, and so with the third; all this while the horse is dashing at full speed along the line of the figures, so that the rider has to keep himself firm in the stirrups while he maneuvers with the promptitude necessary to avoid the getting beyond his mark. From the first figure to the second, the archer has bare time for drawing his arrow, fixing and discharging it, so that when he shoots, he has generally to turn somewhat on his saddle; and as to the third shot, he has to discharge it altogether in the old Parthian fashion. Yet, for a competitor to be deemed a good archer, it is essential that he should fire an arrow into every one of the three figures. "To know how to shoot an arrow," writes a Mantchou author, "is the first and most important knowledge for a Tartar to acquire. Though success therein seems an easy matter, success is of rare occurrence. How many are there who practise day and night? How many are there who sleep with the bow in their arms? and yet how few are there who have rendered themselves famous. How few are there whose names are proclaimed at the matches! Keep your frame straight and firm; avoid vicious postures; let your shoulders be immovable. Fire every arrow into its mark, and you may be satisfied with your skill.

The day after our arrival at the military town of Koukou-Khoton, we repaired on a visit to the mercantile district. Our hearts were painfully affected at finding ourselves in a Mantchou town, and hearing any language spoken there but the Mantchou. We could not reconcile to our minds the idea of a nation renegade of its nationality, of a conquering people, in nothing distinguishable from the conquered, except, perhaps, that they have a little less industry and a little more conceit. When the Thibetian Lama promised to the Tartar chief the conquest of China, and predicted to him that he should soon be seated on the throne at Peking, he would have told him more of truth, had he told him that his whole nation, its manners, its language, its country, was about to be engulfed forever in the Chinese empire. Let any revolution remove the present dynasty, and the Mantchou will be compelled to complete fusion with the empire. Admission to their own country, occupied entirely by the Chinese, will be forbidden to them. In reference to a map of Mantohouria, compiled by the Fathers Jesuits, upon the order of the Emperor Khang-Hi, Father Duhalde says that he abstained from giving the Chinese names of places in the map; and he assigns for this the following reason: "Of what use would it be to a traveler through Mantchouria to be told, for example, that the river Sakhalien-Oula is called by the Chinese Hé-Loung-Kiang, since it is not with Chinese he has there to do; and the Tartars, whose aid he requires, have never heard the Chinese name." This observation might be just enough in the time of Khang-Hi, but now the precise converse would hold good; for in traversing Mantchouria it is always with Chinese you have to deal, and it is always of the Hé-Loung-Kiang that you hear, and never of the Sakhalien-Oula.

Chinese Money Changers.

CHAPTER V.

The Old Blue Town—Quarter of the Tanners--Knavery of the Chinese Traders--Hotel of the Three Perfections--Spoliation of the Tartars by the Chinese--Money Changer's Office—Tartar Coiner--Purchase of two Sheep-skin Robes --Camel Market--Customs of the Cameleers—Assassination of a Grand Lama of the Blue Town--Insurrection of the Lamaseries--Negotiation between the Court of Peking and that of Lha-Ssa--Domestic Lamas—Wandering Lamas—Lamas in Community--Policy of the Mantchou Dynasty with reference to the Lamaseries—Interview with a Thibetian Lama--Departure from the Blue Town.

FROM the Mantchou town to the Old Blue Town is not more than half an hour's walk, along a broad road, constructed through the large market, which narrowed the town. With the exception of the Lamaseries, which rise above the other buildings, you see before you merely an immense mass of houses and shops huddled confusedly together, without any order or arrangement whatever. The ramparts of the old town still exist in all their integrity; but the increase of the population has compelled the people by degrees to pass this barrier. Houses have risen outside the walls one after another until large suburbs have been formed, and now the extra-mural city is larger than the intra-mural.

We entered the city by a broad street, which exhibited nothing remarkable except the large Lamasery, called, in common with the more celebrated establishment in the province of Chan-Si, the Lamasery of the Five Towers. It derives this appellation from a handsome square tower with five turrets, one, very lofty, in the center and one at each angle.

Just beyond this the broad street terminated, and there was no exit but a narrow lane running right and left. We turned down what seemed the least dirty of these, but soon found ourselves in a liquid slough of mud and filth, black, and of suffocating stench—we had got into the Street of the Tanners. We advanced slowly and shudderingly, for beneath the mire lay hid, now a great stone, over which we stumbled, now a hole, into which we sank. To complete our misfortune, we all at once heard before us deafening cries and shouts, indicating that along the tortuosities of the lane in which we were horsemen and carts were about to meet us. To draw back, or to stand aside, were equally impossible, so that our only resource was to bawl on our own account, and, advancing, take our chance. At the next turning we met the cavalcade, and something extremely disagreeable seemed threatening us, when upon sight of our camels, the horses of the other party took fright, and turning right round, galloped off in utter confusion, leaving the way clear before us. Thus, thanks to our beasts of burden, we were enabled to continue our journey without giving the way to any one, and we at last arrived, without any serious accident, in a spacious street, adorned on each side with fine shops.

We looked about for an inn, but fruitlessly; we saw several inns, indeed, but these were not of the kind we sought. In the great towns of Northern China and Tartary each inn is devoted to a particular class of travelers, and will receive no other. "The Corndealers' Arms" inn, for example, will not admit a horse dealer, and so on. The inns which devote themselves to the entertainment of mere travelers are called the taverns of the Transitory Guests. We were pausing, anxiously looking about for one of these, when a young man, hastening from an adjacent shop, came up to us: "You seek an inn, gentlemen travelers," said he; "suffer me to guide you to one; yet I scarcely know one in the Blue City worthy of you. Men are innumerable here, my Lords Lamas; a few good, but, alas! most bad. I speak it from my heart. In the Blue City you would with difficulty find one man who is guided by his conscience; yet conscience is a treasure! You Tartars, you, indeed, know well what conscience is. Ah! I know the Tartars well! excellent people, right-hearted souls! We Chinese are altogether different—rascals, rogues. Not one Chinaman in ten thousand heeds conscience. Here, in this Blue City, everybody, with the merest exceptions, makes it his business to cheat the worthy Tartars, and rob them of their goods. Oh! it's shameful!"

And the excellent creature threw up his eyes as he denounced the knavery of his townsmen. We saw very clearly, however, that the direction taken by the eyes thus thrown up was the camel's back, whereon were two large cases, which our disinterested adviser no doubt took to contain precious merchandise. However, we let him lead us on and chatter as he pleased. When we had been wandering about under his escort for a full hour, and yet had reached no inn, we said to him: "We cannot think of troubling you further, since you yourself seem not to know where we may find that which we need." "Be perfectly easy, my lords," replied he; "I am guiding you to an excellent, a superexcellent hotel. Don't mention a word as to troubling me: you pain me by the idea. What! are we not all brothers? Away with the distinction between Tartar and Chinese! True, the language is not the same, nor the dress; but men have but one heart, one conscience, one invariable rule of justice. Just wait one moment for me, my lords; I will be with you again before you can look round," and so saying he dived into a shop on the left. He was soon back with us, making a thousand apologies for having detained us. "You must be very tired, my lords; one cannot be otherwise when one is traveling. 'Tis quite different from being with one's own family." As he spoke, we were accosted by another Chinese, a ludicrous contrast with our first friend, whose round shining, smiling face was perfectly intense in its aspect of benevolence. The other fellow was meager and lanky, with thin, pinched lips and little black eyes, half buried in the head, that gave to the whole physiognomy a character of the most thorough knavery. "My Lords Lamas," said he, "I see you have just arrived! Excellent! And you have journeyed safely. Well, well! Your camels are magnificent; 'tis no wonder you travel fast and securely upon such animals. Well, you have arrived: that's a great happiness. Se-Eul," he continued, addressing the Chinese who had first got hold of us, "you are guiding these noble Tartars to an hotel. 'Tis well! Take care that the hotel is a good one, worthy of the distinguished strangers. What think you of the 'Tavern of Eternal Equity?'" "The very hotel whither I was leading the Lords Lamas." "There is none better in the empire. By the way, the host is an acquaintance of mine. I cannot do better than accompany you and recommend these noble Tartars to his best care. In fact, if I were not to go with you, I should have a weight upon my heart. When we are fortunate enough to meet brothers who need our aid, how can we do too much for them, for we are all brothers! My lords, you see this young man and myself; well, we two are clerks in the same establishment, and we make it our pride to serve our brothers the Tartars; for, alas! in this dreadful city there is but too little virtue."

Any one, hearing their professions of devoted zeal, would have imagined these two personages to have been the friends of our childhood; but we were sufficiently acquainted with Chinese manners to perceive at once that we were the mark of a couple of swindlers. Accordingly, when we saw inscribed on a door, "Hotel of the Three Perfections; transitory guests on horse and camel entertained, and their affairs transacted with infallible success," we at once directed our course up the gateway, despite the vehement remonstrances of our worthy guides, and rode down a long avenue to the great square court of the hotel. The little blue cap worn by the attendants indicated that we were in a Turkish establishment.

This proceeding of ours was not at all what the two Chinese desired; but they still followed us, and, without appearing disconcerted, continued to act their parts. "Where are the people of the hotel," cried they, with an immense air; "let them prepare a large apartment, a fine, clean apartment? Their Excellencies have arrived, and must be suitably accommodated." One of the principal waiters presented himself, holding by his teeth a key, in one hand a broom, and in the other a watering-pot. Our two protectors immediately took possession of these articles. "Leave everything to us," said they; "it is we who claim the honor of personally waiting upon our illustrious friends; you, attendants of the hotel, you only do things by halves, actuated as you are merely by mercenary considerations." And thereupon they set to work sprinkling, sweeping, and cleaning the room to which the waiter guided us. When this operation was concluded, we seated ourselves on the khang; the two Chinese "knew themselves better than to sit by the side of our Eminent Distinctions," and they accordingly squatted on the floor. As tea was being served, a young man, well attired and of exceedingly elegant address, came into the room, carrying by the four corners a silk handkerchief. "Gentlemen Lamas," said the elder of our previous companions, "this young man is the son of our principal, and doubtless has been sent by his father to inquire after your health, and whether you have so far journeyed in peace." The young man placed his handkerchief upon the table that stood before us. "Here are some cakes my father has sent to be eaten with your tea. When you have finished that meal, he entreats you will come and partake of an humble repast in our poor dwelling." "But why wear your hearts out thus for us mere strangers?" "Oh!" exclaimed all three in chorus, "the words you utter cover us with blushes! What! can we do anything in excess for brothers who have thus honored us with their presence in our poor city!" "Poor Tartars!" said I in French to my colleague, "how thoroughly eaten up they must be when they fall into such hands as these!" These words, in an unknown tongue, excited considerable surprise in our worthy friends. "In which of the illustrious kingdoms of Tartary dwell your Excellencies?" asked one of them. "We are not Tartars at all," was the reply. "Ah! we saw that at once; the Tartars have no such majesty of aspect as yours; their mien has no grandeur about it! May we ask what is the noble country whence you come?" "We are from the West; our native land is far hence." "Quite so," replied the eldest of the three knaves. I knew it, and I said so to these young men, but they are ignorant; they know nothing about physiognomy. Ah! you are from the West. I know your country well; I have been there more than once." "We are delighted to hear this: doubtless, then, you are acquainted with our language?" "Why, I cannot say I know it thoroughly; but there are some few words I understand. I can't speak them, indeed; but that does not matter. You western people are so clever, you know everything, the Chinese language, the Tartarian, the western—you can speak them all. I have always been closely mixed up with your countrymen, and have invariably been selected to manage their affairs for them whenever they come to the Blue Town. It is always I who make their purchases for them."

We had by this time finished our tea; our three friends rose, and with a simultaneous bow, invited us to accompany them. "My lords, the repast is by this time prepared, and our chief awaits you." "Listen," said we, gravely, "while we utter words full of reason. You have taken the trouble to guide us to an inn, which shows you to be men of warm hearts; you have here swept for us and prepared our room; again, in proof of your excellent dispositions, your master has sent us pastry, which manifests in him a benevolence incapable of exhaustion towards the wayfaring stranger. You now invite us to go and dine with you: we cannot possibly trespass so grossly upon your kindness. No, dear friends, you must excuse us; if we desire to make some purchases in your establishment, you may rely upon us. For the present we will not detain you. We are going to dine at the Turkish Eating House." So saying, we rose and ushered our excellent friends to the door.

The commercial intercourse between the Tartars and the Chinese is revoltingly iniquitous on the part of the latter. So soon as Mongols, simple, ingenuous men, if such there be at all in the world, arrive in a trading town, they are snapped up by some Chinese, who carry them off, as it were, by main force, to their houses, give them tea for themselves and forage for their animals, and cajole them in every conceivable way. The Mongols, themselves without guile and incapable of conceiving guile in others, take all they hear to be perfectly genuine, and congratulate themselves, conscious as they are of their inaptitude for business, upon their good fortune in thus meeting with brothers, *Ahatou*, as they say, in whom they can place full confidence, and who will undertake to manage their whole business for them. A good dinner provided gratis in the back shop, completes the illusion. "If these people wanted to rob me," says the Tartar to himelf, "they would not go to all this expense in giving me a dinner for nothing." When once the Chinese has got hold of the Tartar, he employs over him all the resources of the skilful and utterly unprincipled knavery of the Chinese character. He keeps him in his house, eating, drinking; and smoking, one day after another, until his subordinates have sold all the poor man's cattle, or whatever else he has to sell, and bought for him, in return, the commodities he requires, at prices double and triple the market value. But so plausible is the Chinese, and so simple is the Tartar, that the latter invariably departs with the most entire conviction of the immense philanthropy of the former, and with a promise to return, when he has other goods to sell, to the establishment where he has been treated so fraternally.

The next morning we went out to purchase some winter clothing, the want of which began to make itself sensibly felt. But first, in order to facilitate our dealings, we had to sell some ounces of silver. The money of the Chinese consists entirely of small round copper coins, of the size of our halfpenny, with a square hole in the center, through which the people string them, so that they may be more conveniently carried. These coins the Chinese call, tsien; the Tartars, dehos; and the Europeans, sapeks. Gold and silver are not coined at all; they are melted into ingots of various sizes, and thus put into circulation. Gold-dust and gold leaf are also current in commerce, and they also possess bank-notes. The ordinary value of the ounce of silver is 1,700 or 1,800 sapeks, according to the scarcity or abundance of silver in the country.

The money changers have two irregular modes of making a profit by their traffic: if they state the fair price of silver to the customer, they cheat him in the weight; if their scales and their method of weighing are accurate, they diminish the price of the silver accordingly. But when they have to do with Tartars, they employ neither of these methods of fraud; on the contrary, they weigh the silver scrupulously, and sometimes allow a little overweight, and even they pay them above the market price; in fact, they appear to be quite losers by the transaction, and so they would be, if the weight and the price of the silver alone were considered; their advantage is derived, in these cases, from their manner of calculating the amount. When they come to reduce the silver into sapeks, they do indeed reduce it, making the most flagrant miscalculations, which the Tartars, who can count nothing beyond their beads, are quite incapable of detecting, and which they, accordingly, adopt implicitly, and even with satisfaction, always considering they have sold their bullion well, since they know the full weight has been allowed, and that the full market price has been given.

At the money changers in the Blue Town, to which we went to sell some silver, the Chinese dealers essayed, according to custom, to apply this fraud to us, but they were disconcerted. The weight shown by their scales was perfectly correct, and the price they offered us was rather above the ordinary course of exchange, and the bargain between us was so far concluded. The chief clerk took the souan-pan, the calculation table used by the Chinese, and after calculating with an appearance of intense nicety, announced the result of his operation. "This is an exchange-office," said we; "you are the buyers, we the sellers; you have made your calculation, we will make ours: give us a pencil and a piece of paper."—"Nothing can be more just; you have enunciated a fundamental law of commerce," and so saying, they handed us a writing-case. We took the pencil, and a very short calculation exhibited a difference in our favor of a thousand sapeks. "Superintendent of the bank," said we, "your souan-pan is in error by a thousand sapeks."—"Impossible! Do you think that all of a sudden I've forgotten my souan-pan? Let me go over it again;" and he proceeded with an air of great anxiety to appear correct, to set his calculating machine once more in operation, the other customers by our side looking on with great amazement at all this. When he had done: "Yes," said he, "I knew I was right; see, brother;" and he passed the machine to a colleague behind the counter, who went over his calculation; the result of their operations was exactly the same to a fraction. "You see," said the principal, "there is no error. How is it that our calculation does not agree with that which you have written down here?"—"It is unimportant to inquire why your calculation does not agree with ours; this is certain, that your calculation is wrong and ours right. You see these little characters that we have traced on this paper; they are a very different thing from your souan-pan; it is impossible for them to be wrong. Were all the calculators in the world to work the whole of their lives upon this operation, they could arrive at no other result than this; that your statement is wrong by a thousand sapeks."

The money-changers were extremely embarrassed, and began to turn very red, when a bystander, who perceived that the affair was assuming an awkward aspect, presented himself as umpire. "I'll reckon it up for you," said he, and taking the souan-pan, his calculation agreed with ours. The superintendent of the bank hereupon made us a profound bow: "Sirs Lamas," said he, "your mathematics are better than mine." "Oh, not at all," replied we, with a bow equally profound; "your souan-pan is excellent, but who ever heard of a calculator always exempt from error? People like you may very well be mistaken once and a way, whereas poor simple folks like us make blunders ten thousand times. Now, however, we have fortunately concurred in our reckoning, thanks to the pains you have taken." These phrases were rigorously required under the circumstances, by Chinese politeness. Whenever any person in China is compromised by any awkward incident, those present always carefully refrain from any observation which may make him blush, or as the Chinese phrase it, take away his face.

After our conciliatory address had restored self-possession to all present, everybody drew round the piece of paper on which we had cast up our sum in Arabic numerals. "That is a fine souan-pan," said one to another; "simple, sure, and speedy."—"Sirs Lamas," asked the principal, "what do these characters mean? What souan-pan is this?" "This souan-pan is infallible," returned we; "the characters are those which the Mandarins of Celestial Literature use in calculating eclipses, and the course of the seasons."[1] After a brief conversation on the merits of the Arabic numerals, the cashier handed us the full amount of sapeks, and we parted good friends.

[1] The Fathers Jesuits introduced the use of Arabic numerals into the Observatory at Peking.

The Chinese are sometimes victims to their own knavery, and we have known even Tartars catch them in a snare. One day a Mongol presented himself at the counter of a Chinese money-changer, with a youen-pao carefully packed and sealed. A youen-pao is an ingot of silver weighing three pounds—in China there are sixteen ounces to the pound; the three pounds are never very rigorously exacted; there being generally four or five ounces over, so that the usual weight of an ingot of silver is fifty-two ounces. The Tartar had no sooner unpacked his youen-pao than the Chinese clerk resolved to defraud him of an ounce or two, and weighing it, he pronounced it to be fifty ounces. "My youen-pao weighs fifty-two ounces," exclaimed the Tartar. "I weighed it before I left home." "Oh, your Tartar scales are all very well for sheep; but they don't do for weighing bullion." After much haggling, the bargain was concluded, the youen-pao was purchased as weighing fifty ounces, and the Tartar, having first required and obtained a certificate of the stated weight and value of the ingot, returned to his tent with a good provision of sapeks and bank notes.

In the evening the principal of the establishment received the usual report from each clerk of the business done in the course of the day. "I," said one of them with a triumphant air, "bought a youen-pao of silver, and made two ounces by it." He produced the ingot, which the chief received with a smile, soon changing into a frown. "What have you got here?" cried he. "This is not silver!" The ingot was handed round, and all the clerks saw that indeed it was base bullion. "I know the Tartar," said the clerk who had purchased it, "and will have him up before the Mandarin."

The satellites of justice were forthwith dispatched after the roguish Tartar, whose offense, proved against him, was matter of capital punishment. It was obvious that the ingot was base bullion, and on the face of the affair there was clear proof that the Tartar had sold it. The Tartar, however, stoutly repudiated the imputation. "The humblest of the humble," said he, "craves that he may be allowed to put forth a word in his defense." "Speak," said the Mandarin, "but beware how you say aught other than the exact truth." "It is true," proceeded the Tartar, "that I sold a youen-pao at this person's shop, but it was all pure silver. I am a Tartar, a poor, simple man, and these people, seeking to take advantage of me, have substituted a false for my genuine ingot. I cannot command many words, but I pray our father and mother (*i.e.* the Mandarin), to have this false youen-pao weighed." The ingot was weighed, and was found to contain fifty-two ounces. The Tartar now drew from one of his boots a small parcel, containing, wrapped in rags, a piece of paper, which he held up to the Mandarin. "Here is a certificate," cried he, "which I received at the shop, and which attests the value and weight of the youen-pao that I sold." The Mandarin looked over the paper with a roguish smile, and then said: "According to the testimony of the clerk himself who wrote this certificate, this Mongol sold to him a youen-pao weighing fifty ounces; this youen-pao of base bullion weighs fifty-two ounces; this, therefore, cannot be the Mongol's youen-pao; but now comes the question, whose is it? Who are really the persons that have false bullion in their possession?" Every body present, the Mandarin included, knew perfectly well how the case stood; but the Chinese magistrate, tickled with the Tartar's ingenuity, gave him the benefit of the clerk's dull roguery, and dismissed the charge; but not so the accusers, who were well bastinadoed, and would have been put to death as coiners, had they not found means to appease justice by the present of some ingots of purer metal. It is only, however, upon very rare and extraordinary occasions that the Mongols get the better of the Chinese. In the ordinary course of things, they are everywhere, and always, and in every way, the dupes of their neighbors who by dint of cunning and unprincipled machinations, reduce them to poverty.

Upon receiving our sapeks, we proceeded to buy the winter clothing we needed. Upon a consideration of the meagerness of our exchequer, we came to the resolution that it would be better to purchase what we required at some second-hand shop. In China and Tartary no one has the smallest repugnance to wear other people's clothes; he who has not himself the attire wherein to pay a visit or make a holiday, goes without ceremony to a neighbor and borrows a hat, or a pair of trousers, or boots, or shoes, or whatever else he wants, and nobody is at all surprised at these borrowings, which are quite a custom. The only hesitation any one has in lending his clothes to a neighbor, is lest the borrower should sell them in payment of some debt, or, after using them, pawn them. People who buy clothes buy them indifferently, new or second-hand. The question of price is alone taken into consideration, for there is no more delicacy felt about putting on another man's hat or trousers, than there is about living in a house that some one else has occupied before you.

This custom of wearing other people's things was by no means to our taste, and all the less so, that ever since our arrival at the mission of Si-Wang, we had not been under the necessity of departing from our old habits in this respect. Now, however, the slenderness of our purse compelled us to waive our repugnance. We went out, therefore, in search of a second-hand clothes shop, of which, in every town here, there are a greater or less number, for the most part in connection with pawnshops, called in these countries Tang-Pou. Those who borrow upon pledges are seldom able to redeem the articles they have deposited, which they accordingly leave to die, as the Tartars and Chinese express it; or in other words, they allow the period of redemption to pass, and the articles pass altogether from them. The old clothes shops of the Blue Town were filled in this way with Tartar spoils, so that we had the opportunity of selecting exactly the sort of things we required, to suit the new costume we had adopted.

At the first shop we visited they showed us a quantity of wretched garments turned up with sheep-skin; but though these rags were exceedingly old, and so covered with grease that it was impossible to guess at their original color, the price asked for them was exorbitant. After a protracted haggling, we found it impossible to come to terms, and we gave up this first attempt; and we gave it up, be it added, with a certain degree of satisfaction, for our self-respect was somewhat wounded at finding ourselves reduced even to the proposition of wearing such filthy rags. We visited another shop, and another, a third, and a fourth, and still several more. We were shown magnificent garments, handsome garments, fair garments, endurable garments, but the consideration of expense was, in each instance, an impracticable stumbling-block. The journey we had undertaken might endure for several years, and extreme economy, at all events in the outset, was indispensable. After going about the whole day, after making the acquaintance of all the rag-merchants in the Blue Town, after turning over and over all their old clothes, we were fain to return to the second-hand dealer whom we had first visited, and to make the best bargain we could with him. We purchased from him, at last, two ancient robes of sheep-skin, covered with some material, the nature of which it was impossible to identify, and the original color of which we suspected to have been yellow. We proceeded to try them on, and it was at once evident that the tailor in making them had by no means had us in his eye. M. Gabet's robe was too short, M. Huc's too long; but a friendly exchange was impracticable, the difference in height between the two missionaries being altogether too disproportionate. We at first thought of cutting the excess from the one, in order to make up the deficiency of the other; but then we should have had to call in the aid of a tailor, and this would have involved another drain upon our purse; the pecuniary consideration decided the question, and we determined to wear the clothes as they were, M. Huc adopting the expedient of holding up, by means of a girdle, the surplus of his robe, and M. Gabet resigning himself to the exposure to the public gaze of a portion of his legs: the main inconvenience, after all, being the manifestation to all who saw us that we could not attire ourselves in exact proportion to our size.

Provided with our sheep-skin coats, we next asked the dealer to show us his collection of second-hand winter hats. We examined several of these, and at last selected two caps of fox-skin, the elegant form of which reminded us of the shakos of our sappers. These purchases completed, each of us put under his arm his packet of old clothes, and we returned to the hotel of the "Three Perfections."

We remained two days longer at Koukou-Khoton; for, besides that we needed repose, we were glad of the opportunity of seeing this great town, and of becoming acquainted with the numerous and celebrated Lamaseries established there.

The Blue Town enjoys considerable commercial importance, which it has acquired chiefly through its Lamaseries, the reputation of which attracts thither Mongols from the most distant parts of the empire. The Mongols bring hither large herds of oxen, camels, horses, sheep, and loads of furs, mushrooms, and salt, the only produce of the deserts of Tartary. They receive, in return, brick-tea, linen, saddlery, odoriferous sticks to burn before their idols, oatmeal, millet, and kitchen utensils.

The Blue Town is especially noted for its great trade in camels. The camel market is a large square in the center of the town; the animals are ranged here in long rows, their front feet raised upon a mud elevation constructed for that purpose, the object being to show off the size and height of the creatures. It is impossible to describe the uproar and confusion of this market, what with the incessant bawling of the buyers and sellers as they dispute, their noisy chattering after they have agreed, and the horrible shrieking of the camels at having their noses pulled for the purpose of making them show their agility in kneeling and rising. In order to test the strength of the camel, and the burden it is capable of bearing, they make it kneel, and then pile one thing after another upon its back, causing it to rise under each addition, until it can rise no longer. They sometimes use the following expedient: While the camel is kneeling, a man gets upon its hind heels, and holds on by the long hair of its hump; if the camel can rise then, it is considered an animal of superior power.

The trade in camels is entirely conducted by proxy: the seller and the buyer never settle the matter between themselves. They select indifferent persons to sell their goods, who propose, discuss, and fix the price; the one looking to the interests of the seller, the other to those of the purchaser. These "sale-speakers" exercise no other trade; they go from market to market to promote business, as they say. They have generally a great knowledge of cattle, have much fluency of tongue, and are, above all, endowed with a knavery beyond all shame. They dispute, by turns, furiously and argumentatively, as to the merits and defects of the animal; but as soon as it comes to a question of price, the tongue is laid aside as a medium, and the conversation proceeds altogether in signs. They seize each other by the wrist, and beneath the long wide sleeve of their jackets, indicate with their fingers the progress of the bargain. After the affair is concluded they partake of the dinner, which is always given by the purchaser, and then receive a certain

The Camel Market.

number of sapeks, according to the custom of different places.

In the Blue Town there exist five great Lamaseries, each inhabited by more than 2,000 Lamas; besides these, they reckon fifteen less considerable establishments—branches, as it were, of the former. The number of regular Lamas resident in this city may fairly be stated at 20,000. As to those who inhabit the different quarters of the town, engaged in commerce and horse-dealing, they are innumerable. The Lamasery of the Five Towers is the finest and the most famous: here it is that the Hobilgan lives—that is, a Grand Lamá—who, after having been identified with the substance of Buddha, has already undergone several times the process of transmigration. He sits here upon the altar once occupied by the Guison-Tamba, having ascended it after a tragical event, which very nearly brought about a revolution in the empire.

The Emperor Khang-Hi, during the great military expedition which he made in the West against the Oelets, one day, in traversing the Blue Town, expressed a wish to pay a visit to the Guison-Tamba, at that time the Grand Lama of the

Five Towers. The latter received the Emperor without rising from the throne, or manifesting any kind of respect. Just as Khang-Hi drew near to speak to him, a Kian-Kan, or high military Mandarin, indignant at this unceremonious treatment of his master, drew his saber, fell upon the Guison-Tamba, and laid him dead on the steps of his throne. This terrible event roused the whole Lamasery, and indignation quickly communicated itself to all the Lamas of the Blue Town.

They ran to arms in every quarter, and the life of the Emperor, who had but a small retinue, was exposed to the greatest danger. In order to calm the irritation of the Lamas, he publicly reproached the Kian-Kan with his violence. "If the Guison-Tamba," answered the Kian-Kan, "was not a living Buddha, why did he not rise in the presence of the master of the universe? If he was a living Buddha, how was it he did not know I was going to kill him?" Meanwhile the danger to the life of the Emperor became every moment more imminent; he had no other means of escape than that of taking off his imperial robes, and attiring himself in the dress of a private soldier. Under favor of this disguise, and the general confusion, he was enabled to rejoin his army, which was near at hand. The greater part of the men who had accompanied the Emperor into the Blue Town were massacred, and among the rest, the murderer of the Guison-Tamba.

The Mongols sought to profit by this movement. Shortly afterwards it was announced that the Guison-Tamba had reappeared, and that he had transmigrated to the country of the Khalkhas, who had taken him under their protection, and had sworn to avenge his murder. The Lamas of the Great Kouren set actively to the work of organization. They stripped off their red and yellow robes, clothed themselves in black, in memory of the disastrous event of the Blue Town, and allowed the hair and beard to grow, in sign of grief. Everything seemed to presage a grand rising of the Tartar tribes. The great energy and rare diplomatic talents of the Emperor Khang-Hi alone sufficed to arrest its progress. He immediately opened negotiations with the Talé-Lama, Sovereign of Thibet, who was induced to use all his influence with the Lamas for the re-establishment of order whilst Khang-Hi was intimidating the Khalkha kings by means of his troops. Gradually peace was restored; the Lamas resumed their red and yellow robes; but, as a memorial of their coalition in favor of the Guison-Tamba, they retained a narrow border of black on the collar of their robes. Khalkha Lamas alone bear this badge of distinction.

Ever since that period, a Hobilgan has taken the place in the Blue Town of the Guison-Tamba, who himself is resident at the great Kouren, in the district of the Khalkhas. Meanwhile, the Emperor Khang-Hi, whose penetrating genius was always occupied with the future, was not entirely satisfied with these arrangements. He did not believe in all these doctrines of transmigration, and clearly saw that the Khalkhas, in pretending that the Guison-Tamba had reappeared among them, had no other end than that of keeping at their disposal a power capable of contending, upon occasion, with that of the Chinese Emperor. To abolish the office of Guison-Tamba would have been a desperate affair; the only course was, whilst tolerating him, to neutralize his influence. It was decreed, with the concurrence of the Court of Lha-Ssa, that the Guison-Tamba should be recognized legitimate sovereign of the great Kouren; but that after his successive deaths, he should always be bound to make his transmigration to Thibet. Khang-Hi had good reason to believe that a Thibetian by origin would espouse with reluctance the resentments of the Khalkhas against the Court of Peking.

The Guison-Tamba, full of submission and respect for the orders of Khang-Hi and of the Talé-Lama, has never failed since that to go and accomplish his metempsychosis in Thibet. Still, as they fetch him whilst he is yet an infant, he must necessarily be influenced by those about him; and it is said, that as he grows up, he imbibes sentiments little favorable to the reigning dynasty. In 1839, when the Guison-Tamba made that journey to Peking, of which we have spoken, the alarm manifested by the Court arose from the recollection of these events. The Lamas who flock from all the districts of Tartary to the Lamaseries of the Blue Town, rarely remain there permanently. After taking their degrees, as it were, in these quasi universities, they return, one class of them, to their own countries, where they either settle in the small Lamaseries, wherein they can be more independent, or live at home with their families; retaining of their order little more than its red and yellow habit.

Another class consists of those Lamas who live neither in Lamaseries nor at home with their families, but spend their time vagabondizing about like birds of passage, traveling all over their own and the adjacent countries, and subsisting upon the rude hospitality which, in Lamasery and in tent they are sure to receive, throughout their wandering way. Lamasery or tent, they enter without ceremony, seat themselves, and while the tea is preparing for their refreshment, give their host an account of the places they have visited in their rambles. If they think fit to sleep where they are, they stretch themselves on the floor and repose until the morning. After breakfast, they stand at the entrance of the tent, and watch the clouds for a while, and see whence the wind blows; then they take their way, no matter whither, by this path or that, east or west, north or south, as their fancy or a smoother turf suggests, and lounge tranquilly on, sure at least, if no other shelter presents itself by and by, of the shelter of the cover, as they express it, of that great tent, the world; and sure, moreover, having no destination before them, never to lose their way.

The wandering Lamas visit all the countries readily accessible to them:—China, Mantchouria, the Khalkhas, the various kingdoms of Southern Mongolia, the Ourianghai, the Koukou-Noor, the northern and southern slopes of the Celestial Mountains, Thibet, India, and sometimes even Turkestan. There is no stream which they have not crossed, no mountains they have not climbed, no Grand Lama before whom they have not prostrated themselves, no people with whom they have not associated, and whose customs and language are unknown to them. Traveling without any end in view, the places they reach are always those they sought. The story of the Wandering Jew, who is forever a wanderer, is exactly realized in these Lamas. They seem influenced by some secret power, which makes them wander unceasingly from place to place. God seems to have infused into the blood which flows in their veins, something of that motive power which propels them on their way, without allowing them to stop.

The Lamas living in community are those who compose the third class. A Lamasery is a collection of small houses

Vagabond Lamas.

built around one or more Buddhic temples. These dwellings are more or less large and beautiful, according to the means of the proprietor. The Lamas who live thus in community, are generally more regular than the others; they pay more attention to prayer and study. They are allowed to keep a few animals; some cows to afford them milk and butter, the principal materials of their daily food; horses; and some sheep to be killed on festivals.

Generally speaking, the Lamaseries have endowments, either royal or imperial. At certain periods of the year, the revenues are distributed to the Lamas according to the station which they have obtained in the hierarchy. Those who have the reputation of being learned physicians, or able fortune-tellers, have often the opportunity of acquiring possession of the property of strangers; yet they seldom seem to become rich. A childish and heedless race, they cannot make a moderate use of the riches they acquire; their money goes as quickly as it comes. The same Lama whom you saw yesterday in dirty, torn rags, to-day rivals in the magnificence of his attire the grandeur of the highest dignitaries of the Lamasery. So soon as animals or money are placed within his disposition, he starts off to the next trading town, sells what he has to sell, and clothes himself in the richest attire he can purchase. For a month or two he plays the elegant idler, and then, his money all gone, he repairs once more to the Chinese town, this time to pawn his fine clothes for what he can get, and with the certainty that once in the Tang-Pou, he will never, except by some chance, redeem them. All the pawnbrokers' shops in the Tartar Chinese towns are full of these Lama relics. The Lamas are very numerous in Tartary; we think we may affirm, without exaggeration, that they compose at least a third of the population. In almost all families, with the exception of the eldest son, who remains a layman, the male children become Lamas.

The Tartars embrace this profession compulsorily, not of their own free will; they are Lamas or laymen from their birth, according to the will of the parents. But as they grow up, they grow accustomed to this life; and, in the end, religious exaltation attaches them strongly to it.

It is said that the policy of the Mantchou dynasty is to increase the number of Lamas in Tartary; the Chinese Mandarins so assured us, and the thing seems probable enough. It is certain that the government of Peking, whilst it leaves to poverty and want the Chinese Bonzes, honors and favors Lamaism in a special degree. The secret intention of the government, in augmenting the number of the Lamas, who are bound to celibacy, is to arrest, by this means, the progress of the population of Tartary. The recollection of the former power of the Mongols ever fills its mind; it knows that they were formerly masters of the empire,—and in the fear of a new invasion, it seeks to enfeeble them by all the means in its power. Yet, although Mongolia is scantily peopled, in comparison with its immense extent, it could, at a day's notice, send forth a formidable army. A high Lama, the Guison-Tamba, for instance, would have but to raise his finger, and all the Mongols, from the frontier of Siberia to the extremities of Thibet, rising as one man, would precipitate themselves like a torrent wherever their sainted leader might direct them. The profound peace which they have enjoyed for more than two centuries, might seem to have necessarily enervated their warlike character: nevertheless, you may still observe that they have not altogether lost their taste for warlike adventures. The great campaigns of Tsing-Kis-Khan, who led them to the conquest of the world, have not escaped their memory during the long period of leisure of their nomadic life; they love to talk of them, and to feed their imagination with vague projects of invasion.

During our short stay at the Blue Town we had constant conversation with the Lamas of the most celebrated Lamaseries, endeavoring to obtain fresh information on the state of Buddhism in Tartary and Thibet. All they told us only served to confirm us more and more in what we had before learnt on this subject. In the Blue Town, as at Tolon-Noor, every one told us that the doctrine would appear more sublime and more luminous as we advanced towards the West. From what the Lamas said, who had visited Thibet, Lha-Ssa was, as it were, a great focus of light, the rays of which grew more and more feeble in proportion as they became removed from their center.

One day we had an opportunity of talking with a Thibetian Lama for some time, and the things he told us about religion astounded us greatly. A brief explanation of the Christian doctrine, which we gave to him, seemed scarcely to surprise him; he even maintained that our views differed little from those of the Grand Lamas of Thibet. "You must not confound," said he, "religious truths with the superstitions of the vulgar. The Tartars, poor, simple people, prostrate themselves before whatever they see; everything with them is Borhan. Lamas, prayer-books, temples, Lamaseries, stones, heaps of bones,—'tis all the same to them; down they go on their knees, crying, Borhan! Borhan!" "But the Lamas themselves admit innumerable Borhans?" "Let me explain," said our friend, smilingly; "there is but one sole Sovereign of the universe, the Creator of all things, alike without beginning and without end. In Dchagar (India) he bears the name of Buddha, in Thibet, that of Samtche Mitcheba (all Powerful Eternal); the Dcha-Mi (Chinese) call him Fo, and the Sok-Po-Mi (Tartars), Borhan." "You say that Buddha is sole; in that case who are the Talé-Lama of Lha-Ssa, the Bandchan of Djachi-Loumbo, the Tsong-Kaba of the Sifan, the Kaldan of Tolon-Noor, the Guison-Tamba of the Great Kouren, the Hobilgan of Blue Town, the Hotoktou of Peking, the

Chaberon of the Tartar and Thibetian Lamaseries generally?" "They all are equally Buddha." "Is Buddha visible?" "No, he is without a body; he is a spiritual substance." "So, Buddha is sole, and yet there exist innumerable Buddhas: the Talé-Lama, and so on. Buddha is incorporeal; he cannot be seen, and yet the Talé-Lama, the Guison-Tamba, and the rest are visible, and have bodies like our own. How do you explain all this?" "The doctrine, I tell you, is true," said the Lama, raising his arm, and assuming a remarkable accent of authority; "it is the doctrine of the West, but it is of unfathomable profundity. It cannot be sounded to the bottom."

These words of the Thibetian Lama astonished us strangely; the Unity of God, the mystery of the Incarnation, the dogma of the Real Presence seemed to us enveloped in his creed; yet with ideas so sound in appearance, he admitted the metempsychosis, and a sort of pantheism of which he could give no account.

These new indications respecting the religion of Buddha gave us hopes that we should really find among the Lamas of Thibet a symbolism more refined and superior to the common belief, and confirmed us in the resolution we had adopted, of keeping on our course westward.

Previous to quitting the inn we called in the landlord to settle our bill. We had calculated that the entertainment, during four days, of three men and our animals, would cost us at least two ounces of silver; we were therefore agreeably surprised to hear the landlord say, "Sirs Lamas, there is no occasion for going into any accounts; put 300 sapeks into the till, and that will do very well. My house," he added, "is recently established, and I want to give it a good character. You are come from a distant land, and I would enable you to say to your countrymen that my establishment is worthy of their confidence." We replied that we would everywhere mention his disinterestedness; and that our countrymen, whenever they had occasion to visit the Blue Town, would certainly not fail to put-up at the "Hotel of the Three Perfections."

Tchagan-Kouren.

CHAPTER VI.

A Tartar-eater--Loss of Arsalan—Great Caravan of Camels—Night Arrival at Tchagan-Kouren—We are refused Admission into the Inns—We take up our abode with a Shepherd—Overflow of the Yellow River—Aspect of Tchagan-Kouren--Departure across the Marshes—Hiring a Bark—Arrival on the Banks of the Yellow River—Encampment under the Portico of a Pagoda—Embarkation of the Camels—Passage of the Yellow River—Laborious Journey across the Inundated Country—Encampment on the Banks of the River.

We quitted the Blue Town on the fourth day of the ninth moon. We had already been traveling more than a month. It was with the utmost difficulty that our little caravan could get out of the town. The streets were encumbered with men, cars, animals, stalls in which the traders displayed their goods; we could only advance step by step, and at times we were obliged to come to a halt, and wait for some minutes until the way became a little cleared. It was near noon before we reached the last houses of the town, outside the western gate. There, upon a level road, our camels were at length able to proceed at their ease in all the fulness of their long step. A chain of rugged rocks rising on our right sheltered us so completely from the north wind, that we did not at all feel the rigor of the weather. The country through which we were now traveling was still a portion of Western Toumet. We observed in all directions the same indications of prosperity and comfort which had so much gratified us east of the town. Everywhere around substantial villages presented proofs of successful agriculture and trade. Although we could not set up our tent in the cultivated fields by which we were now surrounded, yet, so far as circumstances permitted, we adhered to our Tartar habits. Instead of entering an inn to take our morning meal, we seated ourselves under a rock or tree, and there breakfasted upon some rolls fried in oil, of which we had bought a supply at the Blue Town. The passers-by laughed at this rustic proceeding, but they were not surprised at it. Tartars, unused to the manners of civilized nations, are entitled to take their repast by the roadside even in places where inns abound.

During the day this mode of traveling was pleasant and convenient enough; but, as it would not have been prudent to remain out all night, at sunset we sought an inn: the preservation of our animals of itself sufficed to render this proceeding necessary. There was nothing for them to eat on the wayside, and had we not resorted in the evening to places where we could purchase forage for them, they would, of course, have speedily died.

On the second evening after our departure from Blue Town, we encountered at an inn a very singular personage. We had just tied our animals to a manger under a shed in the great court, when a traveler made his appearance, leading by a halter a lean, rawboned horse. The traveler was short, but then his rotundity was prodigious. He wore on his head a great straw hat, the flapping brim of which rested on his shoulders; a long saber suspended from his girdle presented an amusing contrast with the peaceful joyousness of his physiognomy. "Superintendent of the soupkettle," cried he, as he entered, "is there room for me in your tavern?" "I have but one travelers' room," answered the innkeeper, "and three Mongols who have just come occupy it; you can ask them if they will make room for you." The traveler waddled towards us. "Peace and happiness unto you, Sirs Lamas; do you need the whole of your room, or can you accommodate me?" "Why not? We are all travelers, and should serve one another." "Words of excellence! You are Tartars; I am Chinese, yet, comprehending the claims of hospitality, you act upon the truth, that all men are brothers." Hereupon, fastening his horse to a manger, he joined us, and, having deposited his traveling-bag upon the kang, stretched himself at full length, with the air of a man greatly fatigued. "Whither are you bound?" asked we; "are you going to buy up salt or catsup for some Chinese company?" "No; I represent a great commercial house at Peking, and I am collecting some debts from the Tartars. Where are you going?" "We shall to-day pass the Yellow River to Tchagan-Kouren, and then journey westward through the country of the Ortous." "You are not Mongols, apparently?" "No; we are from the West." "Well, it seems we are both of one trade; you, like myself, are Tartar-eaters." "Tartar-eaters! What do you mean?" "Why, we eat the Tartars. You eat them by prayers; I by commerce. And why not? The Mongols are poor simpletons, and we may as well get their money as anybody else." "You are mistaken. Since we entered Tartary we have spent a great deal, but we have never taken a single sapek from the Tartars." "Oh, nonsense!" "What! do you suppose our camels and our baggage came to us from the Mongols?" "Why, I thought you came here to recite your prayers." We entered into some explanation of the difference between our principles and those of the Lamas, for whom the traveler had mistaken us, and he was altogether amazed at our disinterestedness. "Things are quite the other way here," said he. "You won't get a Lama to say prayers for nothing; and certainly, as for me, I should never set foot in Tartary but for the sake of money." "But how is it you manage to make such good meals of the Tartars?" "Oh, we devour them; we pick them clean. You've observed the silly race, no doubt; whatever they see when they come into our towns they want, and when we know who they are, and where we can find them, we let them have goods upon credit, of course at a considerable advance upon the price, and upon interest at thirty or forty per cent, which is quite right and necessary. In China the Emperor's laws do not allow this; it is only done with the Tartars. Well, they don't pay the money, and the interest goes on until there is a good sum owing worth the coming for. When we come for it, they've no money, so we merely take all the cattle and sheep and horses we can get hold of for the interest, and leave the capital debt and future interest to be paid next time, and so it goes on from one generation to another. Oh ! a Tartar debt is a complete gold mine."

Day had not broken when the Yao-Tchang-Ti (exactor of debts) was on foot. "Sirs Lamas," said he, "I am going to saddle my horse, and proceed on my way,—I propose to travel to-day with you." "'Tis a singular mode of traveling with people, to start before they're up," said we. "Oh, your camels go faster than my horse; you'll soon overtake me, and we shall enter Tchagan-Kouren (White Enclosure) together." He rode off, and at daybreak we followed him. This was a black day with us, for in it we had to mourn a loss. After traveling several hours, we perceived that Arsalan was not with the caravan. We halted, and Samdadchiemba, mounted on his little mule, turned back in search of the dog. He went through several villages which we had passed in the course of the morning, but his search was fruitless; he returned without having either seen or heard of Arsalan. "The dog was Chinese," said Samdadchiemba; "he was not used to a nomadic life, and getting tired of wandering about over the desert, he has taken service in the cultivated district. What is to be done? Shall we wait for him?" "No, it is late, and we are far from White Enclosure." "Well, if there is no dog, there is no dog; and we must do without him." This sentimental effusion of Samdadchiemba gravely delivered, we proceeded on our way.

At first, the loss of Arsalan grieved us somewhat. We were accustomed to see him running to and fro in the prairie, rolling in the long grass, chasing the gray squirrels, and scaring the eagles from their seat on the plain. His incessant evolutions served to break the monotony of the country through which we were passing, and to abridge, in some degree, the tedious length of the way. His office of porter gave him especial title to our regret. Yet, after the first impulses of sorrow, reflection told us that the loss was not altogether so serious as it had at first appeared. Each day's experience of the nomadic life had served more and more to dispel our original apprehension of robbers. Moreover, Arsalan, under any circumstances, would have been a very ineffective guard; for his incessant galloping about during the day sent him at night into a sleep which nothing could disturb. This was so much the case, that every morning, make what noise we might in taking down our tent, loading the camels, and so on, there would Arsalan remain, stretched on the grass, sleeping a leaden sleep; and when the caravan was about to start, we had always to arouse him with a sound kick or two. Upon one occasion, a strange dog made his way into our tent, without the smallest opposition on the part of Arsalan, and had full time to devour our mess of oatmeal and a candle, the wick of which he left contumeliously on the outside of the tent. A consideration of economy completed our restoration to tranquillity of mind: each day we had had to provide Arsalan with a ration of meal, at least quite equal in quantity to that which each of us consumed; and we were not rich enough to have constantly seated at our table a guest with such excellent appetite, and whose services were wholly inadequate to compensate for the expense he occasioned.

We had been informed that we should reach White Enclosure the same day, but the sun had set, and as yet we saw no signs of the town before us. By and by, what seemed clouds of dust made their appearance in the distance, approaching us. By degrees they developed themselves in the form of camels, laden with western merchandise for sale in Peking. When we met the first camel-driver we asked him how far it was from White Enclosure. "You see here," said he with a grin, "one end of our caravan; the other extremity is still within the town." "Thanks," cried we; "in that case we shall soon be there." "Well, you've not more than fifteen lis to go." "Fifteen lis! why you've just told us that the other end of your caravan is still in the town." "So it is, but our caravan consists of at least ten thousand camels." "If that be the case," said we, "there is no time to be lost: a good journey to you, and peace," and on we went.

The cameleers had stamped upon their features, almost blackened with the sun, a character of uncouth misanthropy. Enveloped from head to foot in goat-skins, they were placed between the humps of their camels, just like bales of merchandise; they scarcely condescended to turn even their heads round to look at us. Five months journeying across the desert seemed almost to have brutefied them. All the

camels of this immense caravan wore suspended from their necks Thibetian bells, the silvery sound of which produced a musical

harmony which contrasted very agreeably with the sullen taciturn aspect of the drivers. In our progress, however, we contrived to make them break silence from time to time; the roguish Dchiahour attracted their atten-

tion to us in a very marked manner. Some of the camels, more timid than others, took fright at the little mule, which they doubtless imagined to be a wild beast. In their endeavor to escape in an opposite direction they drew after them the camels next following them in the procession, so that, by this operation, the caravan assumed the form of an immense bow. This abrupt evolution aroused the cameleers from their sullen torpidity; they grumbled bitterly, and directed fierce glances against us, as they exerted themselves to restore the procession to its proper line. Samdadchiemba, on the contrary, shouted with laughter; it was in vain that we told him to ride somewhat apart in order not to alarm the camels; he turned a deaf ear to all we said. The discomfiture of the procession was quite a delightful entertainment for him, and he made his little mule caracole about in the hope of an encore.

The first cameleer had not deceived us. We journeyed on between the apparently interminable file of the caravan, and a chain of rugged rocks, until night had absolutely set in, and even then we did not see the town. The last camel had passed on, and we seemed alone in the desert, when a man came riding by on a donkey. "Elder brother," said we, "is White Enclosure still distant?" "No, brothers," he replied, "it is just before you, there, where you see the lights. You have not more than five lis to go." Five lis! It was a long way in the night, and upon a strange road, but we were fain to resign ourselves. The night grew darker and darker. There was no moon, no stars even, to guide us on our way. We seemed advancing amid chaos and abysses. We resolved to alight, in the hope of seeing our way somewhat more clearly: the result was precisely the reverse; we would advance a few steps gropingly and slowly; then, all of a sudden, we threw back our heads in fear of dashing them against rocks or walls that seemed to rise from an abyss. We speedily got covered with perspiration, and were only happy to mount our camels once more, and rely on their clearer sight and surer feet. Fortunately the baggage was well secured; what misery would it have been had that fallen off amid all this darkness, as it had frequently done before! We arrived at last in Tchagan-Kouren, but the difficulty now was to find an inn. Every house was shut up, and there was not a living creature in the streets, except a number of great dogs that ran barking after us.

At length, after wandering haphazard through several streets, we heard the strokes of a hammer upon an anvil. We proceeded towards the sound, and before long, a great light, a thick smoke, and sparks glittering in the air, announced that we had come upon a blacksmith's shop. We presented ourselves at the door, and humbly entreated our brothers, the smiths, to tell us where we should find an inn. After a few jests upon Tartars and camels, the company assented to our request, and a boy, lighting a torch, came out to act as our guide to an inn.

After knocking and calling for a long time at the door of the first inn we came to, the landlord opened it, and was inquiring who we were, when, unluckily for us, one of our camels, worried by a dog, took it into its head to send forth a succession of those horrible cries for which the animal is remarkable. The innkeeper at once shut his door in our faces. At all the inns where we successively applied, we were received in much the same manner. No sooner were the camels noticed than the answer was, No room; in point of fact, no innkeeper, if he can avoid it, will receive camels into his stables at all: their size occupies great space, and their appearance almost invariably creates alarm among the other animals; so that Chinese travelers generally make it a condition with the landlord before they enter an inn, that no Tartar caravan shall be admitted. Our guide finding all our efforts futile, got tired of accompanying us, wished us good night, and returned to his forge.

We were exhausted with weariness, hunger, and thirst, yet there seemed no remedy for the evil, when all at once we heard the bleating of sheep. Following the sound, we came to a mud enclosure, the door of which was at once opened upon our knocking. "Brother," said we, "is this an inn?" "No, it is a sheep-house. Who are you?" "We are travelers, who have arrived here, weary and hungry; but no one will receive us." As we were speaking, an old man came to the door, holding in his hand a lighted torch. As soon as he saw our camels and our costume, "Mendou! Mendou!" he exclaimed, "Sirs Lamas, enter; there is room for your camels in the court, and my house is large enough for you; you shall stay and rest here for several days." We entered joyfully, fastened our camels to the manger, and seated ourselves round the hearth, where already tea was prepared for us. "Brother," said we to the old man, "we need not ask whether it is to Mongols that we owe this hospitality." "Yes, Sirs Lamas," said he, "we are all Mongols here. We have for some time past quitted the tent, to reside here; so that we may better carry on our trade in sheep. Alas! we are insensibly becoming Chinese!" "Your manner of life," returned we, "may have changed, but it is certain that your hearts have remained Tartar. Nowhere else in all Tchagan-Kouren, has the door of kindness been opened to us."

Observing our fatigue, the head of the family unrolled some skins in a corner of the room, and we gladly laid ourselves down to repose. We should have slept on till the morning, but Samdadchiemba aroused us to partake of the supper which our hosts had hospitably prepared—two large cups of tea, cakes baked in the ashes, and some chops of boiled mutton, arranged on a stool by way of a table. The meal seemed after our long fasting, perfectly magnificent; we partook of it heartily, and then having exchanged pinches of snuff with the family, resumed our slumber.

Next morning we communicated the plan of our journey to our Mongol hosts. No sooner had we mentioned that we intended to pass the Yellow River, and thence traverse the country of the Ortous, than the whole family burst out with exclamations. "It is quite impossible," said the old man, "to cross the Yellow River. Eight days ago the river overflowed its banks, and the plains on both sides are completely inundated." This intelligence filled us with the utmost consternation. We had been quite prepared to pass the Yellow River under circumstances of danger arising from the wretchedness of the ferry boats and the difficulty of managing our camels in them, and we knew, of course, that the Hoang-Ho was subject to periodical overflows; but these occur ordinarily in the rainy season, towards the sixth or seventh month, whereas we were now in the dry season, and, moreover, in a peculiarly dry season.

We proceeded forthwith towards the river to investigate the matter for ourselves, and found that the Tartar had only told us the exact truth. The Yellow River had become, as it were, a vast sea, the limits of which were scarcely visible. Here and there you could see the higher grounds rising above the water, like islands, while the houses and villages looked as though they were floating upon the waves. We consulted several persons as to the course we should adopt. Some said that further progress was impracticable, for that, even where the inundation had subsided, it had left the earth so soft and slippery that the camels could not walk upon it, while elsewhere we should have to dread at every step some deep pool, in which we should inevitably be drowned. Other opinions were more favorable, suggesting that the boats which were stationed at intervals for the purpose would easily and cheaply convey us and our baggage in three days to the river, while the camels could follow us through the water, and that once at the river side, the great ferry-boat would carry us all over the bed of the stream without any difficulty.

What were we to do? To turn back was out of the question. We had vowed that, God aiding, we would go to Lha-Ssa whatever obstacles impeded. To turn the river by coasting it northwards would materially augment the length of our journey, and, moreover, compel us to traverse the great desert of Gobi. To remain at Tchagan-Kouren, and patiently await for a month the complete retirement of the waters and the restoration of solidity in the roads, was, in one point of view, the most prudent course, but there was a grave inconvenience about it. We and our five animals could not live for a month in an inn without occasioning a most alarming atrophy in our already meager purse. The only course remaining was to place ourselves exclusively under the protection of Providence, and to go on, regardless of mud or marsh. This resolution was adopted, and we returned home to make the necessary preparations.

Tchagan-Kouren is a large, fine town of recent construction. It is not marked on the map of China compiled by M. Andriveau-Goujon, doubtless because it did not exist at the time when the Fathers Jesuits residing at Peking were directed by the Emperor Khang-Hi to draw maps of the empire. Nowhere in China, Mantchouria, or in Thibet, have we seen a town like White Enclosure. The streets are wide, clean, and clear; the houses regular in their arrangement, and of very fair architecture. There are several squares, decorated with trees, a feature which struck us all the more that we had not observed it anywhere else in this part of the world. There are plenty of shops, commodiously arranged, and well supplied with Chinese, and even with European goods. The trade of Tchagan-Kouren, however, is greatly checked by the proximity of the Blue Town, to which, as a place of commerce, the Mongols have been much longer accustomed.

Our worthy Tartar host, in his hospitality, sought to divert us from our project, but unsuccessfully; and he even got rallied by Samdadchiemba for his kindness. "It's quite clear," said our guide, "that you've become a mere Kitat (Chinese), and think that a man must not set out upon a journey unless the earth is perfectly dry and the sky perfectly cloudless. I have no doubt you go out to lead your sheep with an umbrella in one hand and a fan in the other." It was ultimately arranged that we should take our departure at daybreak next morning.

Meantime we went out into the town to make the necessary supply of provisions. To guard against the possibility of being inundation-bound for several days, we bought a quantity of small loaves fried in mutton fat, and for our animals we procured a quantity of the most portable forage we could find.

Next morning we departed full of confidence in the goodness of God. Our Tartar host, who insisted upon escorting us out of the town, led us to an elevation whence we could see in the distance a long line of thick vapor which seemed journeying from west to east; it marked the course of the Yellow River. "Where you see that vapor," said the old man, "you will find a great dike, which serves to keep the river in bounds, except upon any extraordinary rise of the waters. That dike is now dry; when you come to it, proceed along it until you reach the little pagoda you see yonder, on your right; there you will find a boat that will convey you across the river. Keep that pagoda in sight, and you can't lose your way." We cordially thanked the old man for the kindness he had shown us and proceeded on our journey.

We were soon up to the knees of the camels in a thick slimy compost of mud and water, covering other somewhat firmer mud, over which the poor animals slowly slid on their painful way; their heads turning alternately right and left, their limbs trembling, and the sweat exuding from each pore. Every moment we expected them to fall beneath us. It was near noon ere we arrrived at a little village, not more than a couple of miles from the place where we had left the old man. Here a few wretched people, whose rags scarce covered their gaunt frames, came round us, and accompanied us to the edge of a broad piece of water, portion of a lake, which they told us, and which, it was quite clear, we must pass before we could reach the dike indicated by the Tartar. Some boatmen proposed to carry us over this lake to the dike. We asked them how many sapeks they would charge for the service:—"Oh, very little; next to nothing. You see we will take in our boats you, and the baggage, and the mule, and the horse; one of our people will lead the camels through the lake; they are too big to come into the boat. When one comes to reckon on all this load, and all the trouble and fatigue, the price seems absolutely less than nothing." "True, there will be some trouble in the affair, no one denies it; but let us have a distinct understanding. How many sapeks do you ask?" "Oh, scarcely any. We are all brothers; and you, brothers, need all our assistance in traveling. We know that; we feel it in our hearts. If we could only afford it, we should have pleasure in carrying you over for nothing; but look at our clothes. We poor fellows are very poor. Our boat is all we have to depend upon. It is necessary that we should gain a livelihood by that; five lis sail, three men, a horse, a mule, and luggage; but come, as you are spiritual persons, we will only charge you 2,000 sapeks." The price was preposterous; we made no answer. We took our animals by the bridle and turned back, pretending that we would not continue our journey. Scarcely had we advanced twenty paces before the ferryman ran after us. "Sirs Lamas, are not you going to cross the water in my boat?" "Why," said we dryly, "doubtless you are too rich to take any trouble in the matter. If you really wanted to let your boat, would you ask 2,000 sapeks?" "2,000 sapeks is the price I ask; but what will you give?" "If you like to take 500 sapeks, let us set out at once; it is already late." "Return, Sirs Lamas; get into the boat;" and he caught hold, as he spoke, of the halters of our beasts. We considered that the price was at last fixed; but we had scarcely arrived on the border of the lake, when the ferryman exclaimed to one of his comrades,—"Come, our fortune deserts us to-day; we must bear much fatigue for little remuneration. We shall have to row five lis, and after all we shall have only 1,500 sapeks to divide between eight of us." "1,500 sapeks!" exclaimed we; "you are mocking us; we will leave you;" and we turned back for the second time. Some mediators, inevitable persons in all Chinese matters, presented themselves, and undertook to settle the fare. It was at length decided that we should pay 800 sapeks; the sum was enormous, but we had no other means of pursuing our way. The boatmen knew this, and took accordingly the utmost advantage of our position.

The embarkation was effected with extraordinary celerity, and we soon quitted the shore. Whilst we advanced by means of the oars, on the surface of the lake, a man mounted on a camel and leading two others after him, followed a path traced out by a small boat rowed by a waterman. The latter was obliged every now and then to sound the depth of the water, and the camel-driver needed to be very attentive in directing his course in the straight trail left by the boat, lest he should be swallowed up in the holes beneath the water. The camels advanced slowly, stretching out their long necks, and at times leaving only their heads and the extremity of their humps visible above the lake. We were in continual alarm; for these animals not being able to swim, there only needed a false step to precipitate them to the bottom. Thanks to the protection of God, all arrived safe at the dike which had been pointed out to us. The boatmen, after assisting us to replace, in a hasty manner, our baggage on the camels, indicated the point whither we must direct our steps. "Do you see, to the right, that small Miao? (pagoda). A little from the Miao, do you observe those wooden huts and those black nets hanging from long poles? There you will find the ferry-boat to cross the river. Follow this dike, and go in peace."

After having proceeded with difficulty for half an hour, we reached the ferry-boat. The boatmen immediately came to us. "Sirs Lamas," said they, "you intend, doubtless, to cross the Hoang-Ho, but you see this evening the thing is impracticable—the sun is just setting." "You are right; we will cross to-morrow at daybreak: meanwhile, let us settle the price, so that to-morrow we may lose no time in deliberation." The watermen would have preferred waiting till the morrow to discuss this important point, expecting we should offer a much larger sum, when just about to embark. At first their demands were preposterous: happily, there were two boats which competed together, otherwise we should have been ruined. The price was ultimately fixed at 1,000 sapeks. The passage was not

Navigation of the Yellow River.

long, it is true, for the river had nearly resumed its bed; but the waters were very rapid, and, moreover, the camels had to ride. The amount enormous in itself, appeared, upon the whole, moderate, considering the difficulty and trouble of the passage. This business arranged, we considered how we should pass the night. We could not think of seeking an asylum in the fishermen's cabins; even if they had been sufficiently large, we should have had a considerable objection to place our effects in the hands of these folks. We were sufficiently acquainted with the Chinese not to trust to their honesty. We looked out for a place whereon to set up our tent; but we could find nowhere a spot sufficiently dry: mud or stagnant water covered the ground in all directions. About a hundred yards from the shore was a small Miao, or temple of idols; a narrow, high path led to it. We proceeded thither to see if we could find there a place of repose. It turned out as we wished. A portico, supported by three stone pillars, stood before the entrance door, which was secured by a large padlock. This portico, made of granite, was raised a few feet from the ground, and you ascended it by five steps. We determined to pass the night here.

Samdadchiemba asked us if it would not be a monstrous superstition to sleep on the steps of a Miao. When we had relieved his scruples, he made sundry philosophical reflections. "Behold," said he, "a Miao which has been built by the people of the country, in honor of the god of the river. Yet, when it rained in Thibet, the Pou-sa had no power to preserve itself from inundation. Nevertheless, this Miao serves at present to shelter two missionaries of Jehovah—the only real use it has ever served." Our Dchiahour, who at first had scrupled to lodge under the portico of this idolatrous temple, soon thought the idea magnificent, and laughed hugely.

After having arranged our luggage in this singular encampment, we proceeded to tell our beads on the shores of the Hoang-Ho. The moon was brilliant, and lit up this immense river, which rolled over an even and smooth bed its yellow and tumultuous waters. The Hoang-Ho is beyond a doubt one of the finest rivers in the world; it rises in the mountains of Thibet, and crosses the Koukou-Noor, entering China by the province of Kan-Sou. Thence it follows the sandy regions at the feet of the Alécha mountains, encircles the country of the Ortous; and after having watered China first from north to south, and then from west to east, it falls into the Yellow Sea. The waters of the Hoang-Ho, pure and clear at their source, only take the yellow hue after having passed the sands of the Alécha and the Ortous. They are almost, throughout, level with the lands through which they flow, and it is this circumstance which occasions those inundations so disastrous to the Chinese. As for the Tartar nomads when the waters rise, all they have to do is to strike their tents, and drive their herds elsewhere.[1]

[1] The bed of the Yellow River has undergone numerous and notable variations. In ancient times, its mouth was situated in the Gulf of Pe-Tchi-Li, in latitude 39.

Though the Yellow River had cost us so much trouble, we derived much satisfaction from taking a walk at night upon its solitary banks, and listening to the solemn murmur of its majestic waters. We were contemplating this grand work of nature, when Samdadchiemba recalled us to the prose of life, by announcing that the oatmeal was ready. Our repast was as brief as it was plain. We then stretched ourselves on our goat-skins, in the portico, so that the three described the three sides of a triangle, in the center of which we piled our baggage; for we had no faith at all that the sanctity of the place would deter robbers, if robbers there were in the vicinity.

As we have mentioned, the little Miao was dedicated to the divinity of the Yellow River. The idol, seated on a pedestal of gray brick, was hideous, as all those idols are that you ordinarily see in Chinese pagodas. From a broad, flat, red face, rose two great staring eyes, like eggs stuck into orbits, the smaller end projecting. Thick eyebrows, instead of describing a horizontal line, began at the bottom of each ear, and met in the middle of the forehead, so as to form an obtuse angle. The idol had on its head a marine shell, and brandished, with a menacing air, a sword like a scythe. This Pou-sa had, right and left, two attendants, each putting out its tongue, and apparently making faces at it.

Just as we were lying down, a man approached us, holding in one hand a small paper lantern. He opened the grating which led to the interior of the Miao, prostrated himself thrice, burned incense in the censers, and lighted a small lamp at the feet of the idol. This personage was not a bonze. His hair, hanging in a tress, and his blue garments, showed him to be a layman. When he had finished his idolatrous ceremonies, he came to us. "I will leave the door open," said he; "you'll sleep more comfortably inside than in the portico." "Thanks," replied we; "shut the door, however; for we shall do very well where we are.

At present it is in the 34th parallel, twenty-five leagues from the primitive point. The Chinese government is compelled annually to expend enormous sums in keeping the river within its bed and preventing inundations. In 1779, the embankment for this purpose cost no less a sum than £1,600,000. Yet, despite these precautions, inundations are of frequent occurrence; for the bed of the Yellow River, in the provinces of Ho-Nan and Kiang-Sou, is higher for 200 leagues than the plain through which it passes. This bed, continuing to rise, with the quantity of mud deposited, there is inevitably impending, at no remote period, an awful catastrophe, involving in death and desolation all the adjacent district.

Why have you been burning incense? Who is the idol of this place?" "It is the spirit of the Hoang-Ho, who inhabits this Miao. I have burned incense before him, in order that our fishing may be productive, and that our boats may float without danger." "The words you utter," cried Samdadchiemba, insolently, "are mere *hou-choue* (stuff and nonsense). How did it happen, that the other day when the inundation took place, the Miao was flooded, and your Pou-sa was covered with mud?" To this sudden apostrophe the pagan churchwarden made no answer, but took to his heels. We were much surprised at this proceeding; but the explanation came next morning.

We stretched ourselves on our goat-skins once more, and endeavored to sleep, but sleep came slowly and but for a brief period. Placed between marshes and the river, we felt throughout the night a piercing cold, which seemed to transfix us to the very marrow. The sky was pure and serene, and in the morning we saw that the marshes around were covered with a thick sheet of ice. We made our preparations for departure, but upon collecting the various articles, a handkerchief was missing. We remembered that we had imprudently hung it upon the grating at the entrance of the Miao, so that it was half in and half out of the building. No person had been near the place, except the man who had come to pay his devotions to the idol. We could, therefore, without much rashness, attribute the robbery to him, and this explained why he had made his exit so rapidly, without replying to Samdadchiemba. We could easily have found the man, for he was one of the fishermen engaged upon the station, but it would have been a fruitless labor. Our only effectual course would have been to seize the thief in the fact.

Next morning, we placed our baggage upon the camels, and proceeded to the riverside, fully persuaded that we had a miserable day before us. The camels having a horror of the water, it is sometimes impossible to make them get into a boat. You may pull their noses, or nearly kill them with blows, yet not make them advance a step; they would die sooner. The boat before us seemed especially to present almost insurmountable obstacles. It was not flat and large, like those which generally serve as ferry-boats. Its sides were very high, so that the animals were obliged to leap over them at the risk and peril of breaking their legs. If you wanted to move a carriage into it, you had first of all to pull the vehicle to pieces.

The boatmen had already taken hold of our baggage, for the purpose of conveying it into their abominable vehicle, but we stopped them. "Wait a moment; we must first try and get the camels in. If they won't enter the boat, there is no use in placing the baggage in it." "Whence came your camels, that they can't get into people's boats?" "It matters little whence they came; what we tell you is that the tall white camel has never hitherto consented to cross any river, even in a flat boat." "Tall camel or short, flat boat or high boat, into the boat the camel shall go," and so, saying, the ferryman ran and fetched an immense cudgel. "Catch hold of the string in the camel's nose," cried he to a companion, "We'll see if we can't make the brute get into the boat." The man in the boat hauled at the string; the man behind beat the animal vehemently on the legs with his cudgel, but all to no purpose; the poor camel sent forth piercing cries, and stretched out its long neck. The blood flowed from its nostrils, the sweat from every pore; but not an inch forward would the creature move; yet one step would have placed it in the boat, the sides of which were touched by its fore legs.

We could not endure the painful spectacle. "No more of this," we cried to the ferryman; "it is useless to beat the animal. You might break its legs or kill it before it would consent to enter your boat." The two men at once left off, for they were tired, the one of pulling, the other of beating. What were we to do? We had almost made up our minds to ascend the banks of the river until we found some flat boat, when the ferryman all at once jumped up, radiant with an idea. "We will make another attempt," cried he, "and if that fails I give the matter up. Take the string gently," he added, to a companion, "and keep the camel's feet as close as ever you can to the side of the boat." Then, going back for some paces, he dashed forward with a spring and threw himself with all his weight upon the animal's rear. The shock, so violent and unexpected, occasioned the camel somewhat to bend its fore legs. A second shock immediately succeeded the first, and the animal, in order to prevent itself from falling into the water, had no remedy but to raise its feet and place them within the boat. This effected, the rest was easy. A few pinches of the nose and a few blows sufficed to impel the hind legs after the fore, and the white camel was at last in the boat, to the extreme satisfaction of all present. The other animals were embarked after the same fashion, and we proceeded on our watery way.

First, however, the ferryman deemed it necessary that the animals should kneel, so that no movement of theirs on the river might occasion an overturn. His proceeding to this effect was exceedingly comic. He first went to one camel and then to the other, pulling now this down, then that. When he approached the larger animal, the creature, remembering the man's treatment, discharged in his face a quantity of the grass ruminating within its jaws, a compliment which the boatman returned by spitting in the animal's face. And the absurdity was, that the work made no progress. One camel was no sooner induced to kneel down than the other got up, and so the men went backwards and forwards, gradually covered by the angry creatures with the green substance, half masticated and particularly inodorous, which each animal in turns spat against him. At length, when Samdadchiemba had sufficiently entertained himself with the scene, he went to the camels, and, exercising his recognized authority over them, made them kneel in the manner desired.

We at length floated upon the waters of the Yellow River; but though there were four boatmen, their united strength could scarcely make head against the force of the current. We had effected about half our voyage, when a camel suddenly rose, and shook the boat so violently that it was nearly upset. The boatmen, after ejaculating a tremendous oath, told us to look after our camels and prevent them from getting up, unless we wanted the whole party to be engulfed. The danger was indeed formidable. The camel, infirm upon its legs, and yielding to every movement of the boat, menaced us with a catastrophe. Samdadchiemba, however, managed to get quickly beside the animal, and at once induced it to kneel, so that we were let off with our fright, and in due course reached the other side of the river.

At the moment of disembarkation, the horse, impatient to be once more on land, leaped out of the boat, but striking, on its way, against the anchor, fell on its side in the mud. The ground not being yet dry, we were fain to take off our shoes, and to carry the baggage on our shoulders to an adjacent eminence; there we asked the boatmen if we should be any great length of time in traversing the marsh and mud that lay stretched out before us. The chief boatman raised his head, and after looking for a while towards the sun, said: "It will soon be noon; by the evening you will reach the banks of the Little River; to-morrow you will find the ground dry." It was under these melancholy auspices that we proceeded upon our journey, through one of the most detestable districts to be found in the whole world.

We had been told in what direction we were to proceed; but the inundation had obliterated every trace of path and even of road, and we could only regulate our course by the nature of the ground, keeping as clear as we could of the deeper quagmires, sometimes making a long circuit in order to reach what seemed firmer ground, and then, finding the supposed solid turf to be nothing more than a piece of water, green with stagnant matter and aquatic plants, having to turn back, and, as it were, grope one's way in another direction, fearful, at every step, of being plunged into some gulf of liquid mud.

By and by our animals, alarmed and wearied, could hardly proceed, and we were compelled to beat them severely and to exhaust our voices with bawling at them before they would move at all. The tall grass and plants of the marshes twisted about their legs, and it was only by leaps and at the risk of throwing off both baggage and riders that they could extricate themselves. Thrice did the youngest camel lose its balance and fall; but on each occasion, the spot on which it fell was providentially dry; had it stumbled in the mud, it would inevitably have been stifled.

On our way, we met three Chinese travelers, who, by the aid of long staves, were making their laborious way through the marshes, carrying their shoes and clothes over their shoulders. We asked them in what direction we were likely to find a better road: "You would have been wiser," said they, "had you remained at Tchagan-Kouren; foot passengers can scarcely make their way through these marshes: how do you suppose you can get on with your camels?"

and with this consolatory assurance, they quitted us, giving us a look of compassion, certain as they were that we should never get through the mud.

The sun was just setting, when we perceived a Mongol habitation; we made our way direct to it, without heeding the difficulties of the road. In fact experience had already taught us that selection was quite out of the question, and that one way was as good as another in this universal slough. Making circuits merely lengthened the journey. The Tartars were frightened at our appearance, covered as we were with mud and perspiration; they immediately gave us some tea, and generously offered us the hospitality of their dwelling. The small mud house in which they lived, though built upon an eminence, had been half carried away by the inundation. We could not conceive what had induced them to fix their abode in this horrible district, but they told us that they were employed to tend the herds belonging to some Chinese of Tchagan-Kouren. After resting for a while, we requested information as to the best route to pursue, and we were told that the river was only five lis off, that its banks were dry, and that we should find there boats to carry us to the other side. "When you have crossed the Paga-Gol" (Little River), said our hosts, "you may proceed in peace; you will meet with no more water to interrupt you." We thanked these good Tartars for their kindness, and resumed our journey.

After half an hour's march, we discovered before us a large extent of water, studded with fishing-vessels. The title, Little River, may, for anything we know, be appropriate enough under ordinary circumstances, but at the time of our visit, the Paga-Gol was a broad sea. We pitched our tent on the bank which, by reason of its elevation, was perfectly dry, and the remarkable excellence of the pasturage determined us upon remaining in this place several days, in order to give rest to our animals, which, since their departure from Tchagan-Kouren had undergone enormous fatigue: we ourselves, too, felt the necessity of some relaxation, after the sufferings which these horrible marshes had inflicted upon us.

Waterfowl and Birds of Passage.

CHAPTER VII.

Mercurial Preparation for the Destruction of Lice—Dirtiness of the Mongols—Lama Notions about the Metempsychosis—Washing—Regulations of Nomadic Life—Aquatic and Passage Birds—The Yuen-Yang—The Dragon's Foot—Fishermen of the Paga-Gol—Fishing Party—Fisherman Bit by a Dog—Kou-Kouo, or, St. Ignatius's Bean—Preparations for Departure—Passage of the Paga-Gol—Dangers of the Voyage—Devotion of Samdadchiemba—The Prime Minister of the King of the Ortous—Encampment.

UPON taking possession of our post our first business was to excavate a ditch round the tent, in order that, should rain occur, the water might be carried into a pond below. The excavated earth served to make a mound round the tent; and, within, the pack-saddles and furniture of the camels formed very comfortable bedsteads for us. Having mode our new habitation as neat as possible, the next business was to make our persons neat also.

We had now been traveling for nearly six weeks, and still wore the same clothing we had assumed on our departure. The incessant pricklings with which we were harassed, sufficiently indicated that our attire was peopled with the filthy vermin to which the Chinese and Tartars are familiarly accustomed, but which with Europeans are objects of horror and disgust,—lice, which of all our miseries on our long journey have been the greatest. Hunger and thirst, fierce winds and piercing cold, wild beasts, robbers, avalanches, menaced death and actual discomfort, all had been as nothing compared with the incessant misery occasioned by these dreadful vermin.

Before quitting Tchagen-Kouren we had bought in a chemist's shop a few sapeks' worth of mercury. We now made with it a prompt and specific remedy against the lice, We had formerly got this receipt from some Chinese, and as it may be useful to others, we think it right to describe it here. You take half-an-ounce of mercury, which you mix with old tea-leaves, previously reduced to paste by mastication. To render this softer, you generally add saliva, water would not have the same effect. You must afterwards bruise and stir it awhile, so that the mercury may be divided into little balls as fine as dust. You infuse this composition into a string of cotton, loosely twisted, which you hang round the neck; the lice are sure to bite at the bait, and they thereupon as surely swell, become red, and die forthwith. In China and in Tartary you have to renew this sanitary necklace once a month, for otherwise, in these dirty countries you could not possibly keep clear from vermin, which swarm in every Chinese house and in every Mongol tent.

The Tartars are acquainted with the cheap and efficacious anti-louse mixture I have described, but they make no use of it. Accustomed from their infancy to live amid vermin, they at last take no heed whatever of them, except, indeed, when the number becomes so excessive as to involve the danger of their being absolutely eaten up. Upon such a juncture they strip off their clothes, and have a grand battue, all the members of the family and any friends who may have dropped in, taking part in the sport. Even Lamas, who may be present, share in the hunt, with this distinction, that they do not kill the game, but merely catch it and throw it away; the reason being, that according to the doctrine of metempsychosis, to kill any living being whatever, is to incur the danger of homicide, since the smallest insect before you may be the transmigration of a man. Such is the general opinion; but we have met with

Lamas whose views on this subject were more enlightened. They admitted that persons belonging to the sacerdotal class should abstain from killing animals; but not, said they, in fear of committing a murder by killing a man transmigrated into an animal, but because to kill is essentially antagonistic with the gentleness which should characterize a man of prayer, who is ever in communication with the Deity.

There are some Lamas who carry this scruple to a point approaching the puerile, so that as they ride along, they are constantly maneuvering their horses in and out, here and there, in order to avoid trampling upon some insect or other that presents itself in their path. Yet, say they, the holiest among them occasion inadvertently, the death, every day, of a great many living creatures. It is to expiate these involuntary murders that they undergo fasting and penitence, that they recite certain prayers, and that they make prostrations.

We who had no such scruples, and whose conscience stood upon a solid basis as to the transmigration of souls, concocted, as effectively as possible, our anti-louse preparation, doubling the dose of mercury in our anxiety to kill the greatest practicable number of the vermin that had been so long tormenting us by day and by night.

It would have been to little purpose merely to kill the present vermin; it was necessary to withhold any sort of shelter or encouragement from their too probable successors, and the first point, with this view, was to wash all our underclothing, which, for some time past, had not been subjected to any such operation. For nearly two months since our departure, we had been wholly dependent, in all respects, upon ourselves, and this necessity had compelled us to learn a little of various professions with which we had been previously unacquainted; becoming our own tailors and shoe menders, for example, when clothes or shoes required repairs. The course of nomadic life now practically introduced us also to the occupation of washermen. After boiling some ashes and soaking our linen in the lye, we next proceeded to wash it in an adjacent pond. One great stone on which to place the linen when washed, and another wherewith to beat it while washing, were our only implements of trade; but we got on very well, for the softness of the pond water gave every facility for cleansing the articles. Before long, we had the delight of seeing our linen once more clean; and when, having dried it on the grass, we folded and took it home to our tent, we were quite radiant with satisfaction.

The quiet and ease which we enjoyed in this encampment, rapidly remedied the fatigue we had undergone in the marshes. The weather was magnificent; all that we could have possibly desired. By day, a gentle, soothing heat; by night, a sky pure and serene; plenty of fuel; excellent and abundant pasturage; nitrous water, which our camels delighted in; in a word, everything to renovate the health and revive the spirits. Our rule of daily life may appear odd enough to some, and perhaps not altogether in harmony with the regulations of monastic houses, but it was in exact adaptation to the circumstances and wants of our little community.

Every morning, with the first dawn, before the earliest rays of the sun struck upon our tent, we rose spontaneously, requiring neither call-bell nor valet to rouse us. Our brief toilet made, we rolled up our goat-skins and placed them in a corner; then we swept out the tent, and put the cooking utensils in order, for we were desirous of having everything about us as clean and comfortable as possible. All things go by comparison in this world. The interior of our tent, which would have made a European laugh, filled with admiration the Tartars who from time to time paid us a visit. The cleanliness of our wooden cups, our kettle always well polished, our clothes not altogether as yet incrusted with grease; all this contrasted favorably with the dirt and disorder of Tartar habitations.

Having arranged our apartment, we said prayers together, and then dispersed each apart in the desert to engage in meditation upon some pious thought. Oh! little did we need, amid the profound silence of those vast solitudes, a printed book to suggest a subject for prayer! The void and vanity of all things here below, the majesty of God, the inexhaustible measures of his Providence, the shortness of life, the essentiality of laboring with a view to the world to come, and a thousand other salutary reflections, came of themselves, without any effort on our parts, to occupy the mind with gentle musings. In the desert the heart of man is free; he is subject to no species of tyranny. Far away from us were all those hollow theories and systems, those utopias of imaginary happiness which men are constantly aiming at, and which as constantly evade their grasp ; those inexhaustible combinations of selfishness and self-sufficiency, those burning passions which in Europe are ever contending, ever fermenting in men's minds and hardening their hearts. Amid these silent prairies there was nothing to disturb our tranquil thoughts, or to prevent us from reducing to their true value the futilities of this world, from appreciating at their lofty worth the things of God and of eternity.

The exercise which followed these meditations was, it must be admitted, far from mystic in its character ; but it was necessary, and not wholly without entertainment in its course. Each of us hung a bag from his shoulders and went in different directions to seek argols for fuel. Those who have never led a nomadic life will, of course, find it difficult to understand how this occupation could possibly develop any enjoyment. Yet, when one is lucky enough to find, half concealed among the grass, an argol, recommendable for its size and dryness, there comes over the heart a gentle joy, one of those sudden emotions which create a transient happiness. The pleasure at finding a fine argol is cognate with that which the hunter feels when he discovers the track of game, with which the boy regards, his eyes sparkling, the linnet's nest he has long sought; with which the fisherman sees quivering at the end of his line a large fish; nay, if we may compare small things with great, one might even compare this pleasure with the enthusiasm of a Leverrier when he has discovered a new planet.

Our sack, once filled with argols, we returned, and piled the contents with pride at the entrance of the tent; then we struck a light and set the fire in movement; and while the tea was boiling in the pot, pounded the meal and put some cakes to bake in the ashes. The repast, it is observable, was simple and modest, but it was always extremely delicious, first, because we had prepared it ourselves, and secondly, because our appetites provided most efficient seasoning.

After breakfast, while Samdadchiemba was collecting round the tent the animals which had dispersed in search of pasturage, we recited a portion of our breviary. Towards noon we indulged in a brief repose, a few minutes of gentle but sound sleep, never interrupted by nightmare or by unpleasant dreams. This repose was all the more necessary that the evenings were prolonged far into the night. It was always with difficulty that we tore ourselves from our walks by moonlight on the banks of the river. During the day all was silent and tranquil around us; but so soon as the shades of night began to overspread the desert, the scene became animated and noisy. Aquatic birds, arriving in immense flocks, diffused themselves over the various pools, and soon thousands of shrill cries filled the air with wild harmony. The cries of anger, the accents of passion, proceeding from those myriads of migratory birds, as they disputed among themselves possession of the tufts of marsh grass in which they desired to pass the night, gave one quite the idea of a numerous people in all the fury of civil war, fighting and clamoring, in agitation and violence, for some supposed advantage, brief as this eastern night.

Tartary is populated with nomadic birds. Look up when you may, you will see them floating high in air, the vast battalions forming, in their systematically capricious flight, a thousand fantastic outlines, dissipating as soon as formed, forming again as soon as dissipated, like the creations of a Kaleidoscope. Oh! how exactly are these migrant birds in their place, amid the deserts of Tartary, where man himself is never fixed in one spot, but is constantly on the move. It was very pleasant to listen to the distant hum of these winged bands, wandering about like ourselves. As we reflected upon their long peregrinations, and glanced in thought over the countries which their rapid flight must have comprehended, the recollections of our native land came vividly before us. "Who knows," we would say to each other, "who knows but that among these birds there are some who have traversed—who have, perhaps, alighted for awhile in our dear France: who have sought transient repose and refreshment in the plains of Languedoc, or on the heights of the Jura. After visiting our own country, they have doubtless pursued their route towards the north of Europe, and have come hither through the snows of Siberia, and of Upper Tartary. Oh! if these birds could understand our words, or if we could speak their tongue, how many questions should we not put to them!" Alas!

we did not then know that for two years more we should be deprived of all communication with our native land. The migratory birds which visit Tartary are for the most part known in Europe; such as wild geese, wild ducks, teal, storks, bustards, and so on. There is one bird which may deserve particular mention: the Youen-Yang, an aquatic bird frequenting ponds and marshes; it is of the size and form of the wild duck, but its beak, instead of being flat, is round, its red head is sprinkled with white, its tail is black, and the rest of its plumage a fine purple; its cry is exceedingly loud and mournful, not the song of a bird, but a sort of clear, prolonged sigh, resembling the plaintive tones of a man under suffering. These birds always go in pairs; they frequent, in an especial manner, desert and marshy places. You see them incessantly skimming over the surface of the waters without the couple ever separating from each other; if one flies away, the other immediately follows; and that which dies first does not leave its companion long in widowhood, for it is soon consumed by sorrow and lonesomeness. Youen is the name of the male, Yang that of the female; Youen-Yang their common denomination.

We remarked in Tartary another species of migratory bird, which offers various peculiarities singular in themselvee, and perhaps unknown to naturalists. It is about the size of a quail; its eyes, of a brilliant black, are encircled by a magnificent ring of azure; its body is of ash color, speckled with black; its legs, instead of feathers, are covered with a sort of long, rough hair, like that of the musk-deer; its feet are totally different from those of any other bird; they exactly resemble the paws of the green lizard, and are covered with scales so hard as to resist the edge of the sharpest knife. This singular creature, therefore, partakes at once of the bird, of the quadruped, and of the reptile. The Chinese call it Loung-Kio (Dragon's Foot). These birds make their periodical appearance in vast numbers from the north, especially after a great fall of snow. They fly with astonishing swiftness, and the movements of their wings makes a loud, rattling noise, like that of heavy hail.

While we had the charge, in Northern Mongolia, of the little christendom of the Valley of Black Waters, one of our Christians, a skilful huntsman, brought us two of these birds which he had caught alive. They were excessively ferocious; no sooner was your hand extended to touch them, than the hair on their legs bristled; and if you had the temerity to stroke them, you instantly were assailed with vehement strokes of the bill. The nature of these Dragon's Feet was evidently so wild as to preclude the possibility of preserving them alive: they would touch nothing we offered them. Perceiving, therefore, that they must soon die of starvation, we determined to kill and eat them; their flesh was of agreeable, pheasant-like savor, but terribly tough.

The Tartars might easily take any number of these migratory birds, especially of the wild geese and ducks, the crowds of which are perfectly prodigious: and take them, moreover, without the expenditure of a single ounce of powder, by merely laying traps for them on the banks of the pools, or by surprising them in the night amongst the aquatic plants; but as we have before observed, the flesh of wild creatures is not at all to the taste of the Tartars; there is nothing to their palates at all comparable with a joint of mutton, very fat and half boiled.

The Mongols are equally disinclined to fishing; and accordingly, the highly productive lakes and ponds which one meets with so frequently in Tartary, have become the property of Chinese speculators, who, with the characteristic knavery of their nation, having first obtained from the Tartar kings permission to fish in their states, have gradually converted this toleration into a monopoly most rigorously enforced. The Paga-Gol (Little River), near which we were now encamped, has several Chinese fishing stations upon its banks. This Paga-Gol is formed by the junction of two rivers, which, taking their source from the two sides of a hill, flow in opposite directions; the one, running towards the north, falls into the Yellow River; the other proceeding southwards, swells the current of another stream, which itself also falls into the Hoang-Ho; but at the time of the great inundations, the two rivers, in common with the hill which separates their course, all alike disappear. The overflowing of the Hoang-Ho reunites the two currents, and that which then presents itself is a large expanse of water, the breadth of which extends to nearly two miles. At this period, the fish which abound in the Yellow River repair in shoals to this new basin, wherein the waters remain collected until the commencement of the winter; and during the autumn, this little sea is covered in all directions with the boats of Chinese fishermen, whose habitations for the fishing season are miserable cabins constructed on either bank.

During the first night of our encampment in this locality, we were kept awake by a strange noise, constantly recurring in the distance, as it seemed to us, the muffled and irregular roll of drums; with daybreak the noise continued, but more intermittent and less loud; it apparently came from the water. We went out and proceeded towards the bank of the lake, where a fisherman, who was boiling his tea in a little kettle, supported by three stones, explained the mystery; he told us that during the night, all the fishermen seated in their barks, keep moving over the water, in all directions, beating wooden drums for the purpose of alarming the fish, and driving them towards the places where the nets are spread. The poor man whom we interrogated had himself passed the whole night in this painful toil. His red, swollen eyes and his drawn face clearly indicated that it was long since he had enjoyed adequate rest. "Just now," he said, "we have a great deal of work upon our hands; there is no time to be lost if we wish to make any money of the business. The fishing season is very short; at the outside not more than three months; and a few days hence we shall be obliged to withdraw. The Paga-Gol will be frozen, and not a fish will be obtainable. You see, Sirs Lamas, we have no time to lose. I have passed all the night hunting the fish about; when I have drunk some tea and eaten a few spoonfuls of oatmeal, I shall get into my boat, and visit the nets I have laid out there westward; then I shall deposit the fish I have taken in the osier reservoirs you see yonder; then I shall examine my nets, and mend them if they need mending; then I shall take a brief repose, and after that, when the old grandfather (the sun) goes down, I shall once more cast my nets; then I shall row over the water, now here, now there, beating my drum, and so it goes on." These details interested us, and as our occupations at the moment were not very urgent, we asked the fisherman if he would allow us to accompany him when he went to raise his nets. "Since personages like you," answered he, "do not disdain to get into my poor boat and to view my unskilful and disagreeable fishing, I accept the benefit you propose." Hereupon we sat down in a corner of his rustic hearth to wait until he had taken his repast. The meal of the fisherman was as short as the preparations for it had been hasty. When the tea was sufficiently boiled, he poured out a basin full of it; threw into this a handful of oatmeal, which he partially kneaded with his forefinger; and then, after having pressed it a little, and rolled it into a sort of cake, he swallowed it without any other preparation. After having three or four times repeated the same operation, the dinner was at an

Fishing Party.

end. This manner of living had nothing in it to excite our curiosity; having adopted the nomad way of living, a sufficiently long experience had made it familiar to us.

We entered his small boat and proceeded to enjoy the pleasure of fishing. After having relished for some moments the delight of a quiet sail on the tranquil water, smooth and unbroken as glass, through troops of cormorants and wild geese, which were disporting on the surface of the expanse, and which, half running, half flying, made a free passage for us as we advanced, we reached the place where the nets lay. At intervals we saw pieces of wood floating on the water, to which the nets were attached which rested at the botfom. When we drew them up we saw the fish glitter as they struggled in the meshes. These fish were generally large, but the fisherman only kept the largest; those that were under half a pound he threw back into the water.

After having examined a few of the nets, he stopped to see if the haul had been productive. Already the two wells, constructed at the extremities of the boat, were nearly full. "Sirs Lamas," said the fisherman, "do you eat fish? I will sell you some if you please." At this proposition, the two poor French missionaries looked at each other without saying a word. In that look you might see that they were by no means averse to trying the flavor of the fish of the Yellow River, but that they dared not, a sufficient reason keeping them in suspense. "How do you sell your fish?" "Not dear, eighty sapeks a pound." "Eighty sapeks! why that is dearer than mutton." "You speak the words of truth; but what is mutton compared with the fish of the Hoang-Ho?" "No matter; it is too dear for us. We have still far to go; our purse is low, we must economize." The fisherman did not insist; he took his oar, and directed the boat towards those nets which had not yet been drawn up from the water. "For what reason," asked we, "do you throw back so much fish? Is it because the quality is inferior?" "Oh, no; all the fish in the Yellow River are excellent, these are too small, that is all." "Ah, just so; next year they will be bigger. It is a matter of calculation; you refrain now, so that in the end you may get more by them." The fisherman laughed. "It is not that," he said; "we do not hope to re-capture these fish. Every year the basin is filled with fresh fish, brought hither by the overflowings of the Hoang-Ho; there come great and small; we take the first; and the others we throw back, because they do not sell well. The fish here are very abundant. We are able to select the best . . . Sirs Lamas, if you like to have these little fish, I will not throw them back." The offer was accepted, and the small fry, as they came, were placed in a little basket. When the fishing was over, we found ourselves possessors of a very respectable supply of fish. Before leaving the boat, we washed an old basket, and having deposited our fish in it, we marched in triumph to the tent. "Where have you been?" exclaimed Samdadchiemba, as soon as he saw us; "the tea is now boiled, and it soon gets cold: I have boiled it up again; it has again got cold." "Pour out some of your tea," answered we. "We will not have oatmeal to-day, but some fresh fish. Place some loaves under the ashes to bake." Our prolonged absence had put Samdadchiemba in an ill humor. His forehead was more contracted than usual, and his small black eyes flashed with displeasure. But when he beheld in the basket the fish which were still in motion, his face relaxed into a smile, and his countenance insensibly grew more cheerful. He opened smilingly the bag of flour, the strings of which were never untied except on rare occasions. Whilst he was busily occupied with the pastry, we took some of the fish, and proceeded to the shore of a lake at a short distance from the tent. We had scarcely got there, when Samdadchiemba ran to us with all his might. He drew aside the four corners of the cloth which contained the fish. "What are you going to do?" said he, with an anxious air. "We are going to cut open and scale this fish." "Oh, that is not well; my spiritual fathers, wait a little; you must not transgress thus." "What are you talking about? Who is committing a sin?" "Why, look at these fish; they are still moving. You must let them die in peace, before you open them: is it not a sin to kill a living creature?" "Go make your bread and let us alone. Are we always to be pestered with your notions of metempsychosis? Do you still think that men are transformed into beasts, and beasts into men?" The lips of our Dchiahour opened for a long laugh. "Bah!" said he, striking his forehead, "what a thick head I have; I did not think of that; I had forgotten the doctrine," and he returned not a little ashamed at having come to give us such ridiculous advice.

The fish were fried in mutton fat, and we found them exquisite.

In Tartary and in the north of China, the fishing continues to the commencement of winter, when the ponds and rivers are frozen. At that time they expose to the air, in the night, the fish they have kept alive in the reservoirs; these immediately freeze, and may be laid up without trouble. It is in this state that they are sold to the fish-mongers. During the long winters of the northern part of the empire, the wealthy Chinese can always, by this means, procure fresh fish; but great care must be taken not to make too large a provision of them to be consumed during the time of the great frosts, for on the first thaw the fish become putrid.

During our few days' rest, we considered the means of crossing the Paga-Gol. A Chinese family having obtained from the King of the Ortous the privilege of conveying travelers across, we were obliged to address ourselves to the master of the boat. He had undertaken to conduct us to the other side, but we had not yet agreed about the fare; he required upwards of 1,000 sapeks. The sum appeared to us exorbitant, and we waited.

On the third day of our halt, we perceived a fisherman coming towards our tent, dragging himself along with great difficulty by the aid of a long staff. His pale and extremely meager face, showed that he was a man in suffering. As soon as he had seated himself beside our hearth, "Brother," said we, "it seems that your days are not happy." "Ah," said he, "my misfortune is great, but what am I to do? I must submit to the irrevocable laws of heaven. It is now a fortnight since, as I was going to visit a Mongol tent, I was bitten in the leg by a mad dog; there has been formed a wound which grows larger and mortifies day by day. They told me that you were from the Western Heaven, and I am come to you. The men of the Western Heaven, say the Tartar Lamas, have an unlimited power. With a single word they are able to cure the most grievous disorders." "They have deceived you, when they said we had such great powers:" and hereupon we took occasion to elucidate to this man the great truths of the faith. But he was a Chinese, and, like all his nation, but little heedful of religious matters. Our words only glanced over his heart; his hurt absorbed all his thoughts. We resolved to treat his case with the Kou-Kouo, or bean of St. Ignatius. This vegetable, of a brown or ashy color, and of a substance which resembles horn, extremely hard, and of intolerable bitterness, is a native of the Philippine Isles. The manner of using the Kou-Kouo is to bruise it in cold water, to which it communicates its bitterness. This water, taken inwardly, modifies the heat of the blood, and extinguishes internal inflammation. It is an excellent specific for all sorts of wounds and contusions, and enjoying a high character in the Chinese Materia Medica, is sold in all chemists' shops. The veterinary doctors also apply it with great success to the internal diseases of cattle and sheep. In the north of China we have often witnessed the salutary effects of the Kou-Kouo.

We infused the powder of one of these beans in some cold water, with which we washed the poor man's wound, and we supplied some clean linen, in place of the disgustingly dirty rags which previously served for a bandage. When we had done all we could for the sufferer, we observed that he still seemed very embarrassed in his manner. His face was red with blushes, he held down his eyes, and he began several sentences which he could not complete. "Brother," said we, "you have something on your mind." "Holy personages, you see how poor I am! you have tended my wound, and you have given me a great mug of healing water to take; I know not what I can offer in exchange for all this." "If this be the subject of your uneasiness," said we, "be at once reassured. In doing what we could for your leg, we only fulfilled a duty commanded by our religion. The remedies we have prepared, we freely give you." Our words evidently relieved the poor fisherman from a very grave embarrassment. He immediately prostrated himself before us, and touched the ground thrice with his forehead, in token of his gratitude. Before withdrawing, he asked us whether we intended to remain where we were for any length of time. We told him that we should gladly depart the next day, but that we had not as yet agreed with the ferryman as to the fare. "I have a boat," said the fisherman, "and since you have tended my wound, I will endeavor to-morrow, to convey you over the water. If my boat belonged entirely to myself, I would at once undertake the matter; but as I have two partners, I must first get their consent. Moreover, we must procure some particulars as to our course; we fishermen are not acquainted with the depth of water at all the points of the passage. There are dangerous places here and there, which we must ascertain the exact nature and locality of beforehand, so that we may not incur some misfortune. Don't say anything more about the matter to the ferry people. I will come back in the course of the evening, and we will talk over the subject."

These words gave us hopes of being able to continue our journey, without too heavy an outlay for the river passage. As he had promised, the fisherman returned in the evening. "My partners," said he, "were not at first willing to undertake this job, because it would lose them a day's fishing. I promised that you would give them 400 sapeks, and so the affair was arranged. To-morrow we will make inquiries as to the best course to follow on the river. Next morning, before sunrise, fold your tent, load your camels, and come down to the river side. If you see any of the ferry people, don't tell them you are going to give us 400 sapeks. As they have the sole right of carrying passengers for hire, they might prosecute us for carrying you, if they knew you had paid us anything."

At the appointed hour, we proceeded to the fisherman's hut. In a minute the baggage was packed in the boat, and the two missionaries seated themselves beside it, attended by the boatman whose wound they had cured. It was agreed that a young companion of his should ride the horse across the shallows, leading the mule, while Samdadchiemba, in like manner, was to conduct the camels over. When all was ready we started, the boat following one course, the horses and camels another, for the latter were obliged to make long circuits in order to avoid the deeper parts of the river.

The navigation was at first very pleasant. We floated tranquilly over the broad surface of the waters, in a small skiff, propelled by a single man with two light sculls. The pleasure of this water party, amid the deserts of Mongolia, was not, however, of long duration. The poetry of the thing, soon at an end, was succeeded by some very doleful prose. We were advancing gently over the smooth water, vaguely listening to the measured dips of the sculls, when, all of a sudden, we were aroused by a clamor behind, of which the shrieks of the camels constituted a prominent share. We stopped, and, looking round, perceived that horse, mule, and camels were struggling in the water, without making any onward progress. In the general confusion we distinguished Samdadchiemba flourishing his arms, as if to recall us. Our boatman was not at all disposed to accept the invitation, reluctant as he was to quit the easy current he had found; but as we insisted, he turned back, and rowed towards the other party.

Samdadchiemba was purple with rage. As soon as we came up to him, he furiously assailed the boatman with invectives: "Did you want to drown us," bawled he, "that you gave us for a guide a fellow that doesn't know a yard of the way. Here are we amid gulfs, of which none of us know the depth or extent." The animals, in fact, would neither advance nor recede; beat them as you might, there they remained immovable. The boatman hurled maledictions at his partner: "If you did not know the way, what did you come for? The only thing to be done now is to go back to the hut, and tell your cousin to get on the horse; he'll be a better guide than you."

To return for a better guide was clearly the safest course, but this was no easy matter; the animals had got so frightened at finding themselves surrounded with such a body of water, that they would not stir. The young guide was at his wits' end; it was in vain that he beat the horse, and pulled the bridle this way and that; the horse struggled and splashed up the water, and that was all; not an inch would it move, one way or the other. The young man, no better horseman than guide, at last lost his balance and fell into the water; he disappeared for a moment, to our increased consternation, and then rose at a little distance, just where he could stand and have his head above water. Samdadchiemba grew furious, but at last, seeing no other alternative, he quietly took off all his clothes as he sat on the camel, threw them into the boat, and slipped down the camel's side into the stream. "Take that man into your boat," cried he to our boatman; "I'll have nothing more to do with him. I'll go back and find some one who can guide us properly." He then made his way back through the water, which sometimes rose up to his neck, leading the animals, whose confidence returned when they saw themselves preceded by the Dchiahour.

Our hearts were filled with gratitude at observing the devotion and courage of this young neophyte, who for our sakes, had not hesitated to plunge into the water which, at that season, was bitterly cold. We anxiously followed him with our eyes until we saw him close upon the shore. "You may now," said the boatman, "be quite at your ease; he will find in my hut a man who will guide him, so as to avoid the least danger."

We proceeded on our way, but the navigation was by no means so agreeable as before; the boatman could not find again the clear path on the waters which he was pursuing when we returned to aid Sàmdadchiemba; and hampered with aquatic plants, the vessel made but very slow progress. We tried to mend matters, by turning to the right and then to the left, but the difficulty only grew greater; the water was so shallow that the boat, in its labored advance, turned up the mud. We were compelled ourselves to take the sculls, while the boatman, getting into the water and passing across his shoulders a rope, the other end of which was tied to the boat, tried to pull us along. We applied our united efforts to the task of moving the vessel, but all in vain; it scarcely advanced a foot. The boatman at last resumed his seat and folded his arms in utter despair: "Since we cannot get on by ourselves," said he, "we must wait here until the passage-boat comes up, and then follow in its course." We waited.

The boatman was evidently altogether disconcerted; he loudly reproached himself for having undertaken this laborious business; while we, on our parts, were angry with ourselves for having permitted a consideration of economy to deter us from proceeding with the ferry-boat. We should have got into the water and waded to the shore, but, besides the difficulty connected with the baggage, the undertaking was dangerous in itself. The ground was so irregular that, while at one moment you passed through water so shallow that it would scarcely float the boat, in the next moment you came to a hole, deep enough to drown you three times over.

It was near noon when we saw three passage-boats passing us, which belonged to the family who enjoyed the monopoly of the ferry. After having, with infinite labor, extricated ourselves from the mud and attained the channel indicated by these boats, we were quietly following their course when they stopped, evidently awaiting us. We recognized the person with whom we had tried to bargain for our passage over, and he recognized us, as we could easily perceive by the angry glances which he directed against us. "You tortoise-egg," cried he to our boatman, "what have these western men given you for the passage? They must have handed over a good bagful of sapeks to have induced you to trespass upon my rights! You and I will have a little talk about the matter, by and by; be sure of that." "Don't answer him," whispered the boatman to us; then raising his voice and assuming an air of virtuous indignation, he cried to the ferryman: "What do you mean? You don't know what you're talking about. Consult the dictates of reason, instead of getting into a fury about nothing. These Lamas have not given me a sapek; they have cured my leg with one of their western specifics, and do you mean to say that in gratitude for such a benefit I am not to carry them over the Paga-Gol? My conduct is perfectly right, and in conformity with religion." The ferryman grumbling between his teeth, pretended to accept the statement thus made.

This little altercation was succeeded by profound silence on both sides. While the flotilla was peaceably advancing, pursuing the thread of a narrow current, just wide enough to admit the passage of a boat, we saw galloping towards us, along the shallows, a horseman whose rapid progress dashed aside the water in all directions. As soon as he came within call he stopped short: "Make haste," cried he, "make haste; lose no time, row with all your might! The Prime Minister of the King of the Ortous is yonder on the prairie with his suite, waiting the arrival of your boat. Row quickly." He who spoke was a Tartar Mandarin, his rank being indicated by the blue button which surmounted his hair cap. After issuing his orders he turned round, whipped his horse, and galloped back the same way he had come. When he was out of sight, the murmurs which his presence had restrained burst out. "Here's a day's labor marked out! A fine thing, truly, to be employed by a Mongol Toudzelaktsi (Minister of State), who'll make us row all day, and then not give us a single sapek for our pains." "As to that, it need not so much matter; but the chances are that this Tcheou-ta-dze will break every bone in our bodies into the bargain." "Well, row away, it can't be helped; after all, we shall have the honor of ferrying over a Toudzelaktsi." This little piece of insolence excited a laugh, but the prevalent expression was that of furious invective against the Mongol authorities.

Our boatman remained silent; at last he said to us: "This is a most unfortunate day for me. I shall be obliged to carry some of this Toudzelaktsi's suite perhaps to Tchagan-Kouren itself. I am by myself, I am ill, and my boat ought this evening to be engaged in fishing." We were truly afflicted at this unlucky turn of affairs, feeling as we did that we were the involuntary occasion of the poor fisherman's misfortune. We knew very well that it was no trifling matter to be called into the service, in this way, of a Chinese or Tartar Mandarin, for whom everything must be done at once, unhesitatingly and cheerfully. No matter what may be the difficulties in the way, that which the Mandarin desires must be done. Knowing the consequences of the meeting to our poor boatman, we determined to see what we could do to relieve him from the dilemma. "Brother," said we, "do not be uneasy; the Mandarin who awaits the passage-boats is a Tartar, the minister of the king of this country. We will endeavor to manage matters for you. Go very slowly, stop now and then; while we are in your boat no one, attendants, Mandarins, not even the Toudzelaktsi himself will venture to say a word to you." We stopped short in our course, and meanwhile the three passage-boats reached the landing-place where the Mongol authorities were waiting for them. Soon two Mandarins, with the blue button, galloped towards us: "What are you stopping there for?" cried they. "Why do you not come on?" We interposed: "Brother Mongols," said we, "request your master to content himself with the three boats already at the shore. This man is ill, and has been rowing a long time; it would be cruel to prevent him from resting himself awhile." "Be it as you desire, Sirs Lamas," replied the horsemen, and they galloped back to the Toudzelaktsi.

We then resumed our course, but very slowly, in order to give time for every person to embark before we reached the shore. By and by, we saw the three ferry-boats returning, filled with Mandarins and their attendants; the horses were fording the river in another direction, under the guidance of one of the boatmen. As the party approached, our boatman grew more and more afraid; he did not venture to raise his eyes, and he scarcely breathed. At last the boats were level with each other; "Sirs Lamas," cried a voice, "is peace with you?" The red button in the cap of the speaker, and the richness of his embroidered dress, indicated that it was the prime minister who addressed to us this Tartar compliment. "Toudzelaktsi of the Ortous," replied we, "our progress is slow, but it is favorable; may peace also attend you." After a few other civilities, required by Tartar forms, we proceeded on our way. When we had attained a safe distance from the Mandarins, our boatman was perfectly relieved; we had extricated him from a most serious difficulty. The ferry-boats, it was probable, would be engaged at least three days in their gratuitous labor, for the Toudzelaktsi not choosing to travel across the marshes, the boats would have to convey him down the Yellow River all the way to Tchagan-Kouren.

After a long, laborious, and dangerous passage, we reached the other side of the waters. Samdadchiemba had arrived long before us, and was awaiting us on the margin of the stream. He was still naked, as to clothes, but then he was covered well nigh up to the shoulders with a thick layer of mud, which gave him a negro aspect. In consequence of the extreme shallowness of the water, the boat could not get within thirty feet of the shore. The boatmen who preceded us had been obliged to carry the Mandarins and their attendants on their shoulders to the boats. We did not choose to adopt the same process, but rather to make use of the animals for our disembarkation. Samdadchiemba accordingly brought them close to the boat; M. Gabet got on the horse, M. Huc on the mule, and so we reached the shore, without having occasion to employ any person's shoulders.

The sun was just about to set. We would willingly have encamped at once, for we were exhausted with hunger and fatigue, but we could not possibly do so, for we had, they told us, fully two lis to journey before we should get out of the mud. We loaded our camels, therefore, and proceeded onward, completing the miserable day in pain and suffering. Night had closed in before we came to a place where we could set up our tent; we had no strength left for preparing the usual meal, so drinking some cold water, and eating a few handfuls of millet, we lay down, after a brief prayer, and fell into a deep slumber.

Election of a Living Buddha.

CHAPTER VIII.

Glance at the Country of the Ortous—Cultivated Lands—Sterile, sandy steppes of the Ortous—Form of the Tartar-Mongol Government—Nobility—Slavery—A small Lamasery—Election and Enthronization of a Living Buddha—Discipline of the Lamaseries—Lama Studies—Violent Storm—Shelter in some Artificial Grottoes—Tartar concealed in a Cavern—Tartaro-Chinese Anecdote—Ceremonies of Tartar Marriages—Polygamy—Divorce—Character and Costume of the Mongol Women.

THE sun was already very high when we rose. On leaving the tent we looked round us, in order to get acquainted with this new country, which the darkness of the preceding evening had not allowed us to examine. It appeared to us dismal and arid; but we were happy, on any terms, to lose sight of bogs and swamps. We had left behind us the Yellow River, with its overflowing waters, and entered the sandy steppes of Ortous.

The land of Ortous is divided into seven banners; it extends a hundred leagues from east to west, and seventy from south to north. It is surrounded by the Yellow River on the west, east, and north, and by the Great Wall on the south. This country has been subjected, at all periods, to the influence of the political revolutions, by which the Chinese empire has been agitated. The Chinese and Tartar conquerors have taken possession of it in turns, and made it the theater of sanguinary wars. During the tenth, eleventh, and twelfth centuries, it remained under the scepter of the kings of Hia, who derived their origin from the Thou-Pa Tartars of the land of Si-Fan. The capital of their kingdom, called Hia-Tcheou, was situated at the foot of the Alécha mountains between the Hoang-Ho and the Great Wall. At present, this town is called Ning-Hia, and belongs to the province Kan-Sou. In 1227 the kingdom of Hia, and afterwards Ortous, were involved in the common desolation by the victories of Tchingghis-Khan, founder of the Tartar dynasty of the Youen.

After the expulsion of the Tartar Mongols by the Ming, the Ortous fell under the power of the Khan of the Tchakar. When the latter submitted to the Mantchou conquerors in 1635, the Ortous followed his example, and were reunited to the empire as a tributary people.

The Emperor Khang-Hi resided for some time among the Ortous in 1696, when he was on his expedition against the Eleuts; and this is what he wrote of this people in a letter to the prince, his son, who had remained at Peking:—"Till now, I never had at all an accurate idea respecting the Ortous: they are a very civilized nation, and have lost nothing of the old manners of the true Mongols. All their princes live in perfect union among themselves, and do not know the difference between *mine* and *thine*. No one ever heard of a thief amongst them, although they take not the slightest precautions for guarding their camels and horses. If by chance one of these animals goes astray, it is taken care of by him who finds it, till he has discovered its owner, to whom he restores it, without the least payment. The Ortous are extremely skilful in breeding cattle; most of their horses are tame and tractable. The Tchakars, north of the Ortous, enjoy the reputation of training them with more care and success; nevertheless, I believe that the Ortous excel them in this point. Notwithstanding these advantages, they are not at all so rich as the other Mongols."

This quotation, which we take from the Abbé Grosier, is

in every point conformable with what we ourselves were able to observe among the Ortous; so that, since the time of the Emperor Khang-Hi, this people has not at all changed in its manners.

The aspect of the country through which we traveled on the first day of our journey seemed affected by the vicinity of the Chinese fishermen, who reside on the banks of the Yellow River. We saw here and there cultivated grounds, but there can be nothing more wretched and bare-looking than this cultivation, except, perhaps, the cultivator himself. These miserable agriculturists are a mixed people, half Chinese, half Tartars, but possessing neither the industry of the former, nor the frank and simple manners of the latter. They live in houses, or rather in dirty sheds built of branches intertwined, rudely covered with mud and cow's excrement. Thirst obliging us to enter one of these habitations to ask for some water, we were able to convince ourselves that the interior did not in any way contradict the misery which appeared outside. Men and animals live together higgledy-piggledy in these abodes, which are far inferior to those of the Mongols, where, at least, the air is not infected by the presence of cattle and sheep.

The sandy soil, which is cultivated by these poor people, beyond a little buckwheat and millet, produces only hemp, but this is very large and abundant. Though, when we were there, the crop was already gathered in, we could nevertheless judge of the beauty of its stem from what remained in the fields. The farmers of Ortous do not pull up the hemp when it is ripe, as is done in China; they cut it off above the ground, so high as to leave a stump of about an inch in diameter. It was accordingly great toil for our camels to traverse those vast fields of hemp; the stumps, occurring at every step beneath their large feet, compelled them to execute all sorts of fantastic movements, which would have excited our mirth, had we not been fearful of seeing them wounded. However, that which so impeded our camels proved of great use to ourselves. When we had set up our tent, these stumps furnished us with a ready and abundant fuel.

We soon entered once more the Land of Grass, if, indeed, one can give this name to such a barren, arid country, as that of the Ortous. Wherever you turn you find only a soil, bare and without verdure; rocky ravines, marly hills, and plains covered with a fine, moving sand, blown by the impetuous winds in every direction; for pasture, you will only find a few thorny bushes and poor fern, dusty and fetid. At intervals only, this horrible soil produces some thin, sharp grass, so firm in the earth, that the animals can only get it up by digging the sand with their muzzles. The numerous swamps, which had been so heavy a desolation to us on the borders of the Yellow River, became matter of regret in the country of the Ortous, so very rare here is water; not a single rivulet is there, not a spring, where the traveler can quench his thirst; at distances only are there ponds and cisterns, filled with a fetid, muddy water.

The Lamas, with whom we had been in communication at Blue Town, had warned us of all the miseries we should have to endure in the country of the Ortous, especially on account of the scarcity of water. By their advice we had bought two wooden pails, which proved indeed of the greatest service to us. Whenever we were lucky enough to find on our way pools or wells dug by the Tartars, we filled our pails, without considering too nicely the quality of the water, which we used with the greatest economy, as if it had been some rare and precious beverage. In spite of all these precautions, it happened more than once that we were obliged to pass whole days without getting a single drop of water wherewith to moisten our lips. But our personal privations were trifling compared with the pain we felt at seeing our animals wanting water almost every day in a country where they had nothing to eat beyond a few plants nearly dried up, and, as it were, calcined by nitre, and where they accordingly fell away visibly. After some days' traveling, the horse assumed a truly wretched appearance; it bent down its head, and seemed, at every step, as though it would sink down with weakness; the camels painfully balanced themselves on their long legs, and their emaciated humps hung over their backs like empty bags.

The steppes of the Ortous, though so destitute of water and good pasture, have not been quite abandoned by wild animals. You often find there gray squirrels, agile yellow goats, and beautifully plumaged pheasants. Hares are in abundance, and are so far from shy, that they did not even take the trouble to move at our approach; they merely rose

The Steppes of Ortous.

on their hind legs, pricked up their ears, and looked at us as we passed with the utmost indifference. The fact is, these animals feel perfectly secure, for, with the exception of a few Mongols who follow the chase, nobody ever molests them.

The herds of the Tartars of the Ortous are not very numerous, and are quite different from those which feed on the rich pastures of the Tchakar, or of Gechekten. The cattle and horses appeared very miserable; the goats, sheep, and camels, however, looked very well, which is undoubtedly the consequence of their predilection for plants impregnated with saltpeter, whereas cattle and horses prefer fresh pastures, and pure and abundant water.

The Mongols of Ortous are very much affected by the wretchedness of the soil upon which they live. In the course of our journey we saw no indication that they had become much richer than they were in the time of the Emperor Khang-Hi. Most of them live in tents made of some rags of felt, or of goat-skins framed on a wretched woodwork. Everything about these tents is so old and dirty, so tattered with time and storms, that you would with difficulty suppose they could serve as abodes for human beings. Whenever we happened to pitch our tent near these poor habitations, we were sure to be visited by a crowd of wretches who prostrated themselves at our feet, rolled on the earth, and gave us the most magnificent titles, in order to extract something from our charity. We were not rich, but we could not abstain from bestowing upon them a part of the modicum which the goodness of Providence had bestowéd upon us. We gave them some leaves of tea, a handful of oatmeal, some broiled millet, sometimes some mutton fat. Alas! we would fain have given more, but we were obliged to give according to our means. The missionaries are themselves poor men, who only live upon the alms distributed among them every year by their brothers in Europe.

Any one not acquainted with the laws by which the Tartars are ruled, would not readily understand why men condemn themselves to spend their lives in the wretched country of the Ortous, whilst Mongolia presents, in every direction, immense uninhabited plains, where water and pasture are to be found in abundance. Although the Tartars are nomads, and incessantly wandering about from one place to another, they are, nevertheless, not at liberty to live in any other country than their own. They are bound to remain in their own kingdom, under the dominion of their own sovereign, for slavery is still maintained among the Mongol tribes with the utmost rigor. In order to attain an accurate idea of the degree of liberty these people enjoy in their desert regions, it is expedient to enter into some details as to the form of their government.

Mongolia is divided into several sovereignties, whose chiefs are subject to the Emperor of China, himself a Tartar, but of the Mantchou race; these chiefs bear titles corresponding to those of kings, dukes, earls, barons, etc. They govern their states according to their own pleasure, none having any right to meddle with their affairs. They acknowledge as sovereign only the Emperor of China. Whenever there arise differences among them, they appeal to Peking. Instead of leveling lances at each other, as used to be done in the middle ages of Europe, among its little sovereigns, so warlike and so turbulent, they always submit with respect to the decision of the Court of Peking, whatever it may be. Though the Mongol sovereigns think it their duty to prostrate themselves, once a year, before the Son of Heaven, Lord of the Earth, they nevertheless do not concede to the Grand-Khan the right of dethroning the reigning families in the Tartar principalities. He may, they say, cashier a king for grave misconduct, but he is bound to fill up the vacant place with one of the superseded prince's sons. The sovereignty belongs, they contend, to such and such a family, by a right which is inalienable, and of which it were a crime to dispossess the owner.

A few years ago, the King of Barains[1] was accused at Peking of having conspired a rebellion against the Emperor; he was tried by the Supreme Tribunal without being heard, and condemned to be "shortened at both ends," the meaning of the decree being, that his head and feet should be cut off. The king made enormous presents to the officials who were sent to superintend the execution of the imperial edict, and they contented themselves with cutting off his braid of hair, and the soles of his boots. They reported at Peking that the order had been executed, and no more was said about the matter. The king however, descended from his throne, and was succeeded by his son.

Although it is a sort of customary right that power shall always remain in the same family, it cannot be said that there is anything precisely fixed in this respect. There can be nothing more vague and indefinite than the relations between the Tartar sovereigns and the Grand-Khan or Emperor of China, whose omnipotent will is above all laws and all customs. In practice, the Emperor has the right to do whatever he chooses to do, and the right is never disputed by any person. If doubtful or disputed cases arise, they are decided by force.

In Tartary, all the families that are in any way related to the sovereign, form a nobility, or a patrician cast, who are proprietors of the whole soil. These nobles, called Taitsi, are distinguished by a blue button surmounting the cap. It is from among them that the sovereigns of the different states select their ministers, who are generally three in number, and called Toutzelaktsi—that is to say, a man who assists or lends his aid. This rank gives them the right of wearing the red button. Below the Toutzelaktsi are the Touchimel, subaltern officers, who are charged with the details of government. Lastly, a certain number of secretaries

[1] Barains is a principality situated north of Peking. It is one of the most celebrated in Mongol Tartary.

or interpreters, who must be versed in the Mongol, Mantchou, and Chinese languages, complete the hierarchy.

In the country of the Khalkhas, to the north of the desert of Gobi, there is a district entirely occupied by Taitsi, who are supposed to be descendants of the Mongol dynasty, that was founded by Tchinggiskhan, and which occupied the imperial throne from 1260 to 1341. After the revolution, which restored the national independence of the Chinese, these people sought refuge among the Khalkhas, obtained, without difficulty, a portion of their immense territory, and adopted the nomad life, which their ancestors had led prior to the conquest of China. These Taitsi live in the greatest independence, liable to no duty, paying no tribute to anyone, and recognizing no sovereign. Their wealth consists in tents and cattle. The country of the Taitsi is, of all the Mongol regions, that wherein the patriarchal manners are found to be most accurately preserved, such as the Bible describes them in the lives of Abraham, Jacob, and the other pastors of Mesopotamia.

The Tartars who do not belong to the royal family, are all slaves, living in absolute subjection to their masters. Besides the rents they pay, they are bound to keep their master's flocks and herds, but they are not forbidden to breed also cattle on their own account. It would be a fallacy to imagine that slavery in Tartary is oppressive and cruel, as amongst some nations; the noble families scarcely differ from the slave families. In examining the relations between them, it would be difficult to distinguish the master from the slave: they live both alike in tents, and both alike occupy their lives in pasturing their flocks. You will never find among them luxury and opulence insolently staring in the face of poverty. When the slave enters his master's tent, the latter never fails to offer him tea and milk; they smoke together, and exchange their pipes. Around the tents the young slaves and the young noblemen romp and wrestle together without distinction; the stronger throws the weaker; that is all. You often find families of slaves becoming proprietors of numerous flocks, and spending their days in abundance. We met many who were richer than their masters, a circumstance giving no umbrage to the latter. What a difference between this slavery and that of Rome, for instance, where the Roman citizen, when he made up the inventory of his house, classed his slaves as furniture. With these haughty and cruel masters the slave did not merit even the name of man; he was called, without ceremony, a domestic thing, *res domestica*. Slavery, with the Mongol Tartars, is even less oppressive, less insulting to humanity, than the bondage of the middle ages. The Mongol masters never give to their slaves those humiliating nicknames which were formerly used to designate serfs; they call them *brothers;* never villeins, never scum, never *gent taillable et corvéable à merci*.

The Tartar nobles have the right of life and death over their slaves. They may administer justice themselves upon their bondsmen, even to sentence of death; but this privilege is never exercised in an arbitrary way. In case a slave has been put to death, a superior tribunal investigates the action of the master, and if it be found that he has abused his right, the innocent blood is revenged. The Lamas who belong to slave families become free, in some degree, as soon as they enter the sacerdotal tribe; they are liable neither to rents nor enforced labor; they are at liberty to quit their country, and ramble through the world at their pleasure, without anybody having the right to stay them.

Although the relations between master and slave are generally full of humanity and good-will, there are, nevertheless Tartar sovereigns who abuse their right, and oppress their people and exact exorbitant tributes. We know one who makes use of a system of oppression that is truly revolting. He selects from among his flocks the oldest and sickliest cattle, camels, sheep and goats, and gives them in charge to the rich slaves in his states, who cannot, of course, object to pasture the cattle of their sovereign master; but are fain to consider it rather an honor. After a few years, the king applies for his cattle, by this time all dead or dying of illness or old age, and selects from the flocks of his slaves the youngest and strongest; often even, not content with this, he demands double or treble the number. "Nothing," says he, "is more just; for in two or three years my beasts must have multiplied, and therefore a great number of lambs, colts, calves and young camels belong to me."

Slavery, however mitigated and softened, can never be in harmony with the dignity of man. It has been abolished in Europe, and we hope will be abolished one day among the Mongol people. But this great revolution will, as everywhere else, be operated by the influence of Christianity. It will not be theory-mongers who will liberate these nomad people. The work will be the work of the priests of Jesus Christ, of the preachers of the Holy Gospel, that Divine Charter, wherein are set forth the true rights of man. So soon as the missionaries shall have taught the Mongols to say, "Our Father who art in Heaven," slavery will fall in Tartary, and the tree of liberty will grow beside the cross.

After some days' march across the sands of the Ortous, we noticed on our way a small Lamasery, richly built in a picturesque and wild situation. We passed on without stopping. We had advanced a gunshot from the place, when we heard behind us the galloping of a horse. On looking round we saw a Lama following us at full speed. "Brothers," he said, "you have passed our *Soumé* (Lamasery) without stopping. Are you in such haste that you cannot repose for a day and offer your adorations to our saint?" "Yes, we are rather in a hurry; our journey is not of a few days; we are going to the West." "I knew very well by your physiognomies that you were not Mongols, and that you came from the West; but as you are going so far, you had better prostrate yourselves before our saint; that will bring you good luck." "We never prostrate ourselves before men; the true creed of the West forbids that." "Our saint is not a mere man; you do not imagine, perhaps, that in our little Lamasery we have the happiness to possess a Chaberon, a living Buddha. It is two years since he deigned to descend from the holy mountains of Thibet; he is now seven years old. In one of his former lives he was Grand Lama of a splendid Lamasery in this vale, which was destroyed, according to the prayer-books, in the time of the wars of Tching-Kis. The saint having reappeared a few years since, we have constructed in haste a small Lamasery. Come, brothers, our saint will hold his right hand over your heads, and luck will accompany your steps!" "The men who know the Holy Doctrine of the West do not believe in all these transmigrations of the Chaberons. We adore only the Creator of Heaven and earth; his name is Jehovah. We believe that the child you have made superior of your Lamasery is destitute of all power. Men have nothing to hope or to fear from him." When the Lama heard these words, which he certainly never expected, he was quite stupefied. By degrees his face became animated, and at last exhibited indignation and anger. He looked at us several times, then, pulling the bridle of his horse, he turned short round and left us hastily, muttering between his teeth some words which we could not exactly hear, but which we were aware did not constitute a benediction.

The Tartars believe with firm and absolute faith in all these various transmigrations. They would never allow themselves to entertain the slightest doubt as to the authenticity of their Chaberons. These living Buddhas are in large numbers, and are always placed at the head of the most important Lamaseries. Sometimes they modestly begin their career in a small temple, and have only a few disciples; but very soon their reputation increases around, and the small Lamasery becomes a place of pilgrimage and devotion. The neighboring Lamas, speculating upon the rising fashion, surround it with their cells; the Lamasery acquires development from year to year, and becomes at last famous in the land.

The election and enthronization of the living Buddhas are conducted in so singular a manner as to be well worth relating. When a Grand Lama has gone, that is to say, is dead, the circumstance is no occasion of mourning in the Lamasery. There are no tears, no lamentations, for everybody knows the Chaberon will very soon reappear. This apparent death is but the beginning of a new existence, as it were, one ring more added to the unlimited, uninterrupted chain of successive lives—a regular palingenesis. While the saint is in a state of chrysalis, his disciples are in the greatest anxiety; for it is their most important affair to discover the place where their master will resume life. A rainbow appearing in the air is considered a signal sent to them by their old Great Lama to aid them in their research. Every one thereupon says his prayers, and while the Lamasery which has lost its Buddha redoubles its fastings and prayers, a troop of elect proceeds to consult the Tchurtchun or augur, famous for the knowledge of things hidden from the common herd. He is informed that on such a day of such a moon the rainbow of the Chaberon has manifested itself on the sky; it made its appearance in such a place; it was more or less luminous, and it was visible so long;

then it disappeared amid such and such circumstances. When the Tchurtchun has received all the necessary indications, he recites some prayers, opens his books of divination, and pronounces at last his oracle, while the Tartars who have come to consult him, listen, kneeling, and full of unction. "Your Great Lama," says he, "has reappeared in Thibet, at such a distance from your Lamasery. You will find him in such a family." When these poor Mongols have heard this oracle, they return full of joy to announce the glad tidings to their Lamasery.

It often happens that the disciples of the defunct have no occasion to trouble themselves at all in order to discover the new birth-place of their Great Lama. He himself takes the trouble to initiate them into the secret of his transformation. As soon as he has effected his metamorphosis in Thibet, he reveals himself at an age when common children cannot yet articulate a single word. "It is I," he says with the accent of authority; "it is I who am the Great Lama, the living Buddha of such a temple; conduct me to my ancient Lamasery. I am its immortal superior." The wonderful baby having thus spoken, it is speedily communicated to the Lamas of the Soumé indicated, that their Chaberon is born in such a place, and they are summoned to attend and invite him home.

In whatever manner the Tartars discover the residence of their Great Lama, whether by the appearance of the rainbow, or by the spontaneous revelation of the Chaberon himself, they are always full of intense joy on the occasion. Soon all is movement in the tents, and the thousand preparations for a long journey are made with enthusiasm, for it is almost always in Thibet that they have to seek their living Buddha, who seldom fails to play them the trick of transmigrating in some remote and almost inaccessible country. Everyone contributes his share to the organization of the holy journey. If the king of the country does not place himself at the head of the caravan, he sends either his own son or one of the most illustrious members of the royal family. The great Mandarins, or ministers of the king, consider it their duty and an honor to join the party. When everything is at last prepared, an auspicious day is chosen, and the caravan starts.

Sometimes these poor Mongols, after having endured incredible fatigues in horrible deserts, fall into the hands of the brigands of the Blue Sea, who strip them from head to foot. If they do not die of hunger and cold in those dreadful solitudes—if they succeed in returning to the place whence they came—they commence the preparations for a new journey. There is nothing capable of discouraging them. At last, when, by dint of energy and perseverance, they have contrived to reach the eternal sanctuary, they prostrate themselves before the child who has been indicated to them. The young Chaberon, however, is not saluted and proclaimed Great Lama without a previous examination. There is held a solemn sitting, at which the new living Buddha is examined publicly, with a scrupulous attention. He is asked the name of the Lamasery of which he assumes to be the Great Lama; at what distance it is; what is the number of the Lamas residing in it. He is interrogated respecting the habits and customs of the defunct Great Lama, and the principal circumstances attending his death. After all these questions, there are placed before him different prayer-books, articles of furniture, teapots, cups, etc., and amongst all these things he has to point out those which belonged to his former life.

Generally this child, at most but five or six years old, comes forth victorious out of all these trials. He answers accurately all the questions that are put to him, and makes without any embarrassment the inventory of his goods. "Here," he says, "are the prayer-books I used; there is the japanned porringer out of which I drank my tea." And so on.

No doubt the Mongols are often dupes of the fraud of those who have an interest in making a Great Lama out of this puppet. Yet we believe that often all this proceeds on both sides with honesty and good faith. From the information we obtained from persons worthy of the greatest credit, it appears certain that all that is said of the Chaberons must not be ranged amongst illusion and deception. A purely human philosophy will, undoubtedly, reject such things, or put them, without hesitating, down to the account of Lama imposture. We Catholic missionaries believe that the great liar who once deceived our first parents in the earthly Paradise still pursues his system of falsehood in the world. He who had the power to hold up in the air Simon

Magus may well at this day speak to mankind by the mouth of an infant, in order to maintain the faith of his adorers.

When the titles of the living Buddha have been confirmed, he is conducted in triumph to the Lamasery, of which he is to be the Grand Lama. Upon the road he takes, all is excitement, all is movement. The Tartars assemble in large crowds to prostrate themselves on his way, and to present to him their offerings. As soon as he is arrived at his Lamasery, he is placed upon the altar; and then, kings, princes, mandarins, Lamas, Tartars, from the richest to the poorest, come and bend the head before this child, which has been brought from the depths of Thibet, at enormous expense, and whose demoniac possessions excite everybody's respect, admiration, and enthusiasm.

There is no Tartar kingdom which does not possess, in one of its Lamaseries of the first class, a living Buddha. Besides this superior, there is always another Grand Lama, who is selected from the members of the royal family. The Thibetian Lama resides in the Lamasery, like a living idol, receiving every day the adorations of the devout, upon whom in return he bestows his blessing. Everything which relates to prayers and liturgical ceremonies, is placed under his immediate superintendence. The Mongol Grand Lama is charged with the administration, good order, and executive of the Lamasery; he governs whilst his colleague is content to reign. The famous maxim, *Le roi règne et ne gouverne pas*, is not, therefore, the grand discovery in politics that some people imagine. People pretend to invent a new system, and merely plunder, without saying a word about it, the old constitution of the Tartar Lamaseries.

Below these two sovereigns, are several subaltern officers, who direct the details of the administration, the revenues, the sales, the purchases, and the discipline. The scribes keep the registers, and draw up the regulations and orders which the governor Lama promulgates for the good keeping and order of the Lamasery. These scribes are generally well versed in the Mongol, Thibetian, and sometimes in the Chinese and Mantchou languages. Before they are admitted to this employment, they are obliged to undergo a very rigorous examination, in presence of all the Lamas and of the principal civil authorities of the country.

After this staff of superiors and officers, the inhabitants

of the Lamasery are divided in Lama-masters and Lama-disciples or Chabis; each Lama has under his direction one or more Chabis, who live in his small house, and execute all the details of the household. If the master possesses cattle, they take charge of them, milk the cows, and prepare the butter and cream. In return for these services, the master directs his disciples in the study of the prayers, and initiates them into the liturgy. Every morning the Chabi must be up before his master; his first task is to sweep the chamber, to light a fire and to make the tea; after that he takes his prayer-book, presents it respectfully to his master, and prostrates himself thrice before him, without saying a single word. This sign of respect is equivalent to a request that the lesson he has to learn in the course of the day may be marked. The master opens the book, and reads some pages, according to the capacity of his scholar, who then makes three more prostrations in sign of thanks, and returns to his affairs.

The Chabi studies his prayer-book, when he is disposed to do so, there being no fixed period for that: he may spend his time, sleeping or romping with the other young pupils, without the slightest interference on the part of his master. When the hour for retiring to bed has arrived, he recites the lesson assigned him in the morning, in a monotonous manner; if the recitation is good, he is looked upon as having done his duty, the silence of his master being the only praise he is entitled to obtain; if, on the contrary he is not able to give a good account of his lesson, the severest punishment makes him sensible of his fault. It often happens, that under such circumstances, the master, laying aside his usual gravity, rushes upon his scholar, and overwhelms him at once with blows and terrible maledictions. Some of the pupils, who are over maltreated, run away and seek adventures far from their Lamasery; but in general they patiently submit to the punishment inflicted on them, even that of passing the night in the open air, without any clothes and in full winter. We often had opportunities of talking with Chabis, and when we asked them whether there was no means of learning the prayers without being beaten, they ingenuously and with an accent manifesting entire conviction, replied, that it was impossible. "The prayers one knows best," they said, "are always those for which one has got most blows. The Lamas who cannot recite prayers, or cure maladies, or tell fortunes, or predict the future, are those who have not been beaten well by their masters."

Besides these studies, which are conducted at home, and under the immediate superintendence of the master, the Chabis may attend, in the Lamasery, public lectures, wherein the books which relate to religion and to medicine are expounded. But these commentaries are mostly vague, unsatisfactory, and quite inadequate to form learned Lamas; there are few of them who can give an exact account of the books they study; to justify their omission in this respect, they never fail to allege the profundity of the doctrine. As to the great majority of the Lamas, they think it more convenient and expeditious to recite the prayers in a merely mechanical way, without giving themselves any trouble about the ideas they contain. When we come to speak of the Lamaseries of Thibet, where the instruction is more complete than in those of Tartary, we shall enter into some details upon Lama studies.

The Thibetian books alone being reputed canonical, and admitted as such by the Buddhist Reformation, the Mongol Lamas pass their lives in studying a foreign idiom, without troubling themselves at all about their own language. There are many of them well versed in the Thibetian literature, who do not even know their own Mongol alphabet. There are indeed a few Lamaseries where the study of the Tartarian idiom receives some slight attention, and where they sometimes recite Mongol prayers, but these are always a translation of Thibetian books. A Lama who can read Thibetian and Mongol is reputed quite a *savant;* he is thought a being raised above mankind, if he has some knowledge of Chinese and Mantchou literature.

As we advanced in the Ortous, the country seemed more and more desert and dismal. To make matters still worse, a terrible storm, solemnly closing in the autumn season, brought upon us the cold of winter.

One day, we were proceeding with difficulty through the arid sandy desert; the perspiration ran down our foreheads, for the heat was stifling; we felt overpowered by the closeness of the atmosphere, and our camels, with outstretched necks and mouths half open, vainly sought in the air a breath of cooling freshness. Towards noon, dark clouds began to gather in the horizon; fearful of being surprised by the storm, we determined to pitch our tent. But where? We looked round on all sides; we ascended to the tops of the hillocks and anxiously sought with our eyes for some Tartar habitation, which might provide us with fuel, but in vain; we had before us on all sides nothing but a mournful solitude. From time to time, we saw the foxes retiring to their holes, and herds of yellow goats running to take repose in the defiles of the mountains. Meantime, the clouds continued to rise and the wind began to blow violently. In the irregularity of its gusts it seemed now to bring us the tempest, now to drive it from us. While we were thus suspended between hope and fear, loud claps of thunder, and repeated flashes of lightning, that seemed to enkindle the sky, gave us notice that we had no other resource than to place ourselves entirely in the hands of Providence. The icy north wind blowing fiercely, we directed our steps to a defile, which opened near us; but before we had time to reach it the storm exploded. At first, rain fell in torrents, then hail, and at last snow half melted. In an instant we were wet through to the skin, and felt the cold seizing upon our limbs. We immediately alighted, hoping that walking would warm us a little, but we had hardly advanced ten steps amidst the deluge of sand, when our legs sank as in mortar. When we found it impossible to go any further we sought shelter by the side of our camels, and crouched down, pressing our arms closely against our sides, in order to attain, if possible, a little warmth.

While the storm continued to hurl against us its fury, we awaited with resignation the fate which Providence destined for us. It was impossible to pitch the tent; it was beyond human power to spread cloth saturated with rain, and half frozen by the north wind. Besides it would have been difficult to find a site for it, since the water streamed in every direction. Amid circumstances so dreadful, we looked at each other in sadness and in silence; we felt the natural warmth of our body diminishing every minute, and our blood beginning to freeze. We offered, therefore, the sacrifice of our lives to God, for we were convinced that we should die of cold during the night.

One of us, however, collecting all his strength and all his

Caves of the Ortous,

energy, climbed up an eminence, which commanded a view of the contiguous defile, and discovered a footpath, leading by a thousand sinuosities into the depths of the immense ravine; he pursued its direction, and after a few steps in the hollow, perceived in the sides of the mountain large openings, like doors. At this sight recovering at once his courage and his strength, he ascended once more the eminence in order to communicate the good news to his companions. "We are saved," he cried; "there are caves in this defile; let us hasten to take refuge in them." These words immediately aroused the little caravan; we left our animals upon the hill, and speedily descended into the ravine. A footpath led to the opening; we advanced our heads, and discovered in the interior of the mountain, not simple caves formed by nature, but fine, spacious apartments excavated by the hand of man. Our first exclamation was an expression of thankfulness for the goodness of Providence. We selected the cleanest and largest of these caverns, and in an instant passed from the utmost misery to the height of felicity. It was like a sudden and unhoped-for transition from death to life.

On viewing these subterranean dwellings, constructed with so much elegance and solidity, we were of opinion that some Chinese families had repaired to this country to cultivate the soil; but that, repelled by its barrenness, they had given up their enterprise. Traces of cultivation, which we perceived here and there, confirmed our conjecture. When the Chinese establish themselves anywhere in Tartary, if they find mountains, the earth of which is hard and solid, they excavate caverns in their sides. These habitations are cheaper than houses, and less exposed to the irregularity of the seasons. They are generally very well laid out; on each side of the door there are windows, giving sufficient light to the interior; the walls, the ceiling, the furnaces, the kang, everything inside is so coated with plaster, so firm and shining, that it has the appearance of stucco. These caves have the advantage of being very warm in winter and very cool in summer; the want of sufficient air, however, sometimes makes a sojourn in them dangerous to the health. Those dwellings were no novelty to us, for they abound in our mission of Si-Wan. However, we had never seen any so well constructed as these of the Ortous.

We took possession of one of those subterranean abodes, and commenced proceedings by making a large fire in the furnaces, with plentiful bundles of hemp-stems, which we found in one of the caves. Never, on our journey, had we at our disposal such excellent fuel. Our clothes dried very soon, and we were so happy at being in this fine hotel of Providence, that we spent the greater part of the night enjoying the delightful sensation of warmth, while Samdadchiemba was never tired of broiling little cakes in mutton fat. It was altogether quite a festival with us, and our flour felt somewhat the effects of it.

The animals were not less happy than we. We found for them stables out in the mountain, and, which was better still, excellent forage. One cave was filled with millet stems and oat-straw. But for this horrible storm, which had nearly killed us, our animals would never have got so grand a treat. After having for a long time enjoyed the poetry of our miraculous position, we yielded to the necessity of taking repose, and laid down upon a well-warmed kang, which made us forget the terrible cold we had endured during the tempest.

Next morning, while Samdadchiemba was using the rest of the hemp stems, and drying our baggage, we went out for a nearer inspection of these numerous subterrenes. We had scarcely gone ten steps, when we beheld, to our great astonishment, whirls of smoke issuing from the door and windows of a cave adjoining our own. As we fancied we were alone in the desert, the sight of this smoke excited a surprise, mingled with fear. We directed our steps to the opening of the cavern, and, on reaching the threshold of the door, perceived within a large fire of hemp stems, whose undulating flame reached the ceiling, so that the place looked like an oven. On further investigation we observed a human form moving amidst the thick smoke; we soon heard the Tartar salute, Mendou! uttered by a sonorous voice; "Come and sit beside this fire." We did not like to advance. This cave of Cacus, that loud voice, presented to our minds something fantastic. Finding that we remained silent and motionless, the inhabitant of this sort of vent-hole of Erebus, rose and came to the threshold. He was neither a devil nor a ghost, but simply a Mongol Tartar, who, the night before, having been surprised by the storm, had fled to this cave, where he had passed the night. After a few words about the rain, wind and hail, we invited him to breakfast with us, and brought him to our dwelling. While Samdadchiemba, aided by our guest, made the tea, we went out again to pursue our researches.

We walked amid these deserted and silent abodes with a curiosity not free from terror. All were constructed upon much the same model, and still preserved their pristine integrity. Chinese characters engraved on the walls, and pieces of porcelain vases, confirmed our impression that these caves had been inhabited not long since by Chinese. Some old woman's shoes, which we discovered in a corner, removed any remaining doubt. We could not shake off a feeling of sadness and melancholy, when we thought of those numerous families, who, after having lived a long time in the entrails of this large mountain, had gone elsewhere to seek a more hospitable soil. As we entered the caves, we alarmed flocks of sparrows, which had not yet left these former dwellings of man, but had, on the contrary, boldly taken possession of these grand nests. The millet and oats strewn around profusely, induced them to remain. "Undoubtedly," said we, "they too will fly away when they no longer find here any more grains, when they find that the old inhabitants of these caves return no more, and they will seek hospitality under the roofs of houses."

The sparrow is a regular cosmopolite; we have found it wherever we have found man; ever with the same vivid, petulant, quarrelsome character; ever with the same sharp, angry cry. It is, however, to be remarked that in Tartary, China, and Thibet it is, perhaps, more insolent than in Europe; because there, nobody makes war upon it, and its nest and brood are piously respected, You see it boldly enter the house, live there on familiar terms, and peck up at its leisure the remnants of man's food. The Chinese call it Kio-nio-eul (bird of the family).

After having inspected about thirty of these caves, which did not present anything remarkable, we returned to our own. At breakfast, the conversation naturally turned upon the Chinese who had excavated these dwellings. We asked the Tartar if he had seen them. "What!" said he, "have I seen the Kitats who inhabited this defile? Why, I knew all of them; it is not more than two years since they left the country. For that matter," he added, "they had no right to remain here; as they were rascals, it was quite proper to turn them out." "Rascals, say you? why, what mischief could they do in this wretched ravine?" "Oh, the Kitats are sly, cheating fellows. At first, they seemed very good; but that did not last long. It is more than twenty years ago that a few of their families sought our hospitality: as they were poor, they got permission to cultivate some land in the vicinity, on condition, that every year after harvest they should furnish some oatmeal, to the Taitsi of the country. By degrees, other families arrived, who also excavated caverns wherein to dwell; and soon this defile was full of them. In the beginning, these Kitats showed a gentle, quiet character; we lived together like brothers. Tell me, Sirs Lamas, is it not well to live together like brothers? Are not all men brothers?" "Yes, that is true; you speak the words of justice; but why did these Kitats go hence?" "Peace did not last long; they soon showed themselves wicked and false. Instead of being content with what had been given them, they extended their cultivation at their pleasure, and took possession of a large territory, without asking any one's leave. When they were rich they would not pay the oatmeal they had agreed to pay as tribute. Every year, when we claimed the rent, we were received with insults and maledictions. But the worst thing was, that these rascally Kitats turned thieves, and took possession of all the goats and sheep that lost their way in the sinuosities of the ravine. At last, a Taitsi of great courage and capacity, called together the Mongols of the neighborbood, and said,—'The Kitats take away our land, they steal our beasts, and curse us; as they do not act or speak as brothers, we must expel them.' Everybody was pleased with these words of the old Taitsi. After a deliberation, it was decided that the principal men of the country should go to the king, and supplicate an order condemning the Kitats to be expelled. I was one of the deputation. The king reproached us for having permitted foreigners to cultivate our lands; we prostrated ourselves before him, observing profound silence. However, the king, who always acts with justice, had the order written, and sealed with his red seal. The ordonnance said, that the king would not permit the Kitats to live any longer in the country; and that they must leave it before the first day of the eighth moon. Three Taitsi rode off to present the ordonnance to the Kitats. They made no answer to the three deputies, but said amongst themselves, 'The king desires us to go; very well.'

"Afterwards we learned that they had assembled and had resolved to disobey the orders of the king and to remain in the country, in spite of him. The first day of the eighth moon arrived, and they still occupied calmly their habitations, without making any preparations for departure. In the morning, before daybreak, all the Tartars mounted their horses, armed themselves with their lances, and drove their flocks and herds upon the cultivated lands of the Kitats, on which the crop was still standing: when the sun rose, nothing of that crop was left. All had been devoured by the animals, or trodden down. The Kitats yelled and cursed us, but the thing was done. Seeing that their position was desperate, they collected, the same day, their furniture and agricultural implements, and went off to settle in the eastern parts of the Ortous, at some distance from the Yellow River, near the Paga-Gol. As you came through Tchagan-Kouren, you must have met on your route, west of the Paga-Gol, Kitats cultivating some pieces of land; well, it was they who inhabited this defile, and excavated all these caves."

Having finished his narrative, the Tartar went out for a moment and brought back a small packet, which he had left in the cavern, where he had passed the night. "Sirs Lamas," he said on his return, "I must depart; but will you not come and repose for a few days in my dwelling? My tent is not far hence: it is behind that sandy mountain which you perceive there towards the north. It is at the utmost not more than thirty lis off." "We are much obliged to you," answered we. "The hospitality of the Mongols of Ortous is known everywhere, but we have a long journey before us; we cannot stop on our way." "What are a few days, sooner or later, in a long journey? Your beasts cannot alway be on their feet; they need a little rest. You yourselves have had much to endure from the weather of yesterday. Come with me; all will then be well. In four days we shall have a festival. My eldest son is going to establish a family. Come to the nuptials of my son; your presence will bring him good fortune." The Tartar, seeing us inflexible, mounted his horse, and after having ascended the pathway which led to the defile, disappeared across the heath and sand of the desert.

Under other circumstances, we should have accepted with pleasure the offer thus made; but we desired to make the shortest possible stay amongst the Ortous. We were anxious to leave behind us that miserable country, where our animals were wasting away daily, and where we had ourselves met with such fatigue and misery. Besides, a Mongol wedding was no new thing to us. Since we had entered Tartary, we had witnessed, more than once, ceremonies of that kind.

The Mongols marry very young, and always under the influence of the absolute authority of the parents. This affair, so grave and important, is initiated, discussed and concluded, without the two persons most interested in it, taking the least part in it. Whatever promises of marriage may take place in youth, or at more advanced age, it is the parents who always settle the contract, without even speaking to their children about it. The two future consorts do not know, perhaps never saw each other. It is only when they are married that they have the opportunity to inquire whether there is sympathy between their characters or not.

The daughter never brings any marriage portion. On the contrary, the young man has to make presents to the family of his bride: and the value of these presents is seldom left to the generosity of the husband's parents. Everything is arranged beforehand and set forth in a public document, with the minutest details. In fact, the matter is less a marriage present than the price of an object, sold by one party and bought by the other. The thing is indeed very clearly expressed in their language; they say, "I have bought for my son the daughter of so and so." "We have sold our daughter to such and such a family." The marriage contract is thus simply a contract of sale. There are mediators, who bargain and haggle, up and down, till at last they come to an agreement. When it is settled how many horses, oxen, sheep, pieces of linen, pounds of butter, what quantity of brandy and wheat-flour shall be given to the family of the bride, the contract is at length drawn up before witnesses, and the daughter becomes the property of the purchaser. She remains, however, with her family till the time of the nuptial ceremonies.

When the marriage has been concluded between the mediators, the father of the bridegroom, accompanied by his nearest relations, carries the news to the family of the bride. On entering, they prostrate themselves before the little domestic altar, and offer to the idol of Buddha a boiled sheep's head, milk, and a sash of white silk. Then they partake of a repast provided by the parents of the bridegroom. During the repast, all the relations of the bride receive a piece of money, which they deposit in a vase filled with wine made of fermented milk. The father of the bride drinks the wine, and keeps the money. This ceremony is called Tahil-Tébihou, "striking the bargain."

The day indicated by the Lamas as auspicious for the marriage having arrived, the bridegroom sends early in the morning a deputation to fetch the girl who has been betrothed to him, or rather whom he has bought. When the envoys draw near, the relations and friends of the bride place themselves in a circle before the door, as if to oppose the departure of the bride, and then begins a feigned fight, which of course terminates with the bride being carried off. She is placed on a horse, and having been thrice led round her paternal house, she is then taken at full gallop to the tent which has been prepared for the purpose, near the dwelling of her father-in-law. Meantime, all the Tartars of the neighborhood, the relations and friends of both families, repair to the wedding-feast, and offer their presents to the new married pair. The extent of these presents, which consists of beasts and eatables, is left to the generosity of the guests. They are destined for the father of the bridegroom and often fully indemnify him for his expenses in the purchase of the bride. As the offered animals come up they are taken into folds ready constructed for them. At the weddings of rich Tartars, these large folds receive great herds of oxen, horses and sheep. Generally the guests are generous enough, for they know that thay will be paid in return, upon a similar occasion.

When the bride has finished dressing, she is introduced to her father-in-law; and while the assembled Lamas recite the prayers prescribed by the ritual, she first prostrates herself before the image of Buddha, then before the hearth, and lastly before the father, mother, and other near relatives of the bridegroom, who, on his part, performs the same ceremonies towards the family of his bride, assembled in an adjacent tent. Then comes the wedding-feast, which sometimes continues for seven or eight days. An excessive profusion of fat meat, infinite tobacco, and large jars of brandy, constitute the splendor and magnificence of these repasts. Sometimes music is added to the entertainment, and they invite Toolholos, or Tartar singers, to give more solemnity to the festival.

The plurality of wives is admitted in Tartary, being opposed neither to the laws, nor to the religion, nor to the manners of the country. The first wife is always the mistress of the household, and the most respected in the family. The other wives bear the name of little spouses (paga ème), and owe obedience and respect to the first.

Polygamy, abolished by the Gospel, and contrary in itself to the happiness and concord of families, may, perhaps, be regarded as a blessing to the Tartars. Considering the present state of society with them, it is, as it were, a barrier opposed to libertinism and corruption of morals. Celibacy being imposed on the Lamas, and the class of those who shave the head and live in lamaseries being so numerous, it is easy to conceive what disorders would arise from this multiplication of young women without support and abandoned to themselves, if girls could not be placed in families in the quality of second wives.

Divorce is very frequent among the Tartars. It takes place without any participation of the civil or ecclesiastical authorities. The husband, who repudiates his wife, has not even occasion for a pretext to justify his conduct. He sends her back, without any formality, to her parents, and contents himself with a message that he does not require her any longer. This proceeding is in accordance with Tartar manners, and does not offend any one. The husband thinks himself entitled to the privilege, in consideration of the oxen, sheep and horses he was obliged to give as nuptial presents. The parents of the repudiated wife do not complain at having their daughter back; she resumes her place in the family till another husband presents himself, in which case, they even rejoice over the profit they make by thus selling the same merchandise twice over.

In Tartary, the women lead an independent life enough. They are far from being oppressed and kept in servitude, as with other Asiatic nations. They may come and go at their pleasure, ride out on horseback, and pay each other visits from tent to tent. Instead of the soft, languishing physiognomy of the Chinese women, the Tartar woman presents in her bearing and manners a power and force well in accordance with her active life and nomad habits, and her attire augments the effect of her masculine, haughty mein.

Large leather boots, and a long green or violet robe fastened round the waist by a black or blue girdle, constitute her dress, except that sometimes she wears over the great robe a small coat, resembling in form our waistcoats, but very large, and coming down to the hips. The hair of the Tartar women is divided in two tresses, tied up in taffetas, and hanging down upon the bosom; their luxury consists in ornamenting the girdle and hair with spangles of gold and silver, pearls, coral, and a thousand other toys, the form and quality of which it would be difficult for us to define, as we had neither opportunity, nor taste, nor patience to pay serious attention to these futilities.

Barbarous Lamanesque Ceremony.

CHAPTER IX.

Departure of the Caravan—Encampment in a fertile Valley—Intensity of the Cold—Meeting with numerous Pilgrims—Barbarous and Diabolical Ceremonies of Lamaism—Project for the Lamasery of Rache-Tchurin—Dispersion and rallying of the little Caravan—Anger of Samdadchiemba—Aspect of the Lamasery of Rache-Tchurin—Different Kinds of Pilgrimages around the Lamaseries—Turning Prayers—Quarrel between two Lamas—Similarity of the Soil—Description of the Tabsoun-Noor or Salt Sea—Remarks on the Camels of Tartary.

THE Tartar who had just taken his leave had informed us, that at a short distance from the caverns we should find in a vale the finest pasturage in the whole country of the Ortous. We resolved to depart. It was near noon already when we started. The sky was clear, the sun brilliant; but the temperature, still affected by the storm of the preceding day, was cold and sharp. After having traveled for nearly two hours over a sandy soil, deeply furrowed by the streams of rain, we entered, on a sudden, a valley whose smiling, fertile aspect singularly contrasted with all that we had hitherto seen among the Ortous. In the center flowed an abundant rivulet, whose sources were lost in the sand; and on both sides, the hills, which rose like an amphitheater, were covered with pasturage and clumps of shrubs.

Though it was still early, we gave up all idea of continuing our journey that day. The place was too beautiful to be passed by: besides, the north wind had risen, and the air became intolerably cold. We pitched our tent, therefore, in a corner, sheltered by the hills. From the interior of the tent, our view extended, without obstruction, down the valley, and we were thus enabled to watch our animals without moving.

After sunset, the violence of the wind increased, and the cold became more and more intense. We thought it advisable to take some measures of security. Whilst Samdadchiemba piled up large stones to consolidate the borders of the tent, we went about the adjacent hills, and made, by aid of a hatchet, an abundant provision of fuel. As soon as we had taken our tea and our daily broth, we went to sleep. But sleep did not last long; the cold became so severe that it soon roused us. "We can't remain so," said the Dchiahour; "if we don't want to die of cold on our goatskins, we must get up and make a large fire." Samdadchiemba's words were full of sense; it was not advisable to sleep at such a time, and accordingly we rose, and added to our usual dress the great sheepskin robes that we had bought at Blue Town.

Our fire of roots and green branches was hardly lighted, when we felt our eyes as it were calcined by the biting acid influence of a thick smoke, which filled the tent. We opened the door; but as this gave admission to the wind, without getting rid of the smoke, we were soon obliged to shut it again. Samdadchiemba was not in any way molested by the thick smoke, which stifled us and drew burning tears from our eyes. He laughed without pity at seeing us crouched by the fire, our heads bending over our knees, and our faces buried in both hands. "My spiritual fathers," he said, "your eyes are large and bright, but they cannot endure a little smoke; mine are small and ugly, but never mind, they perform their service very well." The jests of our camel driver were not much adapted to cheer us up; we suffered dreadfully. Yet, amid our tribulations, we saw occasion to feel our happiness to be very great. We could not reflect without gratitude upon the goodness of Providence, which had led us to caves, whose great value we now fully appreciated. If we had not been able to dry our clothes, if we had been surprised by the cold in the piteous state in which the storm had left us, we certainly could not have lived long; we should have been frozen with our clothes in one immovable block.

We did not think it prudent to proceed amid such severe cold, and to leave an encampment, where at least our animals got sufficient herbage to browse upon, and where fuel was abundant. Towards noon, the weather having grown milder, we went out to cut wood on the hills. On our way we observed that our animals had left the pasturage and collected on the banks of the rivulet. We at once conceived that they were tormented by thirst, and that the stream being frozen, they could not quench it. We bent our steps to them, and found, in fact, the camels eagerly licking the surface of the ice, while the horse and the mule were kicking upon it with their hard hoofs. The hatchet we had brought with us to cut wood, served to break the ice, and to dig a small pond, where our animals could quench their thirst.

Towards evening, the cold having resumed its intensity, we adopted a plan for enabling us to obtain a better sleep than we had in the preceding night. Until morning, the time was divided into three watches, and each of us was charged, in turn, with keeping up a large fire in the tent, while the others slept. Thus we did not feel much of the cold, and slept in peace, without fear of setting our linen house on fire.

After two days of horrible cold the wind abated, and we resolved to proceed on our way. It was only with great difficulty that we got down our tent. The first nail that we tried to draw out, broke like glass under the hammer. The sandy, humid soil on which we had made our encampment, was so frozen that the nails stuck in it as if they had been incrusted in stone. To uproot them, we were obliged to wet them several times with boiling water.

At the time of our departure, the temperature was so

mild that we were fain to take off our skin coats, and to pack them up until further occasion. Nothing is more frequent in Tartary than these sudden changes of temperature. Sometimes the mildest weather is abruptly followed by the most horrible frost. All that is needed for this is the falling of snow, and the subsequent rise of the north wind. Any one not inured to these sudden changes of the atmosphere, and not provided, in traveling, with well-furred robes, is often exposed to dreadful accidents. In the north of Mongolia especially, it is not unusual to find travelers frozen to death amidst the desert.

On the fifteenth day of the new moon, we came upon numerous caravans, following, like ourselves, the direction from east to west. The road was filled with men, women, and children, riding on camels or oxen. They were all repairing, they said, to the Lamasery of Rache-Tchurin. When they had asked whether our journey had the same object, they were surprised at receiving an answer in the negative. These numerous pilgrims, the astonishment they showed upon hearing that we were not going to the Lamasery of Rache-Tchurin, excited our curiosity. At the turn of a defile, we overtook an old Lama, who, laden with a heavy pack, seemed to make his way with great labor and pain. "Brother," said we, "you are old; your black hairs are not so numerous as the gray. Doubtless your fatigue must be extreme. Place your burden upon one of our camels; that will relieve you a little." Upon hearing these words the old man prostrated himself before us, in order to express his gratitude. We made a camel kneel, and Samdadchiemba added to our baggage that of the Lama. So soon as the pilgrim was relieved from the weight which had oppressed him, his walk became more elastic, and an expression of satisfaction was diffused over his countenance. "Brother," said we, "we are from the West, and the affairs of your country not being well known to us, we are astonished at finding so many pilgrims here in the desert." "We are all going to Rache-Tchurin," replied he, in accents full of emotion. "Doubtless," said we, "some grand solemnity calls you together?" "Yes to-morrow will be a great day: a Lama Boktè will manifest his power: Kill himself, yet not die." We at once understood what solemnity it was that thus attracted the Ortous-Tartars. A

Lama was to cut himself open, take out his entrails and place them before him, and then resume his previous condition. This spectacle, so cruel and disgusting, is very common in the Lamaseries of Tartary. The Boktè who is to manifest his power, as the Mongols phrase it, prepares himself for the formidable operation by many days fasting and prayer, pending which, he must abstain from all communication whatever with mankind, and observe the most absolute silence. When the appointed day is come, the multitude of pilgrims assemble in the great court of the Lamasery, where an altar is raised in front of the Temple-gate. At length the Boktè appears. He advances gravely, amid the acclamations of the crowd, seats himself upon the altar, and takes from his girdle a large knife which he places upon his knees. At his feet, numerous Lamas, ranged in a circle, commence the terrible invocations of this frightful ceremony. As the recitation of the prayers proceeds, you see the Boktè trembling in every limb, and gradually working himself up into phrenetic convulsions. The Lamas themselves become excited: their voices are raised; their song observes no order, and at last becomes a mere confusion of yelling and outcry. Then the Boktè suddenly throws aside the scarf which envelopes him, unfastens his girdle, and seizing the sacred knife, slits open his stomach, in one long cut. While the blood flows in every direction, the multitude prostrate themselves before the terrible spectacle, and the enthusiast is interrogated about all sorts of hidden things, as to future events, as to the destiny of certain personages. The replies of the Boktè to all these questions are regarded, by everybody, as oracles.

When the devout curiosity of the numerous pilgrims is satisfied, the Lamas resume, but now calmly and gravely, the recitation of their prayers. The Boktè takes, in his right hand, blood from his wound, raises it to his mouth, breathes thrice upon it, and then throws it into the air, with loud cries. He next passes his hand rapidly over his wound, closes it, and everything after a while resumes its pristine condition, no trace remaining of the diabolical operation, except extreme prostration. The Boktè once more rolls his scarf round him, recites in a low voice, a short prayer; then all is over, and the multitude disperse, with the exception of a few of the especially devout, who remain to contemplate and to adore the blood-stained altar which the Saint has quitted.

These horrible ceremonies are of frequent occurrence in the great Lamaseries of Tartary and Thibet, and we do not believe that there is any trick or deception about them; for from all we have seen and heard, among idolatrous nations, we are persuaded that the devil has a great deal to do with the matter; and moreover, our impression that there is no trick in the operation is fortified by the opinion of the most intelligent and most upright Buddhists whom we have met in the numerous Lamaseries we visited.

It is not every Lama that can perform miraculous operations. Those who have the fearful power to cut themselves open, for example, are never found in the higher ranks of the Lama hierarchy. They are generally lay Lamas of indifferent character, and little esteemed by their comrades. The regular Lamas generally make no scruple to avow their horror of the spectacle. In their eyes, all these operations are wicked and diabolical. Good Lamas, they say, are incapable of performing such acts, and should not even desire to attain the impious talent.

Though these demoniac operations are, in general, decried in well-regulated Lamaseries, yet the superiors do not prohibit them. On the contrary, there are certain days in the year set apart for the disgusting spectacle. Interest is, doubtless, the only motive which could induce the Grand Lamas to favor actions which in their conscience they reprove. The fact is, that these diabolical displays are an infallible means of collecting together a swarm of stupid and ignorant devotees, who communicate renown to the Lamasery, and enrich it with the numerous offerings which the Tartars never fail to bring with them on such occasions.

Cutting open the abdomen is one of the most famous *sié-fa* (supernaturalisms) possessed by the Lamas. There are others of the same class, less imposing, but more common; these are practised in people's houses, privately, and not at the great solemnities of the Lamaseries. For example, they heat irons red-hot, and then lick them with impunity; they make incisions in various parts of the body, which an instant afterwards leave no trace behind, etc. All these operations have to be preceded by the recitation of some prayer.

We knew a Lama who, according to every one's belief, could fill a vase with water, by the mere agency of a prayer; but we could never induce him to try the experiment in our presence. He told us that as we held not the same faith with him, the experiment, in our company, would not be merely fruitless, but would expose him to serious danger. One day, however, he recited to us the prayer of his sié-fa. It was brief, but we readily recognized in it a direct appeal to the assistance of the demon. "I know thee, thou knowest me;" thus it ran: "Come old friend, do what I ask of thee. Bring water, and fill the vase I hold out to thee. To fill a vase with water, what is that to thy vast power! I know thou chargest dear for a vase of water; but never mind: do what I ask of thee, and fill the vase I present to thee. Some time hence we'll come to a reckoning: on the appointed day thou shalt receive thy due." It sometimes happens that the appeal remains without effect: in such cases, praying is discontinued, and the being invoked is assailed with insults and imprecations.

The famous sié-fa that was now attracting so large a number of pilgrims to the Lamasery of Rache-Tchurin, inspired us with the idea of repairing thither also, and of neutralizing, by our prayers, the satanic invocations of the Lamas. Who knows, said we to each other, who knows but that God even now has designs of mercy towards the Mongols of the Ortous land; perhaps the sight of their Lama's power, fettered and overcome by the presence of the priests of Jesus Christ, will strike upon the hearts of these people, and make them renounce the lying creed of Buddha, and embrace the faith of Christianity! To encourage each other in this design, we dwelt upon the history of Simon Magus, arrested in his flight by the prayer of St. Peter, and precipitated from the air to the feet of his admirers. Of course, poor missionaries, such as we, had not the insane pretension to compare ourselves with the prince of the Apostles; but we knew that the protection of God, which is sometimes granted in virtue of the merit and sanctity of him who seeks it, is also often accorded to the omnipotent efficacy in prayer itself.

We resolved, therefore, to go to Rache-Tchurin, to mingle with the crowd, and, at the moment when the diabolical invocations should commence, to place ourselves, fearlessly, and with an air of authority before the Boktè, and to solemnly forbid him, in the name of Jesus Christ, to make a display of his detestable power. We did not disguise from ourselves the possible results of this proceeding; we knew that it would assuredly excite the fury and hatred of the adorers of Buddha; and that perhaps a violent death would be an instant reward for the endeavor to convert these Tartars; "But what matter!" exclaimed we; "let us do courageously our work as missionaries; let us employ fearlessly the power that we have received from on high, and leave to Providence the care of a future which does not appertain to us."

Such were our intentions and our hopes; but the views of God are not always in conformity with the designs of man, even when these appear most in harmony with the plan of His Providence. That very day there happened to us an accident which, carrying us far away from Rache-Tchurin, involved us in the most distressing perplexities.

In the evening, the old Lama who was traveling with us asked us to make the camel kneel, so that he might take his pack from its back. "Brother," said we, "are we not going to journey together to the Lamasery of Rache-Tchurin?" "No; I must follow the path which you see meandering towards the north, along those hills. Behind that sand-hill is a trading place, where, upon festival days, a few Chinese merchants set up their tents and sell goods. As I want to make a few purchases, I cannot continue to walk in your shadow." "Can we buy flour at the Chinese encampment?" "Millet, oatmeal, flour, beef, mutton, tea-bricks, everything is sold there." Not having been able to purchase provisions since our departure from Tchagan-Kouren, we considered this a favorable opportunity for supplying our deficiency in this respect. In order not to fatigue our beasts of burden with a long circuit across stony hills, M. Gabet took the flour-sacks upon his camels, separated from the caravan, and went off at a gallop towards the Chinese post. According to the indications furnished by the old Lama, he was to meet us again in a valley at no great distance from the Lamasery.

After traveling for nearly an hour along a rugged road, continually intersected by pits and quagmires, the Missionary Purveyor reached the small heath, on which he found a number of Chinese encamped, some of their tents serving as shops, and the rest as dwellings. The encampment presented the appearance of a small town full of trade and activity, the customers being the Lamas of Rache-Tchurin and the Mongol pilgrims. M. Gabet speedily effected his purchases; and having filled his sacks with flour, and hung two magnificent sheeps' livers over one of the camel's humps, rode off to the place where it had been arranged the caravan should await him. He soon reached the spot, but he found no person there, and no trace of man or beast having recently passed was visible on the sand. Imagining that perhaps some derangement of the camels' loads had delayed our progress, he turned into the road, which it had been agreed we should follow; but it was to no purpose that he hastened along it, that he galloped here and there, that he ascended every hill he came to,—he could see nothing; and the cries he uttered to attract our attention remained unanswered. He visited several points where various roads met, but he found merely another confusion of the steps of horses, camels, oxen, sheep, tending in every direction, and crossing and recrossing each other, so that he was left, at last, without even a conjecture.

By and by he recalled to mind that our aim, as last resolved, had been the Lamasery of Rache-Tchurin; he turned round, and perceiving the Lamasery in the distance, hurried thither as fast as he could go. When he reached the structure, which stood in the form of an amphitheater upon the slope of a hill, he looked everywhere for us, and asked everybody about us, for here, at least, there was no lack of persons from whom to seek information, and our little caravan was composed in a manner likely to attract the attention of those who saw it at all: two laden camels, a white horse, and, above all, a black mule, that every one we passed stopped to remark, on account of its extreme diminutiveness, and the splendid tint of its skin. M. Gabet inquired and inquired, but to no purpose; no one had seen our caravan. He ascended to the summit of the hill, whence the eye extended over a large expanse, but he could see nothing at all like us.

The sun set, yet the caravan did not appear. M. Gabet, beginning to fear that some serious accident had befallen it, once more set off, and searched in every direction, up hill and down dale, but he could see nothing of us, and learn nothing of us, from the travelers whom he met.

The night advanced, and soon the Lamasery of Rache-Tchurin disappeared in the darkness. M. Gabet found himself alone in the desert, without path and without shelter, fearing alike to advance or to recede, lest he should fall into some abyss. He was fain, therefore, to stop where he was, in a narrow, sandy defile, and to pass the night there. By way of supper, he had to content himself with an *Impression de Voyage*. Not that provisions were wanting, by any means, but fire was, and water. Besides, the feeling of hunger was superseded by the anxieties which afflicted his heart as to the caravan. He knelt on the sand, said his evening prayer, and then lay down his head upon one of the flour-sacks beside the camel, keeping its bridle round his arm lest the animal should stray during the night. It is needless to add that his sleep was neither sound nor continuous; the cold, bare ground is not a very eligible bed, especially for a man preyed upon by dark anxieties.

With the earliest dawn, M. Gabet mounted his camel, and though well-nigh exhausted with hunger and fatigue, proceeded anew in search of his companions.

The caravan was not lost, though it was terribly astray. After M. Gabet had quitted us, in order to visit the Chinese post, we at first exactly followed the right path; but before long we entered upon a vast steppe, all trace of road insensibly faded away amidst sand so fine that the slightest wind made it undulate like sea-waves, there was no vestige upon it of the travelers who had preceded us. By and by the road disappeared altogether, and we found ourselves environed with yellow hills, which presented not the slightest suggestion even of vegetation. M. Huc, fearing to lose himself amid these sands, stopped the cameleer. "Samdadchiemba," said he, "do not let us proceed at random. You see yonder, in the valley, the Tartar horseman driving a herd of oxen; go and ask him the way to Rache-Tchurin." Samdadchiemba raised his head, looked for a moment, closing one eye, at the sun, which was veiled with some passing clouds.— "My spiritual father," said he, "I am accustomed to wander about the desert; my opinion is, that we are quite in the right road: let us continue our course westward, and we cannot go astray." "Well, well, since you think you know the desert, keep on." "Oh, yes; don't be afraid. You see that long, white line on the mountain yonder? that's the road, after its issue from the sands."

On Samdadchiemba's assurance, we continued to advance in the same direction. We soon came to a road, as he had promised, but it was a road disused, upon which we could see no person to confirm or contradict the assertion of Samdadchiemba, who persisted that we were on the way to Rache-Tchurin. The sun set, and the twilight gradually gave place to the darkness of night, without our discovering the least indication of the Lamasery, or, which surprised us still more, of M. Gabet, who, according to the information of the old Lama, ought to have rejoined us long ago. Samdadchiemba was silent, for he now saw that we had lost our way.

It was important to encamp before the night had altogether closed in. Perceiving a well at the end of a hollow, we set up our tent beside it. By the time our linen-house was in order, and the baggage piled, the night had completely set in; yet M. Gabet had not appeared. "Get on a camel," said M. Huc to Samdadchiemba, "and look about for M. Gabet." The Dchiahour made no reply; he was thoroughly disconcerted and depressed. Driving a stake into the ground, he fastened one of the camels to it, and mounting upon the other, departed mournfully in quest of our friend. He had scarcely got out of sight, when the camel that was left behind, finding itself alone, sent forth the most frightful cries; by and by it became furious; it turned round and round the stake, backed to the very limit of the rope and of its long neck, made longer by painful extension, and applied every effort to get rid of the wooden curl that was passed through its nose: the spectacle of its struggle was really frightful. At last it succeeded in breaking the cord, and then dashed off boundingly into the desert. The horse and mule had also disappeared; they were hungry and thirsty; and about the tent there was not a blade of grass, not a drop of water. The well beside which we had encamped was perfectly dry; in fact, it was nothing more than an old cistern which had probably been for years useless.

Thus our little caravan, which for nearly two months had journeyed, without once separating, through the desert plains of Tartary, was now utterly dispersed; man and beast—all had disappeared. There remained only M. Huc, solitary in his little linen-house, and a prey to the most corroding anxieties. For a whole day he had neither eaten nor drunk; but under such circumstances you do not ordinarily feel either hunger or thirst; the mind is too full to give any place to the suggestions of the body; you seem environed with a thousand fearful phantoms: and great indeed were your desolation, but that you have for your safety and your consolation, prayer, the sole lever that can raise from off your heart the weight of somber apprehensions that would otherwise crush it.

The hours passed on, and no one returned. As, in the obscurity of night, persons might pass quite close to the tent, and yet not see it, M. Huc, from time to time, ascended the adjacent hills and rocks, and, in his loudest tones, called out the names of his lost companions, but no one replied; all still was silence and solitude. It was near midnight, when at length the plaintive cries of a camel, apparently remonstrating against being driven so fast, were heard in the distance. Samdadchiemba soon came up. He had met several Tartar horsemen who had no tidings, indeed, of M. Gabet, but from whom he learned that we had gone altogether astray; that the road we were pursuing led to a Mongol encampment, in precisely the contrary direction to Rache-Tchurin. "By daybreak," said Samdadchiemba, "we must raise the tent, and find the right path; we shall there, no doubt, meet the elder spiritual father." "Samdadchiemba, your advice is a bubble; the tent and the baggage must remain here, for the excellent reason that they cannot be moved without animals." "Animals!" exclaimed the Dchiahour, "where, then, is the camel I fastened to the stake?" "It broke the rope and ran away; the horse and the mule have run away too, and I have not the least idea where any of them are to be sought." "This is a pretty business," grumbled the cameleer; "however, when day breaks we must see what can be done. Meanwhile let us make a little tea." "Make tea, by all means, if you can make tea without water, but water there is none; the well is perfectly dry." This announcement completed the discomfiture of poor Samdadchiemba; he sank back quite exhausted upon the baggage, and his weariness soon threw him into deep slumber.

With the first streaks of dawn, M. Huc ascended the adjacent hill in the hope of discovering something or somebody. He perceived, in a distant valley, two animals, one black, one white; he hastened to them, and found our horse and mule browsing on some thin, dusty grass, beside a cistern of soft water. When he led the animals back to the tent, the sun was about to rise, but Samdadchiemba still slumbered, lying in exactly the same position which he had assumed when he went to sleep. "Samdadchiemba," cried M. Huc, "won't you have some tea this morning?" At the word *tea*, our cameleer jumped up as though he had been electrified; he looked round, his eyes heavy with sleep. "Did not the spiritual father mention tea? Where is the tea? Did I dream I was going to have some tea?" "I don't know whether you dreamed it, but tea you may have, if you wish, as there is soft water in the valley yonder, where, just now, I found the horse and the mule. Do you go and fetch some water, while I light the fire." Samdadchiemba joyfully adopted the proposition, and putting the buckets over his shoulders, hastened to the cistern.

When tea was ready, Samdadchiemba became quite comfortable; he was absorbed with his beloved beverage, and seemed to have altogether forgotten the disruption of the caravan. It was necessary, however, to recall the circumstance to him, in order that he might go in search of the camel that had run away.

Nearly one half the day elapsed, yet his companions did not rejoin M. Huc. From time to time there passed Tartar horsemen or pilgrims returning from the festival of Rache-Tchurin. Of these M. Huc inquired whether they had not seen, in the vicinity of the Lamasery, a Lama dressed in a yellow robe and a red jacket, and mounted on a red camel. "The Lama," said he, "is very tall, with a great gray beard, a long pointed nose, and a red face." To this description, there was a general answer in the negative: "Had we seen such a personage," said the travelers, "we should certainly have remarked him."

At length, M. Gabet appeared on the slope of a hill; from its summit he had recognized our blue tent pitched in the valley, and he galloped towards his recovered companion as fast as his camel could go. After a brief, animated conversation, wherein both spoke and neither answered, we burst into a hearty laugh at the misadventure thus happily terminated. The reorganization of the caravan was completed before sunset, by Samdadchiemba's return with the missing camel, which, after a long round, he had found fastened to a tent; the Tartar, who owned the tent, having seen the animal running away, had caught it and secured it until some one should claim it.

Though the day was far advanced, we determined to remove, for the place where we had encamped was miserable beyond all expression. Not a blade of grass was to be seen, and the water I had discovered was at so great a distance, that it involved quite a journey to fetch it. "Besides," said we, "if we can only, before night, manage to get within sight of the right road, it will be a great point gained." Our departure thus determined, we sat down to tea. The conversation naturally turned upon the vexatious mischance which had given us so much fatigue and trouble. Already more than once, on our journey, the intractable, obstinate temperament of Samdadchiemba had been the occasion of our losing our way. Mounted on his little mule, as we have described, it was he who led the caravan, preceding the beasts of burden. Upon his assumption that he thoroughly understood the four cardinal points, and that he was perfectly conversant with the deserts of Mongolia, he would never condescend to inquire the route from persons whom he met, and we not unfrequently suffered from his self opinion. We were resolved, therefore, to convert the accident which had just befallen us, into the basis of a warning to our guide. "Samdadchiemba," said we, "listen with attention to the important advice we are about to impart. Though in your youth you may have traveled a good deal in Mongolia, it does not follow that you are master of all the routes; distrust, therefore, your own conjectures, and be more willing to consult the Tartars whom we meet. If yesterday, for example, you had asked the way, if you had not persisted in your practise of being guided wholly by the course of the sun, we should not have endured so much misery." Samdadchiemba made no reply.

We then got up to make the preparations for departure. When we had put in order the different articles that had been confusedly thrown about the tent, we remarked that the Dchiahour was not occupied, as usual, in saddling the camels. We went to see what he was about, and to our great surprise found him tranquilly seated upon a large stone behind the tent. "Well!" exclaimed we, "has it not been determined that we are to encamp elsewhere this evening? What are you seated on that stone for?" Samdadchiemba made no reply; he did not even raise his eyes, but kept them fixedly directed towards the ground. "Samdadchiemba, what is the matter with you? Why don't you saddle the camels?" "If you wish to go," replied he dryly, "you can go; as for me, I remain here. I cannot any longer accompany you. I am, it seems, a wicked man, devoid of conscience; what occasion can you have for such a person?" We were greatly surprised to hear this from a young neophyte who had seemed so attached to us. We, however, thought it best to attempt no persuasion, lest we should aggravate the sullen pride of his character, and render him still more indocile for the future. We accordingly proceeded to do the necessary work ourselves.

We had already folded the tent and packed it on a camel, not a word being spoken by any of the party. Samdadchiemba remained seated on the stone, covering his face with his hands, and probably watching through his fingers how we got on with the labor which he was accustomed to fulfil. When he saw that we were doing very well without him, he rose, without uttering a word, loaded the other camel, saddled his own mule, mounted it, and led the way as usual. M. Gabet and M. Huc exchanged smiles, but they said nothing, for they feared that any observations at that moment might irritate a temperament which evidently required the greatest care in its management.

We halted in a spot beside the road, not very magnificent, certainly, as a station, but at all events, infinitely preferable to the ravine of desolation in which we had experienced such misery. There was this great blessing, that we were once more united; an immense satisfaction in the desert, and which we had never sufficiently appreciated until the occurrence of the mischance that had for a while separated us. We celebrated the occasion by a splendid banquet, of which the flour and sheep's liver, purchased by M. Gabet, formed the basis. This unaccustomed treat relaxed the frowning brow of Samdadchiemba, who applied himself to the culinary arrangements with absolute enthusiasm, and effected, with very limited resources, a supper of several courses.

Next morning, at daybreak, we were in motion. We had not proceeded far when we discovered before us, outlined on the yellow ground of a sandy hill, several large buildings,

Lamasery of Rache-Tchurin.

surrounded with a multitude of white huts. This was the Lamasery of Rache-Tchurin, which, as we approached it, seemed to us a well-built, well-kept place. The three Buddhist temples which rise from the center of the establishment, are of elegant, of majestic construction. The entrance to the principal temple is through a square tower of colossal proportions, at each angle of which is a monstrous dragon, elaborately carved in stone. We traversed the Lamasery from one end to the other, along the chief streets. There was throughout religious and solemn silence. The only persons we saw were a few Lamas enveloped in their large red scarfs, who, after giving us the salutation of the day in a tone scarce above a whisper, gravely continued their melancholy walk.

Towards the western extremity of the Lamasery, Samdadchiemba's little mule shied, and then dashed off at a gallop, followed in its irregular flight, by the two baggage camels. The animals on which we were mounted were equally alarmed. All this disorder was occasioned by a young Lama, who was stretched at full length in the middle of the street, performing a rite in great vogue among the Buddhists, and which consists in making the circuit of a Lamasery, prostrating yourself, with your forehead to the ground, at every single step you make. Sometimes the number of devotees performing together this painful pilgrimage is perfectly prodigious; they follow each other, in Indian file, along a narrow path which encircles the entire Lamasery and its appendant buildings. Any one who deviates in the slightest degree from the prescribed line, is considered to have failed in his devotion, and loses all the fruit he would otherwise have derived from his previous toil. Where the Lamasery is of any extent, the devotees have hard work to get through the ceremony in the course of a long day; so that the pilgrims, who have undertaken this exercise, and have started early in the morning, think themselves lucky if they can complete the operation by nightfall. For the pilgrimage must be performed without intermission, so strictly, that the pilgrims are not allowed to stop for a moment even to take a little nourishment. If, after commencing the rite you do not complete it off-hand, it does not count; you have acquired no merit, and you are not to expect any spiritual profit.

Each prostration must be perfect, so that the body shall be stretched flat along the ground, and the forehead touch the earth, the arms being spread out before you, and the hands joined, as if in prayer. Before rising, the pilgrim describes each time a semicircle on the ground by means of a goat's horn, which he holds in either hand, the line being completed by drawing the arm down to the side. You cannot but feel infinite compassion when you look upon these wretched creatures, their face and clothes all covered with dust or mud. The most inclement weather will not check their intrepid devotion; they continue their prostrations amid snow and rain and the most piercing cold.

There are various modes of performing the pilgrimage round a Lamasery. Some pilgrims do not prostrate themselves at all, but carry, instead, a load of prayer-books, the exact weight of which is prescribed them by the Great Lama, and the burden of which is so oppressive at times that you see old men, and women, and children absolutely staggering under it. When, however, they have successfully completed the circuit, they are deemed to have recited all the prayers contained in the books they have carried. Others content themselves with simply walking the circuit, telling the beads of their long chaplets, or constantly turning a sort of wheel placed on the right hand, and which whirls about with inconceivable rapidity. This instrument is called Tchu-Kor (turning prayer). You see in every brook a number of these Tchu-Kor, which are turned by the current, and in their movement are reputed to be praying, night and day, for the benefit of those who erect them. The Tartars suspend them over the fireplace, and these in their movements are supposed to pray for the peace and prosperity of the whole family, emblemed by the hearth. The movement itself is effected by the thorough draught occasioned by the openings at the top of the tent.

The Buddhists have another mode of simplifying pilgrimages and devotional rites. In all the great Lamaseries you find at short intervals figures in the form of barrels, and turning upon an axle. The material of these figures is a thick board, composed of infinite sheets of paper pasted together, and upon which are written in Thibetian characters the prayers most reputed throughout the country. Those who have not the taste, or the zeal, or the strength to carry huge boards of books on their shoulders, or to prostrate themselves, step after step, in the dust and mire, or to walk round the Lamasery in winter's cold or summer's heat, have recourse to the simple and expeditious medium of the prayer barrel. All they have to do is to set it in motion; it then turns of itself for a long time, the devotees drinking, eating, or sleeping, while the complacent mechanism is turning prayers for them.

One day, on approaching a prayer barrel, we found two

Turning Prayers.

Lamas quarreling furiously, and just on the point of coming to blows, the occasion being the fervor of each for prayer. One of them having set the prayer automaton in motion, had quietly returned to his cell. As he was entering it he turned his head, doubtless to enjoy the spectacle of the fine prayers he had set to work for himself, but to his infinite disgust, he saw a colleague stopping his prayers, and about to turn on the barrel on his own account. Indignant at this pious fraud, he ran back, and stopped his competitor's prayers. Thus it went on for some time, the one turning on, the other stopping the barrel, without a word said on either side. At last, however, their patience exhausted, they came to high words; from words they proceeded to menaces, and it would doubtless have come to a fight, had not an old Lama, attracted by the uproar, interposed words of peace, and himself put the automaton in motion for the joint benefit of both parties.

Besides the pilgrims whose devotion is exercised within

or about the Lamaseries, you find many who have undertaken fearfully long journeys, which they execute with a prostration at every step. Sad and lamentable is it to see these unhappy victims of error enduring, to no purpose, such terrible and painful labors; one's heart is pierced with grief, and one's soul impressed with yearning for the day when these poor Tartars shall consecrate to the service of the true God that religious energy which they daily waste upon a vain and lying creed. We had hoped to profit by the solemnities at Rache-Tchurin to announce the true faith to the Ortous; but such was doubtless not the will of God, since He had permitted us to lose our way on the very day which seemed most favorable for our project. We accordingly passed through the Lamasery of Rache-Tchurin without stopping, eager as we were to arrive at the very source of that immense superstition, of which, as yet, we had only witnessed a few shallow streams.

At a short distance from Rache-Tchurin we reached a road well marked out, and covered with travelers. It was not, however, devotion that had set these people in motion, as it had the pilgrims whom we saw at the Lamasery; mere matter of business was leading them towards the Dabsoun-Noor, (the Salt Lake), celebrated throughout Western Mantchou, and which supplies with salt not only the adjacent Tartars, but also several provinces of the Chinese Empire.

For a day's journey before you reach Dabsoun-Noor the soil changes by degrees its form and aspect; losing its yellow tint, it becomes insensibly white, as though thinly covered with snow. The earth swelling in every direction, forms innumerable hillocks, cone-shaped, and of a regularity so perfect that you might suppose them to have been constructed by the hand of man. Sometimes they are grouped in heaps, one on the other, like pears piled on a plate; they are of all sizes, some but just created, others old, exhausted, and falling to decay. Around these excrescences grow creeping thorns, long-pointed, without flowers or leaves, which, intertwining spirally, surmount them with a sort of net-work cap. These thorns are never found elsewhere than about these hillocks; upon those of more recent growth they are firm, vigorous, and full of shoots. Upon the elder elevations they are dried up, calcined by the niter, brittle, and in shreds.

As you look upon these numerous mounds, covered with a thick efflorescence of niter, it is obvious to your sense that beneath the surface, and at no great depth, some great chemical operation is in progress. Springs, generally so rare in the Ortous country, are here of frequent occurrence, but the water is for the most part excessively salt. Here and there, however, by the very side of a brackish pool, there is a spring of soft, sweet, delicious water; all such are indicated to travelers by a small flag, fluttering from the end of a long pole.

Dabsoun-Noor is not so much a lake as a reservoir of mineral salt, mixed with nitrous efflorescence. The latter, in color pale white, and crumbling between the fingers, is easily distinguishable from the salt, which is of a gray tint, and glitters like crystal when broken. Dabsoun-Noor is about twenty lis in circumference. Around it, at intervals, are the tents occupied by the Mongols who work it, and the Chinese who have thrust themselves in as partners. It were difficult indeed to find any description of industry or commerce within a certain range of their own country in which the Chinese do not contrive to have a hand. The manipulation to which the salt is subjected requires neither great labor nor great science. All the workers do is to pick it up as it comes in the reservoir, to pile it, and, when the heap is of a certain size, to cover it with a thin coating of potter's earth. When the salt has sufficiently purified itself, the Tartars convey it to the nearest Chinese mart and exchange it for tea, tobacco, brandy, and other commodities. In the locality itself salt is of no value: at every step you see lumps of it, sometimes of remarkable purity. We filled a bag with these for our own use and for that of the camels, which are all very fond of salt. We traversed Dabsoun-Noor throughout its breadth from east to west, and we had to take the utmost precaution as we proceeded over its loose, and at times almost moving, soil. The Tartars recommended us not to deviate in the least from the path we should find marked out, and by all means to avoid any places where we should see the water bubbling up, for there, they informed us, were gulfs which they had frequently endeavored to sound, but without result. This statement induced us to believe that there is a noor, or lake, here, but that it is underground, the place called Dabsoun-Noor being merely the covering or roof of the lake, composed of the saline and saltpetrous matter produced by the constant evaporation of the subterranean waters. Foreign matter, brought by the wind, and consolidated by the rain, would in the lapse of time form a crust upon such a roof strong enough to bear the caravans that incessantly traverse Dabsoun-Noor.

This great salt mine seems to pervade with its influence the whole Ortous district, throughout whose extent the water is brackish, the soil arid, and the surface encrusted with saline matter. This absence of rich pasturage and fresh water is very adverse to the growth of cattle; but the camel, whose robust and hardy temperament adapts itself to the most sterile regions, affords compensation to the Tartars of the Ortous. This animal, a perfect treasure to the dwellers in the desert, can remain a fortnight, or even a month, without eating or drinking. However wretched the land may be on which it is put to feed, it can always find wherewith to satisfy its hunger, especially if the soil be impregnated with salt or niter. Things that no other animal will touch, to it are welcome; briers and thorns, dry wood itself, supply it with efficient food.

Though it costs so little to keep, the camel is of an utility inconceivable to those who are not acquainted with the countries in which Providence has placed it. Its ordinary load is from 700 to 800 lbs., and it can carry this load ten leagues a day. Those, indeed, which are employed to carry despatches, are expected to travel eighty leagues per diem, but then they only carry the despatch bearer. In several countries of Tartary the carriages of the kings and princes are drawn by camels, and sometimes they are harnessed to palanquins; but this can only be done in the level country. The fleshy nature of their feet does not permit them to climb mountains, when they have a carriage or litter of any sort to draw after them.

The training of the young camel is a business requiring great care and attention. For the first week of its life it can neither stand nor suck without some helping hand. Its long neck is then of such excessive flexibility and fragility, that it runs the risk of dislocating it, unless some one is at hand to sustain the head while it sucks the teats of its dam.

The camel, born to servitude, seems impressed from its birth with a sense of the yoke it is destined to bear through life. You never see the young camel playing and frolicking about, as you see kids, colts, and other young animals. It is always grave, melancholy, and slow in its movements, which it never hastens, unless under compulsion. In the night, and often in the day also, it sends forth a mournful cry, like that of an infant in pain. It seems to feel that joy or recreation are not within its portion; that its inevitable career is forced labor and long fastings, until death shall relieve it.

The maturation of the camel is a long affair. It cannot carry even a single rider, until its third year; and it is not in full vigor until it is eight years old. Its trainers then begin to try it with loads, gradually heavier and heavier. If it can rise with its burden, this is a proof that it can carry it throughout the journey. When that journey is only of brief duration, they sometimes load the animal in excess, and then they aid it to rise by means of bars and levers. The camel's capacity for labor endures for a long time. Provided that at certain periods of the year it is allowed a short holiday for pasturing at its leisure, it will continue its service for fully fifty years.

Nature has provided the camel with no means of defense against other animals, unless you may so consider its piercing prolonged cry, and its huge, shapeless, ugly frame, which resembles, at a distance, a heap of ruins. It seldom kicks, and when it does, it almost as seldom inflicts any injury. Its soft, fleshy foot cannot wound, or even bruise you; neither can the camel bite an antagonist. In fact, its only practical means of defense against man or beast is a sort of vehement sneeze, wherewith it discharges, from nose and mouth, a mass of filth against the object which it seeks to intimidate or to annoy.

Yet the entire male camels, *bore* as the Tartars call them, (*temen* being the generic appellation of the animal), are very formidable during the twelfth moon, which is their rutting time. At this period, their eyes are inflamed; an oily, fetid humor exhales from their heads; their mouths are constantly foaming; and they eat and drink absolutely nothing whatever. In this state of excitement they rush at whatever presents itself, man or beast, with a fierceness of precipitation which it is impossible to avoid or to resist; and when they have overthrown the object they have pursued they pound it beneath the weight of their bodies. The epoch passed, the camel resumes its ordinary gentleness, and the routine of its laborious career.

The females do not produce young until their sixth or seventh year; the period of gestation is fourteen months. The Tartars geld most of their male camels, which, by this operation, acquire a greater development of strength, height, and size. Their voices become at the same time thinner and lower, in some instances wholly lost; and the hair is shorter and finer than that of the entire camels.

The awkward aspect of the camel, the excessive stench of its breath, its heavy, ungraceful movements, its projecting hare-lips, the callosities which disfigure various parts of its body, all contribute to render its appearance repulsive; yet its extreme gentleness and docility, and the services it renders to man, render it of pre-eminent utility, and make us forget its deformity.

Notwithstanding the apparent softness of its feet, the camel can walk upon the most rugged ground, upon sharp flints, or thorns, or roots of trees, without wounding itself. Yet, if too long a journey is continuously imposed upon it, if after a certain march you do not give it a few days' rest, the outer skin wears off, the flesh is bared, and the blood flows. Under such distressing circumstances, the Tartars make sheep-skin shoes for it, but this assistance is unavailing without rest; for if you attempt to compel the camel to proceed, it lies down, and you are compelled either to remain with or to abandon it.

There is nothing which the camel so dreads as wet, marshy ground. The instant it places its feet upon anything like mud, it slips and slides, and, generally, after staggering about like a drunken man, falls heavily on its sides.

When about to repose, it kneels down, folds its fore legs symmetrically under its body, and stretches out its long neck before it on the ground. In this position, it looks just like a monstrous snail.

Every year, towards the close of spring, the camel sheds its hair, every individual bristle of which disappears before a single sprout of the new stock comes up. For twenty days the animal remains completely bare, as though it had been closely shaved all over, from the top of the head to the extremity of the tail. At this juncture, it is excessively sensitive to cold or wet; and you see it, at the slightest chillness in the air or the least drop of rain, shivering and shaking in every limb, like a man without clothes exposed on the snow. By degrees the new hair shows itself, in the form of fine, soft, curling wool, which gradually becomes a long, thick fur, capable of resisting the extremest inclemency of the weather. The greatest delight of the animal is to walk in the teeth of the north wind, or to stand motionless on the summit of a hill, beaten by the storm and inhaling the icy wind. Some naturalists say that the camel cannot exist in cold countries; these writers must have wholly forgotten the Tartarian camels, which on the contrary, cannot endure the least heat, and which certainly could not exist in Arabia.

The hair of an ordinary camel weighs about ten pounds. It is sometimes finer than silk, and always longer than sheep's wool. The hair growing below the neck and on the legs of the entire camels is rough, bushy, and in color black, whereas that of the ordinary camel is red, gray, and white. The Tartars make no sort of use of it. In the places where the animals pasture, you see great sheets of it, looking like dirty rags, driven about by the wind, until they are collected in sheltered corners, in the hill sides. The utmost use the Tartars make of it is to twist some of it into cord, or into a sort of canvas, of which they construct sacks and carpets.

The milk of the camel is excellent, and supplies large quantities of butter and cheese. The flesh is hard, unsavory, and little esteemed by the Tartars. They use the hump, however, which, cut into slices, and dissolved in tea, serves the purpose of butter. It is known that Heliogabalus had camel's flesh served up at his banquets, and that he was very fond of camel's feet. We cannot speak as to the latter dish, which the Roman Emperor piqued himself upon having invented, but we can distinctly affirm that camel's flesh is detestable.

Mongol Butcher.

CHAPTER X.

Purchase of a Sheep—A Mongol Butcher—Great Feast *à la Tartare*—Tartar Veterinary Surgeons—Strange Cure of a Cow—Depth of the Wells of the Ortous—Manner of Watering the Animals—Encampment of the Hundred Wells—Meeting with the King of the Alechan—Annual Embassies of the Tartar Sovereigns to Peking—Grand Ceremony in the Temple of the Ancestors—The Emperor gives Counterfeit Money to the Mongol Kings—Inspection of our Geographical Map—The Devil's Cistern—Purification of the Water—A Lame Dog—Curious Aspect of the Mountains—Passage of the Yellow River.

THE environs of the Dabsoun-Noor abound in flocks of goats and sheep. These animals like to browse on the furze and thorny bushes, the sole vegetation of these barren steppes; they especially delight in those nitrous efflorescences which are found here on all sides in the utmost abundance. The soil, miserable as it is in other respects, seems very favorable to the growth of these animals, which enter largely into the consumption of the Tartars, constituting indeed the basis of their food. If bought on the spot, they are of very moderate price. As we calculated that a pound of meat would cost us less than a pound of flour, we resolved, as a matter of economy, to buy a sheep. The thing was not difficult to find; but as it would of course oblige us to stop, at least for a day, we waited till we should come to some place, not quite barren, and where our animals could find some pasturage to browse upon.

Two days after crossing Dabsoun-Noor, we entered a long narrow valley, where some Mongol families had stationed themselves. The earth was covered with a close herb, which, in form and character, had much resemblance to thyme. Our beasts, as they proceeded, browsed furtively, right and left, on this plant, and seemed to be very fond of it. This new pasturage gave us the idea of encamping on the spot. Not far from a tent, a Lama was sitting on a hillock, making ropes with camel's hair. "Brother," said we as we approached him, "the flock upon that hill doubtless belongs to you. Will you sell us a sheep?" "Certainly," he answered, "I will let you have an excellent sheep; as to the price, we shall not quarrel about that. We men of prayer are not like merchants." He indicated to us a spot near his own tent, and unloaded our beasts. The entire family of the Lama, when they heard the cries of our camels, hastened to assist us to encamp. We, indeed, were not allowed to do anything to it; for our new friends took delight in making themselves useful, in unsaddling the beasts, pitching the tent, and putting our baggage in order within.

The young Lama, who had received us with so much kindness, after having unsaddled the horse and the mule, perceived that both these beasts were hurt a little on the back. "Brothers," he said, "here is a bad business; and as you are upon a long journey, it must be remedied, or you will not be able to go on." So saying, he took the knife, which hung from his girdle, sharpened it with rapidity upon his boot-tops, took our saddles to pieces, examined the rough parts of the wood, and pared them away on both sides till he had removed the slightest unevenness. He then put together again, with wonderful skill, all the pieces of the saddles, and returned them to us. "That will do," said he; "now you may travel in peace." This operation was effected rapidly and in the readiest manner possible. The Lama was then about to fetch the sheep; but as it was already late, we said it was unnecessary, for that we should remain a whole day in his valley.

Next morning, before we were awake, the Lama opened

the door of our tent, laughing so loud that he aroused us. "Ah," said he, "I see plainly that you do not intend to depart to-day. The sun is already very high, and you sleep still." We rose quickly, and as soon as we were dressed, the Lama spoke of the sheep. "Come to the flock," he said; "you may choose at your pleasure." "No, go by yourself, and select a sheep for us yourself. At present we have an occupation. With us, Lamas of the Western sky, it is a rule to pray as soon as we rise." "Oh, what a fine thing!" said the Lama; "oh, the holy rules of the West!" His admiration, however, did not make him forget his little affair of business. He mounted his horse and rode towards a flock of sheep which we saw undulating upon the slope of a hill.

We had not yet finished our prayers when we heard the Tartar returning at full gallop. He had fastened the sheep to the back of his saddle, like a portmanteau. Hardly arrived at the door of our tent, he dismounted; and in the twinkling of an eye he had put upon its four legs the poor sheep, quite astounded at the ride it had been favored with. "That is the sheep; is it not fine? Does it suit you?" "Admirably. What is the price?" "One ounce; is that too much?" Considering the size of the animal, we thought the price moderate. "You ask an ounce; here is an ingot, which is just of the weight you require. Sit down for a moment; we will fetch our scales, and you shall ascertain whether this piece of silver really weighs an ounce." At these words the Lama drew back, and cried, stretching out both hands towards us: "Above there is a heaven, below there is the earth, and Buddha is the lord of all things. He wills that men behave towards each other like brothers; you are of the West, I am of the East. Is that any reason why the intercourse between us should not be frank and honorable? You have not cheapened my sheep: I take your money without weighing it." "An excellent principle," said we. "As you will not weigh the money, pray sit, nevertheless, for a moment; we will take a cup of tea together and talk over a little matter." "I know what you mean; neither you nor I may cause the transmigration of this living being. We must find a layman who knows how to kill sheep. Is it not so?" and without awaiting an answer, he added, "another thing; from your appearance, one may easily guess that you are no great hands at cutting up sheep and preparing them." "You are not mistaken," we answered, laughing. "Well, keep the sheep tied to your tent; and for the rest, rely upon me; I shall be back in a minute." He mounted his horse, went off at full gallop and disappeared in a bend of the vale.

According to his promise, the Lama soon returned. He went straight to his tent, tied his horse to a post, took off his saddle, bridle and halter, gave it a cut with his whip, and so sent it off to pasture. He went into his tent for a little while, and then appeared with all the members of his family, that is to say, his old mother and two younger brothers. They advanced slowly towards our tent, in truly ridiculous fashion, just as if they were going to remove all their furniture. The Lama carried on his head a large pot, which covered him as with an enormous hat. His mother had on her back a large basket, filled with argols. The two young Mongols followed with a trivet, an iron spoon, and several other minor kitchen implements. At this sight, Samdadchiemba was full of joy, for he saw before him a whole day of poetry.

When the entire *batterie de cuisine* was arranged in open air, the Lama invited us, in his politeness, to go and repose in our tent for awhile. He judged from our air, that we could not, without derogation, be present at the approaching scene of butchering. The suggestion, however, did not meet our views, and we requested that if we could do so without inconveniencing them, we might sit down on the grass at a respectful distance, and with the promise that we would not touch anything. After some objections, perceiving that we were curious to be spectators, they dispensed with the etiquette of the matter.

The Lama seemed anxious; he kept looking towards the north of the valley, as if expecting some one. "All right," he said at last, with an air of satisfaction, "here he comes." "Who comes? Of whom do you speak?" "I forgot to tell you that I had been just now to invite a layman to come, who is very skilful in killing a sheep. There he is." We rose and perceived, indeed, something moving among the heath of the valley. At first we could not clearly distinguish what it was, for though it advanced with some rapidity, the object did not seem to enlarge. At last the most singular person we had ever met with in our lives presented himself to our view. We were obliged to make the utmost efforts to repress the strong impulse to laughter that came upon us. This layman seemed to be about fifty years old, but his height did not exceed three feet. On the top of his head, which terminated like a sugar-loaf, rose a small tuft of badly combed hair; a gray, thin beard descended in disorder down his chin. Finally, two prominences, one on his back, the other on his breast, communicated to this little butcher a perfect resemblance with Æsop, as he appears in various editions of the "Fables de la Fontaine."

The strong, sonorous voice of the layman was in singular contrast with the exiguity of his thin, stunted frame. He did not lose much time in saluting the company. After having darted his small black eyes at the sheep, which was tied to one of the nails of our tent, he said: "Is this the beast you wish to have put in order?" And while feeling its tail in order to judge its fat, he gave it a turn, and placed it on its back with remarkable dexterity. He next tied together its legs; then while uncovering his right arm by throwing back the sleeve of his leathern coat, he asked whether the operation was to be effected in the tent or outside? "Outside," said we. "Outside, very well, outside;" so saying, he drew from a leathern sheath, suspended from his sash, a knife with a large handle, but whose blade by long use had become thin and narrow. After having examined for a moment its point with his thumb, he plunged it to the hilt into the side of the sheep, and drawing it out quite red, the sheep was dead, dead at once, without making any movement; not a single drop of blood had spouted from the wound. We were greatly astonished at this, and asked the little man how he managed to kill a sheep so very easily and quickly. "We Tartars," he said, "do not kill in the same way as the Kitat; they cut the throat, we go straight to the heart. By our method, the animal suffers less, and all the blood is, as it should be, retained in the interior."

The transmigration once operated, nobody had any further scruples. Our Dchiahour and the Tartar Lama turned back their sleeves and advanced to assist the little butcher. The sheep was skinned with admirable celerity. Meantime the mother of the Lama had made the two pots boil. She now took the entrails of the sheep, washed them pretty clean, and then, with the blood which she took from the interior of the sheep by means of a large wooden spoon, prepared some puddings, the basis of which was the never-failing oatmeal. "Sirs Lamas," said the little layman, "shall I bone the sheep?" Upon our answering in the affirmative, he had the animal hooked upon the tent, for he was not big enough to perform that operation himself; he then mounted upon a large stone, and passing his knife rapidly along the bones, he detached, in one piece, all the meat, so as to leave dangling from the tent a mere skeleton, clean, cleared, and nicely polished.

While the little layman was, according to his expression, putting in order the flesh of the sheep, the rest of the company had prepared a gala in the Tartar fashion. The young Lama was director of the feast. "Now," he cried, "let us all sit round; the great pot is going to be emptied." Forthwith everyone sat down upon the turf. The old Mongol woman plunged both hands into the pot, which was boiling over, and drew out all the intestines—the liver, the heart, the kidneys, the spleen, and the bowels, stuffed with blood and oatmeal. In this gastronomical preparation, the most remarkable thing was, that all the intestines had been retained in their integrity, so that they presented themselves much as they are seen in the living beast. The old woman served up, or rather threw this splendid dish upon the lawn, which was at once our chair, table, plate, and, in case of need, our napkin. It is unnecessary to add, that we used our fingers instead of forks. Every one seized with his hands a portion of the bowels, twisted it from the mass, and devoured it without seasoning or salt.

The two French missionaries were not able, despite their utmost willingness, to do honor to this Tartar dish. First we burned our fingers when we tried to touch the hot and smoking repast. Although our guests urged that it ought not to be allowed to grow cold, we waited a little, afraid of burning our lips also. At last we tasted these puddings of sheep's blood and oatmeal, but after getting down a few mouthfuls, we were quite satisfied. Never, perhaps, had we eaten anything so utterly tasteless and insipid. Samdadchiemba, having foreseen this, had withdrawn from the common dish the liver and the kidneys, which he placed before us, with some salt, which he had previously crushed between two stones. We were thus enabled to keep pace with the company, who, with a devouring appetite, were swallowing the vast system of entrails.

When the whole had disappeared, the old woman brought up the second service, by placing in the midst of us the large pot in which the puddings had been cooked. Instantly all the members of the banquet invited each other, and every one taking from his bosom his wooden porringer, ladled out bumpers of a smoking, salt liquid, which they dignified with the pompous name of sauce. As we did not wish to appear eccentric, or as if we despised the Tartar *cuisine*, we did like the rest. We plunged our porringer into the pot, but it was only by the most laudable efforts that we could get down this green stuff, which gave us the idea of half masticated grass. The Tartars, on the contrary, found it delicious, and readily reached the bottom of the extempore tureen, not stopping for a moment, till nothing was left—not a drop of sauce, not an inch of pudding.

When the feast was finished, the little layman took leave, receiving as his fee the four feet of the sheep. To this fee, fixed by the old custom of the Mongols, we added, as a supplement, a handful of tea leaves, for we desired that he should long remember and talk to his countrymen of the generosity of the Lamas of the Western sky.

Every one having now thoroughly regaled, our neighbors took their kitchen utensils and returned home, except the young Lama, who said he would not leave us alone. After much talk about the east and west, he took down the skeleton, which was still hanging at the entrance of the tent, and amused himself with reciting, or rather singing, the nomenclature of all the bones, large and small, that compose the frame of the sheep. He perceived that our knowledge on this subject was very limited, and this extremely astonished him; and we had the greatest trouble to make him understand, that in our country ecclesiastical studies had for their object more serious and important matters than the names and number of the bones of a sheep.

Every Mongol knows the number, the name, and the position of the bones which compose the frame of animals; and thus they never break the bones when they are cutting up an ox or a sheep. With the point of their large knife they go straight and at once to the juncture of the bones and separate them with astonishing skill and celerity. These frequent dissections, and especially the habit of being every day amongst their flocks, make the Tartars well acquainted with the diseases of animals, and skilful in their cure. The remedies, which they employ internally, are always simples gathered in the prairie, and the decoction of which they make the sick animals drink. For this purpose, they use a large cow-horn. When they have contrived to insert the small end of this into the mouth of the animal, they pour the physic in at the other extremity, as through a funnel. If the beast persists in not opening its mouth, the liquid is administered through the nostrils. Sometimes the Tartars employ a lavement in their treatment of the diseases of animals; but their instruments are still of primitive simplicity. A cow's horn serves for the pipe, and the pump is a great bladder, worked by squeezing it.

Internal remedies, however, are not very often applied; the Tartars make more frequent use of punctures and incisions in different parts of the body. Some of these operations are extremely ludicrous. One day, when we had pitched our tent beside a Mongol dwelling, a Tartar brought to the chief of the family a cow, which, he said, would not eat, and which was pining away day by day. The chief examined the animal, opened its mouth, and rubbed its fore teeth with his nail. "Fool, blockhead," said he to the man who had come to ask his advice, "why did you not come before? Your cow is on the verge of death; there is scarce a day's life more in her. Yet, there may be tried one means; I will attempt it. If your cow dies, you will say it is your own fault; if it recovers, you will regard it as a great favor from Hormousdha, operated by my skill." He called some of his slaves, and ordered them to keep a firm hold of the beast, while he was operating upon it. Then he entered his tent, whence he soon returned, armed with a nail and a great hammer. We waited with impatience this strange chirurgical operation, which was to be performed with a nail and a hammer. While several Mongols held the cow, in order to prevent its running away, the operator placed the nail under its belly, and then drove it in up to the head with a violent stroke of the hammer. Next, he seized with both hands the tail of the cow, and ordered those who were holding it to let go. Instantly, the animal that had been so very singularly operated upon, dashed off, dragging after it the veterinary Tartar, clinging to its tail. In this fashion, they ran nearly a li. The Tartar then quitted his victim, and came quietly back to us, who were quite amazed at this new method of curing cows. He declared there was no further danger for the beast; for he had ascertained, he said, by the stiffness of the tail, the good effect of the ferruginous medicine he had administered.

The Tartar veterinarians sometimes perform their operations at the belly, as we have just seen; but it is more generally, with the head, ears, temple, upper lip, and about the eyes that they deal. The latter operation is principally had recourse to, in the disease which the Tartars call Hen's dung, to which mules are greatly subject. When this disease breaks out, the animals leave off eating, and fall into extreme weakness, so that they can hardly keep themselves on their legs; fleshly excrescences, similar to the excrements of poultry, grow under the lids, in the corners of the eyes. If these excrescences are removed in time, the mules are saved, and recover by degrees their original vigor; if not, they pine for a few days, and then die.

Although cupping and bleeding have great place in the veterinary art of the Tartars, you must not suppose that they have at their disposal fine collections of instruments, such as those of European operators. Most of them have nothing but their ordinary knife, or the small iron awl, which they keep in their girdle, and which they use daily to clear their pipes and mend their saddles and leathern boots.

The young Lama who had sold us the sheep, spent a great part of the day in telling us anecdotes, more or less piquant and curious, about the veterinary science in which he seemed to be very skilful. Moreover, he gave us important instructions concerning the road we had to pursue. He settled the stages we ought to make, and indicated the places where we should encamp, so as to prevent our dying from thirst. We had still before us in the country of the Ortous, a journey of about fourteen days; in all that time we should find neither rivulet nor spring, nor cistern; but only, at certain distances, wells of an extraordinary depth; some of them distant from each other two days' march, so that we should have to carry with us our provision of water.

Next morning, after having paid our respects to the Tartar family, who had shown us so much kindness, we proceeded on our way. Towards evening, when it was nearly time to pitch our tent, we perceived in the distance a large assemblage of various herds. Thinking that one of the indicated wells lay probably there, we bent our steps in the direction, and soon found that we were correct in our anticipations; the water was before us. The beasts were collected from every quarter, waiting to be watered. We halted accordingly, and set up our encampment. As we gazed upon the assembled flocks, and the well, the covering of which was a large stone, we recalled with pleasure the passage of Genesis, which relates the journey of Jacob in Mesopotamia, to Laban, son of Bathuel the Syrian.

"Then Jacob went on his journey, and came into the land of the people of the east.

"And he looked, and behold a well in the field, and, lo, there were three flocks of sheep lying by it; for out of that well they watered the flocks: and a great stone was upon the well's mouth.

"And thither were all the flocks gathered; and they rolled the stone from the well's mouth, and watered the sheep, and put the stone again upon the well's mouth in its place." [1]

The wooden troughs placed around the well, reminded us of the other passage, where the meeting of Rebecca with the servant of Abraham is related.

"And when she had done giving him drink, she said, I will draw water for thy camels also, until they have done drinking.

"And she hasted, and emptied her pitcher into the trough, and ran again unto the well to draw water, and drew for all his camels." [2]

One cannot travel in Mongolia, amongst a pastoral and nomad population, without one's mind involuntarily going back to the time of the first patriarch, whose pastoral life had so close a relation with the manners and customs which we still find amongst the Mongol tribes. But how sad and painful do these coincidences become, when we reflect that these unfortunate people are still ignorant of the God of Abraham, Isaac, and Jacob.

[1] Gen. xxix. 1-3.

[2] Gen. xxiv. 19, 20.

We had scarcely pitched our tent, and arranged our modest kitchen, when we saw several Tartar horsemen advancing at full gallop. They were coming to draw water and give it to the numerous flocks that had been long awaiting them. These animals, which had hitherto stood at a distance, seeing the shepherds approach, hastened to the spot, and soon all were grouped round the well, eager to quench their thirst. This large assemblage of animals, so numerous and so various, created an agitation, a tumult to which we were quite unused amid the silent solitude of the desert; and it was perhaps on account of its novelty that this confusion was, to us, full of entertainment. It was amusing to see the half-tamed horses pushing and struggling to arrive first at the well; then, instead of drinking in peace, biting, quarreling, and even leaving the water in order to pursue each other on the plain. The scene was especially entertaining and picturesque, when an enormous camel came forward, spreading alarm round the well, and driving away the vulgar herd by its despotic presence.

There were four Mongol shepherds; while two of them, armed with a long rod, ran about trying to effect a little order among the flocks, the two others drew the water in a manner which greatly excited our surprise. First, the utensil they used by way of pail, appeared to us very remarkable; it was the entire skin of a goat, solidly fastened at the four feet, the only opening being at the neck. A hoop kept this orifice open; a long, strong rope of camel's hair was fastened at one end to the wooden handle that crossed the diameter of the orifice, and at the other end to the saddle of the horse ridden by one of the Tartars, who, when the skin was filled rode off, and thus hauled up the bucket to the edge of the well, where it was received by another man, who emptied its contents into the troughs.

The well was of astonishing depth; the rope used to raise the bucket seemed more than 200 feet long. Instead of running in a pulley, it went right over a large stone, in which a large groove was already made by the constant friction. Although the drawing up of the water was performed with great activity, it was nearly dark before all the flock had been watered; we then brought our five animals to participate in the general banquet, and the Tartars had the complaisance to draw water also for us; otherwise, it is probable we should never have got it, but have been obliged to suffer thirst beside an abundant well.

These Tartars did not seem contented, like those we had met with in the other parts of Mongolia; we saw they were very depressed at being obliged to spend their lives in such a barren country, where pasturage is so very scarce and water still rarer. They talked to us of the Mongol kingdoms through which we had passed, and where it was so easy, so agreeable indeed, to feed animals. "Oh, how happy are the inhabitants of these countries!" said they. "How fortunate were we, could we spend our days amidst those rich pasturages."

Before they returned to their dwelling, which lay behind a high mountain, these Tartars told us that we ought to depart next morning before daybreak, for that we should not find any water until we came to the Hundred Wells, which was distant a hundred and fifty lis (fifteen leagues).

Dawn had not yet appeared when we left. The country was, as before, sandy, barren, and dismal. About noon we halted, in order to take a little food, and to make tea with the water we had brought with us on one of the camels. Night was setting in before we reached the Hundred Wells; our poor animals could hardly move for hunger and fatigue; yet, at all cost, we were obliged to reach the encampment. To remain where we were would have caused infinite wretchedness. At last we came to the wells, and without troubling ourselves to ascertain whether or no there were a hundred of them, as the Tartar name of the place imported, we hastened to pitch our tent. Happily the well was not so deep as that we had seen the night before. Our first care was to draw some water for the horse and the mule; but when we went to lead them to the trough, we did not find them near the tent, where they usually stood to be unsaddled. This misfortune occasioned us an alarm that made us forget the fatigues of the day. We had, it is true, no fear of robbers, for in this respect no country is more safe than the Ortous; but we thought that our animals, thirsty as they were, had run away in search of water. They will go, meditated we, till they have found water; perhaps they will go without stopping to the frontiers of the Ortous to the very banks of the Yellow River.

The night was quite dark; nevertheless, we thought it

proper to go instantly in search of our horses, while Samdadchiemba was preparing supper. We wandered about for a long time in all directions without seeing anything; ever and anon we stopped to listen whether we could distinguish the sound of the bells suspended from the horse's neck; but our efforts were vain; nothing interrupted the dead silence of the desert. We went on, without losing courage, still hoping to find animals so very necessary to us, and the loss of which would have placed us in such difficulties. Sometimes we fancied we heard in the distance the tinkling of the bells. Then we laid flat down, applying our ears to the earth, in order to catch more readily the slightest noise that might occur; but it was all in vain; our search was fruitless.

The fear of losing our way in a dark night in a country, the bearings of which we had not been able to examine, made us think of retracing our steps. Judge of our consternation when, on turning round, we perceived, apparently in the place where we had pitched our tent, a large volume of flame and smoke rising. We did not doubt for an instant that Samdadchiemba also had set out in search of the animals, and that in his absence the tent had caught fire. Oh, how sad and discouraging was that moment. In the middle of the desert, at two thousand lis distance from our christendom, we contemplated without hope those flames consuming our tent, our sole shelter against the inclemency of the weather. "Alas!" we said, "the tent is certainly destroyed, and doubtless all that was in it has also become a prey to the flames."

We mournfully directed our steps to the place of our encampment. Though anxious to ascertain our misfortune, we advanced slowly, for we were, at the same time, afraid to approach the fearful spectacle, destructive of our plans, and plunging us into misery of every description. As we advanced, we heard loud cries; at last we distinguished the voice of Samdadchiemba, apparently calling for assistance. Imagining that we could still save something from the conflagration, we hastened to the spot, calling out, at the pitch of our voices, that we were coming. When we at last arrived at the encampment, we stood for an instant quite stupefied upon seeing Samdadchiemba quietly seated beside an immense fire, and drinking with the greatest satisfaction bumpers of tea. The tent was untouched, and all our animals lying around it: there had been no conflagration at all. The Dchiahour, having found the horse and the mule, had imagined that, having doubtless got to some distance, we should have a difficulty in finding our way back to the encampment, and therefore he had made a large fire to direct our steps, and sent forth vehement cries inviting us to return. We had so fully believed in the reality of our misfortune that, on beholding our tent again, we seemed to pass at once from the extreme of misery to the height of happiness.

As the night had already made considerable progress, we hastened to eat, with excellent appetite, the soup that Samdadchiemba had prepared, and then laid down upon our goat-skins, where we enjoyed a profound sleep till daybreak.

On getting up next morning a glance around the encampment diffused a shudder of terror through all our limbs; for we found ourselves surrounded on every side by deep wells. We had been, indeed, told that we should not find water until we reached the place called Hundred Wells, but we had never imagined, that this denomination, Hundred Wells, was to be taken literally. When we had pitched our tent the night before, it was too dark for us to remark the presence of these numerous precipices, and accordingly we had taken no precautions. When we went out in search of our stray animals we had, without knowing it, made a thousand turnings and windings amongst these deep pits; and that we had thus walked in a dark night, without any accident, could only be attributed to a special protection of Providence. Before our departure, therefore, we planted a small wooden cross on the brink of one of these wells, as a sign of our thankfulness for the goodness of God.

After having made our usual breakfast, we proceeded. Towards noon we perceived before us a great multitude issuing from a narrow defile, formed by two precipitous mountains. We were lost in conjecture as to what this numerous and imposing caravan could be. Innumerable camels, laden with baggage, advanced in single file, one after the other, escorted on either side by a number of horsemen, who, in the distance, appeared to be richly attired. We slackened our pace, to obtain a nearer view of this caravan, which appeared to us a very strange affair.

Encampment at the Hundred Wells.

It was still a considerable distance off, when four horsemen, who formed a sort of vanguard, galloped on towards us. They were all four Mandarins, as we perceived from the blue button which surmounted their cap of ceremony. "Sirs Lamas," they said, "peace be with you! Towards what point of the earth do you direct your steps?" "We are of the West, and it is to the West we are going. And you, brothers of Mongolia, whither do you travel in so large a troop, and in such magnificent apparel?" "We are from the kingdom of Alechan, and our king is making a journey to Peking to prostrate himself at the feet of Him who dwells above the sky." After these few words the four horsemen rose somewhat in their saddles, saluted, and then returned to their position at the head of the caravan.

We had thus encountered on his way the King of Alechan, repairing to Peking with his gorgeous retinue, to be present at the great meeting of the tributary princes, who, on the first day of the first moon, are bound to offer the compliments of the new year to the Emperor. Behind the vanguard came a palanquin carried by two splendid mules, harnessed, the one before, the other behind, to gilt shafts. The palanquin was square, plain, and by no means elegant; its roof was adorned with some silk fringe, and its four panels were decorated with some pictures of dragons, birds, and nosegays. The Tartar monarch was sitting, not upon a seat, but with his legs crossed, in the oriental fashion. He seemed to be about fifty years old; and his full round features gave to his physiognomy a remarkable air of good nature. As he passed us, we cried: "King of the Alechan, peace and happiness be on your way!" "Men of prayer," he answered, "may you also be at peace," and he accompanied these words with a friendly salute. An old white-bearded Lama, mounted upon a magnificent horse, led the fore mule of the palanquin; he was considered the guide of the whole caravan. Generally, the great marches of the Tartars are under the guidance of the most venerable of the Lamas of the district; for these people are persuaded, that they have nothing to fear on their way, so long as they have at their head, a representative of the divinity, or rather the divinity himself incarnate in the person of the Lama.

A great number of horsemen, who surrounded, as a guard of honor, the royal palanquin, made their horses curvet incessantly, and dash up and down, in and out, from one side to the other, without ever stopping in their rapid movements. Immediately behind the carriage of the king, came a white camel of extraordinary beauty and size; a young Tartar, on foot, led it by a silken string. This camel was not laden. From the tip of each hump, which looked like two pyramids, floated pieces of yellow taffeta. There was no doubt, that this magnificent animal was a present destined for the Chinese Emperor. The remainder of the troop consisted of numerous camels, carrying the baggage, the boxes, tents, pots, the thousand and one utensils, that are always wanted in a country where no tavern is to be found.

The caravan had passed on a long time, when meeting with a well, we resolved to pitch our tent beside it. While we were making our tea, three Tartars, one decorated with the red, the other with the blue button, alighted at the entrance of our dwelling. They asked for news of the caravan of the King of the Alechans. We answered that we had met it a long time since, that it must already be at a considerable distance, and that it would doubtless arrive, before night, at the encampment of the Hundred Wells. "As it is so," they said, "we would rather remain here, than arrive by night at the Hundred Wells, at the risk of falling into some hole. To-morrow, by starting a little before day, we shall reach the caravan."

No sooner said than done: the Tartars forthwith unsaddled their horses, sent them off to seek their fortune in the desert, and without ceremony took their seat beside our fire. They were all Taitsi of the kingdom of the Alechan. One of these, he who wore the cap with the red button, was the king's minister; they all three belonged to the great caravan, but the day before, having started to visit a friend, a prince of the Ortous, they had been left behind by the main body.

The minister of the King of Alechan had an open, frank character, and a very acute understanding; he combined Mongol good nature with vivacious and elegant manners, which he had no doubt acquired in his frequent visits to Peking. He asked many questions about the country which the Tartars call the Western Heaven, and informed us, that every three years a great number of our countrymen, from the different western kingdoms, rendered their homage to the Emperor at Peking.

It is needless to observe that, for the most part, the Tartars do not carry very far their geographical studies. The west means with them simply Thibet and some adjacent countries, which they hear mentioned by the Lamas, who have made the pilgrimage to Lha-Ssa. They firmly believe that beyond Thibet there is nothing; there, say they, is the end of the world; beyond, there is merely a shoreless ocean.

When we had satisfied all the inquiries of the red button, we addressed some to him about the country of the Alechan, and the journey to Peking. "Every third year all the sovereigns of the world," said he, "repair to Peking, for the feast of the new year. Princes who live near, are bound to go thither every year; those who live at the extremities of the earth, go every second or third year, according to the distance they have to travel." "What is your purpose in going every year to Peking?" "We ourselves go as the retinue of our king; the king alone enjoys the happiness of prostrating himself in the presence of the Old Buddha (the Emperor)." He entered then into long details about the the ceremony of the first day of the year, and the relations between the Chinese Emperor and the tributary kings.

The foreign sovereigns, under the dominating influence of the China empire, repair to Peking; first, as an act of obeisance and submission; secondly, to pay certain rents to the Emperor, whose vassals they consider themselves. These rents, which are decorated with the fine name of offerings, are, in fact, imposts which no Tartar king would venture to refuse the payment of. They consist in camels, in horses remarkable for their beauty, and which the Emperor sends to augment his immense herds in the Tchakar. Every Tartar prince is, besides, obliged to bring some of the rarer productions of his country; deer, bear and goat venison; aromatic plants, pheasants, mushrooms, fish, etc. As they visit Peking in the depth of winter, all these eatables are frozen; so that they bear, without danger of being spoiled, the trial of a long journey, and even remain good long after they have arrived at their destination.

One of the Banners of the Tchakar is especially charged with sending to Peking, every year, an immense provision of pheasant's eggs. We asked the minister of the King of the Alechan, whether these pheasant's eggs were of a peculiar flavor, that they were so highly appreciated by the court. "They are not destined to be eaten," he answered; "the Old Buddha uses them for another purpose." "As they are not eaten, what are they used for?" The Tartar seemed embarrassed, and blushed somewhat as he replied that these eggs were used to make a sort of varnish, which the women of the imperial harem used for the purpose of smoothing their hair, and which communicates to it, they say, a peculiar luster and brilliancy. Europeans, perhaps, may consider this pomatum of pheasant's eggs, so highly esteemed at the Chinese court, very nasty and disgusting; but beauty and ugliness, the nice and the nasty, are, as everybody knows, altogether relative and conventional matters, upon which the various nations that inhabit this earth have ideas remotest from the uniform.

These annual visits to the Emperor of China are very expensive and extremely troublesome to the Tartars of the plebeian class, who are overwhelmed with enforced labor, at the pleasure of their masters, and are bound to provide a certain number of camels and horses, to carry the baggage of the king and the nobles. As these journeys take place in the depth of winter, the animals find little food, especially when, after leaving the Land of Grass, they enter upon the districts cultivated by the Chinese; and a great number of them, accordingly, die on the road. Hence, when the caravan returns, it is far from being in such good order and condition as when it started; it presents, one might almost say, merely the skeletons of the animals. Those which have still retained a little strength are laden with the baggage necessary on the way; the others are dragged along by the halter, scarcely able to move one leg before the other. It is a very sad, and, at the same time, singular thing, to see the Mongols walking on foot, and leading behind them horses which they dare not mount for fear of breaking them down.

As soon as the tributary kings are arrived at Peking, they repair to the interior of the city, where they inhabit a quarter especially set apart for them. They are generally two hundred in number, each of whom has his palace or inn, which he occupies, with his retinue. A Mandarin, a grand dignitary of the realm, superintends this quarter, and has it in charge to maintain peace and concord amongst these illustrious visitors. The tributes are transferred to the care of a special Mandarin, whom we may consider as steward of the household.

During their stay at Peking, these monarchs have no communication with the Emperor, no solemn audience. Some of them may perchance obtain admittance to the throne; but it is only upon affairs of the highest importance, above the jurisdiction of the ordinary ministers.

On the first day of the year, however, there is a solemn ceremony, at which these two hundred monarchs are admitted to a sort of contact with their suzerain and master, with him who, as they phrase it, sitting beneath the sky, rules the four seas and the ten thousand nations of the world by a single act of his will. According to the ritual which regulates the state proceedings of the Emperor of

China, he is bound to visit every year, on the first day of the first moon, the temple of his ancestors, and to prostrate himself before the tablet of his fathers. There is before the entrance of this temple a long avenue, wherein the tributary princes, who have come to Peking to render homage to the Emperor, assemble. They range themselves right and left of the peristyle, in three lines, each occupying the place appertaining to his dignity. They stand erect, grave, and silent. It is said to be a fine and imposing spectacle, to witness all these remote monarchs, attired in their silk robes, embroidered with gold and silver, and indicating, by the variety of their costumes, the different countries they inhabit, and the degrees of their dignity.

Meantime the Emperor issues in great pomp from his Yellow Town. He traverses the deserted and silent streets of Peking; for, when the Asiatic tyrant appears, every door must be closed, and every inhabitant of the town must, on pain of death, remain silent within his house. As soon as the Emperor has arrived at the temple of the ancestors, the heralds, who precede the procession, cry out, at the moment he places his foot on the first step of the stairs that lead to the gallery of the tributary kings: "Let all prostrate themselves, for here is the Lord of the earth." To this the two hundred tributary kings respond in unison: "Ten thousand congratulations!" And, having thus wished a happy new year to the Emperor, they all fall down with their faces towards the earth. Then passes through their ranks, the son of heaven, who enters the temple of the ancestors, and prostrates himself, in his turn, thrice before the tablet of his fathers. Whilst the Emperor is offering up his adoration to the spirits of his family, the two hundred monarchs remain prostrate on the earth, and they do not rise until the Emperor has again passed through their ranks; after this they re-enter their litters and return to their respective palaces.

And such is the entire and sole fruit of the long patience of these potentates, after leaving their distant countries, and enduring fatigues and dangers of every description, and a long journey through the desert; they have enjoyed the happiness of prostrating themselves in the path of the Emperor! Such a spectacle would with us Europeans be a matter of pity and disgust, for we could not comprehend

Grand Ceremony at the Ancestral Temple.

how there should be so much humility on one side, so much arrogance on the other. Yet it is the simplest thing in the world to Asiatic nations. The Emperor takes his all-mightiness as a grave matter of course; and the Tartar kings think themselves happy and honored in paying homage to it.

The prime minister of the king of the Alechan told us that a sight of the Emperor is not easily obtained. One year, when his master was ill, he was obliged to take his place at Peking, in the ceremony of the temple of the ancestors, and he then hoped to see the Old Buddha, on his way down the peristyle, but he was altogether mistaken in his expectation. As minister, the mere representative of his monarch, he was placed on the third file, so that, when the Emperor passed, he saw absolutely nothing at all. "Those who are in the first line," he said, "if they are cautiously dexterous, may manage to get a glimpse of the yellow robe of the son of heaven; but they must take heed not to lift up their heads, for such an audacity would be considered a great crime, and be punished very severely."

All the Tartar princes are pensioned by the Emperor; the sum allotted to them is a small matter, but it effects a considerable political result. The Tartar princes, in receiving their pay, consider themselves the slaves, or at least, as the servants of him who pays them; and concede, in consequence, to the Emperor the right of requiring their submission and obedience. It is about the first day of the year that the tributary sovereigns receive, at Peking, the allotted pension, which is distributed by some of the great Mandarins, who are said, by slanderous tongues, to speculate in this lucrative employment, and never fail to make enormous profits at the expense of the poor Tartars.

The minister of the king of the Alechan related, for our edification, that in a particular year, all the tributary princes received their pension in ingots of gilt copper. All found it out at once, but were fain to keep silence, afraid to make public an affair that might result in a catastrophe, compromising, not only the highest dignitaries of the empire, but the Tartar kings themselves. As, in fact, the latter were supposed to receive their money from the hands of the Emperor himself, a complaint would, in some sort, have been to charge the Old Buddha, the son of heaven, with being a coiner. They received accordingly their copper ingots with a prostration, and it was not until they returned into their own countries, that they declared, not indeed that they had been cheated, but that the Mandarins, charged with distributing the money, had been the dupes of the Peking bankers. The Tartar Mandarin who related the adventure, gave us completely to understand that neither the Emperor, nor the courtiers, nor the Mandarins, had anything to do with the affair. We took good care not to undeceive him; as to us, who had no great faith in the probity of the government of Peking, we were convinced that the Emperor had regularly swindled the Tartar kings. We were confirmed in this opinion by the fact that the period of this adventure coincided with the British war; when, as we knew, the Emperor was in the last extremity, and knew not where to get the money necessary to keep from starving the handful of soldiers who were charged with the preservation of the integrity of the Chinese territory.

The visit of the three Mandarins of the Alechan was not

only pleasant on account of the narrative they gave us of the relations of the Tartar kings with the Emperor, but it was of essential utility to us. When they understood that we were directing our steps towards the West, they asked us whether we intended passing through the district of the Alechan. On our answering in the affirmative, they dissuaded us from the project; they told us that our animals would perish there, for not a single pasturage was to be met with. We already knew that the Alechan is a tract still more barren than the Ortous. It consists, in fact, of chains of lofty mountains of sand, where you may travel sometimes for whole days together, without seeing a single blade of vegetation. Some narrow valleys, here and there, alone offer to the flocks a few thorny and wretched plants. On this account the Alechan is very thinly inhabited, even in comparison with the other parts of Mongolia.

The Mandarins told us that this year the drought which had been general throughout Tartary had rendered the district of the Alechan almost uninhabitable. They assured us that at least one-third of the flocks had perished of hunger and thirst, and that the remainder were in a wretched state. For their journey to Peking, they had, they said, chosen the best they could find in the country; and we might have observed that the animals of the caravan were very different indeed from those we had seen in Tchakar. The drought, the want of water and pastures, the destruction of the flocks—all this had given birth to an utter state of misery, whence, again, numerous bands of robbers who were ravaging the country, and robbing travelers. They assured us that, being so few in number, it would not be wise for us to enter upon the Alechan mountains, particularly in the absence of the principal authorities.

On receiving this information, we resolved not to retrace our steps, for we were too far advanced, but to diverge a little from our route. The night was far advanced ere we thought of taking rest; we had scarcely slept a few minutes, in fact, when the day broke. The Tartars saddled their steeds, and after having wished us peace and happiness, dashed off at full gallop, to overtake the great caravan which preceded them.

As for us, before setting out, we unrolled the excellent map of the Chinese Empire, published by M. Andriveau-

Goujon, and sought upon it to what point we ought to direct our steps, so as to avoid the wretched district of the Alechan, without, however, deviating too much from our route. After looking at the map, we saw no other way than to recross the Yellow River, to pass the Great Wall of China, and to travel across the Chinese province of Kan-Sou, until we arrived among the Tartars of the Koukou-Noor. Formerly this determination would have made us tremble. Accustomed as we had been to live privately in our Chinese christendom, it would have seemed to us impossible to enter the Chinese empire alone, and without the care of a catechist. At that time it would have seemed to us clear as the day, that our strangulation, and the persecution of all the Chinese missions, would have been the certain result of our rash undertaking. Such would have been our fears formerly, but the time of our fear was gone. Indurated by our two months' journey, we had come to the persuasion that we might travel in China with as much safety as in Tartary. The stay that we had already made in several large commercial towns, compelled as we had been to manage our own affairs, had rendered the Chinese manners and customs more familiar to us. The language presented to us no difficulties; besides being able to speak the Tartar idiom, we were familiar with the colloquial phrases of the Chinese, a very difficult attainment to those who reside in the missions, because the Christians there seek to flatter them by only employing, in the presence of the missionaries, the short vocabulary of words that they have studied in books. Besides these purely moral and intellectual advantages, our long journey had been useful in a physical point of view; the rain, the wind, and the sun, which had during two months raged against our European tint, had in the end embrowned and tanned it so, that we looked quite like wild men of the wood in this respect. The fear of being recognized by the Chinese now no longer troubled us.

We told Samdadchiemba that we should cease, in a few days, to travel in the Land of Grass, and that we should continue our route through the Chinese empire. "Travel among the Chinese!" said the Dchiahour; "very well. There are good inns there. They boil good tea there. When it rains, you can go under shelter. During the night, you are not disturbed by the blowing of the north wind.

But in China, there are ten thousand roads; which shall we take? Do we know which is the best?" We made him look at the map, pointing out all the places which we should have to pass before we reached Koukou-Noor. We even reduced, for his edification, into lis, all the distances from one town to the other. Samdadchiemba looked at our small geographical chart with perfect enthusiasm. "Oh," said he, "how sincerely I regret that I did not study while I was in the Lamasery; if I had listened to my master, if I had paid more attention, I might perhaps now understand the description of the world, that is here drawn on this piece of paper. With this, one can go everywhere, without asking the way. Is it not so?" "Yes, everywhere," answered we; "even to your own family." "How is that? is my country also written down here?" and as he spoke he bent over the chart, so as entirely to cover it with his huge frame. "Stand aside and we will show you your country. Look; do you see this little space beside that green line? That is the country of the Dchiahours, which the Chinese call the Three Valleys (San-Tchouen). Your village must be here; we shall pass not more than two days' journey from your house." "Is it possible?" cried he, striking his forehead; "shall we pass two days' journey from my house? Do you say so? How can that be? Not more than two days' journey! In that case, when we are near it, I will ask my spiritual fathers' permission to go and see once more my country." "What can you have to do now in the Three Valleys?" "I will go and see what is doing there. It is eighteen years since my departure from my house. I will go and see if my old mother is still there; and if she is alive, I will make her enter into the Holy Church. As for my two brothers, who knows whether they will have enough sense not to believe any longer in the transmigrations of Buddha. Ah, yes," added he after a short pause, "I will make a little tea, and we will talk this matter over again."

Samdadchiemba was no longer with us; his thoughts had flown to his native land. We were obliged to remind him of his real position,—"Samdadchiemba, you need not make any tea; and just now, instead of talking, we must fold up our tent, load the camels, and proceed on our way. Look; the sun is already high in the heavens: if we do not get on, we shall never reach the Three Valleys." "True," cried he; and springing up he set himself busily about making preparations for our departure.

On resuming our route, we abandoned the direction towards the west, which we had strictly followed during our journey, and diverged a little to the south. After having continued our march for half the day, we sat down for a while under a rock to take our repast. As usual, we dined on bread and water; and what bread and water! Dough half baked, and brackish water, which we had to draw up with the sweat of our brow, and to carry about with us during our journey.

Towards the conclusion of our repast, while we were trying to scrape together a few grains of tobacco in our snuff phials, by way of dessert, we saw coming towards us a Tartar on a camel; he seated himself beside us. After having wished each other peace, we let him smell at our empty snuff phial, and then offered him a little loaf baked in the ashes. In an instant he had swallowed the bread, and taken three sniffs of snuff.

We questioned him about the route; he told us that if we followed the same direction we should arrive in two days at the Yellow River, on crossing which, we should enter the Chinese territory. This information gave us great satisfaction, for it perfectly agreed with our map. We asked him if water was far off. "Yes," answered he, "the wells are distant. If you encamp again to-day, you will find a cistern on the way; but there is little water, and that is very bad. Formerly it was an excellent well, but it is now abandoned, for a tchutgour (demon) has corrupted its waters."

This information induced us to proceed at once, for we had no time to lose, if we desired to arrive before night. The Mongol mounted his camel, which bounded across the desert, while our little caravan continued slowly its uniform and monotonous march.

Before sunset, we arrived at the indicated cistern, when we pitched our tent, as there was no hope of finding further on better water; besides, we fancied the cistern might perhaps turn out less diabolical than the Tartar had pretended it to be.

While we were lighting the fire, the Dchiahour went to draw water; he returned in a few moments, saying that it was unfit to be drunk; that it was mere poison. He brought a basin full with him, that we might taste it and judge for ourselves.

The stench of this dirty, muddy water was, indeed, intolerable; and on the surface of the nauseous stuff, we saw floating; a sort of oily drop, which infinitely increased our disgust. We had not the courage to raise it to our lips; we were satisfied with its sight, and, above all, with its smell.

Still we must either drink or die with thirst; we accordingly resolved to make the best we could of this Cistern of the Devil, as it is called by the Tartars. We collected roots, which were growing abundantly around it, half buried in the sand; a few moments' labor supplied us with an ample provision of them. Then, first of all, we made some charcoal which we broke into small pieces; next we filled our kettle with the muddy, stinking water, placed it upon the fire, and when the water boiled, threw in a quantity of the charcoal.

While we were engaged upon this chemical operation, Samdadchiemba, seated beside the kettle, kept every moment asking us what sort of soup we intended to make with all those detestable ingredients. We gave him, by way of reply, a complete dissertation upon the discoloring and disinfecting properties of charcoal. He listened to our scientific statement with patience, but appeared in no degree convinced by it. His eyes were fixed upon the kettle, and it was easy to see, from the skeptical expression of his features, that he had no sort of expectation or idea that the thick water bubbling in the kettle could at all become a clear and limpid fluid.

By and by, we poured out the liquid thus prepared, and filtered it through an impromptu linen sieve. The water realized was not, indeed, delicious, but it was drinkable, having deposited all its salt and all its ill odor. We had more than once, on our journey, used water in no degree superior.

Samdadchiemba was perfectly intoxicated with enthusiasm. Had he not been a Christian, he would assuredly have taken us for living Buddhas. "The Lamas," said he, "pretend they have all knowledge and all power in their prayer-books; but I am certain they would have died of thirst, or been poisoned, had they only had the water of this cistern to make tea with. They have no more notion than a sheep how to render this bad water good." And then he overwhelmed us with all sorts of odd questions about the natural properties of things. In relation to the purification of water which we had just operated, he asked whether by rubbing his face hard with the charcoal, he could make it as white as ours; but then, when his eyes turned to his hands, still black with the charcoal he had just broken up, he himself laughed immensely at the idea he had propounded.

Night had set in before we had completed the distillation of the water we required. We then made abundance of tea, and the evening was occupied in drinking it. We contented ourselves with infusing a few pinches of oatmeal in the tea, for the ardent thirst which devoured us absorbed all desire to eat. After having deluged our inward man, we sought repose.

We had scarcely, however, stretched ourselves on the turf, when an extraordinary and altogether unexpected noise threw us into a state of stupor. It was a long, lugubrious, deep cry that seemed approaching our tent. We had heard the howl of wolves, the roar of tigers and of bears; but these in no way resembled the sound which now affrighted our ears. It was something like the bellowing of a bull, but crossed with tones so strange and unintelligible, that we were utterly panic-stricken. And we were all the more surprised and confounded, because everybody had assured us that there were no wild beasts of any kind in the whole Ortous country.

Our embarrassment was becoming serious. We were in fear not only for our animals, which were tied round the tent, but also on our own account. As the noise did not cease, but, on the contrary, seemed to approach nearer and nearer, we got up, not indeed, to go forth in search of the villainous beast that was thus disturbing our repose, but in order to try to frighten it. To this intent all three of us set to work, shouting at the pitch of our lungs; then we stopped and so did the beast. After a moment's silence, the roaring was heard once more, but at a considerable distance. We conjectured that in our turn we had frightened the animal, and this somewhat reassured us.

The cries once more approaching, we piled up some brushwood at a few paces from the tent, and made a bonfire. The light, instead of deterring the unknown monster, seemed rather to attract it; and before long, by the flame of the brushwood, we could distinguish the outline of what appeared to be a great quadruped, of reddish hue, the aspect of which, however, as near as we could judge, was by no means so ferocious as its voice. We ventured to advance towards it, but as we advanced, it retreated. Samdadchiemba, whose eyes were very sharp, and accustomed to the desert, assured us that the creature was either a dog or a stray calf.

Our animals were, at the very least, as absorbed with the subject as ourselves. The horse and the mule pointed their ears, and dug up the earth with their hoofs, while the camels, with outstretched necks and glaring eyes, did not for an instant remove their gaze from the spot whence these wild cries issued.

In order to ascertain precisely with what creature we had to do, we diluted a handful of meal in a wooden dish, and placing this at the entrance of the tent, withdrew inside. Soon we saw the animal slowly advance, then stop, then advance again. At last it came to the dish, and with the most remarkable rapidity, lapped up the supper we had prepared for it. We now saw that it was a dog of immense size. After having thoroughly licked and polished the empty dish, it lay down, without ceremony, at the entrance of the tent; and we forthwith followed its example, glad to have found a protector in the apprehended foe.

Next morning, upon awaking, we were able to examine at leisure the dog which, after having so alarmed us, had so unreservedly attached itself to us. Its color was red, its size immense; its excessive meagerness showed that it had been wandering about homeless for some time past. A dislocated leg, which it dragged along the ground, communicated to it a sort of swinging motion, which added to its formidable effect. But it was especially alarming when it sent forth its loud fierce voice. Whenever we heard it, we instinctively looked at the animal whence it proceeded, to see whether it really belonged to the canine race.

We resumed our route, and the new Arsalan accompanied us, its general position being a few paces in advance of the caravan, as though to show us the way, with which it appeared to be tolerably familiar.

After two days' journey we reached the foot of a chain of mountains, the summits of which were lost in the clouds.

We set about ascending them, however, courageously, for we hoped that beyond them we should find the Yellow River. That day's journey was very painful, especially to the camels, for every step was upon sharp, rugged rock; and their feet, accordingly, were very speedily bleeding. We ourselves, were too absorbed with the strange, fantastic aspect of the mountains we were traversing to think of the toil they occasioned us.

In the hollows and chasms of the precipices formed by these lofty mountains, you see nothing but great heaps of mica and laminated stones, broken, bruised, and in some cases absolutely pulverized. This wreck of slate and schist must have been brought into these abysses by some deluge, for it in no way belongs to the mountains themselves, which are of granite. As you approach the summits the mountains assume forms more and more fantastic. You see great heaps of rock piled one upon the other, and apparently cemented together. These rocks are almost entirely encrusted with shells and the remains of a plant resembling seaweed; but that which is most remarkable is that these granitic masses are cut and torn and worn in every direction, presenting a ramification of holes and cavities, meandering in a thousand complicated turns and twists, so that you might imagine all the upper portion of each mountain to have been subjected to the slow and destructive action of immense worms. Sometimes in the granite you find deep impressions, that seem the molds of monsters, whose forms they still closely retain.

As we gazed upon all these phenomena, it seemed to us that we were traveling in the bed of some exhausted ocean. Everything tended to the belief that these mountains had undergone the gradual action of the sea. It is impossible to attribute all you see there to the influence of mere rain, or still less to the inundations of the Yellow River, which, however prodigeous they may be, can never have attained so great an elevation. The geologists who affirm that the deluge took place by sinking, and not by a depolarization of the earth, might probably find in these mountains good argument in favor of their system.

On reaching the crest of these mountains we saw beneath us the Yellow River, rolling its waves majestically from south to north. It was now near noon, and we hoped that same evening to pass the river, and sleep in one of the inns of the little town of Che-Tsui-Dze, which we perceived on the slope of a hill beyond the river.

We occupied the whole afternoon in descending the rugged mountain, selecting as we went, the places right and left that seemed more practicable than the rest. At length we arrived, and before nightfall, on the banks of the Yellow River, our passage across which was most successfully effected. In the first place, the Mongol Tartars who rented the ferry oppressed our purse less direfully than the Chinese ferrymen had done. Next, the animals got into the boat without any difficulty. The only grievance was that we had to leave our lame dog on the bank, for the Mongols would not admit it on any terms, insisting upon the rule that all dogs must swim across the river, the boat being destined solely for men, or for animals that cannot swim. We were fain to submit to the prejudice.

On the other side of the Yellow River we found ourselves in China, and bade adieu for awhile to Tartary, to the desert, and to the nomadic life.

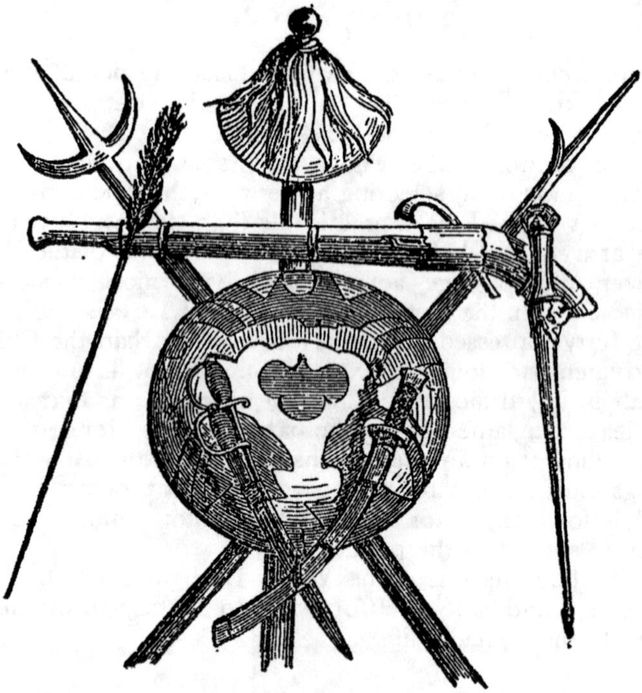

Chinese and Tartar Arms.

CHAPTER XI.

Sketch of the Tartar Nations.

THE Tartars, descended from the ancient Scythians, have preserved to this day the dexterity of their ancestors in archery and horsemanship. The early part of their history is veiled in obscurity, enveloped as they are by the wonders and prodigies of the exploits of their first conqueror, Okhous-Han, who seems to be the Madyes of Herodotus. This illustrious leader of the Scythian hordes carried his arms into Syria, and reached even the confines of Egypt.

The Chinese annals frequently mention certain nomad tribes, which they call Hioung-Nou, and which are no other than the Huns. These wandering and warlike tribes gradually extended themselves, and finished by covering the immense deserts of Tartary from east to west. Thenceforward they made continual incursions on their neighbors, and on several occasions made attacks on the frontiers of the empire. It was on such an occasion that Thisin-Chi-Hoang-Ti had the Great Wall built in the year 213 B. C. About 134 B. C. the Huns, under the conduct of Lao-Chan, their emperor, made an attack on the Tartars Youei-Tchi (the Getæ), who dwelt on the confines of the province of Chen-Si. After a series of long and terrible conflicts, Lao-Chan defeated them, slew their chief, and made of his head a drinking cup, which he wore suspended from his girdle. The Getæ did not choose to submit to the victors, and preferred going elsewhere in search of another country. They divided into two principal bands. One advanced towards the northwest, and took possession of the plains situated upon the banks of the river Ili, beyond the glaciers of the Moussour mountains ; this is that part of Tartary which is now called the Tourgout. The other division marched southwards, associated with it in its course several other tribes, and reached the regions watered by the Indus. There it laid waste the kingdom founded by the successors of Alexander, strove for some time against the Parthians, and finished by establishing itself in Bactriana. The Greeks call these Tartar tribes Indo-Scythians.

Meanwhile divisions arose among the Huns ; and the Chinese, ever politic and cunning, took advantage of this circumstance to enfeeble them. Towards the year 48 of our era, the Tartar empire was divided into northern and southern. Under the dynasty of Han, the Northern Huns were completely defeated by the Chinese armies. They were obliged to abandon the regions wherein they had settled, and proceeded in large numbers towards the west, to the borders of the Caspian Sea ; here they spread themselves over the countries watered by the Volga, and round the Palus Mæotis.

They commenced in 376 their formidable irruptions upon the Roman empire. They began by subduing the territory of the Alani, a nomad and pastoral people like themselves ; some of these sought réfuge in the Circassian mountains, others migrated further west, and finally settled on the shores of the Danube. Later, they drove before them the Suevi, the Goths, the Gepidæ, and the Vandals, and with these advanced to ravage Germany, in the beginning of the fifth century. These large hordes of barbarians resembling waves, one driven on by the other, thus formed, in their destructive course, a fearful torrent, which finally inundated Europe.

The Southern Huns, who had remained in Tartary, were for a long time weakened by the dispersion of their northern countrymen; but they recovered by insensible degrees, and again became terrible to the Chinese: though they did not acquire a political and historical importance till the time of the famous Tchinggiskhan, towards the close of the twelfth century.

The power of the Tartars, long confined within the desert steppes of Mongolia, broke at length its bonds, and innumerable armies might be seen descending from the lofty table-lands of Central Asia, and precipitating themselves with fury on horrified nations. Tchinggiskhan carried pillage and death even to the most remote regions. China, Tartary, India, Persia, Syria, Muscovy, Poland, Hungary, Austria—all these countries successively felt the terrible blows of the victorious Tartar. France, Italy, and the other regions further west, escaped with their fear.

In the year 1260 of our era, Khan-Khoubilai, grandson of Tchinggis, who had commenced the conquest of China, succeeded in subduing that vast empire. It was the first time that it had passed under the yoke of foreigners. Khoubilai died at Peking in the year 1294, aged eighty. His empire was, without dispute, the largest that had ever existed. Chinese geographers state that, under the Mongol dynasty of the Youen, the empire northwards went beyond the In-Chan mountains; westwards it extended beyond the Gobi or sandy desert; to the east, it was terminated by the countries situated on the left of the river Siao; and in the southern direction it reached the shores of the Youé Sea. It is obvious that this description does not include the countries tributary to the empire. Thibet, Turkestan, Muscovy, Siam, Cochin China, Tonking, and Corea, acknowledged the supremacy of the Grand Khan of the Tartars, and faithfully paid him tribute. Even European nations were, from time to time, insolently summoned to acknowledge the Mongol supremacy. Haughty and threatening letters were sent to the Pope, to the King of France, to the Emperor, commanding them to send as tribute the revenues of their states to the depths of Tartary. The descendants of Tchinggiskhan, who reigned in Muscovy, Persia, Bactriana, and Sogdiana, received investiture from the Emperor of Peking, and undertook nothing of importance without first giving him notice. The diplomatic papers which the King of Persia sent, in the thirteenth century, to Philip the Fair, are a proof of this dependence. On these precious monuments, which are preserved to this day in the archives of France, are seals in Chinese characters, which testify the supremacy of the Grand Khan of Peking over the sovereigns of Persia.

The conquests of Tchinggiskhan and of his successors; and, in later times, those of Tamerlan or Timour, which transferred the seat of the Mongol empire to Samarcand, contributed, in as great, and perhaps a greater degree than the Crusades, to renew the intercourse of Europe with the most distant states of the East, and favored the discoveries which have been so useful to the progress of the arts, of the sciences, and of navigation.

On this subject, we will quote in this place, an interesting passage from the Memoirs which M. Abel Rémusat published in 1824, on the political relations of the Christian princes, and particularly of the Kings of France with the Mongol Emperors :—

"The lieutenants of Tchinggiskhan, and of his first successors, on arriving in Western Asia, did not seek at first, to contract any alliance there. The princes, whose domains they entered, silently permitted the impost of a tribute; the rest were required to submit. The Georgians and Armenians were among the first. The Franks of Syria, the Kings of Hungary, the Emperor himself, had to repel their insolent demands. The Pope was not exempted, by the supremacy he enjoyed in relation to the other Christian princes; nor the King of France, by the high renown he enjoyed throughout the East. The terror which the Tartars inspired, precluded a fitting answer to their demands. The course resorted to was conciliation, the seeking their alliance, and the endeavoring to rouse them against the Moslems. The latter attempt would scarcely have been successful, had not the Christians in the East, who, by adhesion as vassals, had obtained credit at the courts of their generals and their princes, zealously employed themselves in the matter. The Mongols were induced at last to undertake war against the Sultan of

Egypt. Such were the relations with this nation during the first period, which lasted from 1224 to 1262.

"In the second period, the Khalifat was destroyed; a Mongol principality was founded in Persia: it bordered on the states of the Sultan of Egypt. A sanguinary rivalry arose between the two countries, which the Eastern Christians did all in their power to irritate. The Mongol empire was divided. Those of Persia had need of auxiliaries, which their Armenian vassals procured for them: these auxiliaries were the Franks. From this time, their power declined more and more; and ere long it was annihilated. Fresh crusades might restore it. The Mongols excited these in the West. They joined their exhortations to those of the Georgians, Armenians, of the wreck of the crusaders, who had taken refuge in Cyprus, and to those of the sovereign pontiffs. The first Tartars had commenced by threats; the last came to offers, and even descended to supplications. Twenty ambassadors were sent by them to Italy, France, and England; and it was no fault of theirs that the fire of the holy wars was not rekindled, and extended over Europe and Asia. These diplomatic attempts, the recital of which forms, so to speak, an epilogue to the transmarine expeditions, scarcely noticed by those who have written their history, and, indeed, unknown to most of them, would deserve perhaps, our fixed attention. We should have to collect facts, resolve difficulties, and place in a clear point of view the political system to which the negotiations with the Tartars belong. Specialties of this class could not be appreciated, whilst they were considered isolately, and without examining them one with another. We might doubt, with Voltaire and De Guignes, that a king of the Tartars had met Saint Louis with offers of service. This fact might seem not tenable, and its recital paradoxical. Yet such skepticism would be unreasonable, after we had seen that the Mongols had acted upon that principle for fifty years; and when we are assured, by reading contemporary writings, and by the inspection of original monuments, that this conduct was natural on their part, that it entered into their views, that it conformed to their interests, and that it is explained by the common rules of reason and policy.

"The series of events which are connected with these negotiations serves to complete the history of the Crusades;

but the part they may have had in the great moral revolution, which soon followed the relations they occasioned between people hitherto unknown to each other, are facts of an importance more general and still more worthy of our particular attention. Two systems of civilization had become established at the two extremities of the ancient continent, as the effect of independent causes, without communication, and consequently without mutual influence. All at once the events of war and political combinations bring into contact these two great bodies, long strangers to each other. The formal interviews of ambassadors are not the only occasions which brought them together. Other occasions more private, but also more efficacious, were established by imperceptible, but innumerable ramifications, by the travels of a host of individuals, attracted to the two extremities of the earth, with commercial views, in the train of ambassadors or armies. The irruption of the Mongols, by throwing everything into agitation, neutralized distance, filled up intervals, and brought the nations together; the events of war transported millions of individuals to an immense distance from the places where they were born. History has recorded the voyages of kings, of ambassadors, of missionaries. Sempad, the Orbelian; Hayton, King of Armenia; the two Davids, Kings of Georgia; and several others were led by political motives to the depths of Asia. Yeroslaf, Grand Duke of Sousdal and vassal of the Mongols, like the other Russian princes, came to Kara-Koroum, where he died of poison, it was said, administered by the Empress herself, the mother of the Emperor Gayouk. Many monks, Italians, French, Flemings, were charged with diplomatic missions to the Grand Khan. Mongols of distinction came to Rome, Barcelona, Valencia, Lyons, Paris, London, Northampton; and a Franciscan of the kingdom of Naples was Archbishop of Peking. His successor was a professor of theology of the Faculty of Paris. But how many others, less celebrated, were led in the train of those men, either as slaves, or impelled by the desire of gain, or by curiosity, to countries hitherto unexplored. Chance has preserved the names of a few. The first envoy who came on the part of the Tartars to the King of Hungary was an Englishman, banished from his country for certain crimes, and who, after having wandered throughout Asia, had finally taken service among the

Mongols. A Flemish Cordelier met in the depth of Tartary a womân of Metz, named Paquette, who had been carried away from Hungary, a Parisian goldsmith whose brother was established in Paris on the Grand Pont, and a young man from the environs of Rouen, who had been present at the capture of Belgrade; he saw there also Russians, Hungarians, and Flemings. A singer, named Robert, after traveling through the whole of Eastern Asia, returned to find a grave in the Cathedral of Chartres. A Tartar was a helmet-maker in the armies of Philip the Fair. Jean de Plan-Carpin met near Gayouk, with a Russian gentleman, whom he calls Temer, who served as interpreter. Several merchants of Breslau, Poland, and Austria, accompanied him in his journey to Tartary; others returned with him through Russia; these were Genoese, Pisans, and two merchants of Venice whom chance had brought to Bokhara. They were induced to go in the suite of a Mongol ambassador, whom Houlagou had sent to Khoubilai. They sojourned several years in China and Tartary, took letters from the Grand Khan to the Pope, and returned to the Grand Khan, bringing with them the son of one of their number, the celebrated Marco-Polo, and quitted once more the Court of Khoubilai to return to Venice. Travels of this kind were not less frequent in the succeeding age. Of this number are those of John de Mandeville, an English physician; of Oderic of Friuli; of Pegoletti; of Guillaume de Boutdeselle, and several others. We may be certain that the journeys which have been recorded are but a small portion of those which were performed, and that there were at that period more people able to make a long journey than to write an account of it. Many of these adventurers must have established themselves and died in the countries they went to visit. Others returned to their country as obscure as when they left it; but with their imaginations full of what they had seen, relating it all to their families and friends, and doubtless with exaggerations; but leaving around them, amidst ridiculous fables, a few useful recollections and traditions productive of advantage. Thus were sown in Germany, in Italy, in France, in the monasteries, among the nobility, and even in the lowest grades of society, precious seeds destined to bud at a later period. All these obscure travelers, carrying the arts of their native country to distant lands, brought back other information about these no less precious, and thus effected, unconsciously, exchanges more productive of good than all those of commerce. By this means not merely the traffic in silks, in porcelains, in commodities from Hindostan, was made more extensive and more practicable, opening new routes to industry and commerce; but, that which was far more valuable, foreign manners and customs of before unknown nations, extraordinary productions, were presented to the European mind, confined, since the fall of the Roman empire, within too narrow a circle. Men began to have an idea that, after all, there was something worthy of notice in the finest, the most populous and the most anciently civilized of the four quarters of the world. People began to think of studying the arts, the religions, the languages of the nations who inhabited it, and there was even a proposition to establish a professorship of the Tartar language in the University of Paris. Romantic narratives, reduced by discussion within reasonable proportions, diffused in all directions juster and more varied information: the world seemed opening towards the East. Geography made immense strides, and ardor of discovery become the new form assumed by the adventurous spirit of Europeans. The idea of another hemisphere ceased, as soon as our own became better known, to present itself to the mind as a paradox destitute of all probability, and it was in going in search of the Zipangri of Marco-Polo that Christopher Columbus discovered the New World.

"I should make too great a digression, were I to investigate what were in the East the effects of the Mongol irruption, the destruction of the Khalifat, the extermination of the Bulgarians, of the Komans, and other northern nations. The decline of the population of Upper Asia, so favorable to the reaction by which the Russians, hitherto the vassals of the Tartars, subdued in their turn all the nomads of the North; the submission of China to a foreign yoke; the definitive establishment of the Indian religion in Thibet and Tartary; all these events deserve to be studied in detail. I will not even pause to inquire what might have been the results, to the nations of Eastern Asia, of the intercourse which they had with the West. The introduction of the Indian numerals into China, a knowledge of the astronomical system of the Moslems, the translation of the New Testament and the Psalms into the Mongol language, executed by the Latin Archbishop of *Khan Balik* (Peking), the foundation of the lamanical hierarchy, framed in imitation of the pontifical court, and produced by the fusion effected between the remnants of the Nestorianism established in Tartary and the dogmas of the Buddhists; such were all the innovations of which there are any traces in Eastern Asia, and therewith the commerce of the Franks has very little to do. The Asiatics are punished for their contempt of the knowledge of Europeans, by the limited results which that very scorn enables them to derive from it. To confine myself to what concerns the people of the West, and to attempt to justify what I said at the commencement of this Memoir, that the effects of the communications with the nations of Upper Asia, in the thirteenth century, had contributed indirectly to the progress of European civilization, I will conclude with a reflection, which I shall offer with the more confidence, that it is not entirely new, while, at the same time, the facts we have just investigated seem calculated to give it a sanction it had not before.

"Before the establishment of the intercourse which, first the Crusades, and then, later, the irruption of the Mongols, caused to spring up between the nations of the East and those of the West, the greater part of those inventions, which distinguished the close of the middle ages, had been known to the Asiatics for centuries. The polarity of the loadstone had been discovered and put into operation in China from the remotest antiquity. Gunpowder had been as long known to the Hindoos and the Chinese, the latter of whom had, in the tenth century, 'thunder carriages,' which seem to have been cannon. It is difficult to account in any other way for the fire-stone throwers, which are so often mentioned in the history of the Mongols. Houlagou, when he set out for Persia, had in his army a body of Chinese artillerymen. Again, the first edition of the classic books engraved on wooden boards is dated in the year 952. The institution of bank-notes, and of banking and exchange offices, took place among the Jou-Tchen in 1154. Bank-notes were adopted by the Mongols established in China; they were known to the Persians by the same name as the Chinese give them, and Josaphat Barbaro was informed in 1450 by an intelligent Tartar whom he met at Asof, and who had been on an embassy to China, that this sort of money was printed in China every year *con nuova stampa*; and this expression is remarkable enough, considering the time when Barbaro made this observation. Lastly, playing cards—into the origin of which so many learned antiquarians would not have busied themselves to inquire, were it not that it marked one of the first applications of the art of engraving on wood—were invented in China in the year 1120.

"There are, besides, in the commencement of each of these inventions, particular features which seem calculated to show their origin. I will not speak of the compass, the ancient use of which, in China, Hager seems to me successfully to have demonstrated, and which passed into Europe by means of the Crusades, previous to the irruption of the Mongols, as the famous passage in Jacques de Vitry, and some others, prove. But the oldest playing cards, those used in the *jeu de tarots*, have a marked analogy in their form, their designs, their size, their number, with the cards which the Chinese made use of. Cannons were the first fire-arms made use of in Europe; they are also, it would appear, the only fire-arms with which the Chinese were acquainted at this period. The question as to paper money appears to have been viewed in its true light by M. Langles, and after him by Hager. The first boards made use of to print upon were made of wood and stereotyped, like those of the Chinese; and nothing is more natural than to suppose that some book from China gave the idea. This would not be more surprising than the fragment of the Bible, in Gothic characters, which Father Martini discovered in the house of a Chinese at Tchang-Tcheou-Fou. We have the instance of another usage, which evidently followed the same route—it is that of the Souan-Pan, or arithmetical machine of the Chinese, which was, doubtless, introduced into Europe by the Tartars of the army of Batou, and which has so extensively pervaded Russia and Poland, that women who cannot read use nothing else in the settlement of their household accounts, and their little commercial dealings. The conjecture which gives a Chinese origin to the primitive idea of European typography is so natural, that it was propounded before there was any opportunity for collecting together all the circumstances which make it so probable.

It is the idea of Paulo Jovio, and of Mendoça, who imagine that a Chinese book may have been brought into Europe before the arrival of the Portuguese in the Indies, by the medium of the Scythians and Muscovites. It was developed by an anonymous Englishman; and carefully putting aside from the consideration the impression in movable types, which is, no doubt, an invention peculiar to the Europeans, one cannot conceive any sound objection to an hypothesis which bears so strongly the stamp of probability. But this supposition acquires a still greater degree of probability when we apply it to the totality of the discoveries in question. All were made in Eastern Asia; all were unheard-of in the West. Communication took place: it was continued for a century and a-half, and ere another century had elapsed, all these inventions were known in Europe. Their origin is veiled in obscurity. The region where they manifested themselves, the men who produced them, are equally a subject of doubt. Enlightened countries were not their theater. It was not learned men who were their authors; it was common men, obscure artisans, who lighted up, one after another, these unexpected flames. Nothing can better demonstrate the effects of a communication; nothing can be more in accordance with what we have said above as to those invisible channels, those imperceptible ramifications, whereby the science of the Eastern nations penetrated into Europe. The greater part of these inventions appear at first in the state of infancy in which the Asiatics have left them; and this circumstance alone, almost prevents our having any doubt as to their origin. Some are immediately put in practice; others remain for some time enveloped in obscurity, which conceals from us their progress, and they are taken, on their appearance, for new discoveries; all are soon brought to perfection, and, as it were, fecundated by the genius of Europeans, operating in concert, communicate to human intelligence the greatest impulse known in history. Thus, by this shock of nations, the darkness of the middle age was dispersed. Calamities, which at first aspect seemed merely destined to afflict mankind, served to arouse it from the lethargy in which it had remained for ages; and the subversion of twenty empires was the price at which Providence accorded to Europe the light of modern civilization."

The Mongol dynasty of the Youen occupied the empire

for a century. After having shone with a brilliancy, the reflection of which spread over the most remote regions, it ended with Chun-Ti, a feeble prince, more mindful of frivolous amusements than of the great inheritance which had been left by his ancestors. The Chinese regained their independence; and Tchou-Youen-Tchang, the son of a laborer, and for some time a servant in a convent of bonzes, was the founder of the celebrated dynasty of the Ming. They ascended the imperial throne in 1368, and reigned in the name of Houng-Wou.

The Tartars were massacred in great numbers in the interior of China, and the rest were driven back to their old country. The Emperor Young-Lo pursued them three several times beyond the desert, more than 200 leagues north of the Great Wall, in order to exterminate them. He could not, however, effect this object, and, dying on his return from his third expedition, his successors left the Tartars in peace beyond the desert, whence they diffused themselves right and left. The principal chiefs of the blood of Tchinggiskhan occupied, each with his people, a particular district, and gave birth to various tribes, which all formed so many petty kingdoms.

These fallen princes, ever tormented by the recollection of their ancient power, appeared several times on the frontiers of the empire, and did not cease to disquiet the Chinese princes, without, however, succeeding in their attempts at invasion.

Towards the commencement of the seventeenth century, the Mantchou Tartars having made themselves masters of China, the Mongols gradually submitted to them, and placed themselves under their sovereignty. The Oelets, a Mongol tribe, deriving their name from Oloutai, a celebrated warrior in the fourteenth century, made frequent irruptions into the country of the Khalkhas, and a sanguinary war arose between these two people. The Emperor Khang-Hi, under the pretense of conciliating them, intervened in their quarrel, put an end to the war by subjecting both parties, and extended his domination in Tartary to the frontiers of Russia; the three Khans of the Khalkhas came to make their submission to the Mantchou Emperor, who convoked a grand meeting near Tolon-Noor. Each Khan presented to him eight white horses, and one white camel; from which circumstance this tribute was called, in the Mongol language *Yousoun-Dchayan* (the nine white) ; it was agreed that they should bring every year a similar present.

At the present time the Tartar nations, more or less subject to the sway of the Mantchou emperors, are no longer what they were in the time of Tchinggiskhan and Timour. Since that epoch Tartary has been disorganized by so many revolutions; it has undergone such notable political and geographical changes, that what travelers and writers said about it in former periods no longer applies to it.

During a length of time geographers divided Tartary into three grand parts—1. Russian Tartary, extending from east to west, from the sea of Kamtchatka to the Black Sea, and from north to south, from the regions inhabited by the Tongous and Samoiede tribes, to the lakes Baikal and Aral. 2. Chinese Tartary, bounded east by the sea of Japan, south by the Great Wall of China, west by the Gobi or great sandy desert; and north, by the Baikal Lake. 3. Independent Tartary, extending to the Caspian Sea, and including in its limits the whole of Thibet. Such a division is altogether chimerical, and without any sound basis. All these immense tracts, indeed, once formed part of the great empires of Tchinggiskhan and Timour. The Tartar hordes made encampments there at their will in the course of their warlike wanderings; but now all this is completely changed, and, to form an exact idea of modern Tartary, it is necessary to modify in a great degree the notions that have been transmitted to us by the mediæval authors, and which, in default of better information, have been adopted by all the geographers, down to Malte-Brun, inclusive. To realize a definite idea about Tartary, we think that the clearest, most certain, and consequently the most reasonable rule, is to adopt the opinions of the Tartars themselves, and of the Chinese, far more competent judges of this matter than Europeans, who, having no connection with this part of Asia, are obliged to trust to conjectures which have often little to do with truth. In accordance with a universal usage, the soundness of which we were enabled to confirm in the course of our travels, we will divide the Tartar people into Eastern Tartars (Toung-Ta-Dze), or Mantchous, and Western Tartars (Si-Ta-Dze), or Mongols. The boundaries of Mantchouria are very distinct, as we have already stated. It is bounded on the north by the Kinggan mountains, which separate it from Siberia; on the south by the gulf of Phou-Hai and Corea; on the east by the sea of Japan; and on the west by the Barrier of Stakes and a branch of the Sakhalien-Oula. It would be a difficult matter to define the limits of Mongolia in an equally exact manner; however, without any serious departure from the truth, we may include them between the 75th and the 118th degrees longitude of Paris, and 35th and 50th degrees of north latitude. Great and Little Boukaria, Kalmoukia, Great and Little Thibet—all these denominations seem to us purely imaginary. We shall enter, by and by, into some details on this subject, in the second part of our travels, when we come to speak of Thibet and of the neighboring people.

The people who are comprised in the grand division of Mongolia, that we have just given, are not all to be indiscriminately considered as Mongols. There are some of them to whom this denomination can only be applied in a restricted sense. Towards the northwest, for instance, the Mongols are frequently confounded with the Moslems; and towards the south, with the Si-Fans, or Eastern Thibetians. The best way clearly to distinguish these people, is to pay attention to their language, their manners, their religion, their costume, and particularly to the name by which they designate themselves. The Mongol Khalkhas are the most numerous, the most wealthy, and the most celebrated in history. They occupy the entire north of Mongolia. Their country is of vast extent, including nearly 200 leagues from north to south, and about 500 from east to west. We will not repeat here what we have already said about the Khalkha district; we will merely add that it is divided into four great provinces, subject to four separate sovereigns. These provinces, are sub-divided into eighty-four banners, in Chinese called Ky, in Mongol Bochkhon. Princes of different ranks are at the head of each banner. Notwithstanding the authority of these secular princes, it may safely be said that the Khalkhas are all dependent on the Guison-Tamba, the Grand Lama, the Living Buddha of all the Mongol Khalkhas, who consider it an honor to call themselves Disciples of the Holy One of Kouren (*Kouré bokte ain Chabi*).

The Southern Mongols have no special designation; they

merely bear the name of the principality to which they belong. Thus they say, "Mongol of Souniout, Mongol of Gechekten," etc. Southern Mongolia comprises twenty-five principalities, which, like those of the Khalkhas, are subdivided into several Bochkhon. The principal are the Ortous, the two Toumet, the two Souniout, the Tchakar, Karatsin Oungniot, Gechekten, Barin, Nayman, and the country of the Elents.

The Southern Mongols, near the Great Wall, have little modified their manners by their constant intercourse with the Chinese. You may remark sometimes in their dress a sort of studied elegance, and in their character pretensions to the refined politeness of the Chinese. Laying aside, on the one hand, the frankness, the good-natured openness of the Mongols of the North, they have borrowed from their neighbors somewhat of their cunning and foppery.

Proceeding to the southeast, we encountered the Mongols of the Koukou-Noor or Blue Lake (in Chinese, Tsing-Hai or Blue Sea). This country is far from possessing the extent which is generally assigned to it in geographical charts. The Mongols of the Koukou-Noor only dwell around the lake, from which they derive their name; and, moreover, they are mixed up to a great extent with Si-Fans, who cannot live secure in their own country, because of the hordes of robbers that are constantly ravaging it.

To the west of the Koukou-Noor is the river Tsaidam, on whose banks encamp the numerous tribes, called Tsaidam-Mongols, who must not be confounded with the Mongols of the Koukou-Noor. Farther still, in the very heart of Thibet, we encounter other Mongol tribes. We shall say nothing about them here, as we shall have occasion to speak of them in the course of our narrative. We will revert, therefore, in some detail to the Mongols of the Koukou-Noor and the Tsaidam.

The Torgot-Tartars, who formerly dwelt near Kara-Koroum, the capital of the Mongols in the time of Tchinggis-khan, are now situated to the northwest of Mongolia. In 1672, the whole tribe, having raised their tents and assembled all their flocks, abandoned the district which had served them as a resting-place, migrated to the western part of Asia, and established themselves in the steppes between the Don and the Volga.

The Torgot princes recognized the sovereignty of the Muscovite emperors, and declared themselves their vassals. But these wandering hordes, passionately attached to the independence of their nomad life, could not long accommodate themselves to the new masters they had selected. They soon felt an aversion to the laws and regular institutions which were becoming established in the Russian empire. In 1770, the Torgots again made a general migration. Led by their chief, Aboucha, they suddenly disappeared, passed the Russian frontiers, and halted on the banks of the river Ili. This flight had been concerted with the government of Peking. The Emperor of China, who had been informed beforehand of the period of their departure, took them under his protection, and assigned to them settlements on the banks of the Ili.

The principality of Ili is now the Botany-Bay of China; thither are sent the Chinese criminals, condemned to exile by the laws of the empire. Before their arrival in these distant regions they are obliged to cross frightful deserts, and to climb the Moussour (glacier) mountains. These gigantic summits are entirely formed of icebergs, piled one on the top of the other, so that travelers cannot advance except by hewing steps out of the eternal ice. On the other side of the Moussour mountains the country, they say, is magnificent; the climate temperate enough, and the soil adapted for every kind of cultivation. The exiles have transported thither a great many of the productions of China; but the Mongols continue to follow their nomad life, and merely to pasture herds and flocks.

We had occasion to travel for some time with Lamas of Torgot; some of them arrived with us at Lha-Ssa. We did not remark, either in their costume, in their manners, or in their language, anything to distinguish them from the Mongols. They spoke a good deal about the *Oros* (Russians), but in a way to make us understand that they were by no means desirous of again becoming subject to their sway. The Torgot camels are remarkably fine, and generally much larger and stronger than those in the other parts of Mongolia.

It would be a very desirable thing to send missionaries to Ili. We believe that there would be found already formed there a numerous and fervent body of Christians. It is well known that for many years past, it is hither that the Christians who have refused to apostatize, have been exiled from all the provinces of China. The missionary who should obtain permission to exercise his zeal in the Torgot, would doubtless have to undergo great privations during his journey thither; but he would be amply compensated, by the thought of carrying the succor of religion to all those generous confessors of the faith, whom the tyranny of the Chinese government has sent to die in these distant regions.

To the southwest of Torgot is the province of Khachghar. At the present day, this district cannot at all be considered a part of Mongolia. Its inhabitants have neither the language, nor the physiognomy, nor the costume, nor the religion, nor the manners of the Mongols; they are Moslems. The Chinese, as well as the Tartars, call them Hoei-Hoei, a name by which they designate the Mussulmen who dwell in the interior of the Chinese empire. This description of Khachghar, is also applicable to the people to the south of the Celestial Mountains, in the Chinese tongue called Tien, Chan, and in Mongol, Bokte-oola (holy mountains).

Not long since the Chinese government had to sustain a terrible war against Khachghar. We are indebted for the following details to some military Mandarins who accompanied this famous and distant expedition.

The Court of Peking kept in Khachghar two grand Mandarins, with the title of Delegates Extraordinary (*Kintchai*), who were charged to guard the frontiers, and to keep an eye on the movements of the neighboring people. These Chinese officers, instead of merely watching, exercised their power with such horrible and revolting tyranny, that they wore out the patience of the people of Khachghar, who, at length, rose in a body, and massacred all the Chinese residents in the country. The news reaching Peking, the Emperor, who knew nothing of the misconduct of his officers, assembled his troops, and marched them against the Moslems. The contest was long and bloody. The Chinese government had several times to send reinforcements. The Hoei-Hoei were commanded by a hero called Tchankoeul; his stature, they say, was prodigious, and he had no weapon but an enormous club. He frequently defeated the Chinese army, and destroyed several grand military Mandarins. At length, the Emperor sent the famous Yang, who put an end to the war. The conqueror of Khachghar is a military Mandarin of the province of Chang-Tong, remarkable for his lofty stature, and above all for the prodigious length of his beard. According to the account we heard of him, his manner of fighting was singular enough. As soon as the action commenced, he tied up his beard in two great knots, in order that it might not get in his way, and then he placed himself behind his troops. There, armed with a long saber, he drove his soldiers on to combat, and massacred, without pity, those who were cowards enough to draw back. This method of commanding an army will seem somewhat peculiar; but those who have lived among the Chinese will see that the military genius of Yang was founded on a thorough knowledge of the soldiers he had to deal with.

The Moslems were defeated, and Tchankoeul was, by means of treachery, made a prisoner. He was conveyed to Peking, where he had to undergo the most barbarous and humiliating treatment, even the being exposed to the people, shut up in an iron cage, like a wild beast. The Emperor Tao-Kouang wished to see this warrior, of whom fame spoke so much, and ordered him to be brought to him. The Mandarins immediately took alarm; they were afraid lest the prisoner should reveal to the Emperor the causes which had brought about the revolt of Khachghar, and the horrible massacres which had followed it. The great dignitaries saw that these revelations would be dangerous for them, and would make them seem guilty of negligence in the eyes of the Emperor, for not having duly observed the conduct of the Mandarins who were placed in charge of distant provinces. To obviate this danger, they made the unfortunate Tchankoeul swallow a draught which took away his speech, and threw him into a disgusting state of stupor. When he appeared in the presence of the Emperor, his mouth, they say, foamed, and his visage was horrible; he could not answer any of the questions which were addressed to him. Tchankouel was condemned to be cut into pieces, and to be served up as food for the dogs.

The Mandarin Yang was loaded with favors by the Emperor, for having so happily terminated the war of Khachghar. He obtained the dignity of Batourou, a Tartar word signifying valorous. This title is the most honorable that a military Mandarin can obtain.

The Batourou Yang was sent against the English, in their last war with the Chinese; but there it would appear his tactics did not avail. During our travels in China we inquired of several Mandarins, how it was that the Batourou Yang had not exterminated the English: the answer everywhere was, that he had had compassion on them.

The numerous principalities of which Mongolia is composed, are all more or less dependent on the Mantchou Emperor, in proportion as they show more or less weakness in their relations with the Court of Peking. They may be considered as so many feudal kingdoms, giving no obedience to their sovereign beyond the extent of their fear or their interest; and indeed, what the Mantchou dynasty fears above all things, is the vicinity of these Tartar tribes. The Emperors are fully aware that, headed by an enterprising and bold chief, these tribes might successfully renew the terrible wars of other times, and once more obtain possession of the empire. For this reason, they use every means in their power to preserve the friendship of the Mongol princes, and to enfeeble the strength of these terrible nomads. It is with this view, as we have already remarked, that they patronize Lamaism, by richly endowing the Lamaseries, and by granting numerous privileges to the Lamas. So long as they can maintain their influence over the sacerdotal tribe, they are assured that neither the people nor the princes will stir from their repose.

Alliances are another means by which the reigning dynasty seeks to consolidate its power in Mongolia. The daughters and nearest relations of the Emperor, intermarrying with the royal families of Tartary, contribute to maintain between the two peoples pacific and friendly relations. Yet these princesses continue to have a great predilection for the pomp and grandeur of the imperial court. The mournful, monotonous life of the desert soon fatigues them, and they sigh for the brilliant fêtes of Peking. To obviate the inconvenience that might attend their frequent journeys to the capital, a very severe regulation has been made to moderate the wandering humor of these princesses. First, for the first ten years after their marriage, they are forbidden to come to Peking, under penalty of having the annual pension the Emperor allows to their husbands suspended. This period having elapsed, they are allowed to go to Peking but never at their own mere fancy. A tribunal is appointed to examine their reasons for temporarily quitting their family. If these are considered valid, they allow them a certain number of days, on the expiration of which they are enjoined to return to Tartary. During their stay at Peking, they are supported at the expense of the Emperor, suitably to their dignity.

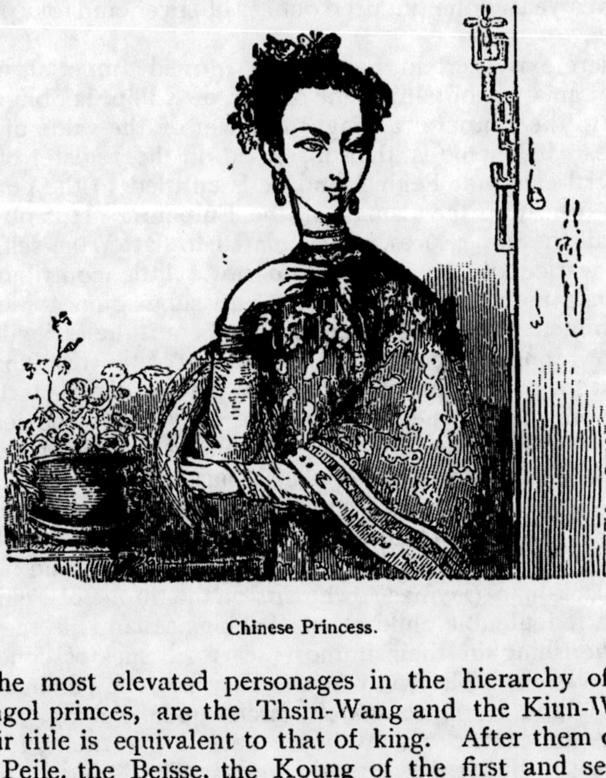

Chinese Princess.

The most elevated personages in the hierarchy of the Mongol princes, are the Thsin-Wang and the Kiun-Wang. Their title is equivalent to that of king. After them come the Peile, the Beisse, the Koung of the first and second class, and the Dchassak. These may be compared to our ancient dukes, barons, etc. We have already mentioned that the Mongol princes are bound to pay certain rents to the Emperor; but the amount of these is so small, that the Mantchou dynasty can only levy it on account of the moral effect that may result. As simple matter-of-fact, it would be nearer the truth to say that the Mantchous are the tributaries of the Mongols; for, in return for the few beasts they receive from them, they give them annually large sums of money, silken stuffs, clothes, and various articles of luxury and ornament, such as buttons, sables, peacocks' feathers, etc. Each Wang of the first degree receives annually 2,500 ounces of silver (about £800), and forty pieces of silk stuff. All the other princes are paid according to the rank they derive from the Emperor. A Dchassak, for example, receives yearly one hundred ounces of silver, and four pieces of silk.

There exist certain Lamaseries, termed Imperial, where each Lama, on obtaining the degree of Kalon, is obliged to offer to the Emperor an ingot of silver of the value of fifty ounces; his name is then inscribed on the register of the imperial clergy at Peking, and he is entitled to the pension given yearly to the Lamas of the Emperor. It is obvious that all these measures, so calculated to flatter the self-love and avarice of the Tartars, do not a little contribute to maintain their feelings of respect and submission towards a government which takes such pains to court their friendship.

The Mongols, however, of the district of the Khalkhas do not seem to be much affected by these demonstrations. They only see in the Mantchous a rival race, in possession of a prey which they themselves have never ceased to desire. We have frequently heard the Mongol Khalkhas use the most unceremonious and seditious language in speaking of the Mantchou Emperor. "They are subject," say they, "to the Guison-Tamba alone, to the *Most Holy*, and not to the black-man (layman), who sits on the throne of Peking." These redoubtable children of Tchinggiskhan still seem to be cherishing in their inmost heart schemes of conquest and invasion. They only await, they say, the command of their Grand Lama to march direct upon Peking, and to regain an empire which they believe to be theirs, for the sole reason that it was formerly theirs. The Mongol princes exact from their subjects or slaves certain tributes, which consist in sheep, and here is the absurd and unjust regulation, in accordance with which this tribute must be paid:

The owner of five or more oxen must contribute one sheep: the owner of twenty sheep must contribute one of them; if he owns forty he gives two; but they need give no more, however numerous their flocks. As may be seen, this tribute really weighs upon the poor only; the wealthy may possess a great number of cattle without being obliged to contribute more than two sheep.

Besides these regular tributes, there are others which the princes are accustomed to levy on their slaves, on some extraordinary occasions; for instance, marriages, burials, and distant voyages. On these occasions, each collection of ten tents is obliged to furnish a horse and a camel. Every Mongol who owns three cows must pay a pail of milk; if he possesses five, a pot of koumis or wine, made of fermented milk. The owner of a flock of 100 sheep furnishes a felt carpet or a tent covering; he who owns three camels must give a bundle of long cords to fasten the baggage. However, in a country where everything is subject to the arbitrary will of the chief, these regulations, as may be supposed, are not strictly observed. Sometimes the subjects are altogether exempted from their operation, and sometimes also there is exacted from them much more than the law decrees.

Robbery and murder are very severely punished among the Mongols; but the injured individuals, or their parents, are themselves obliged to prosecute the prisoner before the tribunals: the worst outrage remains unpunished if no one appears to prosecute. In the ideas of a semi-barbarous people, the man who attempts to take the property or life of any one is deemed to have committed merely a private offense, reparation for which ought to be demanded, not by the public, but by the injured party or his family. These rude notions of justice are common to China and to Thibet; and for that matter, we know that Rome herself had no other until the establishment of Christianity, which caused the right of the community to prevail over the right of the individual.

Mongolia, generally speaking, wears a gloomy and savage aspect; the eye is nowhere recreated by the charm and variety of landscape scenery. The monotony of the steppes is only interrupted by ravines, by vast rents of the earth, or by stony and barren hills. Towards the north, in the district of Khalkhas, nature is more animated; tall forests decorate the summits of the mountains, and numerous rivers water the rich pastures of the plains; but in the long winter season the earth remains buried under a thick bed of snow. Towards the Great Wall, Chinese industry glides like a serpent into the desert. Towns arise on all sides. The Land of Grass is crowned with harvests, and the Mongol shepherds find themselves driven back northwards, little by little, by the encroachments of agriculture.

Sandy plains occupy, perhaps, the greater part of Mongolia; you do not see a single tree there; some short, brittle grass, which seems to have much difficulty in issuing from this unfruitful soil, creeping briers, a few scanty tufts of heath, such is the sole vegetation and pasturage of Gobi. Water is very rarely seen; at long intervals you meet with a few deep wells, dug for the convenience of the caravans that are obliged to cross this dismal tract.

In Mongolia there are only two seasons in the year,—nine months for winter and three for summer. Sometimes the heat is stifling, particularly on the sandy steppes, but it only lasts a few days. The nights, however, are almost invariably cold. In the Mongol countries, cultivated by the Chinese, outside the Great Wall, all agricultural labor must be comprehended within three months. As soon as the earth is sufficiently thawed, they hastily set to work, or rather they do nothing but touch the surface of the ground lightly with the plow; they then immediately sow the seed; the corn grows with astonishing rapidity. Whilst they are waiting for it to come to maturity, the men are incessantly occupied in pulling up the weeds that overrun the plain. . Scarcely have they gathered in the harvest when the winter comes with its terrible cold; during this season they thresh the corn. As the cold makes vast crevices in the earth, they throw water over the surface of the threshing-floor, which freezes forthwith, and creates for the laborers a place always smooth and admirably clean.

The excessive cold which prevails in Mongolia may be attributed to three causes:—to the great elevation of the country, to the nitrous substances with which it is strongly impregnated, and to the almost entire absence of cultivation. In the places which the Chinese have cultivated the temperature has risen in a remarkable degree; the heat goes on increasing, so to speak, from year to year, as cultivation advances; so that particular grain crops, which at first would not grow at all, because of the cold, now ripen with wonderful success.

Mongolia, on account of its immense solitudes, has become the haunt of a large number of wild animals. You see at every step hares, pheasants, eagles, yellow goats, gray squirrels, foxes and wolves. It is remarkable that the wolves of Mongolia attack men rather than animals. They may be seen, sometimes, passing at full gallop through a flock of sheep, in order to attack the shepherd. About the Great Wall they frequently visit the Tartaro-Chinese villages, enter the farms, and disdaining the domestic animals they find in the yard, proceed to the inside of the house, and there select their human victims, whom they almost invariably seize by the throat and strangle. There is scarcely a village in Tartary where, every year, misfortunes of this kind do not occur. It would seem as though the wolves of this country were resolved to avenge on men the sanguinary war which the Tartars make upon their brethren.

The stag, the wild goat, the mule, the wild camel, the yak, the brown and black bear, the lynx, the ounce and the tiger, frequent the deserts of Mongolia. The Tartars never proceed on a journey, unless armed with bows, fusils and lances.

When we consider the horrible climate of Tartary, that climate ever so gloomy and frozen, we should be led to think that the inhabitants of these wild countries must be of an extremely fierce and rugged temperament: their physiognomy, their deportment, the costume they wear, all would seem to confirm this opinion. The Mongol has a flat face, with prominent cheek bones, the chin short and retiring, the forehead sunken, the eyes small and oblique, of a yellow tint, as though full of bile, the hair black and rugged, the beard scanty, the skin of a deep brown, and extremely coarse. The Mongol is of middle height, but his great leathern boots and large sheep-skin robe, seem to take away from his height, and make him appear diminutive and stumpy. To complete this portrait, we must add a heavy and ponderous gait, and a harsh, shrill, discordant language, full of frightful aspirates. Notwithstanding this rough and unprepossessing exterior, the disposition of the Mongol is full of gentleness and good nature; he passes suddenly from the most rollicking and extravagant gaiety to a state of melancholy, which is by no means disagreeable. Timid to excess in his ordinary habits; when fanaticism or the desire of vengeance arouses him, he displays in his courage an impetuosity which nothing can stay; he is candid and credulous as an infant, and he passionately loves to hear marvelous anecdotes and narratives. The meeting with a traveling Lama is always for him a source of happiness.

Aversion to toil and a sedentary life, the love of pillage and rapine, cruelty, unnatural debaucheries, are the vices which have been generally attributed to the Mongol Tartars. We are apt to believe that the portrait which the old writers have drawn of them was not exaggerated, for we always find these terrible hordes, at the period of their gigantic conquests, bringing in their train, murder, pillage, conflagration, and every description of scourge. But are the Mongols the same now that they were formerly? We believe we can affirm the contrary, at least to a great extent.

Wherever we have seen them, we have found them to be generous, frank and hospitable; inclined, it is true, like ill-educated children, to pilfer little things which excite their curiosity, but by no means in the habit of practising what is called pillage and robbery. As to their aversion for toil and a sedentary life, they are just the same as heretofore. It must also be admitted that their manners are very free, but their conduct has more in it of recklessness than of absolute corruption. We seldom find among them those unbridled and brutal debaucheries to which the Chinese are so much given.

The Mongols are strangers to every kind of industry. Some felt carpets, some rudely tanned hides, a little needlework and embroidery, are exceptions not deserving of mention. On the other hand, they possess to perfection the qualities of a pastoral and nomad people. They have the senses of sight, hearing, and scent prodigiously developed. The Mongol is able to hear at a very long distance the trot of a horse, to distinguish the form of objects, and to detect the distant scent of flocks, and the smoke of an encampment.

Many attempts have already been made to propagate Christianity among the Tartars, and we may say that they have not been altogether fruitless. Towards the end of the eighth century and in the commencement of the ninth, Timothy, patriarch of the Nestorians, sent some monks to preach the Gospel to the Hioung-Nou Tartars, who had taken refuge on the shores of the Caspian Sea. At a later period they penetrated into Central Asia, and into China. In the time of Tchinggiskhan and his successors, Franciscan and Dominican missionaries were despatched to Tartary. The conversions were numerous; even princes, it is said, and emperors were baptized. But we must not entirely credit the statements of the Tartar ambassadors, who, the more easily to draw the Christian princes of Europe into a league against the Moslems, never failed to state that their masters had been baptized, and had made profession of Christianity. It is certain, however, that at the commencement of the fourteenth century, Pope Clement V. erected at Peking an archbishopric, in favor of Jean de Montcorvin, a Franciscan missionary who preached the Gospel to the Tartars for forty-two years; he translated into the Mongol language the New Testament and the Psalms of David, and left at his death a very flourishing Christendom. We find on this subject some curious details in "Le livre de l'Estat du Grant Caan" [1] (The book of the State of the Grand Khan), extracted from a manuscript of the National Library, and published in the "Nouveau Journal Asiatique" (vol. vi.), by M. Jacquet, a learned orientalist. We conceive that it may be acceptable to quote a few passages from this production.

OF THE MINORITES WHO DWELL IN THIS COUNTRY OF CATHAY (CHINA).

"In the said city of Cambalech was an archbishop, who was called Brother John of Mount Curvin, of the order of Minorites, and he was legate there for Pope Clement V. This archbishop erected in that city aforesaid, three houses of Minorites, and they are two leagues distant from one another. He likewise instituted two others in the city of Racon, which is a long distance from Cambalech, being a journey of three months, and it is on the sea coast; and in these two places were put two Minorites as bishops. The one was named Brother Andrew of Paris, and the other, Brother Peter of Florence. These brothers, and John the Archbishop, converted many persons to the faith of Jesus

[1] This compilation was made in the fourteenth century by order of Pope John XXII.

Christ. He is a man of irreproachable life, agreeable to God and the world, and very much in the Emperor's favor. The Emperor provided him and all his people with all things necessary, and he was much beloved by both Christians and Pagans; and he certainly would have converted all that country to the Christian and Catholic faith, if the false and misbelieving Nestorian Christians had not prevented it. The archbishop had great trouble in restoring these Nestorians to the obedience of our Holy Mother the Roman Church; without which obedience, he said, they could not be saved; and on this account these Nestorian schismatics disliked him greatly. This archbishop had just departed, as it pleased God, from this life. A great multitude of Christians and Pagans attended his funeral; and the Pagans tore their funeral robes, as is their custom. And these Christians and infidels took, with great reverence, the robes of the archbishop, and held them in great respect, and as relics. He was buried there honorably, in the fashion of the faithful. They still visit his tomb with great devotion."

OF CERTAIN NESTORIAN CHRISTIAN SCHISMATICS WHO DWELL THERE.

"In the said city of Cambalech there is a sort of Christian schismatics whom they call Nestorians. They observe the customs and manners of the Greek Church, and are not obedient to the Holy Church of Rome; but they are of another sect, and are at great enmity with all the Catholic Christians who are loyal to the Holy Church of Rome aforesaid. And when the archbishop, of whom we spoke just now, built those abbeys of Minorites aforesaid, the Nestorians destroyed them in the night, and did them all the mischief in their power; for they dared not injure the said archbishop, or his brethren, or the other faithful Christians publicly and openly, because the Emperor loved them and showed them his favor. These Nestorians dwelling in the said empire of Cathay, number more than 30,000, and are very rich; but many of them fear the Christians. They have very beautiful and very holy churches, with crosses and images in honor of God and of the saints. They receive from the said Emperor several offices, and he grants them many privileges, and it is thought that if they would consent to unite and agree with these Minorites and with other good Christians who reside in this country, they might convert the whole of this country and the Emperor to the true faith."

OF THE EXTRAORDINARY FAVOR WHICH THE GRAND KHAN SHOWS TO THE SAID CHRISTIANS.

"The Grand Khan protects the Christians who in this said kingdom are obedient to the Holy Church of Rome, and makes provision for all their wants, for he shows them very great favor and love; and whenever they require anything for their churches, their crosses, or their sanctuaries, in honor of Jesus Christ, he awards it with great willingness. But they must pray to God for him and his health particularly in their sermons. And he is very anxious that they should all pray for him; and he readily allows the brethren to preach the faith of God in the churches of the infidels, which they call *vritanes,* and he also permits the infidels to hear the brethren preach; so that the infidels go there very willingly, and often with great devotion, and give the brethren much alms; and, likewise, the Emperor lends and sends his servants to aid and assist the Christians when they require their services, and so solicit the Emperor."

While the Tartars remained masters of China, Christianity made great progress in the empire. At the present day (we say it with sorrow), there is not to be found in Mongolia the least vestige of what was done in ages gone by, in favor of these nomad people. We trust, however, that the light of the Gospel will ere long shine once more in their eyes. The zeal of Europeans for the propagation of the faith will hasten the accomplishment of Noah's prophecy. Missionaries, the children of Japheth, will display their courage and devotion; they will fly to the aid of the children of Shem, and will esteem themselves happy to pass their days under the Mongol tents: "God shall enlarge Japheth, and he shall dwell in the tents of Shem."—Genes. cap. ix. v. 27.

Irrigation of the Fields.

CHAPTER XII.

Hotel of Justice and Mercy—Province of Kan-Sou—Agriculture—Great Works for the Irrigation of the Fields—Manner of Living in Inns—Great Confusion in a Town caused by our Camels—Chinese Life-guard—Mandarin Inspector of the Public Works—Ning-Hia—Historical and Topographical Details—Inn of the Five Felicities—Contest with a Mandarin, Tchong-Wei—Immense Mountains of Sand—Road to Ili—Unfavorable aspect of Kao-Tan-Dze—Glance at the Great Wall—Inquiry after the Passports—Tartars traveling in China—Dreadful Hurricane—Origin and Manners of the Inhabitants of Kan-Sou—The Dchiahours—Interview with a Living Buddha—Hotel of the Temperate Climates—Family of Samdadchiemba—Mountain of Ping-Keou—Fight between an Innkeeper and his Wife—Water-mills—Knitting—Si-Ning-Fou—House of Rest—Arrival at Tang-Keou-Eul.

Two months had elapsed since our departure from the Valley of Black Waters. During that period, we had undergone in the desert continual fatigue and privations of every kind. Our health, it is true, was not as yet materially impaired, but we felt that our strength was leaving us, and we appreciated the necessity of modifying, for a few days, our late rough manner of living. In this point of view a country occupied by Chinese could not be otherwise than agreeable, and, in comparison with Tartary, would place within our reach all sorts of comforts.

As soon as we had passed the Hoang-Ho, we entered the small frontier town called Ché-Tsui-Dze, which is only separated from the river by a sandy beach. We proceeded to take up our lodging at the Hotel of Justice and Mercy (*Jeuy-Ting*). The house was large and recently built. With the exception of a solid floor of gray tiles, the whole construction was of wood. The host received us with that courtesy and attention which are always displayed when people desire to give a character to a new establishment; and besides, the man having a most unprepossessing aspect, was anxious, probably, by his amiability of manners, to redeem his ugliness of feature; his eyes, which squinted horribly, were always turned away from the person whom he was addressing. However, if the organ of sight was defective, the organ of speech had marvelous elasticity. In his quality of an old soldier, he had seen much, heard much, and what is more, he remembered much; he was acquainted with all countries, and had had to do with all sorts of men. His loquacity was far from being troublesome to us: he gave us details of every kind, as to the places, great and small, which we had to visit before our arrival at Koukou-Noor. That part of Tartary was well known to him; for, in the military part of his career, he had served against the Si-Fan. The day after our arrival he brought us, early in the morning, a large scroll, on which were written, in order, the names of the towns, villages, hamlets, and places that we had to pass in the province of Kan-Sou; and then he proceeded to give us a description of the localities with so much enthusiasm, so much gesticulation, and in such a loud key, that he made our heads turn.

The time which was not absorbed in long interviews, partly compulsory, partly voluntary, with our host, was occupied in visiting the town. Ché-Tsui-Dze is built in the corner of an angle, formed on one side by the Alechan mountains, and on the other by the Yellow River. On its eastern bank the Hoang-Ho is bordered by dark hills, wherein are abundant coal mines, which the inhabitants work with great activity, and whence they derive their chief wealth. The suburbs of the town are occupied by great potteries, where you observe colossal urns used in families as reservoirs of water, and large stoves of admirable construction, and a large collection of vases of all shapes and sizes. There is in the province of Kan-Sou a large trade in this pottery.

At Ché-Tsui-Dze, provisions are abundant, varied, and of astonishingly moderate price. Nowhere, perhaps, can a person live so economically. At every hour of the day and night, itinerant restaurateurs bring to your house whatever provisions you need: soups, ragouts of mutton and beef, vegetables, pastry, rice, vermicelli, etc. There are dinners for every appetite, and for every purse—from the complicated banquet of the rich, to the simple and clear broth of the beggar. These restaurateurs are coming and going to and fro almost without interval. They are generally Moslems—a blue cap distinguishing them from the Chinese.

After two days repose in the Inn of Justice and Mercy, we proceeded on our way. The environs of Ché-Tsui-Dze are uncultivated. On all sides nothing is to be seen but sand and gravel, drifted by the annual inundation of the Yellow River. However, as you advance, the soil, becoming imperceptibly higher, improves. An hour's distance from the town, we crossed the Great Wall, or rather passed over some miserable ruins that still mark the ancient site of the celebrated rampart of China. The country soon becomes magnificent, and we could not but admire the agricultural genius of the Chinese people. The part of Kan-Sou which we were traversing is especially remarkable by its ingenious and extensive works for facilitating the irrigation of the fields.

By means of creeks cut in the banks of the Yellow River, the waters are conveyed into broad artificial canals; these again supply others of a larger size, which, in their turn, fill the ditches with which all the fields are surrounded. Sluices, great and small, admirable in their simplicity, serve to raise the water and to carry it over all the inequalities of the land. The distribution of the water is perfectly arranged; each landowner waters his fields in his turn, and no one is allowed to open his flood-gate before his regularly appointed time.

Few villages are met with; but you observe, in all directions, farms of various sizes separated from one another by meadows. The eye does not rest upon either groves or pleasure-gardens. Except a few large trees round the dwellings, all the land is devoted to the cultivation of corn;

they do not even reserve a space for stacking the harvest, but pile it up on the tops of the houses, which are always flat-roofed. On the days of the general irrigation, the country gives you a perfect idea of those famous inundations of the Nile, the descriptions of which have become so classic. The inhabitants traverse their fields in small skiffs, or in light carts with enormous wheels, and generally drawn by buffaloes.

These irrigations, so conducive to the fertility of the land, are a great pest to travelers. The roads are generally covered with water and mud, so that you cannot use them, but must labor along the mounds which form the boundaries of the fields. When you have to guide camels over such roads, it is the height of misery. We did not advance a single step without the fear of seeing our baggage fall into the mud; and more than once such an accident did occur, throwing us into infinite embarrassment. In fact, that the misfortune did not oftener befall us, was solely attributable to the skill in mud-walking which our camels had acquired in their apprenticeship amongst the marshes of the Ortous.

In the evening of our first day's march, we arrived at a small village called Wang-Ho-Po; we had expected to find here the same facility in obtaining provisions as at Ché-Tsui-Dze, but we were soon undeceived. The customs were not the same; those amiable restaurateurs, with their baskets of ready-dressed viands, were no longer visible. Forage-dealers were the only persons who came to offer their goods. We therefore commenced by giving the animals their rations, and afterwards went into the village to see if we could find any provisions for our own supper. On our return to the inn, we were obliged to cook our own supper; the host merely furnished us with water, coal, and a meal-kettle. Whilst we were peaceably occupied in appreciating the result of our culinary labors, a great tumult arose in the courtyard of the inn. It was occasioned by a caravan of camels, conducted by Chinese merchants, who were going to the town of Ning-Hia. Destined for the same route as themselves, we soon entered into conversation. They told us that the direct road to Ning-Hia was so bad as to be impracticable, even for the best camels; but they added, they were acquainted with a cross road shorter and less dangerous, and they invited us to go with them. As they were to depart in the night, we called the host in order to settle our account. After the Chinese fashion, when sapeks are in question, on one side they ask much, on the other they offer too little; then there is a long squabble, and after mutual concessions you come to an agreement. As they thought us Tartars, it was quite a matter of course with them to ask us nearly triple the just amount: the result was, that the dispute was twice as long as it ordinarily is. We had to discuss the matter vigorously; first, for ourselves, then for our beasts, for the room, the stabling, the watering, the kettle, the coal, the lamp, for every single item, until at length we got the innkeeper down to the tariff of civilized people. The unfortunate Tartar exterior, which, for other reasons, we had assumed, had been the occasion of our acquiring a certain degree of dexterity in discussions of this kind; for not a day passed, during our journey through the province of Kan-Sou, in which we had not to quarrel, in this manner, with innkeepers. Such quarrels, however, involve no disagreeable results; you dispute, and dispute, and then you come to an agreement, and the matter is over, and you are as good friends as ever with your antagonist.

It was scarcely past midnight when the Chinese camel-drivers were on foot, making with great tumult, their preparations for departure. We rose, but it was to no purpose that we expedited the saddling of our animals; our fellow-travelers were ready before us and went on, promising to proceed slowly till we came up with them. The instant that our camels were ready, we departed. The night was dark; it was impossible to discover our guides. With the aid of a small lamp we sought traces of them, but we were not successful. Our only course, therefore, was to proceed, at chance, across these marshy plains, which were altogether unknown to us. We soon found ourselves so involved in the inundated soil, that we dared advance no farther, and halted at a bank, and there awaited daybreak.

As soon as the day dawned, we directed our steps, by a thousand ins and outs, towards a large walled town that we perceived in the distance; it was Ping-Lou-Hien, a town of the third class. Our arrival in this town occasioned lamentable disorder. The country is remarkable for the number and beauty of its mules; and at this juncture, there was one of these standing, fastened by a halter, before each of the houses of the long street, which we were traversing from north to south. As we proceeded, all these animals, seized with fright at the sight of our camels, reared on their hind legs and dashed with violence against the shops; some broke the halters which confined them, tore off at a gallop, and overthrew, in their flight, the stalls of the street merchants. The people gathered together, sent forth shouts, anathematized the stinking Tartars, cursed the camels, and increased the disorder instead of lessening it. We were grieved to find that our presence had such unfortunate results; but what could we do? We could not render the mules less timid, nor prevent the camels from having a frightful appearance. One of us, at last, determined to run on before the caravan, and inform the people of the approach of the camels. This precaution diminished the evil, which did not, however, entirely cease until we were outside the gates of the town.

We had intended to breakfast at Ping-Lou-Hien; but, not having conciliated the good-will of its inhabitants, we dared not stop there. We had only the courage to purchase some provisions, for which we paid an exorbitant price, the occasion not being favorable for bargaining. At some distance from the town, we came to a guard-house, where we stopped to rest awhile, and to take our morning repast. These guard-houses are very numerous in China, the rule being that there shall be one of them at every half-league, on all the great roads. Of a singular and entirely Chinese construction, these barracks consist of a little edifice either of wood or earth, but always whitewashed. In the center, is a kind of shed entirely without furniture, and with one large opening in front. This is reserved for unfortunate travelers, who, during the night, being overtaken by bad weather, cannot take refuge in an inn. On each side is a little room with doors and windows, and sometimes with a wooden bench painted red, by way of furniture. The exterior of the barrack is decorated with rude pictures, representing the gods of war, cavalry, and fabulous animals; on the walls of the shed are drawn all the weapons used in China, matchlocks, bows and arrows, lances, bucklers, and sabers of every description. At a little distance from the barrack, you see on the right a square tower, and on the left five small posts standing in a line. These denote the five lis which are the distance from one guard-house to another; frequently a large board, on two poles, informs the traveler of the names of the nearest towns in that quarter. The directions on the board now before us were these:—

From Ping-Lou-Hien to Ning-Hia, fifty lis.
Northwards to Ping-Lou-Hien, five lis.
Southwards to Ning-Hia, forty-five lis.

In time of war, the square tower serves during the night for giving signals by means of fireworks, combined in particular ways. The Chinese relate that the Emperor Yeou-Wang, the thirteenth emperor of the Tcheou dynasty, 780 B. C., yielding to the absurd solicitations of his wife, ordered one night the signals of alarm to be made. The Empress wanted at once to amuse herself at the expense of the soldiers, and to ascertain, at the same time, whether these fireworks would really bring the troops to succor the capital. As the signals passed on to the provinces, the governors despatched the military Mandarins and their forces to Peking. When the soldiers learned, on their arrival, that they had been called together for the capricious amusement of a woman, they returned home full of indignation. Shortly afterwards, the Tartars made an irruption into the empire, and advanced with rapidity to the very walls of the capital. This time the Emperor gave the alarm in grave earnest, but throughout the provinces not a man stirred, thinking the Empress was again amusing herself; the consequence was, that the Tartars entered Peking, and the imperial family was massacred.

The profound peace which China has enjoyed so long has much diminished the importance of these guard-houses. When they decay they are seldom repaired; in most cases their doors and windows have been carried off, and no one lives in them at all. On some of the more frequented roads, they keep in repair the direction-boards and the posts.

The barrack where we halted was deserted. After having tied our beasts to a thick post, we entered a room, and took in peace a wholesome refreshment. Travelers looked at us as they passed, and seemed a little surprised to find the place turned into a dining-room. The finer people especially, smiled at these three uncivilized Mongols, as they deemed us. Our halt was brief. The direction-board officially announced that we had yet forty-five lis' march before we reached Ning-Hia, so that, considering the difficulty of the road, and the slowness of our camels, we had no time to lose. We proceeded along the banks of a magnificent canal, supplied by the waters of the Yellow River, and destined for the irrigation of the fields. Whilst the small caravan was slowly marching over a muddy and slippery ground, we saw advancing towards us a numerous party of horsemen. As the retinue came up, the innumerable laborers who were repairing the banks of the canal, prostrated themselves on the earth, and exclaimed, "Peace and happiness to our father and mother!" We at once understood that the person so addressed was a superior Mandarin. In accordance with the strict rules of Chinese etiquette, we ought to have dismounted, and have prostrated ourselves, as the others did; but we considered that, in our quality of priests of the Western Heaven, we might dispense with this troublesome and disagreeable ceremony. We remained, therefore, gravely seated on our steeds, and advanced quietly. At sight of our camels, the other horsemen prudently removed to a respectful distance; but the Mandarin, to show his bravery, spurred his horse, and compelled it to come towards us. He saluted us politely, and made inquiries in Mongol as to our health and our journey. As his horse grew more and more afraid of our camels, he was constrained to cut short the conversation, and to rejoin his retinue, but he went away, triumphant at the reflection that he had found an opportunity of speaking Mongol, and of thus giving the horsemen of his suite a high notion of his knowledge. This Mandarin appeared to us to be a Tartar-Mantchou; he was making an official inspection of the irrigating canals.

We proceeded still some way along the banks of the same canal, meeting nothing on our road but some carriages on large wheels, drawn by buffaloes, and a few travelers mounted on asses of lofty stature. At length, we discerned the lofty ramparts of Ning-Hia, and the numerous kiosks of the pagodas, which looked in the distance like tall cedars. The brick-walls of Ning-Hia are ancient, but well preserved. The antiquity, which has almost entirely covered them with moss and lichen, gives them a grand and imposing aspect. On every side they are surrounded by marshes, where canes, reeds, and water-lilies grow in abundance. The interior of the town is poor and miserable; the streets are dirty, narrow and tortuous; the houses smoke-dried and tottering; you see at once that Ning-Hia is a town of very great antiquity. Although situated near the frontiers of Tartary, the commerce there is considerable.

After having gone nearly half up the central street, as we found we had still a league to go before we reached the other extremity, we resolved to make a halt. We entered a large inn, where we were soon followed by three individuals who impudently demanded our passports. We saw at once that we had to defend our purses against three swindlers. "Who are you that dare to demand our passports?" "We are employed by the great tribunal: it is not lawful for strangers to pass through the town of Ning-Hia without a passport." Instead of replying we called the innkeeper and desired him to write upon a small piece of paper, his name and that of his inn. Our demand greatly surprised him. "What is the good of this writing? what are you going to do with it?" "We shall soon have need of it. We are going to the great tribunal, to inform the Mandarin that three thieves have sought to rob us in your inn." At these words the three collectors of passports took to their heels; the landlord loaded them with imprecations, and the mob, who were already assembled in great numbers, laughed heartily. This little adventure caused us to be treated with especial respect. Next morning, ere day had dawned, we were awakened by a terrible noise, which arose all at once in the courtyard of the inn. Amid the confusion of numerous voices that seemed in violent dispute, we distinguished the words, "Stinking Tartar—camel—tribunal." We hastily dressed ourselves, and proceeded to investigate the nature of this sudden uproar, with which it struck us we had something to do, and so it turned out; our camels had devoured, in the course of the night, two cart-loads of osiers which were in the yard. The remnants still lay scattered about. The owners, strangers at the inn like ourselves, required to be paid the price of their goods, and their demand we considered perfectly just, only, we thought that the landlord alone was bound to repair the damage. Before going to rest, we had warned him of the danger in which the osiers lay. We had told him that he had better place them elsewhere, for that the camels would certainly break their halters in order to get at them. The owners of the carts had joined with us in advising their removal, but the landlord had laughed at our fears, and asserted that camels did not like osiers. When we had sufficiently explained the matter, the mob, the standing jury among the Chinese, decided that the whole loss should be made good by the landlord; however, we had the generosity not to demand the price of the halters of our camels.

Immediately after this impartial judgment had been pronounced, we departed on our way. The southern part of the town seemed to us in even a worse condition than that which we had passed through on the preceding evening. Several portions were altogether pulled down and deserted; the only living things to be seen were a few swine, raking up the rubbish. The inhabitants of this large city were in a state of utter misery. The greater number of them were covered with dirty rags. Their pale visages, haggard and thin, showed that they were often without the necessaries of life. Yet Ning-Hia was once a royal town, and, doubtless, opulent and flourishing.

In the tenth century, a prince of Tartar race, a native of Tou-Pa, at present under the dominion of the Si-Fan, having induced a few hordes to follow him, came, and formed, despite the Chinese, a small state not far from the banks of the Yellow River. He chose for his capital, Hia-Tcheou, which afterwards came to be called Ning-Hia. It was from this town, that this new kingdom was called Hia. It was in a very flourishing state for more than two centuries; but in 1227, it was involved in the common ruin, by the victories of Tchinggiskhan, the founder of the Mongol dynasty. At present, Ning-Hai is one of the towns of the first class in the province of Kan-Sou.

On quitting Ning-Hai, you enter upon a magnificent road, almost throughout bordered by willows and jujube trees. At intervals, you find small inns, where the traveler can rest and refresh himself at small expense. He can buy there tea, hard eggs, beans fried in oil, cakes, and fruit preserved in sugar or salt.

This day's journey was one of absolute recreation. Our camels, which had never traveled except in the deserts of Tartary, seemed thoroughly sensible to the charms of civilization; they turned their heads majestically right and left, observing, with manifest interest, all that presented itself on the way, men and things. They were not, however, so wholly absorbed in the investigations of the industry and manners of China, as to withdraw their attention altogether from its natural productions. The willows, especially, attracted their interest; and when at all within their reach, they did not fail to pluck the tender branches, which they masticated with entire satisfaction. Sometimes, also, expanding their long necks, they would smell the various delicacies displayed over the inn doors, a circumstance which, of course, elicited vehement protests from the innkeepers and other persons concerned. The Chinese were not less struck with our camels, than our camels were with China. The people collected from all directions to see the caravan pass, and ranged themselves on each side of the road; taking care, however, not to approach too near the animals which excited their surprise, and whose strength they instinctively dreaded.

Towards the close of this day's march we arrived at Hia-Ho-Po, a large village without ramparts. We proceeded to dismount at the Hotel of the Five Felicities (*Ou-Fou-Tien*). We were occupied in giving forage to our beasts, when a horseman, bearing a white button on his cap, appeared in the court of the inn. Without dismounting, or making the accustomed salutation, he proceeded to bawl for the landlord. "The great Mandarin is on his way here," cried he, in curt and haughty tones; "let everything be clean and well swept. Let these Tartars go and lodge elsewhere; the great Mandarin will not have camels in the inn." Coming from the courier of a Mandarin, these insolent words did not surprise but they irritated us. We pretended not to hear them, and quietly pursued our occupation. The innkeeper, seeing that we paid no attention to the order that had been made, advanced towards us, and laid before us, with politeness mingled with embarrassment, the state of the case. "Go," we said to him firmly; "go tell this white button that you have received us into your inn, that we will remain there, and that Mandarins have no right to come and take the places of travelers, who are already lawfully established anywhere." The innkeeper was spared the trouble of reporting our words to white button, for they had been pronounced in such a manner that he could hear them himself. He dismounted forthwith; and addressing us directly, said, "The grand Mandarin will soon arrive; he has a large retinue, and the inn is small; besides, how would the horses venture to remain in this yard in presence of your camels?" "A man in the suite of a Mandarin, and, moreover, adorned like you with a white button, should know how to express himself—first, politely, and next, justly. We have a right to remain here, and no one shall expel us; and our camels shall remain tied to the door of our room." "The grand Mandarin has ordered me to come and prepare apartments for him at the Hotel of the Five Felicities." "Very well; prepare them, but don't meddle with our things. If you cannot accommodate yourselves here, reason suggests that you go and seek a lodging elsewhere." "And the great Mandarin?" "Tell your Mandarin that there are three Lamas of the Western Heaven in this place, who are ready to return to Ning-Hia to discuss the matter with him: or before the tribunal, if it be necessary, at Peking; they know their way thither." White button mounted and disappeared. The host came to us immediately, and begged us to be resolute. "If you remain here," said he to us, "I am sure to profit a little by you; but if the Mandarin takes your place, his people will turn my inn upside down, will make us work all night, and then go away in the morning without paying a farthing. And besides that, if I were forced to send you away would not the Hotel of the Five Felicities lose its reputation? Who would afterwards enter an inn where they receive travelers only for the purpose of turning them out again?" Whilst the host was exhorting us to courage, the courier of the Mandarin reappeared; he dismounted and made us a profound bow, which we returned with the best grace possible. "Sirs Lamas," said he, "I have ridden through Hia-Po-Ho; there is no other convenient inn. Who says you are bound to cede to us your place? To speak so were to talk inconsistently with reason! Now, observe, Sirs Lamas; we are all travelers: we are all men far distant from our families; cannot we consult together in a friendly manner and arrange the matter like brothers?" "No doubt," said we, "men ought always to deal together like brothers; that is the true principle. When we travel, we should live like travelers. When each gives way a little, all are, in the end, accommodated." "Excellent saying! excellent saying!" cried the courier; and thereupon the most profound bows recommenced on both sides.

After this brief introduction, which had perfectly reconciled both parties, we deliberated amicably how we should best arrange our common residence in the Hotel of the Five Felicities. It was agreed that we should keep the room in which we were already installed, and that we should tie up our camels in a corner of the court, so that they might not terrify the horses of the Mandarin. The courier was to dispose of the rest of the place as he pleased. We hastened to remove our camels from the door of our room and to place them as had been settled. Just after sunset we heard the Mandarin's party approaching. The two folding doors of the great gate were solemnly opened, and a carriage drawn by three mules advanced into the middle of the court of the inn, escorted by a numerous body of horsemen. In the carriage was seated a man about sixty years old, with gray mustaches and beard, and having his head covered with a red hood. This was the great Mandarin. On entering, he scanned, with a quick and searching glance, the interior of the inn. Perceiving us, and remarking, above all, three camels at the end of the court, the muscles of his lean face were suddenly contracted. When all the horsemen had dismounted they invited him to descend from his vehicle. "What!" cried he in a dry, angry voice; "who are those Tartars? what are those camels? let the landlord be brought to me." On this unexpected summons the host took to his heels, and white button remained for an instant like one petrified: his face turned pale, then red, then olive-color. However, he made an effort, advanced to the carriage, put one knee to the ground, then rose, and approaching the ear of his master, spoke to him for some time, in an undertone. The dialogue ended, the great Mandarin consented to dismount, and after having saluted us with his hand in a protecting manner, he retired like a simple mortal to the small room which had been prepared for him.

The triumph we had thus obtained in a country, admission even to which was prohibited to us under pain of death,[1] gave us prodigious courage. These terrible Mandarins, who had formerly occasioned us such alarm, ceased to be terrible to us the instant that we dared to approach them, and to look at them closely. We saw men puffed up with pride and insolence, pitiless tyrants towards the weak, but dastardly in the extreme before men of energy. From this moment we found ourselves as much at our ease in China as anywhere else, and able to travel without fear, and with our heads erect in the open face of day.

After two days' journey, we arrived at Tchong-Wei, on the banks of the Yellow River, a walled town of moderate size. Its cleanliness, its good condition, its air of comfort, contrasted singularly with the wretchedness and ugliness of Ning-Hia; and judging merely from its innumerable shops, all well stocked, and from the large population crowding its streets, we should pronounce Tchong-Wei to be a place of much commercial importance; yet the Chinese of this district have no notion of navigation, and not a boat is to be seen on the Yellow River in this quarter—a circumstance remarkable in itself, and confirmatory of the opinion that the inhabitants of this part of Kan-Sou are of Thibetian and Tartar origin; for it is well known that the Chinese are everywhere passionately addicted to navigating streams and rivers.

On quitting Tchong-Wei we passed the Great Wall, which is wholly composed of uncemented stones, placed one on top of the other; and we reentered Tartary, for a few days, in the kingdom of the Alechan. More than once the Mongol Lamas had depicted in frightful colors the horrors of the Alechan mountains. We were now in a position to see with our own eyes that the reality exceeds all description of this frightful district. The Alechans are a long chain of mountains, wholly composed of moving sand, so fine, that when you touch it, it seems to flow through your fingers like a liquid. It were superfluous to add that, amid these gigantic accumulations of sand, you do not find anywhere the least trace of vegetation. The monotonous aspect of

[1] At this period there was no French embassy in China, and no treaty in favor of Europeans. All missionaries, therefore, who penetrated into the interior were, *ipso facto*, liable to be put to death.

these immense sands is only relieved by the vestiges of a small insect, that, in its capricious and fantastical sports, describes a thousand arabesques on the moving mass, which is so smooth and fine, that you can trace upon it the meanderings of an ant. In crossing these mountains, we experienced inexpressible labor and difficulty. At each step our camels sank up to the knees; and it was only by leaps that they could advance. The horses underwent still greater difficulties, their hoofs having less purchase on the sand than the large feet of the camels. As for ourselves, forced to walk, we had to keep constant watch that we did not fall from the top of these mountains, which seemed to disappear under our feet, into the Yellow River, whose waters flowed beneath us. Fortunately, the weather was calm. If the wind had blown, we should certainly have been swallowed up and buried alive in avalanches of sand. The Alechan mountains themselves appear to have been formed by the sand which the north wind incessantly sweeps before it from the Chamo, or Great Desert of Gobi. The Yellow River arrests these sandy inundations, and thus preserves the province of Kan-Sou from their destructive assaults. It is to the great quantity of sand that falls into it from the Alechan mountains that this river owes the yellow color which has given to it its name *Hoang-Ho* (Yellow River). Above the Alechan mountains its waters are clear and limpid.

By degrees, hills succeeded to mountains, the sand heaps imperceptibly diminished, and towards the close of the day we arrived at the village of Ever-Flowing Waters (*Tchang-Lieou-Chouy*). Here we found, amidst those sand hills, an oasis of surpassing beauty. A hundred rills disporting through the streets, trees, little houses built of stone, and painted white or red, communicated to the spot an aspect highly picturesque. Weary as we were, we halted at Ever-Flowing Waters with inexpressible delight; but the poetry of the thing vanished when we came to settle with our host. Not only provisions but forage came from Tchong-Wei, and the transport being very difficult, they were dear to a degree that altogether disconcerted our economical arrangements. For ourselves and our animals, we were obliged to disburse 1,600 sapeks, a matter of nearly seven shillings. Only for this circumstance we should perhaps have quitted with regret the charming village of Tchang-Lieou-Chouy; but there is always something which intervenes to aid man in detaching himself from the things of this world.

On quitting Tchang-Lieou-Chouy, we took the road followed by the Chinese exiles on their way to Ili. The country is somewhat less dreadful than that which we had traveled through on the preceding day, but it is still very dismal. Gravel had taken the place of sand, and with the exception that it produced a few tufts of grass, hard and prickly, the soil was arid and barren. We reached, in due course, Kao-Tan-Dze, a village repulsive and hideous beyond all expression. It consists of a few miserable habitations, rudely constructed of black earth, and all of them inns. Provisions are even more scarce there than at Ever-Flowing Waters, and correspondingly dearer. Everything has to be brought from Tchong-Wei, for the district produces nothing, not even water. Wells have been sunk to a very great depth, but nothing has been found except hard, rocky, moistureless earth. The inhabitants of Kao-Tan-Dze have to fetch their water a distance of more than twelve miles, and they accordingly charge travelers a monstrous price for every drop. A single bucket costs sixty sapeks. Had we attempted to water our camels, we should have had to lay out fifty fifties of sapeks; we were therefore forced to be content with drinking ourselves, and giving a draught to our horses. As to the camels, they had to await better days and a less inhospitable soil.

Kao-Tan-Dze, miserable and hideous as it is, has not even the advantage of that tranquillity and security which its poverty and its solitude might reasonably be supposed to give it. It is constantly ravaged by brigands, so that there is not a house in it which does not bear the marks of fire and devastation. At the first inn where we presented ourselves, we were asked whether we desired to have our animals defended against robbers. This question threw us into utter amazement, and we requested further explanation of a point which struck us as so very singular. We were informed that at Kao-Tan-Dze there are two sorts of inns: inns where they fight, and inns where they do not fight; and that the prices at the former sort are four times greater than those at the latter. This explanation gave us a general notion of the matter: but still we requested some details. "How!" said the people. "Don't you know that Kao-

Tan-Dze is constantly attacked by brigands?" "Yes, we know that." "If you lodge in an inn where they don't fight, any brigands that come will drive off your animals, for no one has undertaken to protect them. If, on the contrary, you lodge in an inn where they fight, you have a good chance of preserving your property, unless the brigands are the more numerous party, which sometimes happens." All this seemed to us very singular, and very disagreeable. However, it was necessary to make up our minds on the subject. After grave reflection, we decided upon lodging in an inn where they fought. It occurred to us that the worthy innkeepers of Kao-Tan-Dze had an understanding with the brigands, having for its result the spoliation of travelers, one way or the other, and that therefore it was better, upon the whole, to pay the larger sum, by way of blackmail, than to lose our animals, whose loss would involve our own destruction.

Upon entering the fighting inn, to which we had been directed, we found everything about it on a war footing. The walls were regularly covered with lances, arrows, bows, and matchlocks. The presence of these weapons, however, by no means rendered us perfectly satisfied as to our safety, and we resolved not to lie down at all, but to keep watch throughout the night.

Kao-Tan-Dze, with its robber assailants and its pauper population, was to us an inexplicable place. We could not conceive how men should make up their minds to inhabit a detestably ugly country like this, sterile, waterless, remote from any other inhabited place, and desolated by the constant inroad of brigands. What could be their object? What possible advantage could be their inducement? We turned the matter over in all ways; we framed all sorts of suppositions; but we could achieve no likely solution of the problem. During the first watch of the night, we conversed with the innkeeper, who seemed a frank, open sort of man enough. He related to us infinite anecdotes of brigands, full of battle, murder, and fire. "But," said we, "why don't you leave this detestable country?" "Oh," replied he, "we are not free men; the inhabitants of Kao-Tan-Dze are all exiles, who are only excused from going to Ili on the condition that we remain here for the purpose of supplying with water the Mandarins and soldiers who pass through the place, escorting exiles. We are bound to furnish water gratuitously to all the government officers who come to the village." When we found that we were among exiles, we were somewhat reassured, and began to think that, after all, these people were not in collusion with the brigands; for we learned that a petty Mandarin lived in the village to superintend the population. We conceived a hope that we might find some Christians at Kao-Tan-Dze, but the innkeeper informed us that there were none, for that all exiles on account of the religion of the Lord of Heaven, went on to Ili.

After what the innkeeper had told us, we conceived that we might, without risk, take a brief repose; we accordingly threw ourselves on our goat-skins, and slept soundly till daybreak, the favor of God preserving us from any visit on the part of the brigands.

During the greater part of the day, we proceeded along the road to Ili, traversing with respect, with a degree of religious veneration, that path of exile so often sanctified by the footsteps of the confessors of the faith, and conversing, as we went, about those courageous Christians, those strong souls, who, rather than renounce their religion, had abandoned their families and their country, and gone to end their days in unknown lands. Let us fervently pray that Providence may send missionaries, full of devotion, to bear the consolations of the faith amongst these our exiled brethren.

The road to Ili brought us to the Great Wall, which we passed over without dismounting. This work of the Chinese nation, of which so much is said and so little known, merits brief mention here. It is known that the idea of raising walls as a fortification against the incursions of enemies, was not peculiar, in old times, to China: antiquity presents us with several examples of these labors elsewhere. Besides the works of this kind executed in Syria, Egypt, Media, and on the continent of Europe, there was, by order of the Emperor Septimus Severus, a great wall constructed in the northern part of Britain. No other nation, however, ever effected anything of the sort on so grand a scale as the Great Wall, commenced by Tsin-Chi-Hoang-Ti, A. D. 214. The Chinese call it *Wan-li-Tchang-Tching* (the Great Wall of ten thousand lis). A prodigious number of laborers was employed upon it, and the works of this gigantic enterprise continued for ten years. The Great Wall extends from the westernmost point of Kan-Sou to the Eastern Sea. The importance of this enormous construction has been variously estimated by those who have written upon China, some of whom preposterously exaggerate its importance, while others laboriously seek to ridicule it; the probability being, that this diversity of opinion arises from each writer having judged the whole work by the particular specimen to which he had access. Mr. Barrow, who, in 1793, accompanied Lord Macartney to China, as historiographer to the British embassy, made this calculation: he supposed that there were in England and Scotland 1,800,000 houses, and estimating the masonry work of each to be 2,000 cubic feet, he prepounded that the aggregate did not contain as much material as the Great Wall of China, which, in his opinion, was enough for the construction of a wall to go twice around the world. It is evident that Mr. Barrow adopted, as the basis of his calculation, the Great Wall such as he saw it north of Peking, where the construction is really grand and imposing; but it is not to be supposed that this barrier, raised against the irruptions of the barbarians, is, throughout its extent, equally high, wide, and solid. We have crossed it at fifteen different points, and on several occasions have traveled for whole days parallel with it, and never once losing sight of it; and often, instead of the great double turreted rampart that exists towards Peking, we have found a mere low wall of brickwork, or even earthwork. In some places, indeed, we have found this famous barrier reduced to its simplest expression, and composed merely of flint-stones roughly piled up. As to the foundation wall, described by Mr. Barrow, as consisting of large masses of free-stones cemented with mortar, we can only say that we have never discovered the slightest trace of any such work. It is indeed obvious that Tsin-Chi-Hoang-Ti, in the execution of this great undertaking, would fortify with especial care the vicinity of the capital, as being the point to which the Tartar hordes would first direct their aggressive steps. It is natural, farther, to conceive, that the Mandarins charged with the execution of the Emperor's plan, would, with especial conscientiousness, perfect the works which were more immediately under the Emperor's eye, and content themselves with erecting a more or less nominal wall at remote points of the empire, particularly those where the Tartars were little to be feared, as, for example, the position of the Ortous and the Alechan mountains.

The barrier of San-Yen-Tsin, which stands a few paces beyond the wall, is noted for its great strictness towards the Tartars who seek to enter within the intramural empire. The village possesses only one inn, which is kept by the chief of the frontier guards. Upon entering the courtyard we found several groups of camels assembled there belonging to a great Tartar caravan that had arrived on the preceding evening. There was, however, plenty of room for us, the establishment being on a large scale. We had scarcely taken possession of our chamber than the passport question was started. The chief of the guards himself made an official demand for them. "We have none," replied we. At this answer his features beamed with satisfaction, and he declared that we could not proceed unless we paid a considerable sum. "How! a passport or money? Know that we have traveled China from one end to the other, that we have been to Peking, and that we have journeyed through Tartary, without anything in the shape of a passport, and without having paid a single sapek in lieu of a passport. You, who are a chief of guards, must know that Lamas are privileged to travel wherever they please without passports." "What words are these? Here is a caravan at this very moment in the house, and the two Lamas who are with it have both given me their passports like the rest of the party." "If what you say be true, the only conclusion is, that there are some Lamas who take passports with them and others who do not. We are in the number of those who do not." Finding at last that the dispute was becoming tedious, we employed a decisive course. "Well, come," said we, "we will give you the money you ask, but you shall give us in return a paper signed by yourself, in which you shall acknowledge that, before you would permit us to pass, you exacted from us a sum of money instead of passports. We shall then address ourselves to the first Mandarin we meet, and ask him whether what you have done is consistent with the laws of the empire." The man at once gave up the point. "Oh," said he, "since you have been to Peking, no doubt the Emperor has given you special privileges," and then he added, in a whisper, and smilingly, "Don't tell the Tartars here that I have let you pass *gratis*."

It is really pitiable to observe these poor Mongols traveling in China; everybody thinks himself entitled to fleece them, and everybody succeeds in doing so to a marvelous extent. In all directions they are encountered by impromptû custom-house officers, by persons who exact money from them on all sorts of pretenses, for repairing roads, building bridges, constructing pagodas, etc., etc. First, the despoilers proffer to render them great services, call them brothers and friends, and give them wholesale warnings against ill-designing persons who want to rob them. Should this method not effect an unloosening of the purse-strings, the rascals have recourse to intimidation, frighten them horribly with visions of Mandarins, laws, tribunals, prisons, punishments, threaten to take them up, and treat them, in short, just like mere children. The Mongols themselves materially aid the imposition by their total ignorance of the manners and customs of China. At an inn, instead of using the room offered to them, and putting their animals in the stables, they pitch their tent in the middle of the courtyard, plant stakes about it, and fasten their camels to these. Very frequently they are not permitted to indulge this fancy, and in this case they certainly enter the room allotted to them, and which they regard in the light of a prison; but they proceed there in a manner truly ridiculous. They set up their trivet with their kettle upon it, in the middle of the room, and make a fire beneath with argols, of which they take care to have a store with them. It is to no purpose they are told that there is in the inn a large kitchen where they can cook their meals far more comfortably to themselves; nothing will dissuade them from their own kettle and their own aboriginal fire in the middle of the room. When night comes they unroll their hide-carpets round the fire, and there lay down. They would not listen for a moment to the proposition of sleeping upon the beds or upon the kang they find in the room ready for their use. The Tartars of the caravan we found in the inn at San-Yen-Tsin were allowed to carry on their domestic matters in the open air. The simplicity of these poor children of the desert was so great that they seriously asked us whether the innkeeper would make them pay anything for the accommodation he afforded them.

We continued on our way through the province of Kan-Sou, proceeding to the southwest. The country, intersected with streams and hills, is generally fine, and the people apparently well off. The great variety of its productions is owing partly to a temperate climate and a soil naturally fertile, but above all, to the activity and skill of the agriculturists. The chief product of the district is wheat, of which the people make excellent loaves, like those of Europe. They sow scarcely any rice, procuring almost all the little they consume from the adjacent provinces. Their goats and sheep are of fine breed, and constitute, with bread, the principal food of the population. Numerous and inexhaustible mines of coal place fuel within every one's reach. It appeared to us that in Kan-Sou any one might live very comfortably at extremely small cost.

At two days' distance from the barrier of San-Yen-Tsin we were assailed by a hurricane which exposed us to very serious danger. It was about ten o'clock in the morning. We had just crossed a hill, and were entering upon a plain of vast extent, when, all of a sudden, a profound calm pervaded the atmosphere. There was not the slightest motion in the air, and yet the cold was intense. Insensibly, the sky assumed a dead-white color; but there was not a cloud to be seen. Soon, the wind began to blow from the west; in a very short time it became so violent that our animals could scarcely proceed. All nature seemed to be in a state of dissolution. The sky, still cloudless, was covered with a red tint. The fury of the wind increased; it raised in the air enormous columns of dust, sand, and decayed vegetable matter, which it then dashed right and left, here, there, and everywhere. At length the wind blew so tremendously, and the atmosphere became so utterly disorganized, that, at midday, we could not distinguish the very animals upon which we were riding. We dismounted, for it was impossible to advance a single step, and after enveloping our faces in handkerchiefs in order that we might not be blinded with the dust, we sat down beside our animals. We had no notion where we were; our only idea was that the frame of the world was unloosening, and that the end of all things was close at hand. This lasted for more than an hour. When the wind had somewhat mitigated, and we could see around us, we found that we were all separated from one another, and at considerable distances, for amid that frightful tempest, bawl as loud as we might, we could not hear each other's voices. So soon as we could at all walk we proceeded towards a farm at no great distance, but which we had not before perceived. The hurricane having thrown down the great gate of the court we found no difficulty in entering, and the house itself was open to us with almost equal facility; for Providence had guided us in our distress to a family truly remarkable for its hospitality.

Immediately upon our arrival, our hosts heated some water for us to wash with. We were in a frightful state; from head to foot we were covered with dust which had saturated, so to speak, our clothes and almost our skins. Had such a storm encountered us on the Alechan mountains, we should have been buried alive in the sand, and all trace of us lost forever.

When we found that the worst of the storm was over, and that the wind had subsided to occasional gusts, we proposed to proceed, but our kind hosts would not hear of this; they said they would lodge us for the night, and that our animals should have plenty of food and water. Their invitation was so sincere and so cordial, and we so greatly needed rest, that we readily availed ourselves of their offer.

A very slight observation of the inhabitants of Kan-Sou, will satisfy one that they are not of purely Chinese origin. The Tartaro-Thibetian element is manifestly predominant amongst them; and it displays itself with especial emphasis in the character, manners, and language of the country people. You do not find amongst them the exaggerated politeness which distinguishes the Chinese; but, on the other hand, they are remarkable for their open-heartedness and hospitality. In their particular form of Chinese you hear an infinitude of expressions which belong to the Tartar and Thibetian tongues. The construction of their phrases, instead of following the Chinese arrangement, always exhibits the inversions in use among the Mongols. Thus, for example, they don't say, with the Chinese, open the door, shut the window; but, the door open, the window shut. Another peculiarity is that milk, butter, curds, all insupportably odious to a Chinese, are especially favorite food with the inhabitants of Kan-Sou. But it is, above all, their religious turn of mind which distinguishes them from the Chinese, a people almost universally skeptical and indifferent as to religious matters. In Kan-Sou there are numerous and flourishing Lamaseries in which reformed Buddhism is followed. The Chinese, indeed, have plenty of pagodas and idols of all sorts and sizes in their houses; but with them religion is limited to this external representation, whereas in Kan-Sou every one prays often and long and fervently. Now prayer, as every one knows, is that which distinguishes the religious from the irreligious man.

Besides differing materially from the other peoples of China, the inhabitants of Kan-Sou differ materially amongst themselves, the Dchiahours marking that subdivision, perhaps, more distinctly than any of the other tribes. They occupy the country commonly called *San-Tchouan* (Three Valleys), the birthplace of our cameleer Samdadchiemba. The Dchiahours possess all the knavery and cunning of the Chinese without any of their courtesy, and without their polished form of language, and they are accordingly feared and disliked by all their neighbors. When they consider themselves in any way injured or insulted, they have immediate recourse to the dagger, by way of remedy. With them the man most to be honored is he who has committed the greatest number of murders. They have a language of their own, a medley of Mongol, Chinese, and Eastern Thibetian. According to their own account, they are of Tartar origin. If it be so, they may fairly claim to have preserved, in all its integrity, the ferocious and independent character of their ancestors, whereas the present occupiers of Mongolia have greatly modified and softened their manners.

Though subject to the Emperor of China, the Dchiahours are immediately governed by a sort of hereditary sovereign belonging to their tribe, and who bears the title of Tou-Sse. There are in Kan-Sou, and on the frontiers of the province of Sse-Tchouan, several other tribes, having their own special rulers and their own especial laws. All these tribes are called Tou-Sse, to which each adds, by way of distinction, the family name of its chief or sovereign. Samdadchiemba, for example, belonged to the Ki-Tou-Sse tribe of Dchiahours. Yang-Tou-Sse is the most celebrated and the most redoubtable of all these tribes, and for a long time exercised great influence at Lha-Ssa, the capital of Thibet, but this influence was destroyed in 1845, in consequence of an event which we shall relate by and by.

After thoroughly resting from our fatigue, we departed early next morning. Everywhere, on our way, we saw traces of the tempest, in trees uprooted and torn, houses unroofed, fields devastated and almost entirely deprived of their surface soil. Before the end of the day, we arrived at Tchoang-Long, more commonly called Ping-Fang, an ordinary town, with a tolerable amount of trade, but in no way noticeable, whether for its beauty or for its deformity. We went to lodge at the Hotel of the Three Social Relations (*San-Kan-Tien*), whose landlord was one of the best humored and most amusing persons we had hitherto met with. He was a thorough Chinese: to give us a proof of his sagacity, he asked us, point blank, whether we were not English; and that we might thoroughly understand his question, he added that he understood by Ing-Kie-Li, the sea-devils (*Yang-Kouei-Dze*) who were making war at Canton. "No, we are not English! nor are we devils of any sort, whether of sea or land." An idler who was standing by, interposed to prevent the ill effect of this awkward question. "You," said he to the innkeeper, "you know nothing of physiognomy. How could you suppose that these people are Yang-Kouei-Dze? Don't you know that they have all blue eyes and red hair?" "You're right," returned the host, "I had not thought of that." "No," said we, "clearly you had not thought at all. Do you suppose that sea-monsters could live as we do, on land, and ride on horses?" "You're right, quite so; the Ing-Kie-Li, they say, never venture to quit the sea, for when they're on land they tremble and die like fish out of water." We were favored with a good deal more information of the same class, respecting the manners and characters of the sea-devils, the upshot of which, so far as we were concerned, was the full admission that we did not belong to the same race.

A little before night, an immense bustle pervaded the inn. A Living Buddha had arrived, with a numerous train, on his return from a journey into Thibet, his native country, to the grand Lamasery, of which for many years he had been the superior, and which was situated in the country of the Khalkhas, towards the Russian frontier. As he entered the inn, a multitude of zealous Buddhists, who had been awaiting him in the great courtyard, prostrated themselves before him, their faces to the ground. The Grand Lama proceeded to the apartment which had been prepared for him, and night coming, the crowd withdrew. When the inn had become tolerably clear, this strange personage gave full play to his curiosity; he poked about all over the inn, going into every room, and asking everybody all sorts of questions, without sitting down or staying anywhere. As we expected, he favored us also with a visit. When he entered our chamber, we were gravely seated on the kang; we studiously abstained from rising at his entrance, and contented ourselves with welcoming him by a motion of our hands. He seemed rather surprised at this unceremonious reception, but not at all disconcerted. Standing in the middle of the room, he stared at each of us intently, one after the other. We, like himself, preserving entire silence all the while, exercised the privilege of which he had set us the example, and examined him closely. He seemed about fifty years old; he was enveloped in a great robe of yellow taffeta, and he wore red velvet Thibetian boots, with remarkably thick soles. He was of the middle height, and comfortably stout; his dark brown face denoted extreme good nature, but there was in his eyes, when you attentively examined them, a strange, wild, haggard expression, that was very alarming. At length he addressed us in the Mongol tongue, which he spoke with great facility. In the first instance, the conversation was nothing more than the ordinary phrases exchanged between travelers, about one another's health, destination, horses, the weather, and so on. When we found him prolonging his visit, we invited him to sit down beside us on the kang; he hesitated for a moment, conceiving, no doubt, that in his quality as Living Buddha, it did not become him to place himself on a level with mere mortals like ourselves. However, as he had a great desire for a chat, he at last made up his mind to sit down, and in fact he could not, without compromising his dignity, remain any longer standing while we sat.

A Breviary that lay on a small table beside us, immediately attracted his attention, and he asked permission to examine it. Upon our assenting, he took it up with both hands, admired the binding and the gilt edges, opened it and turned over the leaves, and then closing it again, raised it reverentially to his forehead, saying, "It is your Book of Prayer; we should always honor and respect prayer." By-and by he added, "Your religion and ours are like this," and so saying he put the knuckles of his two forefingers together. "Yes," said we, "you are right; your creed and ours are in a state of hostility, and we do not conceal from you that the object of our journey and of our labors is to substitute our prayers for those which are used in your Lamaseries." "I know that," he replied, smilingly; "I knew that long ago." He then took up the Breviary again, and asked us explanations of the engravings. He evinced no surprise at what we told him, only, when we had related to him the subject of the plate representing the crucifixion, he shook his head compassionately, and raised his joined hands to his head. After he had examined all the prints, he took the Breviary once more in both hands, and raised it respectfully to his forehead. He then rose, and having saluted us with great affability, withdrew, we escorting him to the door.

Upon being left alone, we felt for a moment stupefied as it were at this singular visit. We tried to conceive what thoughts could have filled the mind of the Living Buddha as he sat there beside us, and what impression he had derived from the sketch we gave him of our holy religion. Now, it seemed to us that strange feelings must have arisen in his heart; and then again, we imagined that after all he had felt nothing whatever, but that, a mere ordinary person, he had mechanically availed himself of his position, without reflection, and without himself attaching any real importance to his pretended divinity. We became so interested in the point, that we determined to see this personage once more before we departed. As that departure was fixed for an early hour next morning, we went, accordingly, to return his visit before we slept. We found him in his apartment, seated on thick large cushions, covered with magnificent tiger-skins; before him stood, on a small lacquer table, a silver tea-pot, and a steatite cup in a richly-worked gold saucer. He was evidently in the last stage of ennui, and was correspondingly delighted to see us. For fear he should take it into his head to let us remain standing, we proceeded, upon entering the room, to seat ourselves beside him. His suite, who were assembled in a contiguous room, which opened into their principal's, were extremely shocked at this familiarity, and gave utterance to a murmur of disapprobation. The Buddha himself, however, who passed over the circumstance with a half-angry smile, rang a silver bell, and desired a young Lama, who obeyed the summons, to bring us some tea with milk. "I have often seen your countrymen," said he; "my Lamasery stands at no great distance from your native land; the *Oros* (Russians) often pass the frontier, but I have never known any of them before to advance so far as you." "We are not Russians," said we; "our country is a long way from Russia." This answer seemed to surprise the Buddha; he looked at us closely for some time, and then said, "From what country come you, then?" "We are from the Western Heaven." "Oh! you are Péling,[1] of *Dchou-Ganga* (Eastern Ganges), and your city is Galgata (Calcutta)." The notions of the Living Buddha, it is observable, though not exactly correct, were not altogether destitute of meaning; he could of course only class us among the peoples who were known to him, and in supposing us first Russians and then English, he manifested an acquaintance with geographical terms, by no means contemptible under the circumstances. He would not be persuaded, however, that we were not either Oros or Péling of Galgata. "But after all," said he, "what matters it from what country we come, since we are all brothers? Only let me advise you, while you are in China, to be cautious not to tell everybody who you are. The Chinese are a suspicious and ill-conditioned race, and they might do you a mischief." He then talked to us about Thibet, and the dreadful road thither that we should have to traverse. Judging from our appearance, he said, he doubted very much whether we were strong enough for the undertaking. The words and the manner of the Grand Lama were perfectly affable and kind, but there was a look in his eyes to which we could not reconcile ourselves. We seemed to read there something infernal, fiend-like. But for this circumstance, which perhaps after all was mere fancy on our part, we should have esteemed our Grand Lama friend a most amiable personage.

[1] The Thibetians call the English in Hindostan, Péling, a word signifying stranger, and equivalent to the Chinese y-jin, which the Europeans translate, barbarian, probably with the notion of flattering their self-love by the implied contrast.

From Tchoang-Long, or Ping-Fang, we proceeded to Ho-Kiao-Y, or, as it is named on the maps, Tai-Toung-Fou. The latter is the ancient denomination of the place, and is no longer in popular use. The road was, throughout, covered with oxen, asses, and small carts, all with loads of coal. We resolved to sojourn for a few days at Ho-Kiao-Y, for the purpose of giving rest to our animals, whose strength had become almost exhausted; the horse and the mule, in particular, had tumors on their sides, occasioned by the constant rubbing of the saddle, and it was essential to have these cured before we proceeded further. Having formed this project, our next business was to inspect all the inns in the place, for the purpose of selecting as our abode that which presented the most favorable indications, and the Hotel of the Temperate Climates was ultimately honored with our choice.

Ever since our entry into the province of Kan-Sou, not a day had passed in which Samdadchiemba had not enlarged upon the subject of the Three Valleys and the Dchiahours. Though there was no very immense amount of sentiment about him, he had a great desire to revisit his native place, and to see once more any members of his family who might happen to be surviving there. We could not do otherwise than aid so laudable a purpose; accordingly, when we were established in the Hotel of the Temperate Climates, we granted to our cameleer eight days' leave of absence, wherein to revisit his so long abandoned home. Eight days appeared to him fully sufficient for the purpose: two to go in, two to come back in, and four to be spent in the bosom of his family, relating to them all the marvels he had witnessed abroad. We allowed him the use of a camel, that he might appear among his friends with the greater distinction; and five ounces of silver which we placed in his purse completed his recommendations to a favorable reception.

While awaiting the return of our Dchiahour, we were exclusively occupied in taking care of our animals, and of ourselves. Every day we had to go into the town to buy our provisions, then to cook them, and, morning and evening, to water our cattle at some distance from the inn. The master of the house was one of those good-natured persons who, in their very eagerness to oblige, become troublesome; and whose amiability of intention scarcely induces one to pardon their importunity of attention. The worthy man was incessantly thrusting himself into our room, to give us advice how we ought to do this, that, and the other. After altering the position of everything in the chamber according to his fancy for the moment, he would go up to the furnace, take off the lid of the saucepan, dip his finger into the ragout, and licking it to see how the mess was going on, add salt or ginger, or other condiment, to the infinite annoyance of M. Huc, who was officially charged with the cooking department. At other times he would loudly protest that we knew nothing about making up a fire, that the coals ought to be laid so, and the wood so, and that a draught of air ought to be kept up in this or that direction; and thereupon he would take up the tongs and overturn our fire, to the immense discomfiture of M. Gabet, who presided over that department. At night he appeared to consider himself especially indispensable, and would skip in every quarter of an hour to see that the lamp was burning properly, and that the wick was long enough, or short enough, and what not. At times he had really the air of asking us how it was possible that we had contrived to live without him, the one of us up to thirty-two years of age, the other up to thirty-seven. However, among the exuberance of attentions with which he bored us, there was one which we readily accepted; it was in the matter of warming our beds, the process of which was so singular, so peculiar, that we had never had the opportunity elsewhere of observing it.

The kang, a species of furnace on which you lie, is not in Kan-Sou constructed altogether of brickwork, as is the case in Northern China, but the upper flooring consists of movable planks, placed closely beside one another. When they want to heat the kang for sleeping purposes, they remove the planks, and strew the interior of the kang with horse-dung, quite dry and pulverized. Over this combustible they throw some lighted cinders, and then replace the planks; the fire immediately communicates itself to the dung, which, once lighted, continues to smolder; the heat and the smoke, having no exit, soon warm the planks, and this produces a tepid temperature which, in consequence of the slow combustion of the material, prevails throughout the night. The talent of the kang-heater consists in putting neither too much nor too little dung, in strewing it properly, and in so arranging the cinders that combustion shall commence at different points in the same moment of time, in order that all the planks may equally benefit by the warmth. Ashamed to have our bed warmed for us like children, we one night essayed to perform this service for ourselves, but the result was by no means happy, for while one of us was nearly broiled to death, the other trembled with cold all night long; the fact being, that owing to our want of skill, the fire had actually caught the planks on one side of the kang, while on the other the fuel had not lighted at all. The host of the Hotel of the Temperate Climates was naturally disgusted at the mischance, and in order to prevent its recurrence, he locked the closing plank of the furnace, and himself came every time to light it.

Our various domestic occupations, and the recitation of our Breviary, passed away the time very smoothly at Ho-Kiao-Y. On the eighth day, as had been agreed, Samdadchiemba returned, but not alone; he was accompanied by a lad, whose features bespoke him a brother of our cameleer, and as such Samdadchiemba presented him to us. Our first interview was very brief, for the two Dchiahours had scarcely presented themselves before they disappeared. We imagined, at first, that they were gone to pay their respects to the host, but it was not so, for they almost immediately reappeared with somewhat more solemnity of manner than before. Samdadchiemba marched in first: "Babdcho," said he to his brother, "prostrate thyself before our masters, and present to them the offerings of our poor family." The younger Dchiahour made us three salutations in the Oriental fashion, and then laid before us two great dishes, one of them full of fine nuts, the other laden with three large loaves, in form resembling those made in France. To afford Samdadchiemba the most practical proof in our power that we were sensible to his attention, we forthwith applied ourselves to one of the loaves, which, with some of the nuts, constituted quite a delicious repast, for never since our departure from France had we tasted such excellent bread.

While engaged upon our banquet, we observed that the costume of Samdadchiemba was reduced to its simplest expression; that whereas he had gone decently attired, he had come back half-covered with a few rags. We asked for an explanation of this change, whereupon he gave us an account of the miserable condition in which he had found his family. The father had been dead for some time; his aged mother had become blind, so that she had not enjoyed the happiness of seeing him. He had two brothers, the one a mere child, the other the young man whom he had brought with him, and who, the sole support of the family, devoted his time to the cultivation of a small field which still belonged to them, and to the tending the flocks of other people for hire. This narrative at once explained what Samdadchiemba had done with his clothes; he had given them all to his poor old mother, without even excepting his traveling cloak. We thought it our duty to propose that he should remain, and devote himself to the assistance of his wretched family; but he did not at all adopt the suggestion. "What," said he, "could I have the cruelty to do such a thing as that! Could I ever think of going to devour the little substance that remains to them? They can scarcely subsist themselves: how could they possibly support me; for I myself have no means of making a livelihood there—I cannot labor at the soil, and there is no other way in which I could help them." We considered this resolution neither good nor great; but knowing, as we did, the character of Samdadchiemba, it in no degree surprised us. We did not insist upon his remaining, for we were even better convinced than he himself was, that he could be of no sort of service to his family. We did all we could ourselves to aid these poor people, by giving Samdadchiemba's brother as large an alms as we could spare; and we then proceeded to the preparations for our departure.

During these eight days of repose, the condition of our animals had so improved as to enable us to venture upon the difficult road we had to traverse. The next day after quitting Ho-Kiao-Y, we began the ascent of the high mountain called Ping-Keou, the terribly rugged paths of which interposed almost insurmountable difficulties in the way of our camels. On the ascent, we were obliged to be constantly calling out, at the pitch of our voices, in order to warn any muleteers who might be coming down the road, which was so narrow and dangerous that two animals could not pass each other abreast. Our cries were to enable any persons coming the other way to lead their mules aside, so that they might not take alarm at the sight of our camels, and dash over the precipice. We began the ascent of this mountain before daybreak, and yet it was noon before we reached its summit. There we found a little inn, where, under the denomination of tea, they sold a decoction of burned beans. We stopped at this place for a brief period to take a repast, which hunger rendered very succulent and savory, of some nuts and a slice of the famous bread which the Dchiahour had brought us, and which we expended with the utmost parsimony. A draught of cold water should have been, according to our previous plan, the complement of our feast; but the only water attainable on this mountain was affected with an insupportable stench. We were fain, therefore, to have recourse to the decoction of baked beans, a dreadfully insipid fluid, but for which, notwithstanding, we were charged extortionately.

The cold was by no means so severe as we had expected from the season of the year and the great elevation of the mountain. In the afternoon, indeed, the weather was quite mild; by and by, the sky was overcast, and snow fell. As we were obliged to descend the mountain on foot, we soon got absolutely hot, in the perpetual struggle, of a very laborious kind, to keep from rolling down the slippery path. One of our camels fell twice, but happily in each instance he was stayed by a rock from tumbling over the mountain's side.

Having placed behind us the formidable Ping-Keou, we took up our lodging in the village of the Old Duck (*Lao-Ya-Pou*). Here we found a system of heating in operation different from that of Ho-Kiao-Y. The kangs here are warmed, not with dried horse-dung, but with coal-dust, reduced to paste, and then formed into bricks; turf is also used for the purpose. We had hitherto imagined that knitting was unknown in China; the village of the Old Duck removed this misconception from our minds, and enabled us, indeed, to remove it from the minds of the Chinese themselves in other parts of the empire. We found here in every street men, not women, occupied in this species of industry. Their productions are wholly without taste or delicacy of execution; they merely knit coarse cotton into shapeless stockings, like sacks, or sometimes gloves, without any separation for the fingers, and merely a place for the thumb, the knitting needles being small canes of bamboo. It was for us a singular spectacle to see parties of mustached men sitting before the door of their houses in the sun, knitting, sewing, and chattering like so many female gossips; it looked quite like a burlesque upon the manners of Europe.

From Lao-Ya-Pou to Si-Ning-Fou was five days' march: on the second day we passed through Ning-Pey-Hien, a town of the third order. Outside the western gate, we stopped at an inn to take our morning meal; a great many travelers were already assembled in the large kitchen, occupying the tables which were ranged along the walls; in the center of the room were several furnaces, where the innkeeper, his wife, several children, and some servants were actively preparing the dishes required by the guests. While everybody seemed occupied, either in the preparation or in the consumption of victuals, a loud cry was heard. It was the hostess, thus expressing the pain occasioned by a knock on her head, which the husband had administered with a shovel. At the cry all the travelers looked in the direction whence it proceeded; the woman retreated, with vehement vociferations, to a corner of the kitchen; the innkeeper explained to the company that he had been compelled to correct his wife for insolence, insubordination, and an indifference to the interests of the establishment, which eminently compromised its prosperity. Before he had finished his version of the story, the wife, from her retreat in the corner, commenced hers; she informed the company that her husband was an idle vagabond, who passed his time in drinking and smoking, expending the result of her labors for a whole month in a few days of brandy and tobacco. During this extempore performance, the audience remained imperturbably calm, giving not the smallest indication of approbation or disapprobation. At length the wife issued from her retreat, and advanced with a sort of challenging air to the husband: "Since I am a wicked woman," cried she, "you must kill me. Come, kill me!" and so saying, she drew herself up with a gesture of vast dramatic dignity immediately in front of the husband. The latter did not adopt the suggestion to kill her, but he gave her a formidable box on the ear, which sent her back, screaming at the pitch of her voice, into her previous corner. Hereupon, the audience burst into loud laughter; but the affair, which seemed to them so diverting, soon took a very serious turn. After the most terrible abuse on the one hand, and the most awful threats on the other, the innkeeper at length drew his girdle tight about his waist, and twisted his tress of hair about his head, in token of some decided proceeding. "Since you will have me kill you," cried he, "I will kill you!" and so saying, he took from the furnace a pair of long iron tongs, and rushed furiously upon his wife. Everybody at once rose and shouted; the neighbors ran in, and all present endeavored to separate the combatants, but they did not effect the object until the woman's face was covered with blood, and her hair was all down about her shoulders. Then a man of ripe years, who seemed to exercise some authority in the house, gravely pronounced these words by way of epilogue: "How! what!" said he, "husband and wife fighting thus! and in presence of their children, in presence of a crowd of travelers!" These words, repeated three or four times, in a tone which expressed at once indignation and authority, had a marvelous effect. Almost immediately afterwards the guests resumed their dinner, the hostess fried cakes in nut-oil, and the host silently smoked his pipe.

When we were about to depart, the innkeeper, in summing up our account, coolly inserted fifty sapeks for the animals which we had tied up in the courtyard during our meal. He had evidently an idea of making us pay *en Tartare*. Samdadchiemba was indignant. "Do you think," asked he, "that we Dchiahours don't know the rules of inns? Where did you ever hear of making people pay for fastening their animals to a peg in the wall? Tell me, master publican, how many sapeks are you going to charge us for the comedy we've just witnessed of the innkeeper and his wife?" The burst of laughter on the part of the bystanders which hailed this sarcasm carried the day triumphantly for Samdadchiemba, and we departed without paying anything beyond our personal expenses.

The road thence to Si-Ning-Fou, generally well made and well kept, meanders through a fertile and well cultivated country, picturesquely diversified by trees, hills, and numerous streams. Tobacco is the staple of the district. We saw on our way several water-mills, remarkable for their simplicity, as is the case with all Chinese works. In these mills, the upper story is stationary, while the lower is turned by means of a single wheel, kept in motion by the current. To work these mills, though they are frequently of large proportions, a very small stream suffices, as the stream plays upon the wheel in the form of a cascade, at least twenty feet high.

On the day before arriving at Si-Ning-Fou, we passed over a road extremely laborious, and so dangerously rugged that it suggested frequent recommendations of ourselves to the protection of the Divine Providence. Our course was amid enormous rocks, beside a deep, fierce current, the tumultuous waves of which roared beneath us. There was the gulf perpetually yawning to swallow us up, should we make but one false step; we trembled, above all, for our camels, awkward and lumbering as they were, whenever they had to pass over an uneven road. At length, thanks to the goodness of God, we arrived without accident at Si-Ning. The town is of very large extent, but its population is limited, and itself, in several parts, is falling into absolute decay. The history of the matter is, that its commerce has been in great measure intercepted by Tang-Keou-Eul, a small town on the banks of the Keou-Ho, on the frontier which separates Kan-Sou from Koukou-Noor.

It is the custom, we may say the rule, at Si-Ning-Fou, not to receive strangers, such as the Tartars, Thibetians, and others, into the inns, but to relegate them to establishments called Houses of Repose (*Sie-Kia*), into which no other travelers are admitted. We proceeded accordingly to one of these Houses of Repose, where we were exceedingly well entertained. The Sie-Kia differ from other inns in this important particular, that the guests are boarded, lodged, and served there gratuitously. Commerce being the leading object of travelers hither, the chiefs of the Sie-Kia indemnify themselves for their outlay by a recognized percentage upon all the goods which their guests buy or sell. The persons who keep these Houses of Repose have first to procure a license from the authorities of the town, for which they pay a certain sum, greater or less, according to the character of the commercial men who are expected to frequent the house. In outward show, the guests are well-treated, but still they are quite at the mercy of the landlords, who, having an understanding with the traders of the town, manage to make money of both parties.

When we, indeed, departed from Si-Ning-Fou, the Sie-Kia with whom we had lodged had made nothing by us in the ordinary way, for we had neither bought nor sold anything. However, as it would have been preposterous and unjust on our part to have lived thus at the expense of our neighbors, we paid the host of the House of Repose for what we had had, at the ordinary tavern rate.

After crossing several torrents, ascending many rocky hills, and twice passing the Great Wall, we arrived at Tang-Keou-Eul. It was now January, and nearly four months had elapsed since our departure from the Valley of Dark Waters. Tang-Keou-Eul is a small town, but very populous, very animated, and very full of business. It is a regular tower of Babel, wherein you find collected Eastern Thibetians, *Houng-Mao-Eul* (Long-haired Folk), Elents, Kolos, Chinese, Tartars from the Blue Sea, and Mussulmans, descended from the ancient migrations from Turkestan. Everything in the town bears the impress of violence. Nobody walks the streets without a great saber at his side, and without affecting, at least, a fierce determination to use it on the shortest notice. Not an hour passes without some street combat.

The Jin Seng, a Medicinal Root of China.

TRAVELS IN TARTARY, THIBET AND CHINA

MAUSOLEUM OF A GRAND LAMA OF THIBET.

TRAVELS IN TARTARY, THIBET AND CHINA

DURING THE YEARS 1844-5-6

BY

M. HUC

TRANSLATED FROM THE FRENCH BY W, HAZLITT
SECOND REPRINT EDITION

VOL. II

ILLUSTRATED WITH FIFTY ENGRAVINGS ON WOOD

GYAN

Published by

Gyan Publishing House
5, Ansari Road
Daryaganj, New Delhi-110002
Phone: 011-47034999, 9811692060
E-mail: books@gyanbooks.com

Distribution Network
gyanbooks.com
India, USA, Canada, UK, Australia, France

ISBN : 978-81-212-4154-0 (Set)
ISBN : 978-81-212-4976-8 (HB)
First Published, 1900

2nd Impression 2020

Printed at: Gyan Press, Delhi.

Travels in Tartary, Thibet and China

DURING THE YEARS 1844–5–6

BY M. HUC

TRANSLATED FROM THE FRENCH BY W. HAZLITT

SECOND REPRINT EDITION

VOL. II

ILLUSTRATED WITH FIFTY ENGRAVINGS ON WOOD

CHICAGO
THE OPEN COURT PUBLISHING COMPANY
LONDON AGENTS
KEGAN PAUL, TRENCH, TRUEBNER & CO.
1900

TRAVELS

IN

TARTARY, THIBET, AND CHINA

ILLUSTRATED

BUDDHA

CHICAGO
THE OPEN COURT PUBLISHING COMPANY
LONDON AGENTS
KEGAN PAUL, TRENCH, TRUEBNER & CO.

CONTENTS OF VOLUME II.

CHAPTER IV.

CHAPTER V.

CHAPTER VI.

CHAPTER VII.

CHAPTER VIII.

CHAPTER IX.

LIST OF ILLUSTRATIONS.

Khalkha Tartars

CHAPTER I.

Caravan of Khalkha-Tartars—Son of the King of Koukou-Noor—Sandara the Bearded—Two Thousand Oxen Are Stolen from the Houng-Mao-Eul, or Long Hairs—Fearful Tumult at Tang-Keou-Eul—Description and Character of the Long Hairs—Feasts of the First Day of the Year—Departure for the Lamasery of Kounboum—Arrival at Night—Old Akayé—The Kitat-Lama—The Stammerer—Pilgrims at Kounboum—Description of the Feast of Flowers.

THE Houses of Repose are very numerous in the small town of Tang-Kẹou-Eul, by reason of the great number of strangers, who are drawn thither from all quarters by commerce. It was in one of these establishments, kept by a family of Mussulmans, that we went to lodge. As we had nothing to do with trade, we felt called upon candidly to communicate the fact to the host, and to arrange the terms of our living in his house; it was agreed that we should be there as in a common hotel. All this was very well; but the question was, what we were to do afterwards: what was to become of us? This question incessantly engrossed our minds, and tormented us not a little.

As far as Tang-Keou-Eul we had followed, with sufficient continuity, the route we had traced out for ourselves; we might even say that this portion of our journey had been successful beyond all expectations. Now the business was to carry out our plan, and to penetrate to Lha-Ssa, the capital of Thibet; an undertaking which appeared bristling with almost insuperable difficulties. Tang-Keou-Eul was our columns of Hercules, with their depressing *ne plus ultra* (No farther shalt thou go). However, we had already vanquished too many obstacles, to be easily overcome by discouragement. We heard that almost every year caravans proceeded from Tang-Keou-Eul, and penetrated into the very heart of Thibet. We wanted nothing more to confirm our determination. Whatever other people had undertaken and executed, we assumed also to undertake and to execute, as not being, probably, beyond our power. It was therefore settled that the journey should be carried out to the end, and that no one should say that Catholic missionaries had less courage for the interest of the faith, than merchants for a little profit. The possibility of departure being thus determined we had nothing to seek but the opportunity.

Our great business, therefore, was to collect all possible information respecting this famous route into Thibet. We heard terrible things about it; we should have to travel for four months through a country absolutely without inhabitants, and should have, accordingly, to lay in before our departure all the necessary provisions. In the season of winter, the cold was so horrible that it often happened that travelers were frozen to death or buried beneath the avalanches of snow; while, in summer, a great number were drowned, for they had to cross large streams, without bridge or boat, without other aid than that of animals, which themselves often could not swim. Moreover, there were hordes of brigands, who at certain periods of the year prowled about the desert and stripped travelers and abandoned them, without clothes or food, amidst these frightful plains; in short, there was no end of stories, enough to make our hair stand on end; and these stories, fabulous as they seemed, or, at least, much exaggerated, were the same on every tongue,—were all of a frightful uniformity. Besides, there were to be seen and questioned in the streets of Tang-Keou-Eul, some Tartar-Mongols, who were standing evidence of the truth of these long narratives, being the remnants of a large caravan, which had been attacked in the preceding year by a troop of brigands. These had contrived to escape, but their companions had been left to the mercy of the *Kolo* (brigands). This information, while ineffectual to shake our resolution, induced us to remain where we were, until a favorable opportunity for departure should present itself.

We had been six days at Tang-Keou-Eul, when a small caravan of Tartar-Khalkhas arrived at our House of Repose. It came from the frontiers of Russia, and was on its way to Lha-Ssa to offer up its adorations to a young child, which, the people were informed, was the famous Guison-Tamba newly transmigrated. When the Tartars learned that we were awaiting a favorable opportunity for proceeding towards Thibet, they were delighted, fully appreciating the fact that their troop, in this unexpected accession of three pilgrims, received an accession, also, of three combatants in the event of a fight with the Kolo. Our beards and moustachios inspired them with an exalted idea of our valor, and we were forthwith decorated by them with the title of *Batourou* (braves). This was all exceedingly honorable and seductive; but still, before we finally decided upon joining the cavalcade, we thought it expedient to consider the various aspects of the matter gravely and maturely.

The caravan which occupied the great courtyard of the House of Repose, counted only eight men; the rest was camels, horses, tents, baggage, and kitchen ustensils; but then the eight men, according to their own account, were perfect war dragons. At all events, they were armed up to the teeth, and made a grand display before us of their matchlocks, lances, bows and arrows, and above all, of a piece of artillery, in the shape of a small cannon, of the size of one's arm; it had no carriage, but mounted between the two humps of a camel, it produced a very formidable effect. All this warlike apparatus failed to inspire us with confidence, and, on the other hand, we placed but slight reliance upon the moral effect of our long beards. It was necessary, however, to adopt a decided course; the Tartar-Khalkhas urged us pressingly, assuring us of complete success. Of the lookers-on, disinterested in the matter one way or the other, some told us that the opportunity was altogether eligible, and that we ought by all means to avail ourselves of it; while others assured us that it would be the extreme of imprudence to proceed, for that so small a party would be inevitably eaten up by the Kolo; and that it would be far better, as we were in no immediate hurry, to wait for the great Thibetian embassy.

Now this embassy having only just quitted Peking, would not reach Tang-Keou-Eul for fully eight months, a delay which it seemed absolutely ruinous for us to undergo. How, with our modest means, were we to maintain ourselves and our five animals for so long a time in an inn? After maturely calculating and weighing everything: let us confide in the protection of God, said we, and go forth. We announced our resolution to the Tartars, who were highly delighted. We immediately requested the host of the House of Repose to purchase for us four months' provision of meal. "What do you want with four months' meal?" asked the Tartars. "They say the journey is of at least three months' duration, and it is expedient, therefore, to provide for four months, to meet the chance of accidents." "Ay, the Thibetian embassy occupies a long time on the journey, but we Tartars travel in quite a different manner; we do the distance in a moon and a half at the very outside; we gallop the whole way, so that we get over nearly 200 lis (twenty leagues) a day." This intimation at once caused us to change our resolution. It was manifestly quite impossible for us to keep up with this caravan. In the first place, as to ourselves, never having been accustomed, like the Tartars, to forced marches, we should have been dead in three days; as to our animals, weary and worn with four months' incessant toil, they could not have for any length of time borne up against the pace of our proposed companions. The Tartars having forty camels could afford to knock up one half of them. Indeed, they themselves admitted that with our three camels, it was impossible for us to undertake the journey with them, and they accordingly advised us to buy a dozen others. The advice, excellent in itself, was, with reference to the state of our exchequer, absolutely absurd. Twelve good camels would have cost us three hundred ounces of silver; now the total amount of our funds was under two hundred ounces.

Ceremony of Reception.

The eight Tartar-Khalkhas were all of princely blood, and, accordingly, on the evening preceding their departure, they received a visit from the son of the King of Koukou-Noor, who was then at Tang-Keou-Eul. As the room we occupied was the handsomest in the establishment, it was arranged that the interview should take place there. The young Prince of Koukou-Noor surprised us by his noble mien and the elegance of his manners; it was obvious that he spent considerably more of his time at Tang-Keou-Eul than in the Mongol tent. He was attired in a handsome robe of light blue cloth, over which was a sort of jacket of violet cloth, with a broad border of black velvet. His left ear was decorated, in Thibetian fashion, with a gold earring from which hung several trinkets; his complexion was almost as fair as our own, and his countenance admirably gentle in its expression: in utter contradistinction from ordinary Tartars, his garments were exquisitely clean. As the visit of a Prince of Koukou-Noor was quite an event, we determined to be wholly regardless of expense in celebrating it; and Samdadchiemba received, accordingly, orders to prepare a banquet for his royal highness, that is to say, a great pitcher of good, hot tea, with milk. His royal highness deigned to accept a cup of this beverage, and the remainder was distributed among his staff, who were in waiting outside. The conversation turned upon the journey into Thibet. The prince promised the Tartar-Khalkhas an escort throughout his estates. "Beyond that point," said he, "I can answer for nothing; you must take your chance, good or bad, as shall happen." Then addressing us, he advised us by all means to wait for the Thibetian embassy, in whose company we should be able to travel with greater ease and security. On taking leave, the royal visitor drew from a purse elegantly embroidered, a small agate snuff-box, and graciously offered to each of us a pinch.

Next morning the Tartar-Khalkhas proceeded on their journey. When we saw them depart, a feeling of sorrow came over us, for we would gladly have accompanied them had it been at all practicable; but the sentiment soon subsided, and we applied our thoughts to the best use we should make of our time while we remained at Tang-Keou-Eul. It was at last determined that we should procure a master, and devote ourselves entirely to the study of the Thibetian language and of the Buddhist books.

At eleven leagues from Tang-Keou-Eul there is, in the land of the Si-Fan, or Eastern Thibetians, a Lamasery, whose fame extends not merely throughout Tartary, but even to the remotest parts of Thibet. Thither pilgrims flock from all quarters, venerating; for there was born Tsong-Kaba-Remboutchi, the famous reformer of Buddhism. The Lamasery bears the name of Kounboum, and its Lama population numbers no fewer than 4,000 persons, Si-Fan, Tartars, Thibetians, and Dchiahours. It was determined that one of us should visit this place, and endeavor to engage a Lama to come and teach us for a few months the Thibetian language. M. Gabet, accordingly, departed on this mission, accompanied by Samdadchiemba, while M. Huc remained at Tang-Keou-Eul, to take care of the animals and of the baggage.

After an absence of five days, M. Gabet returned to the House of Repose, eminently successful, having secured at the Lamasery of Kounboum a perfect treasure in the person of a Lama who had passed ten of the thirty-two years of his life in a grand Lamasery at Lha-Ssa itself. He spoke pure Thibetian perfectly, wrote it with facility, and was very learned in the Buddhist books; moreover, he was quite familiar with several other idioms, Si-Fan, Mongol, Chinese, and Dchiahour; in a word, he was a philologist of the first water. This young Lama was a Dchiahour by birth, and a cousin-german of Samdadchiemba; his name was Sandara, and in the Lamasery he was called Sandara the Bearded, by reason of the remarkable length of that appendage in which he luxuriated.

The devotion which Samdadchiemba's cousin forthwith manifested in our favor made us rejoice that we had not adventured with the Tartar-Khalkha caravan, for here we were placed in the precise position for procuring every requisite information about Thibet, and of making ourselves acquainted at the same time with the language and religion of that celebrated region.

We applied ourselves to study with perfect enthusiasm. First, we composed in Mongol two dialogues, comprehending the most familiar conversational phrases. These Sandara translated into Thibetian with scrupulous attention. Every morning he wrote out a page in our presence, giving us a grammatical commentary upon each expression, as he proceeded; this was our lesson for the day, which we first transcribed several times, in order to break our hand into the Thibetian writing, and then chanted, in the manner of the Lamaseries, until the whole page was thoroughly impressed upon the memory. In the evening our master heard us recite the portion of dialogue he had written for us in the morning, and rectified our defects of pronunciation. Sandara acquitted himself of his task with talent and amiability. From time to time in the course of the day he would, by way of recreation, give us details full of interest respecting Thibet and the Lamaseries he had visited. It was impossible to listen to the descriptions given by this young Lama without admiration ; nowhere had we heard a person express himself with greater facility or a more winning manner ; the simplest, commonest things became in his mouth picturesque and full of charm ; he was especially remarkable when he sought to induce upon others any particular view of his own upon some subject in which he really felt an interest. His eloquence was then really powerful.

After having surmounted the first difficulties of the Thibetian language, and familiarized ourselves with the expressions in ordinary use, we proceeded to give our studies an altogether religious direction. We got Sandara to translate for us into the sacred style of his language some of the leading Catholic forms, such as the Lord's Prayer, the Salutation, the Apostles' Creed, the Commandments : and thereupon we took occasion to explain to him the general truths of the Christian religion. He seemed all at once struck with this new doctrine, so different from the vague, incoherent propositions of Buddhism. Before long he attached so much importance to the study of the Christian religion that he entirely laid aside the Lama books he had brought with him, and applied himself to the acquisition of our prayers with an ardor that made us truly joyful.

From time to time in the course of the day he would interrupt what he was about in order to make the sign of the cross, and he practised this religious act in a manner so grave and respectful that we thoroughly believed him to have become a Christian at heart. The excellent tendencies he manifested filled us with the most lively hopes, and we gratefully viewed in Sandara an incipient apostle, destined one day to labor with success in converting the sectaries of Buddha.

While we three, master and pupils, were thus absorbed in studies so important, Samdadchiemba, who had no sort of vocation for things intellectual, passed his time lounging about the streets of Tang-Keou-Eul and drinking tea. Not at all pleased with this occupation of his time, we devised to withdraw him from his idleness, and to utilize him in his special character of cameleer. It was accordingly arranged that he should take the three camels and pasture them in a valley of Koukou-Noor, noted for the excellence and the abundance of its pasturage. A Tartar of the locality promised to receive him into his tent, and we rejoiced in the arrangement, as effecting the double advantage of supplying Samdadchiemba with an occupation in conformity with his tastes, and of giving our camels better and less costly fodder.

By degrees, all the fine things that we had imagined in Sandara, vanished like a dream. This young man, apparently of devotion so pure and disinterested, was in reality a dissipated knave, whose only aim was to ease us of our sapeks. When he thought he had rendered himself essential to us, he threw aside the mask, and placed himself undisguisedly before us in all the detestability of his character : he became insolent, haughty, overbearing. In his Thibetian lessons, he substituted for the mild, gentle, insinuating tone of his former instruction, manners the most insufferably harsh and brutal, such as the worst tempered pedagogue would not betray towards the poorest of his pupils. If we asked him for an explanation which perhaps he had previously given, he would assail us with such amenities as these : "What ! you learned fellows want to have the same thing told you three times over ! Why, if I were to tell a donkey the same thing three times over, he'd remember it." We might easily, no doubt, have cut short these impertinences by sending the man back to his Lamasery ; and, more than once, we were strongly inclined to adopt this course, but, upon the whole, we thought it better to undergo a little humiliation, than to deprive ourselves of the services of a Lama whose talents were indisputable, and who, therefore, might be of the greatest utility to us. His very rudeness, we considered, would aid our progress in acquiring the Thibetian language, for we were sure that he would not pass over the most trivial fault in grammar or pronunciation, but, on the contrary, would rate us for any such defects, in a style eminently calculated to produce an abiding impression. This system, though somewhat tedious, and decidedly displeasing to one's self-love, was incomparably superior to the method practised by the Chinese Christians towards the European missionaries in giving them Chinese lessons. Partly from politeness, partly from religious respect, they affect to be in ecstasies with whatever their spiritual father-pupil says ; and, instead of frankly correcting the faults which naturally occur in his expressions, they are rather disposed to imitate his defective language, so that he may, with the less trouble to himself, understand them, the result of which excessive complaisance is, that the missionaries are put to grave inconvenience when they seek to converse with pagans who, not having the same devotion towards them, do not admit in them a fine pronunciation, or a masterly knowledge of words. Upon such occasions, how one regrets that one had not for a teacher some Sandara the Bearded! Upon such considerations, we resolved to keep our master with all his defects, to endure his abuse, and to make the best and most we could of him. As we found that our sapeks were his object, it was agreed that we should pay him handsomely for his lessons; and, moreover, we made up our minds to wink at his little knaveries, and to affect to have no idea that he had an understanding with the people who sold us our daily provisions.

Samdadchiemba had not been gone many days before he suddenly reappeared amongst us. He had been robbed by brigands who had taken from him his entire provision of meal, butter, and tea. For the last day and a half he had eaten nothing whatever, and of consequence, his voice was hollow, and his face pale and haggard. Only seeing one camel in the courtyard, we imagined that the two others had become the prey of the brigands, but Samdadchiemba relieved us by the assurance that he had confided them to the Tartar family who had granted him their hospitality. Upon hearing this statement, Sandara knitted his brows. "Samdadchiemba," said he, "you are my younger brother, as it were; I have therefore a right to ask you a few questions." And thereupon he submitted the cameleer to an interrogatory characterized by all the depth and subtlety of an able advocate cross-examining some cunning offender. He demanded the minutest details, and applied himself with infinite ingenuity to work up the contradictions into which he involved the questioned party, and to put forward in prominent relief the apparent improbability of his story. How was it, he asked, that the robbers had stolen the butter, yet left the bag in which the butter was carried? How was it they had respected the little snuff-bottle, yet carried off the embroidered purse which served it as a cover. When he had finished his inquiries, he added, with a malicious smile: "I have put these few questions to my brother out of pure curiosity; I attach no importance to them. It is not I who have to disburse the wherewithal to buy him fresh provisions."

Samdadchiemba, meantime, was dying with hunger, so we gave him some sapeks, and he went to dinner in a neighboring eating-house. As soon as he had quitted the room, Sandara proceeded: "Nobody shall ever persuade me that my brother has been robbed. The brigands in this part of the country don't do their work in the way he wants to make out. The fact is, that Samdadchiemba, when he got among the Tartars, wanted to show off, and distributed his provisions right and left in order to make friends. He had no reason to fear being lavish; what he gave away cost him nothing." The probity of Samdadchiemba was a fact so thoroughly impressed upon our convictions, that we altogether repudiated this wicked insinuation, which we clearly saw proceeded at once from Sandara's jealous annoyance at the confidence we reposed in his cousin, and from a cunning desire, in giving us the idea that he was warmly attached to our interests, to divert our attention from his own petty peculations. We gave Samdadchiemba, who did not at all perceive his relative's treachery, some more provisions, and he returned to the pastures of Koukou-Noor.

Next day, the town of Tang-Keou-Eul was the scene of terrible disorder. The brigands had made their appearance in the vicinity, and had driven off 2000 head of cattle belonging to the tribe called *Houng-Mao-Eul* (Long Hairs). These Eastern Thibetians quit once a year the slopes of the Bayan-Khara mountains in large caravans, and come to Tang-Keou-Eul to sell furs, butter, and a kind of wild fruit that grows in their district. While they are engaged in these commercial operations, they leave their large herds in the vast prairies that abut upon the town, and which are under the jurisdiction of the Chinese authorities. There was no example, we heard, of the brigands having ventured to approach so close as this to the frontiers of the Empire. This present audacity of theirs, and more especially the known violence of character of the Long Hairs, contributed to throw the whole town into utter dismay and confusion. Upon hearing of their loss the Long Hairs had tumultuously rushed to the Chinese tribunal, and, their long sabres in their hands, lightning in their eyes, and thunder in their mouths, had demanded justice and vengeance. The terrified Mandarin instantly despatched 200 soldiers in pursuit of the robbers. But the Long Hairs, seeing that these foot soldiers could never overtake the brigands, who were well mounted, threw themselves into their saddles, and dashed off in search of the thieves. They returned next day with no other result attained than that their fury was redoubled. Altogether destitute of foresight, these half-savages had gone off without any provisions whatever, never thinking that, in the desert they would find nothing to eat. Accordingly, after a day's forced march, hunger had compelled them to return. Not so the Chinese soldiers. These worthies, knowing much better what they were about, had provided themselves for their warlike expedition with infinite asses and oxen laden with apparatus for the kitchen, and with ammunition for the mouth. As they felt no sort of desire to go and fight for 2000 cattle that did not belong to them, after a very brief military progress they halted on the bank of a river, where they spent several days, eating, drinking, and amusing themselves, and giving no more heed to the brigands than though there had never been such personages in the world. When they had consumed all their provisions they returned quietly to Tang-Keou-Eul, and declared to the Mandarin that they had scoured the desert without being able to come up with the robbers; that once, indeed, these had seemed within their grasp, but that, availing themselves of their magic powers, they had vanished. At Tang-Keou-Eul everybody is persuaded that the brigands are all more or less sorcerers, and that in order to render themselves invisible, all they had to do is to exhale in a particular manner, or to throw some sheep's treddles behind them. It is probably the Chinese soldiers who have brought these fables into vogue; at all events they certainly make excellent use of them in all their expeditions. The Mandarins, doubtless, are not their dupes; but provided the victims of the robbers are content with these tales, that is all the Chinese authorities care about.

For several days the Houng-Mao-Eul were perfectly furious. They ran about the streets like madmen, flourishing their sabres and vociferating a thousand imprecations against the brigands. All the townspeople got carefully out of their way, respecting their anger with entire veneration. The appearance of these fellows even at their very best, when they are perfectly calm and good-humored, is sufficiently alarming. They are clothed at all seasons of the year in a great sheepskin robe, rudely drawn up round the waist by a thick camel-hair rope. Left to itself this robe would drag along the ground, so that when raised by the cord above the knees it communicates to the chest a most rotund, stuffed, and awkward appearance. They have great leather boots, which come up to just below the knee, so that, as they wear no trousers, their legs are always half bare. Their hair, black and greasy, hangs in long matted locks down their shoulders, and, in fact, falling over the brow, half conceals the face. The right arm is always bare, the sleeve being thrown quite back. A long, broad sabre is passed through their girdle just below the chest, and the right hand scarcely ever quits its hilt. The manners and movements of these inhabitants of the desert are abrupt and jerking, their speech brief and energetic. The tones of their voice have something about them metallic and deafening. Many of them are wealthy, and with these display consists in decorating the sheath of the sword with precious stones, and their own robes with borders of tiger-skin. The horses which they bring to Tang-Keou-Eul are remarkably beautiful, vigorous, well-made, and of great grandeur in the step: in all respects far superior to those of Tartary, and fully justifying the Chinese phrase, *Sima, Toung-nieou* (Western horses—eastern oxen).

The Houng-Mao-Eul, being famous for their bravery and for an independence which amounts to the ferocious, it is they who give the *ton* to the people of Tang-Keou-Eul, who all essay to catch their air and gait, and to acquire a reputation for valor and devil-may-carishness. The result is, that Tang-Keou-Eul bears a strong family resemblance to a great den of thieves. Everybody there makes it his business to have his hair and clothes in utter disorder, everybody bawls at everybody, everybody pushes against everybody, everybody fights everybody, so that everybody from time to time draws everybody's blood. In the depth of winter, though the winter here is desperately cold, people go about with their arms and half their legs bare. To wear clothing adapted to the icy season would be considered a mark of pusillanimity. A good brave fellow, they say, should fear nothing, neither men nor elements. At Tang-Keou-Eul the Chinese themselves have lost much of their urbanity and of the polished forms of their language, having involuntarily undergone the influence of the Houng-Mao-Eul, who converse together in much the same style that we can imagine tigers in the woods to converse. On the day of our arrival at Tang-Keou-Eul, a few minutes before we entered the town, we met a Long Hair who had been giving his horse drink in the river Keou-Ho. Samdadchiemba, who was always attracted by anything having an eccentric air, cautiously approached the man, and saluted him in the Tartar fashion, saying, "Brother, art thou at peace?" The Houng-Mao-Eul turned fiercely towards him: "What business of thine is it, tortoise-egg," cried he, with the voice of a Stentor, "whether I am at peace or at war? And what right hast thou to address as thy brother a man who knows nothing about thee?" Poor Samdadchiemba was taken all aback at this reception, yet he could not help admiring, as something very fine, this haughty insolence of the Long Hair.

Tang-Keou-Eul, in consequence of its dirt and its excessive population, is a very unwholesome place to live in. There is a universal odor of grease and butter about, that is enough to make you sick. In certain quarters, more particularly where the especial poor and the especial vagabonds congregate, the stench is insupportable. Those who have no house wherein to shelter themselves, collect in the nooks of streets and squares, and there they lie, higgledy-piggledy, and half naked, upon filthy straw, or rather, dung-heaps. There are stretched together the sick young, and the infirm old, the dying man, sometimes the dead, whom no one takes the trouble to bury, until at length, putrefaction manifesting itself, the bodies are dragged into the middle of the street, whence the authorities remove them, and have them thrown into some general pit. From amid this hideous misery there pullulates into the bosom of the population, a crowd of petty thieves and swindlers, who, in their address and audacity, leave far behind the Robert Macaires of the western world. The number of these wretched creatures is so great, that authority, weary of contending with them, has left them to take their own course, and the public to guard their own sapeks and goods. These worthies work, as a matter of preference, in the houses of repose and the inns. Their *modus operandi*, is this:—Two of them, associated together for the purpose, hawk about various articles of merchandise, boots, skin-coats, bricks of tea, and what not. They offer these for sale to travelers. While one of them engages the attention of the destined victim, by displaying his goods and bargaining, the other ferrets about and pockets whatever he can lay his hands on. These rascals have inconceivable skill in counting your sapeks for you, in such a way as to finger fifty or a hundred or more of them without your having the slightest notion as to what is going on. One day, two of these little thieves came to offer for our purchase a pair of leathern boots. Excellent boots! said they; boots such as we could not find in any shop in the whole town; boots that would keep out the rain for days; and as to cheapness, perfectly unexampled. If we missed this opportunity, we should never have such another. Only just before they had been offered 1200 sapeks for them! As we did not want boots, we replied that we would not have them at any price. Thereupon the acting merchant assumed a lofty tone of generosity. We were foreigners; we should have them for 1000 sapeks, 900, 800, 700. "Well," said we, "we certainly don't want any boots just now, yet doubtless, as you say, these are very cheap, and it will be worth while to buy them as a reserve." The bargain was accordingly concluded; we took our purse, and counted out 700 sapeks to the merchant who counted them over himself, under our very eyes, pronounced the amount correct, and once more laid the coin before us. He then called out to his companion who was poking about in the courtyard: "Here, I've sold these capital boots for 700 sapeks." "Nonsense," cried the other, "700 sapeks! I won't hear of such a thing." "Very well," said we; "come, take your boots and be off with you." He was off and so quickly that we thought it expedient to count our sapeks once more; there were a hundred and fifty of them gone, and that was not all; while one of these rascals had been pocketing our money under our very nose, the other had bagged two great iron pins that we had driven into the courtyard for the purpose of our camels. Therefore we took a resolution—better late than never—to admit, in future, no merchant whatever into our room.

The House of Repose, as we had already indicated, was kept by Mussulmans. One day, their Mufti, who had recently arrived from Lan-Tcheu, the capital of Kan-Sou, attended at the house, in order to preside over some religious ceremony, the nature and object of which they would not explain to us. Sandara the Bearded, however, had an explanation of his own, which was, that the Grand Lama of the Hoei-Hoei attended on these occasions to teach his sectaries the latest improvements in the art of cheating in trade. For two days, the principal Mussulmans of the town assembled in a large apartment, contiguous to our own. There they remained for a long time, squatting on the ground, with their heads resting on their knees. When the Mufti appeared, all sent forth groans and sobs. After they had sufficiently lamented in this fashion, the Mufti recited, with a perfectly alarming volubility of tongue, several Arabic prayers; then everybody had another turn at lamenting, after which the cheerful assembly separated. This doleful ceremony was performed thrice in each of the two first days. On the morning of the third day, all the Mussulmans ranged themselves in the courtyard round the Mufti, who was seated on a stool, covered with a fine red carpet. Then the host of the House of Repose brought in a fine sheep, adorned with flowers and ribbons. The sheep was laid on its side, the host held it by its head, and two other Mussulmans by the legs, while a fourth presented to the Mufti a knife on a silver dish. He took the knife with great gravity, and approaching the victim, thrust the weapon up to the hilt into its neck. Thereupon cries and groans once more resounded on all sides. These ceasing, the sheep was skinned, cut up, and taken into the kitchen to be cooked, and, by and by, a grand entertainment of boiled mutton, presided over by the Mufti, closed the ceremony.

The Mussulmans, or Hoei-Hoei, are very numerous in China. It is said that they penetrated thither under the dynasty of the Thang, which began in 618, and terminated in 907. They were received by the Emperor, who at that period resided at Si-Ngan-Fou, the present capital of Chan-Si. They were kindly entertained, and the Emperor, struck with their fine features and forms, loaded them with favors, and entreated them to settle in his dominions. At first, it is stated, they were only 200 in number, but they have since so multiplied, that they now constitute a large population, eminently formidable to the Chinese. Kan-Sou, Yun-Nan, Sse-Tchouan, Chan-Si, Chen-Si, Chang-Toung, Pe-Tche-Ly, and Liao-Toung are the provinces in which they are most numerous. In some particular localities, indeed, they form the majority of the population, as compared with the Chinese. They have, however, become so mingled, so fused with the native people, that it would be difficult nowadays to recognize them, were it not for the small blue cap which they all constantly wear, to distinguish themselves from the Chinese. Their physiognomy has retained no vestige of its original type. Their nose has become flat, their eyes have sunk in, their cheek bones started out. They do not know a single word of Arabic—a language which their priests alone are bound to learn, and this only so as to read it. Chinese has become their stepmother tongue; yet they have preserved a certain energy of character which you seldom find among the Chinese. Though few in number, as compared with the enormous general population of the empire, they have ensured for themselves the fear and respect of all about them. Closely united among themselves, the entire community always takes up any matter affecting one of its members. It is to this spirit of association that they owe the religious liberty which they enjoy throughout all the provinces of the empire. No person would venture, in their presence, to cavil at their religious creed, or their religious practises. They abstain from smoking, from drinking wine, from eating pork, from sitting at table with pagans; and no one presumes to find fault with these peculiarities. They do not even hesitate to contravene the laws of the empire, if these contravene their freedom of worship. In 1840, while we were on our mission to Tartary, the Hoei-Hoei of the town of Hada, built a mosque, or Li-Pai-Sse, as the Chinese call it. When it was completed, the Mandarins of the place wanted to demolish it, because, contrary to the law, it rose higher than the Tribunal of Justice. Upon this intention becoming known, all the Mussulmans of the locality rose in arms, assembled, swore to prosecute in common a suit against the Mandarins, to impeach them at Peking, and never to lay down their arms until they had effected the removal of the offending dignitaries. As in China, money has the pre-

2

ponderant influence in all matters of this kind, the Mussulmans of Hada raised a subscription among all their co-religionists in the empire, and by its means defeated the Mandarins, who had desired to demolish their mosques, and effected their deposition and banishment. We have often asked each other how it was that the Christians in China live in a state of oppression, wholly at the arbitrary disposition of the tribunals, while the Mussulmans march about with heads erect, and constrain the Chinese to respect their religion. It certainly is not because the religion of Mahomet is, more than Christianity, in harmony with Chinese manners; quite the contrary, for the Chinese may, without any compromise of their religious duties, live in intimacy with the Pagans, eat and drink with them, interchange presents with them, and celebrate in common with them the Festival of the New Year, all which things are forbidden to the Hoei-Hoei by the despotic and exclusive spirit of their religion. No: that the Christians are everywhere oppressed in China is to be attributed to the great isolation in which they live. If one of them is taken before a tribunal, all his brethren in the locality get out of the way, instead of coming in a body to his aid and awing by their numbers the aggressive Mandarins. Now, more especially, that imperial decrees have been issued favorable to Christianity, if the Christians were to rise simultaneously in all parts of the empire, were energetically to assume possession of their rights, giving publicity to their worship, and exercising fearlessly, and in the face of day, their religious practises, we are satisfied that no one would venture to interfere with them. In China, as everywhere else, men are free who manifest the will to be so; and that will can only be effectively developed by the spirit of association.

We were now approaching the first day of the Chinese year, and in every direction people were preparing for its celebration. The sentences, written on red paper, which decorate the fronts of houses, were renewed; the shops were filled with purchasers; there was redoubled activity of operations in every quarter, while the children, ever eager to anticipate holidays and entertainments, were discharging, each evening, preliminary fireworks in the streets. Sandara informed us that he could not pass the Festival of the New Year at Tang-Keou-Eul, being obliged to return to the Lamasery, where he had duties to fulfil towards his masters and superiors. He added, that on the third day of the new moon, when he had satisfied all his obligations, he would come back and resume his services. He spoke in a tone of intense kindliness, in order to make us forget the daily impertinences he had been guilty of towards us. We did not at all urge him to return. Though delighted at the prospect of renewing our studies with him, we were determined not to seem anxious about the matter, lest we should raise still higher the already preposterous estimate he had of his own importance. We told him that since propriety recalled him to the Lamasery for the first day of the year, he ought by all means to obey the call. We then offered him three rolls of sapeks, saying, according to the custom in such cases, that it was to enable him to drink with his friends a cup of high-colored tea. For some minutes he feigned that he would not accept the coin, but at last we overcame his exquisite delicacy, and he consented to put the sapeks in his pocket. We then lent him Samdadchiemba's mule, and he left us.

The last days of the year are ordinarily, with the Chinese, days of anger and of mutual annoyance; for having at this period made up their accounts, they are vehemently engaged in getting them in; and every Chinese being at once creditor and debtor, every Chinese is just now hunting his debtors and hunted by his creditors. He who returns from his neighbor's house, which he has been throwing into utter confusion by his clamorous demands for what that neighbor owes him, finds his own house turned inside out by an uproarious creditor, and so the thing goes round. The whole town is a scene of vociferation, disputation, and fighting. On the last day of the year disorder attains its height; people rush in all directions with anything they can scratch together, to raise money upon, at the broker's or pawnbroker's, the shops of which tradespeople are absolutely besieged throughout the day with profferers of clothes, bedding, furniture, cooking utensils, and movables of every description. Those who have already cleared their houses in this way, and yet have not satisfied the demands upon them, post off to their relations and friends to borrow something or other which they vow shall be returned immediately, but which immediately takes its way to the Tang-Pou, or pawn-

Pawnbroker's Shop.

broker's. This species of anarchy continues till midnight; then calm resumes its sway. No one, after the twelfth hour has struck, can claim a debt, or even make the slightest allusion to it. You now only hear the words of peace and good-will; everybody fraternizes with everybody. Those who were just before on the point of twisting their neighbor's neck, now twine their friendly arms about it.

The new year is celebrated in much the same way as in Europe. Everybody dresses as fine as he possibly can; formal and informal visits are exchanged; presents circulate; dinners and parties are given; people go to see the play, the jugglers, and so on. Fireworks startle you at every turn; there is nothing going on but merry-making. After a few days, the shops are once more opened, and business imperceptibly resumes its course; at least with those who can carry it on; those who can't, declare themselves bankrupt, or, as the Chinese phrase it, leave the door open.

The Hoei-Hoei do not keep the new year at the same time with the Chinese, for in their special calendar they observe the Hegira of Mahomet. Owing to this circumstance, we passed these days of disorder and tumult in the greatest tranquillity. The epoch assigned for the recovery of debts was, in the place where we lodged, indicated merely by a few disputes, followed immediately by profound quiet. The House of Repose was not even disturbed by fireworks. We availed ourselves of this tranquillity, and of the absence of Sandara, to go thoroughly over our Thibetian lessons. The two dialogues we possessed were analyzed, decomposed, subjected to the intellectual alembic, in every way and in every detail. Housekeeping cares occupied, indeed, a portion of our daytime; but we made up for this by borrowing a few hours from the night, an arrangement which did not at all suit our host, who, finding that it involved him in an extra outlay for light, not only cut off our supplies, by removing the oil bottle, but, like the regular Turk he was, put on a charge per diem for light. As we did not choose to be condemned to darkness in this way, we bought a packet of candles, and constructed, with a long nail and the half of a carrot, a candlestick, not remarkable, indeed, for elegance or costliness, but which perfectly fulfilled its office. When the Turk's dole of oil was consumed, we lighted our candle, and we were thus able to give free course to the ardor of our Thibetian studies. Sometimes we would interrupt our labors to indulge in the relaxation of talking about France; and after this, rambling for awhile in spirit, over our dear native land, it was with a certain amount of difficulty only, that we could resume the realities of our position. It seemed strange, impossible almost, that we two should be seated there, amid the silent night, poring over Thibetian characters, in a country well-nigh at the extremity of the world, and practically unknown to Europeans.

On the third day of the first moon, Sandara the Bearded reappeared. During his absence we had enjoyed such delightful calm, that his aspect occasioned within us a very painful sensation; we felt like schoolboys alarmed at the approach of a severe preceptor. Sandara, however, was charmingly amiable. After gracefully wishing us a happy new year, in the most paternal, the most sentimental of phraseology, he proceeded to discourse upon the little mule we had lent him. First, on their way out, the little mule had thrown him a dozen times, so that at last he had resolved to walk; but then the creature was so droll, so fantastic in its ways, had so amused him, that he had not had time to grow tired. After this and similar small talk, we proceeded to business. Sandara said, that since we were determined to wait for the Thibetian embassy, he invited us to go and reside meanwhile in the Lamasery at Kounboum; and thereupon, with his accustomed eloquence, he descanted upon the advantages presented by a Lamasery to men of study and prayer. The proposition met the very wish of our hearts; but we took care not to manifest any enthusiasm in the matter, contenting ourselves with replying, coldly: "Well, we'll see how we like it."

The next day was devoted to the preparations for departure. Not having our camels with us, we hired a car, on which to transport our baggage. In announcing our departure to the host of the House of Repose, we claimed our tent, which we had lent him twelve days before, for a picnic party that he said he had formed with some friends into the Land of Grass; he replied, that he would send for it immediately to the friend's house, where it was carefully stowed away. We waited, but in vain; night came, the tent did not. At last, the host told us that his friend had left home for a day or two, and that the tent was locked up; but that it should be sent after us so soon as his friend returned. Sandara had hitherto said nothing; but when night came, and he found that we were not ready, he could no longer restrain his impatience. "It's quite obvious," said he to us, "that you are people altogether of another world; why don't you understand that your tent is at the pawnbroker's?" "At the pawnbroker's? Impossible!" "It is not at all impossible; it is considerably more than probable; the Hoei-Hoei wanted money wherewith to pay his debts at the end of the twelfth moon; he was delighted to find you with him in the emergency; he borrowed your tent, and he took it straight—not to the Land of Grass, but to the House of Pledges; and now he hasn't got the money to redeem it with. Just have him up: I'll put the matter to him, and you'll see." We requested the host to come to us. As soon as he entered the chamber, Sandara the Bearded commenced his interrogatory with imposing solemnity. "Listen to me," said he, "this evening I have a few words to say to you. You are a Turk—I a Lama, yet the laws of reason are the same for both of us. You have taken our tent, and you have carried it to the pawnbroker's; if you were in an embarrassed position, you did quite right; we do not reproach you; but we depart to-morrow, and our tent is not yet here. Which of us has reason on his side? we in claiming our property, or you in not restoring it? Do not tell us that the tent is at a friend's: I tell you that it is at the pawnbroker's. If, by the time we have drunk this jug of tea, our tent is not brought back, I will myself go to the magistrate to demand that it be given up to us, and we shall see whether a Lama-Dchiahour is to be oppressed by a Turk." By way of peroration to this harangue, Sandara gave such a thump with his fist upon the table, that our three cups performed a caper in the air. The Turk had nothing to say, and it was manifest that our tent was really at the pawnbroker's. After a moment's pause, the host assured us that we should have our property immediately, and he entreated us earnestly not to mention the matter abroad, lest it should compromise his establishment. We had scarcely quitted our room, before there arose a grand confusion in the courtyard; the attendants were collecting everything they could lay their hands upon, saddles, bedclothes, candlesticks, kitchen utensils, wherewith to redeem the tent, which, before we slept, we saw securely packed on the car which was to convey it to the Lamasery.

Next morning, at daybreak, we proceeded on our journey. The country through which we passed is occupied here by the Si-Fan, who lead a nomad life, and merely use the land as pasturage for their cattle,—whereas the Chinese, as in Eastern Tartary, are gradually encroaching upon the desert, building houses, and bringing into cultivation portions of the Land of Grass. Our brief voyage presented nothing remarkable, except, indeed, that in crossing a small river upon the ice, the car turned over and went to pieces. In France, in order to continue our journey, we should have needed a wheelwright and a smith to repair the damage; but fortunately our Phaeton was a Chinese, that is to say, a man who is never at a loss; and, accordingly, with a large stone, some bits of stick, and some ends of rope, he soon put everything to rights, and we merely lost a little time.

At the distance of a li from the Lamasery we found four Lamas, friends of Sandara, who had come to meet us. Their

Accident on the Ice.

religious costume, the red scarf that enveloped them, their miter-shaped yellow caps, their modest mien, the low, grave tones of their voices, all this produced a marked impression upon us, and we felt as though a perfume of religious and cenobitic life was diffused around us. It was past nine in the evening when we reached the first dwellings of the Lamasery. To avoid disturbing the profound silence which reigned everywhere about, the Lamas made the car-man stop, and filled with straw the interior of the bells which hung from the horses' necks. We then advanced slowly, and without saying a word, along the calm deserted streets of this great Lamanesque city. The moon was not present; but the sky was so clear, so pure, and the stars were so brilliant, that we could perfectly distinguish the cottages of the Lamas spread over the sides of the mountain, and the grand, though fantastic outlines of the Buddhist temples, standing out in the air like gigantic phantoms. That which most struck us at the moment, was the majestic and solemn silence which prevailed throughout the Lamasery, and which was interrupted only by the short sleepy bark of some half-wakened dog, like the scream of the sea-eagle, or the melancholy sound of a marine shell marking, at intervals, the watches of the night. We at length reached Sandara's cottage. As it was too late for us to seek a suitable lodging, our teacher gave us up his own habitation, and himself sought the hospitality of a neighbor. The Lamas who had accompanied us did not withdraw until they had made for us some tea with milk, and set before us some mutton, some fresh butter, and some exquisite rolls. We supped with excellent appetite, for we were thoroughly hungry, and, moreover, we experienced in our inmost heart a feeling of peculiar contentment, for which it seemed difficult to account.

We attempted to sleep, but it was in vain; slumber would not come near us; our minds, indeed, were too full of the strange position in which we now found ourselves. The whole thing appeared quite inconceivable. There were we, in this land of Amdo, unknown to Europe; in this great Lamasery of Kounboum, so famous, so venerated among Buddhists, in the cell of one of its ablest Lamas, amidst conventual manners altogether new to us; all these and analogous considerations whirled through and about the brain, like the vague intangible forms of a dream. We passed the night framing all sorts of plans.

As soon as day began to dawn we were on foot. Around us all was still silent. We offered up our morning prayer, our hearts agitated with sentiments altogether new to us in their peculiar character; with mingled joy and pride that it had been thus vouchsafed to us to invoke the true God in this famous Lamasery, consecrated to a lying and impious worship. It seemed to us as though we were about to grasp universal Buddhism within the paternal arms of the Christian faith.

Sandara soon made his appearance, and prepared for our breakfast some tea with milk, raisins, and cakes fried in butter. While we were occupied with our meal, he opened a small cupboard, and took out a wooden plate, highly polished, and decorated with gilding and flowers, upon a red ground. After wiping it carefully with his scarf, he placed upon it a broad sheet of pink paper, then, upon the paper he symmetrically arranged four fine pears, which he had directed us to buy at Tang-Keou-Eul, and then he covered the whole with a silk handkerchief, of oblong form, called in these countries Khata. "With this," said he, "we will go and borrow a lodging for you."

The Khata, or Scarf of Blessings, is so prominent a feature in Thibetian manners, that we may as well give an account of it. The Khata, then, is a piece of silk, nearly as fine as gauze, and of so very pale a blue as to be almost white. Its length about triples its breadth, and the two extremities are generally fringed. There are Khatas of all sizes and all prices, for a Khata is an object with which neither poor nor rich can dispense. No one ever moves unless provided with a supply. When you go to pay a visit, when you go to ask a favor, or to acknowledge one, you begin with displaying the Khata; you take it in both hands, and offer it to the person whom you desire to honor. When two friends, who have not seen each other for a long time, meet, their first proceeding is to interchange a Khata; it is as much a matter of course as shaking hands in Europe. When you write, it is usual to enclose a Khata in the letter. We cannot exaggerate the importance which the Thibetians, the Si-Fan, the Houng-Mao-Eul, and all the people who dwell towards the western shores of the Blue Sea, attach to the ceremony of the Khata. With them, it is the purest and sincerest expression of all the noblest sentiments. The most gracious words, the most magnificent presents go for nothing, if unaccompanied with the Khata; whereas, with the Khata, the commonest objects become of infinite value. If any one comes, Khata in hand, to ask you a favor, to refuse the favor would be a great breach of propriety. This Thibetian custom is very general among the Tartars, and especially in their Lamaseries; and Khatas accordingly form a very leading feature of commerce with the Chinese at Tang-Keou-Eul. The Thibetian embassy never passes through the town without purchasing a prodigious number of these articles.

When we had finished our modest breakfast, we issued forth in search of a lodging. Sandara the Bearded preceded us, bearing gravely on both hands the famous dish of four pears. This proceeding seemed to us so strange, that we were altogether confused, imagining that the entire population would have their eyes fixed upon us. Nothing of the sort: the Lamas, whom we met, passed silently on, without even turning their heads, or paying the slightest attention to us in any way. The little chabis, harum-scarum rogues in common with schoolboys all over the world, alone seemed to notice our presence. At last we entered a house. The master was in the courtyard, drying horse droppings in the sun. Upon perceiving us, he immediately enveloped himself in his scarf, and entered his cell. We followed him thither, and Sandara presented to him the Khata and the plate of pears, accompanying the present with a harangue in the East Thibetian tongue, of which we did not understand one single word. Meanwhile, we stood humbly apart, like poor wretches incapable even of soliciting a favor for themselves. When the harangue was completed, the host invited us to seat ourselves on the carpet, presented to each a cup of tea with milk, and told us, in Mongol, that he was rejoiced that strangers, come from such a distance, that Lamas of the Western Heaven should deign to cast their eyes upon his poor dwelling. Had he understood our European idioms, our answer would have been: Pray don't mention it; but as we had to speak in Mongol, we told him that we had, indeed, come from a great distance, but that, in great measure, we seemed once more at home, when we had the good fortune to meet with hospitality such as his. After having sipped the tea, and conversed for a while about France, Rome, the Pope, and the cardinals, we got up, in order to visit the place destined for us, which, for poor wanderers like us, seemed perfectly magnificent. Our host assigned to us a large room, with an ample kang, a separate kitchen, with stove, kettle, and other utensils, and, lastly, a stable for the horse and the mule. We almost wept with joy, and infinitely regretted that we had not another Khata at hand, wherewith at once to express our warm gratitude to the excellent Lama.

How potent is the empire of religion over the heart of man, even though that religion be false, and ignorant of its true object! How great was the difference, for example, between these Lamas, so generous, so hospitable, so fraternal towards strangers, and the Chinese, that thorough nation of shopkeepers, with hearts dry as a ship-biscuit, and grasping as a monkey, who will not give a traveler even a cup of water except for money or money's worth. The reception given to us in the Lamasery of Kounboum at once recalled to our thoughts those monasteries, raised by the hospitality of our religious ancestors, in which travelers and the poor ever found refreshment for the body and consolation for the soul.

We moved into our new dwelling the same day, the Lamas, more immediately neighbors of Sandara, cordially giving us their assistance. It was obviously with genuine pleasure that they carried for us, on their shoulders, the various articles composing our baggage; that they swept the room, lighted the fire, and arranged the stable for the reception of the animals. When all these matters were completed, the master of the house had, according to the rules of hospitality, to prepare an entertainment for us, since people who are moving are supposed to have no time for anything else.

Our readers will probably not be displeased at our giving them here a sketch of our new house and of its inhabitants. Immediately within the entrance gate was an oblong court, surrounded with stables commodiously arranged. On the left of the gate, a narrow passage led to a second square court, the four sides of which were occupied with the cells of Lamas. The side opposite the corridor constituted the abode of the master of the house, named *Akayé* (old brother). Akayé was a man of sixty odd years, tall, and so very thin and dry that he seemed a living skeleton. His long face was a mere framework of bones, covered with a baked, wrinkled skin. When he threw aside his scarf, and showed his arms, blackened with the sun, you might very well have taken them for two old bare vine sticks. Though he still managed to keep himself tolerably straight upon his legs, his step itself was tottering. Altogether he looked like some antique piece of mechanism, convulsively put in motion from time to time by the operation of a piston. For thirty-eight years Akayé had been employed in the temporal administration of the Lamasery. He had in this occupation amassed a tolerable fortune, but it had all gone in charitable gifts and in charity-loans never returned, so that he was now reduced to great poverty, nothing remaining to him but this house, which he had built in the time of his prosperity, and which no one would purchase from him. To let it was against the rules of the Lamasery, which admit no medium between absolute sale or absolute gift, except gratuitous loan. To complete his misfortunes, Akayé was unable to profit by the extraordinary offerings which from time to time are distributed among the Lamas who have attained certain grades in the hierarchy. Having been completely occupied throughout life with temporal matters, he had had no time for study, so that he was altogether illiterate, and could neither read nor write. This did not, however, prevent him from praying, morning, noon, and night; he had his chaplet constantly in his hand, and pass him when you might, you would hear him mumbling various forms of prayer. This man was a creature of excellent heart, but nobody seemed to take any heed to him—he was old and penniless.

To the right of Akayé, in another side of the court, lodged a Lama of Chinese origin, who was accordingly called the *Kitat-Lama* (Chinese Lama). Though seventy years old, he was in far better condition than poor Akayé; for though his frame was somewhat bent, it was still comfortably filled out; his face, replete with animation, was adorned with a fine white beard, somewhat yellowish towards the extremity. The Kitat-Lama was a man eminent among the Lama *savans;* he wrote and spoke perfectly Chinese, Mongol, and Thibetian. During a long residence in Thibet and in several kingdoms of Tartary, he had amassed a large fortune; it was said that in his cell were several chests full of silver ingots, yet his avarice continued of the most sordid character; he lived wretchedly, and clothed himself in rags; he was always turning his head about on one side or the other, like a man in perpetual fear of being robbed. In Tartary he had been considered a Grand Lama, but in Kounboum, where Lamanesque notables abound, he was merely one of the crowd. The Kitat Lama had with him a *Chabi* (pupil) eleven years old, a sharp, mischievous little vagabond, though with a good heart at bottom. Every evening we heard him at high words with his master, who regularly reproached him at night for the monstrous extravagances of the day, in respect of too much butter, too much tea, too much oil, too much everything.

Opposite the dwelling of the Kitat-Lama was the lodging of the two French missionaries; and beside their apartment was a small cell, wherein modestly dwelt a young student of medicine, in his second year. This young Lama was a tall, broad-shouldered fellow of twenty-four, whose dull, lead-colored, fat face convicted him of effecting in his small abode a very considerable consumption of butter. We never saw him poking his nose from his hole without thinking of Fontaine's rat, which, out of devotion, had retired into a great Dutch cheese. This young man was afflicted with a convulsive stammering, which sometimes almost choked him when he talked, and this infirmity, in rendering him timid and reserved, had also, perhaps, contributed to develop in him a certain amiability of manner and readiness to oblige. His great horror was the little Chabi, who took a malicious pleasure in imitating his manner of speaking.

The portion of the court which faced the residence of old Akayé was composed of a range of small kitchens, quite separate the one from the other. The master of the house, the Kitat-Lama, the stutterer, the missionaries, each had a kitchen of his own. In the phrase of the Lamasery, we were four distinct families in the house. Notwithstanding the collection of several families within one enclosure, there prevails throughout the most perfect order and silence; the inmates seldom interchange visits, and each attends to his own affairs without in the smallest degree interfering with those of his neighbor. In the house where we were located, we never saw our co-dwellers except on very fine days. It being now the depth of winter, whenever the sun favored our courtyard with its rays, the four families forthwith issued from their respective apartments, and sat themselves down before their doors on their felt carpets. The Kitat-Lama, whose eyes were still very good, would occupy himself in mending his wretched garments with bits of old rags. Akayé would murmur his prayers, scratching all the while his arms, the skin of which was so rough that it almost resounded to the touch. The student in medicine would chant, in order to avoid stammering, his lesson of therapeutics. As to ourselves, it was no easy matter to divert our attention from the singular spectacle around us; we had, indeed, on our knees our book of Thibetian dialogues, but our eyes were more frequently directed to the three families basking in the sun.

The Lamasery of Kounboum contains nearly 4,000 Lamas; its site is one of enchanting beauty. Imagine in a mountain's side a deep, broad ravine, adorned with fine trees, and harmonious with the cawing of rooks and yellow-beaked crows, and the amusing chattering of magpies. On the two sides of the ravine, and on the slopes of the mountain, rise, in an amphitheatrical form, the white dwellings of the Lamas of various sizes, but all alike surrounded with a wall, and surmounted by a terrace. Amidst these modest habitations, rich only in their intense cleanliness and their dazzling whiteness, you see rising, here and there, numerous Buddhist temples with gilt roofs, sparkling with a thousand brilliant colors, and surrounded with elegant colonnades. The houses of the superiors are distinguished by streamers floating from small hexagonal turrets; everywhere the eye is attracted by mystic sentences, written in large Thibetian characters, red or black, upon the doors, upon the walls, upon the posts, upon pieces of linen floating like flags, from masts upon the tops of the houses. Almost at every step you see niches in form resembling a sugar-loaf, within which are burning incense, odoriferous wood, and cypress leaves. The most striking feature of all, however, is to see an exclusive population of Lamas walking about the numerous streets of the Lamasery, clothed in their uniform of red dresses and yellow miters. Their face is ordinarily grave; and though silence is not prescribed, they speak little, and that always in an undertone. You see very few of them at all about the streets, except at the hours appointed for entering or quitting the schools, and for public prayer. During the rest of the day, the Lamas for the most part keep within doors, except when they descend by narrow, tortuous paths to the bottom of the ravines, and return thence, laboriously carrying on their shoulders a long barrel containing the water required for domestic purposes. At intervals you meet strangers who come to satisfy a devotional feeling, or to visit some Lama of their acquaintance.

The Lamasery of Kounboum, indeed, enjoys so high a reputation, that the worshipers of Buddha resort thither in pilgrimage from all parts of Tartary and Thibet, so that not a day passes in which there are not pilgrims arriving and departing. Upon the great festivals, the congregation of strangers is immense, and there are four of these in the year, the most famous of all being the Feast of Flowers, which takes place on the fifteenth day of the first moon. Nowhere is this festival celebrated with so much pomp and solemnity as at Kounboum. Those which take place in Tartary, in Thibet, and even at Lha-Ssa itself, are not at all comparable with it. We were installed at Kounboum on the sixth of the first moon, and already numerous caravans of pilgrims were arriving by every road that led to the Lamasery. The festival was in every one's mouth. The flowers, it was said, were this year of surpassing beauty; the Council of the Fine Arts, who had examined them, had declared them to be altogether superior to those of preceding years. As soon as we heard of these marvelous flowers, we hastened, as may be supposed, to seek information respecting a festival hitherto quite unknown to us. The following are the details with which we were furnished, and which we heard with no little curiosity:—

The flowers of the fifteenth of the first moon consist of representations, profane and religious, in which all the Asiatic nations are introduced with their peculiar physiognomies and their distinguishing costumes. Persons, places, apparel, decorations—all are formed of fresh butter. Three months are occupied in the preparations for this singular spectacle. Twenty Lamas, selected from among the most celebrated artists of the Lamasery, are daily engaged in these butter-works, keeping their hands all the while in water, lest the heat of the fingers should disfigure their productions. As these labors take place chiefly in the depth of the winter, the operators have much suffering to endure from the cold. The first process is thoroughly to knead the butter, so as to render it firm. When the material is thus prepared, the various portions of the butter work are confided to various artists, who, however, all alike work under the direction of a principal who has furnished the plan of the flowers for the year, and has the general superintendence of their production. The figures, etc., being prepared and put together, are then confided to another set of artists, who color them, under the direction of the same leader. A museum of works in butter seemed to us so curious an idea, that we awaited the fifteenth of the moon with somewhat of impatience.

On the eve of the festival the arrival of strangers became perfectly amazing. Kounboum was no longer the calm, silent Lamasery, where everything bespoke the grave earnestness of spiritual life, but a mundane city, full of bustle and excitement. In every direction you heard the cries of the camels and the bellowing of the long-haired oxen on which the pilgrims had journeyed thither; on the slopes of the mountain overlooking the Lamasery arose numerous tents wherein were encamped such of the visitors as had not found accommodation in the dwellings of the Lamas. Throughout the 14th the number of persons who performed the pilgrimage round the Lamasery was immense. It was for us a strange and painful spectacle to view that great crowd of human creatures prostrating themselves at every step, and reciting in undertones their form of prayer. There were among these Buddhist zealots a great number of Tartar-Mongols, all coming from a great distance. They were remarkable, alike, for their heavy, awkward gait, and for the intense devotion and scrupulous application with which they fulfilled the exact rules of the rite. The Houng-Mao-Eul, or Long Hairs, were there too, and, their manners being in no degree better here than at Tang-Keou-Eul, the haughty uncouthness of their devotion presented a singular contrast with the fervent, humble mysticism of the Mongols. They walked proudly, with heads erect, the right arm out of the sleeve and resting on their saber hilts, and with fusils at their backs. The Si-Fan of the Amdo country formed the majority of the pilgrims. Their physiognomy expressed neither the rough recklessness of the Long-Hairs, nor the honest good faith and good nature of the Tartars. They accomplished their pilgrimage with an air of ease and nonchalance which seemed to say, "We are people of the place; we know all about the matter, and need not put ourselves at all out of the way."

The head-dress of the Amdo women occasioned us an agreeable surprise; it was a little bonnet of black or gray felt, the form of which was identical with that of the bonnets which were once all the fashion in France, and which were called if we remember aright, *Chapeaux à la trois pour cent.* The only difference was, that the ribbon by which the bonnet was tied under the chin instead of being black, was red or yellow. The hair was allowed to fall from under the bonnet over the shoulders, in a number of minute braids, decorated with mother-of-pearl and coral beads. The rest of the costume was like that of the Tartar women, the weighty effect of the great sheep-skin robe being, however, mightily modified by the little *Chapeaux à la trois pour cent*, which communicates a most coquettish air. We were greatly surprised to find among the crowd of pilgrims several Chinese who, chaplet in hand, were executing all the prostrations just like the rest. Sandara the Bearded told us they were Khata merchants, who, though they did not believe in Buddha at all pretended intense devotion to him, in order to conciliate custom among his followers. We cannot say whether this was calumny on Sandara's part; but certainly his representation concurred altogether with our knowledge of the Chinese character.

On the 15th, the pilgrims again made the circuit of the Lamasery, but by no means in such numbers as on the preceding days. Curiosity impelled the great majority rather towards the points where preparations were making for the Feast of Flowers. When night fell, Sandara came and invited us to go and see the marvelous butter works of which we had heard so much. We accordingly proceeded with him, accompanied by the Stutterer, the Kitat-Lama, and the Chabi, leaving old Akayé to take care of the house. The flowers were arranged in the open air, before the various Buddhist temples of the Lamasery, and displayed by illuminations of the most dazzling brilliancy. Innumerable vases of brass and copper, in the form of chalices, were placed upon slight frame-work, itself representing various designs; and all these vases were filled with thick butter, supporting a solid wick. The illuminations were arranged with a taste that would have reflected no discredit on a Parisian decorator.

The appearance of the flowers themselves quite amazed us. We could never have conceived that in these deserts, amongst a half savage people, artists of such eminent merit could have been found. From the paintings and sculptures we had seen in various Lamaseries, we had not in the slightest degree been led to anticipate the exquisite finish which we had occasion to admire in the butter works. The flowers were bas-reliefs, of colossal proportions, representing various subjects taken from the history of Buddhism. All the personages were invested with a truth of expression that quite surprised us. The features were full of life and animation, the attitudes natural, and the drapery easy and graceful. You could distinguish at a glance the nature and quality of the materials represented. The furs were especially good. The various skins of the sheep, the tiger, the fox, the wolf, etc., were so admirably rendered, that you felt inclined to go and feel them with the hand, and ascertain whether, after all, they were not real. In each bas-relief you at once recognized Buddha, his face, full of nobleness and majesty, appertained to the Caucasian type; the artists conforming therein to the Buddhist traditions, which relate that Buddha, a native of the Western Heaven, had a complexion fair, and slightly tinged with red, broad, full eyes, a large nose, and long, curling, soft hair. The other personages had all the Mongol type, which the Thibetian, Chinese, Si-Fan, and Tartar shadings, so nicely discriminated that, without any reference whatever to the costume, you recognized at once to what particular tribe each individual belonged. There were a few heads of Hindoos and negroes, excellently represented. The latter excited a good deal of curiosity among the spectators. These large bas-reliefs were surrounded with frames, representing animals and flowers, all in butter, and all admirable, like the works they enclosed, for their delicacy of outline and the beauty of their coloring. On the road which led from one temple to another, were placed, at intervals, small bas-reliefs representing, in miniature, battles, hunting incidents, nomadic episodes, and views of the most celebrated Lamaseries of Thibet and Tartary. Finally, in front of the principal temple, there was a theater, which, with its personages and its decorations, were all of butter. The *dramatis personæ* were a foot high, and represented a community of Lamas on their way to solemnize prayer. At first, the stage is empty, then a marine conch is sounded, and you see issuing from two doors, two files of minor Lamas, followed by the superiors in their state-dresses. After remaining, for a moment, motionless on the stage, the procession disappears at the sides, and the representation is over. This spectacle excited general enthusiasm; but, for ourselves, who had seen rather better mechanism, we regarded these manikins, that moved on the stage and then moved off it without stirring a limb, as decidedly flat. One representation of the play, therefore, amply sufficed for us, and we went about admiring the bas-reliefs.

Whilst we were examining a group of devils, as grotesque, at all events, as those of Callot, we heard behind us a tremendous flourish of trumpets and marine conchs, and, upon inquiry, were informed that the Grand Lama was issuing forth from his sanctuary to visit the flowers. We

The Grand Lama of Kounboum.

desired nothing better, for the Grand Lama of Kounboum was a great object of curiosity with us. He soon reached the place where we stood. He walked in the center of the principal dignitaries of the Lamasery, preceded by minor Lamas, who cleared the way with great black whips. This Living Buddha appeared to us to be, at the outside, forty years old, he was of ordinary size, with a very flat and very common face, and of a very dark complexion. As he passed on he gave a vague glance at the bas-reliefs; when he saw that fine face of Buddha so repeatedly presented to his observation, he must, we thought, have said to himself that by dint of transmigrations he had dolefully degenerated from his original type. If the person of the Grand Lama, however, did not particularly strike us, his costume did, for it was strictly that of our own bishops: he bore on his head a yellow miter, a long staff in the form of a cross was in his right hand, and his shoulders were covered with a mantle of purple colored silk, fastened on the chest with a clasp, and in every respect resembling a cope. Hereafter we shall have occasion to point out numerous analogies between the Roman Catholic worship and the Lamanesque ceremonies.

The spectators generally appeared to give very slight heed to their Living Buddha, their attention being much more closely applied to the Buddhas in butter, which, in truth, were much better worth looking at. The Tartars alone manifested any tokens of devotion; they clasped their hands, bowed their heads in token of respect, and seemed quite afflicted that the pressure of the crowd prevented them from prostrating themselves at full length.

When the Grand Lama had made his circuit, he returned to his sanctuary, a proceeding which was adopted by all the spectators as a signal for abandoning themselves without reserve to transports of the most frantic joy. They sang themselves out of breath, they danced themselves out of breath, they pushed one another about, they shouted and bawled loud enough to frighten the desert itself, they seemed all at once to have become a collection of lunatics. As, with all this disorder, there was risk of the illuminations and the butter works being overturned, Lamas armed with great lighted torches were stationed, at intervals, to stay the waves of the immense mass that rolled to and fro like a sea beaten by the tempest. We could not long endure the pressure, and the Kitat-Lama, perceiving the oppression under which we labored, invited us to return home. We adopted the proposition all the more readily, that the night was far advanced, and we felt the need of repose.

Next morning, when the sun rose, not a trace remained of the Feast of Flowers. All had disappeared; the bas-reliefs had been demolished, and the immense collection of butter had been thrown down a ravine to feed the crows withal. These grand works, on which so much pains, so much time, we may also say, so much genius had been expended, had served merely as a spectacle for a single evening. Every year they make new flowers, and every year upon a new plan.

With the flowers disappeared also the pilgrims. Already, at daybreak, you saw them slowly ascending the tortuous paths of the mountain returning to their homes in the desert sorrowfully and silently; for the heart of man can endure so little of joy in this world that the day succeeding a festival is generally full of bitterness and melancholy.

THE GREAT WALL OF CHINA.

CHAPTER II.

Marvelous Birth of Tsong-Kaba—His Preparation for the Apostleship—He Departs for the West—His Interview with the Grand Lama of Thibet—He Reforms the Lamanesque Worship—Numerous Analogies Between the Catholic Religion and Reformed Buddhism—Origin of these Analogies—Tree of the Ten Thousand Images—Lamanesque Teaching—Faculty of Prayer—Government of the Lamasery of Kounboum—Offerings of the Pilgrims—Industry of the Lamas—The Adventures of Sandara the Bearded—Favorable Deposition of the Lamas Towards Christianity—Singular Practise for the Relief of Travelers—Nocturnal Prayers—Departure for the Lamasery of Tchogorton.

THE country of Amdo, situate south of Koukou-Noor, is inhabited by Eastern Thibetians, who, like the Mongol Tartars, lead a pastoral and nomadic life. The aspect of the country is wild and dismal. In all directions the eye discerns nothing but mountains of red and yellow ocher, almost destitute of vegetation, and intersected by deep ravines. It is only here and there, in this sterile and desolate region, that you find valleys tolerably supplied with pasturage, and hither the nomad tribes lead their flocks.

According to the Lamanesque chronicles, towards the middle of the fourteenth century of our era, a shepherd of the land of Amdo, named Lombo-Moke, had set up his black tent at the foot of a mountain, near the entrance to a deep ravine, through which, over a rocky bed, meandered an abundant stream. Lombo-Moke shared with his wife, Chingtsa-Tsio, the cares of pastoral life. They possessed no numerous flocks; some twenty goats and a few sarligues or long-haired cattle, constituted all their wealth. For many years they had lived alone and childless in these wild solitudes. Each day Lombo-Moke led his animals to the neighboring pastures, while Chingtsa-Tsio, remaining alone in her tent, occupied herself with the various preparations of milk, or with weaving, after the manner of the women of Amdo, a coarse linen with the long hair of the sarligues.

One day, Chingtsa-Tsio, having descended to the bottom of the ravine to draw water, experienced a faintness, and fell senseless on a large stone which bore inscribed on it various characters in honor of the Buddha Chakdja-Mouni. When Chingtsa-Tsio came to herself, she felt a pain in the side, and at once comprehended that the fall had rendered her fruitful. In the year of the Fire Hen (1357), nine months after this mysterious event, she brought into the world a son, whom Lombo-Moke named Tsong-Kaba, from the appellation of the mountain at whose feet his tent had stood for several years past. The marvelous child had, at his birth, a white beard, and his face wore an air of extraordinary majesty. There was nothing childlike about his manners. So soon as he saw the light, he was capable of expressing himself with clearness and precision in the language of Amdo. He spoke little, indeed, but his words always developed a profound appreciation of the nature and destiny of man.

At the age of three, Tsong-Kaba resolved to renounce the world, and to embrace the religious life. Chingtsa-Tsio, full of respect for the holy project of her son, herself shaved his head, and threw his fine long flowing hair outside the tent. From this hair, there forthwith sprung a tree, the wood of which dispensed an exquisite perfume around, and each leaf of which bore, engraved on its surface, a character in the sacred language of Thibet. Tsong-Kaba himself withdrew into the most absolute retirement, avoiding even the presence of his parents. He took up his position on the summits of the wildest mountains, or in the depths of the profoundest ravines, and there passed whole days and nights in prayer and in the contemplation of eternal things. His fastings were long and frequent. He respected the life even of the humblest insect, and rigorously interdicted himself the consumption of any sort of flesh whatever.

While Tsong-Kaba was thus engaged in purifying his heart by assiduity and prayer, and the practises of an austere life, a Lama, from one of the most remote regions of the West, casually visited the land of Amdo, and received the hospitality of Lombo-Moke's tent. Tsong-Kaba, amazed at the science and the sanctity of the stranger, prostrated himself at his feet, and conjured him to become his instructor. The Lamanesque traditions relate that this Lama of the western regions was remarkable not only for his learning, the profundity of which was unfathomable, but for the singularity of his appearance. People especially remarked his great nose, and his eyes that gleamed as with a supernatural fire. The stranger being, on his part, not less struck with the marvelous qualities of Tsong-Kaba, did not hesitate to adopt him as his disciple, and for this purpose took up his abode in the land of Amdo, where, however, he only lived a few years. After having initiated his pupil in all the doctrines recognized by the most renowned saints of the West, he fell asleep one day, on a stone, on the summit of a mountain, and his eyes opened not again.

Tsong-Kaba, deprived of the holy stranger's lessons, became all the more eager for religious instruction, and ere long he formed the resolution of abandoning his tribe, and of going to the further west, to drink at their very source the pure precepts of sacred science. He departed, staff in hand, alone, and without a guide, but his heart filled with superhuman courage. He first proceeded due south, and reached, after long and laborious journeying, the frontiers of the province of Yun-Nan, quite at the extremity of the Chinese empire. Then, instead of pursuing the previous direction, he turned towards the northwest, along the banks of the great river Yarou-Dsangbo. He reached, at length, the sacred town of the kingdom of Oui.[1] As he was about to continue on his way, a *Lha* (spirit), all radiant with light, stayed him, and prohibited his further progress. "Oh, Tsong-Kaba," said he, "all these vast regions belong to the

[1] Oui, in Thibetian, means center, middle; and hence the name was given to the province which occupies the center of Thibet, and the capital of which is Lha-Ssa.

great empire which has been granted to thee. It is here thou art ordained to promulgate the rites of religion and its prayers. It is here will be accomplished the last evolution of thy immortal life." Tsong-Kaba, docile to the supernatural voice, entered the *Land of Spirits* (Lha-Ssa), and selected an humble dwelling, in the most solitary quarter of the town.

The monk of the tribe of Amdo soon attracted disciples; and before long, his new doctrine and the innovations which he introduced into the Lamanesque ceremonies, created considerable excitement. At length, Tsong-Kaba resolutely put himself forward as a reformer, and began to make war upon the ancient worship. His partizans increased from day to day, and became known as the Yellow Cap Lamas, in contradistinction to the Red Cap Lamas, who supported the old system. The king of the country of Oui, and the Chakdja, the Living Buddha, and chief of the local Lamanesque hierarchy, became alarmed at this new sect that was introducing confusion into religious ceremonies. The Chakdja sent for Tsong-Kaba, in order to ascertain whether his knowledge was so profound, so marvelous, as his partizans pretended; but the reformer refused to accept the invitation. Representing a religious system which was to supersede the old system, it was not his business, he considered, to perform an act of submission.

Meantime the Yellow Caps became, by degrees, the predominant sect, and the homage of the multitude was turned towards Tsong-Kaba. The Buddha Chakdja, finding his authority repudiated, made up his mind to go and visit the little Lama of the province of Amdo, as he contumeliously designated the reformer. At this interview, he proposed to have a discussion with his adversary, which he flattered himself would result in the triumph of the old doctrine. He repaired to the meeting with great pomp, surrounded with all the attributes of his religious supremacy. As he entered the modest cell of Tsong-Kaba, his high red cap struck against the beam of the door, and fell to the ground, an accident which everybody regarded as a presage of triumph for the Yellow Cap. The reformer was seated on a cushion, his legs crossed, and apparently took no heed to the entrance of the Chakdja. He did not rise to receive him, but continued gravely to tell his beads. The Chakdja, without permitting himself to be disconcerted either by the fall of his cap, or by the cold reception that was given him, entered abruptly upon the discussion, by a pompous eulogium of the old rites, and an enumeration of the privileges which he claimed under them. Tsong-Kaba, without raising his eyes, interrupted him in these terms: "Let go, cruel man that thou art, let go the louse thou art crushing between thy fingers. I hear its cries from where I sit, and my heart is torn with commiserating grief." The Chakdja, in point of fact, while vaunting his own virtues, had seized a louse under his vest, and in contempt of the doctrine of transmigration, which forbids men to kill anything that has life in it, he was endeavoring to crack it between his nails. Unprovided with a reply to the severe words of Tsong-Kaba, he prostrated himself at his feet, and acknowledged his supremacy.

Thenceforward, the reforms proposed by Tsong-Kaba encountered no obstacle; they were adopted throughout Thibet, and afterwards became, by imperceptible degrees, established in all the kingdoms of Tartary. In 1409, Tsong-Kaba, then 52 years old, founded the celebrated monastery of Kaldan, three leagues from Lha-Ssa; it still flourishes, containing upwards of 8,000 Lamas. In 1419, the soul of Tsong-Kaba, who had become Buddha, quitted the earth and returned to the Celestial Realm, where it was admitted into the Heaven of Rapture. His body, which remained in the Lamasery of Kaldan, preserves to this day, it is alleged, all its original freshness, and, moreover, by a perennial miracle, lies a little above the earth, without being supported or raised upon anything. It is added that the mouth still, from time to time, addresses words of encouragement to those Lamas who have made marked progress towards perfection—words altogether inaudible for the less eminent of the community.

Besides the reformation which Tsong-Kaba introduced into the liturgy, he rendered himself further famous by a new edition of the "Body of Doctrine," left by Chakdja-Mouni. The most important of his other works is entitled *Lam-Rim-Tsien-Bo* (the Progressive Path to Perfection).

Upon the most superficial examination of the reforms and innovations introduced by Tsong-Kaba into the Lamanesque worship, one must be struck with their affinity to

Catholicism. The cross, the miter, the dalmatica, the cope, which the Grand Lamas wear on their journeys, or when they are performing some ceremony out of the temple; the service with double choirs, the psalmody, the exorcisms, the censer, suspended from five chains, and which you can open or close at pleasure; the benedictions given by the Lamas by extending the right hand over the heads of the faithful; the chaplet, ecclesiastical celibacy, spiritual retirement, the worship of the saints, the fasts, the processions, the litanies, the holy water, all these are analogies between the Buddhists and ourselves. Now, can it be said that these analogies are of the Christian origin? We think so. We have indeed found, neither in the traditions nor in the monuments of the country, any positive proof of their adoption, still it is perfectly legitimate to put forward conjectures which possess all the characteristics of the most emphatic probability.

It is known that, in the fourteenth century, at the time of the domination of the Mongol emperors, there existed frequent relations between the Europeans and the peoples of Upper Asia. We have already, in the former part of our narrative, referred to those celebrated embassies which the Tartar conquerors sent to Rome, to France, and to England. There is no doubt that the barbarians who thus visited Europe must have been struck with the pomp and splendor of the ceremonies of Catholic worship, and must have carried back with them into the desert enduring memories of what they had seen. On the other hand, it is also known that, at the same period, brethren of various religious orders undertook remote pilgrimages for the purpose of introducing Christianity into Tartary; and these must have penetrated at the same time into Thibet, among the Si-Fan and among the Mongols on the Blue Sea. Jean de Montcorvin, Archbishop of Peking, had already organized a choir of Mongol monks, who daily practised the recitation of the psalms, and the ceremonies of the Catholic faith. Now, if one reflects that Tsong-Kaba lived precisely at the period when the Christian religion was being introduced into Central Asia, it will be no longer matter of astonishment that we find, in reformed Buddhism, such striking analogies with Christianity.

And may we not proceed to lay down a proposition of a

more positive character? This very legend of Tsong-Kaba, which we heard in the very place of his birth, and from the mouth of several Lamas, does it not materially strengthen our theory? Setting aside all the marvelous features which have been added to the story by the imagination of the Lamas, it may be fairly admitted that Tsong-Kaba was a man raised above the ordinary level by his genius, and also, perhaps, by his virtue; that he was instructed by a stranger from the West; that after the death of the master the disciple, proceeding to the West, took up his abode in Thibet, where he diffused the instruction which he himself had received. May it not be reasonably inferred that this stranger with the great nose was a European, one of those Catholic missionaries who at the precise period penetrated in such numbers into Upper Asia. It is by no means surprising that the Lamanesque traditions should have preserved the memory of that European face, whose type is so different from that of the Asiatics. During our abode at Kounboum, we, more than once, heard the Lamas make remarks upon the singularity of our features, and say, roundly, that we were of the same land with the master of Tsong-Kaba. It may be further supposed that a premature death did not permit the Catholic missionary to complete the religious education of his disciple, who himself, when afterwards he became an apostle, merely applied himself, whether from having acquired only an incomplete knowledge of Christian doctrine, or from having apostatized from it, to the introduction of a new Buddhist Liturgy. The feeble opposition which he encountered in his reformation, would seem to indicate that already the progress of Christian ideas in these countries had materially shaken the faith of Buddha. We shall by and by inquire whether the numerous analogies between the Buddhists and the Catholics are an obstacle or an aid to the propagation of the faith in Tartary and Thibet.

The reformation of Tsong-Kaba triumphed in all the regions comprised between the Himalaya mountains, the frontiers of Russia, and the Great Wall of China. It even made its way into some provinces of the Celestial Empire, into Kan-Sou, for example, Chan-Si, Petche-Li, and all Mantchouria. The Bonzes have retained the ancient rites, with the exception only of a few innovations which have been adopted in particular localities. There is now a regular distinction understood between the two classes of Lamas, the yellow and the gray; that is to say, those who follow the reformation and those who persist in the elder worship. These two sects, which no doubt at one time treated each other as rivals, and made war upon each other, now live in perfect harmony. The Bonzes and the Lamas regard themselves as all of the same family.

The tribe of Amdo, previously altogether obscure and of no importance whatever, has, since the reformation of Buddhism, acquired a prodigious celebrity. The mountain at the foot of which Tsong-Kaba was born, became a famous place of pilgrimage. Lamas assembled there from all parts to build their cells, and thus by degrees was formed that flourishing Lamasery, the fame of which extends to the remotest confines of Tartary. It is called Kounboum, from two Thibetian words signifying Ten Thousand Images, and having allusion to the tree which, according to the legend, sprang from Tsong-Kaba's hair, and bears a Thibetian character on each of its leaves.

It will here be naturally expected that we say something about this tree itself. Does it exist? Have we seen it? Has it any peculiar attributes? What about its marvelous leaves? All these questions our readers are entitled to put to us. We will endeavor to answer as categorically as possible.

Yes, this tree does exist, and we had heard of it too often during our journey not to feel somewhat eager to visit it. At the foot of the mountain on which the Lamasery stands, and not far from the principal Buddhist temple, is a great square enclosure, formed by brick walls. Upon entering this we were able to examine at leisure the marvelous tree, some of the branches of which had already manifested themselves above the wall. Our eyes were first directed with earnest curiosity to the leaves, and we were filled with an absolute consternation of astonishment at finding that, in point of fact, there were upon each of the leaves well-formed Thibetian characters, all of a green color, some darker, some lighter than the leaf itself. Our first impression was a suspicion of fraud on the part of the Lamas; but, after a minute examination of every detail, we could not discover the least deception. The characters all appeared to us portions of the leaf itself, equally with its veins and nerves; the position was not the same in all; in one leaf they would be at the top of the leaf; in another, in the middle; in a third, at the base, or at the side; the younger leaves represented the characters only in a partial state of formation. The bark of the tree and its branches, which resemble that of the plane tree, are also covered with these characters. When you remove a piece of old bark, the

The Tree of Ten Thousand Images.

young bark under it exhibits the indistinct outlines of characters in a germinating state, and, what is very singular, these new characters are not unfrequently different from those which they replace. We examined everything with the closest attention, in order to detect some trace of trickery, but we could discern nothing of the sort, and the perspiration absolutely trickled down our faces under the influence of the sensations which this most amazing spectacle created. More profound intellects than ours may, perhaps, be able to supply a satisfactory explanation of the mysteries of this singular tree; but as to us, we altogether give it up. Our readers possibly may smile at our ignorance; but we care not, so that the sincerity and truth of our statement be not suspected.

The Tree of the Ten Thousand Images seemed to us of great age. Its trunk, which three men could scarcely embrace with outstretched arms, is not more than eight feet high; the branches, instead of shooting up, spread out in the shape of a plume of feathers, and are extremely bushy; few of them are dead. The leaves are always green, and the wood, which is of a reddish tint, has an exquisite odor, something like that of cinnamon. The Lamas informed us that in summer, towards the eighth moon, the tree produces large red flowers of an extremely beautiful character. They informed us also that there nowhere else exists another such tree; that many attempts have been made in various Lamaseries of Tartary and Thibet to propagate it by seeds and cuttings, but that all these attempts have been fruitless.

The Emperor Khang-Hi, when upon a pilgrimage to Kounboum, constructed, at his own private expense, a dome of silver over the Tree of the Ten Thousand Images: moreover, he made a present to the Grand Lama of a fine black horse, capable of traveling a thousand lis a day, and of a saddle adorned with precious stones. The horse is dead, but the saddle is still shown in one of the Buddhist temples, where it is an object of special veneration. Before quitting the Lamasery, Khang-Hi endowed it with a yearly revenue, for the support of 350 Lamas.

The fame of Kounboum, due in the first instance to the celebrity of Tsong-Kaba, is now maintained by the excellent discipline of the Lamasery, and the superiority of its teaching. Its Lamas are deemed students throughout their lives, for religious knowledge is reputed inexhaustible. The students are distributed into four sections, or faculties, according to the nature of the special studies to which they desire to apply themselves. 1. The Faculty of Mysticism, which comprehends the rules of contemplative life, and the examples exhibited in the career of the Buddhist saints. 2. The Faculty of Liturgy, comprising the study of religious ceremonies, with the expounding of all that appertains to Lamanesque worship. 3. The Faculty of Medicine, which applies itself to the four hundred and forty maladies of the human frame, to medical botany, and to the pharmacopœia. 4. The Faculty of Prayers, the most esteemed of all, the best paid, and, as a matter of course, the most numerous.

The voluminous works which serve as the basis of instruction in prayers, are divided into thirteen series, which represent, as it were, so many degrees in the hierarchy. The place which each student occupies in the schoolroom and the temple service, depends upon the series of theological works through which he has passed. Among the Lamas, you see old men proclaiming, by their low position in the hierarchy, their idleness or incapacity; and, on the other hand, mere youths elevated, by their application and their ability, to the highest ranks.

In order to obtain a degree in the Faculty of Prayers, all that is required from the student is to recite, without stopping, the books he has been directed to study. When he believes himself quite up, he gives intimation of this belief to the Grand Lama of prayers, in the form of a rich khata, a dish of raisins, and some ounces of silver, in ingots, the amount depending upon the degree at which he aims; he also makes presents to the Lama-examiners. Although it is, of course, perfectly understood that the judges are incorruptible, yet at Kounboum, as elsewhere, people do say that a few offerings to the academy are not without their effect at any examination. Men are men everywhere!

Before the principal temple of the Lamasery, there is a large square court, paved with broad stones, and surrounded with twisted columns, covered with colored sculptures. It is in this enclosure that the Lamas of the Faculty of Prayers assemble at the lecture hour, which is announced to them by the sound of a marine conch; here they sit, according to their rank, upon the bare stones, undergoing, in winter, the cold, the frost, and the snow; and in summer, the rain and the sun's heat. The professors alone are under shelter; they sit upon a sort of platform, covered with a tent. It is a singular spectacle to see all these Lamas with their red scarfs and great yellow miters, so huddled together that you cannot see the flag-stones on which they sit. After some of the students have given out the lesson of the day, the professors, in turn, give commentaries, vague and incomprehensible as the text itself, but nobody makes any objection; the explanation is quite near enough. Besides, the universal conviction is that the sublimity of a doctrine is in exact proportion to its obscurity and its unintelligibility.

The lesson generally concludes with a thesis, supported by a student previously named for that purpose, and whom the other students are entitled to question, upon whatever subject comes into their heads at the time. There is nothing more preposterous than these theses, which nearly remind one of those famous discussions of the schools in the middle ages, where there were such furious argumentations *de omni re scibili*. At Kounboum the rule is for the conqueror to mount on the shoulders of the conquered, and to be carried by him in triumph right round the walls of the school. One day Sandara the Bearded came home from lecture, his face radiant with unwonted smiles. We soon learned that he had been the hero of the theses; he had defeated his competitor upon the important question why poultry and other winged creatures are destitute of one of the vital functions common to all other animals. We mention this particular instance, because it will give an idea of the elevation and grandeur of Lamanesque education.

At certain periods of the year, the Living Buddha, the Grand Superior of the Lamasery, himself appears in person, and gives, in state, official expoundings of the Sacred Books. These commentaries, though not a bit more learned or more lucid than those of the professors, are received as authority. The Thibetian language is alone used in the schools.

The discipline of the Lamasery is vigilant and severe. In the Faculties, during the lectures, and in the temples, during the recitation of prayers, you see Lama censors leaning upon long iron rods, and maintaining order and silence among the students. The least infraction of the rules is at once visited with a reprimand, and, if necessary, with blows of the iron rod, the old Lamas being equally liable to both the one and the other, with the young Chabis.

A certain number of Lamas form the police of the Lamasery; they are attired in the same manner as the other Lamas, only their dress is gray, and their miter black. Day and night they perambulate the streets of the city, armed with a great whip, and re-establish order wherever their interposition has become necessary. Three tribunals, presided over by Lama judges, have jurisdiction in all matters that are above the immediate authority of the police. Those who are guilty of theft, to however trifling an amount, are first branded on the forehead and on each cheek with a hot iron and then expelled from the Lamasery.

The Buddhist monasteries, though similar in many respects to our own, exhibit essential differences. The Lamas are subject, it is true, to one same rule, and to one same discipline, but it cannot be said that they live in community. You find among them all the graduated shades of poverty and wealth that you see in mundane cities. At Kounboum we often observed Lamas clothed in rags, begging, at the doors of their rich brethren, a few handfuls of barley meal. Every third month the authorities make a distribution of meal to all the Lamas of the Lamaseries, without distinction, but the quantity is altogether inadequate. The voluntary offerings of the pilgrims come in aid, but, besides that these offerings are uncertain, they are divided among the Lamas according to the position which each occupies in the hierarchy, so that there are always a great many who never receive anything at all from this source.

Offerings are of two sorts, tea offerings and money offerings. The first is operated in this fashion: the pilgrim who proposes to entertain the brotherhood, waits upon the superiors of the Lamasery, and, presenting to them a khata, announces that he shall have the devotion to offer to the Lamas a general or special tea. The tea-general is for the whole Lamasery without distinction; the tea-special is given only to one of the four faculties, the selection being with the pilgrim. On the day fixed for a tea-general, after the repetition of morning prayer, the presiding Lama gives a signal for the company to retain their seats. Then forty young Chabis, appointed by lot, proceed to the great kitchen, and soon return, laden with jars of tea with milk; they pass along the ranks, and as they come to each Lama, the latter draws from his bosom his wooden tea-cup, and it is filled to the brim. Each drinks in silence, carefully placing a corner of his scarf before his cup, in order to modify the apparent anomaly of introducing so material a proceeding as tea-drinking into so spiritual a spot. Generally there is tea enough presented to go round twice, the tea being stronger or weaker according to the generosity of the donor. There are some pilgrims who add a slice of fresh butter for each Lama, and magnificent Amphytrions go to the length, further, of oatmeal cakes. When the banquet is over, the presiding Lama solemnly proclaims the name of the pious pilgrim, who has done himself the immense credit of regaling the holy family of Lamas; the pilgrim donor prostrates himself on the earth; the Lamas sing a hymn in his favor, and then march out in procession past their prostrate benefactor, who does not rise until the last of the Lamas has disappeared.

Offerings of this sort are very little for each individual Lama; but when you reflect that on such occasions there are assembled together more than 4,000 tea-drinkers, you may easily estimate that the aggregate expense becomes a very serious affair. In the Lamasery at Kounboum, one single tea-general, without either butter or cakes, costs fifty ounces of silver, or about twenty pounds.

Money offerings are still more expensive, for they are always accompanied with a tea-general. The money is not distributed at service time. After prayers, the presiding Lama announces that such a pilgrim, of such a place, has offered so many ounces of silver to the holy family of Lamas, and that the whole sum equally divided produces such a quotient. In the course of the day, the Lamas proceed to the Offering-office, where their respective proportion is scrupulously delivered to them.

There is no particular period or day fixed for the reception of offerings: they are always welcome; however, at the four great festivals of the year, they are more numerous and more important than at other times, on account of the greater number of pilgrims. After the Feast of Flowers, the King of Souniout, who was at Kounboum, made an offering, before he returned into Tartary, of six hundred ounces of silver, and a tea-general for eight days! with butter and cakes; the total expense amounted to six hundred pounds! When the offering is made by a distinguished personage, it is customary for the Living Buddha to be present at the ceremony, and he receives for his especial share an ingot of silver weighing fifty ounces, a piece of red or yellow silk, a pair of boots, and a miter, arranged in a basket decorated with flowers and ribbons, and covered with a rich khata. The pilgrim prostrates himself on the steps of the altar, where the Living Buddha is seated, and places the basket at his feet. A Chabi takes it up, and in return, presents to the pilgrim a khata in the name of the Living Buddha, whose business throughout is to preserve the impassibility and dignity befitting his assumed divinity.

Besides the distributions and the offerings the Lamas of Kounboum employ various means of improving their temporal condition. Some of them keep cows, and sell to their colleagues the milk and butter which help to season their tea and oatmeal. Others form themselves into a joint-stock company, and undertake the preparation of the teas-general which the pilgrims present to the community; others are tailors, dyers, bootmakers, hatters, and so on, and make up, for a fixed remuneration, the clothes of the Lamas. Lastly, a few of the number have shops, wherein they sell, at enormous profit, various goods, which they procure from Tang-Keou-Eul or Si-Ning-Fou.

In the class of industrial Lamas there is, however, a certain number who derive their livelihood from occupations which seem more conformable with the spirit of a religious life, namely, the printing and transcribing the Lamanesque books. Our readers are, perhaps, aware that the Thibetian writing proceeds horizontally, and from left to right. Though the idiom of the Lamas is alphabetical, much in the manner of our European languages, yet they make no use of movable type; stereotype printing on wood is alone practised. The Thibetian books resemble a large pack of cards; the leaves are movable, and printed on both sides. As they are neither sewn nor bound together, in order to preserve them, they are placed between two thin boards, which are fastened together with yellow bands. The editions of the Thibetian books printed at Kounboum are very rude, the letters are sprawling and coarse, and in all respects very inferior to those which emanate from the imperial printing press at Peking. The manuscript editions, on the contrary, are magnificent; they are enriched with illustrative designs, and the characters are elegantly traced. The Lamas do not write with a brush like the Chinese, but use little sticks of bamboo cut in the form of a pen; their inkstand is a little copper box, resembling a jointed snuff-box, and which is

Buddhic Prayer.

filled with cotton saturated with ink. The Lamas size their paper, in order to prevent its blotting; for this purpose, instead of the solution of alum used by the Chinese, they sprinkle the paper with water mixed with one-tenth part of milk, a simple, ready, and perfectly effective process.

Sandara the Bearded did not belong to any of the classes of industrials that we have enumerated; he had a business of his own, namely, that of *taking in* the strangers whom devotion or other motives brought to the Lamasery. The Mongol-Tartars in particular afforded him profitable employment in this way. On their arrival he would introduce himself in the character of *cicerone*, and, thanks to the easy, seductive elegance of his manners and conversation, he always managed to get engaged as their man of business during their stay. At Kounboum itself Sandara's reputation was by no means unequivocal. The better Lamas shunned him, and some of them went so far as to give us a charitable hint not to confide too much in his fine words, and always to keep an eye upon our purse when in his company.

We learned that, compelled to quit Lha-Ssa for some knavery, he had vagabondized for three years through the provinces of Sse-Tchouen and Kan-Sou, as a strolling player and fortune-teller. We were not at all surprised at this information. We had ourselves remarked that whenever Sandara became frankly himself, his manner was always that of an actor.

One evening, when he seemed in a more amiable humor than ordinary, we thought we could extract from him some of his old adventures. "Sandara," said we, "the chattering Lamas here pretend that on your way from Thibet, you remained three years in China." "The words are truth." "They say, too, that you are a capital hand at stage recitations." Sandara rose, clacked a sort of prelude with his fingers, threw himself into a theatrical attitude, and recited, with emphasis, some Chinese verses. "A Lama comedian!" said we, laughingly; "this is a marvel indeed!" "No, no!" cried he; "I was first a Lama, then a comedian, and now I am a Lama again. "Come," continued he, resuming his accustomed seat, "since the chatterers have spoken to you of my adventures, I will give you the real history of them."

"After remaining for ten years at Lha-Ssa, in the Lamasery of Sera, a longing for my country took possession of my thoughts; the Three Valleys occupied my soul. The malady at length became so powerful, that I could not resist it. I accordingly departed, having as my traveling companions four Lamas of Amdo, who were also returning home. Instead of pursuing the eastern route we proceeded southwards, for in that direction the desert is not wholly uninhabited. We journeyed, pack on back, and staff in hand. If on our way we came to a black tent, we sought its hospitality, otherwise we had to pass the night in the depths of some ravine, or beneath some rock. You know that Thibet is a country covered with great mountains; we had accordingly a continuous series of ascendings and descendings. Although it was summer, we frequently encountered heavy falls of snow. The nights were very cold, but during the day, especially in the valleys, we were almost killed with the heat.

"We walked on merrily, however. We were all in good health and good humor, more particularly when the shepherds had made us a present of a kid, or a good lump of butter. In the country through which we passed, we saw some very singular animals; they were not so big as an ordinary cat, and they were covered with a sort of hair as hard as iron needles. Whenever one of these creatures perceived us, it immediately rolled itself up, so that you could no longer distinguish head, tail, or feet, and became, as it were, a great ball, all bristling with long, hard thorns. At first these beasts frightened us; we could not comprehend at all what they were, for the books of prayer say not a word about them. However, by degrees we got courage enough to examine them closely. As these balls were too prickly to be touched with the hand, we placed a stick horizontally across one of them, and then pressed down both ends, until we made the ball open itself a little, and then there came out a little face like a man's, that looked at us fixedly. We cried out in great terror, and ran away as hard as we could. At last, however, we grew accustomed to the little animals, and they even served for us an amusement, for it was good fun to turn them over and over down the hills, with the iron ends of our staves.

"We also met with worms of a very surprising kind. One day when it was very hot, we were journeying along a little stream that meandered through a valley, in which the grass grew very high. Towards noon, after drinking tea, we lay down and slept on the edge of the stream. You know that, according to the rule of Tsong Kaba, the yellow-mitered Lamas do not wear trousers. When we woke up, we found a number of worms sticking to our legs; they were of a gray color, and as big as one's finger. We tried to get them off, but could not; and as we did not experience any pain from them, we waited to see what would be the end of the affair. By and by the beasts swelled, and when they had become quite round and large, they dropped off themselves. Oh! Thibet is a singular country. You see animals there that are found nowhere else. Lamas who have not traveled in the country won't believe what we tell them about it." "They are wrong, then," said we, "for what you have just said is in perfect conformity with the truth. These curious animals that you describe are not inhabitants of Thibet only; they are very common in our country. Those which are enveloped with sharp thorns, we call hedgehogs; and the great worms we call leeches." "What! have you seen animals of the kind?" "Often." "I'm glad to hear it, for you'll be able to confirm what we say to any Lamas that don't believe us."

"Well, we went on quite comfortably, till we came to the Eul Mountain. This mountain is very lofty, and covered with a great forest of pine and holly; we rested at the foot of it during a whole day in a black tent. When night came, two of our number said: 'The evening is fine, the moon bright; we can't do better than cross the mountain in the cool of the night. In the morning it will grow hot, and we shall find it much more laborious to climb the mountain then.' 'No,' objected the others, 'night is for wild beasts; men should only travel by day.' Thus, you see, we disagreed about the matter. The two first persisted; they took up their iron-pointed staves, fastened their packs on their shoulders, and went on their way. This, you will admit, was an ill step to take. When pilgrims have said: 'Let us journey together,' they should not part company.

"Well, when day broke, we also went on our way—we three who remained of the five. Just as we were reaching the summit of the Eul Mountain, 'Tsong-Kaba,' cried I, 'here is an iron-pointed staff on the ground.' 'Why,' said one of my companions, looking at the staff, 'this is Lobzan's staff.' We examined it closely, and clearly recognized it. 'This,' said we, 'is what people get by traveling at night. They drop something or other, and there is not light enough for them to find it again.' We went on. After a short further and very rugged ascent, we stepped on the plateau of the mountain. We had no sooner done so, than all three sent forth a cry of terror; for we saw before us another iron-pointed staff, Lama's clothes torn in pieces, pieces of human flesh, and bones broken and gnawed. The earth torn up, and the grass trodden down, indicated that a severe struggle had taken place on the spot. It was obvious at once that some wild beasts, tigers or wolves, had killed and devoured our companions. I stood for a moment panic-struck at the horrible spectacle. Then I wept like a child. We rushed down the other side of the mountain with fear-impelled speed. From that moment our journey was a sad and silent one. Only, when we came to a black tent, we would recount to the shepherds the awful catastrophe of our poor comrades, and the relation afforded some slight alleviation of our grief.

"Three moons after our departure from Lha-Ssa, we arrived at the frontier of China. There we separated; the two Lamas of Amdo turned to the north, towards their own country; while I, crossing the Wall of Ten Thousand Lis, entered the province of Sse-Tchouen. After a few days' march, I found in an inn, a company of comedians. All night, these people did nothing but sing, joke, and drink rice-wine. 'In this country of Sse-Tchouen,' said the manager of the company to me, 'there are no Lamas. What do you propose to do with that red robe and that yellow hat of yours?' 'You are quite right,' said I; 'in a country of Lamas, to be a Lama is well; but in a land of comedians, one must be a comedian. Will you take me into your company?' 'Bravo! bravo!' cried everybody; 'you shall be one of us.' And so saying, each made me a low bow, which I returned by putting my tongue in my cheek, and scratching my ear, according to the Thibetian manner of saluting. At first, I took the matter as a joke; but by and by, upon reflecting that I had no means left, I thought I might as well take the manager at his word, and accordingly I became a member of the corps.

"Next day I packed up my religious costume and assumed a mundane suit. As my memory had been long disciplined by the study of prayers, I found little trouble in learning a part in a play and in a few days I became quite a first-rate comedian. We gave representations, during upwards of a year, in all the towns and villages of Sse-Tchouen. The company then resolving to visit the province of Yun-Nan, I quitted them, because that expedition would have carried me too far from my native Three Valleys. After the feast of separation accordingly, I proceeded on my way to the paternal roof. The journey occupied nearly two years. At every place I came to, I stopped a few days and gave representations, practising as a merry-andrew, and making a comfortable thing enough of it, for one always gets more by performing on one's own account. I entered my native village in grand style, mounted on a magnificent ass I had bought at Lan-Tcheou, and with twelve ounces of silver in my pocket. I gave a few representations to my countrymen who were amazed at my skill; but I had soon to give up my new profession.

"One evening when the family were assembled to hear some of my Thibetian stories, my mother maintained profound silence and her face manifested utter grief; soon I observed the tears trickling down her cheeks. 'Mother,' asked I, 'why do you weep? In my story was there anything to excite your tears?' 'Thy story,' she replied, 'produces upon me no impression whatever, agreeable or disagreeable; it strikes upon my ears, but makes no way to my heart. That which moves, that which afflicts me, is the thought that when thou left us fourteen years ago, to visit the Land of Saints, thou wert clothed in the sacred habit of the Lamas, and that now thou art a layman and a buffoon.' These words confounded me. After a moment's silence I rose and cried emphatically: 'It is written in the Holy Doctrine, that it is better to honor one's father and mother than to serve the spirits of heaven and earth. Therefore, mother, say what you would have me do, and your son will reverentially obey you.' 'Throw aside those mundane clothes,' said my mother, 'cut off that tress of hair, and re-enter the family of the saints.' I had nothing to say in reply, but prostrated myself thrice on the ground, in token of submission. When a mother speaks, one must obey; filial piety is the basis of all good doctrine. In translating for you the ten great commandments of Jehovah, I remember that the fourth said: 'Thou shalt honour thy father and thy mother.'

"Next morning I resumed my Lama dress, and a few days after proceeded to Kounboum, where I am laboring to sanctify myself."

These last words of Sandara the Bearded clearly merited to be received with a horse laugh, but we restrained ourselves by dint of biting our lips, for we had experience that, notwithstanding his immense zeal for sanctification, our worthy tutor had not as yet attained any very great results in the matter of patience and mildness.

This summary of the adventures of Sandara, at once explained to us how it was that upon all occasions he manifested such marked predilection for the men and things of China. The rules bequeathed by Tsong-Kaba interdicted to the Lamas the use of garlic, brandy, and tobacco;

garlic being prohibited because it is unbecoming to present one's self before the image of Buddha with bad breath, offensive in itself, and capable of infecting the perfume of the incense; brandy, because this fatal liquor disturbs the reason and excites the passions; and tobacco, because it engenders idleness, and absorbs precious hours that ought to be devoted to the study of prayers and of doctrine. Despite these prohibitions, so soundly based, the Lamas—such of them, at least, as sanctify themselves after the manner of Sandara—do not hesitate to smoke, to drink, and to season their oatmeal with garlic. All this, however, is done secretly, and without the knowledge of the police. In the Lamasery of Kounboum, Sandara was the patron and introducer of the Chinese hawkers who deal in these contraband articles, and aided them in the sale of their goods, for a small commission.

A few days after the Feast of Flowers, we vigorously resumed our Thibetian studies under the direction of Sandara, who came every morning to work with us. We occupied ourselves in the translation of an abridgment of Sacred History from the creation to the preaching of the Apostles. We gave to this work the dialogue form; the two interlocutors being a Lama of Jehovah and a Lama of Buddha. Sandara fulfilled his functions altogether as a matter of business. The favorable tendencies which he at first manifested, when we were at Tang-Keou-Eul, his crossings, his admiration of the Christian doctrine, had been all a mere farce. Religious feelings had no hold upon his grasping, hardened heart. He had acquired, by his long abode among the Chinese, a sneering, cold-blooded, carping incredulity, which he seemed to delight in parading upon all occasions. In his estimation, all religions were so many devices invented by the wise for the more facile and effective despoilment of the witless. Virtue with him, was a vain word, and the man of merit, he who made the most of his fellow-men.

Despite, however, these skeptical and impious opinions, Sandara could not prevent himself from feeling high admiration of the Christian doctrine. He was especially struck with the concatenation of the historical facts which he translated for us. He found in them a character of authenticity, of which the fables accumulated in the Buddhist books are wholly destitute; he admitted this, not unfrequently, but always in an unguarded moment, for his aim was to support in our presence his melancholy part of a free-thinker. When he was with the Lamas, he was more at his ease; and there he did not hesitate to declare that as to religious doctrine, we knew more about it than all the living Buddhas put together.

After some time, we began to make a certain sensation in the Lamasery; the Lamas talked a good deal to one another about the two Lamas of Jehovah, and the new doctrine they taught. It was remarked that we were never seen to prostrate ourselves before Buddha; that, thrice a-day, we said prayers which were not Thibetian prayers; that we had a language of our own, which nobody else understood, but that with other people we talked Tartarian, Chinese, and a little Thibetian. Here was more than enough to excite the curiosity of the Lamanesque public. Every day we had visitors, and the conversation with them always and altogether turned upon religious questions. Among all the Lamas who visited us, we did not find one of the same incredulous stamp with Sandara the Bearded; they all, on the contrary, seemed sincerely religious and full of faith; many of them attached the utmost importance to the study and knowledge of truth; and we found the same men coming again and again to seek instruction from us in our holy religion.

The instruction we communicated was altogether historical in its plan, everything being carefully excluded which could suggest dispute, or arouse the spirit of contention; we gave our friends a simple and concise outline of our religion, leaving them to derive thence, for themselves, conclusions against Buddhism. Proper names and dates, precisely set forth, produced more effect upon them than the most logical reasoning. When they had thoroughly mastered the names of Jesus, of Jerusalem, of Pontius Pilate, the date of four thousand years since the creation of the world, and the names of the twelve Apostles, they had no longer any doubts as to the Redemption, or as to the Preaching of the Gospel. The connection which they observed between the history of the Old Testament and that of the New, amounted, in their eyes, to demonstration. The mysteries and the miracles created no difficulty in their minds.

After all we have seen in our long peregrination, and especially during our abode in the Lamasery of Kounboum, we are persuaded that it is by instruction, and not by controversy, that the conversion of the heathen is to be efficaciously operated. Polemics may reduce an adversary to silence, may often humiliate him, may sometimes irritate him, but they will never convince him. When Jesus Christ sent forth his disciples, he said to them: Go forth and teach all nations, which does not mean: go forth and hold controversies with all nations. In our days, two schools of philosophy, the one recognizing Descartes for its head, the other Lamennais, have much disputed the question whether paganism is a crime or an error; it appears to us to be neither the one nor the other, but simply the effect of ignorance. The spirit of a pagan is enveloped in darkness. Carry light within that darkness, and the darkness will disappear: the pagan needs neither the thesis of the Cartesians, nor the requisitory of the Lamennaisians: all he wants is instruction.

The eagerness of the Lamas to visit us, and especially their favorable tendencies towards Christianity, gave, after a while, umbrage to the zealous tenacity of Sandara; he turned desperately sulky, and after going through the lesson of the day, in the dryest and briefest manner possible, he would say not another word to us for the rest of the twenty-four hours, but observe towards us the most contumelious silence. If we asked him in the humblest manner the Thibetian name of some object, or the meaning of some particular phrase in the Dialogues, he would not condescend to a word of reply. In this extremity we usually had recourse to our neighbor, the young student in medicine, who always gave us the information we needed with the most frank cordiality; and although he was not very learned in Thibetian, we found him of very great utility. His open, good-natured character, moreover, encouraged us to ask him many questions respecting some of the Lama practises, which we desired to understand. In return for these services, we aided, with all our hearts, his desire to become acquainted with the Christian religion. Far different from Sandara, he was full of respect for the truths we announced to him; but his timid, irresolute temperament kept him from openly abjuring Buddhism. His idea was, that he could be, at one and the same time, a good Christian and a fervent Buddhist; in his prayers, he invoked alternately Tsong-Kaba and Jehovah, and he carried his simplicity so far as to ask us sometimes to take part in his religious practises.

One day he proposed to us a service of devotion in favor of all the travelers throughout the whole world. "We are not acquainted with this devotion," said we; "will you explain it to us?" "This is it: you know that a good many

Sending Horses to Travellers.

travelers find themselves, from time to time, on rugged, toilsome roads. Some of these travelers are holy Lamas on a pilgrimage; and it often happens that they cannot proceed by reason of their being altogether exhausted; in this case we aid them by sending horses to them." "That," said we, "is a most admirable custom, entirely conformable with the principles of Christian charity; but you must consider that poor travelers such as we are not in a position to participate in the good work: you know that we possess only a horse and a little mule, which require rest, in order that they may carry us into Thibet." "Tsong-Kaba!" ejaculated the Lisper, and then he clapped his hands together, and burst into a loud laugh. "What are you laughing at? What we have said is the simple truth: we have only a horse and a little mule." When his laughter at last subsided: "It was not that I was laughing at," said he; "I laughed at your misconceiving the sort of devotion I mean; what we send to the travelers are paper horses." And therewith he ran off to his cell, leaving us with an excellent occasion for laughing in our turn at the charity of the Buddhists, which we thus learned consisted in giving paper horses to travelers. We maintained our gravity, however, for we had made it a rule never to ridicule the practises of the Lamas. Presently the Lisper returned, his hands filled with bits of paper, on each of which was printed the figure of a horse, saddled and bridled, and going at full gallop. "Here!" cried the Lisper, "these are the horses we send to the travelers. To-morrow we shall ascend a high mountain, thirty lis from the Lamasery, and there we shall pass the day, saying prayers and sending off horses." "How do you send them to the travelers?" "Oh! the means are very easy. After a certain form of prayer, we take a packet of horses which we throw up into the air, the wind carries them away, and by the power of Buddha they are then changed into real horses, which offer themselves to travelers." We candidly told our dear neighbor what we thought of this practise, and explained to him the grounds upon which we declined to take any part in it. He seemed to approve of our sentiments on the subject; but this approval did not prevent him from occupying a large portion of the night in fabricating, by means of the press, a prodigious number of horses.

Next morning, before daybreak, he went off, accompanied by several colleagues, full, like himself, of devotion for poor travelers. They carried with them a tent, a boiler, and some provisions. All the morning the wind blew a hurricane; when, towards noon, this subsided, the sky became dark and heavy, and the snow fell in thick flakes. We awaited, with anxious impatience, the return of the Stutterer. The poor wretch returned in the evening, quite worn out with cold and fatigue. We invited him to rest for awhile in our tent, and we gave him some tea with milk, and some rolls fried in butter. "It has been a dreadful day," said he. "Yes, the wind blew here with great violence." "I'll venture to affirm it was nothing here to what we found it on the top of the mountain: the tent, the boiler—everything we had with us was carried away by a regular whirlwind, and we were obliged to throw ourselves flat on the ground in order to save ourselves from being carried away too." "It's a sad pity you've lost your tent and boiler." "It is, indeed, a misfortune. However, it must be admitted that the weather was very favorable for conveying horses to the travelers: When we saw that it was going to snow, we threw them all up into the air at once, and the wind whisked them off to the four quarters of the world. If we had waited any longer, the snow would have wetted them, and they would have stuck on the sides of the mountain." Altogether this excellent young man was not dissatisfied with his day's work.

The twenty-fifth of each moon is the day devoted to the transmission of horses to poor travelers. The practise is not a general rule; but is left to the devotion of individuals. The twenty-eighth of the moon is set apart for another species of religious exercise, in which all the Lamas are required to participate. On the twenty-seventh the Stammerer gave us notice of the ceremony in these words: "To-morrow night we shall, perhaps, prevent your sleeping, for we shall have to celebrate our nocturnal prayers." We paid no special attention to this intimation, conceiving that it simply meant that in the course of the night, the Lamas would recite prayers in their cells, as they not infrequently did. We accordingly retired to rest at our usual hour, and fell asleep.

Conformably with the warning of the Stammerer, our slumbers did not remain long uninterrupted. First we seemed to dream that we heard a sort of concert by a great multitude of voices up in the air. Imperceptibly these vague, confused sounds became loud and distinct. We awoke and heard clearly enough the chanting of Lamanesque prayers. In the twinkling of an eye, we were up and dressed and out in the courtyard, which was illumined with a pale light that appeared to descend from above. In his wonted corner sat old Akayé, telling his beads. "Akayé," asked we, "what is this strange noise?" "The nocturnal

5

prayers. If you want to see more of them you had better go on to the terrace." There was a ladder resting in the most accommodating manner against the wall. We hastily ascended it, and became spectators of a most singular sight. The terraces were illuminated by red lanterns suspended from long poles, and all the Lamas, attired in their state mantles and yellow miters, were seated on the roofs of their houses chanting their prayers with a slow and monotonous voice. On the roof of our own house we found the Stammerer, the Kitat-Lama, and his Chabi, wholly absorbed with the ceremony. We took care not to disturb them, and contented ourselves with merely looking on and listening. Those innumerable lanterns, with their red, fantastic glare, the buildings of the Lamasery vaguely illumined by the reflection of their trembling light, the four thousand voices combining in one immense concert, accompanied from time to time by the sound of trumpets and marine conchs—all this produced an effect that agitated the soul with a sort of vague terror.

After having gazed for awhile at this strange spectacle, we descended into the courtyard, where we found old Akayé still in the same place and the same position. "Well," said he, "you have seen the ceremony of nocturnal prayers?" "Yes, but we don't understand what they precisely mean. Would it be troubling you too much to ask from you some explanation of the matter?" "Not at all. These prayers were instituted for the purpose of driving away demons. You must know that this country was once fearfully infested with demons, who caused maladies in the herds and spoiled the milk of the cows; they often invaded the cells of the Lamas, and at times carried their audacity to the excess of penetrating into the temple in the hour of general prayer, their presence being indicated by the confusion and discordance which immediately prevailed in the psalmody. During the night they assembled in large numbers in the ravine, where they frightened everybody with cries and howlings so strange in their character that no man could imitate them. A Lama, full of learning and piety, invented the nocturnal prayers, and the demons have since almost entirely disappeared from the district. A few come here occasionally, but they don't do any mischief as they used to do." "Akayé," asked we, "have you ever chanced to see any of these demons ?" "No, never; and I'm sure you have not seen any of them." "What makes you suppose so ?" "Because the demons only appear to wicked Lamas, and the good Lamas never see them." At this moment the prayer of the Lamas on the house-tops ceased, the trumpets, the bells, the drums, and the marine conchs sounded all at once three different times; the Lamas, then, all sent forth together hideous cries and yells, like those of wild beasts, and the ceremony terminated. The lanterns were extinguished, and silence resumed its sway. We bade old Akayé good night, and once more went to sleep.

We had been residing at Kounboum more than three months, enjoying the friendly sympathies of the Buddhist monks and the protection of the authorities. But for some time past we had been in flagrant opposition to a leading rule of the Lamasery. Strangers who pass through Kounboum, or who merely reside there for a short time, may dress as they please. Those persons, on the contrary, who are connected in any way with the Lamasery, or who are making any stay in the place, are required to wear the sacred dress of the Lamas, that is to say, a red gown, a small dalmatica without sleeves and showing the arm, a red scarf, and a yellow miter. This rule of uniformity is very strictly enforced; and accordingly, one fine morning, the Grand Discipline-Lama sent an official formally to request that we would observe the statutes of the Lamasery. We replied that, not being of the religion of Buddha, we could not adopt the sacred dress of the Lama, without insulting our own holy religion; but that as we did not wish to create the slightest confusion in the establishment, we were ready to quit it, if we could not obtain a dispensation in the matter of costume.

Several days passed without anything further being said on this unpleasant subject. Meantime Samdadchiemba arrived with the three camels, which he had been pasturing in a valley of Koukou-Noor. If we had to remove, it was clear that his return was most opportune. By and by, the Lamanesque government once more sent us their envoy, to say that the rule of the Lamasery was inflexible; that they grieved that our sublime and sacred religion did not permit us to comply with it; but that although we could not remain in the Lamasery of Kounboum, they would gladly retain us in the neighborhood, and that to this end they invited us to go and take up our abode at Tchogortan, where we might wear what dress we pleased.

We had heard a great deal about the little Lamasery of Tchogortan, which serves as a sort of country house and botanical garden for the Faculty of Medicine. It stands within half-an-hour's walk of Kounboum. The Grand Lamas and students of the medical section proceed thither every year, towards the close of summer, and remain generally for about a fortnight, collecting medicinal plants on the surrounding hills. During the remainder of the year most of the houses are empty, and you scarcely see a single soul, except a few contemplative Lamas who have hollowed out cells for themselves in the most rugged declivities of the mountain.

The proposition of the Lamanesque government appeared to us altogether eligible, for the fine weather was just setting in; winter in town, spring in the country—this was admirable! Our three months abode at Kounboum had made us tolerably conversant with Lama manners; we accordingly purchased a khata and a small dish of raisins, with which we repaired to the Lama administrator of Tchogortan, who received us in the most affable manner, and promised at once to give orders for the preparation of a suitable abode for us. After giving a splendid Feast of Farewell to old Akayé, the Kitat-Lama, and the Stammerer, we loaded our camels with our baggage and gaily proceeded on our way to the little Lamasery.

Lamasery of Tchogortan.

CHAPTER III.

Aspect of the Lamasery of Tchogortan—Contemplative Lamas—Lama Herdsmen—The "Book of the Forty-two Points of Instruction, Delivered by Buddha"—Extract from the Chinese Annals, with Relation to the Preaching of Buddhism in China—The Black Tents—Manners of the Si-Fan—Long-Haired Oxen—Adventures of a Stuffed Karba—Lamanesque Chronicle of the Origin of Nations—Alimentary Diet—Valuable Discoveries in the Animal Kingdom—Manufacture of Camel-hair Cord—Frequent Visits to Tchogortan—Classification of Argols—Brigand Anecdote—Elevation of the Pyramid of Peace—The Faculty of Medicine at Tchogortan—Thibetian Physicians—Departure for the Blue Sea.

A HALF hour sufficed for us to effect our removal from Kounboum to Tchogortan. After skirting for some time the arid sides of a lofty mountain, we descended into a broad valley, through which flowed a rivulet, the banks of which were still covered with ice. The place seemed full of good pasturage, but in consequence of the coldness of the climate, vegetation is very slow and very late in the locality. Although it was near the month of May, the nascent germs scarcely as yet colored the surface of the soil.

A Lama, with red, round face, came to meet us, and conducted us to the habitation which the administrator of the Lamasery had prepared for our reception. We were installed in a large apartment which, only the evening before, had served as the abode of sundry juvenile calves, too young and too weak to follow the parent cows to the mountains. Every pains had been taken to clean the apartment, but the success had not been so perfect as to preclude our distinguishing on the floor many traces of the late occupants; however, the authorities had assigned to us the best accommodation that the Lamasery afforded.

Tchogortan is, as we have before stated, the country house of the Faculty of Medicine of Kounboum: its aspect is tolerably picturesque, especially in summer. The habitations of the Lamas, constructed at the foot of a mountain, that terminates in a peak, are shaded by ancient trees, the great branches of which afford a retreat to infinite kites and crows. Some feet below these cottages, runs an abundant stream, interrupted by various dams which the Lamas have constructed for the purpose of turning their tchukor, or praying mills. In the depths of the valley, and on the adjacent hills, you see the black tents of the Si-Fan, and a few herds of goats and long-haired cattle. The rocky and rugged mountain which backs the Lamasery, serves as an abode for five contemplative monks, who, like the eagles, have selected as the site of their eyries the most elevated and most inaccessible points. Some have hollowed out their retreat in the living rock; others dwell in wooden cells, stuck against the mountain like enormous swallows' nests; a few pieces of wood, driven into the rock, form the staircase by which they ascend or descend. One of these Buddhist hermits, indeed, who has entirely renounced the world, has voluntarily deprived himself of these means of communication with his fellows; a bag, tied to a long string, serves as the medium for conveying to him the alms of the Lamas and shepherds.

We had frequent conversations with these contemplative Lamas, but we could never exactly ascertain what it was they contemplated up there in their nests. They themselves could give nothing like a clear idea of the matter; they had embraced this manner of life, they told us, because they had read in their books that Lamas of very great sanctity had lived in that way. However, they were worthy folks, of peaceful, simple, easy temperaments, who passed their waking hours in prayer, and when they were tired of praying relaxed with sleep.

Besides these five hermits, who always dwelt in the rocks above, there were, below, several Lamas who had charge of the unoccupied houses of the Lamasery. These by no means, like the former, looked at life in its refined and mystical aspect; they were, on the contrary, absorbed in the realities of this world; they were, in fact, herdsmen. In the great house where we were installed, there were two big Lamas who poetically passed their time in herding some twenty cattle, in milking the cows, making butter and cheese, and looking after the juvenile calves. These bucolics seemed little to heed contemplation or prayer: they sent forth, indeed, frequent invocations to Tsong-Kaba, but this was always on account of their beasts, because their cows mutinied and would not be milked, or because the calves capered out of bounds over the valley. Our arrival afforded them a little diversion from the monotony of pastoral life. They often paid us a visit in our chamber, and always passed in review the volumes of our small traveling library, with that timid and respectful curiosity which simple and illiterate persons ever manifest towards the productions of the intellect. When they found us writing, they forgot cows, and calves, and milk, and cheese, and butter, and would stand for hours together motionless, their eyes fixed upon our crow-quill as it ran over the paper, and left impressed there characters, the delicacy and novelty of which were matters of ecstatic amazement to these simple creatures.

The little Lamasery of Tchogortan pleased us beyond our hopes. We never once regretted Kounboum any more than the prisoner regrets his dungeon after he has attained liberty. The reason was that we, too, felt ourselves emancipated. We were no longer under the ferule of Sandara the Bearded, of that hard and pitiless taskmaster, who, while giving us lessons of Thibetian, seemed to have undertaken also to discipline us in patience and humility. The desire to attain knowledge had made us submit to his ill-treatment, but our departure from Kounboum afforded a joyful opportunity of throwing off this leech which had, for five whole months obstinately remained stuck to our existence. Besides, the success we had already achieved in the study of the Thibetian tongue, exempted us from the future necessity of having a master at our shoulder; we were quite strong enough now to walk alone and unaided.

Our hours of labor were employed in revising and analyzing our dialogues, and in translating a small Thibetian work, entitled, the "Forty-two Points of Instruction, delivered by Buddha." We possessed a magnificent edition of this work, in four languages, Thibetian, Mongol, Mantchou, and Chinese; so that, thus aided, we had no occasion to recur to the learning of the Lamas. When the Thibetian version presented any difficulty, all we had to do, in order to remove it, was to consult the three other versions, with which we were familiarly acquainted.

The book in question, which is attributed to Chakya-Mouni, is a collection of precepts and sentences, urging men, and especially religious persons, to the practise of piety. In order to give our readers an idea of the morality of the Buddhists, we will extract a few passages from this work, which is of high authority in Lamanism.

I.

"Buddha, the Supreme of Beings, manifesting his doctrine, pronounced these words: There are, in living creatures, ten species of acts which are called good, and there are also ten species of acts which are called evil. If you ask, what are the ten evil acts; there are three which appertain to the body; murder, theft, and impurity. The four appertaining to speech are: words sowing discord, insulting maledictions, impudent lies, and hypocritical expressions. The three appertaining to the will are; envy, anger, and malignant thoughts.

II.

"Buddha, manifesting his doctrine, pronounced these words: The wicked man, who persecutes the good man, is like a madman, who, throwing back his head, spits against heaven; his spittle, incapable of sullying heaven, merely falls back upon himself. And, again, he is like one who, the wind opposing him, throws dust at men; the dust does not touch the men at whom it was aimed, but flies back into the eyes of him who threw it. Beware of persecuting good men lest calamities exterminate you.

III.

"Buddha, etc. Beneath heaven there are twenty difficult things. 1, Being poor and indigent, to grant benefits is difficult. 2, Being rich and exalted, to study doctrine, is difficult. 3, Having offered up the sacrifice of one's life, to die veritably, is difficult. 4, To obtain a sight of the prayers of Buddha, is difficult. 5, To have the happiness to be born in the world of Buddha, is difficult. 6, To compound with voluptuousness and to be delivered from one's passions, is difficult. 7, To behold an agreeable object, and not to desire it, is difficult. 8, To resist a tendency for the lucrative and the exalting, is difficult. 9, To be insulted, and abstain from anger, is difficult. 10, In the whirlwind of business to be calm, is difficult. 11, To study much and profoundly, is difficult. 12, Not to scorn a man who has not studied, is difficult. 13, To extirpate pride from the heart, is difficult. 14, To find a virtuous and able master, is difficult. 15, To penetrate the secrets of nature and the profundities of science, is difficult. 16, Not to be excited by prosperity, is difficult. 17, To leave wealth for wisdom, is difficult. 18, To induce men to follow the dictates of conscience, is difficult. 19, To keep one's heart always in equal motion, is difficult. 20, Not to speak ill of others, is difficult.

IV.

"The man who seeks riches, is like a child that, with the sharp point of a knife, attempt to eat honey; ere he has time to relish the sweetness that has but touched his lips, nothing remains to him but the poignant pain of a cut in the tongue.

V.

"There is no passion more violent than voluptuousness! Nothing exceeds voluptuousness! Happily, there is but one passion of this kind; were there two, not a man in the whole universe could follow the truth.

VI.

"Buddha pronounced these words in the presence of all the Charmanas:[1] 'Beware of fixing your eyes upon women! If you find yourselves in their company, let it be as though you were not present. Take care how you speak with women. If you talk with them, guard well your hearts; let your conduct be irreproachable, and keep ever saying to yourselves: we who are Charmanas, residing in this world of corruption, must be like the flower of the water-lily, which, amid muddy water, contracts no stain.'

VII.

"The man who walks in the path of piety must look upon the passions as dry grass near a great fire. The man who is jealous of his virtue, should flee on the approach of the passions.

VIII.

"A Charmana who passed whole nights chanting prayers, manifested one morning, by his sad suppressed voice, great depression and the desire to withdraw from his calling. Buddha sent for this Charmana, and said to him, 'When you were with your family, what used you to do?' 'I was always playing on the guitar.' Buddha said to him, 'If the strings of the guitar became loose, what happened?' 'I obtained no sound from them.' 'If the strings were too tight, what happened then?' 'The sounds were broken.' 'When the strings obtained the exact equilibrium between tension and flexibility, what happened then?' 'All the sounds accorded in perfect harmony.' Hereupon Buddha

[1] Charmanas (in Sanscrit, S'raman'as) are monks in the Lamanesque hierarchy.

pronounced these words: It is the same with the study of doctrine; after you shall have achieved dominion over your heart, and regulated its movements to harmony, it will attain the acquisition of the truth.

IX.

"Buddha put this question to a Charmana: 'How long a time is fixed for the life of man?' He replied: 'It is limited to a few days.' Buddha pronounced these words: 'You have not yet acquired the knowledge of the doctrine.' Then addressing himself to another Charmana, he put this question: 'How long a time is fixed for the life of man?' He replied: 'It is limited to the time that suffices for a meal.' Buddha pronounced these words: 'So neither hast thou, as yet, the knowledge of the doctrine.' Then addressing himself to a third Charmana, he put to him this question: 'How long a time is fixed for the life of man?' He replied: 'It is limited to the time that suffices to emit a breath.' After he had thus spoken, Buddha pronounced these words: ''Tis well: thou mayest be said to have acquired the knowledge of the doctrine.'

X.

"The man who, practising piety, applies himself to extirpate the roots of his passions, is like a man passing between his fingers the beads of a chaplet. If he proceeds by taking them, one after the other, he easily attains the end; so, by extirpating, one after the other, one's evil tendencies one attains perfection.

XI.

"The Charmana who practises piety, may compare himself with the long-haired ox, which, laden with baggage, is making its way through a marsh; it dares look neither to the right nor to the left, but goes straight on, hoping to get clear of the mud and to reach a place of rest. The Charmana, regarding his passions as more terrible than this mud, if he never diverts his eyes from virtue, will assuredly attain the height of felicity."

We will not prolong these extracts. The few we have given will suffice to convey an idea of the matter and manner of this book, which is accepted as an authority alike by the Bonzes and the Lamas. It was conveyed from India to China, in the 65th year of the Christian era at the epoch when Buddhism was beginning to make its way in the Celestial Empire. The Chinese annals relate this event in the following terms:—

"In the 24th year of the reign of Tchao-Wang, of the dynasty of the Tcheou (which corresponds to the year 1029 B. C.), on the eighth day of the fourth moon, a light, coming from the southwest, illumined the palace of the king. The monarch, beholding this splendor, interrogated concerning it the sages who were skilled in predicting the future. These presented to him the books wherein it was written, that this prodigy would announce that a great saint had appeared in the west, and that in a thousand years after his birth, his religion would spread into those parts.

"In the 53d year of the reign of Mou-Wang, which is that of the Black Ape (951 B. C.), on the fifteenth day of the second moon, Buddha manifested himself (*i. e.* died). A thousand and thirteen years afterwards, under the dynasty of Ming-Ti, of the dynasty of the Han, in the seventh year of the reign of Young-Ping (A. D. 64), on the fifteenth day of the first moon, the king saw in a dream, a man of the color of gold, glittering like the sun, and whose stature was more than ten feet. Having entered the palace of the king, this man said, 'My religion will spread over these parts.' Next day, the king questioned the sages. One of these, named Fou-Y, opening the annals of the time of the Emperor Tchao-Wang, of the dynasty of the Tcheou, pointed out the connection between the dream of the king and the narrative in the annals. The king consulted the ancient books, and having found the passage corresponding with the reign of Tchao-Wang, of the dynasty of the Tcheou, was filled with gladness. Thereupon he despatched the officers Tsa-In and Thsin-King, the man-of-letters, Wang-Tsun, and fifteen other persons, into the west, to obtain information respecting the doctrine of Buddha.

"In the 10th year (A. D. 67), Tsa-In and the rest, having arrived in Central India, among the great Youei-Tchi, met with Kas'yamatanga and Tcho-Fa-Lan, and procured a statue of Buddha, and books in the language of Fan (Fan-Lan-Mo, or Brahma, that is to say, in Sanscrit), and conveyed them on a white horse to the city of Yo-Lang. Kas'yamatanga and Tchou-Fa-Lang, paid a visit to the emperor, attired as religious persons, and were lodged in the Hong-Lon-Ssé, called also Sse Pin-Ssé (Hotel of the Strangers).

"In the 11th year (A. D. 68), the emperor ordered the construction of the monastery of the White Horse, outside the gate Yong-Mon, west of the city of Lo Yang. Matanga there translated the 'Sacred Book of Forty-two Articles.' Six years after, Tsa-In and Tcho-Fa-Lan converted certain Tao-Ssé to Buddhism. Rising afterwards into celestial space they caused the king to hear the following verses:—

"'The fox is not of the race of the lions. The lamp has not the brightness of the sun or moon. The lake cannot be compared with the sea; the hills cannot be compared with the lofty mountains.

"'The cloud of prayer spreading over the surface of the earth, its beneficial dew fecundating the germs of happiness, and the divine rites operating everywhere marvelous changes, all the nations will advance according to the laws of reintegration.'"

Our first days at Tchogortan were entirely devoted to the translation of the "Book of Buddha;" but we soon found ourselves compelled to devote a portion of our time to the occupations of pastoral life. We had remarked that every evening our animals had returned half-starved, that instead of growing fatter and fatter, they were daily becoming leaner and leaner; the simple reason was that Samdadchiemba took no sort of pains to find pasturage for them. After driving them out somewhere or other, he cared not whither he would leave them to themselves on some arid hillside, and himself go to sleep in the sun, or stroll about chattering and tea-drinking in the black tents. It was to no purpose we lectured him; he went on, just the same as before, his reckless, independent character having undergone no modification whatever. Our only mode of remedying the evil, was to turn herdsmen ourselves.

Moreover, it was impossible to remain pertinaciously and exclusively men of letters when all around seemed inviting us to make some concessions to the habits of this pastoral people. The Si-Fan, or Eastern Thibetians, are nomads, like the Tartar-Mongols, and pass their lives solely occupied in the care of their flocks and herds. They do not live, however, like the Mongol tribes, in huts covered with felt. The great tents they construct with black linen, are ordinarily hexagonal in form; within you see neither column nor woodwork supporting the edifice; the six angles below are fastened to the ground with nails, and those above are supported by cords which, at a certain distance from the tent, rest horizontally on strong poles, and then slope to the ground, where they are attached to large iron rings. With all this strange complication of sticks and strings, the black tent of the Thibetian nomads bears no slight resemblance to a great spider standing motionless on its long lanky legs, but so that its great stomach is resting on the ground. The black tents are by no means comparable with the tents of the Mongols; they are not a whit warmer or more solid than ordinary traveling tents. They are very cold, on the contrary, and a strong wind knocks them down without the least difficulty.

It may be said, however, that in one respect the Si-Fan seem more advanced than the Mongols, and to have a tendency for approximating to the manners of sedentary nations. When they have selected an encampment, they are accustomed to erect around it a wall of from four to five feet high, and within their tents they construct furnaces, which are destitute neither of taste nor of solidity. These arrangements, however, do not create in them any attachment to the soil which they have thus occupied. Upon the slightest caprice they decamp, pulling down their walls and other masonry work, and carrying the principal stones with them to their next settlement, as part of their furniture. The herds of the Eastern Thibetians consist of sheep, goats, and long-haired cattle; they do not breed as many horses as the Tartars, but those which they do breed are stronger and better formed; the camels we find in their country, belong, for the most part, to the Tartar-Mongols.

The long-haired cattle, in Chinese Tchang-Mao-Nieou, is called *yak* by the Thibetians, *sarligue* by the Tartars, and *bœuf grognant* by the French naturalists. The cry of this animal does, in fact, resemble the grunting of a hog; but louder in tone, and longer in duration. The yak is short

The Long-haired Ox.

and thick, and not so big as an ordinary ox; its hair is long, fine, and shining, that under the belly actually trailing on the ground. Its hoofs are meager, and crooked, like those of goats; and, like the goats, it delights in clambering up rocks, and impending over the most rugged precipices. When at play, it twists and turns about its tail, which terminates in a broad tuft, like a plume of feathers. The flesh is excellent; the milk delicious, and the butter made of that milk beyond all praise. Malte-Brun, indeed, says, that the milk of this animal smacks of tallow. Matters of taste are generally open questions, but in this particular instance we may anticipate that the presumption will be somewhat in favor of our opinion, since, as we believe, the learned geographer has not had the same opportunities with ourselves of drinking the milk in the black tents, and appreciating its savor at leisure.

Among the herds of the Si-Fan, you find some yellow cattle, which are of the same family with the ordinary cattle of France, but in general poor and ugly. The calf of a long-haired cow and a yellow bull is called Karba; these seldom live. The long-tailed cows are so restive and so difficult to milk, that to keep them at all quiet, the herdsman has to give them a calf to lick meanwhile. But for this device, not a single drop of milk could be obtained from them.

One day, a Lama herdsman, who lived in the same house with ourselves, came, with a long, dismal face, to announce that one of his cows had calved during the night, and that unfortunately the calf was a karba. The calf died in the course of the day. The Lama forthwith skinned the poor beast, and stuffed it with hay. This proceeding surprised us at first, for the Lama had by no means the air of a man likely to give himself the luxury of a cabinet of natural history. When the operation was completed, we remarked that the hay-calf had neither feet nor head; hereupon it occurred to us that, after all, it was merely a pillow that the Lama contemplated. We were in error, but the error was not dissipated until the next morning, when our herdsman went to milk his cow. Seeing him issue forth, his pail in one hand, the hay-calf under the other arm, the fancy occurred to us to follow him. His first proceeding was to put the hay-karba down before the cow; he then turned to milk the cow herself. The mamma at first opened enormous eyes at her beloved infant; by degrees, she stooped her head towards it, then smelt at it, sneezed three or four times, and at last proceeded to lick it with the most delightful tenderness. This spectacle grated against our sensibilities; it seemed to us that he who first invented this parody upon one of the most touching incidents in nature, must have been a man without a heart. A somewhat burlesque circumstance occurred one day to modify the indignation with which this trickery inspired us. By dint of caressing and licking her little calf, the tender parent one fine morning unripped it; the hay issued from within, and the cow, manifesting not the smallest surprise or agitation, proceeded tranquilly to devour the unexpected provender.

The Si-Fan nomads are readily distinguishable from the Mongols by a more expressive physiognomy and by a greater energy of character; their features are not so flat, and their manners are characterized by an ease and vivacity that form a strong contrast with the heavy uncouthness of the Tartars. Merry-makings, noisy songs, and joyous laughter animate their encampments, and banish melancholy; but with this turn for gaiety and pleasure, the Si-Fan are at the same time indomitably brave and exceedingly addicted to warfare. They accordingly manifest the most profound contempt for the Chinese authority and authorities, and though inscribed in the imperial list of tributary nations, they absolutely refuse to render either obedience or tribute. There are among them, indeed, several tribes that constantly exercise their brigandage up to the very frontiers of the empire, the Chinese mandarins never venturing to encounter them. The Si-Fan are good horsemen, though not equal to the Tartars. The care of their herds does not prevent them from carrying on a little trade in the hair of their cattle and the wool of their sheep. They weave a sort of coarse linen, of which they make tents and clothing. When they are assembled round their great pot of milk-tea, they give themselves up, like the Tartars, to their gossiping humor, and their passion for narratives of the adventures of Lamas and brigands. Their memory is full of local anecdotes and traditions; once put them on the track, and they will go on with an interminable series of tales and legends.

One day, while our camels were tranquilly browsing some thorny shrubs in the depths of the valley, we sought an asylum from the north wind in a small tent, whence issued a thick smoke. We found in it an old man who, knees and hands on the ground, was puffing with all his might at a heap of argols which he had just placed on the fire. We seated ourselves on a yak skin. The old man crossed his legs, and held out his hand to us. We gave him our teacups, which he filled with milk tea, saying, "Temouchi" (drink in peace). He then gazed at us, alternately, with an air of some anxiety. "*Aka* (brother)," said we, "this is the first time we have come to seat ourselves in your tent." "I am old," he replied; "my legs will scarce sustain me; otherwise, I should have come to Tchogortan to offer you my khata. According to what the shepherds of the black tents have told me, you are from the farther Western Heaven." "Yes, our country is far hence." "Are you from the kingdom of the Samba, or from that of the Poba?" "From neither; we come from the kingdom of the French." "Ah, you are Franba? I never before heard of them. 'Tis such a great place, that West! The kingdoms there are so numerous. But, after all, it matters not: we are all of the same family, are we not?" "Yes, assuredly all men are brothers, in whatever kingdom each is born." "That is true: what you say is founded on reason; all men are brothers. Yet we know that, under heaven, there exist three great families: we men of the west are all of the great Thibetian family, as I have heard." "Aka, do you know whence come the three great families that are beneath the heaven?" "This is what I have heard about it from Lamas learned in the things of antiquity. In the beginning, there was on the earth but one single man; he had neither house nor tent; for in those days, winter was not cold nor summer hot; the wind did not blow with violence, and there fell neither rain nor snow; tea grew of itself on the mountains, and the cattle had nothing to fear from maleficent animals. This man had three children, who lived a long time with him, feeding upon milk and fruits. After attaining a very great age, this man died. The three children consulted what they should do with the body of their father; they could not agree on the point, for each had a different opinion. One of them wanted to put him in a coffin, and bury him; the second proposed to burn him; the third said it would be better to expose him on the top of a mountain. In the end, they resolved to cut the body into three pieces, to take each of them one piece, and then to separate. The eldest had the head and arms for his share: he was the ancestor of the great Chinese family; and this is why his descendants have become celebrated in arts and industry, and remarkable for their intelligence, and for the devices and stratagems they can invent. The youngest, who was the father of the great Thibetian family, had the chest and stomach for his share, and this is why the Thibetians are full of heart and courage, fearing not to encounter death, and ever having among them indomitable tribes. The middle son, from whom descend the Tartar peoples, received as his inheritance the lower part of the body. You who have traveled much in the deserts of the East, must know that the Mongols are simple and timid, without head and without heart; their only merit consisting in keeping themselves firm on their stirrups, and solid on their saddles. This is how the Lamas explain the origin of the three great families that are beneath heaven, and the difference of their character. This is why the Tartars are good horsemen, the Thibetians good soldiers, and the Chinese good traders." As a return to the old man for his interesting chronicle, we related to him the history of the first man, Adam, of the Deluge, and of Noah and his three children. He was at first extremely pleased to find in our story also his three great families; but his surprise was immense, when he heard us state that the Chinese, the Tartars, and the Thibetians were all children of Shem, and that besides these, there were innumerable nations who composed the two other families of Cham and Japhet. He looked at us fixedly, his mouth half open, and his head, from time to time, thrown up in amazement, as much as to say: I never thought the world was so big.

The time had passed rapidly during this archaiological sitting; so, after saluting the old man, we went to our camels, which we drove home to Tchogortan, where, fastening them to a stake at the door of our residence, we proceeded into our humble kitchen to prepare our evening meal.

Culinarily speaking, we were far better off at Tchogortan than at Kounboum. In the first place, we had milk, curds, butter, and cheese, *à discretion*. Then we had discovered a perfect mine, in a hunter of the vicinity. A few days after our arrival, this Nimrod entered our room, and taking a magnificent hare from a bag he carried at his back, asked us whether the Goucho [1] of the Western Heaven ate the flesh of wild animals. "Certainly," said we; "and we consider hares very nice. Don't you eat them?" "We laymen do, sometimes, but the Lamas, never. They are expressly forbidden by the Book of Prayers to eat black flesh." "The sacred law of Jehovah has prescribed no such prohibition to us." "In that case keep the animal; and, as you like hares, I will bring you as many of them every day as you please; the hills about Tchogortan are completely covered with them."

Just at this point, a Lama chanced to enter our apartment. When he saw, stretched at our feet, the still warm and bleeding form of the hare, "Tsong-Kaba! Tsong-Kaba!" exclaimed he, starting back, with a gesture of horror, and veiling his eyes with both hands. Then, after launching a malediction against the poor hunter, he asked us whether we should dare to eat that black flesh? "Why not," rejoined we, "since it can injure neither our bodies nor our

1 Goucho is a title of honor, given to the Lamas by the Thibetians.

souls?" And thereupon, we laid down certain principles of morality, to the purport that the eating of venison is, in itself, no obstacle to the acquisition of sanctity. The hunter was highly delighted with our dissertation: the Lama was altogether confounded. He contented himself with saying, by way of reply, that in us, who were foreigners and of the religion of Jehovah, it might be no harm to eat hares; but that the Lamas must abstain from it, because, if they failed to observe the prohibition and their dereliction became known to the Grand Lama, they would be pitilessly expelled from the Lamasery.

Our thesis having been thus victoriously sustained, we next proceeded to entertain the proposition of the hunter, to provide us every day with as many hares as we pleased. First, we asked him whether he was in earnest. Upon his replying in the affirmative, we told him that every morning he might bring us a hare, but on the understanding that we were to pay him for it. "We don't sell hares here," replied he; "but since you will not accept them gratuitously, you shall give me for each the value of a gun-charge." We insisted upon a more liberal scale of remuneration, and, at last, it was arranged that for every piece of game he brought us, we should give him forty sapeks, equivalent to about four French sous.

We decided upon eating hares for two reasons. First, as a matter of conscience, in order to prevent the Lamas from imagining that we permitted ourselves to be influenced by the prejudices of the sectaries of Buddha; and, secondly, upon a principle of economy; for a hare cost us infinitely less than our insipid barley-meal.

One day, our indefatigable hunter brought us, instead of a hare, an immense roebuck, which is also black flesh and prohibited. In order not to compound in the least degree with Buddhist superstitions, we purchased the roebuck, for the sum of three hundred sapeks (thirty French sous). Our chimney smoked with venison preparations for eight consecutive days, and all that time Samdadchiemba was in a most amiable frame of mind.

Lest we should contract habits too exclusively carnivorous, we resolved to introduce the vegetable kingdom into our quotidian alimentation. In the desert, this was no easy matter. However, by dint of industry, combined with experience, we ultimately discovered some wild plants, which, dressed in a particular manner, were by no means to be despised. We may be permitted to enter into some details on this subject. The matter in itself is of slight interest; but it may have its use, in relation to travelers who at any future time may have to traverse the deserts of Thibet.

When the first signs of germination begin to manifest themselves, if you scratch up the ground to the depth of about an inch, you will find quantities of creeping roots, long and thin like dog-grass. This root is entirely covered with little tubercles, filled with a very sweet liquid. In order to make an extremely nice dish of this vegetable, you have only to wash it carefully and then fry it in butter. Another dish, not less distinguished in our esteem than the preceding, was furnished by a plant very common in France, and the merit of which has never yet been adequately appreciated: we refer to the young stems of fern; when these are gathered quite tender, before they are covered with down, and while the first leaves are bent and rolled up in themselves, you have only to boil them in pure water to realize a dish of delicious asparagus. If our words were of any effect, we would earnestly recommend to the attention of the Minister of Agriculture this precious vegetable, which abounds, as yet to no purpose, on our mountains and in our forests. We would also recommend to him the nettle (*urtica urens*), which, in our opinion, might be made an advantageous substitute for spinach; indeed, more than once, we proved this by our own experience. The nettle should be gathered quite young when the leaves are perfectly tender. The plant should be pulled up whole, with a portion of the root. In order to preserve your hands from the sharp biting liquid which issues from the points, you should wrap them in linen of close texture. When once the nettle is boiled, it is perfectly innocuous, and this vegetable, so rough in its exterior, then becomes a very delicate dish.

We were able to enjoy this delightful variety of esculents for more than a month. Then, the little tubercles of the fern became hollow and horny, and the stems themselves grew as hard as wood; while the nettles, armed with a long white beard, presented only a menacing and awful aspect. Later in the year, when the season was more advanced, the perfumed strawberry of the mountain and the white mushroom of the valley, became invaluable substitutes for fern and nettle. But we had to wait a long time for these luxuries, the cold in these countries being of protracted duration, and the vegetation, of consequence, exceedingly late. Throughout June there is snow still falling, and the wind is so cold that you cannot, without imprudence, throw aside your fur coats. With the first days of July, the warmth of the sun begins to be felt, and the rain falls in heavy showers; no sooner has the sky cleared up, than a warm vapor rises from the earth, in surprising abundance. You see it first skimming the surface of the valleys and the low hills; then it condenses, and oscillates about somewhat above the surface, becoming, by degrees, so thick that it obscures the light of day. When this vapor has ascended high enough in the air to form great clouds, the south wind rises, and the rain again pours down upon the earth. Then the sky becomes clear once more, and once more the vapor rises and rises, and so it goes on. These atmospheric revolutions continue for a fortnight. Meanwhile, the earth is in a sort of fermentation: all the animals keep crouching on the ground, and men, women, and children feel, in every limb, vague, indescribable discomfort and disability. The Si-Fan call this period the season of land vapors.

Immediately that the crisis is past, the grass in the valley grows visibly, and the mountains and hills around are covered, as by enchantment, with flowers and verdure. The period was also one of palingenesis for our camels. They became wholly divested of their hair, which fell from them in large flakes, like rags, and for a few days they were as bare as though they had been closely shaved from the muzzle of the nose to the tip of the tail. In this condition, they were perfectly hideous. In the shade they shook with cold in every limb, and at night we were obliged to cover them with great pieces of felt to keep them from dying with cold. After four days had elapsed, the hair began to reappear. First, it was merely a red down, extremely fine and curling, like lamb's wool. The intense ugliness of the animals during their state of nudity, made them appear perfectly beautiful in their new attire, which was completed in a fortnight. Thus new dressed, they rushed with ardor to the pasturages, in order to get up respectable dimensions and adequate strength for their autumnal journey. To sharpen their appetites, we had purchased some sea salt, of which we gave them a large dose every morning, before they went into the valley: and every evening, on their return, we gave them another dose, to aid them to ruminate, during the night, the immense mass of forage which they had amassed in their stomachs during the day.

The new coating of our camels had enriched us with an immense quantity of hair; we exchanged one-half of it for barley-meal, and the question then arose, what was the best use we could make of the remainder? A Lama, who was a skilful rope-maker, suggested an excellent idea: he pointed out that during the long journey through Thibet, we should need a large supply of cord wherewith to fasten the luggage, and that ropes made of camel's hair were, on account of their flexibility, the best for cold countries. The suggestion, so full of wisdom, was at once adopted. The Lama gave us, gratuitously, a few lessons in his art, and we set to work. In a very short time, we were able to twist our material tolerably well, so as to give it a form approximately, at least, resembling rope. Every day when we went out to tend our cattle, each of us took under his arm a bundle of camel's hair, which on his way he twisted into the smaller strings, that, on our return, we combined into larger cords.

Samdadchiemba contented himself with looking on as we worked, and with an occasional smile at our slips. Partly through idleness, partly through vanity, he abstained from lending us a hand. "My spiritual fathers," said he, one day, "how can people of your quality demean yourselves by rope-making? Would it not be much more proper to buy what ropes you require, or to give the materials out to be made by persons in the trade?" This question afforded us an opportunity of giving our cameleer a sound rating. After having emphatically impressed upon him that we were in no position to play the fine gentlemen, and that we must closely study economy, we cited to him the example of St. Paul, who had thought it no derogation from his dignity to labor with his hands, in order to avoid being of charge to the faithful. So soon as Samdadchiemba learned that St. Paul had been at the same time a currier and an apostle, he forthwith abdicated his idleness and his self-sufficiency, and applied himself with ardor to rope-making. What was our astonishment, on seeing the fellow at work, to find that he was a first-rate braider, for not an inkling had he ever given us to that effect! He selected the finest wool, and with it wove bridles and halters, that were really quite masterpieces of art. It is almost unnecessary to add that he was forthwith placed at the head of our rope-making establishment, and that we submitted ourselves altogether to his directorship.

The fine weather brought to Tchogortan a great number of visitors from Kounboum, who sought at once change of air, and temporary relaxation from their studies. Our apartment now became a point of pilgrimage, for no one thought of spending a day at Tchogortan without paying a visit to the Lamas of the Western Heaven. Those Lamas, with whom we had formed a more intimate acquaintance at Kounboum, and who had begun there to inform themselves as to the truths of the Christian religion, were attracted by a far higher motive than curiosity; they desired to discourse further of the holy doctrine of Jehovah, and to seek from us explanations of difficulties which had occurred to them. Oh! how our hearts were penetrated with ineffable joy when we heard these Buddhist monks pronounce with respect the sacred names of Jesus and of Mary, and recite, with manifest devotion, the prayers we had taught them. The great God, we doubt not, will place to their favorable account, these first steps in the path of salvation, and will not fail to send shepherds to bring quite home to the fold these poor wandering sheep.

Among the Lamas who came to recreate for a while at Tchogortan, we remarked especially a number of Tartar-Mongols, who, bringing with them small tents, set them up in the valley along the stream, or upon the sides of the most picturesque hills. There they passed whole days reveling in the delight of the independent life of the nomads, forgetting for awhile the constraint and confinement of the Lamanesque life, in the enjoyment of the free life of the tent. You saw them running and frolicking about the prairie like children, or wrestling and exercising the other sports which recalled the days and the land of their boyhood. The reaction with many of these men became so strong, that even fixity of tent became insupportable, and they would take it down and set it up again in some other place, three or four times a day; or they would even abandon it altogether, and taking their kitchen utensils and their pails of water and their provisions on their shoulders, would go, singing and dancing as they went, to boil their tea on the summit of some mountain, from which they should not descend till nightfall.

We observed, also, flocking to Tchogortan, another class of Lamas not less interesting than the Mongols; they always arrived at daybreak; their garments were tucked up to the knees, and on their backs were large osier baskets; all day long they would traverse the valley and the adjacent hills, collecting, not strawberries and mushrooms, but the dung which the herds of the Si-Fan deposit in all directions. On account of this particular occupation, we named these Lamas Lama-Argoleers, from the Tartar word argol, which designates animal excrement, when dried and prepared for fuel. The Lamas who carry on this class of business, are in general idle, irregular persons, who prefer vagabondizing about on the hills to study and retirement; they are divided into several companies, each working under the direction of a superintendent, who arranges and is responsible for their operations. Towards the close of the day, each man brings the portion he has collected to the general depôt, which is always situate at the foot of some well, or in the hollow of some valley. There the raw material is carefully elaborated; it is pounded and molded into cakes, which are placed to dry in the sun, and when completely dessicated, are symmetrically piled, one on the other, the stack, when formed, being covered with a thick layer of dung, to protect it from the dissolving action of the rain. In the winter, this fuel is conveyed to Kounboum, and there sold.

The luxurious variety of combustibles which the civilized nations of Europe enjoy, have exempted us from the necessity of making any very profound researches into the divers qualities of argols. Such has not been the case with the shepherd and nomadic peoples. Long experience has enabled them to classify argols, with a perspicuity of appreciation which leaves nothing to be desired in that particular respect. They have established four grand divisions, to which future generations will scarcely be able to apply any modification.

In the first rank are placed the argols of goats and sheep;

a glutinous substance that enters largely into its composition, communicates to this combustible an elevation of temperature that is truly astonishing. The Thibetians and Tartars use it in the preparation of metals; a bar of iron, placed in a fire of these argols, is soon brought to white heat. The residuum deposited by the argols of goats and sheep after combustion, is a sort of green vitreous matter, transparent, and brittle as glass, which forms a mass full of cavities and very light; in many respects, closely resembling pumice stone. You don't find in this residuum any ash whatever, unless the combustion has been mixed with foreign matter. The argols of camels constitute the second class; they burn easily, and throw out a fine flame, but the heat they communicate is less vivid and less intense than that given by the preceding. The reason of this difference is, that they contain in combination a smaller proportion of glutinous substance. The third class comprehends the argols appertaining to the bovine species; these, when thoroughly dry, burn readily, and produce no smoke whatever. This is almost the only fuel you find in Tartary and Thibet. Last come the argols of horses and other animals of that family. These argols not having, like the others, undergone the process of rumination, present nothing but a mass of straw more or less triturated; they throw out a great smoke when burning, and are almost immediately consumed. They are useful, however, for lighting a fire, filling the office of tinder and paper to the other combustibles.

We perfectly understand that this rapid and incomplete essay on argols is not of a character to interest many readers; but we did not feel justified in either omitting or abridging it, because it has been an object with us to neglect no document that might be of assistance to those who, after us, may venture upon nomadic life for awhile.

The inhabitants of the valley of Tchogortan, though in the apparent enjoyment of profound peace, are, nevertheless, an incessant prey to the fear of the brigands, who, they informed us, make periodical incursions from the mountains, and carry off all the cattle they can find. It was stated that in 1842, these had come in a large body, and devastated the whole of the surrounding country. At a moment when they were least expected, they issued from all the outlets of the mountain, and spread over the valley, sending forth fearful cries, and discharging their matchlocks. The shepherds, terror-struck by this unforeseen attack, had not even thought of the slightest resistance, but had fled in disorder, carrying with them only that which they happened to lay their hands upon at the moment. The brigands, profiting by this panic fear, burned the tents, and collected, in one large enclosure, formed with ropes, all the cattle and sheep they found in and about the place. They then proceeded to the little Lamasery of Tchogortan. But the Lamas had already disappeared, with the exception of the hermits, who remained perched on their nests on the rocks. The brigands carried off or demolished everything they came to; they burned the idols of Buddha, and broke down the dams that had been constructed for the purpose of turning the praying-mills. Three years after the event, we still saw the marked traces of their ferocious devastations. The Buddhist temple, which had stood at the foot of the mountain, had not been rebuilt. Its ruins, blackened with their conflagrations, and some calcined portions of the idols lay strewed upon the grass. The Lama hermits were spared, indeed; but this, no doubt, was simply because the brigands saw it would be too protracted and too arduous a labor to achieve the tormenting them in their lofty and almost inaccessible abodes. The excesses which they perpetrated against the black tents and against the temple of Buddha itself, showed that, if they left the poor recluses unscathed, it was by no means from respect or compassion.

So soon as the news of the arrival of the brigands reached Kounboum, the whole Lamasery was afoot, and in commotion. The Lamas rushed to arms with loud vociferations. They caught up whatever in the shape of a weapon first came to hand, and dashed off, confusedly, toward the Lamasery of Tchogortan. But they arrived there too late; the brigands had disappeared, carrying off all the flocks and herds of the Si-Fan, and leaving behind them in the valley nothing but smoking ruins.

The shepherds who, since this event, had returned and set up their tents amidst the pasturages of Tchogortan, were always on the watch, fearful of a new aggression. From time to time some of them, armed with lances and guns, would patrol the neighborhood; a precaution which though it would certainly have by no means intimidated the

The Pyramid of Peace.

brigands, had at least the advantage of communicating a certain degree of fancied security to the population.

Towards the end of August, while we were quietly occupied in the manufacture of our ropes, sinister rumors began to circulate; by degrees they assumed all the character of certain intelligence and no doubt was entertained that we were threatened with a new and terrible invasion of brigands. Every day we were alarmed with some fresh fact of a formidable nature. The shepherds of such a place had been surprised, their tents burned, and their flocks driven off. Elsewhere there had been a tremendous battle, in which a number of persons had been killed. These rumors became so substantially alarming that the administrators of the Lamasery felt bound to adopt some measures on the subject. They despatched to Tchogortan a Grand Lama and twenty students of the Faculty of Prayers, charged with the task of preserving the locality from any unpleasant occurrence. On their arrival, these Lamas convoked the chiefs of the Si-Fan families, and announced that now they were come, the people had nothing to fear. Next morning, they all ascended the highest mountain in the neighborhood, set up some traveling tents there, and proceeded to recite prayers to the accompaniment of music. They remained in this encampment two whole days, which they occupied in praying, in exorcising, and in constructing a small pyramid of earth, whitened with lime, and above which floated, at the end of a mast, a flag on which were printed various Thibetian prayers. This modest edifice was entitled the Pyramid of Peace. These ceremonies completed, the Lamas, great and small, folded their tents, descended from the mountain, and quietly returned to Kounboun, fully persuaded that they had opposed to the brigands an impassable barrier.

The Pyramid of Peace did not appear, however, to have infused equal confidence into the hearts of the herdsmen; for, one fine morning, they all decamped together, bag and baggage, and went with their herds and flocks to seek a less dangerous position elsewhere. They invited us to follow their example, but we preferred to remain where we were, for in the desert there is scarcely one place more secure than another. The flight of the shepherds, besides, seemed to us a guarantee that our tranquillity would not be disturbed, for we considered that the brigands, when they learned that no flocks remained in the valley of Tchogortan, would feel no interest in paying us a visit. We therefore, in our turn, raised up in our hearts a Pyramid of Peace, in the form of a firm reliance on the divine protection; and, thus fortified, we abode calmly and fearlessly in our adopted home.

For some days we enjoyed the most profound solitude. Since the disappearance of the herds and flocks, the argoleers, having nothing to do, had kept away. We were alone with a Lama, left in charge of the Lamasery. Our animals profited by the change, for now all the pasturages of the valley were theirs; they could browse wherever they liked over the valley, fearless of meeting a single competitor.

The desert, however, became after a time once more alive, and towards the commencement of September, the Lamas of the Faculty of Medicine repaired to Tchogortan, for the purpose of botanizing. The disposable houses received all they could contain, and the rest dwelt in tents, sheltered by the great trees of the Lamasery. Every morning, after they have recited their prayers in common, drunk their buttered tea, and eaten their barley-meal, all the students in medicine tuck up their garments, and go forth on the mountains, under the guidance of one of their professors. They are each provided with a long iron-pointed stick and a small pick-ax; a leathern bag, filled with meal, is suspended from the girdle, and some carry at their backs great tea-kettles, for the Faculty spend the entire day on the mountain. Before sunset, the Lama physicians return laden with perfect fagots of branches, and piles of plants and grasses. As you see them weariedly descending the mountains, supported by their long staves and bearing these burdens, they look more like poaching woodcutters than like future doctors in medicine. We were often obliged to escort in person those of the number who had special charge of the aromatic plants; for our camels, which, attracted by the odor, always put themselves in pursuit of these personages, would otherwise inevitably, and without the smallest scruple, have devoured those precious simples, destined for the relief of suffering humanity. The remainder of the day is occupied in cleaning and spreading out on mats these various products of the vegetable kingdom. The medical harvest lasted eight whole days. Five other days are devoted to the selection and classification of the various articles. On the fourteenth day, a small portion is given to each student, the great bulk remaining the property of the Faculty of Medicine. The fifteenth day is kept as a festival, in the form of a grand banquet of tea with milk, barley-meal, little cakes fried in butter, and boiled mutton. Thus terminates this botanico-medical expedition, and the illustrious Faculty gaily returns to the Grand Lamasery.

The drugs collected at Tchogortan are deposited in the general drug-room of Kounboum. When they have been thoroughly dried in the heat of a moderate fire, they are reduced to powder, and then divided into small doses, which are neatly enveloped in red paper, and labeled with Thibetian characters. The pilgrims who visit Kounboum buy these remedies at exorbitant prices. The Tartar-Mongols never return home without an ample supply of them, having an unlimited confidence in whatever emanates from Kounboum. On their own mountains and prairies they would find exactly the same plants, the same shrubs, the same roots, the same grasses; but then how different must be the plants, shrubs, roots, and grasses that grow and ripen in the birthplace of Tsong-Kaba!

The Thibetian physicians are as empirical as those of other countries—possibly somewhat more so. They assign to the human frame forty hundred and forty maladies, neither more nor less. The books which the Lamas of the Faculty of Medicine are obliged to study and to learn by heart, treat of these four hundred and forty maladies, indicating their characteristics, the means of identifying them and the manner of combating them. These books are a hotch-potch of aphorisms, more or less obscure, and of a host of special recipes. The Lama physicians have not so great a horror of blood as the Chinese physicians have—they bleed sometimes, and cup often. In the latter operation, they first subject the skin of the part to slight excoriations, and afterwards place over it a bullock's horn, open at the point. They exhaust the air within, and when a sufficient vacuum is obtained, stop up the hole with a pellet of chewed paper. When they wish to remove the cup they have only to remove this mastic.

The Lama physicians attach extreme importance to the inspection of the patient's water. They always require various specimens of it, collected at different hours of the day and night. They examine it with the most minute attention, and take the greatest heed to all the changes undergone by its color. They whip it, from time to time, with a wooden spatula, and then put it up to the ear to ascertain what degree, if any, of noise it makes; for in their view, a patient's water is mute or silent, according to his state of health. A Lama physician, to attain the character of thorough ability in his profession, must be able to treat and cure a patient without having ever seen him, the inspection of the water sufficing as a guide in the preparation of his prescriptions.

As we have said elsewhere, in speaking of the Tartar-Mongols, the Lamas introduce many superstitious practices into medicine. Yet, notwithstanding all this quackery, there is no doubt that they possess an infinite number of very valuable recipes, the result of long experience. I were, perhaps, rash to imagine that medical science has nothing to learn from the Tartar, Thibetian, and Chinese physicians, on the pretext that they are not acquainted with the structure and mechanism of the human body. They may, nevertheless, be in possession of very important secrets, which science alone, no doubt, is capable of explaining, but which, very possibly, science itself may never discover. Without being scientific, a man may very well light upon extremely scientific results. In China, Tartary, and Thibet, everybody can make gunpowder; yet it may be safely propounded that not one of these powder-makers can explain scientifically this chemical operation; each man has a good receipt for making the powder, and he makes it.

Towards September, we received the joyful intelligence that the Thibetian embassy had arrived at Tang-Keou-Eul, where it was to remain for several days, in order to lay in a stock of provisions, and arrange its order of march. Thus, then, after long and annoying delay, we were about to proceed to the capital of Thibet. We made, without loss of time, all our necessary preparations. First we had to pay a visit to Kounboum, in order to purchase provisions for four months, since, on the whole route, there was not the least hope of finding anything to buy that we might want. Upon a careful calculation, we found that we should require five bricks of tea, two sheep's paunches of butter, two sacks of flour, and eight sacks of tsamba. Tsamba is the name given here to barley-meal, the insipid article which constitutes the ordinary food of the Thibetians. They take a tea-cup half filled with boiling tea; to this they add some pinches of tsamba, and then mix these materials together with the finger, into a sort of wretched paste, neither cooked nor uncooked, hot nor cold, which is then swallowed, and is considered breakfast, dinner, or supper, as the case may be. If you desire to cross the desert to Lha-Ssa, you must perforce resign yourself to tsamba; 'tis to no avail the French traveler sighs for his accustomed knife and fork, and his accustomed knife and fork dishes: he must do without them.

Persons, full of experience and philanthropy, counseled us to lay in a good store of garlic, and every day to chew several cloves of it, unless we wished to be killed on our way by the deleterious vapors that emanated from certain elevated mountains. We did not discuss the merits of this hygienic advice, but adopted it with absolute confidingness.

Our residence in the valley of Tchogortan had been in a high degree advantageous to our animals, which had become fatter than we had ever before known them; the camels, in particular, were magnificently stout; their humps, made firm with solid flesh, rose proudly on their backs, and seemed to defy the fatigues and privations of the desert. Still, even in their improved condition, three camels were not enough to carry our provisions and our baggage. We accordingly added to our caravan a supplementary camel and horse, which lightened our exchequer to the extent of twenty-five ounces of silver; moreover, we hired a young Lama of the Ratchico mountains, with whom we had become acquainted at Kounboum, and who was admitted into our party in the capacity of pro-cameleer. This appointment, while it raised the social condition of Samdadchiemba, diminished also the fatigues of his functions. According to this new arrangement, the little caravan was disposed in the following order; the pro-cameleer, Charad-chambeul, went on foot, and led after him the four camels, who marched in Indian file, the one fastened to the tail of the other; Samdadchiemba, cameleer-in-chief, rode his little black mule beside the camels, and the two missionaries closed the procession, each mounted on a white horse. After having exchanged infinite khatas with our acquaintance and friends at Kounboum and Tchogortan, we proceeded on our route, directing our march towards the Blue Sea, where we were to await the Thibetian embassy.

From Tchogortan to the Koukou-Noor was four days' march. We passed on our way a small Lamasery, called Tansan, containing at most two hundred Lamas; its site is perfectly enchanting; rocky mountains, covered with shrubs and tall firs, form for it a circular enclosure, in the center of which rise the habitations of the Lamas. A stream, bordered with willows and fine longwort, after tranquilly encircling the Lamasery, dashes over a rocky fall, and continues its course in the desert. The Buddhist monastery of Tansan is, they say, very rich, being largely endowed by the Mongol princes of Koukou-Noor with annual contributions.

On leaving the Lamasery of Tansan, we entered an extensive plain, where numerous Mongol tents and flocks of every kind picturesquely variegated the verdure of the pastures. We met two Lamas on horseback, who were seeking contributions of butter from the wealthy shepherds of the locality. Their course is this: they present themselves at the entrance of each tent, and thrice sound a marine conch. Thereupon, some member of the family, brings out a small roll of butter, which, without saying a word, he deposits in a bag, suspended from the saddle of each Lama's horse. The Lamas never once alight, but content themselves with riding up to each tent, and announcing their presence to the inmates by the sound of the shell.

As we advanced, the country became more fertile and less mountainous, until at length, we reached the vast and magnificent pasturage of Koukou-Noor. There vegetation is so vigorous, that the grass rose up to the stomachs of our camels. Soon we discovered, far before us, quite in the horizon, what seemed a broad silver ribbon, above which floated light vapors that, rising, became lost in the azure of the heavens. Our pro-cameleer informed us that this was the Blue Sea. His words filled us with a tremulous joy; we urged on our animals, and the sun had not set when we planted our tent within a hundred paces of the waters of the great Lake.

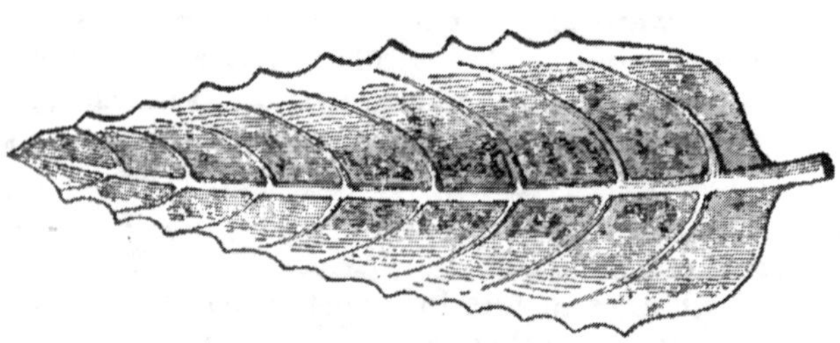

The Leaf of the Tree of Ten Thousand Images.

The Blue Sea.

CHAPTER IV.

Aspect of the Koukou-Noor—Tribes of Kolos—Chronicle of the Origin of the Blue Sea—Description and March of the Great Caravan—Passage of the Pouhain Gol—Adventures of the Altère-Lama—Character of Our Pro-cameleer—Mongols of Tsaidam—Pestilential Vapors of the Bourhan-Bota—Ascent of the Chuga and Bayen-Kharat Mountains—Wild Cattle—Wild Mules—Men and Animals Killed with the Cold—Encounter with Brigands—Plateau of Tant-La—Hot Springs—Conflagration in the Desert—Village of Na-Ptchu—Sale of Camels, and Hiring of Long-tailed Oxen—Young Chaberon of the Kingdom of Khartchin—Cultivated Plains of Pampou—Mountain of the Remission of Sins—Arrival at Lha-Ssa.

THE Blue Lake, in Mongol Koukou-Noor, in Thibetian Tsot-Ngon-Po, was anciently called by the Chinese Si-Haï (Western Sea); they now call it Tsing-Haï (Blue Sea). This immense reservoir of water, which is more than a hundred leagues in circumference, seems, in fact, to merit the title of sea, rather than merely that of lake. To say nothing of its vast extent, it is to be remarked that its waters are bitter and salt, like those of the ocean, and undergo, in a similar manner, flux and reflux. The marine odor which they exhale is smelt at a great distance, far into the desert.

Towards the western portion of the Blue Sea there is a small island, rocky and bare, inhabited by twenty contemplative Lamas, who have built thereon a Buddhist temple, and some modest habitations, wherein they pass their lives, in tranquil retirement, far from the distracting disquietudes of the world. No one can go and visit them, for, throughout the entire extent of the lake, there is not a single boat of any kind to be seen; at all events we saw none, and the Mongols told us that among their tribes no one ever thought of occupying himself in any way or degree with navigation. In the winter, indeed, at the time of the more intense cold, the water is frozen solidly enough to enable the shepherds around to repair in pilgrimage to the Lamasery. They bear to the contemplative Lamas their modest offerings of butter, tea, and tsamba, and receive in exchange, benedictions and prayers for good pasturage and prosperous flocks.

The tribes of the Koukou-Noor are divided into twenty-nine banners, commanded by three Kiun-Wang, two Beïlé, two Beïssé four Koung, and eighteen Paï-Tsi. All these princes are tributaries of the Chinese emperor, and, every second year, repair to Peking, whither they carry, as tribute, furs and gold-dust, which their subjects collect from the sands of their rivers. The vast plains which adjoin the Blue Sea are of very great fertility and of a most agreeable aspect, though entirely destitute of trees; the grass is of prodigious height, and the numerous streams which fertilize the soil, afford ample means to the numerous herds of the desert for satiating their thirst. The Mongols, accordingly, are very fond of setting up their tents in these magnificent pastures. The hordes of brigands harass them in vain; they will not quit the country. They content themselves with a frequent change of encampment, in order to baffle their enemies, but when they can no longer avoid the danger they encounter it with great bravery, and fight gallantly. The necessity under which they permanently exist of defending their property and their lives from the attacks of the Si-Fan, has, at length, rendered them intrepidly courageous. At any hour of the day or night they are ready for battle: they tend their cattle on horseback, lance in hand, fusil in sling, and saber in belt. What a difference between these vigorous shepherds, with their long mustaches, and the languishing fiddle-faddles of Virgil, eternally occupied in piping on a flute, or in decorating with ribbon and flowers their pretty straw hats.

The brigands, who keep the Mongol tribes of the Koukou-Noor always on the alert, are hordes of Si-Fan, or Eastern Thibetians, dwelling in the Bayen-Kharat mountains, towards the sources of the Yellow River. In this part of the country they are known under the generic appellation of Kolo. Their peculiar haunt, it is said, are the deep gorges of the mountain, whither it is impossible to penetrate without a guide, for all the approaches are guarded by impassable torrents and frightful precipices. The Kolos never quit these abodes except to scour the desert on a mission of pillage and devastation. Their religion is Buddhism; but they have a special idol of their own, whom they designate the Divinity of Brigandism, and who, assuredly, enjoys their most intense devotion, their most genuine worship. The chief business of their Lamas is to pray and offer up sacrifices for the success of their predatory expedition. It is said that these brigands are in the revolting habit of eating the hearts of their prisoners, in order to fortify their own courage; but, for that matter, there is no monstrous practise which the Mongols of the Koukou-Noor do not unhesitatingly attribute to these people.

The Kolos are divided into several tribes, each bearing a particular name of its own; and it was only in the nomenclature of these tribes that we ever, in this part of the world, heard of the Khalmouks, or Calmucks. That which we, in Europe, ordinarily conceive to be Khalmoukia, is a purely imaginary distinction; the Khalmouks are very far indeed from enjoying, in Asia, the importance which our books of geography assign to them. In the Khalmoukia of our imagining, no one ever heard of the Khalmouks. It was a long time before we could even discover the existence of the name at all; but, at last, we were lucky enough to meet with a Lama who had traveled extensively in Eastern Thibet, and he told us that among the Kolo, there is a small tribe called Kolo-Khalmouki. It is just possible that at some former period the Khalmouks may have enjoyed great importance, and have occupied a large extent of country; but the great probability, at least, is, that it was the travelers of the thirteenth century, who, relying upon some vague notions they had picked up, represented this petty tribe to be a great nation.

Neither does the Koukou-Noor country itself merit the importance given to it in our geographies: it occupies in the maps a far greater space than it really possesses, Though comprising twenty-nine banners, its limits are restricted: on the north it is bordered by Khilian-Chan, on the south by the Yellow River, on the east by the province of Kan-Sou, on the west by the river Tsaidam, where begins another Tartar country, inhabited by tribes who bear the designation of Mongols of the Tsaidam.

According to the popular traditions of the Koukou-Noor, the Blue Sea did not always occupy its present site: that great mass of water originally covered, in Thibet, the place where the city of Lha-Ssa now stands. One fine day it abandoned its immense reservoir there, and, by a subterranean march, traveled to the place which now serves as its bed. The following is the narrative of this marvelous event that was related to us.

In ancient times the Thibetians of the kingdom of Oui resolved to build a temple in the center of the great valley which they inhabited; they collected, at vast expense, the richest materials, and the edifice rose rapidly; but, just on the point of completion, it suddenly crumbled to pieces, without any one having the least idea as to the cause of this disaster. Next year they made new preparations, and labored upon the construction of the temple with equal ardor; the second temple, when just completed, fell to pieces as the first had done; a third attempt was made, the only result of which was a third catastrophe, exactly the same with the two preceding. Everybody was plunged in utter despair, and there was talk of abandoning the enterprise. The king consulted a famous diviner of the country, who replied that it had not been given to him to know the cause which opposed the construction of the temple, but this he knew; that there was a great saint in the East who possessed a certain secret, which secret, being once extracted from him, the obstacle would forthwith disappear. He could, however, give no exact information as to who the great saint was, or where he lived. After protracted deliberation, a Lama, of excellent address and great courage, was sent on a mission of inquiry. He traversed all the districts east of the kingdom of Oui; he visited all the Tartar tribes, stopping for awhile wherever he heard speak of any man especially noted for his sanctity and knowledge. All his inquiries were fruitless: it was to no purpose he discoursed of the valley of the kingdom of Oui, and of the temple which it had been attempted to raise there: nobody comprehended at all what he was talking about. He was returning home, depressed and disappointed, when, in crossing the great plains which separate Thibet from China, the girth of his saddle broke, and he fell from his horse. Perceiving, near at hand, beside a small pond, a poor, dilapidated tent, he proceeded thither to get his saddle repaired. Having fastened his horse to a stake at the door of the tent, he entered and found within a venerable old man, absorbed in prayer. "Brother," said the traveler, "may peace be ever in thy dwelling." "Brother," replied the old man, without moving, "seat thyself beside my hearth." The Thibetian Lama fancied he saw that the old man was blind. "I perceive, with grief," said he, "that thou hast lost the use of thy eyes." "Yes; 'tis now many years since I was deprived of the happiness of contemplating the brightness of the sun and the verdure of our beautiful plains; but prayer is a great consolation in my affliction. Brother, it seems to me that thy tongue has a peculiar accent: art thou not a man of our tribes?" "I am a poor Lama of the East. I made a vow to visit the temples that have been raised in the Mongol countries, and to prostrate myself before the sainted personages I should meet on my way. An accident has happened to me near this spot; I have broken the girth of my saddle, and I have come to thy tent to mend it." "I am blind," said the old man; "I cannot myself help thee; but look round the tent, there are several straps, and thou canst take that which will best answer thy purpose." While the stranger was selecting a good strap, wherewith to make a new girth, the old man spoke: "O Lama of eastern lands; happy art thou to be able to pass thy days visiting our sacred monuments! The most magnificent temples are in the Mongol countries; the Poba (Thibetians) will never attain anything like them: 'tis in vain they apply their utmost efforts to build such in their beautiful valley; the foundations they put will always be sapped by the waves of a subterranean sea, of which they do not suspect the existence." After a moment's silence the old man added: "I have uttered these words because thou art a Mongol Lama; but thou must lock them up in thy heart, and never communicate them to a single person. If, in thy pilgrimages, thou meetest a Lama of the kingdom of Oui, guard well thy tongue, for the revealing my secret will cause the ruin of our country. When a Lama of the kingdom of Oui shall know that in his valley there exists a subterranean sea, the waters of that sea will forthwith depart thence, and inundate our prairies."

He had scarcely uttered the last word, when the stranger rose and said to him, "Unfortunate old man, save thyself, save thyself in haste: the waters will speedily be here, for I am a Lama of the kingdom of Oui." So saying, he jumped on his horse, and disappeared over the desert.

These words struck like a thunderbolt upon the poor old man. After a moment of dull stupor he gave way to cries and groans. While yielding to this excess of grief his son arrived, bringing home from pasture a small herd of cattle. "My son," cried the old man, "saddle thy horse on the instant, take thy saber, and gallop off towards the West: thou wilt overtake a foreign Lama, whom thou must kill, for he has stolen from me my strap." "How!" exclaimed the young man, terror-struck, "wouldst thou have me commit a murder? Wouldst thou, my father, whom all our tribes venerate for thy great sanctity, order me to kill a poor traveler, because he took from thy tent a strap of which he had, doubtless, need?" "Go, go, my son, hasten, I conjure thee," cried the old man, throwing his arms about in despair; "go and immolate that stranger, unless thou wouldst have us all buried beneath the waves." The young man, believing that his father labored under a temporary fit of insanity, would not contradict him, lest he should exasperate him still more; he therefore mounted his horse and galloped after the Lama of the kingdom of Oui. He came up with him before the evening: "Holy personage," said he, "pardon me, that I interrupt your progress; this morning you rested in our tent, and you took thence a strap, which my father is making a great outcry for; the fury of the old man is so excessive, that he has ordered me to put you to death; but it is no more permissible to execute the orders of a raving old man than it is to fulfil those of a child. Give me back the strap, and I will return to appease my father." The Lama of the kingdom of Oui dismounted, took off the girth of his saddle, and gave it to the young man, saying, "Your father gave me this strap, but, since he regrets the gift, carry it back to him; old men are fanciful, but we must, nevertheless, respect them, and carefully avoid occasioning them any annoyance." The Lama took off his own girdle, made a saddle-girth of it, and departed, the young man returning in all haste to his tent.

He arrived in the night time, and found his dwelling surrounded by a multitude of shepherds, who, unable to comprehend the lamentations of the great saint of their district, were awaiting, in much anxiety, the return of his son. "My father, my father," cried the young man, dismounting, "be calm, here is what thou wantedst." "And the stranger?" asked the old man, "hast thou put him to death?" "I let him depart in peace for his own country. Should I not have committed a great crime, had I murdered a Lama who had done you no evil? Here is the strap he took from you." And, so saying, he put the strap into his father's hands. The old man shuddered in every limb, for he saw that his son had been overreached: the same word in Mongol signifies both strap and secret. The old man had meant that his son should kill the man who had stolen his secret from him: but when he saw that his son brought back to him a strap, he cried: "The West triumphs; 'tis the will of heaven!" He then told the shepherds to flee with their cattle and sheep in all haste, unless they desired to be swallowed up by the waters. As to himself, he prostrated himself in the center of his tent and there resignedly awaited death.

Day had scarce dawned when there was heard underground a rumbling but majestic sound, similar to the tumult of torrents rolling their waves over the mountain sides. The sound advanced with fearful rapidity, and the water of the pond, beside which the old man lived, was seen to be in great commotion; then the earth opened with terrible shocks, and the subterranean waters rose impetuously, and spread, like a vast sea, over the plain, destroying infinite numbers of men and beasts who had not time to escape. The old man was the first who perished beneath the waves.

The Lama, who bore the secret of this great catastrophe, upon arriving in the kingdom of Oui, found his countrymen in utter consternation at fearful sounds they had heard beneath them in the valley, and the nature and cause of which no one could explain. He related the story of the blind old man, and all immediately comprehended that the uproar which had so alarmed them had been occasioned by the subterranean sea, on its removal to the East. They resumed, with enthusiasm, the labors of construction they had abandoned, and raised a magnificent temple, which is still standing. An immense number of families settled around the temple, and, by degrees, there was created a great city, which took the name of Lha-Ssa (Land of Spirits).

This singular chronicle of the origin of the Blue Sea was first related to us in Koukou-Noor; it was afterwards repeated to us at Lha-Ssa, in almost precisely the same terms; but we could nowhere discover traces of any historical fact with which the singular fable might be supposed to correspond.

We abode in Koukou-Noor for nearly a month. Continual rumors of the brigands compelled us to move our encampment five or six times, in order to follow the Tartar tribes, who, at the least suggestion of approaching assailants, change their quarters, taking care, however, never to remove altogether from the rich pastures which border the Blue Sea.

Towards the end of October, the Thibetian embassy arrived, and we joined the immense body, already swollen on its previous way by a great number of Mongol caravans, which, like ourselves, availed themselves of this favorable escort to Lha-Ssa. Formerly, the Thibetian government sent an embassy every year to Peking. That of 1840 was attacked on its journey by a large body of Kolos. The engagement lasted a whole day, but, in the end, the Thibetians were victorious over their assailants, and continued their journey. Next morning, however, it was discovered that they had no longer amongst them the Tchanak-Kampo,[1] a Grand Lama, who accompanies these embassies to Peking, in the character of representative of the Talé-Lama. For several days he was sought all around, but to no effect, and the only conclusion was that during the fight

[1] Tchanak is the Mongol name of Peking; Kampo means Pontiff.

he had been taken prisoner by the Kolos, and carried off. The embassy, however, proceeded on its way, and arrived at Peking without its official head. The emperor, of course, was tremendously afflicted.

In 1841, there was another battle with the brigands, and another catastrophe. This time, the Tchanak-Kampo was not carried off by the brigands, but he received from them a gash in the chest, of which he died in a few days afterwards. The emperor, on hearing these melancholy tidings, was, it is affirmed, altogether inconsolable, and forthwith sent despatches to the Talé-Lama, setting forth that, considering the difficulties and dangers of the journey, he would henceforth require the compliment of an embassy only once in three years. Accordingly, the present embassy was the first which had been despatched from Lha-Ssa since 1841. On its journey out it had been fortunate enough to encounter no brigands, and, consequently, its Tchanak-Kampo had been neither stolen nor stabbed.

Next day, after our departure from Koukou-Noor, we placed ourselves at the van of the caravan, and then halted on one side, in order to see the immense procession defile before us, and so make acquaintance with our traveling companions. The men and animals composing the caravan might be thus estimated: 1500 long-haired oxen, 1200 horses, 1200 camels, and 2000 men. Thibetians and Tartars, some on foot, some on ox-back, but most of them on horses and camels. All the cavalry were armed with lances, sabers, bows and arrows, and matchlocks. The foot-men, designated Lakto, were charged with the conduct of the files of camels and of the capricious and disorderly march of the cattle. The Tchanak-Kampo traveled in a large litter, carried by two mules. Besides this multitude, whose journey extended to Lha-Ssa, there was an escort of 300 Chinese soldiers, furnished by the province of Kan-Sou, and 200 brave Tartars, charged by the princes of Koukou-Noor, with the protection of the holy embassy of the Talè-Lama, to the frontiers of Thibet.

The soldiers of the province of Kan-Sou fulfilled their functions like thorough Chinese. In order to avoid any disagreeable encounter, they carefully kept at the rear of the caravan, where they sang, smoked, and joked at their ease, giving no sort of heed to any possible brigands. Every day they exhibited the remarkable peculiarity of waiting until the rest of the caravan had filed off, when they carefully searched all over the night's encampment in order to pick up anything that might have been left behind, and, of course, traveling somewhat in the rear of the rest, they were further able to realize any matters that those preceding them might drop during the progress of the day. The Tartar soldiers pursued a conduct precisely the reverse: they were ever in the van, and at the sides of the caravan, dashing about to

The Tchanak-Kampo, and the Caravan.

the tops of the hills and the depths of the valleys to see that no ambush of brigands lay in wait there.

The general march and particular movements of the caravan were executed with tolerable order and precision, especially at the outset. Generally, we started every morning two or three hours before sunrise, in order that we might encamp about noon, and give the animals full time to feed during the remainder of the day; the *reveillé* was announced by a cannon shot; forthwith, everybody rose, the fires were lighted, and while some of each particular party loaded the beasts of burden, the others boiled the kettle and prepared breakfast; a few cups of tea were drunk, a few handfuls of tsamba eaten, and then the tent was taken down, folded, and packed. A second cannon-shot gave the signal for departure. A few of the more experienced horsemen took the lead as guides; these were followed by long files of camels, and then came the long-haired cattle, in herds of two or three hundred beasts each, under the care of several lakto. The horsemen had no fixed place in the procession; they dashed here and there, up and down, just as their caprice suggested. The plaintive cries of the camels, the roaring of the bulls, the lowing of the cows, the neighing of the horses, the talking, bawling, laughing, singing of the travelers, the whistling of the lakto to the beasts of burden, and, above all, the innumerable bells tinkling from the necks of the yaks and the camels, produced together an immense, undefinable concert, which, far from wearying, seemed, on the contrary, to inspire everybody with fresh courage and energy.

The caravan went on thus across the desert, stopping each day in plains, in valleys and on the mountain-sides, improvising, with its tents, so numerous and so varied in form and color, a large town, which vanished each morning, to reappear further on each evening. What an astonishing thing it must have been for these vast and silent deserts, to find themselves, all of a sudden, traversed by so numerous and so noisy a multitude! When we viewed those infinite traveling tents, those large herds, and those men, in turns shepherds and warriors, we could not help frequently reflecting upon the march of the Israelites, when they went in search of the Promised Land, through the solitudes of Madian.

On quitting the shore of the Blue Sea, we directed our steps towards the west, with a slight inclination, perhaps, southward. The first days of our march were perfect poetry; everything was just as we could have wished; the weather was magnificent, the road excellent, the water pure, the pastures rich and ample. As to brigands, we lost all thought of them. In the night, it was, indeed, rather cold; but this inconvenience was easily obviated by the aid of our sheepskin coats. We asked one another what people could mean by representing this Thibet journey as something so formidable; it seemed to us impossible for any one to travel more comfortably, or more agreeably. Alas! this enchantment was not of long duration.

Six days after our departure, we had to cross the Pouhain-Gol, a river which derives its source from the slopes of the Nan-Chan mountains, and throws itself into the Blue Sea. Its waters are not very deep, but being distributed in some dozen channels, very close to one another, they occupy altogether a breadth of more than a league. We had the misfortune to reach the first branch of the Pouhain-Gol long before daybreak; the water was frozen, but not thickly enough to serve as a bridge. The horses which arrived first grew alarmed and would not advance; they stopped on the bank, and gave the cattle time to come up with them. The whole caravan thus became assembled at one point, and it would be impossible to describe the disorder and confusion which prevailed in that enormous mass, amid the darkness of night. At last, several horsemen, pushing on their steeds and breaking the ice, actually and figuratively, the whole caravan followed in their train: the ice cracked in all directions, the animals stumbled about and splashed up the water, and the men shouted and vociferated; the tumult was absolutely fearful. After having traversed the first branch of the river, we had to maneuver, in the same way, over the second, and then over the third, and so on. When day broke, the holy Embassy was still dabbling in the water: at length, after infinite fatigue and infinite quaking, physical and moral, we had the delight to leave behind us the twelve arms of the Pouhain-Gol, and to find ourselves on dry land; but all our poetical visions had vanished, and we began to think this manner of traveling perfectly detestable.

And yet everybody about us was in a state of jubilation, exclaiming that the passage of Pouhain-Gol had been admirably executed. Only one man had broken his legs, and only two animals had been drowned. As to the articles lost or stolen, during the protracted disorder, no one took any heed to them.

When the caravan resumed its accustomed march, it persented a truly ludicrous appearance. Men and animals were all, more or less, covered with icicles. The horses walked on, very dolefully, evidently much incommoded by their tails, which hung down, all in a mass, stiff and motionless, as though they had been made of lead instead of hair. The long hair on the legs of the camels had become magnificent icicles, which knocked one against the other, as the animals advanced, with harmonious discord. It was very manifest, however, that these fine ornaments were not at all to the wearers' taste, for they endeavored, from time to time, to shake them off by stamping violently on the ground. As to the long-haired oxen, they were regular caricatures; nothing can be conceived more ludicrous than their appearance, as they slowly advanced, with legs separated to the utmost possible width, in order to admit of an enormous system of stalactites which hung from their bellies to the ground. The poor brutes had been rendered so perfectly shapeless by the agglomeration of icicles with which they were covered, that they looked as though they were preserved in sugar-candy.

During the first few days of our march we were somewhat isolated and lonely amid the multitude; without friends or even acquaintance. However, we soon acquired companions for there is nothing like traveling to bring men together. The companions whom we entered into association with, and beside whose tent we each day set up our own, were neither merchants, nor pilgrims, nor members of the embassy itself, nor simple travelers, like ourselves; they were four Lamas, who constituted a category altogether apart. Two of them were from Lha-Ssa, one from Further Thibet, and the fourth from the kingdom of Torgot. On our way, they related to us their long and picturesque history, of which the following is an outline.

The three Thibetian Lamas had become the disciples of a Grand Lama, named Altère, who proposed to erect, in the vicinity of Lha-Ssa, a Buddhist temple, which, in extent and magnificence, was to surpass all those previously existing. One day he announced to his three disciples that all his plans were formed, and that they must all now proceed upon a grand quest for subscriptions wherewith to defray the enormous expenses of the sacred construction. They accordingly all four set forth, with hearts full of zeal and devotion. They first directed their steps towards the north, and traversing all Central Asia, reached the kingdom of Torgot, close to the Russian frontier. On their way, they called at all the

Lamasaries, and at the abode of all the Thibetian and Tartar princes that lay near the route. Everywhere, they received considerable offerings, for, besides that their object was of itself calculated to excite the warmest interest in well-disposed minds, Altère-Lama had letters of recommendation from the Talé-Lama, from the Bandchan-Remboutchi, and from the heads of all the most famous Lamaseries of Thibet. In Torgot, a rich Mongol Lama, touched with the devotion of these intrepid collectors, offered them all his herds, and entreated Altère-Lama to admit him among his disciples, so that he might aid them in their mission through the countries of Tartary. Altère-Lama, on his part, moved with a zeal so pure, a disinterestedness so entire, consented to accept both his offerings and himself. The Lama collectors thus became five in number.

From Torgot they directed their march towards the east, going from one tribe to another, and everywhere augmenting their herds of cattle, sheep, and horses. On their way they passed through the country of the Khalkhas, where they stayed for some time in the Lamasery of the Great Kouren, the offerings of the Tartary pilgrims flowing in abundantly. Hence, they turned south, to Peking, where they converted into gold and silver the innumerable animals which they had collected together from all parts. After an extended residence in the capital of the Chinese empire, they resumed their operations in the deserts of Tartary, and still seeking subscriptions, and still receiving them, arrived at Kounboum. In this famous and sainted Lamasery, capable of appreciating the merit of good Lamas, the zeal and devotion of the celebrated questors attained a colossal reputation; they became the objects of the public veneration, and the professors, who aimed at perfection in their pupils, proposed to them these five men as models.

Altère-Lama, after three years of so meritorious a quest, now only sighed for the hour when he should return to Lha-Ssa and consecrate to the construction of his temple all the rich offerings he had succeeded in collecting. Great, therefore, was his joy, when he heard the intelligence that the Thibetian embassy was at hand. He resolved to avail himself of its escort, on its return from Peking, so as securely to convey his gold and silver through the dangerous district of the Kolo. Meanwhile, he announced, he would apply all his attention to the preparations required for this important journey.

But, alas! the projects of men are often frustrated at the very moment when they seem on the point of succeeding in the most triumphant manner. One fine day there arrived at Si-Ning-Fou an imperial courier extraordinary, bearing despatches by which the Grand Mandarin of that town was ordered to arrange with the superior of the Lamasery of Kounboum, for the immediate arrest of Altère-Lama, charged with having, during the past three years, committed the most comprehensive swindling, by means of certain letters of recommendation, falsely attributed to the Talé-Lama. The orders of his imperial majesty were executed. One may easily imagine the stupefaction, on the occasion, of the poor Altère-Lama, and especially of his four disciples, who throughout the affair, had acted with the most entire good faith. The very embassy, on the protection of which Altère-Lama had so relied, was directed by the Thibetian government to take charge of the Grand Questor, whose marvelous successes had been published at Lha-Ssa, by the indiscreet laudations of the pilgrims.

Altère-Lama, having been arrested on the spot, was immediately forwarded, under safe escort, to Lha-Ssa, the route taken by his guard being that of the imperial couriers, through the province of Sse-Tchouan. Upon his arrival in the capital of Thibet, his case was to be investigated by his natural judges. Meanwhile, his prodigious receipts were confiscated to the benefit of the Talé-Lama; for, obviously, nothing could be more just than that he should be placed in possession of the gold and the silver which had been raised under the all-potent influence of his name. As to the Grand Questor's four disciples, it was arranged that they should await the return of the Thibetian embassy, and proceed with it to Lha-Ssa, taking with them fifty-eight magnificent camels which the Altère-Lama had procured, and which were to be at the disposal of the Thibetian government.

These four unfortunate disciples were the traveling companions whom good fortune had thrown in our way. The recollection of their fallen master was ever in their minds, but the sentiments which that recollection excited in them were not always the same. Sometimes they regarded their master as a saint, sometimes as a swindler; one day they would pronounce his name with veneration, raising their clasped hands to their forehead; another day, they would curse him, and spit in the air, to show their contempt for him. The Lama of Torgot, however, always made the best of the matter. He reproached himself, sometimes, for having made an offering of all his herds to a man who now developed, pretty manifestly, every appearance of a rogue; but still he consoled himself that after all the man's knavery had been the occasion of his seeing a good deal of the world, and visiting the most celebrated Lamaseries. These four young men were excellent fellows, and capital traveling companions. Every day they gave us some fresh details of their varied adventures, and their narratives frequently contributed to make us forget, for awhile, the fatigues and miseries of the journey.

A permanent cause of the sufferings we had to endure was our pro-cameleer Charadchambeul. At first, this young Lama appeared to us a budding saint, but before long we found that we had got amongst us a complete little demon with a human face. The following adventure opened our eyes to his character, and showed us what we should have to endure on his account.

The day after the passage of the Pouhain-Gol, when we had been marching for a part of the night, we remarked, on one of our camels, two great packages carefully enveloped in wrappers, which we had not before seen. We thought, however, that some traveler, who had not been able to find room for them on his own sumpter animal, had asked Charadchambeul to take charge of them during the journey; and we, accordingly, quietly pursued our way, without, at the time, recurring to the circumstance. When we reached our encampment for the night, so soon as the baggage was taken down, we saw, to our great surprise, our Lama of Ratchico mountains take the two packets, envelop them mysteriously in a piece of felt, and hide them in a corner of the tent. There was evidently something here which required explanation; and we accordingly desired Charadchambeul to inform us what was this new luggage that we saw in the tent. He approached us, and in a whisper, as though fearing to be heard, told us that during the night Buddha had bestowed on him a special grace, in enabling him to find on the road a good thing, and then he added, with a knavish smile, that at Lha-Ssa, this good thing would sell for at least ten ounces of silver. We frowned, and required to see this same good thing. Charadchambeul, having first carefully closed the door of the tent, uncovered, with infinite emotion, his pretended godsend. It consisted of two great leathern jars, full of a sort of brandy, that is distilled in the province of Kan-Sou, and which is sold at a high price. On these two jars were Thibetian characters indicating the well-known name of the proprietor. We had the charity to reject the thought that Charadchambeul had stolen these jars during the night, and preferred to suppose that he had picked them up on the road. But our pro-cameleer was a casuist of very loose morality. He pretended that the jars belonged to him, that Buddha had made him a present of them, and that all which now required to be done was carefully to conceal them, lest the previous proprietor should discover them. Any attempt to reason such a worthy as this into morality and justice would have been simply lost labor and time. We therefore emphatically declared to him that the jars were neither ours nor his, that we would neither receive them into our tent nor place them on our camels during the journey, and that we had no desire whatever to arrive at Lha-Ssa with the character of being thieves. And in order that he might labor under no sort of misconception as to our feelings, we added, that unless he forthwith removed the jars from our tent, we should instantly proceed and give information of the circumstance to the proprietor. He seemed somewhat shaken by this intimation, and in order effectually to induce him to restitution, we advised him to carry what he had "found" to the ambassador, and request him to return it to the owner. The Tchanak-Kampo, we said, would not fail to be affected by his probity, and even if he did not give him a reward in hand, would bear him in mind, and when we reached Lha-Ssa would doubtless benefit him in some way. After an animated opposition, this advice was adopted. Charadchambeul presented himself before the Tchanak-Kampo, who said to him, on receiving the jars: "Thou art a good Lama. A Lama who has justice in his heart is acceptable to the spirits." Charadchambeul returned perfectly furious, vehemently exclaiming that we had induced him to commit an imbecility in giving up the jars to the ambassador, who had presented him with nothing in return but empty words. From that moment he vowed an implacable hatred towards us. He did his work how and when he pleased; he took a delight in wasting our provisions; every day he loaded us with abuse, and in his rage often turning upon the poor animals, he would beat them about the head till he had half killed them. To discharge the wretch there, amid the desert, was impossible. We were fain therefore to arm ourselves with patience and resignation, and to avoid irritating still more the man's untamed ferocity.

Five days after the passage of the Pouhain-Gol, we reached Toulain-Gol, a narrow, shallow river, which we crossed without any difficulty. The caravan halted shortly afterwards near a Lamasery, which had the appearance of former prosperity, but which was, at present, wholly deserted. The temples and the Lamas' cells, all tumbling in pieces, had become the abode of bats and of enormous rats. We heard that this Buddhist monastery, after having been besieged for three days by the brigands, had been taken by them, the greater portion of the inmates massacred, and the place itself plundered and demolished. From that time forth, no Lama had ventured to settle in the spot. The vicinity, however, was not so entirely uninhabited as we at first supposed. In walking over some rocky hills close by, we found a herd of goats and three miserable tents, concealed in a ravine. The poor inmates came out and begged for a few leaves of tea and a little tsamba. Their eyes were hollow, and their features pale and haggard. They knew not, they said, where to take refuge, so as to live in peace. The fear of the brigands was so powerful over them, that it divested them even of the courage to flee away.

Next day the caravan continued its route, but the Chinese escort remained encamped on the bank of the river; its task was completed, and after a few days' rest, it would return home. The Thibetian merchants, so far from being distressed at the circumstance, said that now the Chinese soldiers were no longer with them, they should be able to sleep at night, freed from the fear of thieves.

On the 15th November, we quitted the magnificent plains of the Koukou-Noor, and entered upon the territory of the Mongols of Tsaidam. Immediately after crossing the river of that name, we found the aspect of the country totally changed. Nature becomes all of a sudden savage and sad; the soil, arid and stony, produces with difficulty a few dry, saltpetrous bushes. The morose and melancholy tinge of these dismal regions seems to have had its full influence upon the character of its inhabitants, who are all evidently a prey to the spleen. They say very little, and their language is so rude and guttural that other Mongols can scarcely understand them. Mineral salt and borax abound on this arid and almost wholly pastureless soil. You dig holes two or three feet deep, and the salt collects therein, and crystallizes and purifies of itself, without your having to take any trouble in the matter. The borax is collected from small reservoirs, which become completely full of it. The Thibetians carry quantities of it into their own country, where they sell it to the goldsmiths, who apply it to facilitate the fusion of metals. We stayed two days in the land of Tsaidam, feasting upon tsamba and some goats which the shepherds gave in exchange for some bricks of tea. The long-tailed oxen and the camels regaled themselves with the nitre and salt which they had everywhere about for the picking up. The grand object with the whole caravan was to get up its strength as much as possible, with a view to the passage of the Bourhan-Bota, a mountain noted for the pestilential vapors in which, as we were informed, it is constantly enveloped.

We started at three in the morning, and after infinite sinuosities and meanderings over this hilly country, we arrived, by nine o'clock, at the foot of the Bourhan-Bota. There the caravan halted for a moment, as if to poise its strength; everybody measured, with his eyes, the steep and rugged paths of the lofty ascent, gazed with anxiety at a light, thin vapor, which we were told was the pestilential vapor in question, and for awhile the entire party was completely depressed and discouraged. After having taken the hygienic measures prescribed by tradition, and which consist in masticating two or three cloves of garlic, we began to clamber up the side of the mountain. Before long, the horses refused to carry their riders, and all, men as well as animals, advanced on foot, and step by step; by degrees, our faces grew pale, our hearts sick, and our legs incapable of supporting us; we threw ourselves on the ground, then rose again to make another effort; then once more prostrated ourselves, and again rose to stumble on some paces farther; in this deplorable fashion was it that we ascended the famous Bourhan-Bota. Heavens! what wretchedness it was we went through; one's strength seemed exhausted, one's head turning round, one's limbs dislocated; it was just like a thoroughly bad sea-sickness; and yet, all the while, one has to retain enough energy, not only to drag one's self on, but, moreover, to keep thrashing the animals which lie down at every step, and can hardly be got to move. One portion of the caravan, as a measure of precaution, stopped half way up the mountain, in a gully where the pestilential vapors, they said, were not so dense; the other portion of the caravan, equally as a measure of precaution, exerted their most intense efforts in order to make their way right up to the top, so as to avoid being asphyxiated by that dreadful air, so completely charged with carbonic acid. We were of the number of those who ascended the Bourhan-Bota at one stretch. On reaching its summit, our lungs dilated at their ease. The descent of the mountain was mere child's play, and we were soon able to set up our tent far from the murderous air we had encountered on the ascent.

The Bourhan-Bota mountain has this remarkable particularity, that the deleterious vapor for which it is noted, is only found on the sides facing the east and the north; elsewhere, the air of the mountain is perfectly pure and respirable. The pestilential vapors themselves would appear to be nothing more than carbonic acid gas. The people attached to the embassy told us that when there is any wind, the vapors are scarcely perceptible, but that they are very dangerous when the weather is calm and serene. Carbonic acid gas being, as the reader is aware, heavier than the atmospheric air, necessarily condenses on the surface of the ground, and remains fixed there until some great agitation of the air sets it in movement, disperses it in the atmosphere, and neutralizes its effects. When we crossed the Bourhan-Bota, the weather was rather calm than otherwise. We remarked, that when we were lying on the ground, respiration was much more difficult; when, on the contrary, we raised ourselves on horseback, the influence of the gas was scarcely felt. The presence of the carbonic acid rendered it very difficult to light a fire; the argols burned without flame, and threw out great quantities of smoke. As to the manner in which the gas is formed, or as to whence it comes, we can give no sort of idea. We will merely add, for the benefit of those who are fond of seeking explanations of things in their names, that Bourhan-Bota means Kitchen of Bourhan; Bourhan being a synonym of Buddha.

During the night we passed on the other side of the mountain, there fell a frightful quantity of snow. Our companions, who had not ventured to ascend the entire mountain at once, rejoined us in the morning; they informed us that they had effected the ascent of the upper portion of the mountain easily enough, the snow having dispersed the vapor.

The passage of the Bourhan-Bota was but a sort of apprenticeship. A few days after, Mount Chuga put our strength and courage to a still more formidable test. The day's march being long and laborious, the cannon shot, our signal for departure, was heard at one o'clock in the morning. We made our tea with melted snow, ate a good meal of tsamba, seasoned with a clove of garlic, cut up into small bits, and started. When the huge caravan first set itself in motion, the sky was clear, and a brilliant moon lit up the great carpet of snow with which the whole country was covered. Mount Chuga being not very steep in the direction where we approached it, we were able to attain the summit by sunrise. Almost immediately afterwards, however, the sky became thickly overcast with clouds, and the wind began to blow with a violence which grew constantly more and more intense. The opposite sides of the mountain we found so encumbered with snow, that the animals were up to their girths in it; they could only advance by a series of convulsive efforts, which threw several of them into gulfs from which it was impossible to extricate them, and where they accordingly perished. We marched in the very teeth of a wind so strong and so icy, that it absolutely at times choked our respiration, and despite our thick furs, made us tremble lest we should be killed with the cold. In order to avoid the whirlwinds of snow which the wind perpetually dashed in our faces, we adopted the example of some of our fellow travelers, who bestrode their horses' backs with their faces to the tail, leaving the animals to follow the guidance of their instinct. When we reached the foot of the mountain, and could use our eyes, we found that more than one face had been frozen in the descent. Poor M. Gabet, among the rest, had to deplore the temporary decease of his nose and ears. Everybody's skin was more or less chapped and cut.

The caravan halted at the foot of Mount Chuga, and each member of it sought refuge for awhile in the labyrinths of a number of adjacent defiles. Exhausted with hunger, and our limbs thoroughly benumbed, what we wanted to bring us to, was a good fire, a good supper, and a good, well-warmed bed; but the Chuga is far from possessing the comfortable features of the Alps; no Buddhist monks have as yet bethought themselves of taking up their abode there for the solace and salvation of poor travelers. We were, consequently, fain to set up our tent amid the snow, and then to go in search of what argols we could burn. It was a spectacle worthy of all pity to see that multitude, wandering about in all directions, and rummaging up the snow, in the hope of lighting upon some charming thick bed of argols. For ourselves, after long and laborious research, we managed to collect just enough of the article to melt three great lumps of ice, which we extracted by aid of a hatchet, from an adjacent pond. Our fire not being strong enough to boil the kettle, we had to content ourselves with infusing our tsamba in some tepid water, and gulping it down in order to prevent its freezing in our hands. Such was all the supper we had after our frightful day's journey. We then rolled ourselves up in our goatskins and blankets, and, crouching in a corner of the tent, awaited the cannon-shot that was to summon us to our delightful *Impressions de Voyage*.

We left in this picturesque and enchanting encampment, the Tartar soldiers who had escorted us since our departure from Koukou-Noor; they were no longer able to extend to us their generous protection, for, that very day, we were about to quit Tartary, and to enter the territory of Hither Thibet. The Chinese and Tartar soldiers having thus left us, the embassy had now only to rely upon its own internal resources. As we have already stated, this great body of 2,000 men was completely armed, and every one, with the merest exception, had announced himself prepared to show himself, upon occasion, a good soldier. But somehow or other the whilome so martial and valorous air of the caravan had become singularly modified since the passage of the Bourhan-Bota. Nobody sang now, nobody joked, nobody laughed, nobody pranced about on his horse; everybody was dull and silent; the moustachios which heretofore had been so fiercely turned up, were now humbly veiled beneath the lambskins with which all our faces were covered up to the eyes. All our gallant soldiers had made up their lances, fusils, sabres, bows and arrows, into bundles, which were packed upon their sumpter animals. For that matter, the fear of being killed by the brigands scarcely occurred now to any one: the point was to avoid being killed by the cold.

It was on Mount Chuga that the long train of our real miseries really began. The snow, the wind, and the cold there set to work upon us, with a fury which daily increased. The deserts of Thibet are certainly the most frightful country that it is possible to conceive. The ground continuing to rise, vegetation diminished as we advanced, and the cold grew more and more intense. Death now hovered over the unfortunate caravan. The want of water and of pasturage soon destroyed the strength of our animals. Each day we had to abandon beasts of burden that could drag themselves on no further. The turn of the men came somewhat later. The aspect of the road was of dismal auspice. For several days, we traveled through what seemed the excavations of a great cemetery. Human bones, and the carcases of animals presenting themselves at every step, seemed to warn us that, in this fatal region, amidst this savage nature, the caravans which had preceded us, had preceded us in death.

To complete our misery, M. Gabet fell ill, his health abandoning him just at the moment when the frightful difficulties of the route called for redoubled energy and courage. The excessive cold he had undergone on the passage of Mount Chuga, had entirely broken up his strength. To regain his previous vigor, he needed repose, tonic drinks, and a substantial nourishment, whereas all we had to give him was barley-meal, and tea made with snow water; and, moreover, notwithstanding his extreme weakness, he had every day to ride on horseback, and to struggle against an iron climate. And we had two months more of this traveling before us, in the depth of winter. Our prospect was, indeed, somber!

Towards the commencement of September, we arrived in sight of the Bayen-Kharat, a famous chain of mountains, extending from southeast to northwest, between the Hoang-Ho and the Kin-Cha-Kiang. These two great rivers, after running a parallel course on either side of the Bayen-Kharat, then separate, and take opposite directions, the one towards the north, the other towards the south. After a thousand capricious meanderings in Tartary and Thibet, they both enter the Chinese empire; and after having watered it from west to east, they approach each other, towards their mouths, and fall into the Yellow Sea very nearly together. The point at which we crossed the Bayen-Kharat is not far from the sources of the Yellow River; they lay on our left, and a couple of days' journey would have enabled us to visit them; but this was by no means the season for pleasure trips. We had no fancy for a tourist's excursion to the sources of the Yellow River: how to cross the Bayen-Kharat was ample occupation for our thoughts.

From its foot to its summit the mountain was completely enveloped in a thick coat of snow. Before undertaking the ascent, the principal members of the embassy held a council. The question was not whether they should pass the mountain: if they desired to reach Lha-Ssa, the passage of the mountain was an essential preliminary; nor was it the question, whether they should await the melting of the snow; the point was simply whether it would be more advantageous to ascend the mountain at once or to wait till next day. The fear of avalanches filled every one's mind, and we should all have gladly subscribed to effect an assurance against the wind. After the example of all the councils in the world, the council of the Thibetian embassy was soon divided into two parties, the one contending that it would be better to start forthwith, the other insisting that we ought, by all means, to wait till the morrow.

To extricate themselves from this embarrassment, they had recourse to the Lamas, who had the reputation of being diviners. But this expedient did not combine all minds in unity. Among the diviners there were some who declared that this day would be calm, but that the next day there would be a terrible wind, and there were others who announced an exactly contrary opinion. The caravan thus became divided into two camps, that of movement and that of non-movement. It will at once be understood that in our character of French citizens, we instinctively placed ourselves in the ranks of the progressists; that is to say, of those who desired to advance, and to have done with this villainous mountain as soon as possible. It appeared to us, moreover, that reason was altogether on our side. The weather just then was perfectly calm; but we knew not what it might be on the morrow. Our party, therefore, proceeded to scale these mountains of snow, sometimes on horseback, but more frequently on foot. In the latter case, we made our animals precede us, and we hung on to their tails, a mode of ascending mountains which is certainly the least fatiguing of all. M. Gabet suffered dreadfully, but God, of his infinite goodness, gave us strength and energy enough to reach the other side. The weather was calm throughout, and we were assailed by no avalanche whatever.

Next morning, at daybreak, the party who had remained behind advanced and crossed the mountain with entire success. As we had had the politeness to wait for them, they joined us, and we entered together a valley where the temperature was comparatively mild. The excellence of the pasturage induced the caravan to take a day's rest here. A deep lake, in the ice of which we dug wells, supplied us with abundance of water. We had plenty of fuel, too, for the embassies and pilgrimages being in the habit of halting in the valley, after the passage of the Bayen-Kharat, one is always sure to find plenty of argols there. We all kept up great fires throughout our stay, burning all the burnable things we could find, without the smallest consideration for our successors, leaving it to our 15,000 long-haired oxen to supply the deficit.

We quitted the great valley of Bayen-Kharat, and set up our tents on the banks of the Mouroui-Oussou, or, as the Thibetians call it, Polei-Tchou (river of the Lord). Towards its source, this magnificent river bears the name of Mouroui-Oussou (tortuous river); further on it is called Kin-Cha-Kiang (river of golden sand), and arrived in the province of Sse-Tchouan, it becomes the famous Yang-Dze-Kiang (blue river). As we were passing the Mouroui-Oussou, on the ice, a singular spectacle presented itself. We had previously, from our encampment, observed dark, shapeless masses, ranged across this great river; and it was not until we came quite close to these fantastic islets that we could at all make head or tail of them. Then we found out that they were neither more nor less than upwards of fifty wild cattle, absolutely encrusted in the ice. They had no doubt attempted to swim across the river, at the precise moment of the concretion of the waters, and had been so hemmed in by the flakes as to be unable to extricate themselves. Their fine heads, surmounted with great horns, were still above the surface; the rest of the bodies were enclosed by the ice, which was so transparent as to give a full view of the form and position of the unlucky animals, which looked as though they were still swimming. The eagles and crows had pecked out their eyes.

Wild cattle are of frequent occurrence in the deserts of Hither Thibet. They always live in great herds, and prefer the summits of the mountains. During the summer, indeed, they descend into the valleys in order to quench their thirst in the streams and ponds; but throughout the long winter season, they remain on the heights feeding on snow, and on a very hard rough grass they find there. These animals, which are of enormous size, with long black hair, are especially remarkable for the immense dimensions and splendid form of their horns. It is not at all prudent to hunt them, for they are said to be extremely ferocious. When, indeed, you find two or three of them separated from the main herd, you may venture to attack them; but the assailants must be numerous, in order to make sure of their game, for if they do not kill the animal at once there is decided danger of his killing them. One day we perceived one of these creatures licking up the niter in a small place encircled with rocks. Eight men, armed with matchlocks, left the caravan, and posted themselves in ambush, without being detected by the bull. Eight gun-shots were fired at once; the bull raised his head, looked round with fiery eyes in search of the places whence he had been assailed, and then dashed over the rocks into the plain, where he tore about furiously, roaring awfully. The hunters affirmed that he had been wounded, but that, intimidated by the appearance of the caravan, he had not ventured to turn upon his assailants.

Wild mules are also very numerous in Hither Tartary. After we had passed the Mouroui-Oussou we saw some almost every day. This animal, which our naturalists call *cheval hémione*, a horse half-ass, is of the size of an ordinary mule; but its form is finer and its movements more graceful and active; its hair, red on the back, grows lighter and lighter down to the belly, where it is almost white. The head, large and ugly, is wholly at variance with the elegance of

Wild Mules of Tartary.

its body; when in slow motion, it carries its head erect, and its long ears extended; when it gallops, it turns its head to the wind, and raises its tail, which exactly resembles that of the ordinary mule; its neigh is ringing, clear, and sonorous, and its speed so great that no Thibetian or Tartar horseman can overtake it. The mode of taking it is to post oneself in ambush near the places that lead to the springs where they drink, and to shoot it with arrows or bullets; the flesh is excellent, and the skins are converted into boots. The hémiones are productive, and their young, from generation to generation, are always of the same species. They have never been tamed to domestic purposes. We heard of individuals having been taken quite young, and brought up with other foals; but it has always been found impracticable to mount them or to get them to carry any burden. With the first opportunity, they run away, and resume their wild state. It did not, however, appear to us that they were so extremely fierce as they were represented: we have seen them frolicking about with the horses of our caravans, when pasturing; and it was only on the approach of man, whom they see and scent at a great distance, that they took to flight. The lynx, the chamois, the reindeer, and the wild goat abound in Hither Tartary.

Some days after the passage of the Moroui-Oussou, the caravan began to break up; those who had camels went on ahead, refusing to be any longer delayed by the slow progress of the long-haired oxen. Besides, the nature of the country no longer permitted so large a body to encamp on one spot. The pasturages became so scarce and meager, that the animals of the caravan could not travel all together, without the danger of starving all together. We joined the camel party, and soon left behind us the long-haired oxen. The camel party itself was before long fain to subdivide; and the grand unity once broken, there were formed a number of petty caravans, which did not always concur, either as to the place of encampment or the hour of departure.

We were imperceptibly attaining the highest point of Upper Asia, when a terrible north wind, which lasted fifteen days, combined with the fearful severity of the temperature, menaced us with destruction. The weather was still clear; but the cold was so intense that even at midday we scarcely felt the influence of the sun's rays, and then we had the utmost difficulty in standing against the wind. During the rest of the day, and more especially during the night, we were under constant apprehension of dying with cold. Everybody's face and hands were regularly plowed up. To give something like an idea of this cold, the reality of which, however, can never be appreciated, except by those who have felt it, it may suffice to mention a circumstance which seemed to us rather striking. Every morning, before proceeding on our journey, we ate a meal, and then we did not eat again until the evening, after we had encamped. As tsamba is not a very toothsome affair, we could not get down, at a time, as much as was required for our nourishment during the day; so we used to make three or four balls of it, with our tea, and keep these in reserve, to be eaten, from time to time, on our road. The hot paste was wrapped in a piece of hot linen, and then deposited in our breasts. Over it, were all our clothes; to wit, a thick robe of sheepskin, then a lambskin jacket, then a short fox-skin cloak, and then a great wool overall; now, upon every one of the fifteen days in question, our tsamba cakes were always frozen. When we took them out, they were merely so many balls of ice, which, notwithstanding, we were fain to devour, at the risk of breaking our teeth, in order to avoid the greater risk of starvation.

The animals, overcome with fatigue and privation, had infinite difficulty in at all resisting the intensity of the cold. The mules and horses, being less vigorous than the camels and long-haired oxen, required especial attention. We were obliged to pack them in great pieces of carpet, carefully fastened round the body, the head being enveloped in rolls of camel's hair. Under any other circumstances this singular costume would have excited our hilarity, but just then, we were in no laughing mood. Despite all these precautions, the animals of the caravans were decimated by death.

The numerous rivers that we had to pass upon the ice were another source of inconceivable misery and fatigue. Camels are so awkward and their walk is so uncouth and heavy, that in order to facilitate their passage, we were compelled to make a path for them across each river, either by strewing sand and dust, or by breaking the first coat of ice with our hatchets. After this, we had to take the brutes, one by one, and guide them carefully over the path thus traced out; if they had the ill-luck to stumble or slip, it was all over with them; down they threw themselves on the ice, and it was only with the utmost labor they could be got up again. We had first to take off their baggage, then to drag them with ropes to the bank, and then to stretch a carpet on which they might be induced to rise; sometimes all this labor was lost: you might beat the obstinate animals, pull them, kick them; not an effort would they make to get on their legs; in such cases, the only course was to leave them where they lay, for it was clearly impossible to wait, in those hideous localities, until the pig-headed brute chose to rise.

All these combined miseries ended in casting the poor travelers into a depression bordering on despair. To the mortality of the animals, was now added that of the men, who, hopelessly seized upon by the cold, were abandoned, yet living, on the road. One day, when the exhaustion of our animals had compelled us to relax our march, so that we were somewhat behind the main body, we perceived a traveler sitting on a great stone, his head bent forward on his chest, his arms pressed against his sides, and his whole frame motionless as a statue. We called to him several times, but he made no reply, and did not even indicate, by the slightest movement, that he heard us. "How absurd," said we to each other, "for a man to loiter in this way in such dreadful weather. The wretched fellow will assuredly die of cold. We called to him once more, but he remained silent and motionless as before. We dismounted, went up to him, and recognized in him a young Mongol Lama, who had often paid us a visit in our tent. His face was exactly like wax, and his eyes, half-opened, had a glassy appearance; icicles hung from his nostrils and from the corners of his mouth. We spoke to him, but obtained no answer; and for a moment we thought him dead. Presently, however, he opened his eyes, and fixed them upon us with a horrible expression of stupefaction: the poor creature was frozen, and we comprehended at once that he had been abandoned by his companions. It seemed to us so frightful to leave a man to die, without making an effort to save him, that we did not hesitate to take him with us. We took him from the stone on which he had been placed, enveloped him in a wrapper, seated him upon Samdadchiemba's little mule, and thus brought him to the encampment. When we had set up our tent, we went to visit the companions of this poor young man. Upon our informing them what we had done, they prostrated themselves in token of thanks and said that we were people of excellent hearts, but that we had given ourselves much labor in vain, for that the case was beyond cure. "He is frozen," said they, "and nothing can prevent the cold from getting to his heart." We ourselves did not participate in this despairing view of the case, and we returned to our tent, accompanied by one of the patient's companions, to see what further could be done. When we reached our temporary home, the young Lama was dead.

More than forty men of the caravan were abandoned still living, in the desert, without the slightest possibility of our aiding them. They were carried on horseback and on camel-back so long as any hope remained, but when they could no longer eat, or speak, or hold themselves up, they were left on the wayside. The general body of the caravan could not stay to nurse them, in a barren desert, where there was hourly danger of wild beasts, of robbers, and worse than all, of a deficiency of food. Yet, it was a fearful spectacle to see these dying men abandoned on the road! As a last token of sympathy, we placed beside each, a wooden cup and a small bag of barley meal, and then the caravan mournfully proceeded on its way. As soon as the last straggler had passed on, the crows and vultures that incessantly hovered above the caravan, would pounce down upon the unhappy creatures who retained just enough of life to feel themselves torn and mangled by these birds of prey.

The north wind greatly aggravated M. Gabet's malady. From day to day his condition grew more alarming. His extreme weakness would not permit him to walk, and being thus precluded from warming himself by means of a little exercise; his feet, hands, and face were completely frozen; his lips became livid, and his eyes almost extinct; by and by he was not able to support himself on horseback. Our only remedy was to wrap him in blankets, to pack him upon a camel, and to leave the rest to the merciful goodness of Divine Providence.

One day, us we were following the sinuosities of a valley, our hearts oppressed with sad thoughts, all of a sudden we perceived two horsemen make their appearance on the ridge of an adjacent hill. At this time, we were traveling in the company of a small party of Thibetian merchants, who, like ourselves, had allowed the main body of the caravan to precede them, in order to save their camels the fatigue of a too-hurried march. "Tsong-Kaba," cried the Thibetians, "see, there are horsemen yonder, yet we are in the desert, and every one knows that there are not even shepherds in this locality." They had scarcely uttered these words, when a number of other horsemen appeared at dif-

9

ferent points on the hills, and, to our extreme alarm, dashed down towards us at a gallop. What could these horsemen be doing in so barren a region? What could they want with us? The case was clear: we had fallen into the hands of thieves. Their appearance, as they approached, was anything but reassuring: a carbine slung at the saddle-bow, two long sabers in the girdle, thick black hair falling in disorder over the shoulders, glaring eyes, and a wolf's skin stuck on the head by way of cap; such was the portrait of each of the gentlemen who now favored us with their company. There were twenty-seven of them, while we numbered only eighteen, of which eighteen all were by no means practised warriors. However, both armies alighted, and a valorous Thibetian of our party advanced to parley with the chief of the brigands, who was distinguished from his men by two red pennants which floated from his saddle back. After a long and somewhat animated conversation: "Who is that man?" asked the chief of the Kolo, pointing to M. Gabet, who, fastened upon his camel, was the only person who had not alighted. "He is a Grand Lama of the western sky," replied the Thibetian merchant; "the power of his prayers is infinite." The Kolo raised his clasped hands to his forehead, in token of respect, and looked at M. Gabet, who, with his frozen face, and his singular envelope of many-colored wrappers, was by no means unlike those alarming idols that we see in pagan temples. After contemplating for a while the famous Lama of the western sky, the brigand addressed some further words, in an undertone, to the Thibetian merchant; then, making a sign to his companions, they all jumped into their saddles, set off at a gallop, and soon disappeared behind the mountains. "Do not let us go any further to-day," said the Thibetian merchant; "but set up our tents where we are; the Kolo are robbers, but they have lofty and generous souls; when they see that we place ourselves without fear in their hands, they will not attack us. Besides," added he, "I believe they hold in much awe the power of the Lamas of the western sky." We adopted the counsel of the Thibetian merchant and proceeded to encamp.

The tents were scarcely set up, when the Kolo reappeared on the crest of the mountain, and once more galloped down upon us with their habitual impetuosity. The chief alone entered the encampment, his men awaiting him at a short distance outside. The Kolo addressed the Thibetian who had previously conversed with him. "I have come," said he, "for an explanation of a point that I don't at all understand. You know that we are encamped on the other side of the mountain, yet you venture to set up your tents here, close by us. How many men, then, have you in your company?" "We are only eighteen; you, I believe, are twenty-seven in number; but brave men never run away." "You'll fight, then?" "If there were not several invalids amongst us, I would answer, Yes; for I have already shown the Kolo that I am not afraid of them." "Have you fought with the Kolo? When was it? What's your name?" "It's five years ago, at the affair of the Tchanak-Kampo, and here's a little reminiscence of it;" and, throwing back the sleeve of his right arm, he showed the cicatrice of a great saber cut. The brigand laughed, and again requested his interlocutor's name. "I am called Rala-Tchembe," said the merchant; "you ought to know the name." "Yes, all the Kolos know it; it is the name of a brave man." So saying, he dismounted, and taking a saber from his girdle, presented it to the Thibetian. "Here," said he, "accept this saber; 'tis the best I have; we have fought one another before; in future, when we meet, it shall be as brothers." The Thibetian received the brigand's present, and gave him, in return, a handsome bow and quiver which he had bought at Peking.

The Kolo, who had remained outside the camp, upon seeing their chief fraternize with the chief of the caravan, dismounted, fastened their horses to each other, two and two, by the bridles, and came to drink a friendly cup of tea with the travelers, who now, at length, began to breathe freely. All these brigands were extremely affable, and they asked us various questions about the Tartar-Khalkhas, whom, they said, they were particularly anxious to see, by reason that, in the preceding year, these warriors had killed three of their companions, whom they were eager to avenge. We had a little chat about politics too. The brigands affirmed that they were warm friends of the Talé-Lama, and irreconcilable enemies to the Emperor of China; on which account they seldom failed to pillage the embassy on its way to Peking, because the Emperor was unworthy to receive gifts from the Talé-Lama, but that they ordinarily respected it on its return, because it was altogether fitting that the Emperor should send gifts to the Talé-Lama. After having done honor to the tea and tsamba of the caravan, the brigands wished us a good journey, and returned to their own encampment. All these fraternal manifestations did not prevent our sleeping with one eye open; our repose, however, was not disturbed, and in the morning we resumed our way in peace. Of the many thousands of pilgrims who have performed the journey to Lha-Ssa, there are very few who can boast of having had so close a view of the robbers, at so small a cost.

We had escaped one great danger; but another awaited us, we were informed, far more formidable in its character, though different in kind. We were beginning to ascend the vast chain of the Tant-La mountains, on the plateau of which, our traveling companions assured us, the invalids would die, and those who were now well would become invalids, with but a small chance of living. The death of M. Gabet was considered quite a matter of certainty. After six days' laborious ascent of several mountains, placed amphitheatrically, one above another, we at length reached the famous plateau, the most elevated point, perhaps, on the earth's surface. The snow there appeared an incrustation, an ordinary portion of the soil. It cracked beneath our feet, but the feet left scarcely any impression upon it. The entire vegetation consisted of an occasional tuft of a low, sharp-pointed, smooth grass, ligneous within, and as hard as iron, but not brittle; so that it might very well be converted into mattress needles. The animals were, however, so famishing, that they were fain to attack even this atrocious forage, which absolutely cracked between their teeth, and could be realized at all only by vigorous efforts and at the cost of infinite lip bleeding.

From the brow of this magnificent plateau we could see below us the peaks and needles of numerous ridges, the ramifications of which were lost in the horizon. We had never witnessed anything at all comparable with this grand, this gigantic spectacle. During the twelve days that we were journeying along the heights of Tant-La, we enjoyed fine weather; the air was calm, and it pleased God to bless us each day with a warm, genial sunshine, that materially modified the ordinary coldness of the atmosphere. Still the air, excessively rarified at that enormous altitude, was very piercing, and monstrous eagles, which followed the track of the caravan, were daily provided with a number of dead bodies. The small caravan of the French mission itself paid its tribute to death; but, happily, that tribute was only in the shape of our little black mule, which we abandoned at once with regret and with resignation. The dismal prophecy that had been announced with reference to M. Gabet was falsified. The mountains, which were to have been fatal to him, proved, on the contrary, highly favorable, restoring to him, by degrees, health and strength. This blessing, almost unexpected by us, even at the hands of the God of Mercy, made us forget all our past miseries. We resumed all our courage, and firmly entertained the hope that the Almighty would permit us to accomplish our journey.

The descent of Tant-La, though long in duration, was rapid in itself. Throughout four whole days we were going down, as it seemed, a gigantic staircase, each step of which consisted of a mountain. At the bottom, we found some hot springs, of an extremely magnificent description. Amongst huge rocks, you see a great number of reservoirs, hollowed out by the hand of nature, in which the water boils and bubbles, as in a vast cauldron over a fierce fire. Sometimes the active fluid escapes through the fissures of the rocks, and leaps, in all directions, by a thousand capricious jets. Every now and then the ebullition, in particular reservoirs, grows so furious, that tall columns of water rise into the air, as though impelled by some tremendous pumping machinery. Above these springs, thick vapors, collecting in the air, condense into white clouds. The water is sulphureous. After bubbling and dashing about in its huge granite reservoirs, it boils over, and quitting the rocks, which had seemed to wish to keep it captive, pours down by various currents into a small valley below, where it forms a large stream flowing over a bed of flints, yellow as gold. These boiling waters do not long preserve their fluidity. The extreme rigor of the atmosphere cools them so rapidly, that within a mile and a half from its source, the stream they have thus formed is almost frozen through. These hot springs are of frequent occurrence in the mountains of Thibet, and the Lama physicians, who attribute to them considerable medicinal virtue, constantly prescribed their use, both internally and externally

From the Tant-La mountains to Lha-Ssa, the ground constantly declines. As you descend, the intensity of the cold diminishes, and the earth becomes clothed with more vigorous and more varied vegetation. One evening, we encamped in a large plain, where the pasturage was marvelously abundant, and as our cattle had been for some time past on very short commons indeed, we determined to give them the full benefit of the present opportunity, and to remain where we were for two days.

Next morning, as we were quietly preparing our tea, we perceived in the distance a troop of horsemen galloping towards our encampment at full speed. The sight seemed to freeze the very blood in our veins; we stood for a moment perfectly petrified. After the first moment of stupor, we rushed out of our tent, and ran to Rala-Tchembé. "The Kolo! the Kolo!" cried we; "here's a great body of Kolo advancing against us." The Thibetian merchants, who were boiling their tea and mixing their tsamba, laughed at our alarm, and told us to sit down quite at our ease. "Take breakfast with us," said they; "there are no Kolo to fear here; the horsemen you see yonder are friends. We are now entering upon an inhabited country; hehind the hill there, to the right, are a number of black tents, and the horsemen, whom you take to be Kolo, are shepherds." These words restored our equanimity, and with our equanimity returned our appetite, so that we were very happy to accept the invitation to breakfast with which we had been favored. We had scarcely taken up a cup of buttered tea before the horsemen made their appearance at the door of the tent. So far from being brigands, they were worthy fellows who came to sell us butter and fresh meat; their saddles were regular butchers' stalls hung with joints of mutton and venison, which rested on the sides of their horses. We purchased eight legs of mutton, which, being frozen, were easily susceptible of transport. They cost us an old pair of Peking boots, a Peking steel, and the saddle of our defunct mule, which luckily could also boast of Peking origin. Everything coming from Peking is highly prized by the Thibetians, more especially by that portion of the population which has not advanced beyond the pastoral and nomadic life. The merchants who accompany the caravan take care, accordingly, to label every package "Goods from Peking." Snuff is especially an object of earnest competition among the Thibetians. All the shepherds asked us whether we had not snuff from Peking. M. Huc, who was the only snuff-taker of our party, had formerly possessed a quantity of the precious commodity, but it had all departed, and for the last eight days he had been reduced to the necessity of filling his snuff-box and his nose with a frightful mixture of dust and ashes. Those who are devotees of snuff will at once comprehend all the horrors to poor M. Huc of this deplorable position.

Condemned for the two last months to live upon barley-meal, moistened with tea, the mere sight of our legs of mutton seemed to fortify our stomachs and invigorate our emaciated limbs. The remainder of the day was occupied in culinary preparations. By way of condiment and seasoning, we had only a little garlic, and that little so frozen and dried, that it was almost imperceptible in its shell. We peeled, however, all we had, and stuck it into two legs of mutton, which we set to boil in our great cauldron. The argols, which abounded in this blessed plain, supplied ample materials for cooking our inestimable supper. The sun was just setting, and Samdadchiemba, who had been inspecting one of the legs of mutton with his thumb-nail, had triumphantly announced that the mutton was boiled to a bubble, when we heard in all directions, the disastrous cry, "Fire! fire!" (*Mi yon! mi yon!*) At one bound we were outside our tent, where we found that the flame, which had caught some dry grass, in the interior of the encampment, and menaced to assail also our linen tents, was spreading about, in all directions, with fearful rapidity. All the travelers, armed with their felt carpets, were endeavoring to stifle the flame, or at all events to keep it from reaching the tents, and in this latter effort they were quite successful. The fire, repulsed on all sides, forced an issue from the encampment, and rushed out into the desert, where, driven by the wind, it spread over the pasturages, which it devoured as it went. We thought, however, that we had nothing further to fear; but the cry, "Save the camels! save the camels!" at once reminded

Fire in the Camp.

us how little we knew of a conflagration in the desert. We soon perceived that the camels stolidly awaited the flame, instead of fleeing from it, as the horses and oxen did. We hereupon hastened to the succor of our beasts, which, at the moment, seemed tolerably remote from the flame. The flame, however, reached them as soon as we did, and at once surrounded us and them. It was to no purpose we pushed and beat the stupid brutes; not an inch would they stir; but there they stood phlegmatically gaping at us with an air that seemed to ask us, what right we had to come and interrupt them at their meals. We really felt as if we could have killed the impracticable beasts. The fire consumed so rapidly the grass it encountered, that it soon assailed the camels, and caught their long, thick hair; and it was with the utmost exertion that, by the aid of the felt carpets we had brought with us, we extinguished the flame upon their bodies. We got three of them out of the fire, with only the end of their hair singed, but the fourth was reduced to a deplorable condition; not a bristle remained on its entire body; the whole system of hair was burned down to the skin, and the skin itself was terribly charred.

The extent of pasturage consumed by the flame might be about a mile and a quarter long by three quarters of a mile broad. The Thibetians were in esctasies at their good fortune in having the progress of conflagration so soon stayed, and we fully participated in their joy, when we learned the full extent of the evil with which we had been menaced. We were informed that if the fire had continued much longer it would have reached the black tents, in which case the shepherds would have pursued and infallibly massacred us. Nothing can equal the fury of these poor children of the desert when they find the pastures, which are their only resource, reduced to ashes, no matter whether by malice or by mischance. It is much the same thing to them as destroying their herds.

When we resumed our journey the broiled camel was not yet dead, but it was altogether incapable of service; the three others were fain to yield to circumstances, and to share among them the portion of baggage which their unlucky traveling companion had hitherto borne. However, the burdens of all of them had very materially diminished in weight since our departure from Koukou-Noor; our sacks of meal had become little better than sacks of emptiness; so that, after descending the Tant-La mountains we had been compelled to put ourselves upon an allowance of two cups of tsamba per man, *per diem*. Before our departure we had made a fair calculation of our reasonable wants, *in prospectu*; but no such calculation could cover the waste committed upon our provender by our two cameleers; by the one through indifference and stupidity, by the other through malice and knavery.

Fortunately we were now approaching a large Thibetian station, where we should find the means of renewing our stores.

After following, for several days, a long series of valleys, where we saw, from time to time, black tents and great herds of yaks, we at last encamped beside a large Thibetian village. It stands on the banks of the river Na-Ptchu, indicated on M. Andriveau-Goujon's map, by the Mongol name of Khara-Oussou, both denominations equally signifying black waters. The village of Na-Ptchu is the first Thibetian station of any importance that you pass on this route to Lha-Ssa. The village consists of mud-houses and a number of black tents. The inhabitants do not cultivate the ground. Although they always live on the same spot, they are shepherds like the nomadic tribes, and occupy themselves solely with the breeding of cattle. We were informed that at some very remote period, a king of Koukou-Noor made war upon the Thibetians, and having subjugated them to a large extent, gave the district of Na-Ptchu to the soldiers whom he had brought with him. Though these Tartars are now fused

View of Na-Ptchu.

with the Thibetians, one may still observe among the black tents, a certain number of Mongol huts. This event may also serve to explain the origin of a number of Mongol expressions which are used in the country, having passed within the domain of the Thibetian idiom.

The caravans which repair to Lha-Ssa, are necessitated to remain several days at Na-Ptchu, in order to arrange a fresh system of conveyance; for the difficulties of an awfully rocky road do not permit camels to proceed further. Our first business, therefore, was to sell our animals; but they were so wretchedly worn that no one would look at them. At last, a sort of veterinary surgeon, who, doubtless, had some recipe for restoring their strength and appearances, made us an offer, and we sold him the three for fifteen ounces of silver, throwing in the grilled one into the bargain. These fifteen ounces of silver just sufficed to pay the hire of six long-haired oxen, to carry our baggage to Lha-Ssa.

A second operation was to discharge the Lama of the Ratchico mountains. After having settled with him on very liberal terms, we told him that if he proposed to visit Lha-Ssa, he must find some other companions, for that he might consider himself wholly freed from the engagements which he had contracted with us; and so, at last, we got rid of this rascal, whose misconduct had fully doubled the trouble and misery that we had experienced on the way in his company.

Our conscience imposes upon us the duty of here warning persons whom any circumstances may lead to Na-Ptchu, to be carefully on their guard there against thieves. The inhabitants of this Thibetian village are remarkable for their peculations, robbing every Mongol or other caravan that comes to the place, in the most shameful manner. At night, they creep into the travelers' tents, and carry off whatever they can lay hands upon; and in broad day itself they exercise their deplorable ingenuity in this line, with a coolness, a presence of mind, and an ability which might arouse envy in the most distinguished Parisian thieves.

After having laid in a supply of butter, tsamba, and legs of mutton, we proceeded on our way to Lha-Ssa, from which we were distant now only fifteen days' march. Our traveling companions were some Mongols of the kingdom of Khartchin, who were repairing in pilgrimage to Mouche-Dehot (the Eternal Sanctuary) as the Tartars call Lha-Ssa, and who had with them their Grand Chaberon; that is to say, a Living Buddha, the superior of their Lamasery. The Chaberon was a young man of eighteen, whose manners were agreeable and gentlemanly, and whose face, full of ingenuous candor, contrasted singularly with the part which he was constrained habitually to enact. At the age of five he had been declared Buddha and Grand Lama of the Buddhists of Khartchin, and he was now about to pass a few years in one of the Grand Lamaseries of Lha-Ssa, in the study of prayers and of the other knowledge befitting his dignity. A brother of the King of Khartchin and several Lamas of quality were in attendance to escort and wait upon him. The title of Living Buddha seemed to be a dead weight upon this poor young man. It was quite manifest that he would very much have liked to laugh and chat and frolic about at his ease; and that, *en route*, it would have been far more agreeable to him to have dashed about on his horse, whither he fancied, than to ride, as he did, solemnly between two horsemen, who, out of their extreme respect, never once quitted his sides. Again, when they had reached an encampment, instead of remaining eternally squatted on cushions, in a corner of his tent, apeing the idols in the Lamasery, he would have liked to have rambled about the desert, taking part in the occupations of nomadic life; but he was permitted to do nothing of the sort. His business was to be Buddha, and to concern himself in no degree with matters which appertained to mere mortals.

The young Chaberon derived no small pleasure from an occasional chat in our tent; there, at all events, he was able to lay aside, for a time, his official divinity, and to belong to mankind. He heard with great interest what we told him about the men and things of Europe; and questioned us, with much ingenuity, respecting our religion, which evidently appeared to him a very fine one. When we asked him, whether it would not be better to be a worshipper of Jehovah than a Chaberon, he replied that he could not say. He did not at all like us to interrogate him respecting his interior life, and his continual incarnations; he would blush when any such questions were put to him, and would always put an end to the conversation by saying that the subject was painful to him. The simple fact was that the poor lad found himself involved in a sort of religious labyrinth, the meanderings of which were perfectly unknown to him.

The road which leads from Na-Ptchu to Lha-Ssa is, in general, rocky and very laborious, and when it attains the chain of the Koïran mountains it become fatiguing in the highest degree. Yet as you advance, your heart grows lighter and lighter, at finding yourself in a more and more populous country. The black tents that speckle the background of the landscape, the numerous parties of pilgrims repairing to Lha-Ssa, the infinite inscriptions engraved on the stones erected on each side of the way, the small caravans of long-tailed oxen that you meet at intervals—all this contributes to alleviate the fatigues of the journey.

When you come within a few days' march of Lha-Ssa, the exclusively nomadic character of the Thibetians gradually disappears. Already, a few cultivated fields adorn the desert; houses insensibly take the place of black tents. At length, the shepherds vanish altogether, and you find yourself amidst an agricultural people.

On the fifteenth day after our departure from Na-Ptchu, we arrived at Pampou, which on account of its proximity to Lha-Ssa is regarded by the pilgrims as the vestibule of the holy city. Pampou, erroneously designated Panctou on the map, is a fine plain watered by a broad river, a portion of whose stream, distributed in canals, diffuses fertility all around. There is no village, properly so called; but you see, in all directions, large farmhouses with handsome terraces in front, and beautifully white with lime-wash. Each is surrounded with tall trees, and surmounted with a little tower, in the form of a pigeon-house, whence float banners of various colors, covered with Thibetian inscriptions. After traveling for more than three months through hideous deserts, where the only living creatures you meet are brigands and wild beasts, the plain of Pampou seemed to us the most delicious spot in the world. Our long and painful journeying had so nearly reduced us to the savage state, that anything in the shape of civilization struck us as absolutely marvelous. We were in ecstasies with everything: a house, a tree, a plow, a furrow in the plowed field, the slightest object seemed to us worthy of attention. That, however, which most forcibly impressed us, was the prodigious elevation of the temperature which we remarked in this cultivated plain. Although it was now the end of January, the river and its canals were merely edged with a thin coat of ice, and scarcely any of the people wore furs.

At Pampou, our caravan had to undergo another transformation. Generally speaking, the long-haired oxen are here replaced by donkeys, small in size, but very robust, and accustomed to carry baggage. The difficulty of procuring a sufficient number of these donkeys to convey the baggage of the Khartchin-Lamas, rendered it necessary for us to remain two days at Pampou. We availed ourselves of the opportunity to arrange our toilet, as well as we could. Our hair and beards were so thick, our faces so blackened with the smoke of the tent, so plowed up with the cold, so worn, so deplorable, that, when we had here the means of looking at ourselves in a glass, we were ready to weep with compassion at our melancholy appearance. Our costume was perfectly in unison with our persons.

The people of Pampou are for the most part in very easy circumstances, and they are always gay and frolicsome accordingly. Every evening they assemble, in front of the different farms, where men, women, and children dance to the accompaniment of their own voices. On the termination of the *bal champêtre*, the farmer regales the company with a sort of sharp drink, made with fermented barley, and which, with the addition of hops, would be very like our beer.

After a two days' hunt through all the farms of the neighborhood, the donkey-caravan was organized, and we went on our way. Between us and Lha-Ssa there was only a mountain, but this mountain was, past contradiction, the most rugged and toilsome that we had yet encountered. The Thibetians and Mongols ascend it with great unction, for it is understood amongst them that whoever attains its summit, attains, *ipso facto*, a remission of all his or her sins. This is certain, at all events, that whoever attains the summit has undergone on his way a most severe penance; whether that penance is adequate to the remission of sins, is another question altogether. We had departed at one o'clock in the morning, yet it was not till ten in the forenoon that we reached this so beneficial summit. We were fain to walk nearly the whole distance, so impracticable is it to retain one's seat on horseback along the rugged and rocky path.

The sun was nearly setting when, issuing from the last of the infinite sinuosities of the mountain, we found ourselves in a vast plain, and saw on our right Lha-Ssa, the famous metropolis of the Buddhic world. The multitude of aged trees which surround the city with a verdant wall; the tall white houses, with their flat roofs and their towers; the numerous temples with their gilt roofs, the Buddha-La, above which rises the palace of the Talé-Lama—all these features communicate to Lha-Ssa a majestic and imposing aspect.

At the entrance of the town, some Mongols with whom we had formed an acquaintance on the road, and who had preceded us by several days, met us, and invited us to accompany them to lodgings which they had been friendly enough to prepare for us. It was now the 29th January, 1846; and it was eighteen months since we had parted from the Valley of Black Waters.

Chinese and Tartar Male Head-dresses.

View of Lha-Ssa.

CHAPTER V.

Lodgings in a Thibetian House—Appearance of Lha-Ssa—Palace of the Talé-Lama—Picture of the Thibetians—Monstrous Toilet of the Women—Industrial and Agricultural Productions of Thibet—Gold and Silver Mines—Foreigners Resident at Lha-Ssa—The Pebouns—The Katchis—The Chinese—Position of the relations between China and Thibet—Various Speculations of the Public Respecting us—We Present Ourselves to the Authorities—Form of the Thibetian Government—Grand Lama of Djachi-Loumbo—Society of the Kalons—Thibetian Prophecy—Tragical Death of Three Talé-Lamas—Account of Ki-Chan—Condemnation of the Nomekhan—Revolt of the Lamasery of Sera.

After eighteen months' struggle with sufferings and obstacles of infinite number and variety, we were at length arrived at the termination of our journey, though not at the close of our miseries. We had no longer, it is true, to fear death from famine or frost in this inhabited country; but trials and tribulations of a different character were, no doubt, about to assail us, amidst the infidel populations, to whom we desired to preach Christ crucified for the salvation of mankind. Physical troubles over, we had now to undergo moral sufferings; but we relied, as before, on the infinite goodness of the Lord to aid us in the fight, trusting that He who had protected us in the desert against the inclemency of the seasons, would continue to us His divine assistance against the malice of man, in the very heart and capital of Buddhism.

The morning after our arrival at Lha-Ssa, we engaged a Thibetian guide, and visited the various quarters of the city, in search of a lodging. The houses at Lha-Ssa are for the most part several stories high, terminating in a terrace slightly sloped, in order to carry off the water; they are whitewashed all over, except the bordering round the doors and windows, which are painted red or yellow. The reformed Buddhists are so fond of these two colors, which are, so to speak, sacred in their eyes, that they especially name them Lamanesque colors. The people of Lha-Ssa are in the habit of painting their houses once a year, so that they are always perfectly clean, and seem, in fact, just built; but the interior is by no means in harmony with the fine outside. The rooms are dirty, smoky, stinking, and encumbered with all sorts of utensils and furniture, thrown about in most disgusting confusion. In a word, the Thibetian habitations are literally whited sepulchers; a perfect picture of Buddhism and all other false religions, which carefully cover, with certain general truths and certain moral principles, the corruption and falsehood within.

After a long search, we selected two rooms, in a large house, that contained in all fifty lodgers. Our humble abode was at the top of the house, and to reach it we had to ascend twenty-six wooden stairs, without railing, and so steep and narrow that in order to prevent the disagreeable incident of breaking our necks, we always found it prudent to use our hands as well as our feet. Our suite of apartments consisted of one great square room and one small closet, which we honored with the appellation of cabinet. The larger room was lighted, northeast, by a narrow window, provided with three thick wooden bars, and above, by a small round skylight, which latter aperture served for a variety of purposes;

first it gave entrance to the light, the wind, the rain, and the snow: and secondly, it gave issue to the smoke from our fire. To protect themselves from the winter's cold, the Thibetians place in the center of their rooms a small vessel of glazed earth, in which they burn argols. As this combustible is extremely addicted to diffuse considerably more smoke than heat, those who desire to warm themselves, find it of infinite advantage to have a hole in the ceiling, which enables them to light a fire without incurring the risk of being stifled by the smoke. You do, indeed, undergo the small inconvenience of receiving, from time to time, a fall of snow, or rain, on your back; but those who have followed the nomadic life are not deterred by such trifles. The furniture of our larger apartment consisted of two goatskins spread on the floor, right and left of the fire dish; of two saddles, our traveling tent, some old pairs of boots, two dilapidated trunks, three ragged robes, hanging from nails in the wall, our night things rolled together in a bundle, and a supply of argols in the corner. We were thus placed at once on the full level of Thibetian civilization. The closet, in which stood a large brick stove, served us for kitchen and pantry, and there we installed Samdadchiemba, who, having resigned his office of cameleer, now concentrated the functions of cook, steward, and groom. Our two white steeds were accommodated in a corner of the court, where they reposed after their laborious but glorious campaign, until an opportunity should present itself of securing new masters; at present the poor beasts were so thoroughly worn down, that we could not think of offering them for sale, until they had developed some little flesh between the bone and the skin.

As soon as we were settled in our new abode, we occupied ourselves with inspecting the capital of Thibet, and its population. Lha-Ssa is not a large town, its circuit being at the utmost two leagues. It is not surrounded like the Chinese towns with ramparts; formerly, indeed, we were told it had walls, but these were entirely destroyed in a war which the Thibetians had to sustain against the Indians of Boutan. At present not a trace of wall remains. Around the suburbs, however, are a great number of gardens, the large trees in which form, for the town, a magnificent wall of verdure. The principal streets of Lha-Ssa are broad, well laid out, and tolerably clean, at least when it does not rain: but the suburbs are revoltingly filthy. The houses, as we have already stated, are in general large, lofty, and handsome; they are built some with stone, some with brick, and some with mud, but they are all so elaborately covered with lime-wash that you can distinguish externally no difference in the material. In one of the suburban districts there is a locality where the houses are built with the horns of oxen and sheep. These singular constructions are of extreme solidity and look very well. The horns of the oxen being smooth and white, and those of the sheep, on the contrary, rough and black, these various materials are susceptible of infinite combinations, and are arranged accordingly, in all sorts of fantastic designs; the interstices are filled up with mortar. These houses are the only buildings that are not lime-washed; the Thibetians having taste enough to leave the materials in their natural aspect, without seeking to improve upon their wild and fantastic beauty. It is superfluous to add, that the inhabitants of Lha-Ssa consume an immense quantity of beef and mutton; their horn-houses incontestably demonstrate the fact.

The Buddhist temples are the most remarkable edifices in Lha-Ssa. We need not here describe them, for they all closely resemble those which we have already had occasion to portray. We will only remark, therefore, that the temples of Lha-Ssa are larger, richer, and more profusely gilt than those of other towns.

The palace of the Talé-Lama merits, in every respect, the celebrity which it enjoys throughout the world. North of the town, at the distance of about a mile, there rises a rugged mountain, of slight elevation and of conical form, which, amid the plain, resembles an islet on the bosom of a lake. This mountain is entitled Buddha-La (mountain of Buddha, divine mountain), and upon this grand pedestal, the work of nature, the adorers of the Talé-Lama have raised the magnificent palace wherein their Living Divinity resides in the flesh. This palace is an aggregation of several temples, of various size and decoration; that which occupies the center is four stories high, and overlooks all the rest; it terminates in a dome, entirely covered with plates of gold, and surrounded with a peristyle, the columns of which are, in like manner, all covered with gold. It is here that the

Talé-Lama has set up his abode. From the summit of this lofty sanctuary he can contemplate, at the great solemnities, his innumerable adorers advancing along the plain or prostrate at the foot of the divine mountain. The secondary palaces, grouped round the great temple, serve as residences for numerous Lamas, of every order, whose continual occupation it is to serve and do honor to the Living Buddha. Two fine avenues of magnificent trees lead from Lha-Ssa to the Buddha-La, and there you always find crowds of foreign pilgrims, telling the beads of their long Buddhist chaplets, and Lamas of the court, attired in rich costume, and mounted on horses splendidly caparisoned. Around the Buddha-La there is constant motion; but there is, at the same time, almost uninterrupted silence, religious meditations appearing to occupy all men's minds.

In the town itself the aspect of the population is quite different; there all is excitement, and noise, and pushing, and competition, every single soul in the place being ardently occupied in the grand business of buying and selling. Commerce and devotion incessantly attracting to Lha-Ssa an infinite number of strangers, render the place a rendezvous of all the Asiatic peoples; so that the streets, always crowded with pilgrims and traders, present a marvelous variety of physiognomies, costumes, and languages. This immense multitude is for the most part transitory; the fixed population of Lha-Ssa consists of Thibetians, Pebouns, Katchis, and Chinese.

The Thibetians belong to the great family which we are accustomed to designate by the term Mongol race; they have black eyes, a thin beard, small, contracted eyes, high cheek-bones, pug noses, wide mouths, and thin lips; the ordinary complexion is tawny, though, in the upper class, you find skins as white as those of Europeans. The Thibetians are of the middle height; and combine, with the agility and suppleness of the Chinese, the force and vigor of the Tartars. Gymnastic exercises of all sorts and dancing are very popular with them, and their movements are cadenced and easy. As they walk about, they are always humming some psalm or popular song; generosity and frankness enter largely into their character; brave in war, they face death fearlessly; they are as religious as the Tartars, but not so credulous. Cleanliness is of small estimation among them; but this does not prevent them from being very fond of display and rich sumptuous clothing.

The Thibetians do not shave the head, but let the hair flow over their shoulders, contenting themselves with clipping it, every now and then, with the scissors. The dandies of Lha-Ssa, indeed, have of late years adopted the custom of braiding their hair in the Chinese fashion, decorating the tresses with jewelry, precious stones, and coral. The ordinary head-dress is a blue cap, with a broad border of black velvet surmounted with a red tuft; on high days and holidays, they wear a great red hat, in form not unlike the Basquebarret cap, only larger and decorated at the rim with long, thick fringe. A full robe fastened on the right side with four hooks, and girded round the waist by a red sash, red or purple cloth boots, complete the simple, yet graceful costume of the Thibetian men. Suspended from the sash is a green taffeta bag, containing their inseparable wooden cups, and two small purses, of an oval form and richly embroidered, which contain nothing at all, being designed merely for ornament.

The dress of the Thibetian women closely resembles that of the men; the main difference is, that over the robe, they add a short many-colored tunic, and that they divide their hair into two braids, one hanging down each shoulder. The women of the humbler classes wear a small yellow cap, like the cap of liberty that was in fashion in France at the time of our first republic. The head decoration of the ladies is a graceful crown composed of pearls. The Thibetian women submit, in their toilet, to a custom, or rather rule, doubtless quite unique, and altogether incredible to those who have not actually witnessed its operation; before going out of doors, they always rub their faces over with a sort of black, glutinous varnish not unlike currant jelly; and the object being to render themselves as ugly and hideous as possible, they daub this disgusting composition over every feature, in such a manner as no longer to resemble human creatures. The origin of this monstrous practise was thus related to us: Nearly 200 years ago, the Nomekhan, a Lama king, who ruled over Hither Thibet, was a man of rigid and austere manners. At that period, the Thibetian women had no greater fancy for making themselves ugly than other women; on the contrary, they were perfectly mad after all sorts of luxury and finery, whence arose fearful disorders, and immorality that knew no bounds. The contagion, by degrees, seized upon the holy family of the Lamas; the Buddhist monasteries relaxed their ancient and severe discipline, and were a prey to evils which menaced them with complete and rapid dissolution. In order to stay the progress of a libertinism which had become almost general, the Nomekhan published an edict, prohibiting women from appearing in public otherwise than with their faces bedaubed, in the manner we have described. Lofty, moral, and religious considerations were adduced in support of this strange law, and the refractory were menaced with the severest penalties, and above all, with the wrath of Buddha. There needed, assuredly, more than ordinary courage to publish such an edict as this; but the most extraordinary circumstance of all is, that the women were perfectly resigned and obedient. Tradition has handed down not the least hint of any insurrection, or the slightest disturbance even, on the subject, and conformably with the law, the women have blackened themselves furiously and uglified themselves fearfully, down to the present time. In fact, the thing has now come to be considered a point of dogma, an article of devotion; the women who daub themselves most disgustingly being reputed the most pious. In the country places the edict is observed with scrupulous exactitude, and to the entire approbation of the censors; but at Lha-Ssa, it is not unusual to meet in the streets women who, setting law and decency at defiance, actually have the impudence to show themselves in public with their faces unvarnished, and such as nature made them. Those, however, who permit themselves this license, are in very ill odor, and always take care to get out of the way of the police.

It is said that the edict of the Nomekhan has been greatly promotive of the public morality. We are not in a position to affirm the contrary, with decision, but we can affirm that the Thibetians are far indeed from being exemplary in the matter of morality. There is lamentable licentiousness amongst them, and we are disposed to believe that the blackest and ugliest varnish is powerless to make corrupt people virtuous. Christianity can alone redeem the pagan nations from the shameful vices in which they wallow.

At the same time, there is one circumstance which may

induce us to believe that in Thibet there is less corruption than in certain other pagan countries. The women there enjoy very great liberty. Instead of vegetating, prisoners in the depths of their houses, they lead an active and laborious life. Besides fulfilling the various duties of the household, they concentrate in their own hands all the petty trade of the country, whether as hawkers, as stall-keepers in the streets, or in shops. In the rural districts, it is the women who perform most of the labors of agriculture.

The men, though less laborious and less active than the women, are still far from passing their lives in idleness. They occupy themselves especially with spinning and weaving wool. The stuffs they manufacture, which are called poulou, are of a very close and solid fabric; astonishingly various in quality, from the coarsest cloths to the finest possible Merino. By a rule of reformed Buddhism, every Lama must be attired in red poulou. The consumption of the article in Thibet itself is very large, and the caravans export considerable quantities of it to Northern China and Tartary. The coarser poulou is cheap, but the superior qualities are excessively dear.

The pastile-sticks, so celebrated in China, under the name of Tsan-Hiang (perfumes of Thibet), are an article of leading commerce with the people of Lha-Ssa, who manufacture them with the ash of various aromatic trees mixed with musk and gold dust. Of these various ingredients, they elaborate a pink paste, which is then molded into small cylindrical sticks, three or four feet long. These are burned in the Lamaseries, and before the idols which are worshiped in private houses. When these pastile-sticks are once lighted, they burn slowly, without intermission, until they are completely consumed, diffusing all around a perfume of the most exquisite sweetness. The Thibetian merchants, who repair every year to Peking in the train of the embassy, export considerable quantities of it, which they sell at an exorbitant price. The Northern Chinese manufacture pastile-sticks of their own, which they sell equally under the name of Tsan-Hiang; but they will sustain no comparison with those which come from Thibet.

The Thibetians have no porcelain, but they manufacture pottery of all sorts in great perfection. As we have already observed, their own breakfast, dinner, and tea-service, consist simply and entirely of a wooden cup, which each person carries either in his bosom, or suspended from his girdle in an ornamental purse. These cups are made of the roots of certain fine trees that grow on the mountains of Thibet. They are graceful in form, but simple and without any sort of decoration, other than a slight varnish which conceals neither their natural color nor the veins of the wood. Throughout Thibet, every one, from the poorest mendicant up to the Talé-Lama, takes his meals out of a wooden cup. The Thibetians, indeed, make a distinction of their own, unintelligible to Europeans, between these cups, some of which are bought for a few small coins, while others cost up to a hundred ounces of silver, or nearly £40. If we were asked what difference we had discerned between these various qualities of cups, we should reply, most conscientiously, that they all appeared to us pretty nearly of the same value, and that with the best disposition in the world to be convinced, we had utterly failed to perceive any distinction of moment between them. The first quality cups, however, according to the Thibetians, have the property of neutralizing poisons.

Some days after our arrival at Lha Ssa, desirous of renewing our meal service, which had become somewhat worn, we went into a cup shop. A Thibetian dame, her face elaborately varnished with black, sat behind the counter. The lady, judging from our exotic appearance, probably, that we were personages of distinction, opened a drawer and took out two small boxes, artistically executed, each of which contained a cup, thrice enveloped in soft paper. After examining the goods with a certain degree of suspense, we asked the price : "Tchik-la, gatse resi ?" (How much a piece ?) "Excellency, fifty ounces of silver each." The words came upon us like a thunder-clap, that filled our ears with a buzzing noise, and our eyes with a conviction that the shop was turning round. Our entire fortune would scarcely have purchased four of these wooden cups. Upon coming somewhat to ourselves, we respectfully restored the two precious bowls to their respective boxes, and passed in review the numerous collection that was unceremoniously displayed on the shelves of the shop. "And these, how much are they each ?" "Excellency, two for an ounce of silver." We forthwith disbursed the ounce of silver, and carried off, in triumph, the two wooden cups, which appeared

Thibetian cup-shop.

to us precisely the same as those for which we had been asked £20 a-piece. On our return home, the master of the house, to whom we showed our purchase, gratified us with the information, that for an ounce of silver we ought to have had at least four such cups as the two we had received.

Poulou, pastile-sticks, and wooden-cups, are the three principal branches of industry which the Thibetians successfully prosecute. Their other manufactures are so poor and coarse as to be unworthy of any special mention. Their agricultural productions scarcely merit notice. Thibet, almost entirely covered with mountains, or cut up with impetuous torrents, affords to its population very little cultivable space. It is only in the valleys that anything like a harvest can be expected. The Thibetians cultivate little wheat, and still less rice. The chief production is Tsing-Kou, or black barley, of which is made the tsamba, that basis of the aliment of the entire Thibetian population, rich and poor. The town of Lha-Ssa itself is abundantly supplied with sheep, horses, and oxen. There is excellent fish, also, sold there, and pork, of most exquisite flavor; but for the most part so dear as to be quite out of the reach of the humbler classes. In fact, the Thibetians, as a rule, live very poorly. Their ordinary repast is buttered tea and tsamba, mixed coarsely together with the finger. The richest people observe the same diet; it is quite pitiable to see them swallowing such miserable provender out of cups, some of which have cost £40. Meat, when eaten at all, is not eaten with the ordinary repasts, but apart, as a luxurious specialty, in the same way that elsewhere people eat costly fruit, or extra fine pastry, on these occasions. There are usually served up two plates, one with boiled meat, the other with raw meat, which the Thibetians devour with equal appetite, unassisted by any seasoning whatever. They have, however, wit enough not to eat without drinking. From time to time they fill their dear wooden cups with a sort of acid liquor, made of fermented barley, not at all disagreeable to the palate.

Thibet, so poor in agricultural and manufacturing products, is rich, beyond all imagination, in metals. Gold and silver are collected there so readily, that the common shepherds have become acquainted with the art of purifying these precious metals. You often see them, in the ravines, or in the hollows of the mountains, seated round a fire of argols, amusing themselves with purifying in a rude crucible the gold-dust they have found while tending their herds. The result of this abundance of the precious metals is, that specie is of low value, and that, consequently, goods always maintain a very high price. The monetary system of the Thibetians consists entirely of silver coins, which are somewhat larger, but not so thick as our francs. On one side they bear inscriptions in Thibetian, Parsee, or Indian characters; on the other, a crown composed of eight small, round flowers. To facilitate commerce, these coins are cut into pieces, the number of flowers remaining on each piece determining its value. The entire coin is called Tchan-Ka. A Tche-Ptche is one-half of the Tchan-Ka; or, in other words, is a piece of four flowers only. The Cho-Kan has five flowers, the Ka-Gan three. In the larger commercial operations, they employ silver ingots, which are weighed in a Roman balance, upon the decimal system. Generally speaking, the Thibetians reckon up accounts upon their beads; some people, however, and especially the merchants, use the Chinese Souan-pan, while the learned employ the numerals which the Europeans call Arabic, and which appear to have been of very ancient date in Thibet. We have seen several Lamanesque manuscripts, illustrated with astronomical figures and diagrams, all of them represented by Arabic numerals, which were also used in the paging of the volumes. Some of these figures differed slightly from the Arabic numerals used in Europe; the most marked difference we noticed was that of the 5, which, in these manuscripts, was turned upside down, thus: ꞩ.

From the few details we have thus given as to the productions of Thibet, it may be concluded that this country is perhaps the richest, and, at the same time, the poorest in the world; rich in gold and silver, poor in all that constitutes the well-being of the masses. The gold and silver collected by the people is absorbed by the great people, and especially by the Lamaseries, those immense reservoirs, into which flow, by a thousand channels, all the wealth of these vast regions. The Lamas, invested with the major part of the currency, by the voluntary donations of the faithful, centruple their fortunes by usury that puts even Chinese knavery to the blush. The offerings they receive are converted, as it were, into hooks, with which they catch the purses out of every one's pocket. Money being thus accumulated in the coffers of the privileged classes, and, on the other hand, the necessaries of life being only procurable at a very high price, it results from this capital disorder, that a great proportion of the population is constantly plunged in the most frightful destitution. At Lha-Ssa the number of mendicants is very considerable. They go from door to door, soliciting a handful of tsamba, and enter any one's house, without the least ceremony. Their manner of asking charity is to hold out the closed hand, with the thumb raised. We must add, in commendation of the Thibetians, that they are generally very kind and compassionate, rarely sending away the poor unassisted.

Among the foreigners settled at Lha-Ssa, the Pebouns are the most numerous. These are Indians from the vicinity of Boutan, on the other side of the Himalaya mountains. They are of slight frame, but very vigorous, active, and animated; their features are rounder than those of the Thibetians: the complexion very dark, the eyes small, black, and roguish; the forehead is marked with a dark, cherry-colored spot, which they renew every morning. They are all attired in a uniform robe of pink poulou, with a small felt cap of the same color, but of somewhat darker tint. When they go out, they add to their costume a long red scarf, which twice encircles the neck like a great collar, and the two ends of which are thrown back over the shoulders.

The Pebouns are the only workers in metals at Lha-Ssa. It is in their quarter that you must seek the iron-smiths, the braziers, the plumbers, the tinmen, the founders, the goldsmiths, the jewelers, the machinists, and even the physicians and chemists. Their workshops and laboratories are nearly underground. You enter them by a low, narrow opening, down three or four steps. Over the doors of all their houses, you see a painting representing a red globe, and below it a white crescent. These manifestly signify the sun and moon; but the particular allusions conveyed we omitted to ascertain.

You find, among the Pebouns, artists very distinguished in metallurgy. They manufacture all sorts of vases, in gold and silver, for the use of the Lamaseries, and jewelry of every description that certainly would reflect no discredit upon European artists. It is they who construct for the Buddhist temples those fine roofs of gilt plates, which resist all the inclemencies of the seasons, and always retain a marvelous freshness and glitter. They are so skilful at this class of work, that they are sent to the very interior of Tartary to decorate the great Lamaseries. The Pebouns are also the dyers at Lha-Ssa. Their colors are vivid and enduring; stuffs upon which they have operated may wear out, but they never lose their color. They are only permitted, however, to dye the poulou. All stuffs coming from foreign countries must be worn as they are, the government absolutely prohibiting the dyers from at all exercising their industry upon them. The object of this prohibition is probably the encouragement of the stuffs manufactured at Lha-Ssa.

The Pebouns are in disposition extremely jovial and childlike. In their hours of relaxation they are full of laughter and frolic; and even while at work they are constantly singing. Their religion is Indian Buddhism. Although they have not adopted the reformation of Tsong-Kaba, they respect the Lamanesque ceremonies and rites. They never fail, on all the more solemn occasions, to prostrate themselves at the feet of the Buddha-La, and to offer their adorations to the Talé-Lama.

Next to the Peboun, you remark at Lha-Ssa, the Katchi, or Mussulmans, from Cashmere—their turban, their large beard, their grave, solemn step, their physiognomy full of intelligence and majesty, the neatness and richness of their attire,—everything about them presents an emphatic contrast with the peoples of inferior race, by whom they are surrounded. They have at Lha-Ssa a governor, to whom they are immediately subject, and whose authority is recognized by the Thibetian government. This officer is, at the same time, the local head of the Mussulman religion; so that his countrymen consider him, in this foreign land, at once their pasha and their mufti. The Katchi have been established at Lha-Ssa for several centuries, having originally abandoned their own country, in order to escape the persecutions of a certain pasha of Cashmere, whose despotism had become intolerable to them; and the children of these first emigrants found themselves so well off in Thibet, that they never thought of returning to their own country. The descendants still keep up a correspondence with Cashmere, but the intelligence they receive thence is little calculated to give them any desire to renounce their adopted country. The Katchi governor, with whom we got upon very intimate terms, told us that the Pelings of Calcutta (the English), were now the real masters of Cashmere. "The Pelings," said he, "are the most cunning people in the world. Little by little they are acquiring possession of all the countries of India, but it is always rather by stratagem than by open force. Instead of overthrowing the authorities, they cleverly manage to get them on their side, to enlist them in their interest. Hence it is that, in Cashmere, the saying is: The world is Allah's, the land the Pasha's; it is the company that rules."

The Katchi are the richest merchants at Lha-Ssa. All the establishments for the sale of linen, and other goods for personal and other use, belong to them. They are also money-changers, and traffic in gold and silver: hence it is that you almost always find Parsee characters on the Thibetian coinage. Every year, some of their number proceed to Calcutta for commercial operations, they being the only class who are permitted to pass the frontiers to visit the English. On these occasions they are furnished with a passport from the Talé-Lama, and a Thibetian escort accompanies them at the foot of the Himalaya mountains. The goods, however, which they bring from Calcutta, are of very limited extent, consisting merely of ribbons, galloons, knives, scissors, and some other articles of cutlery and ironmongery, and a small assortment of cotton goods, The silks and linens in their warehouses, and of which they have a large sale at Lha-Ssa, come from Peking by the medium of the caravans; the linen goods, being Russian, come to them much cheaper than they buy them at Calcutta.

The Katchi have a mosque at Lha-Ssa, and are rigid observers of the law of Mahomet—openly and even ostentatiously expressing their contempt for all the superstitious practises of the Buddhists. The first Katchi who arrived at Lha-Ssa married Thibetian wives, whom they compelled to renounce their own religion, and to embrace Mahomedanism. But now, the rule with them is only to contract marriage alliances among themselves; so that there has imperceptibly become formed, in the heart of Thibet, a small nation apart, having neither the costume, nor the manners, nor the language, nor the religion of the natives. As they do not prostrate themselves before the Talé-Lama, and do not pray in the Lamaseries, everybody says they are infidels; but as, for the most part, they are rich and powerful, people stand aside in the streets to let them pass, and put out their tongues to them in token of respect. In Thibet, when you desire to salute any one, you take off your hat, put out your tongue, and scratch the right ear, all three operations being performed simultaneously.

The Chinese you find at Lha-Ssa are for the most part soldiers or officers of the tribunals; those who fix their residence in this town are very few in number. At all times the Chinese and the Thibetians have had relations more or less important: they frequently have waged war against each other, and have tried to encroach upon one another's rights. The-Tartar-Mantchou dynasty, as we have already remarked elsewhere, saw from the commencement of their elevation the great importance of conciliating the friendship of the Talé-Lama, whose influence is all-powerful over the Mongol tribes; consequently, they have never failed to retain at the court of Lha-Ssa two Grand Mandarins invested with the title of Kin-Tchai, which signifies ambassador, or envoy-extraordinary. The ostensible mission of these individuals is to present, under certain fixed circumstances, the homage of the Chinese Emperor to the Talé-Lama, and to lend him the aid of China in any difficulties he may have with his neighbors. Such, to all appearance, is the purport of this permanent embassy; but in reality they are only in attendance to flatter the religious belief of the Mongols, and to bind them to the reigning dynasty, by making them believe that the government of Peking has great veneration for the divinity of the Budda-La. Another advantage of this embassy is, that the two Kin-Tchais can easily, at Lha-Ssa, watch the movements of the people on the confines of the empire, and send information of them to their government.

In the thirty-fifth year of the reign of Kien-Long, the court of Peking had at Lha-Ssa two Kin-Tchai, or ambassadors, the one named Lo, the other Pou; by a combination of the two names, these men were called the Kin-Tchais (*Lo-Pou*). The word Lo-Pou signifying in Thibetian "radish." This term was, to a certain extent, an insult, and the people of Lha-Ssa, who had never regarded with a pleased eye the presence of the Chinese in the country, were delighted to take up this denomination. Besides, for some time past, the two Chinese Mandarins had given, by their behavior, umbrage to the Thibetians; they interfered every day, more and more, in the affairs of the state, and openly encroached on the rights of the Talé-Lama. At last, as a climax of annoyance, they ordered numerous Chinese troops into Thibet, under the pretext of protecting the Talé-Lama from certain Nepaulese tribes who were giving him uneasiness. It was easy to see that China sought to extend its empire and dominion into Thibet. The opposition of the Thibetian government was, they say, terrible, and the Nomekhan exerted all his authority to check the usurpation of the two Kin-Tchai. One day, as he was going to the palace of the Chinese ambassadors, a young Lama threw a note into his litter, on which were written the words, *Lo Pou, ma, sa*, which signifies, Do not eat radishes—abstain from radishes. The Nomekhan clearly saw, that by this play upon words, some one wished to advise him to be on his guard against the Kin-Tchais (Lo-Pou) ; but as the warning was not clear or precise, he went on. Whilst he was in secret conversation with the two delegates of the court of Peking, some satellites suddenly entered the apartment, poniarded the Nomekhan, and cut off his head. A Thibetian cook, who was in an adjoining room, ran, on hearing the victim's cries, took possession of

Insurrection of the Thibetians at Lha-Ssa.

the bleeding head, stuck it on a pike, and ran through the streets of Lha-Ssa, crying, "Vengeance—death to the Chinese!" The whole town was raised; all rushed to arms, and went tumultuously to the palace of the Kin-Chai, who were cut in pieces. The fury of the people was so great, that they attacked, indiscriminately, all the Chinese, and hunted them down like wild beasts—not only at Lha-Ssa, but also at the other places in Thibet, where they had established military stations, making a ruthless butchery of them.

The Thibetians, it is said, did not lay down their arms till they had pitilessly pursued and massacred all the Chinese to the very frontiers of Sse-Tchouen and Yun-Nan.

The news of this frightful catastrophe having reached the court of Peking, the emperor Kien-Long immediately ordered large levies of troops throughout the empire, and had them marched against Thibet. The Chinese, as in almost all the wars they have waged with their neighbors, were worsted, but they were successful in negotiation. Matters were replaced on their former footing, and since then, peace has never been seriously disturbed between the two governments.

The military force which the Chinese keep up in Thibet is inconsiderable. From Sse-Tchouen to Lha-Ssa, they have, at each stage, miserable barracks, designed to facilitate the journeys of the imperial couriers. In the town of Lha-Ssa, their garrison consists of a few hundred soldiers, whose presence contributes to adorn and protect the position of the ambassadors. From Lha-Ssa, going towards the south as far as Boutan, they have also a line of barracks, very badly kept. On the frontiers they guard, conjointly with the Thibetian troops, the high mountains which separate Thibet from the first English stations. In the other parts of Thibet there are no Chinese, their entrance thither being strictly forbidden.

The soldiers and the Chinese Mandarins established in Thibet are in the pay of the government of Peking; they generally remain three years in the country. When this time has elapsed others are sent to replace them, and they return to their respective provinces. There are some of them, however, who, on the termination of their service, obtain leave to settle at Lha-Ssa, or in the towns on the road to Sse-Tchouen. The Chinese at Lha-Ssa are very few in number; and it would be rather difficult to say to what profession they attach themselves to make their living. Generally speaking, they are jacks-of-all-trades, having a thousand ways of transferring to their own purses the tchankas of the Thibetians. Many of them take a wife in the country; but the bonds of marriage are inadequate to fix them for life in their adopted country. After a certain number of years, when they consider they have accumulated enough, they return to China, and leave behind them wife and children, excepting the sons, whom they would scruple to abandon. The Thibetians fear the Chinese, the Katchi despise them, the Peboun laugh at them.

Of the several classes of strangers sojourning at, or merely visiting Lha-Ssa, there was no one to which we seemed to

Chinese Mandarin and his Wife.

belong; we resembled no one. Accordingly, from the first day of our arrival, we observed that the strangeness of our physiognomy attracted general attention. When we passed along the streets the people looked at us with astonishment, and then advanced, in an under tone, various hypotheses as to our nation. At one time, they took us for two Muftis lately come from Cashmere; at another time for two Indian Brahmins; some said we were Lamas from the north of Tartary; others maintained that we were merchants from Peking, and that we had disguised ourselves in order to accompany the Thibetian embassy. But all these suppositions soon vanished, for we formally declared to the Katchi that we were neither Mufti nor Cashmerians; to the Peboun, that we were neither Indians nor Brahmins; to the Mongols, that we were neither Lamas nor Tartars; to the Chinese, that we were neither merchants, nor from the Central Kingdom. When all were fully convinced that we did not belong to any of these categories they began to call us White Azaras. The denomination was very picturesque, and rather pleased us; we were not, however, inclined to adopt it before getting some information on the point. We therefore asked what they meant by White Azaras. The answer we got was that the Azaras were the most fervent of all the adorers of Buddha, that they were a large tribe of Indians, and that out of devotion they often made a pilgrimage to Lha-Ssa. It was added, that as we were neither Thibetians, nor Katchi, nor Peboun, nor Tartars, nor Chinese, we must certainly be Azaras. There was only this little difficulty in the way, that the Azaras who had previously been at Lha-Ssa, were black; it had become necessary, therefore, in order to solve the difficulty, to call us White Azaras. We again rendered homage to the truth, and declared that we were not Azaras of any kind, white or black. All these doubts about our origin were at first amusing enough; but they soon became serious. Some ill-disposed persons went on to consider that we must be Russians or English, and ultimately almost everybody honored us with the latter qualification. It was set forth, without further hesitation, that we were Pelings from Calcutta, that we had come to investigate the strength of Thibet, to make maps, and to devise means to get possession of the country. All national prejudice apart, it was very annoying to us to be taken for the subjects of her Britannic Majesty. Such a *quid-pro-quo* could not but render us very unpopular, and, perhaps, end in our being cut to pieces; for the Thibetians, why, we know not, have taken it into their heads that the English are an encroaching people, who are not to be trusted.

To cut short the various chatter circulated about us, we

resolved to conform to a regulation in force at Lha-Ssa, and which commands all strangers, who are desirous of staying in the town, to present themselves to the authorities. We went accordingly to the chief of police, and declared to him that we belonged to the Western Heaven, to a great kingdom called France, and that we had come to Thibet to preach the Christian religion, of which we were the ministers. The person to whom we made this declaration was cold and impenetrable as became a bureaucrat. He phlegmatically drew his bamboo quill from behind his ear, and began to write, without the slightest observation, what we had told him. He contented himself with repeating twice or thrice, between his teeth, the words "France," and "Christian religion," like a man who does not know what you mean. When he had done writing, he wiped his pen, still wet with ink, in his hair, and replaced it behind his right ear, saying, "*Yak pose*" (very well); "*Temou chu*" (dwell in peace), we replied, and putting out our tongues at him, we left him, delighted at having placed ourselves on a proper footing with the police. We then walked about the streets of Lha-Ssa with a firmer and more assured step, and regardless of the remarks that continually assailed our ears. The lawful position we had established raised us in our own eyes, and restored our courage. What a happiness at length to find ourselves in a hospitable land, and to be able to breathe a free air, after living so long in China; always in restraint, always outside the law, always occupied with plans for tricking the government of his Imperial Majesty.

The sort of indifference with which our declaration was received by the Thibetian authorities did not surprise us in the least. From the information we had received of the position of strangers at Lha-Ssa, we were convinced we should have no difficulty in the matter. The Thibetians do not profess, in regard to other people, those principles of exclusion which constitute the distinctive character of the Chinese nation. Every one is allowed to enter Lha-Ssa; every one can go and come, and engage in commerce and industrial pursuits without the least restraint. If entrance into Thibet is forbidden to the Chinese, this prohibition must be attributed to the government of Peking, which, to show its complete adherence to its narrow and suspicious policy, forbids its subjects to penetrate among other nations.

It is probable that the English would not be excluded more than any other nation, had not their invasive march into Hindostan inspired the Talé-Lama with a natural terror.

We have already mentioned the many and striking analogies between the Lamanesque worship and the Catholic rites—Rome and Lha-Ssa—the pope and the Talé-Lama,[1] might furnish further analogies. The Thibetian government, being purely Lamanesque, seems in some sort framed upon the ecclesiastical government of the Pontifical states. The Talé-Lama is the political and religious head of all the Thibetian countries; in his hands is all the legislative, executive, and administrative power. The common law and some rules left by Tsong-Kaba, serve to direct him in the exercise of his immense authority. When the Talé-Lama dies, or, in the language of the Buddhists, when he transmigrates, a child is selected who is to continue the imperishable personification of the Living Buddha. This election is made by the grand assembly of the Houtouktou Lamas, whose sacerdotal dignity is only inferior to that of the Talé-Lama. By and by we will enter more fully into the form and rules of this singular election. As the Talé-Lama is not only the religious and political sovereign of the Thibetians, but also their visible deity, it is obvious that he cannot, without seriously compromising his divinity, descend from the height of his sanctuary, to meddle, on all occasions, with human affairs. He has, therefore, reserved to himself the matters of primary importance, content to reign much, and to govern very little. The exercise of his authority wholly depends on his will and pleasure. There is no charter or constitution to regulate his conduct.

After the Talé-Lama, whom the Thibetians also call Kian-Ngan-Remboutchi (sovereign treasure), comes the Nomekhan, or Spiritual Emperor. The Chinese give him the name of Tsan-Wang, king of Thibet. This personage is nominated by the Talé-Lama, and must be selected from the class of Chaberon Lamas. He retains office for life, and can only be overthrown by some state stroke. All the affairs of the government are managed by the Nomekhan, and four ministers called Kalons. The Kalons are chosen by the Talé-

[1] Dalae-Lama is altogether an erroneous form of this designation; the words are Talé-Lama. Talé, in Thibetian, means sea, and the appellation has been applied to the Grand Lama of Thibet, because this personage is locally supposed to be a sea of wisdom and power.

Lama, from a list of candidates made out by the Nomekhan; they do not belong to the sacerdotal tribe, and may marry: the duration of their power is unlimited. When they render themselves unworthy of their office, the Nomekhan sends a report to the Talé-Lama, who dismisses them, if he thinks proper. The subaltern functionaries are selected by the Kalons, and most frequently belong to the class of Lamas.

The provinces are divided into several principalities, which are governed by Houtouktou Lamas. These petty ecclesiastical sovereigns receive their investiture from the Talé-Lama, and recognize his sovereign authority. Generally they are of a warlike turn, and frequently engage with their neighbors, in hostile skirmishes, which are always accompanied by pillage and conflagration.

The most potent of these Lama sovereigns is the Bandchan-Remboutchi. He resides at Djachi-Loumbo (mountain of oracles), capital of Further Thibet. This town is situated south of Lha-Ssa, and is only eight days' journey from it. The celebrity of the present Bandchan is prodigious; his partisans assert that his spiritual power is as great as that of the Talé-Lama, and that the sanctuary of Djachi-Loumbo does not yield in sanctity to that of the Buddha-La. It is generally, however, admitted, that the temporal power of the Talé-Lama is superior to that of the Bandchan-Remboutchi. Great rivalry will not fail to manifest itself, sooner or later, between Lha-Ssa and Djachi-Loumbo, and occasion dismal dissensions among the Thibetians.

The present Bandchan-Remboutchi is sixty years of age; he is, they say, of a fine and majestic frame, and astonishingly vigorous for his advanced age. This singular personage states himself to be of Indian origin, and that it is already some thousands of years since his first incarnation took place in the celebrated country of the Azaras. The physiognomists who, at our first coming to Lha-Ssa, took us for white Azaras, failed not to urge us to go and offer our devotions to the Djachi-Loumbo, assuring us, that in our quality of countrymen of the Bandchan-Remboutchi, we should have a very good reception. The learned Lamas, who occupy themselves with Buddhic genealogies, explain how the Bandchan, after numerous and marvelous incarnations in Hindostan, ended by appearing in Further Thibet, and fixing his residence at Djachi-Loumbo. Whatever may be his biography, which, fortunately we are not bound to believe in, it is certain that this able Lama has managed to establish an astonishing reputation. The Thibetians, the Tartars, and the other Buddhists call him by no other name than the Great Saint, and never pronounce his name without clasping their hands and raising their eyes to heaven. They pretend that his knowledge is universal. He knows how to speak, they say, all the languages of the universe without having ever studied them, and can converse with pilgrims from all parts of the world. The Tartars have so strong a faith in his power, that they invoke him continually. In dangers, in afilictions, in all matters of difficulty, they have in their mouths the magic word *bokte* (saint).

The pilgrims who come to Thibet never fail to visit the Djachi-Loumbo, to prostrate themselves at the feet of the saint of saints, and to present to him their offerings. No one can form a notion of the enormous sums which the Tartar caravans bring him every year. In return for the ingots of gold and silver which he shuts up in his coffers, the Bandchan distributes among his adorers shreds of his old clothes, bits of paper printed with Mongol or Thibetian sentences, earthen statuettes, and red pills of infallible efficaciousness against all sorts of maladies. The pilgrims receive with veneration these trifles, and deposit them religiously in a bag which they always have hanging from their necks.

Those who make the pilgrimage to Djachi-Loumbo, seculars or Lamas, men or women, all enroll themselves in the society of Kalons, instituted by the Bandchan-Remboutchi. Almost all the Buddhists aspire to the happiness of becoming members of this association, which will give rise, some day, to some important event in Upper Asia. All minds, even now, are vividly occupied with the presentiment of a grand catastrophe. Here are some of the strange prophecies that are current on this subject.

When the saint of Djachi-Loumbo, when the Bandchan-Remboutchi dies, he will not transmigrate, as heretofore, in Further Thibet. His new incarnation will take place to the north of Lha-Ssa, in the steppes inhabited by the Ouri-anghai, in the country called Thien-Chan-Pé-Lou, between the Celestial Mountains and the chains of the Altai. While he remains there, a few years incognito, preparing himself by retirement, prayer, and good works, for the great events of the future, the religion of Buddha will continue to grow weaker and weaker in all men's hearts; it will only exist in the bosoms of the brotherhood of the Kalons. At this disastrous epoch the Chinese will gain influence in Thibet; they will spread themselves over the mountains and through the valleys, and will seek to possess themselves of the empire of the Talé-Lama. But this state of things will soon pass away; there will be a general rise of the people; the Thibetians will take up arms, and will massacre in one day all the Chinese, young and old, and not one of them shall repass the frontiers.

A year after this sanguinary day, the Chinese Emperor will raise innumerable battalions, and will lead them against the Thibetians. There will be a terrible reaction; blood will flow in torrents, the streams will be red with gore, and the Chinese will gain possession of Thibet. But this triumph will not be of long duration. Then it will be that the Bandchan-Remboutchi will manifest his power. He will summon all the Kalons of the holy society. Those who shall have already died will return to life, and they will all assemble in a vast plain of Thien-Chan-Pé-Lou. There the Bandchan will distribute arrows and fusils to all of them, and will form of this multitude a formidable army of which he himself will take the command. The society of Kalons will march with the Saint of Saints, and will throw themselves on the Chinese, who will be cut to pieces. Thibet will be conquered, then China, then Tartary, and finally, the vast empire of the Oros. The Bandchan will be proclaimed universal sovereign, and under his holy influence Lamanism will be soon restored to its pristine vigor, superb Lamaseries will rise everywhere, and the whole world will recognize the infinite power of Buddhic prayers.

These predictions, of which we content ourselves with giving a mere summary, are related by every one in most minute detail; but what is most surprising is, that no one seems to entertain the least doubt of the full accomplishment of the events they foretell. Every one speaks of them as of things certain and infallible. The Chinese residing at Lha-Ssa seem likewise to attach credit to the prediction, but they take good care not to trouble their heads much about it; they hope that the crisis will not come for a long while, that by that time they may be dead, or at least be able to anticipate it. As for the Bandchan-Remboutchi, they say he is preparing himself vigorously for the grand revolution of which he is destined to be the soul. Although already advanced in years he often practises military exercises; every moment which is not absorbed by his high functions as Living Buddha he employs in making himself familiar with his future position of generalissimo of the Kalons. They affirm that he shoots an arrow very skilfully, and that he handles with great dexterity the lance and the matchlock. He breeds large herds of horses for his future cavalry, and packs of enormous dogs, which, combining prodigious strength with superior intelligence, are destined to play an important part in the grand army of the Kalons.

These absurd and extragavant ideas have so made their way with the masses, and particularly with those who belong to the society of the Kalons, that they are very likely, at some future day, to cause a revolution in Thibet. It is never without result that people thus preoccupy their minds with the future. After the death of the Grand Lama of Djachi-Loumbo, a reckless adventurer will only have to proceed to Thien-Chan-Pé-Lou, boldly proclaim himself Bandchan-Remboutchi, and summon the Kalons together—nothing more will, probably, be required to raise these fanatical people.

An actual and immediate result of this society of the Kalons is to give the Bandchan-Remboutchi an importance which seems by slow degrees to be compromising the supremacy of the Talé-Lama. This result is the more feasible, that the sovereign of Lha-Ssa is a child of nine years old, and that his three predecessors have fallen victims to a violent death before attaining their majority, which is fixed by the laws at twenty years of age. The Bandchan-Remboutchi, who seems to be an able and ambitious man, will not have failed to take advantage of these four minorities to confiscate to his own advantage a portion of the spiritual and temporal power of the Talé-Lama.

The violent death of the three Talé-Lamas, the immediate predecessors of the reigning sovereign, gave rise in the year 1844, to an event which occupied the attention of all Thibet, Tartary, and even China, and which, on account of its importance, deserves, perhaps, a brief notice here. The unprecedented phenomenon of three Talé-Lamas dying successively in the flower of their age, had plunged the inhabitants of Lha-Ssa into a state of mournful consternation. Gradually, dark rumors began to circulate, and soon the words "crime," "assassination," were heard. The thing went so far that they related in the streets of the town and the Lamaseries all the circumstances of these dismal events. It was said that the first Talé-Lama had been strangled, the second crushed by the roof of his sleeping apartment, and the third poisoned with his numerous relations, who had come to settle at Lha-Ssa. The superior Lama of the Grand Lamasery of Kaldan, who was very much attached to the Talé-Lama, had suffered the same fate. The public voice denounced the Nomekhan as the author of all these crimes. The four ministers had no doubt about the matter, knowing the whole truth; but they found themselves unable to avenge the death of their sovereign; they were too weak to struggle with the Nomekhan, who was supported by numerous and powerful friends.

This Nomekhan was a Si-Fan, a native of the principality of Yang-Tou-Sse, in the province of Kan-Sou. The supreme dignity of Tou-Sse was hereditary in his family, and a great number of his relations, settled at Lha-Ssa for several generations, exercised great influence over the affairs of Thibet. The Nomekhan of Yang-Tou-Sse, was still very young when he was invested with an authority inferior only to that of the Talé-Lama. They say that a few years after his elevation to power, he manifested his ambitious sentiments and a boundless desire for domination. He used his own great wealth and the influence of his relations, to surround himself with dependents wholly devoted to his interest. He took particular care to secure partisans among the Lamas; and, to this end, he took under his immediate protection the famous Lamasery of Sera, situated half a league from Lha-Ssa, and containing upwards of 15,000 Buddhist monks. He loaded it with presents, granted it infinite privileges and revenues, and placed, in its different departments, a great number of his creatures. The Lamas of Sera failed not to acquire great enthusiasm for the Nomekhan; they regarded him as a saint of the first degree, and compiled an enumeration of his perfections as extensive and pompous as that of the perfections of Buddha. Supported by the powerful party he had got together, the Nomekhan withdrew all bounds from his projects of usurpation. It was then that he caused the three young Lamas to be murdered in succession, in order to keep for himself the position of Regent. Such was the Nomekhan of Yang-Tou-Sse, or rather, such was he represented to us during our stay at Lha-Ssa.

It was not easy, as may be seen, to overthrow a personage whose power was so solidly based. The Kalon ministers, unequal to an open struggle with the Nomekhan, resolved to dissimulate, and to work, meanwhile, in secret, at the downfall of this execrable man. The assembly of the Houtouktou elected a new Talé-Lama, or rather indicated the child into whose body the soul of the Living Buddha had transmigrated. Now he was enthroned at the summit of the Buddha-La. The Nomekhan, like the other dignitaries, proceeded to throw himself at his feet, worshiped him with all devotion, but with the full resolution, doubtless, to make him undergo a fourth transmigration, when he should think proper.

The Kalons secretly adopted measures to prevent a new catastrophe. They consulted with the Bandchan-Remboutchi of Djachi-Loumbo, and it was determined that, to check the infamous projects of the Nomekhan, they should call to their aid the irresistible power of the Emperor of China. A request was accordingly drawn up and signed by the Bandchan and the four Kalons, and privately sent to Peking by the embassy of 1844. For three special reasons the government of Peking could not dispense with granting to the Thibetians the protection they demanded under these grave circumstances. In the first place the Tartaro-Mantchou dynasty had solemnly declared itself protector of the Talé-Lama; in the second place, the Nomekhan, as being a native of Yang-Tou-Sse, in the province of Kan-Sou, was in some degree amenable to the Chinese Emperor; finally, politically speaking, it was an excellent opportunity for the court of Peking to establish its influence in Thibet, with a view to the realization of its projects of usurpation.

The request sent to Peking by the Bandchan-Remboutchi and the four Kalons, was received with all the favor that could be desired, and the government there determined to send to Lha-Ssa an ambassador of energy and prudence, capable of overthrowing the power of the Nomekhan. The

Emperor thought of the Mandarin Ki-Chan, and charged him with this difficult mission.

Before proceeding further, it will not, perhaps, be superfluous to give a sketch of this Ki-Chan, a very celebrated personage in China, who has played an important part in the affair of the English at Canton. Ki-Chan is of Tartaro-Mantchou origin; he commenced his career as a scrivener in one of the six grand tribunals of Peking. His rare capacity was soon remarked, and although he was still very young, he rapidly mounted all the steps of the magistracy. At the age of twenty-two he was governor of the province of Ho-Nan; at the age of twenty-five he was its viceroy, but he was dismissed from this charge for not having been able to foresee an overflow of the Yellow River, which caused great disasters in the province that was entrusted to him. His disgrace did not last long; he was reinstated in his former dignity, and sent, successively, in quality of viceroy, to the provinces of Chan-Tong-Sse Tchouen, and Pe-Tche-Ly. He was decorated with the red button, the peacock's feather, and the yellow tunic, with the title of Heou-Ye (imperial prince). At length, he was nominated Tchoung-Tang, the highest dignity to which a Mandarin can ever aspire. They have only eight Tchoung-Tangs in the empire; four Mantchous and four Chinese; these compose the privy council of the Emperor, and have the right of direct correspondence with him.

Towards the close of the year 1839, Ki-Chan was sent to Canton, as viceroy of the province, and with the title of imperial commissioner he had full powers to treat, in the name of his government, with the English, and to re-establish the peace which had been disturbed by the foolish and violent proceedings of his predecessor Lin. That which most emphatically proves the capacity of Ki-Chan is that on his arrival at Canton he recognized the infinite superiority of the Europeans over the Chinese, and saw that war was impossible. He, accordingly, forthwith commenced negotiations with Mr. Elliott, the English plenipotentiary, and peace was concluded, on the consideration of the cession of the small island of Hong-Kong. To cement the good understanding that had been established between the Emperor Tao-Kouang and Queen Victoria, Ki-Chan gave the English authorities a magnificent banquet, at which was present M. de Rosamel, the commander of the corvette *Danaide*, which had arrived a few days before in the roads of Macao. Every one was enchanted with the graceful and affable manners of the commissioner-general.

A few days only elapsed before the intrigues worked at Peking by the former imperial commissioner, Lin, occasioned the disallowance by the Emperor of the treaty that had just been concluded at Canton. Ki-Chan was accused of having allowed himself to be corrupted by English gold, and of having sold to the "sea devils" the territory of the Celestial Empire. The Emperor sent him a furious letter, declaring him worthy of death, and ordering him to repair to Peking forthwith. The poor imperial commissioner had not his head cut off, as every one expected. The Emperor, in his paternal mildness, gave him his life, and merely degraded him from all his titles, withdrew all his decorations, confiscated his property, razed his house, sold his wives by public auction, and banished him to the depths of Tartary. The numerous and influential friends whom Ki-Chan had at court, did not desert him in his reverses; they labored with courage and perseverance to reinstate him in the good graces of the Emperor. In 1844, he was, at length, recalled, and sent to Lha-Ssa as envoy-extraordinary in the matter of the Nomekhan. He departed, decorated with the blue button, instead of the red one, which he wore before his fall; they restored to him the peacock's feather, but the privilege of wearing the yellow tunic was still withheld. His friends at Peking clubbed together and built for him a magnificent house. The post of Kin-Tchai, amid the mountains of Thibet, was still considered banishment; but it was a step towards a glorious and complete reinstatement. Immediately upon his arrival at Lha-Ssa, Ki-Chan concerted with the Bandchan-Remboutchi, and had the Nomekhan arrested. He then proceeded to examine all the persons attached to the service of the accused, and, in order to facilitate their declaration of the truth, he had long bamboo needles thrust under their nails; by this means, as the Chinese phrase it, "truth was separated from falsehood," and the conduct of the Nomekhan was brought to light. The wretched man avowed his crimes voluntarily, in order to avoid the torture. He acknowledged himself guilty of taking away three lives from the Talé-Lama, of having used violent means to make him transmigrate, the first time by strangulation, the second time by suffocation, and the third by poison. A confession was drawn up in the Tartar, Chinese, and Thibetian languages; the Nomekhan and his accomplices signed it; the Bandchan-Remboutchi, the four Kalons, and the Chinese ambassador set their seals to it; and it was immediately forwarded to Peking by a courier-extraordinary. All this was done in secret. Three months afterwards, the capital of Thibet was thrown into a state of the greatest agitation; there was seen placarded on the great gate of the Nomekhan's palace, and in the principal streets of the town, an imperial edict, in three languages, on yellow paper, and with borders representing winged dragons. After a long flourish about the duties of kings, and of sovereigns, great and small, and an exhortation to the potentates, monarchs, princes, magistrates, and people of the four seas, to walk in the paths of justice and virtue, under pain of incurring the wrath of heaven and the indignation of the Grand Khan, the Emperor recounted the crimes of the Nomekhan, and comdemned him to perpetual banishment on the banks of the Sakhalien-Oula, in the depths of Mantchouria. At the end was the usual formula: "Tremble and obey."

The inhabitants of Lha-Ssa collected round these strange placards, which they were unused to see on the walls of their town. The report of the condemnation of the Nomekhan spread rapidly among the people. Numerous groups began to form, who discussed the point with vehemence, but in whispers. All faces were animated, and from every quarter there rose a deep murmur. This agitation among the Thibetian people arose not so much from the merited downfall of the Nomekhan, as from the interference of the Chinese authorities, an interference which every one felt to be very humiliating.

At the Lamasery of Sera, opposition manifested itself with an altogether different sort of energy. As soon as they had notice there of the imperial edict, the insurrection was spontaneous and general. Those 15,000 Lamas, who were all devoted to the cause of the Nomekhan, armed themselves hastily with lances, fusils, sticks, whatever came first to hand, and threw themselves into Lha-Ssa, which was only half a league distant. The thick clouds of dust which they raised in their disorderly course, and the terrible shouts they sent forth, announced their arrival to the inhabitants of Lha-Ssa—"The Lamas of Sera! Here are the Lamas of Sera!" Such was the cry which resounded through the town, and inspired all hearts with fear. The Lamas burst like an avalanche upon the house of the Chinese ambassador, and dashed in the door with shouts of "Death to Ki-Chan! death to the Chinese!" But they found no one upon whom they could vent their rage. The ambassador, forewarned in time of their arrival, had run and concealed himself in the house of a Kalon, and the people of his train were dispersed over the town. The multitude of Lamas then divided itself into several bands, some took their way to the palace of the Nomekhan, and others besieged the dwellings of the Kalons, demanding loudly that they should give up to them the Chinese ambassador. There was, on this point, a long and fierce contest, in which one of the four Thibetian ministers was torn to pieces, and the others received wounds more or less dangerous.

Whilst they were contending with the Kalons for possession of the person of Ki-Chan, the most numerous party of the Lamas had broken into the prison where the Nomekhan was confined, and wanted to bear him in triumph to the Lamasery of Sera. The Nomekhan, however, strongly opposed this intention, and exerted all his influence to calm the excitement of the Lamas. He told them that their inconsiderate revolt aggravated his position instead of ameliorating it. "I am," said he, "the victim of a conspiracy. I will go to Peking; I will explain the whole affair to the Emperor, and will return in triumph amongst you. At present we have only to obey the imperial decree. I will depart, as I have been commanded. Do you go back quietly to your Lamasery." These words did not shake the resolution of the Lamas, but, night falling, they returned tumultuously to Sera, promising themselves a better plan for the morrow. When day broke, the Lamas began to move about in their vast monastery, and to prepare themselves for a fresh invasion of the town of Lha-Ssa, but, to their great astonishment, they perceived in the plain, round about the Lamasery, numerous tents and a multitude of Chinese and Thibetian soldiers, armed to the teeth, and prepared to bar their passage. At this sight, all their valor evaporated: the marine conch was sounded, and these extempore soldiers, throwing aside their arms, re-entered their cells, took their books under their arms, and quietly proceeded to the choir, to recite, as usual, their matins.

A few days afterwards, the Nomekhan, accompanied by a strong escort, took the road to Sse-Tchouen, and proceeded like a sheep, to the place of exile that had been assigned him. They could never understand at Lha-Ssa how the man, who had not hesitated to murder three Talé-Lamas, had not chosen to take advantage of the insurrection of the Lamas of Sera. Certain it is, that, with a single word, he might have annihilated all the Chinese at Lha-Ssa, and most probably set all Thibet in a blaze; but the Nomekhan was not formed to play such a part; he had the cowardly energy of an assassin, but not the audacity of a revolutionist.

Ki-Chan, encouraged by his triumph, wanted to extend his power to the Thibetian accomplices of the Nomekhan. This claim, however, did not suit the Kalons, who told him that to them alone belonged the right of judging men who in no wise were subject to China, and against whom they had not asked for the protection of the Emperor. The Kin-Tchai did not press the point; but, not to appear to yield to the Thibetian authorities, he replied to them officially, "that he left to them these inferior assassins, who were below the notice of the representative of the Emperor."

A new Nomekhan was elected in the place of the exile. The person selected for this important charge was the Chaberon of the Lamasery of Ran-Tchan, a young man of eighteen years of age. The Talé-Lama and the new Nomekhan being minors, at the time that we arrived at Lha-Ssa, the regency was entrusted to the first Kalon. All the solicitude of the Regent was applied to the erection of barriers against the encroachments and usurpation of the Chinese ambassador, who sought, by all possible means, to avail himself of the present feebleness of the Thibetian government.

The Spies.

CHAPTER VI.

Visit of Five Spies—Appearance Before the Regent—Ki-Chan Makes us Undergo an Examination—Supper at the Expense of the Government—A Night of Imprisonment with the Regent—Confidential Communications of the Governor of the Katchi—Domiciliary Visit—Seals Affixed to all Our Effects—Sinico-Thibetian Tribunal—Inquiry About the Geographical Maps—Homage Paid to Christianity, and to the French Name—The Regent Assigns to Us One of His Houses—Erection of a Chapel—Preaching of the Gospel—Conversion of a Chinese Doctor—Religious Conferences with the Regent—Recreation with a Magnifying Glass—Conversations with Ki-Chan—Religious Character of the Thibetians—Celebrated Formula of the Buddhists—Buddhist Pantheism—Election of the Talé-Lama—The Small-pox at Lha-Ssa—Sepultures in Use Among the Thibetians.

As soon as we had presented ourselves to the Thibetian authorities, declaring our characters and the object which had brought us to Lha-Ssa, we availed ourselves of the semi-official position we had thus taken, to enter into communication with the Thibetian and Tartar Lamas, and thus, at last, to begin our work as missionaries. One day, when we were sitting beside our modest hearth, talking of religious questions with a Lama who was well versed in Buddhist learning, a Chinese dressed in exquisite style suddenly appeared before us, saying that he was a merchant and very desirous of buying our goods. We told him we had nothing to sell. "How, nothing to sell?" "Not anything, except indeed these two old saddles, which we do not want any longer." "Ah, exactly; that is just what I am looking for; I want saddles." Then, while he examined our poor merchandise, he addressed to us a thousand questions about our country and the places we had visited before we came to Lha-Ssa. Shortly afterwards there arrived a second Chinese, then a third, and at last two Lamas, in costly silk scarves. All these visitors insisted upon buying something from us; they overwhelmed us with questions, and seemed, at the same time, to scrutinize with distrust all the corners of our chamber.

We might say, as often, as we liked, that we were not merchants—they insisted. In default of silk, drapery, or hardware, they would like our saddles; they turned them round and round in every way, finding them now perfectly magnificent, now abominable. At last, after long haggling and cross-questioning, they went off, promising to return.

The visit of these five individuals occasioned much serious reflection; their manner of acting and speaking was not at all natural. Although they came one after the other, yet they seemed perfectly to understand each other, and to aim at the same end by the same means. Their desire of buying something from us was evidently a mere pretext for disguising their intentions; these people were rather swindlers or spies, than real merchants. "Well," we said, "let us wait quietly; sooner or later we shall see clearly into this affair."

As it was dinner time, we sat down to table, or rather, we remained at the fireside, contemplating the pot, in which a good cut of beef had been boiling for some hours. Samdadchiemba, in his quality of steward, brought this to the surface of the liquid by means of a large wooden spoon, seized it with his nails, and threw it on the end of a board, where he cut it into three equal pieces; each then took his portion in his cup, and with the aid of a few rolls baked in the ashes, we tranquilly commenced our dinner without troubling ourselves very much about swindlers or spies. We were at our dessert—that is to say, we were about to rinse our cups with some buttered tea, when the two Lamas, the pretended merchants, made their reappearance. "The Regent," they said, "awaits you in his palace; he wants to speak to you." "But," cried we, "does the Regent, perchance, also want to buy our old saddles?" "It is not a question about either saddles or merchandise. Rise at once, and follow us to the Regent." The matter was now beyond a doubt; the government was desirous of meddling with us —to what end? Was it to do us good or ill, to give us liberty, or to shackle us? to let us live or to make us die? This we could not tell. "Let us go to the Regent," we said, "and trust for the rest to the will of our Heavenly Father."

After having dressed ourselves in our best, and put on our majestic caps of fox-skin, we said to our apparitor, "We are ready." "And this young man," he said, pointing to Samdadchiemba, who had turned his eyes upon him with no very affectionate expression. "This young man, he is our servant, he will take care of the house in our absence." "No, no, he must come too; the Regent wishes to see all three of you." Samdadchiemba shook, by way of making his toilet, his great robe of sheepskin, placed, in a very insolent manner, a small black cap over his ear, and we departed all together, after padlocking the door of our lodging.

We went at a rapid pace for about five or six minutes, and then arrived at the palace of the First Kalon, the Regent of Thibet. After having crossed a large courtyard, where were assembled a great number of Lamas and Chinese, who began to whisper when they saw us appear, we were stopped before a gilt door, the folds of which stood ajar; our leader passed through a small corridor on the left, and an instant after the door was opened. At the farther end of an apartment, simply furnished, we perceived a personage sitting with crossed legs on a thick cushion covered with a tiger's-skin: it was the Regent. With his right hand he made us a sign to approach. We went close up to him, and saluted him by placing our caps under our arms. A bench covered with a red carpet stood on our right; on this we were invited to sit down—we complied immediately. Meantime the gilt door was closed, and there remained in the saloon only the Regent and seven individuals, who stood behind him—namely, four Lamas of a modest and composed bearing, two sly-looking, mischievous-eyed Chinese, and a person whom, by his long beard, his turban, and grave countenance, we recognized to be a Mussulman. The Regent was a man of fifty years of age; his large features, mild and remarkably pallid, breathed a truly royal majesty; his dark eyes, shaded by long lashes, were intelligent and gentle. He was dressed in a yellow robe, edged with sable; a ring, adorned with diamonds, hung from his left ear, and his long, jet black hair was collected together at the top of his head, and fastened by three small gold combs. His large red cap, set with pearls and surmounted by a coral ball, lay at his side on a green cushion.

When we were seated, the Regent gazed at us for a long while in silence, and with a minute attention. He turned his head alternately to the right and left, and smiled at us in a half mocking, half friendly manner. This sort of pantomime appeared to us at last so droll, that we could not help laughing. "Come," we said in French, and in an undertone, "this gentleman seems a good fellow enough; our affair will go on very well." "Ah!" said the Regent, in a very affable tone, "what language is that you speak? I did not understand what you said?" "We spoke the language of our country." "Well, repeat aloud what you said just now." "We said, 'This gentleman seems a good-natured fellow enough.'" The Regent, turning to those who were standing behind him, said, "Do you understand this language?" They all bowed together, and answered that they did not understand it. "You see, nobody here understands the language of your country. Translate your words into the Thibetian." We said, that in the physiognomy of the First Kalon there was expressed much kindliness. "Ah! you think I have much kindliness; yet I am very ill-natured. Is it not true that I am very ill-natured?" he asked his attendants. They answered merely by smiling. "You are right," continued the Regent; "I am kind, for kindness is the duty of a Kalon. I must be kind towards my people, and also towards strangers." He then addressed to us a long harangue, of which we could comprehend only a few sentences. When he had finished, we told him that, not being much accustomed to the Thibetian language, we had not fully penetrated the sense of his words. The Regent signed to a Chinese, who, stepping forward, translated to us his harangue, of which the following is the outline. We had been summoned without the slightest idea of being molested. The contradictory reports that had circulated respecting us since our arrival at Lha-Ssa, had induced the Regent to question us himself, in order to know where we came from. "We are from the western sky," we said to the Regent. "From Calcutta?" "No; our country is called France." "You are, doubtless, Peling?" "No, we are Frenchmen." "Can you write?" "Better than speak." The Regent, turning round, addressed some words to a Lama, who disappearing, returned in a moment with paper, ink, and a bamboo point. "Here is paper," said the Regent; "write something." "In what language—in Thibetian?" "No, write some letters in your own country's language." One of us took the paper on his knees, and wrote this sentence: "What avails it to man to conquer the whole world, if he lose his soul?" "Ah, here are characters of your country! I never saw any like them; and what is the meaning of that?" We wrote the translation in Thibetian, Tartar, and Chinese, and handed it to him. "I have not been deceived," he said; "you are men of great knowledge. You can write in all languages, and you express thoughts as profound as those we find in the prayer-books." He then repeated, slowly moving his head to and fro, "What avails it to man to conquer the whole world if he lose his own soul?"

While the Regent and his attendants were indulging in their raptures at our wonderful knowledge, we heard on a sudden, in the courtyard of the palace, the cries of the crowd and the sonorous noise of the Chinese tamtam. "Here is the ambassador of Peking," said the Regent, "he wishes to examine you himself. Tell him frankly what concerns you, and rely on my protection; it is I who govern the country." This said, he quitted the saloon with his retinue through a small secret door, and left us alone in this judgment-hall.

The idea of falling into the hands of the Chinese made at first a disagreeable impression upon us; and the picture of those horrible persecutions which at different times have afflicted the christendoms of China, seized upon our imagination; but we soon recovered our spirits in the reflection that we were alone, and isolated as we were in the midst of

Thibet, could not compromise any one. This thought gave us courage. "Samdadchiemba," we said to our young neophyte, "now must we show that we are brave men, that we are Christians. This affair will perhaps proceed to great lengths; but let us never lose sight of eternity. If we are treated well, we shall thank God for it; if we are maltreated, we shall thank him nevertheless, for we shall have the happiness of suffering for the faith. If we are killed, the martyrdom will be a splendid crowning of all our labors. To arrive, after a journey of only eighteen months, in heaven, were not that a good journey? were not that happiness? What do you say, Samdadchiemba?" "I have never been in fear of death; if I am asked whether I am a Christian, you will see if I tremble."

This excellent frame of mind in Samdadchiemba filled our hearts with joy, and completely dissipated the unpleasant impressions which this misadventure had occasioned. We thought for a moment of considering the questions that would probably be put to us, and the answers we should give; but we rejected this counsel of mere human prudence, reflecting that the moment had come for us to keep strictly to the injunction which our Saviour addressed to his disciples, that "when they were brought before the synagogues, governors, and kings, they should take no thought how or what they should speak;" only it was agreed that we should salute the Mandarin in the French way, and that we should not kneel before him. We thought that, having the honor to be Christians, missionaries, and Frenchmen, we might very fairly insist on standing erect before any Chinese whatsoever.

After waiting a few moments, a young Chinese, elegantly dressed, and of very graceful manners, came to inform us that Ki-Chan, grand ambassador of the grand Emperor of China, wished to examine us. We followed our amiable apparitor and were ushered into a saloon decorated in the Chinese style, where Ki-Chan was seated upon a sort of throne, about three feet high, and covered with red cloth. Before him was a small table of black laque, upon which were an inkstand, some pens, some sheets of paper, and a silver vase filled with snuff. Below the throne were four scribes, two on the right, and two on the left; the rest of the saloon was occupied by a great number of Chinese and Thibetians, who had put on their holiday dresses to attend the inquiry.

Ki-Chan, although sixty years old, seemed to us full of strength and vigor. His face is, without contradiction, the most noble, elegant, and intellectual we have seen amongst the Chinese. When we took off our caps to him, and made him one of our best bows, "'Tis well, 'tis well," he said; "follow your own customs. I have been told you speak correctly the language of Peking. I want to talk with you for a moment." "We make many blunders in speaking, but your marvelous understanding will know how to remedy the obscurity of our words." "Why, that is pure Pekinese. You Frenchmen possess a great facility for all learning. You are Frenchmen, are you not?" "Yes, we are Frenchmen." "Oh, I know the French; there were formerly a great many of them at Peking; I used to see some of them." "You must have known them, too, at Canton, when you were imperial commissioner?" This reminiscence furrowed the forehead of our judge; he took an abundant pinch of snuff out of his box, and threw it up his nose in a very bad humor. "Yes, that is true; I have seen many Europeans at Canton. You are of the religion of the Lord of Heaven, are you not?" "Certainly we are; moreover, preachers of that religion." "I know, I know; you have come hither, doubtless, to preach that religion?" "We have no other object." "Have you already traveled over a great number of countries?" "We have traveled over all China, Tartary, and now we are in the capital of Thibet." "With whom did you live when you were in China?" "We do not answer questions of that sort." "And if I command you to do so?" "We should not obey." Here the irritated judge struck the table with his fist. "You know," we said, "that Christians have no fear; why seek, then, to intimidate us?" "Where did you learn Chinese?" "In China." "In what place?" "A little everywhere." "And the Tartar, you know it? where did you learn it?" "In Mongolia, in the Land of Grass."

After some other trifling questions, Ki-Chan, telling us that we must be tired, invited us to seat ourselves. Then suddenly changing his tone and manner, he addressed Samdadchiemba, who, with his hand on his hip, had been standing a little behind us. "And you," he said, in a dry and angry voice, "whence are you?" "I am from Ki-Tou-Sse." "What is Ki-Tou-Sse? who knows that?" "Ki-Tou-Sse is in San-Tchouen." "Ah, you are from San-Tchouen, in the province of Kan-Sou. Son of the central nation, on your knees!" Samdadchiemba turned pale, his hand left his hip, and his arm modestly glided down along his leg. "On your knees," repeated the Mandarin, in a thundering voice. Samdadchiemba fell on his knees saying, "On my knees, standing or sitting, 'tis all the same to me: a man of labor and fatigue, as I am, is not accustomed to take his ease." "Ah, you are from Kan-Sou," said the judge, taking large pinches of snuff; "ah! you are from Kan-Sou; you are a child of the central nation! Very well; in that case, it is within my province to deal with you. Son of the central nation, answer your father and mother, and take heed how you tell lies. Where did you meet with these two foreigners? How did you become attached to their service?" Samdadchiemba gave, with perfect self-confidence, a long history of his life, which seemed to interest the auditory; he then related how he had made our acquaintance in Tartary, and the reasons that had induced him to follow us. Our young neophyte spoke with dignity, and, moreover, with a prudence which we had not expected. "Why did you adopt the religion of the Lord of Heaven? Don't you know that this is forbidden by the grand Emperor?" "The *entirely humble* [1] adopted that religion, because it is the only true religion. How could I suppose that the grand Emperor proscribed a religion which orders man to do good and to avoid evil?" "That is true, the religion of the Lord of Heaven is holy; I know it. Why did you enter the service of these foreigners? Don't you know that the laws forbid that?" "How should an ignorant man, as I am, know who is a foreigner, and who not? These men always showed kindness to me, always exhorted me to practise virtue; why was I not to follow them?" "How much wages do they pay you?" "If I accompany them, it is to save my soul, and not to get money. My masters have never let me want rice and clothes, and with that I am satisfied." "Are you married?" "As I was a Lama, before entering the religion of the Lord of Heaven, I have never been married." The judge then laughingly addressed an indelicate question to Samdadchiemba, who lowered his eyes

[1] *Siao-ti*, an expression used by the Chinese when they speak of themselves in the presence of Mandarins.

and remained silent. One of us rising, said to Ki-Chan: "Our religion not only prohibits the commission of impure actions, but also the thinking or speaking of them; it is even not permitted to us to listen to indecent expressions." These words pronounced with calmness and solemnity, raised a slight blush on the face of his excellency the ambassador of China. "I know," he said, "I know the religion of the Lord of Heaven is holy; I know it, for I have read its books of doctrine; he who should strictly keep all its precepts would be a man without reproach." He made a sign to Samdadchiemba to rise; then, turning to us, he said: "It is night, you must be tired; it is time to take supper; you may go; to-morrow if I want you, I will send for you."

The ambassador Ki-Chan was quite right, it was very late, and the various emotions which had been furnished to us in the course of the evening had not by any means supplied the place of supper. On leaving the Sinico-Thibetian pretorium, we were accosted by a venerable Lama, who informed us that the First Kalon awaited us. We crossed the court, illuminated by some red lanterns; turned on the right, to a perilous staircase, which we ascended, prudently holding on by our conductor's robe; then, after traversing a long terrace, in the dubious light of the stars, we were introduced to the Regent. The large and lofty room was splendidly lighted by butter-oil lamps, the walls, the ceiling, even the floor, were all covered with gilding and brilliant colors. The Regent was alone; he bade us sit down near himself on a rich carpet, and endeavored to express by his words, and still more by his gestures, how deep an interest he felt in us. Above all, we clearly understood that he was making arrangements to keep us from starving. Our pantomime was interrupted by the arrival of a person, who left, upon entering, his slippers at the door; it was the governor of the Cashmerian Mussulmans. After having saluted the company, by raising his hand to his forehead, and pronouncing the formula "Salamalek" he leaned against a column, in the center of the room, which supported the ceiling. The Mussulman governor spoke Chinese very well; and the Regent had accordingly sent for him to act as interpreter. Immediately upon his arrival, a servant placed before us a small table, and supper was served up to us at the expense of the

Thibetian government. We shall not say anything here as to the Regent's *cuisine;* firstly, because our keen appetite did not permit us to pay sufficient attention to the quality of the dishes; secondly, because that day our minds were more occupied with politics than with gastronomy. All of a sudden we missed Samdadchiemba; we asked what had become of him: "He is with my servants," answered the Regent; "do not trouble yourselves on his account, he shall not want for anything."

During, and after the repast, there was much inquiry about France and the countries we had visited. Then the Regent, pointing to the pictures that adorned his room, asked whether we could ourselves paint any such. "We cannot paint," was our answer; "study, and the preaching of the doctrine of Jehovah are our only occupations." "Oh, don't tell me you cannot paint; I know that the people of your country are very skilful in that art." "Yes, those who make it their employment; but our clergymen are not in the habit of exercising it." "Though you may not follow this art specially, yet you are not quite unacquainted with it; you can, doubtless, draw geographical maps?" "No, we cannot." "How! on your journey did you never sketch, did you never make a map?" "Never." "Oh, that is impossible!" The pertinacity of the Regent in questioning us on this subject, made us pause to reflect; presently we expressed the surprise we felt at all these inquiries, "I see," he said, "that you are straightforward, honest men; I will speak frankly to you. The Chinese are very suspicious, you are aware of that: you have been long enough in China to know it as well as I do; well, they believe that you are traveling through foreign kingdoms on purpose to draw maps of them and to explore them. If you do draw, if you do make geographical maps, admit it without fear; rely on my protection." Evidently the Regent was afraid of an invasion; he fancied, perhaps, that we were charged with laying down the route for some formidable army, ready to overwhelm Thibet. We endeavored to dissipate his fears, and to assure him of the extremely peaceful views of the French government. We admitted, however, that amongst our effects there was a great number of drawings and geographical maps, and that we had even a map of Thibet. At these words, the face of the Regent was suddenly contracted; but we hastened to add, in order to quiet him, that all our drawings and maps were printed, and that we were not their authors. We took the opportunity to speak to the Regent and the Cashmerian governor, of the geographical knowledge of the Europeans. They were greatly astonished when we told them that, with us, children of ten and twelve years old possessed an exact and complete idea of all the kingdoms of the world.

The conversation extended far into the night. At last the Regent rose, and asked us whether we did not feel in want of a little repose. "We only awaited," we answered, "for the permission of the Kalon, to return to our lodgings." "Your lodgings! I have ordered an apartment to be prepared for you in my palace; you will sleep here to-night: to-morrow, you can return to your house." We sought to excuse ourselves from accepting the kind offer of the Regent; but soon became aware that we were not at liberty to refuse what we had been simple enough to consider a compliment. We were regular prisoners. We took leave of the Regent rather coolly, and followed an individual, who, after crossing a great many rooms and corridors, ushered us into a sort of closet, which we might fairly call a prison, as we were not permitted to leave it for any other place.

There had been prepared for us two couches, which, no doubt, were infinitely superior to our own beds; nevertheless, we regretted our poor pallets, whereon we had so long enjoyed a free and independent sleep throughout our travels in the desert. Lamas and attendants of the Regent came in great numbers to see us. Those who had gone to bed got up, and soon we heard, in this vast palace, lately so calm and silent, doors opened and shut, and the rapid steps of the curious sounding in the passages. Crowds thronged around us and examined us with insupportable avidity. In all those eyes staring at us there was neither sympathy nor ill-will; they simply expressed vapid curiosity. To all these individuals around us, we represented merely a kind of zoological phenomenon. Oh, how hard it is to be exposed thus to an indifferent multitude! When we thought that these troublesome people had sufficiently stared and whispered, and ought now to be satisfied, we informed them that we were going to bed, and that we should feel extremely obliged if they would be kind enough to retire. Every one bowed: some of them even were polite enough to put out their tongues at us; but nobody stirred. It was evident that they had a mind to know how we should behave on going to bed. This desire seemed to us somewhat misplaced; but we thought we would submit to it up to a certain point. Accordingly we knelt down, made the sign of the cross, and recited, aloud, our evening prayer. As soon as we commenced, the whispering ceased, and a religious silence prevailed. When the prayer was finished, we once more invited the crowd to leave us, and, in order to add efficacy to our words, we extinguished the light. The crowd, thus plunged into deep darkness, adopted the course of first having a hearty laugh, and then retiring gropingly. We closed the door of our prison and laid down to rest.

When stretched on the beds of the First Kalon, we felt much more disposed to talk than to sleep. We experienced a certain pleasure in recapitulating the adventures of the day. The feigned merchants who wanted to purchase our saddles, our appearance before the Regent, the examination we had undergone by the ambassador, Ki-Chan, our supper at the expense of the public treasury, our long conversation with the Regent: all this appeared to us a phantasmagoria. It seemed as though our whole day had been a long nightmare. Our journey itself, our arrival at Lha-Ssa, everything seemed incredible. We asked one another whether it was true, that we, missionaries, Frenchmen, were really in the states of the Talé-Lama, in the capital of Thibet, sleeping in the very palace of the Regent. All these events, past and present, clashed in our heads. The future, especially, appeared to us enveloped in dark, thick clouds. How was all this to end? Would they say to us, "You are free; go wherever you please?" Would they keep us in this prison? or would they strangle us? These reflections were well calculated to chill the heart, and to cause a headache. But trust in God is a grand thing in such trials! How happy is one in feeling one's-self supported by Providence, when one is thus left alone, abandoned, and destitute of succor. "Oh," said we to each other, "let us be prepared for the worst, relying upon the protection of our Heavenly Father! Not a single hair will fall from our heads without his permission."

We went to sleep amid these considerations, but our slumber was light and disturbed. As soon as dawn appeared, the door of our cell was gently opened, and the governor of the Katchi entered. He took a seat at our side, between the two couches, and asked us in kind, affectionate tones, whether we had spent a good night. He

The Governor of Katchi.

then presented to us a basket of cakes, made by his family, and some dried fruits from Ladak. We were deeply touched by this attention, which seemed to announce that we had met with a sincere and devoted friend.

The governor of the Katchi was thirty-two years old; his face full of nobleness and majesty, breathed at the same time, a kindness and candor well calculated to arouse our confidence. His looks, his words, his deportment, everything about him, seemed to express that he felt a very lively interest in us. He had come to acquaint us with what would be done during the day, with reference to us. "In the morning," he said, "the Thibetian authorities will go with you to your lodgings. They will put a seal upon all your effects, which will then be brought before the tribunal, and be examined by the Regent and the Chinese ambassador, in your presence. If you have no manuscript maps in your baggage you need fear nothing; you will not be molested in any way. If, on the contrary, you have any such maps, you would do well to let me know beforehand, as in this case, we may perhaps find some way to arrange the affair. I am very intimate with the Regent (this we had, indeed, observed the night before during our supper); and it is he himself who directed me to make to you this confidential communication." He then added, in an under voice, that all these difficulties were got up against us by the Chinese, against the will of the Thibetian government. We answered the governor of Katchi, that we had not a single manuscript map; and we then gave him, in detail, a statement of all the articles that were in our trunks. "Since they are to be examined to-day, you will judge for yourself whether we are people to be believed." The countenance of the Mussulman brightened. "Your words," he said, "quite reassure me. None of the articles you have described can at all compromise you. Maps are feared in this country—extremely feared, indeed; especially since the affair of a certain Englishman named Moorcroft, who introduced himself into Lha-Ssa, under the pretense of being a Cashmerian. After a sojourn there of twelve years, he departed; but he was murdered on his way to Ladak. Amongst his effects they found a numerous collection of maps and plans, which he had drawn during his stay at Lha-Ssa. This circumstance has made the Chinese authorities very suspicious on this subject. As you do not draw maps, that is all right; I will now go and tell the Regent what I have heard from you."

When the governor of Katchi had left us, we rose, for we had remained in bed, without ceremony, during his long visit. After having offered up our morning prayer, and prepared our hearts to patience and resignation, we ate the breakfast which had been sent to us by order of the Regent. It consisted of a plate of rolls stuffed with sugar and minced meat, and a pot of richly-buttered tea. But we gave the preference to the cakes and dried fruit, which the governor of Katchi had presented to us.

Three Lama ushers soon came and announced to us the order of the day; viz., that our luggage was to be inspected. We submitted respectfully to the orders of the Thibetian authority, and proceeded to our lodgings, accompanied by a numerous escort all the way. From the palace of the Regent to our habitation we observed great excitement; they were sweeping the streets, removing the dirt, and decorating the fronts of the houses with large strips of poulou, yellow and red. We asked ourselves what all this meant? for whom were all these demonstrations of honor and respect? Suddenly we heard behind us loud acclamations, and turning round we saw the Regent, who was advancing, mounted on a magnificent white charger, and surrounded by numerous horsemen. We arrived at our lodgings nearly at the same time with him. We opened the padlock by which the door was fastened, and requested the Regent to honor us by entering the apartments of the French missionaries.

Samdadchiemba, whom we had not seen since our audience with the Chinese ambassador, was there too. He was quite stupefied, for he could not comprehend these proceedings. The servants of the Regent, with whom he had passed the night, could not give him any information. We said to him some words of encouragement, giving him to understand that we were not yet quite on the eve of martyrdom.

The Regent took a seat in the middle of our room on a gilded chair, which had been brought from the palace for this purpose, and asked whether what he saw in our room was all we possessed? "Yes; that is all we possess; neither more nor less. These are all our resources for invading Thibet." "There is satire in your words," said the Regent; "I never fancied you such dangerous people. What is that?" he added, pointing to a crucifix we had fixed against the wall. "Ah, if you really knew what that was, you would not say that we were not formidable; for by that we design to conquer China, Tartary, and Thibet." The Regent laughed, for he only saw a joke in our words, which yet were so real and serious.

A scribe sat down at the feet of the Regent, and made

an inventory of our trunks, clothes, and kitchen implements. A lighted lamp was brought, and the Regent took from a small purse which hung from his neck, a golden seal, which was applied to all our baggage. Nothing was omitted; our old boots, the very pins of our traveling tent, were all daubed with red wax, and solemnly marked with the seal of the Talé-Lama.

When this long ceremony was completed, the Regent informed us that we must now proceed to the tribunal. Some porters were sent for, and found in very brief time. A Lama of the police had only to present himself in the street and summon, in the name of the law, all the passers by, men, women, and children, to come into the house immediately and assist the government. At Lha-Ssa, the system of enforced labor is in a most prosperous and flourishing state; the Thibetians coming into it with entire willingness and good grace.

When enough laborers were collected, all our goods were distributed among them, and the room was completely cleared, and the procession to the tribunal set out with great pomp. A Thibetian horse soldier, his drawn sword in hand, and his fusil at his side, opened the procession; after him came the troop of porters, marching between two lines of Lama satellites; the Regent, on his white charger, surrounded by a mounted guard of honor, followed our baggage; and last, behind the Regent, marched the two poor French missionaries, who had, by way of suite, a no very agreeable crowd of gapers. Our mien was not particularly imposing. Led, like malefactors, or, at least, like suspected persons, we could only lower our eyes, and modestly pass through the numerous crowd that thronged on our way. Such a position was, indeed, very painful and humiliating; but the remembrance of our holy Saviour, dragged to the pretorium, through the streets of Jerusalem, was sufficient to mitigate the bitterness with which we were afflicted. We prayed to him to sanctify our humiliations by his own, and to accept them in remembrance of his Passion.

When we arrived at the tribunal, the Chinese ambassador attended by his staff, was already in his place. The Regent addressed him: "You want to examine the effects of these strangers; here they are; examine them. These men are

Carrying Goods to the Tribunal.

neither rich, nor powerful, as you suppose." There was vexation in the tone of the Regent, and, at bottom, he was naturally enough annoyed at this part of policeman which he had to play. Ki-Chan asked us if we had no more than two trunks. "Only two; everything has been brought here; there remains in our house not a rag, not a bit of paper." "What have you got in your two trunks?" "Here are the keys; open them, empty them, and examine them at your pleasure." Ki-Chan blushed, and moved back. His Chinese delicacy was touched. "Do these trunks belong to me?" he said, with emotion. "Have I the right to open them? If anything should be missed afterwards, what would you say?" "You need not be afraid; our religion forbids us rashly to judge our neighbor." "Open your trunks yourselves; I want to know what they contain; it is my duty to do so; but you alone have the right to touch what belongs to you."

We broke the seal of the Talé-Lama, the padlock was removed, and these two trunks, which had been pierced by all eyes for a long time past, were at last opened to the general gaze. We took out the contents, one after another, and displayed them on a large table. First came some French and Latin volumes, then some Chinese and Tartar books, church linens, ornaments, sacred vases, rosaries, crosses, medals, and a magnificent collection of lithographs. All the spectators were lost in contemplation at this small European museum. They opened large eyes, touched each other with the elbow, and smacked their tongues in token of admiration. None of them had ever seen anything so beautiful, so rich, so marvelous. Everything white they considered silver, everything yellow, gold. The faces of all brightened up, and they seemed entirely to forget that we were suspected and dangerous people. The Thibetians put out their tongues and scratched their ears at us; and the Chinese made us the most sentimental bows. Our bag of medals, especially, attracted attention, and it seemed to be anticipated that, before we left the court, we should make a large distribution of these dazzling gold pieces.

The Regent and Ki-Chan, whose minds were elevated above those of the vulgar, and who certainly did not covet our treasure, nevertheless forgot their character as judges. The sight of our beautiful colored pictures transported them quite out of themselves. The Regent kept his hands joined, and preserved a continuous stare with his mouth open, whilst Ki-Chan, showing off his knowledge, explained how the French were the most distinguished artists in the world. "At one time," he said, "he knew, at Peking, a French missionary, who painted portraits that were quite alarmingly like. He kept his paper concealed in the sleeve of his robe, took the likeness as it were by stealth, and, in a whiff, all was done." Ki-Chan asked us if we had not watches, telescopes, magic-lanterns, etc., etc. We thereupon opened a small box which no one had hitherto remarked, and which contained a microscope. We adjusted its various parts, and no one had eyes but for this singular machine, in pure gold, as they took it to be, and which, certainly, was about to perform wondrous things. Ki-Chan alone knew what a microscope was. He gave an explanation of it to the public, with great pretension and vanity. He then asked us to put some animalculæ on the glass. We looked at his excellency out of the corner of the eye, and then took the microscope to pieces, joint by joint, and put it in the box. "We thought," said we to Ki-Chan, with a formal air, "we thought, that we came here to undergo judgment, and not to play a comedy." "What judgment!" exclaimed he, abruptly; "we wished to examine your effects, ascertain really who you were, and that is all." "And the maps: you do not mention them." "Oh, yes—yes! that is the great point; where are your maps?" "Here they are;" and we displayed the three maps we had; a map of the world, the two hemispheres upon the projection of Mercator, and a Chinese empire.

The appearance of these maps seemed to the Regent a clap of thunder; the poor man changed color three or four times in the course of a minute, as if we had shown our death warrant. "It is fortunate for us," said we to Ki-Chan, "that we have met with you in this country. If, by ill luck, you had not been here, we should have been utterly unable to convince the Thibetian authorities that these maps are not our own drawing. But an instructed man like yourself, conversant with European matters, will at once see that these maps are not our own work." Ki-Chan was evidently much flattered by the compliment. "Oh, it is evident," said he, at the first glance, "that these maps are printed. Look here," said he to the Regent; "these maps were not drawn by these men; they were printed in the kingdom of France. You cannot distinguish that, but I have been long used to objects, the productions of the Western Heaven." These words produced a magical effect on the Regent. His face became radiant, and he looked at us with a look of satisfaction, and made a gracious movement with his head, as much as to say, "It is well; you are honest people."

We could not get off without a little geographical lecture. We yielded charitably to the wishes of the Regent and the Chinese ambassador. We indicated with our fingers on the map of Mercator, China, Tartary, and Thibet, and all the other countries of the globe. The Regent was amazed at seeing how far we were from our native land, and what a long journey we had been obliged to make, by land and water, to come and pay him a visit in the capital of Thibet. He regarded us with astonishment, and then raised the thumb of his right hand, saying, " You are men like that," signifying, in the figurative language of the Thibetians: you are men of a superlative stamp. After recognizing the principal points of Thibet, the Regent inquired whereabouts was Calcutta? "Here," we said, pointing to a little round speck on the borders of the sea. "And Lha-Ssa; where then is Lha-Ssa?" "Here it is." The eyes and finger of the Regent went from Lha-Ssa to Calcutta, and from Calcutta to Lha-Ssa. "The Pelings of Calcutta are very near our frontiers," said he, making a grimace, and shaking his head. "No matter," he added, "here are the Himalaya mountains."

The course of geography being ended, the maps were folded up again, placed in their respective cases, and we passed on to religious subjects. Ki-Chan had long since become acquainted with these matters. When he was viceroy of the province of Pe-Tche-Ly, he had sufficiently persecuted the Christians, to have numerous opportunities of making himself familiar with everything connected with the Catholic worship; and he according now displayed his knowledge. He explained the images, the sacred vases, the ornaments. He even informed the company that in the box of holy oils there was a famous remedy for people at death's door. During all these explanations the Regent was thoughtful and abstracted; his eyes were constantly turned towards a large host-iron. These long pincers, terminating in two large lips, seemed to act powerfully on his imagination. He gave us an inquiring look, seeming to ask us if this frightful implement was not something like an infernal machine. He was only reassured upon viewing some wafers that he kept in a box, for he then comprehended the use of this strange object.

The worthy Regent was all joyous and triumphant, when he saw that we had nothing in our possession calculated to compromise us. "Well," said he to the Chinese ambassador with a sneer, "what do you think of these men? What must we do with them? These men are Frenchmen, they are ministers of the religion of the Lord of Heaven, they are honest men; we must leave them in peace." These flattering words were received in the saloon with a murmur of approbation, and the two missionaries said, from the bottom of their hearts, *Deo gratias*.

The porters shouldered our luggage, and we returned to our lodging with undoubtedly greater alacrity and lighter hearts than when we had left it. The news of our reinstatement soon spread through the town, and the Thibetian people hastened from all quarters to congratulate us. They saluted us heartily, and the French name was in every one's mouth. Thenceforward the white Azaras were entirely forgotten.

When we had refurnished our apartments we gave some Tchang-Ka to the porters, in order that they might drink our health in a pot of Thibetian small beer, and appreciate the magnanimity of the French, in not making people work for nothing.

Every one having gone away, we resumed our accustomed solitude, and solitude inducing reflection, we discovered two important things. In the first place, that we had not yet dined, and in the second, that our horses were no longer in the stable. Whilst we were considering how to get something quickly cooked, and how to find where our horses were, we saw at the threshold of our door the governor of the Katchi, who relieved us from the double embarrassment. This excellent man having foreseen that our attendance at the court of inquiry would not allow us time to make our pot boil, came, followed by two servants carrying a basket of provisions, with an ovation he had prepared for us. "And our horses—can you give us any information about them? We no longer see them in the court?" "I was going to tell you about them; they have been since yesterday evening in the Regent's stables. During your absence they have felt neither hunger nor thirst. I heard you say you intended to sell them—is it so?" "Oh, quite so, these animals ruin us; and yet they are so thin, no one will buy them." "The Regent wants to buy them." "The Regent!" "Yes, the Regent himself. Do not smile, it is no jest." "How much do you want for them?" "Oh, whatever he likes to give." "Well, then, your horses are purchased," and so saying, the Cashmerian unrolled a small packet he had under his arm, and laid upon the table two silver ingots, weighing ten ounces each." "Here," said he, "is the price of your two horses." We thought our beasts, worn and attenuated as they were, not worth the money, and we conscientiously said so to the governor of the Katchi; but it was impossible to modify the transaction which had been all settled and concluded beforehand. The Regent made out that our horses, although thin, were of an excellent breed, since they had not succumbed beneath the fatigues of our long journey. Besides, they had, in his eyes, a special value, because they had passed through many countries, and particularly because they had fed on the pastures of Kounboum, the native place of Tsong-Kaba. Twenty extra ounces of silver in our low purse was almost a fortune. We could be generous with it; so, on the spot, we took one of the ingots and placed it on Samdadchiemba's knees. "This is for you," we said; "you will be able with it to clothe yourself in holiday dress from head to foot." Samdadchiemba thanked us coldly and awkwardly; then the muscles of his face became distended, his nostrils swelled, and his large mouth assumed a smile. At last, he could not restrain his joy; he rose and made his ingot leap in the air twice or thrice, crying, "This is a famous day!" And Samdadchiemba was right. This day, so sadly begun, had been fortunate beyond anything we could have expected. We had now, at Lha-Ssa, an honorable position, and we were to be allowed to labor freely in the propagation of the gospel.

The next day was still more lucky for us than its predecessor; putting, as it were, a climax to our prosperity. In the morning we proceeded, accompanied by the Cashmerian governor, to the palace of the Regent, to whom we desired to express our gratitude for the manifestations of interest with which he had honored us. We were received with kindness and cordiality. He told us, in confidence, that the Chinese were jealous of our being at Lha-Ssa; but that we might count on his protection, and reside freely in the country, without any one having a right to interfere with us. "You are very badly lodged," added he; "your room seemed to me dirty, small, and uncomfortable. I would have strangers like you, men come from so great a distance, well treated at Lha-Ssa. In your country of France, do they not treat strangers well?" "They treat them excellently." "Oh, if you could but go there some day, you would see how our Emperor would receive you."

"Strangers are guests; you must leave your present abode; I have ordered a suitable lodging to be prepared for you in one of my houses." We accepted this generous offer with grateful thanks. To be lodged comfortably and free of expense was not a thing for men in our position to despise; but we appreciated, above all, the advantage of residing in one of the Regent's own houses. So signal a favor, such emphatic protection, on the part of the Thibetian authorities, could not but give us with the inhabitants of Lha-Ssa great moral influence, and facilitate our apostolic mission.

On leaving the palace, we proceeded, without loss of time, to visit the house which had been assigned to us; it was superb—charming. The same evening we effected our removal, and took possession of our new dwelling.

Our first care was to erect in our house a small chapel. We selected the largest and best apartment; we papered it as neatly as possible, and we then adorned it with holy images. Oh! how our hearts flowed with joy, when we were at length allowed to pray publicly at the foot of the cross, in the very heart of the capital of Buddhism, which, perhaps, had never before beheld the sign of our redemption. What a comfort to us to be able, at length, to announce the words of life to the ears of these poor people, sitting for so many ages in the shadow of death. This little chapel was certainly poor, but it was to our minds that hundredfold which God has promised to those who renounce all things for his service. Our hearts were so full, that we thought we had cheaply bought the happiness we now enjoyed, by two years of suffering and tribulation in the desert.

Every one at Lha-Ssa visited the chapel of the French Lamas; many, after satisfying themselves with asking us a few explanations as to the meaning of the images they beheld, went away, putting off till some other time further instruction in the holy doctrine of Jehovah; but several felt inwardly struck, and seemed to attach a great importance to the study of the truths we had come to announce. Every day they came to us regularly, they read with attention the summary of the Christian religion, which we had composed at the Lamasery of Kounboum, and entreated us to tell them the "true prayers."

The Thibetians were not the only persons who seemed

zealous to study our holy religion. Among the Chinese, the secretaries of the ambassador Ki-Chan often came to visit us, to hear about the great doctrine of the west; one of them, to whom we lent some works written in Tartaro-Mantchou, was convinced of the truth of Christianity and of the necessity of embracing it, but he had not courage enough to make an open profession of faith, whilst he was attached to the embassy; he wished to wait until he should be free to return to his country. God grant that his good intention may not vanish.

A physician, a native of the province of Yun-Nan, displayed more courage. This young man, since his arrival at Lha-Ssa, had led so strange a life, that every one called him the Chinese hermit. He never went out except to visit his patients, and ordinarily he only visited the poor. The wealthy in vain solicited his attendance; he disdained to notice their invitations, unless compelled by necessity to obtain some aid, for he never took anything from the poor, to whose service he had devoted himself. The time not absorbed in visiting his patients, he consecrated to study; he passed, indeed, the greater part of the night over his books. He slept little, and only took throughout the day, one single meal of barley meal, never eating meat. You needed, indeed, only to see him to be convinced that he led a hard and self-denying life; his face was extremely pale and thin, and although he was not more than thirty years old, his hair was almost entirely white.

One day, he paid us a visit while we were repeating our breviary in our little chapel; he stopped short a few steps from the door, and awaited in grave silence. A large colored image, representing the Crucifixion, had no doubt fixed his attention; for as soon as we had finished our prayers, he asked us abruptly and without staying to make the usual salutations, to explain to him the meaning of that image. When we had answered his question, he crossed his arms upon his chest, and without uttering a single word, remained motionless, his eyes fixed upon the image of the Crucifixion; he retained this position for nearly half-an-hour; at length his eyes were filled with tears. He extended his arms toward the Christ, fell on his knees, struck the earth thrice with his forehead, and rose, exclaiming, "That is the only Buddha that men ought to worship." He then turned to us, and after making a profound bow, added, "You are my masters, accept me as your disciple."

All this surprised us greatly. We could not help believing that a powerful impulse of grace had moved his heart. We briefly explained to him the principal points of the Christian religion, and to all we told him, he simply replied with an expression of faith truly astonishing, "I believe!" We presented to him a small crucifix of gilt copper, and asked him if he would accept it. His only answer was an earnest inclination of the head. As soon as he had the crucifix in his hand, he solicited us to give him a cord, and he immediately hung the cross round his neck; he then asked what prayer he ought to recite before the cross? "We will lend you," we said, "some Chinese books, wherein you will find explanations of the doctrine, and numerous forms of prayer." "My masters, that is well; but I wish to have a short and easy prayer, which I can learn immediately, and repeat often and everywhere." We taught him to say, "Jesus, Saviour of the world, have mercy on me." For fear of forgetting these words, he wrote them on a piece of paper, which he placed in a small purse, suspended from his girdle; he then went away, assuring us that the recollection of this day would never be effaced from his memory.

This young physician applied himself with ardor to learn the truths of the Christian religion; but the most remarkable circumstance was, that he took no pains to hide the faith he had in his heart. When he came to visit us, or when we met him in the streets, he always had the crucifix glittering on his breast, and he never failed to approach us with the words, "Jesus, Saviour of the world, have mercy on me." It was the form of saluting us which he had adopted.

Whilst we were making efforts to spread the evangelical seed amongst the population of Lha-Ssa, we did not neglect the endeavor to sow the divine seed also in the very palace of the Regent, and this not without the hope of reaping there one day a precious harvest. Since our trial, so to speak, our intercourse with the Regent had become frequent, and even intimate. Almost every evening, when he had finished his labors of ministry, he invited us to partake with him his Thibetian repast, to which he always added for ourselves some dishes cooked in the Chinese fashion. Our conversations generally extended far into the night.

The Regent was a man of extraordinary capacity; of humble extraction, he had raised himself gradually, and by his own merits, to the dignity of First Kalon. This had occurred three years before. Up to that time he had always fulfilled arduous and laborious functions; he had

The Regent of Lha-Ssa.

frequently traversed, in all directions, the immense regions of Thibet, either to make war or to negotiate with the neighboring states, or to inspect the conduct of the Houtouktou governors of the various provinces. So active, so busy a life, so apparently incompatible with study, had not prevented him from acquiring a profound knowledge of Lamanesque works. Every one concurred in saying that the knowledge of the most renowned Lamas was inferior to that of the Regent. The facility with which he conducted public business was matter of especial admiration. One day we were with him, when they brought him a great many rolls of paper, despatches from the provinces; a sort of secretary unrolled them one after the other, and gave them to him to read, bending on one knee. The Regent hastily ran his eye over them, without interrupting the conversation with us. As soon as he had gathered the contents of a despatch, he took his bamboo stile, and wrote his orders at the bottom of the roll, and thus transacted all his affairs with promptitude, and as if for amusement. We are not competent to judge of the literary merit that was attributed to the First Kalon. We can only say that we never saw Thibetian writing so beautiful as his.

The Regent was very fond of engaging in religious discussions, and they most frequently formed the subject of our conversations. At the commencement, he said to us these remarkable words:—"All your long journey you have undertaken solely with a religious object. You are quite right, for religion is the thing most essential to man. I see that the French and the Thibetians have the same view on that subject. We do not at all resemble the Chinese, who hold the soul of no account; yet your religion is not the same as ours. It is important we should ascertain which is the true one. Let us, then, examine both carefully and sincerely; if yours is right, we will adopt it; how could we refuse to do so? If, on the contrary, ours is the true religion, I believe you will have the good sense to follow it." This arrangement seemed to us excellent; we could not at the time desire better.

We commenced with Christianity. The Regent, always amiable and polished in his conversation with us, said that, as we were his guests, our belief ought to have the honor of priority. We successively reviewed the dogmatical and moral truths. To our great astonishment, the Regent did not seem surprised at anything we said. "Your religion," he incessantly repeated, "is conformable with ours; the truths are the same: we only differ in the explanations. Of what you have seen and heard in Tartary and Thibet, there is, doubtless, much to blame; but you must not forget that the numerous errors and superstitions you may have observed, were introduced by ignorant Lamas, and that they are rejected by well-informed Buddhists." He only admitted, between him and us, two points of difference —the origin of the world, and the transmigration of souls. The belief of the Regent, though it here and there seemed to approximate to the Catholic doctrine, nevertheless resulted in a vast pantheism; but he affirmed that we also arrived at the same result, and he did his best to convince us of this.

The Thibetian language, essentially religious and mystic, conveys with much clearness and precision all the ideas respecting the human soul and divinity. Unfortunately, we were not sufficiently versed in this language, and were compelled, in our conversations with the Regent, to have recourse to the Cashmerian governor to interpret for us; but, as he himself was not very skilful in rendering metaphysical ideas into Chinese, it was often difficult to understand each other. One day, the Regent said to us, "The truth is clear in itself, but if you envelope it in obscure words, one cannot perceive it. So long as we are obliged to communicate in Chinese, it will be impossible to make ourselves intelligible to each other. We shall never be able to discuss the matter to advantage, till you speak the Thibetian language fluently." We quite concurred in the justice of this observation. We replied to the Regent, that the study of the Thibetian tongue was a great object of solicitude with us, and that we labored hard at it every day. "If you like," said he, "I will facilitate your acquisition of it." And thereupon he called a servant and said to him a few words which we did not understand.

A youth, elegantly dressed, immediately came, and saluted us with much grace. "This is my nephew," said the Regent; "I present him to you as at once tutor and pupil; he will pass the whole day with you, and you will thus have the opportunity of practising the Thibetian language; in return, you will give him some lessons in Chinese and Mantchou." We gratefully adopted this proposition, and were enabled, by this means, to make rapid progress in the language of the country. The Regent was very fond of talking about France, during our long visits; he asked us a number of questions about the manners, customs, and productions of our country. All we told him of the steamboats, the railways, the balloons, gas, telegraphs, daguerrotype, our industrial productions, completely amazed him, and gave him an immense idea of the grandeur and power of France. One day when we were talking to him of observatories and astronomical instruments, he asked if we would allow him to examine closely the strange and curious machine which we kept in a box; he meant the microscope. As we were in a better humor and infinitely more amiable than when the officers inspected our property, we readily satisfied the curiosity of the Regent. One of us ran to our residence, and returned immediately with the wonderful instrument. While adjusting, we tried to give our auditor, as well as we could, some notions of optics, but seeing that the theory did not excite much enthusiasm, we proceeded at once to the practise. We asked if one of the company would be so good as to procure us a louse. The article was easier to find than a butterfly. A noble Lama, secretary to his excellency the First Kalon, had merely to put his hand under his silk dress to his armpit, and an extremely vigorous louse was at our disposition. We seized it by the sides with our nippers, but the Lama forthwith opposed this proceeding, and insisted upon putting a stop to the experiment, on the ground that we were going to cause the death of a living being. "Do not be afraid," we said, "your louse is only taken by the skin; besides, he seems strong enough to get over the pressure, even were it greater." The Regent, who, as we have before mentioned, had religious theories superior to those of the common herd, told the Lama to be silent, and to allow us to proceed. We continued the experiment, and fixed in the glass the poor little beast, that struggled, with all its might, at the extremity of the nippers. We then requested the Regent to apply his right eye, shutting his left, to the glass at the top of the machine. "Tsong-Kaba!" exclaimed the Regent, "the louse is as big as a rat." After looking at it for a moment, he raised his head and hid his face with both hands, saying it was horrible to look at. He tried to dissuade the others from examining it; but his influence failed to make any impression. Every one, in his turn, looked through the miscroscope, and started back with cries of horror. The Lama secretary, seeing that his little animal scarcely moved, advanced a claim in his favor. We removed the nippers, and let the louse fall into the hands of its owner. But, alas! the poor victim did not move. The

Regent said laughingly, to his secretary, "I think your louse is unwell; go and see if you can get it to take some physic, otherwise it will not recover."

No one wishing to see other living creatures, we continued the entertainment, by passing a small collection of microscopical pictures before the eyes of the spectators. Every one was charmed, and exclaimed with admiration, "What prodigious capacity the French have!" The Regent told us, "Your railways and your aerial ships no longer astonish me so much; men who can invent such a machine as that, are capable of anything."

The First Kalon was so delighted with the productions of our country, that he took a fancy to study the French language. One evening we brought him, in accordance with his wish, a French alphabet, each letter of which had the pronunciation written beneath it in Thibetian characters. He ran his eye over it, and when we proposed to give him some explanations, he replied, that they were not necessary, as what we had written was quite clear.

The next day, as soon as we appeared in his presence, he asked us what was the name of our emperor. "Our emperor is called Louis Philippe." "Louis Philippe! Louis Philippe! very well." He then took his style, and began to write. An instant afterwards he gave us a piece of paper, on which was written, in very well formed characters, LOUY-FILIPE.

During the brief period of our prosperity at Lha-Ssa, we had also tolerably intimate communication with the Chinese ambassador Ki-Chan. He sent for us twice or thrice, to talk politics, or, as the Chinese phrase it, to speak idle words. We were much surprised to find him so intimately acquainted with the affairs of Europe. He spoke a good deal about the English and Queen Victoria. "It appears," said he, "that this woman has great abilities; but her husband, in my opinion, plays a very ridiculous part; she does not let him meddle with anything. She laid out for him a magnificent garden full of fruit-trees and flowers of all sorts, and there he is always shut up, passing his time walking about. They say that in Europe there are other countries where women rule. Is it so? Are their husbands also shut up in gardens? Have you in the kingdom of France any such usage?" "No, in France the women are in the gardens, and the men in the state." "That is right, otherwise all is disorder."

Ki-Chan inquired about Palmerston; and whether he was still at the head of foreign affairs. "And Ilu,[1] what has become of him? Do you know him?" "He was recalled; your fall involved his." "That is a pity. Ilu had

Portrait of Ki-Chan.

an excellent heart, but he was devoid of prompt resolution. Has he been put to death or banished?" "Neither the one nor the other. In Europe they do not proceed to such extremities as you at Peking." "Ay, truly; your Mandarins are more fortunate than we: your government is better than ours: our Emperor cannot know everything, and yet he judges everything, and no one may presume to object. Our Emperor tells us, That is white; we prostrate ourselves and answer, Yes, that is white; he then points to the same thing, and says, That is black; we again prostrate ourselves and reply, Yes, that is black." "But if you were

[1] The Chinese name for Mr. Elliot, the English Plenipotentiary at Canton, at the commencement of the Anglo-Chinese war.

to say that a thing cannot be at once white and black?" "The Emperor would perhaps say to a person who exhibited such courage, You are right; but, at the same time, he would have him strangled or beheaded. Oh, we have not like you a general assembly of the chiefs (Tchoung-Teou-Y; so Ki-Chan designated the Chamber of Deputies). If your Emperor wished to act contrary to justice, your Tchoung-Teou-Y would be there to stop him."

Ki-Chan related to us the strange manner in which the great affair of the English in 1839 had been managed at Peking. The Emperor convoked the eight Tchoung-Tang who constituted his privy council, and spoke to them of the events that had occurred in the south. He told them that some adventurers from the western seas had manifested themselves rebellious and insubordinate; that they must be taken and punished severely, in order to give an example to all who might be tempted to imitate their misconduct. After thus stating his opinion, the Emperor asked the advice of his council. The four Mantchou Tchoung-Tang prostrated themselves and said, "Tché, tché, tché, Tchou-Dze-Ti, Fan-Fou." (Yes, yes, yes; such is the command of the master.) The four Chinese Tchoung-Tang prostrated themselves in their turn, and said, "Ché, ché, ché, Hoang-Chang-Ti, Tien-Ngen." (Yes, yes, yes; it is the celestial benefit of the Emperor.) After this, nothing further had to be said, and the council was dismissed. This anecdote is perfectly authentic, for Ki-Chan is one of the eight Tchoung-Tang of the empire. He added that, for his part, he was persuaded that the Chinese were incapable of contending against the Europeans, unless they altered their weapons and changed their old habits; but that he should take care not to say so to the Emperor, because, besides that the suggestion would be futile in itself, it would perhaps cost him his life.

Our frequent conferences with the Chinese ambassador, the Regent, and the Cashmerian governor, contributed not a little to secure for us the confidence and consideration of the inhabitants of Lha-Ssa. On seeing the number of those who came to visit us, and to be instructed in our holy religion, augment from day to day, we felt our hopes enlarge and our courage increase. Yet, amidst these consolations, one thought constantly vexed us; it was that we could not present to the Thibetians the inspiring spectacle of the pompous and touching festivals of Catholicism. We were convinced that the beauty of our ceremonies would have a powerful influence over the minds of these people, so eager after all that appertains to external worship.

The Thibetians, as we have already observed, are eminently religious; but, with the exception of a few contemplative Lamas, who withdraw to the summits of mountains and pass their lives in the hollows of rocks, they are very little disposed to mysticism. Instead of confining their devotion within their inner hearts, they like, on the contrary, display by outward acts; and accordingly pilgrimages, noisy ceremonies in the Lamaseries, prostrations on the tops of their houses, are practises extremely to their taste. They always have in their hands the Buddhist rosary, turning and twisting it, and incessantly murmur prayers, even when they are engaged in business.

There exists at Lha-Ssa a very touching custom, and which we felt a sort of jealousy at finding among infidels. In the evening, just as the day is verging on its decline, all the Thibetians stay business, and meet together, men, women and children, according to their sex and age, in the principal parts of the town, and in the public squares. As soon as groups are formed, every one kneels down, and they begin slowly and in undertones to chant prayers.

The religious concerts produced by these numerous assemblages create throughout the town an immense solemn harmony, which operates forcibly on the soul. The first time we witnessed this spectacle, we could not help drawing a painful comparison between this pagan town, where all prayed together, and the cities of Europe, where people would blush to make the sign of the cross in public. The prayer which the Thibetians chant in these evening assemblies, varies according to the seasons of the year; that, on the contrary, which they repeat on their rosary, is always the same and only consists of six syllables—*Om mani padme houm.* This formula, which the Buddhists call, by abbreviation, the *mani,* is not only in every one's mouth, but you see it written everywhere about, in the streets, in the squares, and in houses. On all the flags that float above the doors, or from the summit of the public edifices, there is always a mani printed in Landza, Tartar, and Thibetian characters.

Certain rich and zealous Buddhists maintain, at their own expense, companies of Lama sculptors, whose business it is to diffuse the mani. These singular missionaries travel, chisel and mallet in hand, over hill, dale, and desert, engraving the sacred formula upon the stones and rocks.

According to the opinion of the celebrated orientalist Klaproth, "Om mani padme houm" is merely the Thibetian transcription of a Sanscrit formula brought from India to Thibet. Towards the middle of the seventh century of our era, the famous Hindoo Tonmi-Sambhodha introduced writing into Thibet; but as the Landza alphabet, which he had at first adopted, seemed to King Srong-Bdzan-Gombo too complex and too difficult to learn, he invited the learned personage to draw up an easier writing, better adapted to the Thibetian tongue. Accordingly, Tonmi-Sambhodha shut himself up for awhile, and composed the Thibetian writing now in use, and which is merely a modification of Sanscrit characters. He also initiated the king into the mysteries of Buddhism, and communicated to him the sacred formula "Om mani padme houm," which spread rapidly through all the countries of Thibet and Mongolia.

This formula has, in the Sanscrit language, a distinct and complete meaning, which cannot be traced in the Thibetian idiom. Om is, among the Hindoos, the mystic name of the Divinity, with which all their prayers begin. It is composed of A, the name of Vishnu; of O, that of Siva; and of M, that of Brahma. This mystic particle is also equivalent to the interjection O, and expresses a profound religious conviction; it is, as it were, a formula of the act of faith; mani signifies a gem, a precious thing; padma, the lotus; padme, the vocative of the same word. Lastly, houm, is a particle expressing a wish, a desire, and is equivalent to our Amen. The literal sense, then, of this phrase is this:

Om mani padme houm.
O the gem in the lotus, Amen.

The Buddhists of Thibet and Mongolia have not been content with this clear and precise meaning, and have tortured their imaginations in their endeavors to find a mystic interpretation of each of the six syllables composing the sentence.

They have written an infinity of voluminous books, wherein

they have piled one extravagance on another, to explain their famous mani. The Lamas are wont to say that the doctrine contained in these marvelous words is immense, and that the whole life of a man is insufficient to measure its breadth and depth. We were anxious to know what the Regent thought of this formula. This is what he said on the subject: "Living beings, in Thibetian *semdchan*, and in Mongol *amitan*, are divided into six classes—angels, demons, men, quadrupeds, birds, and reptiles.[1] These six classes of living beings correspond to the six syllables of the formula 'Om mani padme houm.' Living beings, by continual transformations, and according to their merit or demerit, pass about in these six classes until they have attained the apex of perfection, when they are absorbed and lost in the grand essence of Buddha; that is to say, in the eternal and universal soul, whence emanate all souls, and wherein all souls, after their temporary evolutions, are destined to meet and become fused.

"Living beings have, according to the class to which they belong, particular means of sanctifying themselves, of rising to a superior class, of obtaining perfection, and arriving, in process of time, at the period of their absorption. Men who repeat very frequently and devotedly 'Om mani padme houm,' escape falling, after death, into the six classes of animate creatures corresponding to the six syllables of the formula, and obtain the plenitude of being by their absorption into the eternal and universal soul of Buddha."

We know not whether this explanation, which was given to us by the Regent himself, is generally adopted by the learned Buddhists of Thibet and Mongolia. We may, however, observe, as it appears to us, that it bears some analogy with the literal meaning: Oh, the gem in the lotus, Amen. The gem being the emblem of perfection, and the lotus of Buddha, it may perhaps be considered that these words express the desire to acquire perfection in order to be united with Buddha, to be absorbed in the universal soul. The symbolic formula, Oh, the gem in the lotus, Amen, might then be paraphrased thus: Oh, may I obtain perfection, and be absorbed in Buddha. Amen.

According to the explanation of the Regent, the mani

[1] The class of reptiles comprehends fish, mollusks, and all animals that are neither quadrupeds nor birds.

would be, as it were, the summary of a vast pantheism, the basis of the whole belief of the Buddhists. The learned Lamas say that Buddha is the necessary, the independent Being, the Beginning and End of all things. The earth, the stars, mankind, everything that exists is a partial and temporal manifestation of Buddha. Everything was created by Buddha; in this sense, that everything proceeds from him, as light proceeds from the sun. All creatures sprung from Buddha, have had a beginning, and will have an end; but in the same way that they have necessarily sprung from the universal essence, they will necessarily return to it. It is as the rivers and the torrents produced by the waters of the sea, and which, after a course, more or less long, proceed again to lose themselves in its immensity. So Buddha is eternal; his manifestations also are eternal; but in this sense, that there have been manifestations, and that there always will be manifestations, though taken separately, they have a beginning and an end.

Without inquiring too nicely whether this agrees or not with what precedes, the Buddhists admit, besides, an unlimited number of divine incarnations. They say that Buddha assumes a human body, and comes to dwell among men, in order to aid them in acquiring perfection, and to facilitate for them their reunion with the universal soul. These Living Buddhas constitute the numerous class of Chaberons, whom we have frequently noticed before. The most celebrated Living Buddhas are—at Lha-Ssa, the Talé-Lama; at Djachi-Loumbo, the Bandchan-Remboutchi; at the Grand Kouren, the Guison-Tamba; at Peking, the Tchang-Kia-Fo, a sort of grand almoner of the imperial court; and in the country of the Ssamba, at the foot of the Himalaya mountains, the Sa-Dcha-Fo. This last has, they say, a somewhat singular mission. He prays night and day, in order to get the snow to fall continuously on the summit of the Himalaya; for, according to a Thibetian tradition, there exists behind these lofty mountains a savage and cruel people, who only await the subsidence of the snow to come over and massacre the Thibetian tribes, and to take possession of the country.

Although all the Chaberons are, without distinction, Living Buddhas, there is, nevertheless, among them, a hierarchy, of which the Talé-Lama is the head. All the rest acknowledge, or ought to acknowledge, his supremacy. The present Talé,Lama, as we have said, is a child of nine years old, and he has now for six years occupied the palace of the Buddha-La. He is a Si-Fan by birth, and was taken from a poor and obscure family of the principality of Ming-Tchen-Tou-Sse.

When the Talé-Lama dies, or to speak Buddhickly, when he has laid aside his human envelope, they proceed to the election of his successor, in the following manner: Prayers are directed to be offered up, and fasts to be performed in all the Lamaseries. The inhabitants of Lha-Ssa especially, as being the most interested in the affair, redouble their zeal and devotion. Every one goes a pilgrimage round the Buddha-La and the "City of Spirits." The Tchu-Kors are perpetually turning in everybody's hands, the sacred formula of the mani re-echoes day and night, in all the streets of the town, and perfumes are burnt in profusion everywhere. Those who think they possess the Talé-Lama in their family, give information of the belief to the authorities of Lha-Ssa, in order that there may be established, in the children so indicated, their quality of Chaberons. In order to be able to proceed to the election of the Talé-Lama, there must be discovered three Chaberons, authentically recognized as such. The candidates come to Lha-Ssa, and the Houtouktous of the Lamanesque states meet in assembly. They shut themselves up in a temple of the Buddha-La, and pass six days in retirement, fasting and praying. On the seventh day, they take a golden urn, containing three fish, likewise of gold, upon which are engraved the names of the three little candidates for the functions of the divinity of the Buddha-La. They shake the urn, the eldest of the Houtouktous draws out a fish, and the child whose name is thus designated by lot is immediately proclaimed Talé-Lama. He is then conducted, in great pomp, to the street of the City of Spirits, every one devoutly prostrating himself on his passage, and is placed in his sanctuary.

The two Chaberons in swaddling clothes, who have contested for the place of Talé-Lama, are carried back by their nurses to their respective families; but to compensate them for not having succeeded, government makes them a present of 500 ounces of silver.

The Talé-Lama is venerated by the Thibetians and the Mongols like a divinity. The influence he exercises over the Buddhist population is truly astonishing; but still it is going too far to say that his excrements are respectfully collected, and made into amulets which devotees enclose in pouches and carry round their necks. It is equally untrue that the Talé-Lama has his arms and head encircled with serpents, in order to strike the imagination of his worshippers. These assertions, which we read in some geographies, are entirely without foundation. During our stay at Lha-Ssa, we asked a good many questions on this point, and every one laughed in our faces. Unless it could be made out that, from the Regent to our argol merchant, all conspired to hide the truth from us, it must be admitted that the narratives, which have given circulation to such fables, were written with but very little caution.

It was not possible for us to get a sight of the Talé-Lama; not that there is any great difficulty made in admitting the curious, or devotees, to see him, but we were prevented by a rather singular circumstance. The Regent had promised to take us to Buddha-La, and we were upon the point of fulfilling this notable visit, when all of a sudden an alarm was started that we should give the Talé-Lama the smallpox. This malady had in fact, just manifested itself at Lha-Ssa, and the people declared that it had been brought from Peking, by the great caravan which arrived a few days before. As we had formed part of that caravan, we were asked whether it would not be better to postpone our visit, in order that we might not expose the Talé-Lama to the risk of catching the disease. The proposition was too reasonable to admit of our making any objection.

The fear which the Thibetians have of the smallpox is something inconceivable. They never mention its name even, without a sort of stupor, as though they were speaking of the greatest scourge that could by possibility desolate mankind. And, indeed, there is no year in which this malady does not make fearful ravages at Lha-Ssa, and the only remedy which has hitherto suggested itself to the government as a preservative for the population against this fearful epidemic, is to proscribe the wretched families who are seized with it. As soon as the smallpox has declared itself in a house, all the inhabitants must dislodge, and repair, whether they will or not, far from the city to the summits of the mountains, or the depths of the valleys. No one may hold any communication whatever with the poor wretches, who soon die of hunger and privation, or become the prey of wild beasts. We did not fail to make the Regent acquainted with the precious means used by the European nations to preserve themselves from the disorder; and one of the chief circumstances which procured for us the good-will and protection of the Regent, was his hope that we might one day introduce vaccination into Thibet. The missionary who should be fortunate enough to endow the Thibetians with so invaluable a blessing, would assuredly acquire over their minds an influence capable of competing with that of the Talé-Lama itself. The introduction of vaccination into Thibet by the missionaries would, not improbably, be the signal of the downfall of Lamanism, and of the establishment of the Christian religion among these infidel tribes.

People afflicted with the itch and leprosy, are numerous at Lha-Ssa. These cutaneous diseases are engendered by the want of cleanliness, more peculiarly prevalent among the lower classes of the population. Cases of hydrophobia are not unfrequent among the Thibetians; and one is only surprised that this horrible malady does not commit greater ravages, when one bears in mind the terrible multitudes of gaunt, famishing dogs that are always prowling about the streets of Lha-Ssa. These animals, in fact, are so numerous in that city, that the Chinese contemptuously say, that the three great products of the capital of Thibet, are Lamas, women, and dogs—Lama, Ya-Teou, Keou.

This marvelous infinitude of dogs arises from the extreme respect which the Thibetians have for these animals, and the use to which they apply them in burying the dead. There are four different species of sepulture practised in Thibet; the first, combustion; the second, immersion in the rivers and lakes; the third, exposure on the summit of mountains; and the fourth, which is considered the most complimentary of all, consists in cutting the dead body in pieces, and giving these to be eaten by the dogs. The last method is by far the most popular. The poor have only as their mausoleum the common vagabond dogs of the locality; but the more distinguished defunct are treated with greater ceremony. In all the Lamaseries, a number of dogs are kept *ad hoc*, and within them the rich Thibetians are buried.[1]

[1] Strabo, speaking of the customs of the nomadic Scythians, as retained among the Sogdians and Bactrians, writes: "In the capital of Bactria, they breed dogs, to which they give a special name, which name, rendered into our language, means buriers. The business of these dogs is to eat up all persons who are beginning to fall into decay, from old age or sickness. Hence it is that no tomb is visible in the suburbs of the town, while the town itself is all filled with human bones. It is said that Alexander abolished this custom."

Cicero attributes the same custom to the Hyrcanians, in his "Tusculan Questions" (Lib. i. § 45): "In Hyrcania plebs publicos alit canes; optimates, domesticos. Nobile autem genus canum illud scimus esse. Sed pro sua quisque facultate parat, à quibus lanietur: eamque optimam illi esse censent sepulturam."

Justin also says of the Parthians: "Sepultura vulgo aut avium aut canum laniatus est. Nuda demum ossa terrà obruunt."

Chinese and Tartar Female head-dresses.

Thibetian Theater.

CHAPTER VII.

Notice of Moorcroft the English Traveler—Routes between Lha-Ssa and Europe—Discussion with the Chinese Ambassador—Contest between the Regent and Ki-Chan about us—Our expulsion from Lha-Ssa determined on—Protest against this arbitrary measure—Report of Ki-Chan to the Emperor of China—System of Chronology in use in Thibet—New Thibetian Year—Festivals and rejoicings—Buddhist Monasteries of the Province of Oui—Khaldan—Preboung—Sera—Farewell of the Regent—Separation from Samdadchiemba—Ly, the Pacificator of Kingdoms—Triple Address of the Chinese Ambassador—Picturesque adieu between the Ly-Kouo-Ngan and his Wife—Departure from Lha-Ssa for Canton—Crossing a River in a Leathern Boat.

WE have already referred to the travels of Moorcroft in Thibet, in noticing the excessive fear with which the designers and makers of geographical charts inspire the Thibetian government. One day, the governor of the Cashmerians brought to us one of his fellow countrymen, named Nisan, who had been for a long time the servant of Moorcroft at Lha-Ssa. He talked to us at some length about his old master, and the details he gave us confirmed all that had already been related to us. The adventures of this English traveler appearing to us too singular to be passed over wholly in silence, we have thought proper to give a short review of them.

According to the statements collected in the capital of Thibet itself, Moorcroft arrived from Ladak at Lha-Ssa in the year 1826; he wore the Mussulman dress, and spoke the Farsie language, expressing himself in that idiom with so much facility that the Cashmerians of Lha-Ssa took him for one of their countrymen. He hired a house in the town, where he lived for twelve years with his servant Nisan, whom he had brought from Ladak, and who himself thought that his master was a Cashmerian. Moorcroft had purchased a few herds of goats and oxen, which he had confided to the care of some Thibetian shepherds, who dwelt in the gorges of the mountains, about Lha-Ssa. Under the pretext of inspecting his herds, the feigned Mussulman went freely about the country, making drawings and preparing his geographical charts. It is said that never having learnt the Thibetian language, he abstained from holding direct communication with the people of the country. At last, having dwelt for twelve years at Lha-Ssa, Moorcroft took his way back to Ladak, but whilst he was in the province of Ngari, he was attacked by a troop of brigands who assassinated him. The perpetrators of this murder were pursued and arrested by the Thibetian government, who recovered a portion of the property of the English traveler, among which was a collection of geographical designs and charts. It was only then, and upon sight of these objects, that the authorities of Lha-Ssa found out that Moorcroft was an Englishman.

Before separating from his servant, Moorcroft had given him a note, telling him to show it to the inhabitants of Calcutta, if he ever went to that city, and that it would suffice to make his fortune. It was doubtless a letter of recommendation. The seizure of the effects of Moorcroft created such a disturbance in Thibet, that Nisan, afraid of being compromised, destroyed his letter of recommendation. He told us himself that this note was written in characters exactly similar to ours.

The facts we have here related, we derive from the Regent, from the Cashmerian governor, from Nisan, and from several other inhabitants of Lha-Ssa. Before reaching this town, we had never heard of Moorcroft; it was there we first learned the name of this English traveler. From what we have stated, it may be considered established that Moorcroft really went to Lha-Ssa in 1826, that he resided there for twelve years, and that he was afterwards assassinated on the road to Ladak from Lha-Ssa.

Let us turn now, however, to other information, extremely discrepant from that which was given us in the capital of Thibet. According to the "Universal Geography" of Charles Ritter,[1] Moorcroft made first a journey in 1812, which lasted two months; he was afterwards directed by the Company to procure horses from Turkestan, wherewith to improve the breed of horses in India. For this purpose he undertook a second journey in November, 1819; he got as far as Ladak, where he remained two years. In the month of October, 1822, he left that town for Cashmere, and on the 25th of August, 1825, died at Andkou, on the way from Herat to Balk. The death of Moorcroft, at the date and place stated by Charles Ritter, was announced by his fellow-traveler, M. Tribeck, in a letter dated Balk, 6th September, 1825, and addressed to Captain Wade, the resident at Loudiana.[2]

We confess that we cannot possibly reconcile such opposite statements. If Moorcroft was really not at Lha-Ssa, how is it that he was so well known there, and that the people there speak of his residence among them in terms so precise? What interest could the Thibetians have in forging such a tale? On the other hand, if Moorcroft was at Lha-Ssa, how can we explain that letter of M. Tribeck, which announces that his fellow-traveler died in 1825, exactly at the time when, according to the other hypothesis, he was on his way to the capital of Thibet?

Without pretending to reconcile these contradictions, we will cite a fact which concerns ourselves, and which will, perhaps, seem to bear some relation to the affair of Moorcroft. Some time after our arrival at Macao, we read the following

[1] "Asia," vol. v., p. 800, German edition, 1833–1837.

[2] See "Asiatic Journal of London," vol. xxi., p. 786, and vol. xxii., p. 596. A notice of Moorcroft's manuscripts was inserted in the "Journal of the Geographical Society of London," 1831.

article in the "Bengal Catholic Herald,"[1] a journal printed at Calcutta. "Canton the 12th September. The French missionaries of our city have lately received the news of the deplorable death of two fathers of their mission in Mongol-Tartary." After a cursory sketch of the Mongol-Chinese territory, the writer of the article proceeds thus :—" A French Lazarist called Huc arrived, about three years ago, amongst some Chinese families, who were established in the valley of Black Waters, about two hundred leagues journey from the Great Wall. Another Lazarist, whose name is unknown to me,[2] joined him in the plan of forming a mission among the Mongol Buddhists. They studied the Mongol language with the Lamas of the neighboring Lamaseries. It seems that they were taken for foreign Lamas, and were treated in a friendly manner, particularly by the Buddhists, who are very ignorant, and who mistook the Latin of their breviaries for Sanscrit, which they do not understand, but for which they have a secret veneration, because the rites of their religious books, in Mongol, translated from the Sanscrit, are printed in red ink.

"When the missionaries thought themselves sufficiently learned in the language, they advanced into the interior, with the intention of commencing their work of conversion. From that time only uncertain rumors were heard about them, but in May last, from the interior of Mongol-Tartary, the news came that they had been tied to horses' tails and so dragged to death. The real causes of this event are not as yet known."

Whilst they were thus announcing our death so positively, we were approaching the termination of our long journey, and were close upon Canton, happily enjoying a health fully capable of refuting the news thus propagated concerning us. But if, by chance, we had perished among the mountains of Thibet, if we had been murdered there, the world would have remained convinced that we had been tied to horses' tails and had died in Mongolia. It would probably have never been believed that we had reached the capital of Thibet; and if, at some later time, some European traveler had visited Lha-Ssa, and had been informed of our abode in that town, it would have been, perhaps, just as difficult to reconcile these statements, as those respecting Moorcroft.

[1] Vol. xii., No. 9, p. 120. [2] M. Gabet.

Although the death of the English traveler is a matter which we cannot clear up, we did not conceive that we could omit to say what we knew of it, without pretending to invalidate, by the accounts collected at Lha-Ssa, the documents set forth in the scientific London journals.

We were scarcely a month at Lha-Ssa before the numerous inhabitants of this town grew accustomed to speak with respect and admiration of the holy doctrine of Jehovah, and of the great kingdom of France. The peace and tranquillity we enjoyed, the distinguished protection which the Thibetian government extended to us, the sympathy with which the people seemed to surround us, all inspired us with the hope, that, by the aid of God, we might lay in the very capital of Buddhism the foundation of a mission, the influence of which would soon extend itself among the nomad tribes of Mongolia. The moment seemed to have come when the Tartar pilgrims might at length learn, at Lha-Ssa, the only doctrine which can save men's souls, and civilize nations.

As soon as we considered our position at Lha-Ssa confirmed, we turned our thoughts to the means of renewing our communications with Europe in the speediest manner. The path of the desert was impracticable. We had, certainly, managed to cross once, and as it were by a miracle, these steppes infested by brigands and wild beasts; but it was out of the question to think of organizing a service of couriers along that frightful route. Supposing, besides, the fullest security that could be desired, the mere length of the journey was a thing to make one shudder. The road by India seemed alone practicable. From Lha-Ssa to the first English station is not quite a month's journey. By establishing one correspondent on the other side of the Himalaya mountains, and one at Calcutta, our communication with France would become, if not prompt and easy, at all events feasible. As this plan could only be put into execution with the consent of the Thibetian government, we communicated it to the Regent, who immediately entered into our views, and it was agreed that in the summer M. Gabet should undertake the journey to Calcutta, with a Thibetian escort, which was to accompany him as far as Boutan.

Such were the plans we were forming for the establishment of a mission at Lha-Ssa; but at this very moment the enemy to all good was hard at work to ruin our projects, and to remove us from a country which he seems to have chosen for the seat of his empire. Having heard here and there words of evil auspice, we comprehended that the Chinese ambassador was secretly plotting our expulsion from Thibet. The vague rumor of this persecution had, in fact, nothing about it to surprise us. From the outset we had foreseen that if difficulties assailed us, they would emanate from the Chinese Mandarins. Ki-Chan, in fact, could not bear to see the Thibetian government receive with so much favor a religion and strangers, whom the absurd prejudices of China have so long driven from her frontiers. Christianity and the French name excited too forcibly the sympathy of the people of Lha-Ssa, not to arouse Chinese jealousy. An agent of the court of Peking could not, without anger, reflect on the popularity which strangers enjoyed in Thibet, and on the influence which they might one day exercise in a country which China has every interest in keeping under her dominion. It was determined, therefore, that the preachers of the religion of the Lord of Heaven should be driven from Lha-Ssa.

One day, the ambassador, Ki-Chan, sent for us, and after sundry attempts at cajolery, ended by saying that Thibet was too cold, too poor a country for us, and that we had better think of returning to our kingdom of France. Ki-Chan addressed these words to us, with a sort of indifferent, careless manner, as though he supposed there could be no sort of objection to them. We asked him if, in speaking thus, he proposed to us advice or command. "Both the one and the other," he replied, coldly. "Since it is so, we have first to thank you for the interest which you seem to have in our welfare, in telling us that this country is cold and miserable. But you must know, that men such as we do not regard the good and conveniences of this world; were it not so, we should have remained in our own kingdom of France. For know, there is not anywhere a country comparable with our own. As for the imperative portion of your words, this is our answer: 'Admitted into Thibet by the local authority, we recognize no right in you, or in any other person, to disturb our abode here.'" "How! you, who are strangers, presume still to remain here?"

"Yes, we are strangers, but we know that the laws of Thibet are not like those of China. The Peboun, the Katchi, the Mongols, are strangers like us, and yet they are permitted to live here in peace; no one disturbs them. What, then, is the meaning of this arbitrary proceeding of yours, in ordering Frenchmen from a country open to all people? If foreigners are to quit Lha-Ssa, why do you stay here? Does not your title of Kin-Tchai (ambassador) distinctly announce that you yourself are but a foreigner here?" At these words, Ki-Chan bounded on his velvet cushion. "I a foreigner!" cried he, "a foreigner! I, who bear the authority of the Grand Emperor, who, only a few months since, condemned and exiled the Nomekhan." "We are acquainted with that affair. There is this difference between the Nomekhan and us, that the Nomekhan came from Kan-Sou, a province of the empire, and we come from France, where your Grand Emperor is nobody; and that the Nomekhan assassinated three Talé-Lamas, while we have done no injury to any man. Have we any other aim than to make known to men the true God, and to teach them the way to save their souls?" "Ay, as I have already said to you, I believe you to be honest people; but then the religion you preach has been declared wicked, and prohibited by our Grand Emperor." "To these words, we can only reply thus: The religion of the Lord of Heaven does not need the sanction of your Emperor to make it a holy religion, any more than we, of its mission, need it to come and preach in Thibet." The Chinese ambassador did not think it expedient to continue this discussion; he dryly dismissed us, declaring that we might rest assured he would make us quit Thibet. We hastened to the Regent, in order to acquaint him with the melancholy interview we had had with Ki-Chan. The chief Kalon had been made aware of the projects of persecution which the Chinese Mandarins were hatching against us. He endeavored to reassure us, and told us, that protecting in the country thousands of strangers, he was powerful enough to give us the protection which the Thibetian government extended to all. "Besides," added he, "even though our laws did prohibit strangers from entering our country, those laws could not affect you. Religious persons, men of prayer, belonging to all countries, are strangers nowhere; such is the doctrine taught by our holy books. It is written: 'The yellow coat has no country, the Lama no family.' Lha-Ssa being the peculiar assembling-place and abode of men of prayer, that title of itself should always secure for you liberty and protection." This opinion of the Buddhists, which constitutes a religious man a cosmopolite, is not merely a mystic idea written in books, but we have found it recognized in the manners and customs of the Lamaseries; when a man has had his head shaved, and assumes the religious habit, he renounces his former name to take a new one. If you ask a Lama of what country he is, he replies, "I have no country, but I pass my time in such a Lamasery." This manner of thinking and acting is even admitted in China, amongst the bonzes and other classes of religionists, who are called by the generic name of Tchou-Kia-Jin (a man who has left his family).

There was, respecting us, a controversy of several days' duration, between the Thibetian government and the Chinese ambassador. Ki-Chan, in order to insure better success to his aim, assumed the character of defender of the Talé-Lama. This was his argument: Sent to Lha-Ssa by his Emperor, to protect the Living Buddha, it was his duty to remove from him whatever was calculated to injure him. Certain preachers of the religion of the Lord of Heaven, animated, no doubt, by excellent intentions, were propagating a doctrine which, in the end, tended to destroy the authority and power of the Talé-Lama. Their avowed purpose was to substitute their religious belief for Buddhism, and to convert all the inhabitants of Thibet of every age, condition, and sex. What would become of the Talé-Lama when he had no worshipers? The introduction into the country of the religion of the Lord of Heaven, does it not lead directly to the destruction of the sanctuary of the Buddha-La, and consequently, to the downfall of the Lamanesque hierarchy and the Thibetian government? "I," said he, "who am here to protect the Talé-Lama, can I permit, at Lha-Ssa, men who propagate such formidable doctrines? When those doctrines have taken root, and it is no longer possible to extirpate them, who will be responsible for such a misfortune? What shall I reply to the Grand Emperor, when he shall reproach me with my negligence and cowardice? You Thibetians," said he to the Regent, "you do not comprehend the gravity of this matter. Because these men are virtuous and irreproachable, you think they are harmless—it is a mistake. If they remain long at Lha-Ssa, they will spell-bind you. Among you, there is not a man capable of disputing with them upon religion. You will not be able to keep from adopting their belief, and then the Talé-Lama is undone."

The Regent did not enter at all into these apprehensions, with which the Chinese ambassador endeavored to inspire him. He maintained that our presence at Lha-Ssa could not in any way be prejudicial to the Thibetian government. "If the doctrine which these men hold," said he, "is a false doctrine, the Thibetians will not embrace it; if, on the contrary, it is true, what have we to fear? How can the truth be prejudicial to men? These two Lamas of the kingdom of France," he added, "have not done any harm; they are animated with the best intentions towards us. Can we, without good ground, deprive them of the liberty and protection which we extend here to all strangers, and particularly to men of prayer? Can we make ourselves guilty of an actual and certain injustice, through an imaginary fear of some possible evil to come?"

Ki-Chan reproached the Regent with neglecting the interests of the Talé-Lama, and the Regent on his part accused Ki-Chan of taking advantage of the minority of the sovereign to tyrannize over the Thibetian government. For our parts, in this unfortunate contest, we refused to acknowledge the authority of the Chinese Mandarin, and declared that we would not quit the country without a formal order from the Regent, who assured us that they should never extort from him any such thing.

The quarrel became more and more exacerbate every day. Ki-Chan resolved to take on himself to expel us from the country. Matters had come to such a crisis, that prudence obliged us to yield to circumstances, and to oppose no further resistance, for fear of compromising the Regent, and of becoming, perhaps, the cause of lamentable dissensions between China and Thibet. By further opposing this unjust persecution, we might irritate too vehemently the Chinese, and furnish pretexts for their project of usurping the Thibetian government. If, on our account, a rupture unhappily broke out between Lha-Ssa and Peking, we should inevitably be held responsible for it; we should become odious in the eyes of the Thibetians, and the introduction of Christianity into these countries would be encountered hereafter with greater difficulties than ever. We therefore considered that it would be better to submit, and to accept with resignation the crown of persecution. Our conduct should prove to the Thibetians, that at least we had come among them with peaceful intentions, and that we did not intend to establish ourselves there by violence.

Another consideration helped to confirm our resolution. It occurred to us that this very tyranny which the Chinese exercised against us might perhaps be the ultimate occasion of our missionaries establishing themselves in Thibet with security. In our simplicity, we imagined that the French government would not see with indifference this monstrous assumption of China, in daring to persecute Christianity and the French name even among foreign nations, and at a distance of more than a thousand leagues from Peking. We were persuaded that the representative of France at Canton, could not omit to make emphatic remonstrances to the Chinese authorities, and that he would obtain just reparation for the violence with which we had been treated. In thinking thus, we poor and obscure missionaries were far from wishing to give ourselves, in our own eyes, the least personal importance; but we do not disguise it, we were proud in the belief that our position as Frenchmen would be a sufficient title for our obtaining the protection of the government of our country.

After having maturely considered these points, we proceeded to the Regent. On learning that we had determined to leave Lha-Ssa, he seemed sad and embarrassed. He told us he greatly wished he had it in his power to secure for us a free and tranquil abode in Thibet; but that alone, and without the support of his sovereign, he had found himself too weak to resist the tyranny of the Chinese, who for several years past, taking advantage of the infancy of the Talé-Lama, had assumed unprecedented claims in the country. We thanked the Regent for his good-will, and left him to wait upon the Chinese ambassador.

We told Ki-Chan that, at a distance from all protection, we had resolved to leave Lha-Ssa, since he was determined to compel us to do so; but that we protested against this violation of our rights. "Well, well," answered Ki-Chan, "you cannot do better; you must depart; it will be better for you, better for the Thibetians, better for me, better for everybody." He then told us that he had ordered all preparations to be made for our departure; that the Mandarin and escort who were to accompany us had been selected. It had even been arranged that we should depart in eight days, and that they should take us along the route which leads to the frontiers of China. This last arrangement excited at once our indignation and surprise; it was inconceivable how they could have the cruelty to condemn us to a journey of eight months, whilst by proceeding towards India twenty-five days' march would suffice to carry us to the first European station, whence we could not fail to find means, both secure and easy, for reaching Calcutta. We forthwith and vehemently protested against the project, but our protest was disregarded, as was the request for some few additional days' rest, after the long journey we had just made, and to give time for the closing of the great wounds caused by the cold of the desert. All we could say to mollify the cruelty of the Chinese ambassador was unavailing.

We then laid aside our suppliant tone, and declared to the delegate of the court of Peking, that we yielded to violence, but that we would denounce to our government: first, that the Chinese ambassador, installed at Lha-Ssa, had arbitrarily and violently driven us thence, under the vain pretext that we were strangers and preachers of the Christian religion, which he called wicked and repudiated by his Emperor. In the second place, that in opposition to all right and all justice, he had prevented us from pursuing an easy and direct route, of only twenty-five days' journey, to drag us tyrannically into the interior of China, and make us undergo the hardships of an eight months' journey. Finally, that we would denounce to our government the barbarity with which they forced us to set out, without allowing us a little rest, a barbarity which, in our then state, we had a right to consider as an attempt upon our life. Ki-Chan replied that he had nothing to do with what the French government might think or do, that in his conduct he had only to regard the will of his Emperor. "If my master," he said, "knew that I had permitted two Europeans freely to preach the religion of the Lord of Heaven in Thibet, I should be lost. It would not be possible for me to escape death."

The next day, Ki-Chan sent for us in order to communicate to us a report he had drawn up on the subject of our affairs; and which he proposed to lay before the Emperor. "I did not wish," said he, "to let it go without reading it to you previously, for fear there should have escaped me in it any expressions inexact in themselves or distasteful to you." Having attained his chief object, Ki-Chan had resumed his amiable and conciliatory manner towards us. His report was unmeaning enough; what it said about us was neither good nor bad; it simply set forth a dry nomenclature of the countries we had passed through, since our departure from Macao. "Is this report as you like it?" said Ki-Chan; "do you see anything in it to alter?" M. Huc answered, that he had an observation to make of great importance. "Speak, I listen." "What I have to say to you does not interest us in the least; but it affects you very nearly." "Let us hear what it is." "My communication must be private: let your people withdraw." "These men are my servants; they all belong to my household; fear nothing." "Oh, it is not we who have anything to fear; all the danger is to you." "The danger to me! No matter, the officers of my suite may hear all." "If you will, you can repeat to them what I have to say; but I cannot speak in their presence." "Mandarins cannot hold secret conversations with strangers; it is forbidden by the laws." "In that case, I have nothing to tell you; send the report just as it is; but if it brings misfortune upon you, only blame yourself." The Chinese ambassador became pensive; he took infinite pinches of snuff, one after another, and then, as the result of long reflection, told his suite to retire, and to leave us alone with him.

When every one had gone, M. Huc began: "Now," said he to Ki-Chan, "you will understand why I wished to speak to you in private, and how important it is to you that no one should hear what I have to tell you. You will judge if we are dangerous men, we who fear even to injure our persecutors." Ki-Chan was pale and disconcerted. "Let us hear," said he; "explain yourself—let your words be candid and clear; what would you say?" "In your report, there is an inexactitude; you make me set out from Macao with my brother Joseph Gabet, and yet I did not enter China till four years after him." "Oh, if that is all, it is easy to correct it." "Yes, very easy. This report, you say, is for your Emperor; is it not so?" "Certainly." "In that case, it is your duty to tell the Emperor the truth and nothing but the truth." "Oh, nothing but the truth; let us correct the report. At what period did you enter China?" "In the twentieth year of Tao-Kouang (1840)." Ki-Chan took his pencil and wrote in the margin—twentieth year of Tao-Kouang. "What moon?" "The second moon." Ki-Chan hearing us speak of the second moon, laid down his pencil and looked at us with a fixed stare. "Yes, I entered the Chinese empire in the twentieth year of Tao-Kouang, in the second moon; I passed through the province of Canton, of which you were at that time viceroy. Why do you not write? are you not to tell all the truth to the Emperor?" The face of Ki-Chan contracted. "Do you see now why I wished to talk to you in private?" "Yes, I know the Christians are good people—does any one here know of this matter?" "No, not any one." Ki-Chan took the report, tore it up; he wrote a fresh one, entirely different from the first. The dates of our first entry into China were not exactly set forth, and there was a pompous eulogium on our knowledge and sanctity. The poor man had been simple enough to believe that we attached a great importance to his Emperor's good opinion of us.

In accordance with the orders of Ki-Chan, we were to set out after the festivals of the Thibetian new year. We had only been at Lha-Ssa two months, and we had already passed the new year twice, first the European new year, and then the Chinese; it was now the turn of the Thibetian. Although at Lha-Ssa, they reckon the year as in China, according to the lunar system, yet the calendars of these two countries do not agree: that of Lha-Ssa is always a month behind that of Peking. It is known that the Chinese, the Mongols, and most of the peoples of Eastern Asia, make use in their chronological calculations of a sexagenary cycle, composed of ten signs called trunks, and of twelve signs which bear the name of branches. Among the Tartars and Thibetians, the signs of the denary cycle are expressed by the names of the five elements repeated twice, or by the names of the five colors with their shades. The names of twelve animals denote the duodenary cycle.

DENARY CYCLE.

Mongol.	Thibetian.	
1. Moto.	Cheng.	Wood.
2. Moto.	Cheng.	Wood.
3. Gal.	Mé.	Fire.
4. Gal.	Mé.	Fire.
5. Chéré.	Sa.	Earth.
6. Chéré.	Sa.	Earth.
7. Témur.	Dchak.	Iron.
8. Témur.	Dchak.	Iron.
9. Oussou.	Tchon.	Water.
10. Oussou.	Tchon.	Water.

DUODENARY CYCLE.

Mongol.	Thibetian.	
1. Khouloukhana.	Chi-wa.	Mouse.
2. Oukhere.	Lang.	Ox.
3. Bara.	Tak.	Tiger.
4. Tolé.	Yen.	Hare.
5. Lou.	Dchouk.	Dragon.
6. Mokhé.	Phroul.	Serpent.
7. Mori.	Rta.	Horse.
8. Khoui.	Lonk.	Ram.
9. Betchi.	Preou.	Monkey.
10. Takia.	Chia.	Fowl.
11. Nokhé	Dchi.	Dog.
12. Khakhé.	Phak.	Pig.

To form the sexagenary cycle, the two first cycles are combined in the following manner:—

SEXAGENARY CYCLE.

Mongol.	
1. Moto khouloukhana.	Wooden mouse.
2. Moto oukere.	Wooden ox.
3. Gal bara.	Fire tiger.
4. Gal tolé.	Fire hare.
5. Chéré lou.	Earth dragon.
6. Chéré Mokhé.	Earth serpent.

MONGOL. (*Continued.*)

7. Temur mori.	Iron horse.
8. Temur knoui.	Iron ram.
9. Oussou betchi.	Water monkey.
10. Oussou takia.	Water fowl.
11. Moto nokhé.	Wooden dog.
12. Moto khakhé.	Wooden pig.
13. Gal khouloukhana.	Fire mouse.
14. Gal oukhere.	Fire ox.
15. Chéré bara.	Earth tiger.
16. Chéré tolé.	Earth hare.
17. Témur lou.	Iron dragon.
18. Témur mokhé.	Iron serpent.
19. Oussou mori.	Water horse.
20. Oussou khoui.	Water ram.
21. Moto betchi.	Wooden monkey.
22. Moto takia.	Wooden fowl.
23. Gal nokhé.	Fire dog.
24. Gal khakhé.	Fire pig.
25. Chéré khouloukhana.	Earth mouse.
26. Chéré oukhéré.	Earth ox.
27. Temur bara.	Iron tiger.
28. Temur tolé.	Iron hare.
29. Oussou lou.	Water dragon.
30. Oussou makhé.	Water serpent.
31. Moto mori.	Wooden horse.
32. Moto khoui.	Wooden ram.
33. Gal betchi.	Fire monkey.
34. Gal takia.	Fire chicken.
35. Chéré nokhé.	Earth dog.
36. Chéré khakhé	Earth pig.
37. Temur khouloukhana.	Iron mouse.
38. Temur oukhere.	Iron ox.
39. Oussou bara.	Water tiger.
40. Oussou tolé.	Water hare.
41. Moto lou.	Wooden dragon.
42. Moto mokhé.	Wooden serpent.
43. Gal mori.	Fire horse.
44. Gal khoui.	Fire ram.
45. Chéré betchi.	Earth monkey.
46. Chéré takia	Earth fowl.
47. Temur nokhé.	Iron dog.
48. Temur khakhé.	Iron pig.

MONGOL. (*Continued.*)

49. Oussou khouloukhana.	Water mouse.
50. Oussou oukhere.	Water ox.
51. Moto bara.	Wooden tiger.
52. Moto tolé.	Wooden hare.
53. Gal lou.	Fire dragon.
54. Gal mokhé.	Fire serpent.
55. Chéré mori.	Earth horse.
56. Chéré khoui.	Earth ram.
57. Temur betchi.	Iron monkey.
58. Temur takia.	Iron fowl.
59. Oussou nokhé.	Water dog.
60. Oussou khakhé.	Water pig.

As this cycle returns periodically every sixty years, it may be imagined that great confusion might occur in chronology, if they had not a sure method of fixing the past sexagenary cycles. To obviate this inconvenience, the sovereigns give to each year of their reign a particular name, and by this means the cyclic epochs are fixed in a way to leave no doubt. Thus the Mongols say, "The twenty-eighth year Tao-Kouang, which is that of the fiery ram (1848)." In China, the present sexagenary cycle commenced with the year 1805, and the years Tao-Kouang date from 1820, the epoch when the Emperor now reigning mounted the throne. It is to be observed that Chun-Tchi, Khang-Hi, Young-Tching, Kien-Long, Kia-King, Tao-Kouang, are not at all the names of the six first Emperors of the Mantchou dynasty, but special denominations to denote the years of their reign.

The Thibetians have adopted the use of the denary and duodenary cycles. But by making them undergo more numerous combinations than the Mongols, they obtain a cycle of 252 years. The twelve first years merely bear the names of twelve animals; then these same names are combined with those of the five elements, repeated twice up to the 72d year of the cycle. They then add to these combinations the word *po* (male), which carries them up to the 132d year; then the word *mo* (female), which takes it up to the 192d year; finally, they alternate the words *po* and *mo* to the end of the cycle.

This chronological system, too complicated for the use of

the lower classes, is confined to the Lamaseries, where it is studied and understood by the more learned Lamas. The masses live on from day to day, without an idea even of the existence of this method of combining the cycles. Except the Regent, we found no one at Lha-Ssa who could tell us in what year we were. They seemed generally to be wholly unaware of the importance of denoting dates and years by particular names. One of the highest functionaries of Lha-Ssa, a very celebrated Lama, told us that the Chinese method of counting the years was very embarrassing, and not at all comparable with the simplicity of the Thibetian method; he thought it more natural to say plainly, this year, last year, twenty or a hundred years ago, and so on. When we told him that this method would only serve to make history an inextricable confusion, "Provided we know," said he, "what occurred in times gone by, that is the essential point. What is the good of knowing the precise date of the occurrences? Of what use is that?"

This contempt, or rather this indifference for chronology, is observable, in fact, in most of the Lamanesque works; they are frequently without order or date, and merely present to the reader a hotch-potch of anecdotes piled one on another, without any precision, either about persons or events. Fortunately the history of the Thibetians being continually mixed up with that of the Chinese and the Tartars, one can apply the literature of these latter peoples to the introduction of a little order and precision into the Thibetian chronology.

During our stay at Lha-Ssa, we had occasion to remark that the Thibetians are very bad chronologists, not only with respect to leading dates, but even in the manner of reckoning each day the age of the moon. Their almanac is in a state of truly melancholy confusion, and this confusion entirely proceeds from the superstitious ideas of the Buddhists respecting lucky and unlucky days; all the days reputed unlucky, which occur in the course of the moon, are omitted, and do not count. Thus, for example, if the fifteenth day of the moon is a day of ill-omen, they count the fourteenth twice over, and pass on direct to the sixteenth. Sometimes several days of ill-omen occur one after the other; but that is of no consequence; they cut them all off just the same, until they come to a lucky day.

The Thibetians do not seem to find the least inconvenience in such a method.

The renewal of the year is, with the Thibetians, as with all people, a season of festivals and rejoicings. The last days of the twelfth moon are consecrated to the preparations for it; people lay in supplies of tea, butter, tsamba, barley wine, and some joints of beef and mutton. The holiday clothes are taken from the wardrobes; they remove the dust under which the furniture is generally hidden; they furbish up, clean, sweep, and try, in a word, to introduce into the interior of their houses a little order and neatness. The thing only happening once a year, all the households assume a new aspect; the domestic altars are the objects of especial care; they repaint the old idols, and they make, with fresh butter, pyramids, flowers, and various ornaments designed to deck the little sanctuaries where the Buddhas of the family reside.

The first Louk-So, or Rite of the Festival, commences at midnight, so that every one sits up, impatiently awaiting this mystical and solemn hour, which is to close the old year, and open the course of the new. As we were not anxious to catch the exact point of intersection which separates the two Thibetian years, we went to sleep at our usual hour. We were in a deep slumber, when we were suddenly awakened by the cries of joy which issued from all sides, in all quarters of the town. Bells, cymbals, marine conchs, tambourines, and all the instruments of Thibetian music, were set to work, and operated the most frightful uproar imaginable; it seemed as though they were receiving the new-born year with a charivari. We had once a good mind to get up, to witness the happiness of the merry inhabitants of Lha-Ssa, but the cold was so cutting, that after serious reflection, we opined that it would be better to remain under our thick woolen coverlets, and to unite ourselves in heart only with the public felicity. Repeated knocks on the door of our house, threatening to dash it into splinters, warned us that we must renounce our project. After several excuses, we were at last fain to leave our warm beds; we donned our clothes, and the door being opened, some Thibetians of our acquaintance rushed into our room, inviting us to the new year's banquet. They each bore in their hands a small vessel made of baked earth, in which floated, on boiling water, balls composed of honey and flour. One of these visitors offered us a long silver needle, terminating in a hook, and invited us to fish in his basin. At first, we sought to excuse ourselves, objecting that we were not in the habit of taking food during the night, but they entreated us in so engaging a manner, they put out their tongues at us with so friendly a grace, that we were obliged to resign ourselves to the Louk-So. We each hooked a ball, which we then crushed between our teeth to ascertain its flavor. We looked at each other, making grimaces; however, for politeness' sake, we had to swallow the dose. If we could only have got off with this first act of devotion! But the Louk-So was inexorable; the numerous friends we had at Lha-Ssa succeeded each other almost without interruption, and we had perforce to munch Thibetian sweatmeats till daybreak.

The second Louk-So also consists in making visits, but with a different ceremony. As soon as the dawn appears, the Thibetians walk through the streets of the town, carrying in one hand a pot of buttered tea, and in the other a large gilt and varnished plate, filled with tsamba, piled up in the form of a pyramid, and surmounted by three ears of barley. On these occasions, it is not allowed to pay visits without the tsamba and the buttered tea. As soon as you have entered the house of a person to whom you propose to wish a happy year, you first of all make three prostrations before the domestic altar, which is solemnly adorned and illuminated; then, after having burnt some leaves of cedar, or other aromatic tree, in a large copper censer, you offer to every one present a cup of tea, and hand the plate, from which each takes a pinch of tsamba. The people of the house reciprocate the compliment to the visitors. The inhabitants of Lha-Ssa have a saying, the Thibetians celebrate the festival of the new year with tsamba and buttered tea; the Chinese with red paper and crackers; the Katchi with delicate meats and tobacco; the Peboun with songs and sports.

Although this popular saying is correct enough, the Pebouns do not altogether monopolize the gaiety of the period. The Thibetians also enliven their new years' fêtes with noisy rejoicings, in which the song and the dance always play a large part. Groups of children, with numerous bells hung from their green dresses, pervade the streets, giving, from house to house, concerts that are not wanting in harmony. The song, generally sweet and melancholy, is interspersed with animated choruses. During the strophe, all these little singers keep marking the time, by making, with their bodies, a slow and regular movement like the swinging of a pendulum; but when they come to the chorus, they vigorously stamp their feet on the ground in exact time. The noise of the bells, and of the nailed boots, produces a kind of wild accompaniment that strikes upon the ear not disagreeably, especially when it is heard at a certain distance. These youthful *dilettanti* having performed their concert, it is usual with those for whom they have sung to distribute among them cakes fried in nut-oil, and some balls of butter.

On the principal squares, and in front of the public monuments, you see, from morning till night, troops of comedians and tumblers amusing the people with their representations. The Thibetians have not, like the Chinese, collections of theatrical pieces; their comedians remain altogether and continuously on the stage, now singing and dancing, now exhibiting feats of strength and agility. The *ballet* is the exercise in which they seem to excel the most. They waltz, they bound, they tumble, they *pirouette* with truly surprising agility. Their dress consists of a cap, surmounted by long pheasants' plumes, a black mask adorned with a white beard of prodigious length, large white pantaloons, and a green tunic coming down to the knees, and bound round the waist by a yellow girdle. To this tunic are attached, at equal distances, long cords, at the end of which are thick tufts of white wool. When the actor balances himself in time, these tufts gracefully accompany the movements of his body; and when he whirls round they stick out horizontally, form a wheel round the performer, and seem, as it were, to accelerate the rapidity of his *pirouettes*.

You also see at Lha-Ssa a sort of gymnastic exercise called the Dance of the Spirits. A long cord, made of leathern straps, strongly plaited together, is attached to the top of the Buddha-La, and descends to the foot of the mountain. The dancing sprites go up and down this cord, with an agility only to be compared with that of cats or monkeys. Sometimes, when they have reached the top, they fling out their arms as if about to swim, and let themselves slide down the rope with the velocity of an arrow. The inhabitants of the province of Ssang are reputed the most skilful in this kind of exercise.

The most singular thing we observed at Lha-Ssa, during the new year's festival, is what the Thibetians call the Lha-Ssa-Morou, that is, the total invasion of the town, and its environs, by innumerable bands of Lamas. The Lha-Ssa-Morou commences on the third day of the first moon. All the Buddhist monasteries of the province of Oui open their doors to their numerous inhabitants, and you see great bodies of Lamas, on foot, on horseback, on asses, on oxen, and carrying their prayer-books and cooking utensils, arriving tumultuously by all the roads leading to Lha-Ssa. The town is soon overwhelmed at all points, by these avalanches of Lamas, pouring from all the surrounding mountains. Those who cannot get lodgings in private houses, or in public edifices, encamp in the streets and squares, or pitch their little traveling tents in the country. The Lha-Ssa-Morou lasts six entire days. During this time, the tribunals are closed, the ordinary course of justice is suspended, the ministers and public functionaries lose in some degree their authority, and all the power of the government is abandoned to this formidable army of Buddhist monks. There prevails in the town an inexpressible disorder and confusion. The Lamas run through the streets in disorderly bands, uttering frightful cries, chanting prayers, pushing one another about, quarreling, and sometimes having furious contests with their fists.

Although the Lamas generally show little reserve or modesty during these festive days, it is not to be supposed that they go to Lha-Ssa merely to indulge in amusements incompatible with their religious character; it is devotion, on the contrary, which is their chief motive. Their purpose is to implore the blessing of the Talé-Lama, and to make a pilgrimage to the celebrated Buddhist monastery called Morou, which occupies the center of the town. Hence the name of Lha-Ssa-Morou given to these six festive days.

The monastery of Morou is remarkable for the splendor and wealth displayed in its temples. The order and neatness which always prevail here, make it as it were, the model and example for the other monasteries of the province. West of the principal temple, there is a vast garden surrounded by a peristyle. In this is the printing establishment. Numerous workmen, belonging to the Lamasery, are daily occupied in engraving blocks and printing Buddhist books. Their process being the same as that of the Chinese, which is sufficiently understood, we shall dispense with describing it. The Lamas who pay their annual visit to the festival of the Lha-Ssa-Morou, take the opportunity to purchase the books they require.

In the district of Lha-Ssa alone, they reckon more than thirty large Buddhist monasteries.[1] Those of Khaldhan, of Preboung and Sera are the most celebrated and the most populous. Each of them contains nearly 15,000 Lamas.

Khaldhan, which means in Thibetian "celestial beatitude," is the name of a mountain situated east of Lha-Ssa about four leagues. It is on the summit of this mountain that the Lamasery of Khaldhan stands. According to the Lamanesque books, it was founded in the year 1409 of our era, by the famous Tsong-Kaba, reformer of Buddhism, and founder of the sect of the yellow cap. Tsong-Kaba fixed his residence there, and it was there he quitted his human envelope, when his soul was absorbed in the universal essence. The Thibetians pretend that they still see his marvelous body there, fresh, incorruptible, sometimes speaking, and, by a permanent prodigy, always holding itself in the air without any support. We have nothing to say about this belief of the Buddhists, because the too short stay we made at Lha-Ssa did not permit us to visit the monastery of Khaldhan.

The Lamasery of Preboung (ten thousand fruits) is situate two leagues west of Lha-Ssa; it is built on the site of a lofty mountain. In the center of the monastery rises a sort of kiosk, magnificently ornamented, and all shining with gold and paintings. It is reserved for the Talé-Lama, who repairs thither once a year, to explain to the monks the contents of the sacred volumes. The Mongol Lamas, who come to Thibet to perfect themselves in the science of prayer, and to obtain the degrees of the Lamanesque hierarchy, generally fix themselves at Preboung, which, on that

[1] In the province of Oui there are three thousand.

account, is sometimes called in the country a Monastery of the Mongols.

Sera is situated north of Lha-Ssa not more than half a league from the town. The Buddhist temples and the residences of the Lamas stand on the slope of a mountain planted with hollies and cypresses. The road followed by the pilgrims who come from Tartary passes by these houses. At a distance, these monuments, ranged in the form of an amphitheater one above the other, and standing out upon the green base of the mountain, present an attractive and picturesque sight. Here and there, in the breaks of the mountain, and quite above the religious city, you see a great

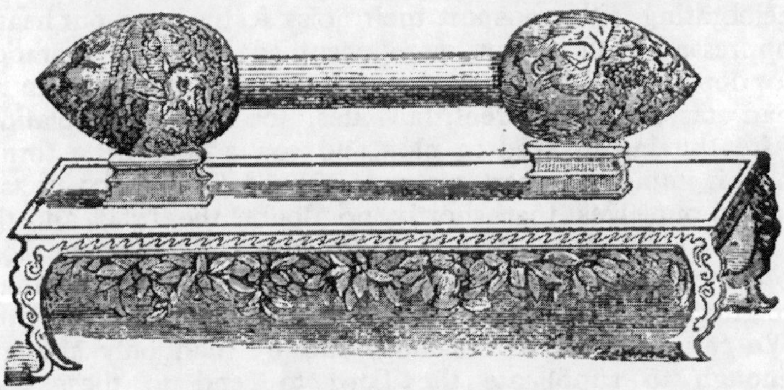

The Tortche, or Sanctifying Instrument.

number of cells inhabited by contemplative Lamas, and which you can only reach with great difficulty. The monastery of Sera is remarkable for three large temples of several stories high, all the rooms of which are entirely gilt. Hence it is that the Lamasery has acquired the name of Sera, from the Thibetian word *ser*, which signifies gold. In the chief of these three temples, they religiously preserve the famous *tortché*, or sanctifying instrument, which, in the belief of the Buddhists, came from India through the air, to place itself, of its own accord, in the monastery of Sera. This instrument is of bronze, in form resembling a pestle; the middle, by which you hold it, is in one piece, and cylindrical; the two extremities swell out in oval form, and are covered with symbolical figures. Every Lama must possess a small *tortché*, made on the model of that which marvelously came from

India. When they repeat their prayers, and during the religious ceremonies, this instrument is indispensable to them: they must sometimes hold it, sometimes lay it on their knees; then take hold of it again, and turn it in their hand, according to the rules of the ritual. The *tortché* of Sera is the object of great veneration. The pilgrims never fail to go and prostrate themselves before the niche, wherever it lies. At the new year's festival, it is carried in procession, with great pomp, to Lha-Ssa, to be presented to the adoration of the people of the town.

While the innumerable Lamas of Lha-Ssa-Morou were celebrating with transport their noisy festival, we, our hearts oppressed with sorrow, were occupied in the preparation for departure. We took down the little chapel wherein we had tasted such sweet, but alas, too short, consolation. After having essayed to plow and sow a poor little corner of this immense desert, we were obliged to abandon it, saying to ourselves that shortly, no doubt, the briar and the thorn would spring forth in abundance, and suffocate those precious germs of salvation, which were already beginning to grow. Oh, how bitter and depressing were these thoughts! We felt our hearts breaking, and we had only strength enough to supplicate the Lord to send to these poor children of darkness, missionaries more worthy of bearing to them the light of the faith.

The evening before our departure, one of the secretaries of the Regent entered our lodging, and presented to us, in his name, two great ingots of silver. This attention on the part of the first kalon affected us deeply, but we considered we ought not to accept this sum. In the evening, on going to his palace to bid him adieu, we took back to him the two ingots. We laid them before him on a small table, protesting to him that this proceeding resulted from no ill-feeling on our part; that, on the contrary, we should always remember, with gratitude, the good treatment we had received from the Thibetian government, during the short stay we had made at Lha-Ssa; that we had no hesitation in expressing our belief that if it had depended on the Regent, we should throughout have enjoyed in Thibet the most tranquil and honorable repose; but that, as to this money, we could not receive it without compromising our conscience as missionaries and the honor of our nation.

The Regent did not seem in any degree irritated by this proceeding. He told us that he understood our conduct, and could appreciate the objection we had expressed; that he would not insist on our accepting this money, but that still he should be very glad to make us some present upon separating. Then pointing to a dictionary in four languages, which he had often observed us turning over with interest, he asked us if this work would be agreeable to us. We thought we might receive this present without compromising in any way the dignity of our character, and we, on our parts, expressed to the Regent how happy we should be if he would deign to accept, as a reminiscence of France, the microscope which had so excited his curiosity; our offer was kindly received.

At the moment of separation, the Regent rose and addressed to us these words:—"You are going away, but who can know future events? You are men of astonishing courage. Since you have been able to get thus far, I know you have in your hearts a great and holy resolve. I think you will never forget it: for my part, I shall always bear it in mind. You understand me: circumstances will not permit me to say more." "We understand," we replied to the Regent, "the full bearing of your words, and we will implore our God to realize one day the purpose they express." We then parted, our heart bursting with grief, from this man who had been so kind to us, and by whose means we had formed the hope of making known, with God's help, the truths of Christianity to these poor people of Thibet.

When we re-entered our house, we found the Cashmerian governor awaiting us; he had brought us some provision for our journey; some excellent dried fruits from Ladak, cakes made of flour, butter, and eggs. He insisted upon passing all the evening with us, to assist us in packing our trunks. As he intended shortly to visit Calcutta, we charged him to give intelligence of us to the first Frenchman he should meet in the English possessions in India. We also gave him a letter, which we entreated him to get forwarded to the representative of the French government at Calcutta. In this letter we briefly explained the circumstances of our stay in the capital of Thibet, and the reasons of our departure.

It seemed to us advisable to take this measure, when we were about to commence a journey of a thousand leagues, along frightful roads continually bordered with precipices. We thought that, if it should be the will of God for us to be buried amid the mountains of Thibet, our friends in France would at least know what had become of us.

The same evening, Samdadchiemba came to bid us adieu. On the day that the Chinese ambassador had resolved to make us leave Thibet, our dear neophyte had been taken from us. It is needless to say how hard and painful this trial was; but to this measure, we could not, either the Regent or ourselves, offer any objection. Samdadchiemba was a native of the province of Kan-Sou, directly subject to the Chinese authority. Although our influence with Ki-Chan was not very great, yet we got him to promise that Samdadchiemba should suffer no injurious treatment, and should be sent back safe to his family. Ki-Chan promised this, and we have since ascertained that he was true to his word. The Regent was full of kindness towards our neophyte. As soon as he was separated from us, he took care that he should want for nothing; he even gave him a sum of money to provide for his journey. With what circumstances allowed us to add to this, Samdadchiemba was enabled to amass a small fortune, and to place himself in a position to return in a fitting manner to his paternal dwelling. We recommended him to go to his aged mother, and fulfil the duties which filial affection dictates, to instruct her in the mysteries of the Christian faith, and to cause her to enjoy at her last moments the benefit of baptismal regeneration; then, when he had closed her eyes, to return and pass his days among the Christians.

To say the truth, Samdadchiemba was not an amiable young man; sour, savage, and sometimes saucy, he was by no means an agreeable fellow-traveler; yet he had in him a groundwork of honesty and devotion, quite capable, in our opinion, of compensating for the perversities of his nature. We felt at parting from him a deep affliction, and all the more so, that we had never suspected the existence, at the bottom of our hearts, of so strong an attachment to this young man. But we had made together a long and painful journey; we had endured together so many privations, and so much misery, that, unconsciously, our existence was, so to speak, fused with his. The law of affinity which unites men to each other, acts with much more power amidst suffering, than in prosperity.

On the day appointed for our departure, two Chinese soldiers came, early in the morning, to inform us that the Ta-Lao-Ye, Ly-Kouo-Ngan; that is to say, his Excellency Ly, pacificator of kingdoms, awaited us at breakfast. This personage was the Mandarin whom the ambassador Ki-Chan had appointed to accompany us to China. We fulfilled his invitation; and, as the departure was to take place from his house, we had our luggage transported thither.

Ly, the pacificator of kingdoms, was a native of Tchang-Tou-Fou, capital of the province of Sse-Tchouen; he belonged to the hierarchy of the military mandarins. For twelve years he had served in Gorkha, a province of Boutan, where he obtained rapid promotion, and reaching the dignity of Tou-Sse, with the general command of the troops guarding the frontiers bordering on the English possessions, he was decorated with the blue button, and enjoyed the privilege of wearing in his cap seven sable tails. Ly-Kouo-Ngan was only forty-five years old, but you would have taken him for seventy; so broken and battered was he; he had hardly any teeth left in his head; his scanty hair was gray; his dull and glassy eyes endured a strong light with difficulty; his flabby wrinkled face, his totally withered hands, and his enormous legs, upon which he could scarcely support his frame, all bespoke a man exhausted by great excesses. We thought at first that this premature senility resulted from an immoderate use of opium, but he informed us himself, in our very first conversation, that it was brandy which had reduced him to this state. Having obtained permission to quit the service, he was now about to seek, in the bosom of his family, and by a careful and severe diet, the restoration of his shattered health. The ambassador Ki-Chan had in fact hurried our departure in order that we might go in company with this Mandarin, who, in his quality of Tou-Sse, was entitled to an escort of fifteen soldiers.

Ly-Kouo-Ngan was very well instructed for a military Mandarin; the knowledge he had of the Chinese literature, and above all, his eminently observant character, rendered his conversation effective and full of interest. He spoke slowly, almost in a drawling manner, but he had the faculty of giving to his stories and general conversation a dramatic and picturesque turn. He was very fond of philosophical and religious discussions; he had even, he said, magnificent projects of perfection for the time, when quiet and unembarrassed in his family, he should have nothing to do but to play at chess with his friends, or go and see the play. He believed neither in the Bonzes nor in the Lamas; as to the doctrine of the Lord of Heaven, he scarcely knew what it was, and required to be initiated in it before he embraced it. Meanwhile, all his religion consisted in a fervent veneration for the Great Bear. He affected aristocratic manners and exquisite polish; unfortunately, he happened sometimes to forget himself and to expose his altogether plebeian origin. It is superfluous to add that his excellency the pacificator of kingdoms was passionately fond of silver ingots; otherwise it would have been difficult to recognize in him a Chinese, much less a Mandarin. Ly-Kouo-Ngan had a luxurious breakfast prepared for us; and his table seemed to us all the finer, as for two years we had been used to live almost like savages. The habit of eating with our fingers had nearly made us forget the use of the Chinese chop-sticks. When we had finished, Ly-Kouo-Ngan informed us that everything was ready for departure, but, that before setting out, it was his duty to go to the palace of the ambassador, with his company of soldiers, to take leave. He asked us if we would not accompany him. "By all means," we replied, "let us go together to the residence of the ambassador; you will fulfil your duty, and we a politeness."

We entered, our guide and ourselves, the apartment where Ki-Chan sat. The fifteen soldiers drew up in file at the threshold of the door, after prostrating themselves thrice and striking the earth with their foreheads. The pacificator of kingdoms did the same, but the poor wretch could not himself get up again without our assistance. According to our custom, we saluted by placing our caps under our arms. Ki-Chan opened the discourse, and addressed a short speech to each of us.

Addressing us first, he assumed a wheedling tone: "You," said he, "are going to return to your country; I do not think you have any complaint to make of me; my conduct towards you has been irreproachable. I do not allow you to stay here, but this is the will of the Grand Emperor, not mine. I do not suffer you to go to India, because the laws of the empire forbid it; if it were otherwise, I, old as I am, would accompany you myself to the frontiers. The road you are about to travel is not so horrible as you are led to imagine; you will have, it is true, a little snow, you will pass some high mountains, and some of the days will be cold. You see I do not conceal the truth from you. Why should I try to mislead you? but at all events, you will have attendants to wait upon you, and every evening you will have a lodging for the night ready for you; you will have no need to put up a tent. Is not this traveling better than that on your way hither? You will be obliged to travel on horseback; I cannot give you a palanquin; there are none to be got in this country. The report I am going to address to the Grand Emperor will be sent in a few days. As my couriers go day and night they will pass you. When you have reached in safety the capital of Sse-Tchouen, the viceroy, Pao, will take charge of you, and my responsibility will be at an end. You may depart in confidence and with joyful hearts. I have sent on orders that you shall be well treated throughout. May the star of happiness guide you in your journey from beginning to end." "Although we consider ourselves oppressed," replied we to Ki-Chan, "we do not the less on that account offer up wishes for your prosperity. Since it is to dignities you aspire, may you recover all those you have lost, and attain still higher." "Oh, my star is unlucky! my star is unlucky!" cried Ki-Chan, taking a vigorous pinch of snuff from his silver box.

Then addressing himself to the pacificator of kingdoms, his voice assumed a grave and solemn tone. "Ly-Kouo-Ngan," said he, "since the Grand Emperor allows you to return to your family, you depart; you will have these two fellow-travelers, and this circumstance ought to cause you great joy, for the way, you know, is long and tedious. The character of these men is full of justice and gentleness; you will therefore live with them in perfect harmony. Take care never to sadden their hearts, by word or deed. Another important thing I have still to say: As you have served the empire for twelve years on the frontiers of Gorkha, I have commanded the paymaster to send you 500 ounces of silver; it is a present from the Grand Emperor." At these words Ly-Kouo-Ngan, finding all at once an unwonted suppleness in his legs, threw himself on his knees with vehemence : "The heavenly beneficence of the great Emperor," said he, "has always surrounded me on every side, but, unworthy servant that I am, how could I receive a further signal favor without blushing? I address my heartfelt supplications to the ambassador, that I may hide my face from him, and withdraw myself from this undeserved graciousness." Ki-Chan replied: "Do you imagine the Grand Emperor will thank you for your disinterestedness? What are a few ounces of silver? Go, receive this small sum, as it is offered to you; it will furnish you with tea to offer to your friends; but when you get home, take care not to begin drinking brandy again. If you wish to live a few years longer, you must deny yourself brandy. I say to you this, because a Father and Mother ought to give their children good advice." Ly-Kouo-Ngan struck the earth thrice with his forehead, and then rose up and placed himself beside us. Ki-Chan then harangued the soldiers, and changed his tone for the third time. His voice was sharp, abrupt, and sometimes bordering on anger. "And you soldiers!" At these words the fifteen soldiers, as though moved by one string, fell together on their knees, and retained that position all the time of the harangue. "Let me see, how many are there of you? You are fifteen, I think," and at the same time he counted them with his finger; "yes, fifteen men; you, fifteen soldiers, are about to return to your own province; your service is fulfilled; you will escort your Tou-Sse to Sse-Tchouen, as also these two strangers. On the way you will serve them faithfully, and take care to be always respectful and obedient. Do you clearly understand what I say?" "Yes, we do." "When you pass through the villages of the *Poba* (Thibetians) beware that you do not oppress the people. At the stations take care not to rob or pillage the property of any person. Do you clearly understand?" "Yes, we do." "Do not injure the flocks, respect the cultivated fields, do not set fire to the woods. Do you clearly understand me?" "Yes, we do." "Among yourselves let there always be peace and harmony. Are you not all soldiers of the empire? Do not then abuse or quarrel with one another. Do you understand clearly?" "Yes, we do." "Whoever conducts himself badly, let him not hope to escape chastisement; his crime will be investigated attentively, and severely

Adieu of Ki-Chan.

punished. Do you clearly understand?" "Yes, we do." "As you understand, obey and tremble." After this brief but energetic peroration, the fifteen soldiers struck the ground with their foreheads thrice and rose.

Just as we were leaving the residence of the ambassador, Ki-Chan drew us apart, to say a few words in private. "In a little while," said he, "I shall leave Thibet, and return to China.[1] In order that I may not be too much encumbered with luggage, on my departure, I am going to send two large cases with you; they are covered with the hide of a long-haired ox." He then told us the characters with which they were marked. "These two cases," added he, "I recommend to your care. Every evening, when you reach the station, have them deposited in the place where you yourselves pass the night. At Tching-Tou-Fou, capital of Sse-Tchouen, you will commit them to the care of Pao-Tchoung-Tang, viceroy of the province. Keep a good eye

[1] Ki-Chan, in fact, is now viceroy of the province of Sse-Tchouen.

on your own property, for in the route you will pursue, there are many petty thieves." Having assured Ki-Chan that we would observe his recommendation, we rejoined Ly-Kouo-Ngan, who was waiting for us on the threshold of the great entrance gate.

It was rather curious that the Chinese ambassador should think fit to confide his treasure to us, whilst he had at his disposal a Grand Mandarin, who was naturally called upon by his position to render him this service. But the jealousy which Ki-Chan felt towards strangers did not make him forget his own interests. He considered, no doubt, that it would be more safe to trust his cases to missionaries than to a Chinese, even though the Chinese was a Mandarin. This token of confidence gave us great pleasure. It was a homage rendered to the probity of Christians, and, at the same time, a bitter satire upon the Chinese character.

We proceeded to the house of Ly-Kouo-Ngan, where eighteen horses, ready saddled, were awaiting us in the courtyard. The three best were standing apart, reserved for the Tou-Sse and ourselves. The fifteen others were for the soldiers, and each was to take the one which fell to him by lot.

Before we mounted, a strong-limbed Thibetian female, very fairly dressed, presented herself: she was the wife of Ly-Kouo-Ngan. He had been married to her six years, and was about to leave her forever; he only had one child by her, which had died in its infancy. As these two conjugal halves were never again to see each other, it was but natural that at the moment of so afflicting a separation, there should be a few words of adieu. The thing was publicly done, and in the following manner: "We are going to part," said the husband, "do you stay here and sit quietly in your room." "Go in peace," replied the wife, "go hence in peace, and take care of the swellings in your legs." She then put her hand before her eyes, to make believe she was crying. "Look here," said the pacificator of kingdoms, turning to us, "they are odd people these Thibetian women. I leave her a well-built house, and plenty of furniture almost new, and yet she is going to cry—is she not content?"

After this adieu, so full of unction and tenderness, every one mounted, and the party set out down the streets of

Lha-Ssa, taking care to select those less encumbered with Lamas.

When we were out of the town, we perceived a large group awaiting us. They were those inhabitants of Lha-Ssa with whom we had had more intimate acquaintance, during our stay in that town. Many of them had begun to learn the truths of Christianity, and seemed to us sincerely

Parting of Li-Kouo-Ngan with his wife.

disposed to embrace our holy religion; they had assembled on our road to salute us and offer us a farewell khata. We observed, amongst them, the young physician, still wearing on his breast the cross we had given him. We dismounted, and addressed to these Christian hearts a few words of consolation; we exhorted them courageously to renounce the superstitious worship of Buddha, to adore the God of the Christians, and ever to have full trust in his infinite mercy. Oh, how cruel was that moment, when we were obliged to part from these well-beloved Catechumens, to whom we had as yet only pointed out the path of eternal salvation without being able to guide their first steps! Alas! we could do nothing further for them, except to implore Divine Providence to have compassion on these souls redeemed by the blood of Jesus Christ.

As we were remounting, we saw a horseman advancing towards us at full gallop. It was the governor of the Cashmerians, who had resolved to accompany us as far as the river Bo-Tchou. We were extremely touched by so friendly an attention, which, however, did not surprise us at all on the part of a sincere and devoted friend, who had given us repeated proofs of his attachment during our stay at Lha-Ssa.

The arrival of the governor of the Cashmerians occasioned us to ride on slowly, for we had much to say. At length, after an hour's march, we reached the borders of the Bo-Tchou. We found there a Thibetian escort, which the Regent had ordered to conduct us to the frontiers of China; it was composed of seven men and a Grand Lama, bearing the title of Dheba (governor of a district). With the Chinese escort, we formed a caravan of twenty-six horsemen, without counting the drivers of a large herd of oxen that carried our baggage.

Two large ferry-boats were ready to receive the horsemen and the horses; the latter jumped in at a single bound, and drew up in a line, one beside the other. It was easy to see this was not the first time they had performed this maneuver. The men then entered, with the exception of the Dheba, Ly-Kouo-Ngan, and ourselves. We saw that they were going to convey us across the river in a rather more aristocratic manner; we looked in every direction, but saw no means of transit. "How, then, are we to go over?" "Look below there," they replied, "see the boat coming." We turned our eyes in the direction indicated, and we perceived, in fact, a boat and a man coming across the fields, but, contrary to the usual practice, it was the boat that was carried by the man, and not the man by the boat. This boatman, running with his back laden with a large boat, was a thing monstrous to behold. As soon as he reached the river side, he quietly set down his load, and pushed the boat into the water without the least effort. It was clearly one thing or the other: either the man was of prodigious strength, or the boat of extreme lightness. We looked at the man, and saw nothing extraordinary in him; we approached the boat, examined it, touched it, and the problem was solved. This large boat was made of ox-hide solidly sewn together; inside, a few light bamboo sticks served to keep it in shape.

After having heartily shaken hands with the Cashmerian governor, we entered the boat, but we nearly burst it the first step we made. They had forgotten to tell us that we must only tread on the bamboo rods. When we were all embarked, the boatman pushed off with a long pole, and in the twinkling of an eye we were on the other side of the river; we sprang ashore, and the owner taking the boat on his back, went off across the fields.

These hide-boats have the disadvantage of not remaining long in the water without rotting. Each time they are done with, the boatmen take care to turn them upside down on the beach, to let them dry. Perhaps by varnishing them well, they might be preserved from the action of the water, and rendered capable of enduring a longer navigation.

When we were mounted, we cast a last look on the town of Lha-Ssa, still visible in the distance, and said in our hearts: "Oh, my God, thy will be done!" and followed in silence the progress of the caravan. It was the 15th of March, 1846.

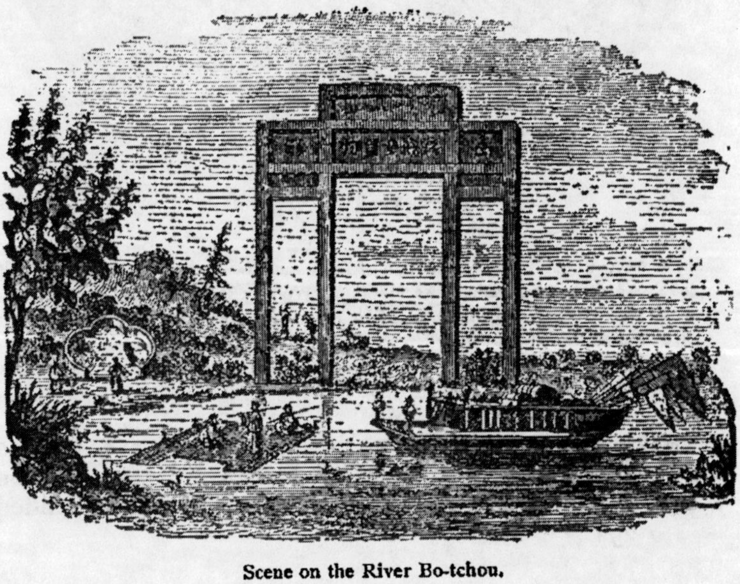

Scene on the River Bo-tchou.

Bridge of Ghiamda.

CHAPTER VIII.

Chinese Account of Thibet—Mountain of Loumma-Ri—Arrival at Ghiamda—Visit of Two Military Mandarins—Accident on a Wooden Bridge—The Unicorn—Passage of a Glacier—Appearance of Lha Ri—Ascent of Chor-Kou-La—Frightful Road to Alan-To—Village of Lang-Ki-Tsoung—Famous Mountain of Tanda—Catastrophe of Kia-Yu-Kiao—Passage of the Celebrated Plateau of Wa-Ho—Arrival at Tsiamdo.

Leaving Lha-Ssa we traveled for several days, amid a large valley entirely cultivated, and where we remarked on every side numerous Thibetian farms, generally surrounded by trees. The labors of agriculture had not yet commenced, for in Thibet the winters are always long and severe. Herds of goats and bellowing oxen were wandering dejectedly about the dusty fields, biting every now and then at the hard roots of the tsing-kou, with which the ground was covered; this species of barley is the chief culture of these poor regions.

The entire valley is composed of a number of small fields, separated from one another by thick low fences, made of large stones. The clearing of this stony ground doubtless costs the original cultivators much fatigue. These enormous stones had to be dug out of the ground one after the other, and rolled with labor to the borders of the fields.

At the time of our passing, the country presented a dull and melancholy aspect. The landscape, however, was animated at intervals by caravans of Lamas, who, singing and dancing, were going to the solemn festival of the Lha-Ssa-Morou. Shouts of joy and laughter issued now and then from the farmhouses on the roadside, and informed us that the rejoicings for the new year were not yet at an end.

Our first stage was a short one. We stopped some time before sunset, at Detsin-Dzoug, a large village, six leagues (60 lis) distant from Lha-Ssa.

A large house had been previously got ready for the accommodation of the caravan. As soon as we had alighted, we were introduced, by the governor of the village, to a room, in the midst of which flamed a magnificent fire of argols, in a large earthen basin. We were invited to seat ourselves on thick cushions of green Pou-Lou, and we were served immediately with buttered tea. We were, in fact, surrounded by such care and attention, that our hearts began to open. This kind of traveling seemed marvelous to us. What a contrast to the hard and laborious life we had spent in the desert, where a halt was only an aggravation of misery to us. To travel without being obliged to pitch a tent, and to see to the animals, without being put to any straits for fuel and food, seemed the realization of a brilliant utopia. As soon as we dismounted, to find a warm room, and a large pitcher of buttered tea, was for us absolute sybaritism.

Soon after our arrival we received the official visit of the Grand Lama, whom the Regent had appointed to accom-

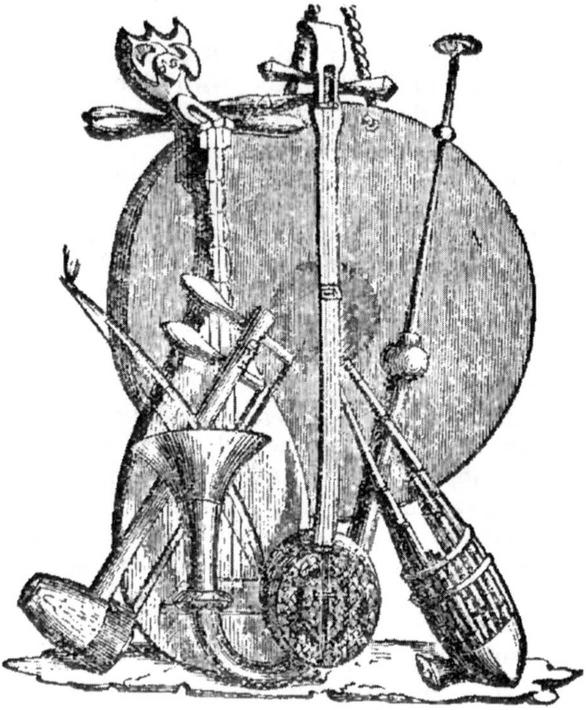

Chinese Musical Instruments.

pany us to the frontiers of China, and with whom we had as yet merely exchanged a few compliments as we crossed the river. This individual called Dsiamdchang, that is to say, the musician, was a thick-set man, about 50 years of age, who had fulfilled administrative functions in several parts of Thibet. Before being recalled to Lha-Ssa, he occupied the post of Dheba-general, in a district some little distance from Ladak; his large and somewhat wrinkled countenance was full of good nature. His character partook of the frankness and open disposition of a child. He told us that the Regent had commanded him to come here expressly on our account, that he might see we wanted nothing, during the time we were in the regions subject to the Talé-Lama. He then presented to us two young Thibetians, on whom he pronounced a long and pompous eulogium. "These two men," said he, "have been specially appointed to serve you on the way. Whatever you command them to do, that they must do punctually. As to your refreshments," added he, "as you are not accustomed to the Thibetian cookery, it has been arranged that you shall take them with the Chinese Mandarin."

After a brief conversation with the Lama Dsiamdchang, we had, in fact, the honor to sup in the company of Ly, the pacificator of kingdoms, who lodged in a chamber contiguous to our own. Ly-Kouo-Ngan was very complaisant, and gave us a great deal of information about the route we were to pursue, and which he himself was now traveling for the eighth time. That we might be enabled to have every day correct notions of the countries through which we were passing, he lent us a Chinese work, containing an itinerary from Tching-Tou, the capital of Sse-Tchouen to Lha-Ssa. This book is entitled "Oui-Tsang-Thou-Tchi," that is to say, "A description of Thibet, with engravings." This compilation, from various Chinese notices of Thibet, was drawn up by a Mandarin named Lou-Houa-Tchou, who, in the 51st year of Kien-Long (1786), was charged with the commissariat of the Chinese army. Father Hyacinthe, the Russian archimandrite at Peking, published a translation of this sort of geography of Thibet. M. Klaproth, after having revised, corrected, and enriched with notes the work of the Russian translator, inserted it in the *Journal Asiatique*.[1] The portion of this Chinese work which concerns the route from Lha-Ssa to the province of Sse-Tchouen, and which we had daily before us during our journey, is extraordinarily exact; but this dry and laconic itinerary can be of no interest except to persons occupying themselves specially with geography, or who travel through the places it mentions. It is merely an arid nomenclature, stage by stage, of the places you find on the way. To give an idea of it, we will transcribe the article relative to our first day's journey.

"From Detsin-Dzoug to the halt of Tsai-Li.
"From Tsai-Li to the inn at Lha-Ssa.

"At Detsin-Dzoug there are several inns, in which travelers generally stop for some time; near the

[1] *Nouveau Journal Asiatique*, 1st series, tome iv. and vi.

road is a post-house. Thence a journey of 40 lis takes you to the convent of Tsai-Li.............. 40 lis.

"At Tsai Li, there is a Dheba who supplies travelers with wood and hay; this district is separated only by a river from the territory of Lha-Ssa; you reach this last place, after a journey of 20 lis; there is a military commandant there..................... 20 lis.

Total.......60 lis."

We set out from Detsin-Dzoug before daybreak, for we had a long way to go. We followed the same valley we had entered, on quitting the town of Lha-Ssa. But as we advanced, the mountains, with which this large plain is surrounded, rose insensibly in the horizon, and seemed to draw near us; the valley grew narrower and narrower; the ground became more and more stony; the farms less frequent; and the population lost by degrees that appearance of refinement and civilization which is always observable in the environs of large towns. After a rapid and uninterrupted march of 80 lis we stopped to take a little repose and refreshment in a large and ruinous Buddhist convent, which served as a residence for some old ragged Lamas. The poverty in which they lived rendered them unable to offer to the staff of the caravan anything but tea with milk, a pot of beer, and a small roll of butter. However, by adding to these provisions some biscuit and a leg of mutton which the cook of Ly-Kouo-Ngan had been civil enough to prepare for us on the previous evening, we realized a sufficiently substantial repast.

As soon as we had satisfied our appetite and refreshed our limbs, we thanked these poor religious Buddhists with a khata, or scarf of blessings, and then remounted our horses. It was already late, and we had yet 40 lis to go before we reached our night stage. It was pitch-dark when we arrived at Midchoukoung. Our first care was to summon our Thibetian grooms, and bid them get ready our beds as soon as possible. We considered that after a long journey on a bad horse, we might dispense with ceremony. After partaking of a light repast, and saying our prayers, we wished a good night to the Pacificator of Kingdoms, and to the Lama musician, and proceeded to bury ourselves under the coverlid.

Next day, when we put our heads out of bed, the sun was already shining in all its splendor, yet all was quiet in the courtyard of the inn; we could hear neither the bellowing of the yaks, nor the neighing of the horses, nor anything indicating preparations for the departure of a caravan. We rose, and after rubbing our eyes, opened the door of our room to see how matters stood. We found Ly-Kouo-Ngan and the Lama Dsiamdchang seated in a corner of the courtyard, quietly basking in the rays of the sun. As soon as they saw us they approached, and told us in an infinitely roundabout manner, that we should be obliged to halt for one day, as there were difficulties in procuring horses and a change of oxen. "This is very bad news," said they; "this mischance is very unfortunate, but we cannot help it; the circumstances of the new-year's festival is the sole cause of this delay." "On the contrary," said we, "this is excellent news; we are in no sort of hurry. Let us go quietly, and rest frequently on the way, and all will go well." These words relieved our two guides from a great embarrassment. These good people imagined that we should quarrel with them, because it was necessary to make a day's halt; they were prodigiously mistaken. If, in our previous travels, delays had been sources of grievous vexation to us, the reason was that we had an object in view, and that we were eager to attain it. But now this was not the case, and we wished, as much as possible, to travel like gentlemen. We felt, besides, that it was not logical to go at a running pace from a place from which we had been expelled.

Midchoukoung is a stage where you change your *oulah,* that is, the horses, beasts of burden, and guides. These services are kept up by the Thibetian government, all the way from Lha-Ssa to the frontiers of China. The Chinese or Thibetian public officers, who make official inspections of the roads, are alone allowed to avail themselves of these sources. The government of Lha-Ssa gives them a passport upon which is stated the number of men and animals that the villages, subject to the contribution of the oulah, must furnish.

The Chinese account of Thibet gives the following account of this compulsory service: "As respects the local service called oulah, all those who have any fortune, whether men or women, are compelled to supply it; even those who come from the most distant countries, if they occupy a house to themselves, are not exempt from it. The number of men each person must furnish for this service is regulated by the fortune of each individual. The elders and the Dhebas determine, according to the size of each house, the number of men, etc., it must furnish to the oulah; each village provides three, four, and sometimes as many as ten men. The smaller families employ poor people as substitutes, paying them wages. People beyond sixty years of age are exempt from the burden. If the public service requires it, they exact oxen and horses, asses and mules from the dwellings of the rich; the poor people club together, and three or four houses give one beast."

The Chinese Mandarins, who always try to make money out of everything, find means to speculate in the oulah with which the Thibetian government furnishes them. Before leaving Lha-Ssa, they maneuver, by all imaginable means, to have set forth on their road-bill a great number of animals; they then take as many as are actually necessary, and receive, instead of the rest, a compensation in money, which the wealthy Thibetians much prefer to give them than to expose their animals to the perils of the road. Others claim the whole oulah, and employ it to transport into China Thibetian merchandise. Ly-Kouo-Ngan, whom we had heard declare so energetically his disinterestedness, when the ambassador Ki-Chan offered him a present on the part of the Emperor, showed feelings much less generous in relation to the oulah.

During the day we passed at Midchoukoung, his road-bill accidentally fell into our hands, and we were much surprised to read there that we had been allotted two horses and twelve long-haired oxen. Yet our entire baggage was two portmanteaus and a few bed things. "What do all these oxen mean?" inquired we of the Pacificator of Kingdoms; "do we need twelve beasts to carry two portmanteaus?" "Oh, it's a mistake of the secretary," replied he; and out of politeness, we affected to be perfectly satisfied with the answer.

It often happens, however, that the Chinese make gross mistakes as to their speculations in the oulah; they find, on the way, for example, some Thibetian tribes who are not at all disciplined to this kind of contribution. It is in vain they point out to these rude and fierce mountaineers the road-bill sealed with the seal of the Talé-Lama and that of the Chinese ambassador; they remain inexorable. To everything that is said to them, as an inducement to submit to the law, they have but this answer: "For a guide you will give so much; for a horse, so much; for a yak, so much;" until, at last, Chinese diplomacy is pushed into a corner, and the oulah is paid. The inhabitants of the district of Midchoukoung treated us with great politeness and courtesy: the chiefs of the village had a spectacle got up for us, by a troop of buffoons, who were assembled for the new-year's festival. The large courtyard of the inn, where we lodged, served for a theater: first, the artists, masked, and fantastically dressed, performed for some time, wild, deafening music, in order to summon to the play the inhabitants of the neighborhood. When all were come, and arranged in a circle round the stage, the Dheba of Midchoukoung approached in a solemn manner to offer to our two guides, and to ourselves, a scarf of blessings, and invited us to take our places on four thick cushions which had been placed at the foot of a large tree, that rose from an angle of the court. As soon as we were seated, all the troop of players put themselves in motion, and executed to the sound of music a sort of satanic round, the rapidity of which nearly made our heads swim; then came leaping, jumping, pirouetting, feats of strength, combats with wooden sabers; the whole accompanied alternately by songs, dialogues, music, and imitations of the cries of wild beasts. Among this troop of comedians, there was one more grotesquely masked than the others, who acted as a sort of clown to the ring, monopolizing the jests and repartees. We had not knowledge enough of the Thibetian language to appreciate his sallies; but judging from the stamping of feet, and the shouts of laughter of the audience, he seemed to acquit himself wonderfully as a wit. Altogether, the exhibition was amusing enough; the Thibetians were perfectly enthusiastic. When they had danced, leaped, and sung for upwards of two hours, the performers ranged themselves in a semicircle around us, took off their masks, and put their tongues in their cheeks at us, with profound bows. Each of us presented to the chief of the troop a scarf of blessings, and the curtain fell.

In the afternoon, we invited Ly-Kouo-Ngan to a short walk. Notwithstanding the indifferent elasticity possessed by his legs, he acceded to our proposal with good grace, and we proceeded together to explore the country. The village of Midchoukoung is populous; but everything announces that its inhabitants are living in anything but a state of comfort. The houses are generally built of stones strongly cemented with glazed earth; a great many are crumbling away, the ruins serving as a retreat for troops of large rats. Some small Buddhist altars, carefully lime-washed, are the only constructions that exhibit any cleanliness, and their whiteness presents a remarkable contrast with the gray, smoky hue of the village. Midchoukoung has a Chinese guard, composed of four soldiers and an under corporal. These men keep a few horses, and their barracks serve as a stage for the couriers who carry the despatches of the Chinese government.

On reentering the inn, we found in the courtyard, which in the morning had been used as a theater, a noisy assembly of men and beasts. They were occupied in collecting our oulah, which was settled at twenty-eight horses, seventy oxen, and twelve guides. At the commencement of the night, the Dheba came to inform us that all was done in accordance with the sacred ordinance of the Talé-Lama, and that on the morrow we could depart at an early or late hour as we pleased. At the dawn of day we mounted our horses, and bade adieu to Midchoukoung. After some hours' journey, we left, as through the extremity of a large funnel, the great valley in which we had been traveling since we left Lha-Ssa, and emerged into a wild uncultivated region. For five days we journeyed on in a labyrinth, now to the right, now to the left, and sometimes retracing our steps, in order to avoid abysses and inaccessible mountains. We were perpetually in the depths of ravines, or on the precipitous and rocky banks of torrents; our horses rather leaped than walked. The most vigorous animals, not accustomed to these dreadful places, could not resist for any length of time the fatigues of such a route. For half a day only could we travel with any pleasure and security. We came again to the river we had crossed on quitting Lha-

Ssa; it was tranquilly flowing over a slightly inclined bed, and its broad banks offered an easy and even path to travelers. Amid these wild regions, you find no place wherein to pass the night, except cold, damp hovels, exposed to all the winds of heaven. However, you arrive there so overcome by fatigue, that you always sleep profoundly.

Before reaching the town of Ghiamda, we crossed the mountain Loumma-Ri. "This mountain," says the Chinese itinerary, "is high and somewhat declivitous; it extends over a space of about forty lis. The snow, ice, and menacing peaks which travelers meet with on the way, before reaching this mountain, and which intimidate the heart and dim the eye, may cause this to be regarded, in comparison, as a plain easily traversed." The summit of Mount Loumma-Ri, although very lofty, is, in fact, very easy of access. We reached it by an easy slope, without being obliged to dismount once, a very remarkable circumstance in the mountains of Thibet. We found, however, on the other side of the mountain a somewhat serious difficulty, on account of the snow, which fell that day in abundance. The animals frequently slipped, sometimes their hind feet came suddenly in contact with their fore feet, but they never fell. The only result to the horsemen was a sort of jerking swing, to which we grew gradually accustomed.

The Pacificator of Kingdoms took it into his head to dismount, and walk, to warm himself a little; but after a few stumbling steps, he staggered for an instant on his poor legs, fell, and made in the snow a broad, deep furrow. He rose in a fury, ran to the nearest soldier, and loaded him with curses and cuts of his whip, because he had not dismounted to support him. All the Chinese soldiers immediately jumped from their steeds, and fell at the feet of their colonel, making excuses. All, in fact, had been deficient in their duty; for, according to the Chinese code of politeness, when a chief sets his foot on the ground, all the subalterns must on the instant dismount.

When we were at the base of the mountain of Loumma-Ri, we continued our march along a little river, which meandered through a forest of firs so thick that the light of day scarce penetrated it; the snow lay deeply on the broad branches of the trees, whence the wind shook them in thick flakes on the caravan. These small avalanches, falling unexpectedly upon the horsemen, made them start, and utter cries of surprise; but the animals, which, doubtless, had crossed the forest before in similar weather, were in no degree affected. They continued at their ordinary pace, without taking fright, contenting themselves with quietly shaking off the snow from their ears whenever it incommoded them.

We had scarcely emerged from the forest when we were all obliged to dismount, for the purpose of scaling, during a full hour, some horrible rocks. When we had reached the summit, we laid the bridles on the necks of the horses, and left the animals to the sagacity of their instinct as a guide over this rapid and precipitous descent. The men descended, now backwards, as down a ladder, now seated, and letting themselves slide down the snow; every one extricated himself victoriously from this dangerous position, and arrived at the bottom, without breaking or bruising arms or legs.

We still went on five lis more, in a narrow valley, and then perceived, at the foot of a high mountain, a large collection of houses, amongst which rose two Buddhic temples of colossal proportions. This was the station of Ghiamda. A little before reaching the town, we found on the road, a company of eighteen soldiers, drawn up in file, and having at their head two petty Mandarins, decorated with the white button. Mandarins and soldiers had their sabers drawn and their bows in their shoulder-belts. It was the garrison of Ghiamda, which, under arms and in full uniform, awaited Ly, the Pacificator of Kingdoms, to pay him military honors. When the caravan had come within proper proximity, the eighteen soldiers and the two Mandarins fell on their knees, turning the points of their sabers to the ground, and crying out with one voice, "To the Tou-Sse, Ly-Kouo-Ngan, the humble garrison of Ghiamda wishes health and prosperity." At these words, Ly-Kouo-Ngan, and the soldiers of his suite, stopped their horses, dismounted, and ran to the garrison, to invite them to rise. On both sides there was an infinity of bowing, during which we quietly continued our journey. On entering the town, we had, in our turn, our little official reception. Two Thibetians, in holiday attire, seized, to do us honor, the bridles of our horses, and conducted us to the house which had been prepared for our reception. There the Dheba, or chief magistrate of the district, awaited us; he offered us a scarf of blessings, and led us into an apartment where was a table already laid out with tea, butter, cakes, and dried fruits. In all these marks of friendship and attention, we could not help discerning the effect of orders forwarded by the Regent. Whilst we were doing honor to this modest collation we were informed that we should be obliged to stop two days at Ghiamda, because the Dheba of the district, having received only that morning the announcement of our approaching arrival, had not had time to send for the animals, which were grazing, at a great distance from the town. This news was very welcome to us; but it plunged Ly-Kouo-Ngan and the Lama Dsiamdchang into despair. We essayed to console them, by telling them, that when one cannot direct events, one bears them with resignation. Our two conductors acknowledged our doctrine to be very fine in theory, but the practise was not to their taste. However, they were obliged to admit afterwards, that this delay was very opportune, as, during the two days that we remained at Ghiamda, the sky was so overcast, the north wind blew with so much violence, and the snow fell so abundantly, that, in the opinion of the Ghiamdians, we could not have proceeded with safety in such boisterous weather. In fact, judging from what passed in the valley, it was easy to imagine that a frightful storm must have laid waste the mountains.

The day after our arrival at Ghiamda we received a visit from the two Chinese officers stationed in the town. The one bore the title of Pa-Tsoung, and the other that of Wei-Wei. The Pa-Tsoung was a fine man, strongly made, with a sounding voice and quick movement. A large scar across his face, and great black mustaches, contributed not a little to give him a highly military look. For four years he had served in the Kachkhar as a private soldier, and had returned thence with the title of Pa-Tsoung and the decoration of the peacock's feather. The Wei-Wei, a young man of two-and-twenty, was also a well-built person, but his languid and effeminate mien presented a singular contrast with the manly bearing of his colleague. His face was pale, flabby, and extremely delicate, his eyes were constantly humid and languishing. We asked him if he was ill. "No," replied he, with a scarcely audible voice; "my health is excellent;" and, as he spoke, his cheeks were slightly tinged with an angry redness. We saw that we had been guilty of an indiscretion, and we turned to another subject of conversation. This poor young man was an insane smoker of opium. When they were gone, Ly-Kouo-Ngan said, "The Pa-Tsoung is a man born under a very favorable star; he will ascend rapidly the grades of the military mandarinship; but the Wei-Wei was born under a cloud. Since he has become addicted to the European smoke, heaven has forsaken him. Before a year has elapsed he will have said good-by to the world."

The torrents of rain which fell almost without interruption during our stay at Ghiamda prevented us from visiting in detail this populous and commercial town. You find a great number of Pebouns or Indians of Boutan, who monopolize here, as at Lha-Ssa, all that appertains to the arts and industry. The agricultural products of the country are next to nothing. They cultivate in the valley some black barley, but scarcely sufficient for the consumption of the inhabitants. The wealth of the district is derived from its wool and goat's-hair, out of which they manufacture large quantities of stuffs. It appears that amid these frightful hills, there are excellent pastures, where the Thibetians feed numerous flocks. The lapis lazuli, stag's horn, and rhubarb are also materials of a great commercial intercourse with Lha-Ssa and the provinces of Sse-Tchouen and Yun-Nan. They affirm here, that it is in the mountains about Ghiamda that the best rhubarb grows. This district abounds in game of every description. The forest, which we crossed after leaving Mount Loumma-Ri, was full of partridges, pheasants, and several varieties of wild fowl. The Thibetians have no idea how to make the best of these meats, so admired by the gourmands of Europe. They eat them boiled, and without any kind of seasoning. The Chinese, in this respect as in every other, are much more advanced than their neighbors. The cook of Li-Kouo-Ngan dressed our venison in a manner that left us nothing to desire.

The appointed day of departure having arrived, the oulah was ready early in the morning. The wind had fallen, and the rain had ceased, yet the weather was by no means fine; a cold and thick fog enveloped the valley and intercepted the view of the surrounding mountains. We resolved, however, to proceed, for the people of the place agreed in saying that, for the time of year, the weather was all that could be expected. "So long as you are in the valley," they said, "you will not see very distinctly, but once on the heights, the obscurity will disappear; as a general rule, whenever there is a fog in the valley, snow is falling on the mountains." These words were far from encouraging. We were fain, however, to be resigned to our position, fortifying ourselves against the snow, for every one assured us that from Ghiamda to the frontiers of China, every day, without a single exception, we should have it on our road. Just as we were mounting, the Dheba of Ghiamda made us a present of two pairs of spectacles to protect our eyes from the dazzling whiteness of the snow. We could not, at first, help laughing at the sight of these optical instruments, so entirely novel to us was their form.

The place occupied by glass in ordinary spectacles, was here occupied by a sort of gauze horsehair work, carved out like a half walnut-shell. To fasten these two lids against the eyes, there was on each side a string which passed behind the ears, and was then tied under the chin. We thanked the excellent Dheba most heartily; for under the circumstances, the present was inestimable. On crossing the mountain of Loumma-Ri, we had already suffered much from the reflection of the snow.

On quitting the town, we found, as on entering it, the soldiers of the garrison awaiting Ly-Kouo-Ngan, in order to give him the military salute. These men, ranged in file, in the fog, and holding in their hands a saber that gleamed in the obscurity, had so odd an appearance, that almost all the horses in the caravan shied at them. These military salutes were renewed, on the way, wherever there was a Chinese garrison, to Ly-Kouo-Ngan's extreme exasperation. As he was unable, on account of his diseased legs, to dismount and remount with facility, these ceremonies were a regular torment to him. It was in vain that at each point he sent forward one of his soldiers to direct the garrison not to come out to receive him. This made them only more eager and more earnest for display, thinking that it was mere modesty prompted him to withdraw himself from the honors due to his rank.

Four lis from Ghiamda, we crossed a large and rapid torrent, over a bridge composed of six enormous trunks of fir trees, not planed, and so badly joined, that you felt them shake under your feet. No one ventured to cross on horseback, and the precaution was most valuable to one of our soldiers; his horse, slipping over the wet and trembling bridge, one of its legs passed between two trees, and stuck there as in a vice. If the man had been on it, he would have inevitably been precipitated into the torrent, and dashed to pieces on the rocks. After long and painful efforts, we managed to extricate the unfortunate animal from its frightful position: to the astonishment of every one, it had not broken its leg, nor even received the least wound.

Beyond this wretched bridge, we resumed our wild pilgrimage across rugged and snow-clad mountains. For four days we did not find in these wild regions a single Thibetian village. Every evening we lay in the Chinese guard-houses, around which were grouped a few shepherds' huts, made with the bark of trees. During these four days, however, we changed the oulah three several times without experiencing the least delay. The orders had been so well given beforehand, that on our arrival at each stage, we found everything ready arranged for our departure on the morrow.

If we had not known that in these countries, desert in appearance, there were shepherds living in the gorges of the mountains, it would have been impossible for us to understand this prompt organization of the oulah. Generally speaking, it was only in large towns that the service of the caravan experienced delays and difficulties.

On the fourth day of our departure from Ghiamda, after having crossed a great lake on the ice, we stopped at the station Atdza, a small village, the inhabitants of which cultivate a few acres of land, in a little valley encircled by mountains, the tops of which are covered with hollies and pines. The Chinese Itinerary says, on the subject of the lake you see before your arrival at Atdza: "The unicorn, a very curious animal, is found in the vicinity of this lake, which is 40 lis long."

The unicorn, which has long been regarded as a fabulous creature, really exists in Thibet. You find it frequently

The Unicorn.

represented in the sculptures and paintings of the Buddhic temples. Even in China, you often see it in the landscapes that ornament the inns of the northern provinces.[1] The inhabitants of Atdza spoke of it, without attaching to it any greater importance than to the other species of antelopes which abound in their mountains. We have not been fortunate enough to see the unicorn during our travels in Upper Asia. But all we were there told about it serves to confirm the curious details which M. Klaproth has published on this subject in the new *Journal Asiatique*. We think it not irrelevant to give here an interesting note which that learned orientalist has added to his translation of the "Itinerary of Lou-Hoa-Tchou."

"The unicorn of Thibet is called, in the language of this country, serou; in Mongol, kere; and in Chinese, tou-kio-

[1] We had for a long time a small Mongol treatise on natural history, for the use of children, in which a unicorn formed one of the pictorial illustrations.

cheou: which means the one-horned animal, or kio-touan, the straight horn. The Mongols sometimes confound the unicorn with the rhinoceros, called in Mantchou, bodi-gourgou; and in Sanscrit, khadga; calling the latter also, kere."

The unicorn is mentioned, for the first time, by the Chinese, in one of their works, which treats of the history of the first two ages of our era. It is there said that the wild horse, the argali, and the kio-touan are animals foreign to China; that they belong to Tartary, and that they use the horns of the latter to make the bows called unicorn bows.

The Chinese, Mahometan, and Mongol historians agree in the following tradition, relative to a fact which took place in 1224, when Tchinggiskhan was preparing to attack Hindostan. "This conqueror having subdued Thibet," says the Mongol history, "set out to penetrate into Enedkek (India.) As he was ascending Mount Djadanaring, he perceived a wild beast approaching him, of the species called serou, which has but one horn on the top of the head. This beast knelt thrice before the monarch, as if to show him respect. Every one being astonished at this event, the monarch exclaimed: 'The Empire of Hindostan is, they say, the birthplace of the majestic Buddhas and the Buddhistavas, and also of the powerful Bogdas or princes of antiquity. What then can be the meaning of this dumb animal saluting me like a human being?' Having thus spoken, he returned to his country." Although this circumstance is fabulous, it demonstrates, nevertheless, the existence of a one-horned animal on the upper mountains of Thibet. There are further, in this country, places deriving their names from the great number of these animals, which, in fact, live there in herds; for example, the district of Serou-Dziong, which means, the village of the land of unicorns, and which is situate in the eastern part of the province of Kham, towards the frontier of China.

A Thibetian manuscript, which the late Major Lattre had an opportunity of examining, calls the unicorn the one-horned tsopo. A horn of this animal was sent to Calcutta: it was fifty centimeters[1] in length, and twelve centimeters in circumference from the root; it grew smaller and smaller, and terminated in a point. It was almost straight, black,

[1] A centimeter is 39-100 of an inch.

and somewhat flat at the sides. It had fifteen rings, but they were only prominent on one side.

Mr. Hodgson, an English resident in Nepaul, has at length achieved the possession of a unicorn, and has put beyond doubt the question relative to the existence of this species of antelope, called tchirou, in Southern Thibet, which borders on Nepaul. It is the same word with serou, only pronounced differently, according to the varying dialects of the north and of the south.

The skin and the horn, sent to Calcutta by Mr. Hodgson, belonged to a unicorn that died in a menagerie of the Rajah of Nepaul. It had been presented to this prince by the Lama of Digourtchi (Jikazze), who was very fond of it.

The persons who brought the animal to Nepaul informed Mr. Hodgson that the tchirou mostly frequented the beautiful valley or plain of Tingri, situated in the southern part of the Thibetian province of Tsang, and watered by the Arroun. To go from Nepaul to this valley, you pass the defile of Kouti or Nialam. The Nepaulese call the valley of Arroun Tingri-Meidam, from the town of Tingri, which stands there on the left bank of the river; it is full of salt-beds, round which the tchirous assemble in herds. They describe these animals as extremely fierce, when they are in their wild state; they do not let any one approach them, and flee at the least noise. If you attack them, they resist courageously. The male and the female have generally the same aspect.

The form of the tchirou is graceful, like that of all the other animals of the antelope tribe, and it has likewise the incomparable eyes of the animals of that species; its color is reddish, like that of the fawn in the upper parts of the body, and white below. Its distinctive features are, first a black horn, long and pointed, with three slight curvatures, and circular annulations towards the base; these annulations are more prominent in front than behind; there are two tufts of hair which project from the exterior of each nostril, and much down round the nose and mouth, which gives the animal's head a heavy appearance. The hair of the tchirou is rough, and seems hollow, like that of all the animals north of the Himalaya that Mr. Hodgson had the opportunity of examining. The hair is about five centimeters long, and so thick that it seems to the touch a solid mass.

Beneath the hair, the body of the tchirou is covered with a very fine and delicate down, as are almost all the quadrupeds that inhabit the lofty regions of the Himalaya mountain, particularly the famous Cashmere goats.

Doctor Abel has proposed to give to the tchirou the systematic name of *Antelope Hodgsonii*, after the name of the learned person who has placed its existence beyond a doubt.[1]

At Atdze we changed our oulah, although we had only fifty lis to go before we reached the residence of Lha-Ri. We required fresh animals accustomed to the dreadful road we had below us. One single mountain separated us from Lha-Ri, and to cross it it was, we were told, necessary to set out early in the morning, if we wished to arrive before night. We consulted the Itinerary, and we found there the following agreeable account of the place: "A little further on you pass a lofty mountain, the summits of which rise in peaks. The ice and snow never melt here throughout the year. Its chasms resemble the declivitous shores of the sea; the wind often fills them with snow; the paths are almost impracticable, the descent is so rapid and slippery." It is obvious that this brief but emphatic sketch did not hold out to us any very agreeable pleasure trip for the morrow. Oh, how readily we would have given up our places to some of those intrepid tourists, whom the love of ice and snow, or rocks and precipices, leads every year amidst the Alps, those mountains of Thibet in miniature.

Another thing, very little calculated to encourage us, was, that the people of the caravan, the villagers, everybody seemed anxious and uneasy. They asked one another whether the snow, which had fallen in abundance for five days, and had not had time to settle, would not render the mountains impassable; whether there was not a danger of being buried in the chasms, or of being overwhelmed by the avalanches; whether, in a word, it would not be prudent to wait a few days, in the hope that the snow would be dispersed by the wind, or partly melted by the sun, or con-

[1] The unicorn antelope of Thibet is probably the oryx-capra of the ancients. It is still found in the deserts of Upper Nubia, where it is called Ariel. The unicorn (Hebrew, reem; Greek, monoceros), that is represented in the Bible, and in Pliny's "Natural History," cannot be identified with the oryx-capra. The unicorn of holy writ would appear rather to be a pachydermous creature, of great strength and formidable ferocity. According to travelers, it still exists in Central Africa, and the Arabs call it Aboukarn.

solidated by the cold. To all these questions, the answers were anything but encouraging. In order to guard against the effects of mere pusillanimity of presumption, we held, before going to bed, a council, to which we summoned the old mountaineers of the country. After long deliberation, it was decided first, that if, on the morrow, the weather was calm and serene, we might set out without temerity; secondly, that in the supposition of departure, the long-haired oxen laden with the baggage, and conducted by some people of the district, should precede the horsemen, in order to trace out for them, in the snow, a more easy path. The matter being thus determined, we tried to take a little rest, relying little on the advantages of this plan, and much on the Divine protection.

When we rose, a few stars were still shining in the heaven, contending with the first rays of light; the weather was wonderfully beautiful. We quickly made our preparations for departure, and as soon as the last shades of night were dissipated, we began to ascend the formidable Mountain of Spirits (*Lha-Ri*). It rose before us like a huge block of snow, whereon we perceived not a single tree, not a blade of grass, not a dark spot to interrupt the uniformity of the dazzling whiteness. As had been arranged, the long-haired oxen, followed by their drivers, went first, advancing one after the other; next came the horsemen, in single file, in their steps, and the long caravan, like a gigantic serpent, slowly developed its sinuosities on the mountain side. At first the descent was by no means rapid, for we encountered frightful quantities of snow, that threatened every instant to bury us. We saw the oxen at the head of the column, advancing by leaps, anxiously seeking the least perilous places, now to the right, now to the left, sometimes disappearing all at once in some deep rut, and struggling amidst those masses of moving snow, like porpoises amid the billows of the ocean. The horsemen who closed the cavalcade found a more solid footing. We advanced slowly along the steep and narrow furrows traced out for us between the walls of snow, that rose to the height of our breasts. The air resounded with the bellowing of the oxen; the horses panted loudly, and the men, to keep up the courage of the caravan, raised, every now and then, a simultaneous shout like that of mariners at the capstan. Gradually the route became so steep, so precipitous, that the caravan seemed suspended from the mountain's side. It was impossible to remain on horseback; every one dismounted, and each clinging to his horse's tail, resumed his march with renewed ardor. The sun, shining in all its splendor, darted its rays on these vast piles of snow, and caused them to emit innumerable sparks, the flashing of which dazzled the eyes. Fortunately, our visuals were sheltered by the inestimable glasses that the Dheba of Ghiamda had given us.

After long and indescribable labor, we arrived, or rather, were hauled up to the summit of the mountain. The sun was already on the decline. We stopped for an instant, both to readjust the saddles and fasten the baggage, and to remove from the soles of our boots the masses of snow that had accumulated upon them, and become consolidated into the form of cones reversed. Every one was transported with joy. We felt a sort of pride in being mounted so high, and in finding ourselves standing on this gigantic pedestal. We took a pleasure in following with our eyes the deep and tortuous path that had been hollowed out in the snow, and the reddish tint of which was markedly outlined in the otherwise spotless white of the mountain.

The descent was more precipitous than the ascent, but it was much shorter, and did not require the exertion we had been obliged to make on the other side of the mountain. The extreme steepness of the way assisted us, on the contrary, in the descent, for we had merely to let ourselves go; the only danger was that of rolling down too fast, or of stepping out of the beaten path, and being thus forever buried in the bottom of some abyss. In a country such as this, accidents of this description are by no means chimerical. We descended easily then, now standing, now seated, and without any other mischance than a few falls and some protracted slides, more calculated to excite the merriment than the fear of travelers.

Shortly before arriving at the base of the mountain, the whole caravan halted on a level spot, where stood an Obo, or Buddhic monument, consisting of piled up stones, surmounted by flags and bones covered with Thibetian sentences. Some enormous and majestic firs, encircling the Obo, sheltered it with a magnificent dome of verdure.

"Here we are, at the glacier of the Mountain of Spirits," said Ly-Kouo-Ngan. "We shall have a bit of a laugh now." We regarded with amazement the Pacificator of Kingdoms. "Yes, here is the glacier; look here." We proceeded to the spot he indicated, bent over the edge of the plateau, and saw beneath us an immense glacier jutting out very much, and bordered with frightful precipices. We could distinguish, under the light coating of snow, the greenish hue of the ice. We took a stone from the Buddhic monument, and threw it down the glacier. A loud noise was heard, and the stone gliding down rapidly, left after it a broad green line. The place was clearly a glacier, and we now comprehended partly Ly-Kouo-Ngan's remark, but we saw nothing at all laughable in being obliged to travel over such a road. Ly-Kouo-Ngan, however, was right in every point, as we now found by experience.

They made the animals go first, the oxen, and then the horses. A magnificent long-haired ox opened the march; he advanced gravely to the edge of the plateau; then, after stretching out his neck, smelling for a moment at the ice, and blowing through his large nostrils some thick clouds of vapor, he manfully put his two front feet on the glacier, and whizzed off as if he had been discharged from a cannon. He went down the glacier with his legs extended, but as stiff and motionless as if they had been made of marble. Arrived at the bottom, he turned over, and then ran on, bounding and bellowing over the snow. All the animals, in turn, afforded us the same spectacle, which was really full of interest. The horses, for the most part, exhibited, before they started off, somewhat more hesitation than the oxen; but it was easy to see that all of them had been long accustomed to this kind of exercise.

The men, in their turn, embarked with no less intrepidity and success than the animals, although in an altogether different manner. We seated ourselves carefully on the edge of the glacier, we stuck our heels close together on the ice, as firmly as possible, then using the handles of our whips by way of helm, we sailed over these frozen waters with the velocity of a locomotive. A sailor would have pronounced us to be going at least twelve knots an hour. In our many travels, we had never before experienced a mode of conveyance at once so commodious, so expeditious, and, above all, so refreshing.

At the foot of the glacier, each caught his horse as soon as he could, and we continued our journey in the ordinary style. After a somewhat rapid descent, we left behind us the Mountain of Spirits, and entered a valley, sprinkled here and there with patches of snow, that had withstood the rays of the sun. We rode for a few minutes along the frozen banks of a small river, and reached at length the station of Lha-Ri. We had, at the gate of this town, as at Ghiamda, a military reception. The Dheba of the place came to offer us his services, and we proceeded to occupy the lodging that had been prepared for us, in a Chinese pagoda, called Kouang-Ti-Miao,[1] which means the temple of the god of war. From Lha-Ssa to Lha-Ri, they reckon 1,010 lis (101 leagues); we had been fifteen days traveling the distance.

As soon as we were installed in our residence, it was agreed unanimously, among Ly-Kouo-Ngan, the Lama Dsiamdchang, and ourselves, that we should stop one day at Lha-Ri. Although the oulah was all ready, we considered it better to make a brief halt, in order to reinstate, by a day's repose, the strength we should require for climbing another formidable mountain, that lay in our way.

The large village of Lha-Ri is built in a gorge, surrounded by barren and desolate mountains; this district does not exhibit the least signs of cultivation, so that the people have to get their flour from Tsing-Kou. The inhabitants are nearly all shepherds; they breed sheep, oxen, and, especially, goats, the fine silky hair of which is used in the fabric of poulou of the first quality, and of those beautiful manufactures, so well known by the name of Cashmere shawls. The Thibetians of Lha-Ri are much less advanced in civilization than those of Lha-Ssa; their physiognomy is hard and rugged; they are dirty in their clothing; their houses are merely large, shapeless hovels, made of rough

[1] Kouang-Ti, was a celebrated general who lived in the third century of our era, and who, after many and famous victories, was put to death with his son. The Chinese, indeed, say that he did not really die, but that he ascended to heaven, and took his place among the Gods. The Mantchous, who now reign in China, have named Kouang-Ti the tutelary spirit of their dynasty, and raised a great number of temples in his honor. He is ordinarily represented seated, having on his left hand his son Kouang-Ping, standing, and on his right, his squire, a man with a face so very dark, as to be almost black.

stone, and rudely plastered with lime. You remark, however, on the side of the mountain, a little above the village, a vast Buddhic monastery, the temple of which is fine enough. A Kampo is the superior of this Lamasery, and, at the same time, temporal administrator of the district. The numerous Lamas of Lha-Ri lead an idle, miserable life; we saw them, at all hours of the day, squatting in the different quarters of the town, trying to warm, in the rays of the sun, their limbs, half covered with a few red and yellow rags,—it was a disgusting sight.

At Lha-Ri, the Chinese government maintained a magazine of provisions, under the management of a learned Mandarin, bearing the title of Leang-Tai (purveyor), and decorated with the button of white crystal. The Leang-Tai has to pay the various garrisons quartered on his line of road. There are, between Lha-Ssa and the frontiers of China, six of these provision magazines. The first and most important is at Lha-Ssa; the Leang-Tai of which town superintends the five others, and receives an annual salary of seventy ounces of silver, whereas his colleagues have only sixty. The maintenance of the provisional magazine at Lha-Ssa cost the Chinese government 40,000 ounces of silver per annum; while that at Lha-Ri costs only 8,000 ounces. The garrison of the latter town consists of 130 soldiers, having at their head a Tsien-Tsoung, a Pa-Tsoung, and a Wei-Wei.

The day after our arrival at Lha-Ri, the Leang-Tai, or purveyor, instead of coming to pay an official visit to the staff of the caravan, contented himself with sending us, by way of card, a leaf of red paper on which were inscribed the letters of his name; he added, by the mouth of his messenger, that a severe illness confined him to his room. Ly-Kouo-Ngan said to us, in a whisper, and with a sly laugh, "The Leang-Tai will recover as soon as we are gone." When we were left alone, he said, "Ah, I knew how it would be: every time a caravan passes, Leang-Tai-Sue (the name of the Mandarin) is at death's door; that is well understood by everybody. According to the usages of hospitality, he should have prepared for us to-day a feast of the first class, and it is to avoid this that he feigns illness. The Leang-Tai-Sue is the most avaricious man imaginable; he never dressed better than a palanquin bearer; he eats tsamba like a barbarian of Thibet. He never smokes, he never plays, he never drinks wine; in the evening his house is not lighted; he gropes his way to bed in the dark, and rises very late in the morning, for fear of being hungry too early. Oh, a creature like that is not a man; 'tis a mere tortoise-egg! The ambassador Ki-Chan is resolved to dismiss him, and he will do well. Have you any Leang-Tais of this kind in your country?" "What a question! The Leang-Tais of the kingdom of France never go to bed without a candle, and when the oulah passes through their town, they never fail to get ready a good dinner." "Ah, that is the thing! those are the rites of hospitality! but this Sue-Mou-Tchou—" at these words we burst into a hearty fit of laughter. "By the by," asked we, "do you know why the Leang-Tai-Sue is called Sue-Mou-Tchou; the name seems to us somewhat ignoble?" "Ignoble, indeed; but it has reference to a very singular anecdote. Leang-Tai-Sue, before he was sent to Lha-Ri, exercised the functions of Mandarin in a small district of the province of Kiang-Si. One day, two laborers presented themselves at his tribunal, and besought him to give judgment in the matter of a sow, which they both claimed. Judge Sue pronounced thus his decision: 'Having separated truth from fiction, I see clearly that this sow belongs neither to you, nor to you; I declare, therefore, that it belongs to me: respect this judgment.' The officers of the court proceeded to take possession of the sow, and the judge had it sold in the market. Since that occurrence, Mandarin Sue has been always called Sue-Mou-Tchou (Sue the sow)." The recital of this story made us deeply regret that we must depart without seeing the physiognomy of this interesting individual.

We left the town of Lha-Ri in changeable weather; our first day's march was only sixty lis, and offered nothing remarkable, except a large lake which they say is eight lis in breadth and ten in length: it was frozen, and we crossed it easily, thanks to a slight coating of snow with which it was covered. We lodged in a miserable hamlet, called Tsa-Tchou-Ka, near which are hot springs. The Thibetians bathe there, and do not fail to attribute to them marvelous properties.

The next day was a day of great fatigue and tribulation; we crossed the mountain Chor-Kou-La, which, for its height and ruggedness, may well rival that of Lha-Ri. We began its ascent, our hearts full of anxiety, for the clouded and lowering sky that hung over us seemed to presage wind or snow; the mercy of God preserved us from both the one and the other. Towards mid day, there rose a light north wind, the cutting cold of which soon chapped our faces; but it was not strong enough to raise the thick coat of snow which covered the mountain.

As soon as we had reached the summit, we rested for a moment under the shade of a large stone obo, and dined on a pipe of tobacco. During this frugal repast, the Mandarin Ly-Kouo-Ngan told us, that in the time of the wars of Kien-Long against Thibet, the Chinese troops, exasperated by the fatigues and privations of a long journey, mutinied as they were passing Chor-Kou-La. "On this plateau," said he, "the soldiers arrested their officers, and after having bound them, threatened to precipitate them into this gulf, unless they promised them increased pay. The generals, having agreed to do right to the claims of the army, the sedition was appeased, the Mandarins were set at liberty, and they quietly continued their march to Lha-Ri. As soon as they arrived in this town, the generals made good their promise, and increased the pay; but, at the same time, these insubordinate soldiers were mercilessly decimated." "And what did the soldiers say?" inquired we of Ly-Kouo-Ngan. "Those upon whom the lot did not fall laughed heartily, and declared that their officers had shown great ability."

On quitting the summit of Chor-Kou-La, you follow a somewhat inclined path, and continue for several days on an extensive, high ground, the numerous ramifications of which stretch afar their pointed tops and the sharp needles of their peaks. From Lha-Ssa to the province of the Sse-Tchouen, through all this long route, nothing is to be seen but immense chains of mountains, intersected with cataracts, deep gulfs, and narrow defiles. These mountains are now all heaped up together, presenting to the view the most varied and fantastic outlines; now they are ranged symmetrically, one against the other, like the teeth of a huge saw. These regions change their aspect every instant, and offer to the contemplation of travelers landscapes of infinite variety; yet, amidst this inexhaustible diversity, the continuous sight of mountains diffuses over the route a certain uniformity which after awhile becomes tiresome. A detailed account of a journey in Thibet being extremely susceptible of monotony, we abstain, that we may not fall into unnecessary repetitions from describing the ordinary mountains. We shall content ourselves with mentioning the most celebrated—those which, in the Chinese phrase, "claim the life of travelers." This method, besides, will be conformable with the style of the inhabitants of these mountainous countries, who call whatever is not lost in the clouds, *plain;* whatever is not precipice and labyrinth, *level road.*

The high grounds we traversed, after surmounting the Chor-Kou-La, are considered by the natives level ground. "Thence to Alan-To," said the Thibetian escort to us, "there is no mountain; the path is all like that," showing us the palm of their hand. "Yet," said they, "it is necessary to use a good deal of precaution, for the paths are sometimes very narrow and slippery." Now hear what, in reality, was this same road, "as flat as the palm of your hand." As soon as you have quitted the summits of Chor-Kou-La, you encounter a long series of frightful chasms, bordered on each side by mountains cut perpendicularly, and rising up like two vast walls of living rock. Travelers are obliged to pass these deep abysses by following, at a great height, so narrow a ledge, that the horses frequently find only just enough room to plant their feet. As soon as we saw the oxen of the caravan making their way along this horrible path, and heard the low roar of the waters rising from the depths of those gulfs, we were seized with fear, and dismounted, but every one at once told us immediately to remount, saying that the horses, accustomed to the journey, had surer feet than we; that we must let them go their own way, contenting ourselves with keeping firmly in our stirrups, and not looking about us. We recommended our souls to God, and followed in the wake of the column. We were soon convinced that, in point of fact, it would have been impossible for us to keep our equilibrium on this slippery and rugged surface; it seemed as though, at every moment, an invisible force was drawing us towards those fathomless gulfs. Lest we should get giddy, we kept our heads turned towards the mountain, the declivity of which was sometimes so perpendicular, that it did not even offer

The Defile of Alan-To.

a ledge for the horses to plant their feet on. In such places we passed over large trunks of trees, supported by piles fixed horizontally in the mountain side. At the very sight of these frightful bridges we felt a cold perspiration running from all our limbs. It was essential, however, to advance, for to return or to dismount were two things beyond possibility.

After having been for two days constantly suspended between life and death, we at length got clear of this route, the most dreadful and most dangerous imaginable, and arrived at Alan-To. Every one was rejoiced, and we congratulated each other on not having fallen into the abyss. Each recounted, with a sort of feverish excitement, the terrors he had experienced in the most difficult parts of the passage. The Dheba of Alan-To, on hearing that no one had perished, expressed his opinion that the caravan had been unprecedentedly fortunate. Three oxen laden with baggage had indeed been swallowed up, but these mischances were not worth talking about. Ly-Kouo-Ngan told us that he had never passed the defile of Alan-To without witnessing frightful accidents. In his previous journey, four soldiers had been precipitated from the top of the mountain with the horses they rode. Every one was able to recount catastrophes, the mere recital of which made our hair stand on end. They had forborne to mention them before, for fear of our refusing to continue the journey. In fact, if we could have seen at Lha-Ssa the frightful abysses of Alan-To, it is probable that the ambassador Ki-Chan would scarcely have succeeded in inducing us to attempt this journey.

From Alan-To, where we changed oulah, we descended through a thick forest of firs, into a valley where we stopped, after eighty lis march, at a village called Lang-Ki-Tsoung. This post is one of the most picturesque and most agreeable we had met throughout our journey. It is situated amidst the center of a plain, bounded on all sides by low mountains, the sides of which are covered with trees of fine growth. The country is fertile, and the Thibetians of the district seem to cultivate it with much care. The fields are watered by an abundant stream, the waters of which drift down a large quantity of gold sand, for which reason the Chinese give this valley the name of Kin-Keou (gold).

The houses of Lang-Ki-Tsoung are very singularly constructed; they are absolutely nothing more than trunks of trees, stripped of their bark, and with the two extremities cut off; so that they may be nearly of the same size throughout. Enormous piles are first driven into the earth to a great depth; the part remaining above ground being at most two feet in height. Upon these piles they arrange horizontally, one beside the other, the trunks of fir which they have prepared; these form the foundation and the floor of the house. Other fir trees similarly prepared, and laid one upon the other, serve to form walls remarkable for their thickness and solidity. The roof is likewise formed of trunks, covered with large pieces of bark, arranged like slates. These houses exactly resemble enormous cages, the bars of which are closely fixed against each other. If between the joints they discover any cracks they stop these up with argols. They sometimes build in this fashion very large houses, of several stories high, very warm, and always free from damp. Their only inconvenience is their having very uneven and disagreeable floors. If the inhabitants of Lang-Ki-Tsoung ever take it into their heads to give balls, they will, it is most likely, be obliged to modify their plan of house construction. Whilst we were waiting patiently and in silence in our big cage until they should please to serve up supper, the Dheba of Lang-Ki-Tsoung, and the corporal of the Chinese guard, came to tell us that they had a little point to settle with us. "What point?" cried Ly-Kouo-Ngan, with an important air, "what point?" "Oh, I see, the oulah is not ready." "It is not that," answered the Dheba. "Never at Lang-Ki-Tsoung has any one to wait for his oulah; you shall have it this evening, if you like, but I must warn you that the mountain of Tanda is impassable; for eight consecutive days, the snow has fallen in such abundance that the roads are not yet open." "We have passed the Chor-Kou-La, why should we not with equal success pass the Tanda?" "What is the Chor-Kou-La to the Tanda? these mountains are not to be compared with each other. Yesterday, three men, of the district of Tanda, chose to venture upon the mountain, two of them have disappeared in the snow, the third arrived here this morning alone and on foot, for his horse was also swallowed up. However," said the Dheba, "you can go when you like; the oulah is at your service, but you will have to pay for the oxen and horses that will die on the way." Having thus stated his ultimatum, the Thibetian diplomatist put out his tongue at us, scratched his ear, and withdrew. Whilst the Pacificator of Kingdoms, the Lama Dsiamdchang, and a few other experienced persons belonging to the caravan, were discussing earnestly the question of departure, we took up the Chinese Itinerary, and read there the following passage: "The mountain of Tanda is extremely precipitous and difficult of ascent; a stream meanders through a narrow ravine: during the summer it is miry and slippery, and during the winter it is covered with ice and snow. Travelers, provided with sticks, pass it, one after the other, like a file of fish. It is the most difficult passage on the whole way to Lha-Ssa." On reading this last sentence, the book fell from our hands. After a moment's stupor, we resumed the book, in order to assure ourselves that we had read correctly. We were right; there it was written: "It is the most difficult passage on all the way to Lha-Ssa." The prospect of having to pursue a still more arduous route than that of Alan-To was enough to stagnate the blood in our veins. "The ambassador Ki-Chan," said we to ourselves, "is evidently a cowardly assassin. Not having dared to kill us at Lha-Ssa, he has sent us to die in the midst of the snow." This fit of depression lasted but for an instant; God, in his goodness, gradually restored to us all our energies, and we rose to take part in the discussion which was proceeding around us, and the result of which was that, on the morrow, a few men of the caravan should set out before daybreak to sound the depth of the snow, and to assure themselves of the real state of the case. Towards midday the scouts returned, and announced that Mount Tanda was impassable. These tidings distressed all of us. We ourselves, although in no great hurry, were annoyed. The weather was beautiful, and we apprehended that if we did not profit by it, we should soon have fresh snow, and thus see our departure indefinitely adjourned. Whilst we were anxiously deliberating what we should do, the Dheba of the place came to relieve us from our embarrassment. He proposed to send a herd of oxen to trample down, for two days, the snow that encumbered the path up the mountain. "With this precaution," said he, "if the weather continues fine, you may, without fear, depart on your journey." The proposition of the Dheba was eagerly and gratefully adopted.

Whilst we waited until the long-haired oxen had made us a path, we enjoyed at Lang-Ki-Tsoung, a few days of salutary and agreeable repose. The Thibetians of this valley were more kindly and civilized than those we had encountered since our departure from Lha-Ri. Every evening and morning they furnished us abundantly with the appliances of cookery, they brought us pheasants, venison, fresh butter, and a sort of small sweet tubercle which they gather on the mountains. Prayer, walks, and some games of chess contributed to the delights of these days of leisure. The chessmen which we used had been given to us by the Regent of Lha-Ssa; the pieces were made of ivory, and represented various animals sculptured with some delicacy. The Chinese, as is known, are passionately fond of chess, but their game is very different from ours. The Tartar and the Thibetians are likewise acquainted with chess; and singularly enough, their chessboard is absolutely the same as our own; their pieces, although differently formed, represent the same value as ours and follow the same moves, and the rules of the game are precisely the same in every respect. What is still more surprising, these people cry *chik* when they check a piece, and *mate* when the game is at an end. These expressions, which are neither Thibetian nor Mongol, are nevertheless used by every one, yet no one can explain their origin and true signification. The Thibetians and the Tartars were not a little surprised, when we told them that, in our country, we said in the same way, *check* and *mate*.

It would be curious to unravel the archæology of the game of chess, to seek its origin and its progress amongst various nations, its introduction into Upper Asia, with the same rules and the same technical phrases that we have in Europe. This labor appertains, of right, to the *Palamede, Revue française des échecs*. We have seen among the Tartars first-rate players of chess; they play quickly, and with less study, it seemed to us, than the Europeans apply, but their moves are not the less correct.

After three days' rest, the Dheba of Lang-Ki-Tsoung having announced to us that the long-haired oxen had sufficiently trampled down the mountain paths, we departed; the sky was clouded, and the wind blew briskly. When we reached the foot of Tanda, we perceived a long dark line moving, like a huge caterpillar, slowly along the precipitous sides of the mountain. The guides of Lang-Ki-Tsoung told us that it was a troop of Lamas returning from a pilgrimage to Lha-Ssa-Morou, and who had encamped for the night at the other end of the valley. The sight of these numerous travelers restored our courage, and we resolutely undertook the ascent of the mountain. Before we reached the top, the wind began to blow violently, and drove about the snow in every direction. It seemed as though the whole mountain was falling to pieces; the ascent became so steep, that neither men nor animals had strength enough to climb up. The horses stumbled at almost every step, and if they had not been kept up by the large masses of snow, on more than one occasion they would have been precipitated into the valley of Lang-Ki-Tsoung. M. Gabet, who had not yet recovered from the illness which our first journey had occasioned him, could scarcely reach the top of Tanda; not having sufficient strength to grasp the tail of his horse, he fell from exhaustion, and became almost buried in the snow. The Thibetian escort went to his assistance, and succeeded, after long and painful exertion, in getting him to the top, where he arrived more dead than alive; his face was of a livid paleness, and his heaving breast sent forth a sound like the death-rattle.

We met on the top of the mountain the Lama pilgrims, who had preceded us; they were all lying in the snow, having beside them their long iron-feruled sticks. Some asses, laden with baggage, were packed one against the other, shivering in the cold wind, and hanging down their long ears. When all had sufficiently recovered breath, we resumed our march. The descent being almost perpendicular, we had only to sit down, and leave it to our own weight to secure our making a rapid journey. The snow, under these circumstances, was rather favorable than otherwise; it formed on the asperities of the ground a thick carpet which enabled us to slide down with impunity. We had only to deplore the loss of an ass, which, choosing to get out of the beaten path, was precipitated into an abyss.

As soon as we reached Tanda, the Mandarin, Ly-Kouo-Ngan, shook off the snow which covered his clothes, put on his hat of ceremony, and proceeded, accompanied by all his soldiers, to a small Chinese pagoda we had seen on our entrance into the village. It is reported that at the time of the wars of Kien-Long against the Thibetians, one of the Leang-Tai, charged with victualing the Chinese army, crossed during the winter the mountain of Tanda on his way to Lha-Ri. On passing the brink of an abyss filled with snow, a long-haired ox let fall a coffer of silver with which it was laden. On seeing this, the Leang-Tai sprang from his horse, threw himself upon the coffer, which he grasped in his arms, and rolled, without relaxing his hold of the treasure, to the bottom of the gulf. Tradition adds, that in the spring, the snow having melted, they found the Leang-Tai standing on his coffer of money. The Emperor Kien-Long, in honor of the devotion of this faithful commissary, who had so faithfully abided by his trust, named him the Spirit of the Mountain of Tanda, and raised a pagoda to him in the village. The Mandarins who journey to Lha-Ssa never fail to visit this temple, and to prostrate themselves thrice before the idol of the Leang-Tai. The Chinese emperors are in the habit of deifying in this manner

Pagoda of Tanda.

civil or military officers whose life has been signalized by some memorable act, and the worship rendered to these constitutes the official religion of the Mandarins.

On leaving the village of Tanda, you travel for sixty lis on a plain called Pian-Pa, which, according to the Chinese Itinerary, is the most extensive in Thibet. If this statement be correct, Thibet must be a very detestable country; for, in the first place, this so-called plain is constantly intercepted by hills and ravines, and in the second place, it is so limited in extent, that any one in the center of it can easily distinguish a man at the foot of the surrounding mountains. After passing the plain of Pian-Pa, you follow, for fifty lis, the serpentine course of a small mountain stream, and then reach Lha-Dze, where you change the oulah.

From Lha-Dze to the stage of Barilang is 100 lis journey; two-thirds of the way are occupied by the famous mountain of Dchak-Da, which is of the number of those that are reputed murderous, and which, for that reason, the Chinese call Yao-Ming-Ti-Chan; that is to say *Mountain that claims, life*. We effected its ascent and descent without any accident. We did not even get tired, for we were becoming used, by daily practise, to the hard employment of scaling mountains.

From Barilang we pursued a tolerably easy route, whence we observed, rising here and there, the smoke from a few poor Thibetian dwellings, insulated in the gorges of the mountains. We saw some black tents, and numerous herds of long-haired oxen. After a journey of 100 lis we reached Chobando.

Chobando is a small town, the houses and lamaseries of which, painted with a solution of red ochre, present, in the distance, a singular and not disagreeable appearance. The town is built on the slope of a mountain, and is enclosed, in front, by a narrow but deep river, which you cross on a wooden bridge, that shakes and groans under the feet of travelers, and seems every moment about to break down. Chobando is the most important military station you find after quitting Lha-Ri; its garrison consists of twenty-five soldiers and of an officer bearing the title of Tsien-Tsoung. This military Mandarin was an intimate friend of Ly, the pacificator of kingdoms; they had served together for several years on the frontiers of Gorkha. We were invited to sup with the Tsien-Tsoung, who managed to give us, amidst these wild and mountainous regions, a splendid repast, where were displayed Chinese delicacies of every description. During supper the two brothers-in-arms enjoyed the satisfaction of recounting to each other their former adventures.

Just as we were going to bed, two horsemen, having belts adorned with bells, came into the courtyard of the inn; they stopped for a few minutes, and then set off again at full gallop. We were informed that it was the courier-extraordinary, bearing dispatches from the ambassador Ki-Chan to Peking. He had quitted Lha-Ssa only six days before, so that he had already traveled more than 2,000 lis (200 leagues). Ordinarily, the dispatches only occupy thirty days between Lha-Ssa and Peking. This speed will, doubtless, seem in no way prodigious when compared with that of the couriers of Europe; but, making allowance for the excessive difficulties of the journey, it will perhaps be considered surprising. The express couriers, who carry the mails in Thibet, travel day and night; they always go in twos, a Chinese soldier and a Thibetian guide. At about every hundred lis, they find on the road a change of horses, but the men are not relieved so often. These couriers travel fastened to their saddles by straps; they are in the habit of observing a day of rigorous fast before mounting their horses, and all the time they are on duty, they content themselves with swallowing two raw eggs at every stage. The men who perform this arduous labor rarely attain an advanced age; many of them fall into the abysses or remain buried in the snow. Those who escape the perils of the road fall victims to the diseases which they readily contract in these dreadful regions. We had never been able to conceive how these couriers traveled by night among these mountains of Thibet, where almost at every step you find frightful precipices.

You see at Chobando two Buddhic monasteries, where numerous Lamas reside, belonging to the sect of the Yellow Cap. In one of these monasteries there is a great printing press, which furnishes sacred books to the Lamaseries of the province of Kham.

From Chobando, after two long and arduous days' march, in the turnings and windings of the mountains, and through immense forests of pine and holly, you reach Kia-Yu-Kiao. This village is built on the rugged banks of the river Souk-Tchou, which flows between two mountains, and the waters of which are wide, deep, and rapid. On our arrival we found the inhabitants of Kia-Yu-Kiao in a state of profound grief. Not long before, a large wooden bridge, thrown over the river, had broken down, and two men and three oxen that were upon it at the time perished in the waters. We could still see the remains of this bridge, built of large trunks of trees; the wood, completely rotten, showed that the bridge had fallen from decay. At sight of these sad ruins, we thanked Providence for having kept us three days on the other side of the mountain of Tanda. If we had arrived at Kia-Yu-Kiao before the fall of the bridge, it would probably have sunk under the weight of the caravan.

Contrary to our expectation, this accident caused us no delay. The Dheba of the place hastened to construct a raft, and on the morrow we were able, at daybreak, to resume our march. The men, baggage, and saddles crossed the river on the raft, the animals swimming.

Thirty lis from Kia-Yu-Kiao, we came to a wooden bridge, suspended over a frightful precipice. Having our imaginations still full of the accident at Kia-Yu-Kiao, we felt at sight of this perilous pass, a cold shudder of terror pervade all our limbs. As a matter of precaution, we made the animals pass first, one after the other; the bridge trembled and shook under them, but held firm; the men went next. They advanced gently on their toes, making themselves as light as possible. All passed safely, and the caravan proceeded again in its usual order. After having surmounted a rocky and precipitous hill, at the foot of which roared an impetuous torrent, we stayed for the night at Wa-Ho-Tchai, a station composed of a barracks, a small Chinese temple, and three or four Thibetian huts.

Immediately after our arrival the snow began to fall in great flakes. In any other place, such weather would have been merely disagreeable; at Wa-Ho-Tchai, it was calamitous. We had next day to travel a stage of 150 lis, on a plateau famous throughout Thibet. The Itinerary gave us the following details as to this route: "On the mountain Wa-Ho there is a lake. That people may not lose themselves in the thick fogs which prevail here, there have been fixed on the heights wooden signals. When the mountain is covered with deep snow you are guided by these signals; but you must take care not to make a noise; you must abstain from even uttering a word, otherwise the ice and snow will fall upon you in abundance, and with astonishing rapidity. Throughout the mountain you find neither beast nor bird, for it is frozen during the four seasons of the year. On its sides, and within 100 lis distance there is no dwelling. Many Chinese soldiers and Thibetians die there of cold."

The soldiers of the garrison of Wa-Ho-Tchai, finding that the weather seemed really made up for snow, opened the gates of the little pagoda, and lighted a number of small red candles in front of a formidable-looking idol, brandishing a sword in its right-hand, and holding in the other a bow and a bundle of arrows. They then struck, with repeated blows, on a small tam-tam, and executed a flourish on a tambourine. Ly-Kouo-Ngan assumed his official costume, and went to prostrate himself before the idol. On his return we asked in whose honor this pagoda had been raised.

"It is the pagoda of Kiang-Kian [1] Mao-Ling." "And what did Kiang-Kian do, that he is thus honored?" "Oh, I see that you are ignorant of these events of times gone by. I will tell you about him. In the reign of Khang-Hi the empire was at war with Thibet. Mao-Ling was sent against the rebels in the rank of generalissimo. Just as he was going to pass the mountain Wa-Ho with a body of 4,000 men, some of the people of the locality who acted as guides warned him that every one, in crossing the mountain, must observe silence, under penalty of being buried beneath the snow. Kiang-Kian issued forthwith an edict to his soldiers, and the army proceeded in the most profound silence. As the mountain was too long for the soldiers, laden with baggage, to cross it in a single day, they encamped on the plateau. Conformably with the established rule in large towns of the empire, and of camps in time of war, as soon as it was night they fired off a cannon, Mao-Ling not daring to infringe this rule of military discipline. The report of the cannon had scarcely subsided, when enormous blocks of snow came pouring down from the sky upon the mountain. Kiang-Kian and all his men were buried beneath the fall, and no one has ever since discovered their bodies. The only persons saved were the cook and three servants of Kiang-Kian, who had gone on before, and arrived that same day in the village where we are. The Emperor Khang-Hi created Kiang-Kian Mao-Ling tutelary genius of the mountain Wa-Ho, and had this pagoda erected to him, on the condition of protecting travelers from the snow."

Ly-Kouo-Ngan having finished his story, we asked him who was the potent being that sent down these terrible masses of snow, ice, and hail, when any one presumed to

[1] The Kiang-Kian are the highest dignitaries of the military hierarchy in China; they are decorated with the red button. Each province has a Kiang-Kian, who is its military governor, and a Tsoung-Tou, or viceroy, who is its chief literary Mandarin.

make a noise in crossing the mountain Wa-Ho? "Oh, that is perfectly clear," answered he; "it is the Spirit of the Mountain, the Hia-Ma-Tching-Chin" (the deified toad). "A deified toad!" "Oh, yes; you know that on the top of Wa-Ho there is a lake." "We have just read so in the Itinerary." "Well, on the borders of this lake there is a great toad. We can scarcely ever see him, but you often hear him croaking 100 lis round. This toad has dwelt on the borders of the lake since the existence of heaven and earth. As he has never quitted this solitary spot, he has been deified, and has become the Spirit of the Mountain. When any one makes a noise and disturbs the silence of his retreat, he becomes exasperated against him, and punishes him by overwhelming him with hail and snow." "You seem to speak quite in earnest; do you think that a toad can be deified and become a spirit?" "Why not, if he makes a point every night of worshiping the Great Bear?" When Ly-Kouo-Ngan came to his singular system of the Great Bear, it was futile to reason with him. We contented ourselves with smiling at him and holding our tongues. "Ah!" said he, "you laugh at me because I speak of the Seven Stars; and, indeed, as you do not believe in their influence, it is wrong in me to speak to you of them. I ought merely to have told you that the toad of Wa-Ho was deified, because he had always lived in solitude, on a wild mountain, inaccessible to the foot of man. Is it not the passions of man that pervert all the beings of the creation, and prevent them from attaining perfection? Would not animals in the course of time become spirits if they did not breathe an air poisoned by the presence of man?" This argument seeming to us somewhat more philosophical than the first, we vouchsafed the honor of a serious answer. Ly-Kouo-Ngan, who possessed a fair judgment, when he was not confused with this Great Bear, doubted at length the power of the deified toad, and the protection of Kiang-Kian Mao-Ling. Just as we were going to repeat our evening prayer, Ly-Kouo-Ngan said to us: "Whatever may be the actual case with the toad and Kiang-Kian, this is certain, that our journey to-morrow will be fatiguing and perilous; since you are Lamas of the Lord of Heaven, pray to him to protect the caravan." "That is what we do every day," answered we; "but on account of to-morrow's journey, we shall do so in an especial manner this evening." We had scarcely slept two hours when one of the soldiers noisily entered our room, hung on a peg in the wall a large red lantern, and announced that the cock had already crowed once. We had, therefore, to rise, and make, with expedition, the preparations for departure, for we had 150 lis to march before we reached the next stage. The sky was studded with stars, but the snow had fallen the evening before in such abundance, that it had added to former layers another of a foot thick. This was precisely what we wanted, by way of carpet, to facilitate the passage of Wa-Ho, a mountain perpetually covered with frozen snow, almost as slippery as a glacier.

The caravan set out long before daybreak; it advanced slowly and silently along the tortuous paths of the mountain, sufficiently lighted up by the whiteness of the snow and the luster of the stars. The sun was beginning to tinge the horizon with red when we reached the plateau. The fear of the Great Toad having dissipated with the night, every one now broke the silence to which he had been condemned. First the guides commenced vituperating the long-haired oxen that were wandering beyond the beaten path. By and by the travelers themselves hazarded some reflections on the mildness of the air and the unexpected facility of the route. At length we altogether scorned the anger of the Toad, and every one talked, hallooed, chattered, or sang, without seeming in the least apprehensive of the fall of snow or hail. Never, perhaps, had the caravan been so noisy as on this occasion.

The aspect of the plateau of Wa-Ho is extremely melancholy and monotonous. As far as the eye can reach, nothing is to be seen but snow; not a single tree, not even a trace of wild animals, interrupts the monotony of this immense plain. Only, at intervals, you come to a long pole, blackened by time, which serves to guide the march of caravans. Throughout this extended mountain travelers do not find even a place to prepare their tea and take refreshment. Those who have not strength enough to pass twenty hours without eating or drinking, swallow, as they go, a few handfuls of snow, and a little tsamba previously prepared.

Throughout the day the sky was pure and serene, not a single cloud obscuring for a moment the rays of the sun. This excess of fine weather was to us the source of the greatest suffering; the glare of the snow was so intensely dazzling, that the hair spectacles did not suffice to keep our eyes from severe inflammation.

When darkness began to spread over the mountain, we had reached the edge of the plateau. We descended by a narrow, rugged path, and after a thousand twistings and turnings in a deep gorge, we reached at length the stage of Ngenda-Tchai, where we passed the night in intolerable suffering. Everybody was continually crying and groaning as though his eyes had been torn out. Next day it was impossible to proceed. The Lama Dsiamdchang, who knew something of physic, made a general distribution of medicine and eye-salve, and we all spent the day with our eyes bandaged.

Thanks to the drugs of the Lama, the next day we were able to open our eyes and continue our journey. Three stages separated us from Tsiamdo; and they were very laborious and annoying stages, for we were obliged to cross a number of those odious wooden bridges, suspended over torrents, rivers, and precipices. The recollection of the recent catastrophe at Kia-Yu-Kiao haunted us incessantly. After having pursued for twenty lis a narrow path on the rugged banks of a large river called the Khiang-Tang-Tchou, we at length reached Tsiando. Thirty-six days had elapsed since our departure from Lha-Ssa. According to the Chinese Itinerary we had traveled 2,500 lis (250 leagues).

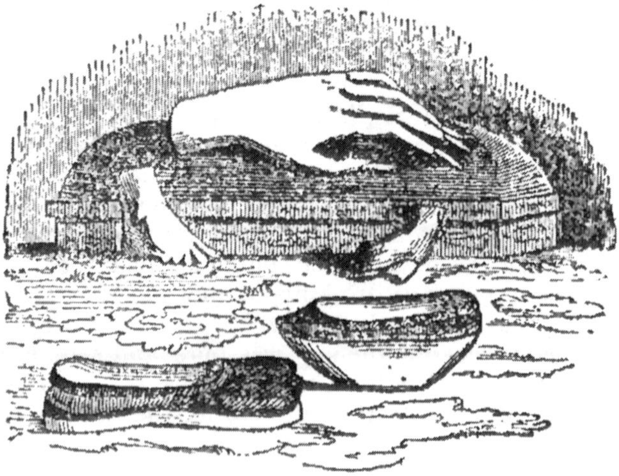

Chinese hand, foot, shoes, &c.

Proul-Tamba, a celebrated Thibetian Chief.

CHAPTER IX.

Glance at Tsiamdo—War Between the Living Buddhas—We Meet a Small Caravan —Calcareous Mountains—Death of the Mandarin Pey—The Great Chief Proul-Tamba—Visit to the Castle of Proul-Tamba—Buddhist Hermit—War Among the Tribes—Halt at Angti—Thibetian Museum—Passage of the Mountain Angti—Town of Djaya—Death of the Son of the Mandarin Pey—Musk Deer —River with Gold Sands—Plain and Town of Bathang—Great Forest of Ta-So—Death of Ly-Kouo-Ngan—Interview with the Mandarins of Lithang—Various Bridges of Thibet—Arrival on the Frontiers of China—Residence at Ta-Tsien-Lou—Departure for the Capital of the Province of Sse-Tchouen.

THE Chinese government has established at Tsiamdo[1] a magazine of provisions, the management of which is confided to a Liang-Tai. The garrison is composed of about 300 soldiers and four officers, a Yeou-Ki, a Tsien-Tsoung, and two Pa-Tsoung. The maintenance of this military station, and of the garrisons dependent upon it, amounts annually to the sum of 10,000 ounces of silver.

Tsiamdo, the capital of the province of Kham, is built in a valley surrounded by high mountains. Formerly it was enclosed by a rampart of earth, now broken down everywhere, and the remnants of which are taken away every day to repair the floors of the houses. Tsiamdo, indeed, has little need of fortifications; it is sufficiently de-

[1] On Andriveau-Goujon's map, this place is called Chamiton.

fended by two rivers, the Dza-Tchou and the Om-Tchou, which, after flowing, the one to the east, the other to the west of the town, unite on the south, and form the Ya-Long-Kiang, which crosses, from north to south, the province of Yun-Nan and Cochin-China, and falls at length into the sea of China. Two large wooden bridges, one over the Dza-Tchou, the other over the Om-Tchou, to the right and left of the town, lead to two parallel roads, the first called the Sse-Tchouen road, the other the Yun-Nan road. The couriers who convey the mails from Peking to Lha-Ssa, and all the civil and military servants of the Chinese government, are obliged to use the Sse-Tchouen road; that of Yun-Nan is almost deserted. You only see there, from time to time, a few Chinese merchants, who purchase, from the Mandarins of their provinces, the privilege of going to Thibet to sell their merchandise.

The military stations which the court of Peking has established in the states of the Talé-Lama were at one time maintained and managed by the joint authorities of Sse-Tchouen and Yun-Nan. This combination having been, for a long time, the source of dissensions and quarrels between the Mandarins of the two provinces, it was determined that the viceroy of Sse-Tchouen should be sole director of the Chinese resident in Thibet.

Tsiamdo presents the appearance of an ancient town in decay; its large houses, constructed with frightful irregularity, are scattered confusedly over a large tract, leaving on all sides unoccupied ground or heaps of rubbish. Except a few buildings of later date, all the rest bear the stamp of great antiquity. The numerous population you see in the different quarters of the town are dirty, uncombed, and wallow in profound idleness.

We could not divine what were the means of existence of the inhabitants of Tsiamdo; they are without arts, industry, and, we may add, almost without agriculture. The environs of the town present, generally speaking, nothing but sands, unfavorable to the cultivation of corn. They grow, however, some poor crops of barley, but these are, doubtless, insufficient for the supply of the country. Possibly musk, skins of wild beasts, rhubarb, turquoises, and gold-dust provide the population with the means of a petty commerce, and thus with the necessaries of life.

Although Tsiamdo is not a place remarkable for its luxury or elegance, you admire there a large and magnificent Lamasery standing towards the west, on an elevated platform which commands the rest of the town. It is inhabited by about 2000 Lamas, who, instead of each having his small house, as in the other Buddhic monasteries, live all together in the large buildings, with which the principal temple is surrounded. The sumptuous decorations that ornament this temple make it regarded as one of the finest and most wealthy in Thibet. The Lamasery of Tsiamdo has for its ecclesiastical superior a Houtouktou Lama, who is at the same time temporal sovereign of the whole province of Kham.

Five lis from Tsiamdo, towards the frontiers of China, there is a town called Djaya, which, with the countries dependent on it, is subject to a Grand Lama, bearing the title of Tchaktchouba. This Lamanesque dignity is somewhat inferior to that of Houtouktou. At the time we were in Thibet, there arose a great contest between the Houtouktou of Tsiamdo and the Tchaktchouba of Djaya. The latter, a young, bold, and enterprising Lama, had declared himself Houtouktou, in virtue of an old diploma, which he affirmed had been granted to him, in one of his former lives, by the Talé-Lama. He asserted, accordingly, his rights to supremacy, and claimed the see of Tsiamdo and the government of the province of Kham. The Houtouktou of Tsiamdo, a Lama advanced in years, did not choose to resign his authority, and, on his side, alleged authentic titles, sent by the court of Peking, and confirmed by the Grand Lama of Lha-Ssa. All the tribes, and all the Lamaseries of the province, entered into this quarrel, and took part, some with the young Lama, some with the old. After long and futile discussions, written and verbal, they resorted to arms, and for a full year these wild and fanatic tribes were engaged in bloody conflicts. Whole villages were destroyed, and their inhabitants cut in pieces. In their terrible fury, these ferocious combatants devastated everything; they pursued into the desert, with arrows and fusils, the herds of goats and long-haired oxen, and in their destructive course, set fire to the forests they found on their way.

When we arrived at Tsiamdo the war had ceased some

days, and all parties had consented to a truce, in hopes of effecting a reconciliation. Thibetian and Chinese negotiators had been sent by the Talé-Lama and the ambassador Ki-Chan conjointly. The youthful Houtouktou of Djaya had been summoned to this congress, and fearful of treachery, he had come with a formidable escort of his bravest partisans. Several conferences had been held without producing any satisfactory result. Neither the one nor the other of the two pretenders would withdraw his claims; the parties were irreconcilable, and everything presaged that the war would be soon resumed with fresh fury. It appeared to us that the party of the young Houtouktou had every chance of success, because it was the most national, and consequently the most popular and strongest. Not that his title was really better founded or more valid than that of his competitor, but it was easy to see that the old Houtouktou of Tsiamdo had hurt the pride of his tribes by invoking the arbitration of the Chinese, and relying upon the aid of the government of Peking. All foreign intervention is odious and detestable. This is truth, alike in Europe and in the mountains of Thibet, wherever people care for their independence and their dignity.

Our residence at Tsiamdo was quite exempt from the irritation and rage that reigned about us. We were treated with all those marks of attention and kindness which we had experienced on all our journey since our departure from Lha-Ssa. Both the young and the old Houtouktou sent us a scarf of blessing, with a good provision of butter and quarters of mutton.

We stayed at Tsiamdo three days; for our guide, the Pacificator of Kingdoms, had great need of rest. The fatigues of this arduous route had sensibly affected his health. His legs were so swollen that he could not mount or dismount from his horse without the assistance of several persons. The physicians and sorcerers of Tsiamdo, whom he consulted, gave answers, the clearest meaning of which was, that if the malady diminished, it would be no great matter; but that if it should grow worse, it might become a serious affair. The most reasonable counselors advised Ly-Kouo-Ngan to continue his journey in a palanquin. A Chinese Mandarin of the place offered to sell him his own, and to engage carriers. This advice was perfectly prudent;

but avarice interposed, and the sick man protested that he should be more fatigued in a palanquin than on horseback.

To the illness of Ly-Kouo-Ngan was added another source of delay. A Chinese caravan which had left Lha-Ssa a few days after us had arrived at Tsiamdo on the same evening with ourselves. This caravan consisted of a Liang-Tai, or commissary, of his son, a young man of eighteen, and of a numerous suite of soldiers and servants. We wanted to let these pass on before, for, if we traveled in company, it was to be feared that we should not find lodgings and oulah sufficient for so great a number. The Liang-Tai and his son traveled in palanquins; but, notwithstanding the conveniences of this mode of conveyance, the two illustrious travelers were so extenuated with fatigue, and so languid, that it was the general impression their strength would not suffice to carry them into China. The literary Mandarins being used to an easy life, are little adapted for supporting the innumerable miseries of the journey into Thibet. Among those who are sent to fulfil the duties of commissary, few are fortunate enough to return to their country.

The day of our departure, the old Houtouktou of Tsiamdo sent us an escort of four Thibetian horsemen, to guard us until we reached the territory of the Tchaktchouba of Djaya. On quitting the town, we passed over a magnificent bridge entirely built of large trunks of fir, and we then found ourselves on the Sse-Tchouen road, which meanders along the sides of a high mountain, at the base of which runs the rapid river Dza-Tchou. After proceeding twenty lis, we met, at a turn of the mountain, in a deep and retired gorge, a little party of travelers, who presented a picture full of poetry. The procession was opened by a Thibetian woman astride a fine donkey, and carrying an infant, solidly fastened to her shoulders by large leathern straps. She led after her, by a long cord, a pack-horse, laden with two panniers, which hung symmetrically on its sides. These two panniers served as lodgings for two children, whose laughing joyous faces we saw peeping out from little windows in their respective baskets. The difference in the age of these children seemed slight; but they could not be of the same weight, for to keep the equilibrium between them, a large stone was tied to the side of one of the panniers. Behind the horse laden with these child-boxes followed a horseman,

Thibetian Travelers.

whom one easily recognized, by his costume, as a retired Chinese soldier. He had behind him, on the crupper, a boy of twelve years old. Last of all an enormous red-haired dog, with squinting eyes, and an expression altogether of decided bad temper, completed this singular caravan, which joined us, and took advantage of our company as far as the province of Sse-Tchouen.

The Chinese was an ex-soldier of the garrison of Tsiamdo. Having performed the three years' service required by law, he had obtained leave to remain in Thibet, and to engage in commerce. He had married, and after having amassed a little fortune, he was returning to his country with all his family.

We could not but admire the fortitude, the energy, and the devotion of this brave Chinese, so different from his selfish countrymen, who never scruple to leave their wives and children in foreign lands. He had to bear up, not only against the dangers and fatigues of a long journey, but also against the raillery of those who themselves had not the heart to follow his good example. The soldiers of our escort soon began to turn him into ridicule. "This man," said they, "is evidently insane; to bring from foreign countries money and merchandise, that is reasonable; but to bring into the central nation a large-footed woman and all these little barbarians, why, it is contrary to all established usages. Has the fellow an idea of making money by exhibiting these animals of Thibet?"

More than once observations of this kind excited our indignation. We always made a point of defending this worthy father, of commending his honorable conduct, and of reproving loudly the barbarity and immorality of the Chinese customs.

Shortly after we had admitted into our caravan the interesting little party from Tsiamdo, we left the river Dza-Tchou to our right, and ascended a high mountain covered with large trees and enormous rocks, themselves covered with thick coats of lichen. We afterwards again came upon the river, and proceeded along its banks, by a rugged path, for a few lis, till we arrived at Meng-Phou. We had traveled scarcely eight leagues, but we were overcome with fatigue. The three days' rest we had taken at Tsiamdo had modified our equestrian powers, so that we had some difficulty in getting our legs into riding order again. Meng-Phou consists of seven or eight huts, built of rough stone, in a large and deep ravine.

Next day we traveled along the crest of a lofty mountain, having continually to mount and dismount, in order to get from one eminence to another. On this route we had frequently to cross precipices on wooden bridges, which, to use the expression of the Chinese Itinerary, are "suspended in the region of the clouds." After a march of 60 lis we reached Pao-Tun, where we changed the oulah, and where we began to find the Thibetians less complaisant and docile than on the other side of Tsiamdo. Their mien was haughtier and their manner more abrupt. On the other hand, the Chinese of the caravan became more humble, less exacting, and prudently abstained from speaking in a domineering fashion. All the way from Pao-Tun to Bagoung, you see nothing for ten leagues but calcareous mountains, entirely bare and rough. No trees are to be seen, nor grass, nor even moss. Below you only remark, in the fissures of the rocks, a little verdant stone-crop, which seems to protest against the desolate sterility around. One of these mountains, which the Chinese call Khou-Loung-Chan, which means the perforated mountain, presents a very singular appearance. You see here a great number of holes and hollows, in infinite variety of form and size. Some of these apertures resemble huge doorways. The smaller look like bells, some like round and oval skylights.

The mountain being in the peak form, we were not able to go and visit these caverns. However, we approached sufficiently near to them to be able to judge that they are all of a considerable depth. These numerous cavities resulting, probably, from old volcanic eruptions, are attributed by the Chinese to the Kouei, or evil genii. The Thibetians, on the contrary, affirm that they were dug by the tutelary deities of the country; that, in ancient times, some Lamas of great sanctity made them their retreat, and that therein they were transformed into Buddha; and that at certain periods of the year you still hear within the mountain the murmur of Lama prayers.

In Thibet, we had never observed on our route other mountains than those of a granitic nature, always remarkable for masses of enormous stones, heaped upon one another, generally assuming a form originally quadrangular, but rounded at the angles by the incessant action of the wind and rain. These enormous calcareous masses, which we observed on our way to Bagoung, could not fail to fix our attention. In fact, the country began entirely to change its aspect. For more than a fortnight we saw nothing but calcareous mountains, producing a marble as white as snow, of a fine and very close grain. The shepherds of these regions are in the habit of cutting from them large slabs, on which they carve the image of Buddha, or the formula "Om mani padme houm," and which they afterwards place on the roadside. These carvings remain for many years, without being in the least defaced, for this marble having a great quantity of silex closely intermixed with carbonate of chalk, is extremely hard. Before our arrival at Bagoung, we journeyed for four or five lis, along a road bordered on both sides by two unbroken lines of these Buddhic inscriptions. We saw some Lamas engraving the *mani* on marble slabs.

We reached the little village of Bagoung a little before nightfall, and proceeded to dismount at a Chinese barracks, composed of a few huts built of magnificent fragments of white marble, cemented with mud and dung. As soon as we arrived, they announced to us the death of the Liang-Tai, named Pei, who had overtaken us at Tsiamdo. It was two days before, that his caravan had passed through Bagoung. Having reached the barracks, the bearers of the Mandarin, after setting down the palanquin, had opened the curtains, as usual, to invite his excellency to enter the apartment that had been prepared for him. But in the palanquin, they only found a corpse. In accordance with the Chinese usages, the son of the departed could not leave the body of his father in a foreign land, but must take it to his family, in order to deposit it in the sepulcher of his ancestors. Now, we were still in the heart of Thibet, and the family of the Mandarin Pei was in the province of Tche-Kiang, altogether at the extremity of China. The route, as has been seen, was difficult and long; but hesitation in the matter was out of the question: filial piety had to surmount all obstacles. A coffin, ready made, was, by chance, in the guard-house. The son of the Mandarin bought it at a high price from the soldiers; he deposited therein the remains of his father. They adapted the shafts of the palanquin to the coffin, and the carriers, in consideration of increased pay, agreed to carry to the frontiers of China, a dead instead of a living man. The caravan had quitted Bagoung the evening preceding our arrival.

The announcement of this death astonished and affected all of us.

Ly-Kouo-Ngan particularly, who was in no satisfactory state of mind, was thunderstruck. The fear he felt prevented him from taking any supper; but, in the evening, another matter occurred to divert his attention from these sad thoughts of death. The chief of the Thibetian village came to the guard-house, to announce to the travelers, that it had been resolved in that country, that thereafter they would not supply the oulah gratuitously; that for a horse, people must pay one ounce of silver, and for a yak half an ounce. "The caravan which passed yesterday," added he, "was obliged to agree to this." . . . To make it manifest that this regulation would not admit of any discussion, he abruptly put his tongue in his cheek at us, and withdrew.

A manifesto so plain and definite was a complete thunderbolt to the Pacificator of Kingdoms. He entirely forgot the melancholy death of the poor Liang-Tai, in the thought of this frightful catastrophe which threatened his purse. We charitably participated in his affliction, and tried, as well as we could, to conform our words to his somber thoughts. But, in reality, it was a matter of utter indifference to us. If they refused to supply us with the means of continuing our journey, we should merely have to stay in Thibet, which, after all, was a result to which we should without difficulty become reconciled. Meantime, we went to bed, and left the people of the escort to discuss politics and social economy.

The next day, when we rose, we found neither oxen nor horses in the court of the barracks. Ly-Kouo-Ngan was in utter despair. "Shall we have the oulah?" inquired we; "shall we depart to-day?" "These barbarians," answered he, "do not comprehend the merit of obedience. I have resolved to address myself to Proul-Tamba; I have sent a deputation to him; I have known him a long time, and I hope he will procure the oulah for us." This Proul-Tamba was a person of whom we had already heard a great deal. He was at the head of the party of the young Tchaktchouba of Djaya, and consequently the avowed enemy of Chinese influence. He was, we were informed, learned as the most learned Lamas of Lha-Ssa. No one came up to him in valor; never in battle had he experienced defeat. Accordingly, among all the tribes of the province of Kham, his name alone had potency, and acted like a talisman on the minds of the multitude. Proul-Tamba was, in some measure, the Abd-el-Kader of these wild mountaineers.

The dwelling of Proul-Tamba was distant from Bagoung not more than five or six lis. The deputation that had been sent to him soon returned, and announced that the great chief himself was coming. This unexpected news put in commotion the whole Thibetian village, and the soldiers. Every one said to every one, excitedly, "The great chief is coming, we are going to see the great chief!" Ly-Kouo-Ngan hastened to attire himself in his best clothes, his silk boots, and his hat of ceremony. The Chinese soldiers, also improved, as well as they could, their toilet. Whilst the Thibetians ran to meet their chief, Ly-Kouo-Ngan selected from his baggage a magnificent khata, or scarf of blessing, and then posted himself on the threshold of the door, to receive the illustrious Proul-Tamba. As for us the department we selected was to study the physiognomy of the different parties. The most interesting was, doubtless, that of the Pacificator of Kingdoms. It was curious to see this Chinese Mandarin, generally so haughtily insolent in the presence of Thibetians, become all at once humble and modest, and awaiting, tremblingly, the arrival of a man whom he deemed strong and potent.

At last the great chief appeared; he was on horseback, escorted by a guard of honor, consisting or four horsemen. As soon as all had dismounted, the Pacificator of Kingdoms approached Proul-Tamba, made him a low bow, and offered him the scarf of blessing. Proul-Tamba motioned to one of his attendants to receive the present, and without saying a word, quickly crossed the court, and went straight to the room prepared for his reception, and where we awaited him with the Lama Dchiamdchang. Proul-Tamba made us a slight bow, and sat down without ceremony, in the place of honor, on a carpet of gray felt. Ly-Kouo-Ngan placed himself on his left, the Lama Dchiamdchang on his right, and we in front of him. Between us five there was such a respectful distance, that we formed a sort of large circle. Some Chinese soldiers and a crowd of Thibetians stood behind us.

There was a minute of profound silence. The great chief (Proul-Tamba) was at most forty years of age; he was of middle height, and his sole attire was a large robe of green silk, bordered with beautiful wolf-fur, and fastened at the waist by a red girdle. Large purple leather boots, an alarming fox-skin cap, and a broad, long saber, passed through the girdle horizontally, completed his costume. Long hair, black as ebony, which hung down over his shoulders, gave to his pale, thin face, a marked expression of energy. The eyes were, however, the most remarkable features in the physiognomy of this man; they were large, glittering, and seemed to breathe indomitable courage and pride. The whole appearance and bearing of Proul-Tamba denoted a man of real superiority, born to command his fellows. After having attentively looked at us, one after the other, his hands resting one on each end of his saber, he drew from his bosom a packet of little khatas, and had them distributed amongst us by one of his men. Then turning to Ly-Kouo-Ngan: "Ah, thou art back again," said he, with a voice that resounded like a bell; "if they had not told me this morning it was thee, I should not have recognized thee. How thou hast aged since thy last visit to Bagoung." "Yes, thou art right," answered the Pacificator of Kingdoms, in soft and insinuating tones, drawing himself along the felt carpet nearer to his interlocutor; "yes, I am very feeble; but thou art more vigorous than ever." "We live in circumstances under which it is necessary to be vigorous; there is no longer peace in our mountains." "True, I heard yonder that you have had here amongst you a little dispute." "For more than a year past, the tribes of Kham have been waging a bloody war, and thou callest that a little dispute. Thou hast only to open thy eyes, on thy way, and thou wilt behold, on every side, villages in ruins, and forests burnt down. In a few days, we shall be obliged to resume our work, for no one will hear the words of peace. The war, indeed, might have been brought to a conclusion after a few skirmishes; but, since you Chinese have chosen to meddle in our affairs, the parties have become irreconcilable. You Chinese Mandarins are good for nothing but to bring disorder and confusion into these countries. It cannot go on in this way. We have let you alone for some time, and now your audacity knows no bounds. I cannot, without shuddering all over, think of that affair of the Nomekhan of Lha-Ssa. They pretend that the Nomekhan committed great crimes. It is false: these great crimes, it is you that invented them. The Nomekhan is a saint, a Living Buddha. Who ever heard that a Living Buddha could be tried and exiled by Ki-Chan, a Chinese, a layman?" "The order came from the Grand Emperor!" answered Ly-Kouo-Ngan in a low and tremulous voice. "The Grand Emperor!" cried Proul-Tamba, turning with an angry air to his interrupter, "thy Grand Emperor is only a layman. What is thy Grand Emperor compared with a Grand Lama, a Living Buddha? The great chief to the province of Kham inveighed for a length of time against the domination of the Chinese in Thibet. He assailed in turns the Emperor, the viceroy of Sse-Tchouen, and the ambassador of Lha-Ssa."

Throughout these energetic philippics, he frequently reverted to the affair of the Nomekhan. One could see that he felt a deep interest in the fate of the Grand Lama, whom he regarded as a victim of the court of Peking. The Pacificator of Kingdoms took care not to contradict him; he affected to concur in the sentiments of Proul-Tamba, and received each proposition with an inclination of the head. At length he hazarded a word as to departure and the oulah.

"The oulah," replied Proul-Tamba; "henceforth, there will be none for the Chinese, unless they pay the price for them. It is enough that we allow the Chinese to penetrate into our country, without adding the folly of furnishing them with the oulah gratuitously. However, as thou art an old acquaintance, we will make an exception in favor of thy caravan. Besides, thou art conducting two Lamas of the Western Heaven, who have been recommended to me by the chief Kalon of Lha-Ssa, and who are entitled to my services. Where is the Dheba of Bagoung? Let him advance."

The individual who, the evening before, had come to tell us, "no more money, no more oulah," presented himself. He bent his knee before the great chief, and respectfully put his tongue in his cheek at him. "Let them get ready the oulah immediately," cried Proul-Tamba, "and let every one do his duty." The Thibetians, who were in the courtyard, sent forth a simultaneous shout of submission, and ran off to the adjacent village.

Proul-Tamba rose, and after having invited us to take tea in his house, which stood on our road, sprang on his horse, and returned home at full gallop. The oulah soon appeared, and the caravan found itself organized, as it were, by magic. After half an hour's march, we reached the residence of the great chief. It was a lofty, large structure, not unlike a stronghold of the feudal times. A broad canal, bordered with large trees, encircled it. A drawbridge descended for us. We dismounted to cross it, and entered, through an immense gateway, a square court, where my lord Proul-Tamba awaited us. They tied the horses to posts planted in the middle of the court, and we were introduced into a vast saloon, which seemed to serve as the domestic temple, or castle chapel. The enormous beams which supported the roof were entirely gilt. The walls were hung with flags of all colors, covered with Thibetian inscriptions.

At the end of the saloon were three colossal statues of Buddha, before which were placed large butter lamps and censers. In a corner of the temple, they had prepared a low table, with four thick cushions, covered with red stuff. Proul-Tamba graciously invited us to take our places, and as soon as we were seated, the chatelaine made her appearance in state costume, that is to say, with her face frightfully daubed over with black, her copious tresses adorned with spangles, red coral beads, and small mother-of-pearl buttons.

In her right hand she carried a majestic tea-pot, the vast circumference of which rested on her left arm. Each of us presented his cup, which was filled with a bumper of tea, on the surface of which floated a thick coat of butter: the tea was of the best quality. While we were sipping the hot fluid, our hostess reappeared, bearing two dishes of gilt wood, the one full of raisins, the other of nuts. "These are fruits of our country," said Proul-Tamba to us; "they grow in a fine valley not far distant. In the Western Heaven, have you fruits of this kind?" "Oh, yes, plentifully; and you cannot conceive how much pleasure you give us in presenting to us these fruits, for they recall to us our country," and, as we spoke, we took a handful of raisins from the gilt plate. Unfortunately, they were only remarkable for a tough and sour skin, and for a number of pips, which cracked under our teeth like gravel. We turned to the nuts, which were of a magnificent size, but were again deceived; the kernel was so solidly fixed in its hard shell, that it was as much as we could do to extract a few morsels with the tips of our nails. We returned to the raisins, then again to the nuts, traveling from one plate to the other in search, but vainly, of something wherewith to quiet the gnawings of our stomach. We were growing convinced that Mrs. Proul-Tamba had resolved to play us a trick, when we saw two vigorous Thibetians approach, carrying another table, on which was a whole kid, and a superb haunch of venison. This unexpected apparition gladdened our hearts, and an involuntary smile must have announced to our Amphitryon how favorably his second service was received. They removed the skins of raisins and the nut shells; Thibetian beer took the place of the buttered tea, and we set to work with incomparable energy. When we had triumphantly achieved this Homeric repast, we offered to the grand chief a scarf of blessing, and remounted our horses. Not far from the feudal castle of the illustrious Proul-Tamba, we came to a calcareous hill, with great apertures on its summit, and on its rugged sides numerous Buddhic sentences cut in gigantic characters. All the Thibetians stopped, and prostrated themselves thrice to the

The Hermit of the Mountain.

ground. This mountain was the retreat of a hermit Lama, for whom all the tribes of the province of Kham entertained profound veneration. According to the statement of the natives, this holy Lama had withdrawn, twenty-two years before, to one of the caverns of the mountain; since that time, he had remained in it, without quitting it once, passing day and night in prayer, and in the contemplation of the ten thousand virtues of Buddha. He allowed no one to visit him. Every three years, however, he gave a grand audience of eight days, and, during that period, the devout might present themselves freely at his cell, and consult him about things past, present, and to come. At this time, large offerings failed not to pour in from every quarter: the sainted Lama kept none for himself, but distributed them among the poor of the district. What did he want with riches and the good things of this world? His cell, dug out of the living rock, never required the least repair; his yellow robe, lined with sheepskin, served him alike in all seasons of the year. On every sixth day only did he take a repast, consisting of a little tea and barley-meal, which charitable persons in the vicinity passed to him by means of a long cord, which descended from the top of the grotto to the foot of the mountain.

Several Lamas had placed themselves under the direction of this hermit, and had resolved to adopt his manner of life. They dwelt in cells, dug near that of their master. The most celebrated of his disciples was the father of the great Proul-Tamba. He, also, had been a famous warrior, and ever at the head of the people of this country. Having reached an advanced age, and seeing his son capable of being his successor, he had conferred on him the title of Grand Chief. Then shaving his head, and assuming the sacred habit of the Lamas, he had retired into solitude, leaving to younger and more vigorous hands the charge of terminating the contest which had commenced between the two Houtouktous of the province of Kham.

The sun had not set when we reached the station of Wang-Tsa, fifty lis from Bagoung. Wang-Tsa is a small village built at the foot of a hill of black loam, covered with thickets of holly and cypress. The houses, built of the black soil, communicate to the village an extremely somber and funereal aspect. At Wang-Tsa, we began to observe traces of the civil war, which was laying waste these countries. The Chinese barracks, built of large fir planks, had been entirely burned; its remains, half-charred, which lay about, served throughout the evening to keep up a magnificent fire. Upon setting out next morning, we observed a singular alteration in the caravan. The horses and oxen were the same that we had taken from Bagoung, but all the Thibetian guides had vanished; not one of them remained: women of Wang-Tsa had taken their place. Upon inquiring the meaning of this new and surprising arrangement: "To-day," answered the Lama Dchiamdchang, "we shall reach Gaya, which is a hostile village. If the Bagoung men went there, there would inevitably be a fight, and the inhabitants of Gaya would seize the animals of the caravan. The oulah being conducted by women, we have nothing to fear. Men, who would have the cowardice to fight with women, and take the animals confided to their care, would be despised by the whole world. Such is the usage of these countries." We were not a little surprised to find, among the wild mountains of Thibet, sentiments so like those of our own country. This was pure French chivalry. We were eager to see in what courteous and gallant fashion the ladies of Wang-Tsa would be received by the gentlemen of Gaya.

After passing a lofty mountain, covered with large masses of rock, partly buried in old layers of snow, we entered a valley thoroughly cultivated, and of a mild temperature. We perceived in the distance, in a hollow, the houses of Gaya. They were high, flanked with watch-towers, and not unlike castles. When we were some hundred paces from this large village, there issued from it all at once a formidable squadron of cavalry, who dashed forward to meet the caravan. The horsemen, armed with fusils and long lances, seemed quite disposed for a skirmish. Their martial humor, however, vanished, when they perceived that the caravan was conducted by women; and they contented themselves with hearty shouts of laughter, and with expressions of contempt at the cowardice of their foes. As we entered Gaya, men, women, and children, were all in motion, and sending forth cries, that seemed to us anything but amicable. No mischance, however, occurred. We dismounted in the court of a large three-storied house, and as soon as they had unsaddled the horses, and unyoked the long-haired oxen, the ladies of Wang-Tsa drank hastily a cup of buttered tea, which was courteously handed round to each, and immediately returned with their oulah.

We found at Gaya a tolerably comfortable lodging, but we did not know on what conditions we should proceed. The important question of the oulah occupied every one's mind, yet no one ventured to put the question openly, and we went to bed, leaving the consideration of serious matters to the morrow.

It was scarce day when the court of the house where we lodged was filled with a crowd of Thibetians, who had come to deliberate on the degree in which they should tax our caravan. From a second-floor balcony, we could enjoy at our leisure the singular spectacle which this council presented. Of the immense multitude, there was not an individual who was not an orator; everybody spoke at once; and, judging from the sounding altitude of the voices, and the impetuous animation of the gestures, there must certainly have been some very fine speeches there. Some orators mounted upon the luggage that was piled in the court, and made of it a pulpit, whence they overlooked the multitude. Sometimes it seemed that the eloquence of words was insufficient to convey conviction to the minds of the audience, for the disputants would fight and pull each other's hair, and beat each other without mercy, until an orator of superior influence came and called the honorable members to order. This calm, however, would not be of long duration; the tumult and disorder would soon recommence with increased vigor. The thing became so serious, that we were convinced these people would end with drawing their sabers, and massacring each other. We were mistaken. After the assembly had vociferated, gesticulated, and manipulated for more than an hour, there was a great shout of laughter; the council rose, and everybody withdrew perfectly calm. Two deputies then ascended to the second-floor, where the staff of the caravan lodged, and informed Ly-Kouo-Ngan that the chiefs of the family of Gaya, after deliberating on the organization of the oulah, had decided that they would furnish gratuitously animals for the two Lamas of the Western Heaven, and for the Thibetians of Lha-Ssa; but that the Chinese must pay half-an-ounce of silver for a horse, and a quarter for a long-haired ox. At this intimation, Ly-Kouo-Ngan collected his strength, and inveighed with energy against what he called a tyranny, an injustice. The Chinese soldiers of the caravan, who were present, co-operated with loud cries and menaces, for the purpose of intimidating the delegates of the national assembly of Gaya; but the latter preserved an attitude deliciously haughty and contemptuous. One of them advanced a step, placed, with a sort of wild dignity, his right hand on the shoulder of Ly-Kouo-Ngan, and after piercing him with his great black eyes, shaded with thick eyebrows, "Man of China," said he, "listen to me; dost thou think that with an inhabitant of the valley of Gaya, there is much difference between cutting off the head of a Chinese and that of a goat? Tell thy soldiers, then, not to be too fierce, and not to talk big words. Who ever saw the fox that could terrify the terrible yak of the mountains? The oulah will be ready presently; if you do not take it, and go to-day, to-morrow the price will be doubled." The Chinese, perceiving that violence would only involve disagreeable results, had recourse to cajolery, but to no purpose. Ly-Kouo-Ngan found no resource except that of opening his strong-box, and weighing out the required sum. The oulah soon arrived, and we occupied ourselves busily with the organization of the caravan, in order to leave as soon as possible this village of Gaya, which the Chinese deemed barbarous and uninhabitable, but which seemed to us extremely picturesque.

From Gaya to Angti, where we were to change the oulah, was only a short stage of thirty lis. The Chinese were in despair at having been obliged to spend so much money to effect so short a distance; but they had only come to the commencement of their miseries; for we were destined to meet with Thibetian tribes, still less tractable than those of Gaya.

The snow, which had given us a few days' respite since our departure from Tsiamdo, again assailed us on the very evening of our arrival at Angti. During the night, and the following day, it fell in such abundance that we were unable to go out without having it up to our knees. As a climax of misfortune, we had, on leaving Angti, to ascend one of the rugged and most dangerous mountains on this route. The Chinese Itinerary thus describes it: "At Angti, you cross a great snow-clad mountain; the road is very steep; the accumulated snows resemble a silvery vapor. The fog which the mountain exhales penetrates the body, and makes the Chinese ill."

According to a popular tradition of the country, in the olden time, a chief of the tribe of Angti, a famous warrior, held in awe by all his neighbors, was buried under an avalanche one day when he was crossing the mountain. All the efforts to recover his body were fruitless. A holy Lama of the period, having declared that the chief had become the genius of the mountain, they raised a temple to him, which still exists, and where travelers never fail to burn a few incense sticks, before proceeding on their way. In tempests, when the wind blows with violence, the genius of Mount Angti never fails to appear; there is no one about who has not seen him several times. He is always seen mounted upon a red horse, clothed in large white robes, and quietly sauntering upon the crest of the mountain. If he meets any traveler, he takes him on his crupper, and vanishes forthwith at full gallop. The red horse being so light that he leaves no trace, even on the snow, no one, to this day, has been able to discover the retreat of the White Knight, for so they call him in the country.

As to us, we were not much concerned about the red horse and the white knight. What we feared was the mountain itself. We could not help shuddering at the sight of the frightful quantity of snow which had fallen, and which would render the road extremely dangerous. We were obliged to await the return of fine weather, and then to send, as we had before done under similar circumstances, a herd of long-haired oxen to trample down the snow, and trace out a path over the mountain.

We stayed five days at Angti. Ly-Kouo-Ngan took advantage of this long halt to doctor his legs, the malady in which assumed every day a more alarming character. The question of the oulah, long discussed in several assemblies, was resolved, at last, in the same way as at Gaya; a result which did not fail greatly to annoy the Chinese, and to elicit from them infinite clamor.

What we found most remarkable at Angti was, certainly, the Dheba, or chief of the tribe. This individual, named Bomba, was at most three feet high; the saber which he carried in his girdle was, at least, twice his own length; notwithstanding this, the man had a magnificent chest, and a face, broad, energetic in its expression, and beautifully regular in its features. The exiguity of his stature arose from an entire abortion of the legs, which, however, did not in the least affect his feet; nor did the almost total absence of legs prevent the chief of the tribe of Angti from being surprisingly active. He was always running about with as much agility as the longest legged of his people; he could not, indeed, make very extended strides, but he compensated for this by the rapidity of his movements. By dint of working about right and left, skipping and jumping, he always arrived as soon as any one else; he was, they said, the most expert horseman and the most intrepid warrior of the tribe. When they had once hoisted him on his horse, where he held on, at once standing and seated, he was invincible. In the popular assemblies, which the mountaineers of these regions are in the habit of holding very frequently, and always in the open air, to discuss all questions of public and private interest, the chief Bomba always made himself remarkable by the ascendency of his eloquence and his resolute character. When they were discussing at Angti the tax on the oulah, no one was seen, no one heard, but the astonishing Bomba. Perched on the shoulders of a big, tall Thibetian, he pervaded, like a giant, the tumultuous assembly, and dominated it, by word and gesture, still more than by his factitious stature.

The chief of Angti omitted no opportunity of giving us special proofs of kindness and sympathy. One day, he invited us to dine with him. This invitation served the double end of exercising towards us the duty of hospitality, and, in the next place, of piquing the jealousy of the Chinese, whom he hated and despised with all his soul. After dinner, which offered nothing remarkable but a profusion of uncooked and boiled meat, and tea richly saturated with butter, he asked us to go and see a saloon full of pictures and armor of every description. The pictures which lined the walls consisted of portraits, rudely colored, representing the most illustrious ancestors of the family of Bomba. We observed there a numerous collection of Lamas of every age and dignity, and some warriors in war costume. The arms were numerous and in great variety. There were lances, arrows, two-edged sabers, spiral and scythe-shaped; tridents; long sticks with large iron rings, and matchlocks, the stocks of which were of most singular shapes. The defensive arms were round bucklers of the hide of the wild yak, ornamented with red copper nails; armlets and greaves of copper, and coats of mail of iron wire, of a thick and close web, but, notwithstanding, very elastic. The chief Bomba told us that these coats of mail were the armor of very ancient times, which had been put aside since the use of the gun had become general in their country. The

Thibetians, as we have said, are too indifferent in matters of chronology to be able to assign the time when they began to make use of firearms. It may be presumed, however, that they were not acquainted with gunpowder until towards the thirteenth century, in the time of the wars of Tchingghiskhan, who had, as we know, artillery in his army. A rather remarkable circumstance is, that in the mountains of Thibet, as well as in the Chinese empire and the plains of Tartary, there is no one but knows how to make powder. Every family makes it for its own use. In passing through the province of Kham, we often remarked women and children busily employed in pounding coal, sulphur, and saltpeter. The powder thus made is certainly not so good as that of Europe, yet, when it is put in a fusil, with a ball upon it, it is sufficiently potent to project the ball, and make it kill stags in hunting and men in battle.

After five days' repose, we resumed our route. Immediately at the outset, the caravan began to ascend the lofty mountain of Angti. We met neither red horse nor white knight, and no genius took us on his crupper, to bear us away to his solitary abode. On every side we saw only snow, but that snow was so abundant that even on the most noted mountains, we had never found so frightful a quantity. Frequently the guides, mounted upon long-haired oxen, entirely disappeared in gulfs, from which they could only disengage themselves with great difficulty. More than once we were on the point of retracing our steps, and giving up all hopes of reaching the summit.

The small Sinico-Thibetian caravan that had joined us at Tsiamdo, and that had never left us since, presented a spectacle worthy of the utmost compassion. We forgot, in some degree, our own sufferings, when we saw these poor little creatures almost at every step buried in the snow, and with hardly strength enough to cry. We admired the intrepid energy of the Thibetian mother, who, so to speak, multiplied herself, in order to rush to the assistance of her numerous offspring, and who derived, from maternal tenderness, superhuman strength.

The mountain of Angti is so lofty and steep, that it took us the whole day to ascend and descend it. The sun had already set when we managed to roll to the bottom. We halted a few minutes, under some black tents inhabited by nomad shepherds, swallowed a few handsful of tsamba, diluted with brackish tea, and then resumed our route along a rocky valley where the snow was all melted. We followed for two hours, in utter darkness, the steep banks of a river, of which we heard the waters without seeing them. Every instant we trembled lest we should be precipitated into it; but the animals, which knew the road, and which we left to their instinct, conducted us safely to Djaya.

Our arrival in the middle of the night put all the town in commotion. The dogs, by their fierce barking, gave the alarm. Soon after, the doors of the houses were opened, and the inhabitants of the town rushed out in a crowd into the streets, with horn lanterns, torches, and weapons of every description, the general impression being that there was an invasion of the enemy. However, when they observed the peaceful and even timid bearing of the caravan, their apprehensions were quieted, and each person returned home. It was past midnight before we were able to get to sleep, having previously resolved to stay a day at Djaya, with a view to take a few hours' rest after crossing the famous mountain of Antgi,—not more than was necessary.

Djaya is, as we have stated already, the residence of the young Lama Houtouktou, who at the time was warring with the Houtouktou of Tsiamdo. The town, situated in a beautiful valley, is tolerably large; but, at the time we passed through it, it was half in ruins; scarce twenty days had elapsed since it had been attacked by the partisans of the Grand Houtouktou. The two parties, we were informed, had had terrific combats, wherein on both sides the victims had been numerous. In passing through the town, we found whole quarters laid waste by fire; nothing remained but enormous heaps of calcined stones, and woodwork reduced to ashes. All the trees of the valley had been cut down, and the trampling of horses had utterly laid waste the cultivated fields. The celebrated Lamasery of Djaya was deserted, the cells of the Lamas and the walls, for more than 400 yards in circuit, which surrounded them, had been demolished, and presented nothing but a terrible mass of ruins. The assailants had only respected the principal temples of Buddha.

The Chinese government keeps at Djaya a small garrison, composed of twenty soldiers, commanded by a Tsien-Tsoung and a Pa-Tsoung. These military gentlemen wore anything but a satisfied aspect. They seemed to be very indifferently pleased in this country, a prey to all the horrors of civil war. The warlike attitude of the mountaineers left them no rest, day or night. It was in vain they tried to preserve neutrality, or rather to have the appearance of belonging to both parties; they none the less found themselves constantly between two fires. It would appear, indeed, that Djaya has never furnished to the Chinese an easy and agreeable residence. At all times, Chinese domination has met with invincible resistance from the fierce tribes around it. The Chinese Itinerary, which was written in the reign of the Emperor Kien-Long, expresses itself thus concerning these countries: "The Thibetians, who inhabit the district of Djaya, are of a haughty and fierce character; all attempts to subdue them have been fruitless, they are considered very ferocious; it is their natural character." What the Chinese writer calls "fierce character," is nothing more in reality than ardent patriotism, and a very just hatred of a foreign yoke.

A day's rest having sufficiently repaired our strength, we quitted Djaya. It is unnecessary to add that the Chinese were obliged to pay, and in ready money, for the hire of the oulah. The Thibetians of the country were too ferocious to furnish us gratuitously with oxen and horses. We traveled for two days, through a country extremely low, where we frequently found small villages and black tents grouped in the valleys. We were often obliged to traverse wooden bridges, in order to cross sometimes calm and quiet streams, and at other times torrents, the impetuous waters of which rolled on with a terrible noise. Shortly before our arrival at the station of Adzou-Thang, we overtook the party which was accompanying the coffin of the deceased Liang-Tai to Bagoung. The son also had just died in a black tent, after a few hours' frightful agony. The caravan, having no chief, was in a complete state of disorganization; most of the soldiers of the escort had dispersed, after pillaging the baggage of their Mandarin; three only had remained, who were devising the best means of effecting the conveyance of the two bodies to China. They despaired of being able to continue their journey in so small a number; so that the arrival of our caravan extricated them from a great difficulty.

The conveyance of the father's body had been arranged at Bagoung; that of the son remained unsettled. The carriers of this palanquin had refused to undertake the carriage, for they foresaw that there would not be money enough to pay them for their trouble. To place the coffin on an ox was impracticable; there was no inducing a Thibetian guide to allow one of their animals to carry a corpse, much less the corpse of a Chinese. We were obliged to have recourse to stratagem. The body of the last deceased Mandarin was secretly cut into four pieces, and then packed in a box, which we put among the general luggage, making the Thibetians believe that in honor of filial piety, the body of the son had been laid beside that of his father, in the same coffin.

The two corpses, that had become our fellow-travelers, communicated to the caravan a mournful aspect, which had great influence upon the Chinese imagination. Ly, the Pacificator of Kingdoms, whose strength decreased daily, was particularly alarmed by the circumstance; he would fain have removed the sad spectacle, but this he could not effect without exposing himself to the terrible accusation of having impeded the sepulture of two Mandarins, who had died in a foreign country.

From Adzou-Thang, we went on to sleep and change oulah in a small village of the valley of Che-Pan-Keou (Valley of States). According to the testimony of the Chinese Itinerary, the inhabitants of this valley are a rude, wicked, and obstinate people; that is to say, in other words, they do not fear the Chinese, and are in the habit of making them pay a good price for the yaks and horses with which they furnish them.

The valley of Che-Pan-Keou, as its name indicates, abounds in quarries of argillaceous schist. The Thibetians of these countries raise from them beautiful slate, which they use in tiling their houses; they also raise very thick pieces, upon which they engrave images of Buddha with the form, "Om mani padme houm." This slate is of very fine texture. The small portions of mica or talc which they contain give them a brilliant and silky luster.

The stream which flows through the center of the valley contains a large quantity of gold dust, which the natives do not neglect to collect and refine. As we walked along the stream, we found fragments of crucibles, to which were still attached a few particles of gold; we showed them to the Pacificator of Kingdoms, and this sight seemed to reanimate his strength, and to renew the bonds which attached him to life. The blood suddenly rushed into his face; his eyes, which had been almost extinct, shone with an unwonted fire. One would have said that the sight of a few grains of gold had made him completely forget both his malady and the two corpses which accompanied him.

Musk deer abound in this schistous valley. Although that animal, addicted to cold climates, is met with on almost all the mountains of Thibet, nowhere, perhaps, is it seen in such large numbers as in the neighborhood of Che-Pan-Keou. The pines, cedars, hollies, and cypresses, which cover this country, contribute, no doubt, a good deal to attract these animals thither, peculiarly fond, as they are, of the roots of these trees, which have a strong aromatic perfume.

The musk deer is of the height of a goat; it has a small head; its nose is pointed, and ornamented with long white mustaches; its legs are small, its haunches large and thick; two long crooked teeth, which grow out of the upper jaw, enable it to tear up from the ground the odoriferous roots, upon which it subsists; its hair is generally from two to three inches long, and is hollow, like that of almost all the animals which live north of the Himalaya mountains; extremely rough, and always bristling; its color is black below, white in the middle, and inclining to gray above. A bladder, suspended from the belly, near the navel, contains the precious substance, the musk.

The inhabitants of the schistous valley capture in the chase such a number of these musk deer, that you see nothing in their houses but the skins of these animals, hung on the walls by pegs. They use the hair to stuff the thick cushions, on which they sit during the day, and the sort of mattress which serves them for a bed; they have in the musk the source of a very lucrative trade with the Chinese.

The day after our arrival at Che-Pan-Keou, we bade farewell to the inhabitants of the valley, and proceeded on our way. At the three next stations they were quite inexorable on the question of the oulah. The Chinese were disgusted at the behavior of these rude mountaineers, who, as they said, did not comprehend hospitality, and had no notion of what was right and what was wrong. As to us, on the contrary, we sympathized with these men and their rude, spirited temperament; their manners, it is true, were not refined, but their natural disposition was generosity and frankness itself, and in our eyes matter was of more moment than manner. At length we reached Kiang-Tsa, and the Chinese now began to breathe more freely, for we were entering upon a less hostile district. Kiang-Tsa is a very fertile valley, the inhabitants of which seem to live in plenty. We remarked among them, besides the soldiers of the garrison, a great number of Chinese from the provinces of Sse-Tchouen and Yun-Nan, who keep a few shops and exercise the primary arts and trades. A few years, they say, enable them, in this country, to amass a tolerably large fortune. The two military Mandarins of Kiang-Tsa, who had been companions in arms of Ly-Kouo-Ngan, were alarmed at the deplorable state in which they found him, and advised him strongly to continue his journey in a palanquin. We joined our entreaties to theirs, and we were fortunate enough to triumph over the avarice of the Pacificator of Kingdoms. He appeared at last to comprehend that a dead man had no need of money, and that first of all he should see to the saving of his life. The son of the Mandarin Pei seemed to have died just in the nick of time for placing at Ly-Kouo-Ngan's disposal, his palanquin and his eight Chinese bearers, all of whom were at Kiang-Tsa. We halted for one day to repair the palanquin and to give the bearers time to prepare their traveling sandals.

The countries which we passed to the south of Kiang-Tsa, seemed to us less cold and less barren than those we had journeyed through previously. The ground perceptibly declined; we were still, indeed, completely surrounded by mountains, but they gradually lost their savage and mournful aspect. We no longer saw those threatening forms, those gigantic masses of granite with sharp and perpendicular declivities. High grass and forests showed themselves on every side, cattle became more numerous, and everything announced that we were rapidly advancing towards more temperate climes; only the tops of the mountains still preserved their crowns of snow and ice.

Four days after our departure from Kiang-Tsa, we reached the banks of the Kin-Cha-Kiang (River of Gold-dust), which we had already crossed on the ice with the Thibetian ambassador, two months before our arrival at Lha-Ssa. Amid the beautiful plains of China, this magnificent river rolls on its blue waves with an imposing majesty; but among the mountains of Thibet, it is ever bounding about, throwing the great mass of its waters to the bottom of gorges and valleys, with terrible impetuosity and noise. At the spot where we came to the river, it was enclosed between two mountains, the sharp flanks of which, rising perpendicularly on its banks, made for it a narrow but extremely deep bed; the waters ran rapidly, sending forth a low and lugubrious sound. From time to time, we saw huge masses of ice approach, which, after having whirled round in a thousand eddies, at last were dashed to pieces against the sharp projections of the mountain.

We followed the right bank of the Kin-Cha-Kiang for half a day. Towards noon, we reached a small village, where we found everything prepared beforehand for crossing the river. The caravan divided itself among four flat boats, and, in a little while, we were on the opposite bank. Near it, at the entrance to a narrow valley, was the station of Tchon-Pa-Loung. The Dheba of the place furnished us, by way of supper, with some excellent fresh fish; and, for sleeping, with a very snug wind-tight chamber, and thick mattresses stuffed with the hair of the musk deer.

Next day we traveled along a small river, which subsequently joins the River of Gold-dust. Our hearts were lighter than usual, for we had been told that we should arrive the same day in a charming country. As we went along, we accordingly looked first on one side and then on the other, with an uneasy curiosity; from time to time we rose on our stirrups in order to see further; but the landscape was a long time before it became poetical. On our left we had still the aforesaid river, prosaically running over great stones, and on our right a large red mountain, dismal, bare, and cut up in all directions by deep ravines; masses of white clouds, driven onward by a cutting wind, flitted over the sides of the mountain, and formed, ahead of us, a somber horizon of mist.

Towards midday, the caravan halted at some ruins, to drink a cup of tea and eat a handful of tsamba; we then clambered to the top of the red mountain, and from the height of this great observatory, admired on our right the magnificent, the enchanting plain of Bathang.[1] We found ourselves all at once transported, as it were by magic, into the presence of a country which offered to our view all the wonders of the richest and most varied vegetation. The contrast, above all, was striking. On one side, a somber, barren, mountainous region, almost throughout a desert; on the other, on the contrary, a joyous plain, where numerous inhabitants occupied themselves in fertile fields, in the labors of agriculture. The Chinese Itinerary says: "The canton of Bathang is a beautiful plain, a thousand lis in length, well watered by streams and springs; the sky there is clear, the climate pleasant, and everything gladdens the heart and the eyes of man." We quickly descended the mountain, and continued our journey in a real garden, amid flowering trees and verdant rice fields. A delicious warmth gradually penetrated our limbs, and we soon felt our furred dresses oppressive; it was nearly two years since we had perspired, and it seemed very odd to be warm without being before a good fire.

Near the town of Bathang, the soldiers of the garrison were drawn up in line, to do military honors to the Pacificator of Kingdoms, who, perched up, at the bottom of his palanquin, went through the ranks in a very unwarlike manner. The Thibetian population, who were all on foot, accompanied the caravan to a beautiful Chinese pagoda which was to serve for our lodging. The same evening, the Mandarins of the Chinese garrison and the Grand Lamas of the town came to pay us a visit, and to offer us some beef and mutton, butter, corn, candles, bacon, rice, nuts, raisins, apricots, and other products of the country.

At Bathang there is a magazine of provisions, the fourth from Lha-Ssa; it is, like all the others, managed by a literary Mandarin, bearing the title of Liang-Tai. The Chinese garrison, consisting of three hundred soldiers, is commanded by a Cheou-Pei, two Tsien-Tsoung, and a Pa-Tsoung. The annual maintenance of the Chinese troops, who belong to this post, amounts to nine thousand ounces of silver, without reckoning the rations of rice and tsamba. We observed, among the population of Bathang, a very great number of Chinese; they are engaged in various arts and trades;

[1] Bathang signifies in Thibetian, plain of cows.

several of them, indeed, occupy themselves with agriculture, and make the most of the Thibetian farms. This plain, which you find, as by enchantment, amid the mountains of Thibet, is wonderfully fertile: it produces two harvests each year. Its principal products are, rice, maize, barley, wheat, peas, cabbages, turnips, onions, and several other varieties of vegetable. Of fruits, you find grapes, promegranates, peaches, apricots, and watermelons. Honey is also very abundant there. Lastly, you find there mines of cinnabar (sulphur of mercury), from which they extract a large quantity of mercury. The Thibetians get the mercury in all its purity, by disengaging the sulphur by combustion, or by combining it with slack-lime.

The town of Bathang is large and very populous, and its inhabitants seem to be well off. The Lamas there are very numerous, as they are in all the Thibetian towns. The principal Lamasery, which they call the Grand Monastery of Ba, has for its superior a Khampo, who holds his spiritual authority from the Talé-Lama of Lha-Ssa.

The temporal power of the Talé-Lama ends at Bathang. The frontiers of Thibet, properly so called, were fixed in 1726 on the termination of a great war between the Thibetians and the Chinese. Two days before you arrive at Bathang, you pass, on the top of the Mang-Ling mountain, a stone monument, showing what was arranged at that time between the government of Lha-Ssa and that of Peking, on the subject of boundaries. At present, the countries situate east of Bathang are independent of Lha-Ssa in temporal matters. They are governed by the Tou-Sse, a sort of feudal princes, originally appointed by the Chinese Emperor, and still acknowledging his paramount authority.

These petty sovereigns are bound to go every third year to Peking, to offer their tribute to the Emperor.

We halted at Bathang three days, the illness of our guide Ly-Kouo-Ngan being the cause of this delay. The daily fatigues of this long journey had so overpowered the poor Mandarin, that he was in an almost hopeless state. His best plan was to take advantage of the fine climate of Bathang, and to let the caravan proceed on its way. His friends advised him to do so, but without success. He insisted upon continuing his journey, and sought, in every way, to deceive himself as to the serious nature of his malady.

As for us, we considered his case so dangerous, that we felt it our duty to profit by the repose we enjoyed at Bathang, to talk seriously to him on the subject of his soul and of eternity. Our previous conversations on the way had already sufficiently enlightened him as to the principal truths of Christianity. Nothing now remained but to make him clearly perceive his position, and to convince him of the urgency of entering frankly and fully into the path of salvation. Ly-Kouo-Ngan altogether concurred with us, admitting our observations to be replete with reason. He himself spoke with great eloquence on the frailty and brevity of human life, of worldly vanities, of the impenetrability of God's decrees, of the importance of salvation, of the truth of the Christian religion, and of the obligation on all mankind to embrace it. He said to us, on all these subjects, some very sensible and very touching things; but when it came to the point, to the practical result, to the declaring himself Christian, there was a dead stand; he must absolutely wait till he had returned to his family, and had abdicated his mandarinate. It was in vain that we represented to him the danger he incurred by postponing this important matter; all was useless. "So long as I am a Mandarin of the Emperor," said he, "I cannot serve the Lord of Heaven," and he had got this absurd idea so deep in his brain, that it was impracticable to dislodge it.

On leaving the station of Bathang, we were obliged to turn for some distance, quite northward, in order to resume an eastern direction; for since our departure from Tsiamdo, we had continually progressed towards the south during twenty consecutive days. The caravans are compelled to lengthen this route considerably, in order to reach a secure passage across the great river Kin-Cha-Kiang.

Our first day's march from Bathang was full of charms, for we traveled, in a delightful temperature, through a country of an infinite variety of landscape. The narrow path we followed was throughout bordered with willows and apricot trees in flower. Next day, however, we again found ourselves amid all the horrors and dangers of our old route. We had to ascend a very high mountain, upon which we were mercilessly assailed by the snow and the north wind. It was a complete reaction against the Sybaritism we had enjoyed in the warm and flowery plain of Bathang. At the foot of the mountain, the snow was succeeded by torrents of cold rain, which seemed to filter through into the very marrow of our bones. As a climax of misfortune, we were obliged to pass the night in a habitation, the roof of which, cracked in several places, gave free passage to the wind and rain. We were, however, so exhausted with fatigue that this did not prevent our sleeping. The next day we awoke in the mire; we found our bedclothes entirely soaked, and our limbs stiff with cold. We were obliged to rub ourselves violently with pieces of ice, in order to restore circulation to the blood. The abominable village, which afforded us this horrible lodging, bears the name of Ta-So. On emerging from the valley of Ta-So, you ascend, by a narrow gorge, an elevated plain, which we found covered with snow. Here we entered a magnificent forest, the finest we had seen in the mountains of Thibet. The pines, cedars, and hollies entwined their vigorous branches, and formed a dome of verdure impenetrable to the sun, and under which there is much better protection from the rain and snow than in the houses of Ta-So. The trunks and branches of these large trees are covered with thick moss, which extends in long and extremely delicate filaments. When this stringy moss is new, it is of a beautiful green hue; but when it is old, it is black, and bears an exact resemblance to long tufts of dirty and ill-combed hair. There is nothing more grotesque or fantastic than the appearance of these old pines, with this very long hair suspended from their branches. The prickly holly that grows on the mountains of Thibet is remarkable for the extraordinary development it attains. In Europe, it never exceeds the size of a shrub, but here it always grows to the size of a large tree. If it does not rise as high as the pine, it equals it in the size of its trunk, and it is even superior to it in the richness and abundance of its foliage.

This day's march was long and fatiguing. The night had set in when we reached the station of Samba, where we were to change the oulah. We were just going to bed, when we missed a Thibetian, belonging to the escort, precisely the very man who had been assigned as our servant. We sought him, but without success, in every corner of the small village in which we had arrived. We concluded he had lost his way in the forest. We at first thought of sending in search of him, but in so dark a night, how could one possibly find a man in that vast and thick forest? We contented ourselves with going in a body to a neighboring hill, where we shouted and lit a large fire. Towards midnight, the lost man reappeared, almost dead with fatigue. He carried on his back the saddle of his horse, which, no doubt, finding the journey too long, had thought fit to lie down in the midst of the forest, and it had been impossible to get him up again. The return of this poor young man filled every one with joy, and we all then went to rest.

The next day we rose late. Whilst the inhabitants of Samba were bringing the horses and the beasts of burden to form the caravan, we went for a little walk, and to have a view of the place, which we had reached over night. The village of Samba is a collection of thirty small houses, built of large flint stones, rudely cemented, some with argols, others with mud. The aspect of the village is mournful, but the environs are tolerably cheerful. Two streams, one coming from the west, the other from the south, join near the village, and form a river, the transparent waters of which flow over a vast prairie. A small wooden bridge, painted red, herds of goats and long-haired cattle, which sported amid the pastures, some storks and wild ducks, fishing for their breakfast on the banks of the water, a few gigantic cypresses here and there, even the smoke which rose from the Thibetian cottages, and which the wind gently wafted over the adjacent hills, all contributed to give life and charm to the landscape. The sky was clear and serene. Already the sun, having risen a little above the horizon, promised us a fine day and a mild temperature.

We returned to our lodgings, walking slowly. The caravan was ready, and on the point of departure; the beasts were laden with their burdens; the horsemen, their robes tucked up, and whip in hand, were ready to mount. "We are behindhand," said we, "let us make haste," and at a run we were in our places. "Why are you in such a hurry?" said a Chinese soldier, "Ly-Kouo-Ngan is not ready; he has not yet opened the door of his room." "To-day," answered we, "there is no great mountain ahead; the weather is fine: there is no objection to our starting a little later; go, however, and tell the Mandarin that the caravan is ready." The soldier pushed open the door, and entered the chamber of Ly-Kouo-Ngan; he rushed out again pale and with haggard eyes. "Ly-Kouo-Ngan is dead!" said he to us, in a low tone. We rushed into the room, and saw the unfortunate Mandarin, stretched on his bed, his mouth open, his teeth clenched, and his eyes shrunk up by death. We placed our hands on his heart, which gently moved. He had yet a spark of life in him, but all hope was vain; the dying man had altogether lost the use of his senses; there was another rattle or two in his throat, and he expired. The humors with which his legs were swollen had gone up to his chest, and suffocated him.

The death of our guide had not been unexpected; there was nothing in it to surprise us, but it occurred in such a sudden, melancholy manner, that every one of us was greatly agitated. As for ourselves, in particular, we were afflicted at it beyond all expression. We bitterly regretted that it had not been our good fortune to assist at the last moments of this unfortunate man, whom we had so desired to bring from the darkness of paganism into the light of the faith. Oh, how impenetrable are the decrees of God! Some hope, however, mingled with our but too just grounds for fear. As this poor soul had been sufficiently enlightened as to the truths of religion, it is permissible to suppose that God, of his infinite mercy, perhaps accorded to him, in his last moments, the grace of the baptism of volition.

That day the caravan did not proceed on its march, the animals were unsaddled and sent out to pasture; and then the soldiers of the escort made all the necessary preparations, according to the Chinese rites, for conveying the body of their Mandarin to his family. We will not enter here into the details of what was done in this matter, for whatever concerns the manners, customs and ceremonies of the Chinese will find a place elsewhere. We will merely say that the defunct was enveloped in a large white pall, which had been given him by the Living Buddha of Djachi-Loumbo, and which was covered with Thibetian sentences, and with images of Buddha, printed in black.

The Thibetians, and other Buddhists, have unlimited confidence in the printed winding-sheets which are distributed by the Talé-Lama and the Bandchan-Remboutchi. They are persuaded that those who are fortunate enough to be buried in them cannot fail to have a happy transmigration.

By the demise of Ly-Kouo-Ngan, the caravan found itself without a leader and without a guide. There was, to be sure, the Lama Dsiamdchang, to whom the power should have fallen by right, and by legitimate succession; but the Chinese soldiers being very little disposed to acknowledge his authority, we passed from the monarchic state to the republican, democratic form. This state of things lasted at most half-a-day. Perceiving that the men of the caravan, both Thibetians and Chinese, were not yet prepared for so perfect a government, and considering that anarchy was developing itself in every direction, and that matters threatened to go to rack and ruin, consulting only the public interest and the safety of the caravan, we assumed the dictatorship. We immediately issued several decrees, in order that everything might be in readiness for us to proceed on the morrow at daybreak. The necessity of being governed was so completely understood, that no one made any opposition, and we were obeyed punctually.

At the appointed time we left Samba. The caravan bore a sad and melancholy aspect. With its three corpses, it absolutely resembled a funeral procession. After three days' march across mountains, where we generally found wind, snow, and cold, we arrived at the station of Lithang (copper plain). The Chinese government keeps here a magazine of provisions, and a garrison consisting of 100 soldiers. The Mandarins of Lithang are: a Liang-Tai, a Cheou-Pei, and two Pa-Tsoung. A few minutes after our arrival, these gentlemen came to pay us a visit. In the first place, the illness and death of our guide were discussed at full length; then we were required to state our quality, and by what authority and in what position we were in the caravan. By way of answer, we simply showed him a large scroll, fortified with the seal and signature of the ambassador Ki-Chan, and containing the instructions which had been given to Ly-Kouo-Ngan about us. "Good, good," said these persons to us, "the death of Ly-Kouo-Ngan will make no change in your position; you shall be well treated wherever you go. Up to this time you have always lived peaceably with the men of the caravan, doubtless this good understanding will continue to the end." We hoped so too. Yet, as considering human frailty, difficulties might possibly arise on the way, particularly among the Chinese soldiers, we wished to have with us a responsible Mandarin. We made this request, and were informed that of the four Mandarins who were at Lithang, not one could be spared to conduct us; that we could go along quietly enough as far as the frontiers, with our Thibetian and Chinese escort; and that there we should readily find a Mandarin to conduct us to the capital of Ssa-Tchouen. "Very well," said we, "as you cannot give us a Mandarin we shall travel as we think fit, and go where we please. We are not even sure that on quitting this place we shall not return to Lha-Ssa. You see that we deal freely with you; reflect upon the point." Our four magistrates rose, saying that they would deliberate on this important matter, and that in the evening we should have an answer.

During our supper, at Pa-Tsoung, one of the four Mandarins, presented himself in his state robes. After the usual compliments, he told us that he had been selected to command our escort as far as the frontiers; that he had never, in his dreams of ambition, imagined he should have the honor of conducting people such as we; that he was ashamed on the first day of seeing us, to have to ask us a favor; it was, that we would rest for two days at Lithang, in order to recover our strength, which must be exhausted by so long and arduous a journey. We perceived that our friend had need of two days to arrange some affairs of his own, previous to a journey which he had not expected. "Ah," we replied, "already how full of solicitude is your heart for us. We will rest then two days as you wish it." Authority having been thus reorganized, our dictatorship was at an end. But we thought we perceived that this was anything but agreeable to our people, who would much rather have had to do with us than with a Mandarin.

The town of Lithang is built on the sides of a hill which rises in the middle of a plain, broad but almost sterile. Nothing grows there but a little barley, and a few poor herbs, which serve for pasturage to some miserable herds of goats and yaks. Seen from a distance, the town has some promise. two large Lamaseries, richly painted and gilt, which are built quite on the top of the hill, especially contribute to give it an imposing aspect. But, when you pass through the interior, you find nothing but ugly, dirty, narrow streets, so steep that your legs must be accustomed to mountain traveling, to keep their equilibrium. This side of the River of Gold-dust, you observe among the tribes a rather remarkable modification in the manners, customs, costume, and even in the language. You see that you are no longer in Thibet, properly so called. As you approach the frontiers of China, the natives have less ferocity and rudeness in their character; you find them more covetous, flattering, and cunning; their religious faith is no longer so vivid, nor so frank. As to the language, it is no longer the pure Thibetian that is spoken at Lha-Ssa, and in the province of Kham: it is a dialect closely connected with the idiom of the Si-Fan, and in which you remark various Chinese expressions. The Thibetians of Lha-Ssa who accompanied us had the greatest difficulty in the world in understanding and being understood. The costume, for the most part, only differs as to the head-dress. The men wear a hat of gray or brown felt, somewhat similar to our own felt hats when they first come from the hatter's board and have not been rounded to the form. The women form with their hair a number of small tresses, which flow over their shoulders. They then place on their heads a large silver plate, somewhat similar to a dinner-plate. The more elegant wear two of these, one on each side, so that the two ends meet above the head. The precept of daubing the face with black does not apply to the women of Lithang. This kind of toilet operates only in the countries temporally subject to the Talé-Lama.

The most important of the Lamaseries of Lithang possesses a great printing press for Buddhic books, and it is hither that, on holidays, the Lamas of the neighboring countries come for their supplies. Lithang carries on also a large trade in gold-dust, in chaplets of black beads, and in cups made with the roots of the vine and box-tree. As we departed from Lithang, the Chinese garrison was under arms, to render military honors to Ly-Kouo-Ngan. They acted just as if he had been alive. When the coffin passed, all the soldiers bent their knees and exclaimed: "To the Tou-Sse, Ly-Kouo-Ngan, the poor garrison of Lithang wishes health and prosperity." The petty Mandarin, with the white button, who had become our guide, saluted the garrison in the name of the deceased. This new commander of the caravan was a Chinese of Moslem extraction; but one could find nothing about him which seemed to belong in the least to the fine type of his ancestors: his puny, stunted person, his pointed smiling face, his shrill treble voice, his trifling manners, all contributed to give him the air of a shop-boy, and not in the least that of a military Mandarin. He was a prodigious talker. The first day he rather amused us, but he soon became a bore. He thought himself bound, in his quality of Mussulman, to talk to us, on all occasions, about Arabia, and of its horses that are sold for their weight in gold; about Mahomet, and his famous saber that cut through metals; about Mecca and its bronze ramparts.

From Lithang to Ta-Tsien-Lou, a frontier town of China, is only 600 lis, which are divided into eight stages. We found the end of that frightful route to Thibet exactly like its middle and its beginning. We in vain climbed mountains; we found still more and more before us, all of a threatening aspect, all covered with snow and rugged with precipices; nor did the temperature undergo any perceptible change. It appeared to us, that, since our departure from Lha-Ssa, we had been doing nothing but move round and round in the same circle. Yet, as we advanced, the villages became more frequent, without, however, losing their Thibetian style. The most important of these villages is Makian-Dsoung, where some Chinese merchants keep stores for supplying the caravans. One day's journey from Makian-Dsoung, you pass in a boat the Ya-Loung-Kiang, a large and rapid river. Its source is at the foot of the Bayen-Kharat mountains, close to that of the Yellow River. It joins the Kin-Cha-Kiang, in the province of Sse-Tchouen. According to the traditions of the country, the banks of the Ya-Loung-Kiang were the first cradle of the Thibetian nation. As we were passing the Ya-Loung-Kiang in a boat, a shepherd crossed the same river on a bridge merely composed of a thick rope of yak skin tightly stretched from one bank to the other. A sort of wooden stirrup was suspended by a solid strap to a movable pulley on the rope. The shepherd had only to place himself backwards under this strange bridge, with his feet on the stirrup, and hold on to the rope with both his hands; he then pulled the rope gently; the mere weight of his body made the pulley move, and he reached the other side in a very short time. These bridges are very common in Thibet, and are very convenient for crossing torrents and precipices; but one must be accustomed to them. We ourselves never ventured on them. Iron chain bridges also are much in use, particularly in the provinces of Ouei and Dzang. To construct them, as many iron hooks are fixed on both sides of the river as there are

Iron Chain Bridge.

to be chains, then the chains are fastened, and on the chains planks, which are sometimes covered with a coating of earth. As these bridges are extremely elastic, they are furnished with hand-rails.

We arrived at length safe and sound at the frontiers of China, where the climate of Thibet gave us a very cold farewell. In crossing the mountain which precedes the town of Ta-Tsien-Lou, we were almost buried in the snow, it fell so thick and fast; and which accompanied us into the valley where stands the Chinese town, which, in its turn, received us with a pelting rain. It was in the early part of June, 1846, and three months since we had departed from Lha-Ssa; according to the Chinese Itinerary, we had traveled 5,050 lis.

Ta-Tsien-Lou signifies the forge of arrows, and this name was given to the town, because in the year 234 of our era, General Wou-Heou, while leading his army against the southern countries, sent one of his lieutenants to establish there a forge of arrows. This district has by turns belonged to the Thibetians and to the Chinese; for the last hundred years it has been considered as an integral part of the empire.

"The walls and fortifications of Ta-Tsien-Lou," says the Chinese Itinerary, "are of freestone. Chinese and Thibetians dwell there together. It is thence that the officers and troops which are sent to Thibet quit China. Through it passes also a large quantity of tea coming from China, and destined to supply the provinces of Thibet, it is at Ta-Tsien-Lou that is held the principal tea fair. Although the inhabitants of this canton are very addicted to the worship of Buddha, they seek to get a little profit; yet they are sincere and just, submissive and obedient, so that nothing, even death, can change their natural good nature. As they have been long accustomed to the Chinese domination, they are the more attached to it.

We rested three days at Ta-Tsien-Lou, and each day had several quarrels with the principal Mandarin of the place, who would not consent to our continuing our route in a palanquin. However, he had at length to give way, for we could not bear even the idea of mounting once more on horseback. Our legs had bestrided so many horses of every age, size, quality, and color, that they refused to have anything further to do with horses at all, and were full of an irresistible resolution to stretch themselves at ease in a palanquin. This was granted them, thanks to the perseverance and energy of our remonstrances.

The Thibetian escort which had accompanied us so faithfully during the long and arduous route, returned after two days' rest. We gave the Lama Dchiamdchang a letter for the Regent, in which we thanked him for having assigned us so devoted an escort, and which had throughout kept in our memory the good treatment we had received at Lha-Ssa. On parting from these good Thibetians we could not help shedding tears, for insensibly, and as it were without our knowledge, ties had been formed between us which it was painful to sever. The Lama Dchiamdchang secretly told us that he had been charged to remind us, at the moment of separation, of the promise we had made to the Regent. He asked us if they might reckon on seeing us again at Lha-Ssa. We replied that they might, for at that time we were far from anticipating the nature of the obstacles that were to prevent our return to Thibet.

The next morning, at daybreak, we entered our palanquins, and were conveyed, at the public expense, to the capital of the province of Sse-Tchouen, where, by order of the Emperor, we were to undergo a solemn judgment before the Grand Mandarins of the Celestial Empire.

POSTSCRIPT.

After a few months journey through China, we arrived at Macao, in the early part of October, 1846. Our long and painful journey was at an end; and at last we were able, after so many tribulations, to enjoy a little quiet and repose. During two years we applied our leisure moments to the preparation of the few notes made in our journey. Hence these "Reminiscences of Travel," which we address to our European brethren, whose charity will no doubt be interested in the trials and fatigues of the missionaries.

Our entrance into China, for the purpose of returning to our mission in Mongol-Tartary, compels us to leave unfinished the labor we had undertaken. It remains for us to speak of our relations with the Chinese tribunals and Mandarins, to give a sketch of the provinces we have traversed, and to compare them with those which we had occasion to visit in our former travels in the Celestial Empire. This omission we will endeavor to supply in the leisure hours we may be able to snatch from the labors of the sacred ministry. Perhaps we shall be in a position to give some correct notions about a country, of which, at no time, certainly, have men's ideas been so erroneous as they are at this day. Not that we are without abundant books about China and the Chinese. On the contrary, the number of works on these subjects that have appeared in France, and particularly in England, within the last few years, is really prodigious. But the zeal of a writer will not always suffice to describe countries in which he has never set his foot. To write travels in China, after a saunter or two through the factories of Canton and the environs of Macao, involves the danger of speaking of things that one is not thoroughly acquainted with. Although it has been the good fortune of the learned orientalist, J. Klaproth, to discover the Potocki Archipelago without quitting his closet, it is, generally speaking, rather difficult to make discoveries in a country which one has not visited.

Chinese Ornamental Ware.

INDEX.

N. B.—The volumes are indicated by small Roman numerals, and each, page-number refers to the volume-mark last preceding it.